W9-CFQ-434

ADMINISTRATIVE OFFICE MANAGEMENT
An Introduction

Sixth Edition

Zane K. Quible

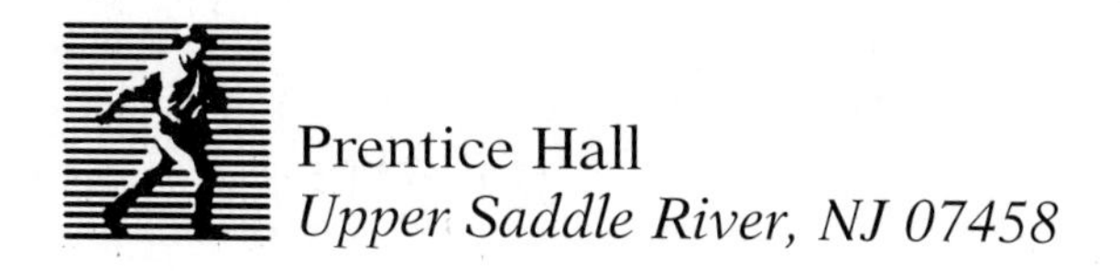

Prentice Hall
Upper Saddle River, NJ 07458

Library of Congress Cataloging-in-Publication Data

Quible, Zane K.
Administrative office management / Zane Quible.—6th ed.
p. cm.
Includes index.
ISBN 0-13-349457-8
1. Office management. I. Title.
HF5547.Q49 1996
651.3—dc20 95-22506
CIP

Acquisitions editor: Elizabeth Sugg
Managing editor: Mary Carnis
Director of production and manufacturing: Bruce Johnson
Editorial/production supervision: Tally Morgan, WordCrafters Editorial Services, Inc.
Cover design: Bruce Kenselaar
Manufacturing buyer: Ed O'Dougherty
Formatting/page makeup: University Graphics
Printer/binder: Courier Westford

Printed in the United States of America
10 9 8 7 6 5 4 3 2 1

ISBN 0-13-349457-8

Prentice-Hall International (UK) Limited, *London*
Prentice-Hall of Australia Pty, Limited, *Sydney*
Prentice-Hall Canada Inc., *Toronto*
Prentice-Hall Hispanoamericana, S.A., *Mexico*
Prentice-Hall of India Private Limited, *New Delhi*
Prentice-Hall of Japan, Inc., *Tokyo*
Simon & Schuster Asia Pte. Ltd., *Singapore*
Editora Prentice-Hall do Brasil, Ltda., *Rio De Janeiro*

To Patricia and Chris

CONTENTS

II MANAGEMENT OF THE OFFICE ENVIRONMENT

III MANAGEMENT OF OFFICE EMPLOYEES

PREFACE

Administrative office management is continually experiencing change, often as a result of technological advances. As technology changes, work processes and procedures often need to be adapted. New developments arising from this change are reflected in this sixth edition of *Administrative Office Management*.

The attention the business world is focusing on administrative office management is encouraging. This interest is intensified by more high-level executives becoming cognizant of the need to (and advantages of) managing their offices in a more professional, efficient manner. As a result, there is an increased number of opportunities for those who wish to pursue a career in administrative office management. A lack of concern for the efficient management of offices will result in higher than average operating costs. Administrative office management has a significant impact on the bottom line.

TEXT STRUCTURE

These topics included in each of the five units that comprise this text:

I: *Principles of Administrative Office Management* consists of three chapters concerned with the managerial process, the organizing process, and the communication process.

II: *Management of the Office Environment* contains three chapters concerned with office layout, office environment, and office equipment and furniture.

III: *Management of Office Employees* has ten chapters concerned with selecting office employees, developing office employees, supervising office employees, motivating, performance appraisal, job analysis, job evaluation, salary administration, work measurement, and productivity.

IV: *Management of Office Systems* has six chapters covering such topics as systems analysis, telecommunications, word processing, electronic data processing, records management and micrographics, and office automation.

V: *Management of Office Functions* contains four chapters dealing with forms design and control, office reprographics and mail services, quality and quantity control, and budgetary and cost control.

A partial list of topics new to this text include: facilities management, multicultural diversity, Total Quality Management (TQM), costing of office space, ergonomic considerations, résumé databanks, outsourcing, Civil Rights Act of 1991, distance learning, team building, employee promotion, Family Medical Leave Act of 1993, computer phones, e-mail, computer networks, color laser printers, color ink-jet printers, image processing, voice annotation, optical cards, electronic document management, electronic forms, digital color copying, and digital duplicators.

The instructor has considerable flexibility in changing the order of chapter coverage. Doing so should not impede learner understanding, as chapter content is not interdependent.

CHAPTER FEATURES

Several features are found in each chapter, including the chapter outline, chapter terms, chapter aim, marginal notations, review questions, discussion questions, projects and activities, a minicase, and a case.

The chapter outline lists the primary and secondary headings found in the chapter. The chapter terms section gives the important terms found within the chapter. Each of these terms is shown in bold type at the point of first reference in the chapter. The chapter aim identifies the knowledge the student should possess after studying the chapter. A number of marginal notations are also found in each chapter; these ask a question about the material presented.

The **review questions** at the end of each chapter provide questions that can be used to determine how well the material has been mastered. The **discussion questions** are also designed to help the learner more quickly grasp the important concepts of administrative office management. The **projects and activities** are designed to provide an enrichment and/or growth opportunity. The **minicase** in each chapter presents a situation, followed by two or three items or statements requiring learner response. The **case** presents details about a situation, along with a list of items to which the learner is to respond. The minicase and case in each chapter are designed as an opportunity to apply important chapter concepts.

SUPPLEMENTARY MATERIALS

The supplementary materials that accompany this text include a teacher's manual and a student guide. The teacher's manual contains a variety of information, including suggested time schedules for a two-term course, a semester course, or a term course, as well as sample course objectives and suggested teaching procedures. Other content includes supplementary teaching material, helpful software packages, answers to review questions and discussion questions, examination questions, solutions to the minicase and case, lecture notes with examination questions, and transparency masters for the lecture notes.

The study guide contains an application problem for each chapter, an in-basket simulation to facilitate decisionmaking, and a major comprehensive case that ties together many of the concepts presented.

DISTINCTIVE FEATURES OF THIS TEXT

Among the distinctive features of this text are:

- Retention of the highly readable writing style found in each of the five earlier editions. Closely related to this is presentation of technical material in a readily understandable manner.
- Inclusion of material that was up to the minute as the book went into production.
- Emphasis on and recognition of the human element, the critical link in any office.

A NOTE OF THANKS

To Elizabeth Sugg, the Prentice Hall acquisitions editor, and Tally Morgan, the WordCrafters (Sterling, VA) production editor.

And to my wife Patricia, whose love, support, and understanding sustained me throughout this project.

Zane K. Quible
Stillwater, OK

CHAPTER

THE MANAGERIAL PROCESS

CHAPTER AIMS

After studying this chapter, you should be able to develop an appropriate management strategy for use by an administrative office manager, taking into consideration the evolutionary nature of the broader field of management.

CHAPTER OUTLINE

- Current Thrust
- Administrative Office Management
  - Function
  - Objectives
- A Career in Administrative Office Management
- The Administrative Office Manager
  - Responsibilities
  - Challenges
  - Qualifications
  - Professionalism
  - Educational Background
  - Profile
- Evolution of Management Theory
  - Scientific Management Movement
  - Administrative Movement
  - Human Relations Movement
  - Modern Movement
- Implications for the Administrative Office Manager

CHAPTER TERMS

- Administrative movement
- Behavioral science approach
- Certified Administrative Manager (C.A.M.)
- Hawthorne Studies
- Human relations movement
- Information management
- Management functions
- Modern movement
- Motion study
- Office automation
- Operations approach
- Scientific management movement
- Systems analysis
- Theory Z
- Time study
- Total Quality Management (TQM)

How is today's administrative office management function different from yesterday's office management area?

Over the years, the administrative office management function with organizations has experienced profound change, with the current function being much different than its predecessor—office management. A half-century ago, the office management function was much more limited in scope than its successor. Administrative office management today permeates the entire organization. With the broadening of the function has come the broadening of the role of the administrative office manager.

Today's technology and the ever-broadening scope of administrative office management are responsible for significant changes in many of its functional components. Whereas office management was primarily concerned with the creation, processing, and retention of forms and records, administrative office management is concerned with information. Fewer paper forms are being created as more information is stored electronically. Today's emphasis is on a systems approach encompassing people, equipment, and procedures. In the early days of office management, less emphasis was put on the interaction between people, equipment, and procedures.

Being a service area, administrative office management generates no revenue for the organization. Rather, it provides specialized support for individuals and organizational units—revenue generating and service areas, alike—resulting in cost-effective operations. Various functions and services of administrative office management relieve individuals of several administrative responsibilities, giving them additional time to devote to other tasks for which they have primary responsibility.

CURRENT THRUST

What is the most significant new thrust in administrative office management?

The most significant thrust in administrative office management continues to be its involvement in creating, processing, storing, and retrieving organizational information. The **information management** thrust makes the administrative office management area more crucial to organizational success now than ever before. Increasingly, the systems being installed to manage organizational information are using a variety of electronic devices that result in greater levels of automation.

Regardless of their field of specialization, managers often consider information to be their most important managerial tool as well as a fundamental and precious organizational resource. Never before have managers had so much information available to support their decision-making efforts. Administrative office management makes a significant contribution to organizational success by providing specialized support in the management of information.

The explosion of technology is primarily responsible for the rapid increase in the amount of information accessible to managers. Although the technology does not necessarily create vast amounts of new information, it makes existing information more readily available, accessible, and convenient to use. The technology largely responsible for the increased amount of available and accessible information is generally the same technology used in the successful management of the information.

The efficiency with which an organization manages its information is affected by several factors directly related to the administrative office management function, including the following: office environment, office employees, office systems, and a variety of office functions. The important role the administrative office manager plays in each of the areas is thoroughly covered in this text.

ADMINISTRATIVE OFFICE MANAGEMENT FUNCTION

The nature of the background and role of administrative office management makes it the most logical of all organizational areas to assume responsibility for the management of information. The background and expertise of administrative office managers make them well qualified to assume these crucial information management responsibilities. Increasingly, the administrative office management function and administrative office managers are being recognized and credited for their contribution to the well-being of many organizations of varying size.

In what ways does administrative office management impact on office employees?

Administrative office management has a significant impact on employees throughout the organization, perhaps most significantly by enabling them to enhance their productivity. In addition to relieving employees of responsibility for certain tasks, this position helps them maximize the efficiency of other designated tasks. Also, administrative office management helps provide employees with the information they need, when they need it, and in the format they desire. This partially explains why the administrative office management function in most organizations transcends all units and departments.

The current practice of centralizing many of the office functions and services found in the modern organization has added a new perspective to the administrative office management function. In the early days of office management, only a few functions and services were centralized. Today, administrative office management has a significant impact in some way on virtually every white-collar worker in the organization.

The increased use of **office automation** has considerably broadened the scope of administrative office management. Various elements of office au-

1. To ensure that relevant organizational activities are designed to minimize individual and unit productivity.
2. To provide effective management of the organization's information.
3. To maintain reasonable quantity and quality standards.
4. To develop effective work processes and procedures.
5. To provide a satisfactory physical and mental working environment for the organization's employees.
6. To help define duties and responsibilities of employees assigned within the administrative office management functional area.
7. To develop satisfactory lines of communication among employees within the administrative office management functional area and between these employees and employees in other areas within the organization.
8. To help employees maintain a high level of work effectiveness.
9. To enhance the effective supervision of office personnel.
10. To assure the efficient and proper use of specialized office equipment.

Figure 1-1 Objectives of administrative office management.

tomation, which contributes significantly to organizational productivity, are discussed in several chapters in this text.

In the future, office functions and services will become even more systems oriented and will use even greater amounts of technology. As a result, today's administrative office management function likely will evolve as tomorrow's information systems function. Today's administrative office manager will likely become tomorrow's manager of information systems.

Objectives

Administrative office management, like any other managerial area, has a common core of objectives. Some of the more common ones are illustrated in Figure 1-1.

A CAREER IN ADMINISTRATIVE OFFICE MANAGEMENT

What is the nature of the new career opportunity for middle-level managers?

Paralleling the rapid growth in organizational information is the increased number of career opportunities in administrative office management. Managers are readily discovering that an effective way for their organizations to become more profitable is to scrutinize closely the cost of their office operations and to develop efficient work methods and procedures. Accordingly, the number of career opportunities in administrative office management increases proportionately to the ever-growing contribution this field makes to organizational success.

Administrative office management is generally considered to be within the middle-management level of the organizational hierarchy. In some organizations, especially in larger ones, administrative office management typically is an important component of one of the functional areas, such as the administrative services area. A vice president of administrative services (or a vice president with some other similar title) is likely to be responsible for the area, and several middle-level managers are likely to report to this individual. While one manager may be responsible for systems analysis and design, another manager may be responsible for data processing, and a third manager responsible for word processing.

The structure shown in Figure 1-2 identifies the nature of a new career opportunity for middle-level managers—the vice presidency of the functional area. In the illustration, this individual's title is vice president of administrative services. Increasingly, individuals who started in a low-level office job can now become a vice president of administrative services. Such opportunities make a career in administrative office management challenging and rewarding.

Another new career opportunity found attractive by individuals who have training and/or a background in administrative office management is in facility management. Individuals who serve their organization as a facility manager are concerned with efficient utilization of facilities and control of operating costs associated with the organization's facilities. Another important responsibility involves various aspects of the work environment, especially the compliance with federal, state, and local regulations involving the environment. Other areas with which facility managers are concerned are efficient utilization of work space, especially when the workforce expands or contracts. With the increasing use of facility managers, administrative office managers have expanded career opportunities.

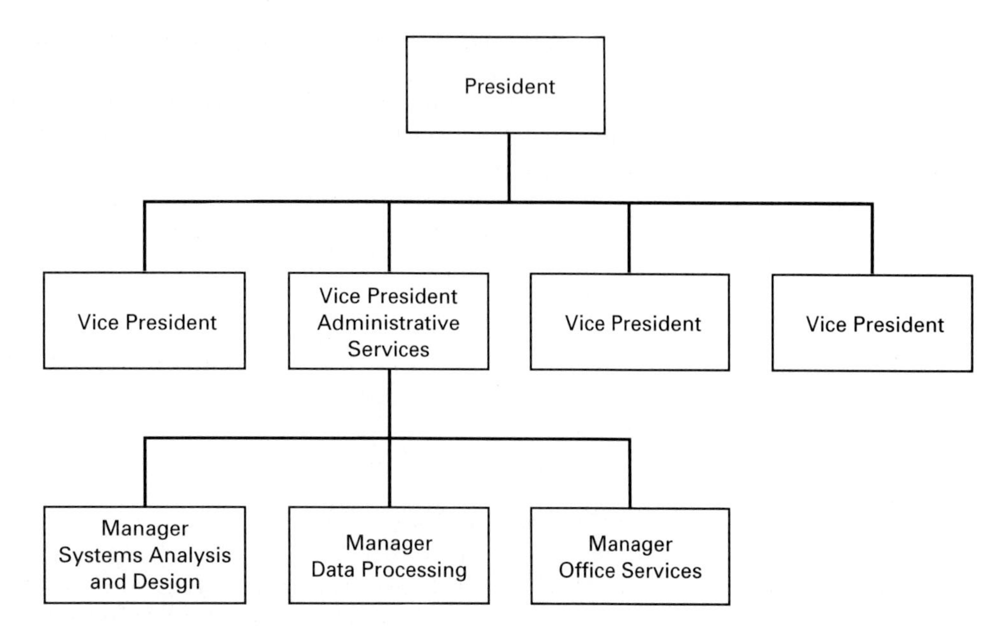

Figure 1-2 Hierarchical structure of administrative office management.

THE ADMINISTRATIVE OFFICE MANAGER

The broad nature of the responsibilities of administrative office managers creates considerable diversity in their positions. In fact, finding two administrative office managers with identical job responsibilities is virtually impossible.

The job responsibilities of administrative office managers, as well as the titles of their jobs, are diverse. Among the job titles found are the following: administrative office manager, administrative manager, office manager, office administrator, manager of office support, and director of administrative services. Although the title administrative office manager will be used throughout the remainder of this text when referring to a person with these job responsibilities, other job titles would have been just as appropriate.

Responsibilities.

Administrative office managers have several important job responsibilities within each of the five basic **management functions** of planning, organizing, staffing, directing, and controlling. Some of the more common responsibilities are presented in Figure 1-3.

Challenges.

What is the nature of the challenges affecting administratve office managers?

Administrative office managers are performing an important new role as change agents. Among their important responsibilities are implementing a variety of new systems and helping employees overcome their resistance to these systems. Ability to cope with change and to help others accept change will continue to create—into the foreseeable future—a challenge for administrative office managers.

Another significant challenge will be brought about by a vast increase in new technology used in offices, most of which will be found in such areas as

Planning function

1. Developing goals and objectives for each of the office functions and services, including layout, environment, telecommunications, word processing, automation, electronic data processing, records management, forms design, reprographics, mail services, and control.
2. Keeping abreast of new developments in the field and determining what changes should be made in existing functions and services to maintain a state-of-the-art position.
3. Assessing the need for designing and implementing totally new functions and services.
4. Developing policies that will help assure the attainment of goals and objectives.
5. Determining the most effective means of implementing desired changes.
6. Developing the unit's budget.
7. Determining personnel requirements.
8. Determining space and equipment needs.
9. Designing new operating systems.

Organizing function

1. Determining the most effective means of organizing resources to achieve goals and objectives.
2. Determining the most effective way for employees to perform specific tasks.
3. Designing efficient work methods and procedures.
4. Assuring the maximum utilization of the organization's office equipment.
5. Developing techniques for maximizing organizational and individual productivity.
6. Developing effective methods and techniques when implementing changes.
7. Developing effective procedures for evaluating equipment being considered for acquisition.

Staffing function

1. Assuring the use of efficient employee selection procedures including placement and orientation.
2. Providing sufficient growth opportunities and experiences for employees.
3. Providing appropriate training experiences.
4. Assuring effective appraisal of employee performance.
5. Assuring the realistic description of employees' jobs.

Directing function

1. Using effective techniques to supervise employees.
2. Using effective techniques to motivate employees.
3. Designing effective lines of communication within the unit.
4. Assuring employee compliance with organizational policies and procedures.
5. Assuring that employee performance meets expectations.
6. Helping employees solve work-related problems.
7. Using a fair, objective approach for adjusting employees' salaries.

Controlling function

1. Developing efficient procedures for controlling the quantity and quality of work processed in areas for which the administrative office manager is responsible.
2. Developing efficient procedures for scheduling work.
3. Developing efficient procedures

Figure 1-3 Responsibilities of the administrative office manager.

for use in readily determining the status of unfinished work.
4. Maintaining the unit's budget.
5. Assuring that methods and procedures are cost-effective.
6. Motivating employees to be cost-conscious.
7. Developing effective assessment procedures for use in determining why actual results fail to conform with anticipated results.
8. Developing effective procedures for dealing with employees who fail to comply with organization's rules and policies.
9. Developing effective strategies for taking corrective action when and where necessary.

Figure 1-3 Continued.

data processing, word processing, reprographics, and telecommunications. Although some of the new technology will result in more sophisticated versions of existing equipment, much of the technology that will likely be common in a few years is currently in the developmental stage.

A variety of government regulations will continue to create a challenge for administrative office managers. In many organizations, this manager is responsible for creating the data needed to complete a variety of required compliance reports as well as for maintaining the data banks in which this information is stored.

Organizational productivity is another area in which administrative office managers will continue to be challenged. Managers will be responsible for continually developing efficient systems that enable employees to maximize their productivity as well as for designing strategies that motivate office employees to want to be productive.

Another challenge confronting an increasing number of administrative office managers results from the discovery that some of the newly implemented office systems have not performed according to expectations. Increasingly, a variety of different brands of equipment and technology constitute these systems, with some of the hybrid systems not performing as anticipated. When this happens, the administrative office manager has either primary or secondary responsibility for making systems modification.

As the workforce becomes more multiculturally diverse, administrative office managers will also be challenged by having to become familiar with ways to accommodate the diversity. The customs, beliefs, habits, and attitudes of culturally diverse individuals make managerial acceptance—and subsequent accommodation—of the diversity more important now than ever before.

Qualifications.

What are the important qualifications of administrative office managers?

Administrative office managers must possess a thorough understanding of various business fundamentals. Because administrative office management is primarily supportive in nature and is designed to help others achieve personal or organizational goals, a solid background in such areas as accounting, marketing, management, statistics, economics, and psychology is desirable. Administrative office managers responsible for systems analysis and design will find helpful a thorough understanding of such functional areas as production, marketing, and finance.

A specialized knowledge of the following areas is also important: work simplification, work measurement, work standards, records management, forms design, data processing, job analysis, job evaluation, office layout, office equipment, cost control, performance appraisal, employee selection, productivity improvement, word processing, and office automation.

Leadership is another important qualification. As supervision responsibilities increase, so does the need for well-developed leadership skills. Effective leadership skills enable one to inspire and motivate employees and to instill in subordinates the desire to act in the best interests of the organization, to be loyal to the organization, and to be cooperative. In addition, interpersonal behavior and human relations skills are crucial for the administrative office manager.

A commitment to ethical behavior is another qualification administrative office managers must possess. Increasingly, organizations are becoming concerned about ethics and the display of ethical behavior among employees. Over the past decade, lack of ethical behavior among employees has been quite costly—both in dollars and reputation—to a number of organizations.

The ability to delegate responsibility is another important qualification of the administrative office manager, as well as effective decision making and communication skills. The administrative office manager must also be able to accept the viewpoint of others and to exercise good judgment. Furthermore, the administrative office manager must have the initiative and desire to continue to learn and develop professionally.

Professionalism.

How can administrative office managers become professional?

An excellent way for administrative office managers to increase their professionalism is to participate in professional organizations and associations. For example, the **Certified Administrative Manager (C.A.M.)**, a program sponsored by the Administrative Management Society Foundation, is another means for the administrative office manager to become a more professional manager. Individuals who meet the requirements for the C.A.M. program become members of the Academy of Certified Administrative Managers. Certification requirements are shown in Figure 1-4.

Professional organizations of interest to administrative office managers are the American Records Management Association, Association for Systems Management, Data Processing Management Association, National Microfilm Association, Office Automation Management Association, Society of Office

1. Pass the C.A.M. examination, which covers personnel management concepts, finance, administrative services, and information systems, in addition to the case study.
2. Have a minimum of three years of administrative management experience.
3. Provide proof of possessing high standards of personal and professional conduct.
4. Make a contribution to administrative management effectiveness.
5. Provide evidence of leadership ability.

Figure 1-4 Certified Administrative Manager certification requirements.

Automation Professionals, Association for Information Systems Professionals, Society for Advancement of Management, International Facility Management Association, Office Systems Research Association, and the Business Forms Management Association.

An abundance of professional literature of interest to administrative office managers also exists. Some of the more useful periodicals include *Managing Office Technology*, *Words*, *Office Systems*, *Office Technology Management*, *Records Management Quarterly*, *The Office*, *OSRA Journal*, and *Supervisory Management*.

Educational Background.

What educational background is needed by administrative office managers?

To be successful as an administrative office manager, certain minimal educational requirements are needed, coupled with appropriate work experience. Traditionally, a position in administrative office management has not been a job-entry position. Although an individual may have the needed educational requirements for becoming an administrative office manager, most organizations require a certain amount of related work experience. For this reason, many administrative office managers have "come up through the ranks," having served previously as a supervisor of employees in one of the functional areas of administrative office management, such as data processing, for example.

Some of the college-level courses that administrative office managers find helpful are accounting, economics, business law, finance, statistics, office systems, and oral and written communication, as well as administrative office management. Also helpful are courses in psychology, sociology, and human relations.

Profile.

The profile of the typical administrative office manager includes the following characteristics: male, although the number of female managers is rapidly increasing; between forty and fifty years of age; salary ranging between $48,000 and $54,000; a bachelor's degree; supervisor of three to fourteen employees; ten to fifteen years of prior work experience; and employment as an administrative office manager for five or fewer years.

An increasing number of educational institutions are offering office systems and administrative office management curricula, resulting in the opportunity for students to major in this important specialized area. Therefore, younger and less-experienced individuals will be able to begin a career as an administrative office manager. Individuals who wish a career in this area will find that specializing enables them to perform more efficiently and with greater effectiveness than has been the case with some of their predecessors.

EVOLUTION OF MANAGEMENT THEORY

An understanding of the evolution of management theory is essential for a complete appreciation of the managerial process. The administrative office management area is firmly grounded in the theory of management that has evolved during the last 100 years. This evolution has progressed through four rather distinct phases, beginning with the **scientific management movement** in the early 1900s, and continuing with the **administrative movement** of the 1930s, the **human relations movement** of the 1940s and 1950s, and the current **modern movement**.

Scientific Management Movement.

What are the characteristics of the scientific management movement?

Generally regarded as the founder of scientific management, Frederick W. Taylor was greatly concerned during the late 1800s and early 1900s with the emphasis that organizations placed on production. Taylor believed that any major problem confronting an organization could be resolved if management would scientifically determine and communicate to employees their expected output levels. Scientific management, as conceived by Taylor, was designed to increase the output of the employees and to improve the operating efficiency of management.

Taylor viewed workers as an economic entity whose motivation to work stemmed from their financial needs. He also believed that workers had to produce more at a lower cost and that they should be paid on a piecework basis, which would enable them to increase their earnings.

According to Taylor, the cornerstone of scientific management was the use of time and motion study for increasing workers' efficiency in using machines. **Time study** is concerned with the amount of time it takes to complete a task, while **motion study** is concerned with the efficiency of the motion involved in performing a task.

Taylor and his followers believed in the need to identify one best way to do a job. Because the mechanical and physiological aspects of work were emphasized, the workers' psychological and social needs were often neglected.

Administrative Movement.

Popular during the 1930s, the administrative movement focused on the firm as a whole or total entity rather than on specific isolated functions. During this movement, the following specific management functions were identified: planning, organizing, commanding, coordinating, and controlling.

Henri Fayol, a French geologist and engineer, was one of the more important proponents of the administrative philosophy. Fayol and his followers believed that management, regardless of the specialized area, was comprised of the following universal principles:

What principles constituted the administrative movement?

1. Division of labor
2. Authority
3. Discipline
4. Unity of command
5. Unity of direction
6. Subordination of the individual interest to the general interest
7. Remuneration
8. Centralization
9. Scalar chain (line of authority)
10. Order
11. Equity
12. Stability of tenure of personnel
13. Initiative
14. Esprit de corps[1]

Human Relations Movement.

Emerging during the 1940s and 1950s, the human relations movement was largely a response to the failure of organizations to treat their employees in a humane manner. Rather than focusing on the whole organization, which was the philosophy of the administrative movement, the human relations era was primarily concerned with individuals and groups. Especially important in the human relations movement was the relationship between the superior and subordinate, particularly in terms of interpersonal relations and communication. Much of the work that evolved out of the human relations movement was concerned primarily with the lower levels of management.

One of the main proponents of the human relations movement was Elton Mayo. The well-known **Hawthorne Studies**, conducted in the late 1920s and early 1930s by Mayo and other researchers from Harvard University, provided the primary impetus for the development of the human relations movement. Undertaken at Western Electric's plant in Hawthorne, Illinois, the Hawthorne Studies were concerned with determining the effects that such factors as lighting, heating, fatigue, and layout had on productivity.

What was the major finding of the Hawthorne Studies?

One phase of the study determined the relationship between the illumination level of the employees' work area and their output. As the illumination level was increased, the output also predictably increased. Unexpectedly, however, the output continued to increase even when the illumination level was decreased. The researchers concluded that the human element had greater impact on determining output and reaction to change than did the technical factor. Those advocating human relations strongly believed, therefore, that the treatment of employees in a humane manner had a greater effect on operating efficiency and output than did any of the technical factors.

During this era, three individuals gained prominence for their research that examined the relationship between employees and their jobs. These individuals are Abraham Maslow (Hierarchy of Needs), Douglas McGregor (Theory X-Theory Y), and Frederick Herzberg (Motivation-Hygiene Theory).

Modern Movement.

The fourth phase in the evolution of management theory, the modern movement, began in the early 1950s and continues today. The modern movement consists of two approaches: the quantitative approach and the nonquantitative approach. The quantitative approach is also known as the **operations approach**, while the nonquantitative approach is frequently called the **behavioral sciences approach**.

How does the operations approach differ from the behavioral approach?

The operations approach is concerned primarily with the making of decisions, especially decisions about which operations should be undertaken and about how they should be carried out.

Systems analysis is closely related to the operations approach, with the following basic differences: systems analysis depends more on judgment and premonition, whereas the operations approach depends more on quantitative methods and mathematical models. Systems analysis is more subjective, whereas the operations approach is more objective.

The behavioral sciences approach is the scientific study of observable and verifiable human behavior. The effects of behavioral sciences can be observed at the individual, group, and organizational levels. The individual level is concerned with such factors as motivation, attitudes, and personality. The group level is concerned with interactions, interrelationships, group norms, and group leadership. The organizational level is concerned with such areas as bureaucracy and the effect of the system's design on employee behavior.

Other comparisons can be made between the behavioral sciences approach and the operations approach. The behavioral sciences approach is concerned with the manner in which decisions are made, whereas the operations approach is concerned with the way they ought to be made. This approach uses psychology, sociology, and anthropology as its base, whereas the operations approach is more concerned with mathematics, computer science, and statistical applications.

What is TQM?

Although not a new management concept—but one that is currently receiving considerable attention—**Total Quality Management (TQM)** has important implications for administrative office management. Rather than emphasizing hierarchical structures and managerial control of employees and work processes, TQM puts emphasis on the following: teamwork, empowerment of employees, and organization-wide recognition and acceptance of the critical need to serve its customers.

Adherence to the TQM philosophy effectively diminishes the adversity common in many organizations, replacing it with a spirit of cooperation. Rather than employees' energies being wasted dealing with subversive and divergent behaviors, their energies are expended toward the organization's better serving its customers. TQM results in a 100 percent commitment of 100 percent of the employees to 100 percent quality 100 percent of the time.

Although TQM programs found in organizations vary in their approach—sometimes quite extensively—they possess the following common elements:

1. Focus on customer satisfaction.
2. On-going improvement of the organization's products and/or services.
3. Workteams based on trust and cooperation.
4. Statistical measurement techniques designed to identify causes of production problems.

What are the major concepts of Theory Z?

The most recent management theory that has evolved is **Theory Z**, which was developed by William G. Ouchi. This theory is based heavily on the Japanese style of management. Among the important Theory Z concepts are those shown in Figure 1-5.

1. Employees are assumed to have lifetime employment. They need not be concerned about layoffs.
2. Employees are hired for their specific talents. The nature of an employee's job will be determined by his or her specific talents rather than by using a job to determine what talents an employee should have.
3. Decision making uses a consensus process that eventually results in widespread agreement on all decisions.
4. Managers and workers trust one another and are loyal to one another.
5. Managers are genuinely concerned about their subordinates' well-being.

Figure 1-5 Theory Z concepts.

IMPLICATIONS FOR THE ADMINISTRATIVE OFFICE MANAGER

Many administrative office management elements impact both directly and indirectly on the organization's ability to operate in a cost-effective manner. A failure by organizations to enhance the efficiency of their office operations results in operating costs that are higher than they otherwise would have to be.

The administrative office management function permeates the entire organization. For this reason, administrative office managers need to have a broad understanding of the various business functions as well as an excellent grasp of the various areas that comprise the administrative office management function.

Developments in the administrative office management area closely parallel the evolution of management theory. In the 1930s and 1940s, office managers readily adopted various principles that emerged from the human relations movement. As the modern movement surfaced in the 1950s, the administrative office management area again responded quickly to new beliefs, philosophies, and developments.

NOTE

1. Henri Fayol, *General and Industrial Management* (London: Sir Isaac Pitman and Sons Ltd., 1949), pp. 19–42.

REVIEW QUESTIONS

1. What is the new thrust of administrative office management?
2. What factor is primarily responsible for the increasing number of career opportunities in administrative office management?
3. What is the nature of the challenges that administrative office managers will likely confront during the 1990s?
4. What is the nature of the educational qualifications that are needed by administrative office managers?
5. What opportunities are available to help administrative office managers further their professional development?
6. During the scientific management movement, what technique or process was used to help increase workers' efficiency in using machines?
7. In what ways does the scientific management movement differ from the administrative movement?
8. What impact have the Hawthorne Studies had on the development of management theory?
9. How do systems analysis and the operations approach of the modern movement differ from one another?
10. What organizational elements does TQM emphasize?
11. What are some of the basic elements of Theory Z?

DISCUSSION QUESTIONS

1. Discuss the various ways in which administrative office management is a service function.
2. Assume you have been asked to prepare a list of the qualifications that should be possessed by the "ideal" administrative office manager. Use the following for categorizing each qualification: educational experience, background experience, areas of expertise, and personality characteristics. Be as specific as possible in preparing the wording of each qualification.
3. Although each of the five manage-

ment functions is important for any management position, select the one you believe to be the most important for an administrative office manager. Outline the reasons for your choice. Be able to defend your reasoning.
4. Assume the scientific management theory prevails today. Also assume you are currently an administrative office manager. Discuss how the various concepts of scientific management will impact on your managerial style.
5. Assume that you could have been a manager during either the administrative movement era or the human relations era. If you could choose the era that is most consistent with your philosophy of management, which would you choose? Why?
6. You are responsible for identifying the characteristics of what you consider to be the ideal management philosophy. In identifying these characteristics, you decide to select one or more characteristics from each of the four movements discussed in this chapter. As you select the characteristics that embody your concept of the ideal management philosophy, keep in mind that the characteristics have to be consistent with one another. What characteristics will your list comprise?

STUDENT PROJECTS AND ACTIVITIES

1. Interview an administrative office manager to determine the nature of his or her specific job duties and the nature of his or her educational preparation.
2. Scan through the oldest general management journals you can find in the library at your school. What kinds of topics were included in the articles pertaining to management theory?
3. With another student in the class, engage in a debate of the pros and cons of two of the management theories presented in this chapter.
4. From each of the management theories presented in this chapter, select two characteristics that you fully support. Which characteristics will your list comprise?

MINICASE

You are the administrative assistant to Mary Chial, the administrative office manager at Baskin Company. She is a frequent guest speaker at a variety of local professional associations in the Chicago area. Ms. Chial has been asked to address the members of a local administrative personnel group on the topic of the modern movement of management theory. Because she spent all last week attending a seminar in New York City, she has run out of time to research her topic. As her assistant, you have been asked to do her research for her. She has asked specifically that you prepare for her a written list of the differences between the operations approach and the behavioral sciences approach.

1. What differences are you going to point out between the two areas?
2. Are there any similarities between the two areas about which she should be made aware?

CASE

You are a student in an administrative office management class at the local university. To give the students an opportunity to gain practical, firsthand experience in solving business problems, the class is divided into several teams ; each group works in a consulting capacity with a local company.

The company your team works with is a manufacturer of replacement auto parts, such as starters and alternators. The company, which is only twelve years old, has grown quite rapidly the last seven years. In fact, in your initial conversation with the company's president, he made the following statements: "Many of our administrative practices have not developed as rapidly as they should have or as rapidly as circumstances warrant. We now have evidence that a certain percentage of our profit margin is being lost because of this situation. To be more specific, last week the Production Department spent many hours generating data that only three weeks ago had been generated by another department. Because Production didn't know the data had already been created, considerable effort was wasted. This same problem occurs all too often."

You and your team members are now ready to put together the report regarding your analysis of the situation. The report will be shared with the president.

1. Which of the five management functions is (are) not working as it (they) should, resulting in the situation discussed by the president?
2. What suggestion(s) are you going to mention in your report that help(s) ensure this situation or a similar one won't occur in the future?
3. Assume the president has accepted and begun to implement your suggestion(s). How can the effectiveness be evaluated six months after implementation?

CHAPTER

2

THE ORGANIZING PROCESS

CHAPTER AIM

After studying this chapter, you should be able to develop an appropriate philosophy regarding the organizing function of administrative office management.

CHAPTER OUTLINE

CHAPTER TERMS

Authority
Centralization
Chain of command
Committee structure
Decentralization
Employee participation
Functional areas
Functional structure
Informal organization
Line and staff structure
Line structure
Matrix structure
Organization chart
Organizational principles
Product structure
Responsibility
Span of control
Unity of command

In what ways is the organizing function helpful?

As one of the five managerial functions introduced in Chapter 1, the organizing function is vital to the operational effectiveness of all organizations. In fact, the organizing function is a significant determinant of how efficiently organizations use their resources.

Among the ways the organizing function is helpful to organizations are the following: assures more efficient use of the organization's resources; provides better, more thorough understanding by employees of their job duties and responsibilities; improves employee morale; and provides a sense of direction for each of the organization's functional areas.

The **organizational principles** managers use today originated in the various management theories that have evolved during the last one hundred years. These principles provide basic guidelines useful in designing and structuring various organizational activities. Furthermore, these principles play an important role in guiding organizations toward the successful achievement of their goals.

ORGANIZATIONAL PRINCIPLES

The organizational principles discussed in this chapter apply to any type of firm and to nearly every activity found within a firm. Adherence to the principles results in more efficient use of the firm's resources, especially the human and financial resources.

Definition of Objectives

For objectives to be meaningful, they must be clearly defined, understood, and accepted by each individual who is concerned with their attainment. Objectives devoid of these characteristics hinder the managerial process. Determining whether objectives have been attained is accomplished more easily when they are stated in numerical terms that involve quantity or time elements. For example, an objective of the word processing center may be to increase its output 5 percent between January 1 and June 30. The numerical elements found in this objective are helpful in determining if and when the desired level was attained. Objectives can be either short or long range, and some will involve only a few of the organization's employees, whereas others concern virtually the entire workforce.

Span of Control

What is meant by span of control?

The number of subordinates an individual is able to supervise effectively is known as **span of control**. Although no formula exists for determining an appropriate span, several factors should be considered. For example, the nature of the work being performed is important. Some office activities require a greater amount of supervision than do others. Another factor is the capability of supervisors and subordinates. Skilled supervisors generally are more able to work with a greater number of subordinates than are supervisors whose skills are less well developed. Likewise, if subordinates are well trained, supervisors may be able to increase their span of control because less time will be consumed helping employees. Other factors affecting span of control are the leadership style, the latitude extended to the subordinates in decision making, and the nature of interpersonal relationships inherent in each situation.

The nature of the responsibilities of the supervisor can be significant in determining an appropriate span of control. If the individual has numerous responsibilities in addition to supervising subordinates, the span of control will likely have to be smaller. The hierarchical level of the supervisor is also an important determinant. Generally, higher-level supervisors tend to supervise fewer employees than do lower-level supervisors.

Interrelated Functions

Most organizations are no longer composed of mutually exclusive **functional areas**. Rather, such areas as sales, production, finance, marketing, and personnel are becoming more interrelated—and sometimes intricately so. Consequently, problems that emerge in one functional area will often expand to or influence other areas. For example, if the marketing function is experiencing difficulties, the sales function will likely experience problems as well. The interrelated nature of these areas requires that the objectives of one area be consistent with those of other areas. Furthermore, related activities should be grouped together in one functional area. Otherwise, coordination of activities cannot be maximized.

Chain of Command

What is the essence of chain of command?

The formal identification of who reports to whom within the organization is known as **chain of command**. Each employee within an organization should be familiar with the chain as it affects him or her. Lack of adherence to the chain may cause the communication process to break down. Generally, simple chains are more effective than complex ones because they are more readily understood and because communication moves through a simple chain more rapidly than through a complex one. Furthermore, simple chains provide the benefit of being more clear-cut and definitive than their complex counterparts.

Unity of Command

What is the essence of unity of command?

The chain of command principle is closely related to the organizational principle which states that an employee should be directly responsible to only one supervisor. This principle is known as **unity of command**. An employee who has more than one supervisor is likely to be put into a precarious situation, especially when receiving conflicting orders or directions from two or more supervisors. Difficulties arise when both supervisors give the employee work to do at the same time and then one supervisor expects the employee to fulfill his or her request first. The absence of unity of command produces job-related frustration, job dissatisfaction, and loss of morale.

Commensurate Authority and Responsibility

Why do authority and responsibility have to be commensurate?

Another organizational principle states that individuals who are given the **responsibility** to undertake a task must also be given an appropriate amount of **authority** to ensure task completion. Otherwise, they cannot be held accountable for the ultimate outcome. The inability to delegate authority is a common problem for some supervisors. The result, consequently, is their performing many duties that could be effectively assigned to their subordinates. The failure of supervisors to delegate often prevents their performing at an optimum level. Subordinates, therefore, experience a loss of morale because they are unable to exercise full authority over those situations for which they are responsible.

Among the reasons supervisors avoid delegating authority are the following: (1) they lack confidence in their subordinates; (2) they lack understanding of the nature of the supervisory role; (3) they believe that unless they do the work, they cannot "stay on top" of the situation; and (4) they lack technical competence.

Occasionally, subordinates assume too much authority, resulting in their taking excessive liberties or control. Although this does not occur as frequently as the failure of supervisors to delegate authority, the results may be just as disastrous. Usually, when a subordinate is allowed to assume too much authority, the cohesion of the work group deteriorates, and the cooperation among the group members diminishes.

Work Assignment

When making work assignments, special strengths and talents of each individual should be considered. This helps ensure that each person's work assignment is consistent with his or her ability and interest. The absence of clearly defined job duties and responsibilities makes it more difficult to hold an employee accountable for unsatisfactory performance.

An individual's work assignment should be determined before he or she is hired. Defining a new employee's job duties and responsibilities once a person is on the job is not recommended.

Employee Participation

Why should employees be encouraged to participate in decision-making processes?

Employees should be encouraged to participate as much as possible in decision-making processes. Many administrative office managers have recognized the advantages of **employee participation**. Because employees are often more familiar with a given situation than a manager or supervisor is, their insight and suggestions are invaluable in the decision-making process. The recognition employees receive from the participation process has a positive impact on their motivation. Even though employees are given an opportunity to participate in the decision-making process, ultimate responsibility for the outcome of decisions rests with the manager or supervisor.

ORGANIZATIONAL STRUCTURES

The organization's internal structure determines the authority relationships among its employees. Common structures are line structure, line and staff structure, functional structure, product structure, committee structure, and matrix structure. The typical organization uses a combination of two or more of these structures.

Line Structure

Why is line structure not found in large organizations?

In **line structure**—the oldest and simplest of the structures—direct authority flows vertically from the top hierarchical levels, through the middle levels, and on to the bottom levels. The activities characteristic of line structure are directly associated with the attainment of the organization's primary objectives. Line organization is sometimes called military or scalar organization.

Because of the growing complexity of most organizations, the line structure is generally found only in small organizations or in those recently founded. Typically, owners or managers in small or new organizations have time to perform duties directly related to the primary objectives of the organization as well as those not directly related. As the organization increases in size and managerial duties become more complex, however, the hiring of additional support staff becomes necessary. When this happens, the line structure is no longer "pure." In some large organizations, a line structure is used for certain activities even though one of the other structures is predominate.

The direct authority characteristic of the line organizational structure makes each employee directly responsible for the performance of designated duties. Although direct line authority gives the supervisor the right to take disciplinary action against subordinates who fail to carry out reasonable orders and directions, supervisors do not have direct authority over individuals in other units or departments.

Advantages of line structure Use of the line structure results in several advantages. Because of direct authority and clearly defined areas of responsibility, employees are fully aware of the boundaries of their jobs. Decision making is expedited because bureaucratic buck passing is virtually eliminated. Also, employees readily understand the simplicity of line structure. Finally, because employees are familiar with their duties and responsibilities, they can be held directly accountable when their performance is less than expected.

Disadvantages of line structure The most serious disadvantage of line structure is its failure to provide the specialization needed by organizations when they become larger and more complex. Line managers have to perform certain specialized activities themselves because staff assistance is unavailable. As a manager's line duties expand, other duties will eventually have to be slighted. The line structure occasionally fails to provide for the adequate replacement of key managerial personnel because, in some cases, the limited nature of employees' duties prevents their getting the broad experiences they need for moving into managerial positions.

Line and Staff Structure

How does line structure differ from line and staff structure?

The **line and staff structure** is similar to the line structure, with one added dimension. The direct authority characteristic of line structure is still present, as are those line activities concerned with the attainment of the primary objectives of the organization. The new dimension is the addition of specialized staff activities that support line activities. Staff employees assist the line function by facilitating the attainment of the organization's primary objectives.

Line activities in one organization may be staff activities in another organization. Determining the appropriate classification of each type of activity can be done by answering the following question: Does the activity contribute directly to the attainment of the primary objectives of the organization? Line activities make a direct contribution; staff activities do not.

Managers or supervisors of staff units possess line authority over their subordinates. For example, the office services area of most organizations is considered to be a staff unit; when administrative office managers are given line authority to issue orders, however, they have line authority over their subordinates. Typically, they have only an advisory relationship with all other employees. Giving administrative office managers line authority over the employees in their units enhances the operational effectiveness of the office services area.

A partial organization chart depicting line and staff organizational relationships is illustrated in Figure 2-1. The shaded boxes are line positions; the unshaded boxes are staff positions.

In the illustration, the vice presidents for production and sales are line managers because their activities contribute directly to the attainment of the organization's primary objective: to make a profit on the products it manufactures and sells. The vice presidents for finance and corporate affairs perform support staff activities.

What are the advantages of line and staff structure?

Advantages of line and staff structure The most distinct advantage of line and staff structure is the freeing of line employees from their having to perform specialized activities that can be assigned to staff employees. Consequently, line managers have more time to perform activities that contribute directly to the attainment of the organization's primary objectives. Also beneficial is the use of the specialized assistance of staff personnel. The flexibility of most staff units enables them to undertake and successfully complete new projects within a minimum amount of time. Rarely is this flexibility possible in pure line structures. Many individuals use their staff experience as preparation for moving into a line position.

What are the disadvantages of line and staff structure?

Disadvantages of line and staff structure Conflict between line and staff employees may become troublesome. For example, because staff employees perform primarily in supportive or advisory capacities, line employees may ignore their input. In other instances, staff employees have added to line-staff conflict by usurping line authority. In addition, some line managers continually suppress the talents of capable staff employees, which hampers the development of an effective line-staff working relationship.

Functional Structure

What rights does functional authority provide?

Organizations that use **functional structure** are built around specialized areas. For example, in a manufacturing organization, the specialized areas might be production, sales, marketing, finance, corporate relations, and so forth. A specialist, perhaps with the title of vice president, manages each functional area. These managers have both line authority and functional authority: line authority over the subordinates in their own unit and functional authority over activities in other departments that relate to their own specialized areas.

The functional structure is most commonly found in small- and medium-sized organizations. It tends to centralize decision making at the top levels of the organization. The functional structure is illustrated in Figure 2-2.

For example, in the partial organization chart illustrated in Figure 2-2, the manager of office services has line authority over the office workers in the office services unit and functional authority over the office workers found in the other functional areas. The manager has the right to issue orders and to take disciplinary action against those over whom he or she has line authority. Although the manager cannot take disciplinary action against individuals for

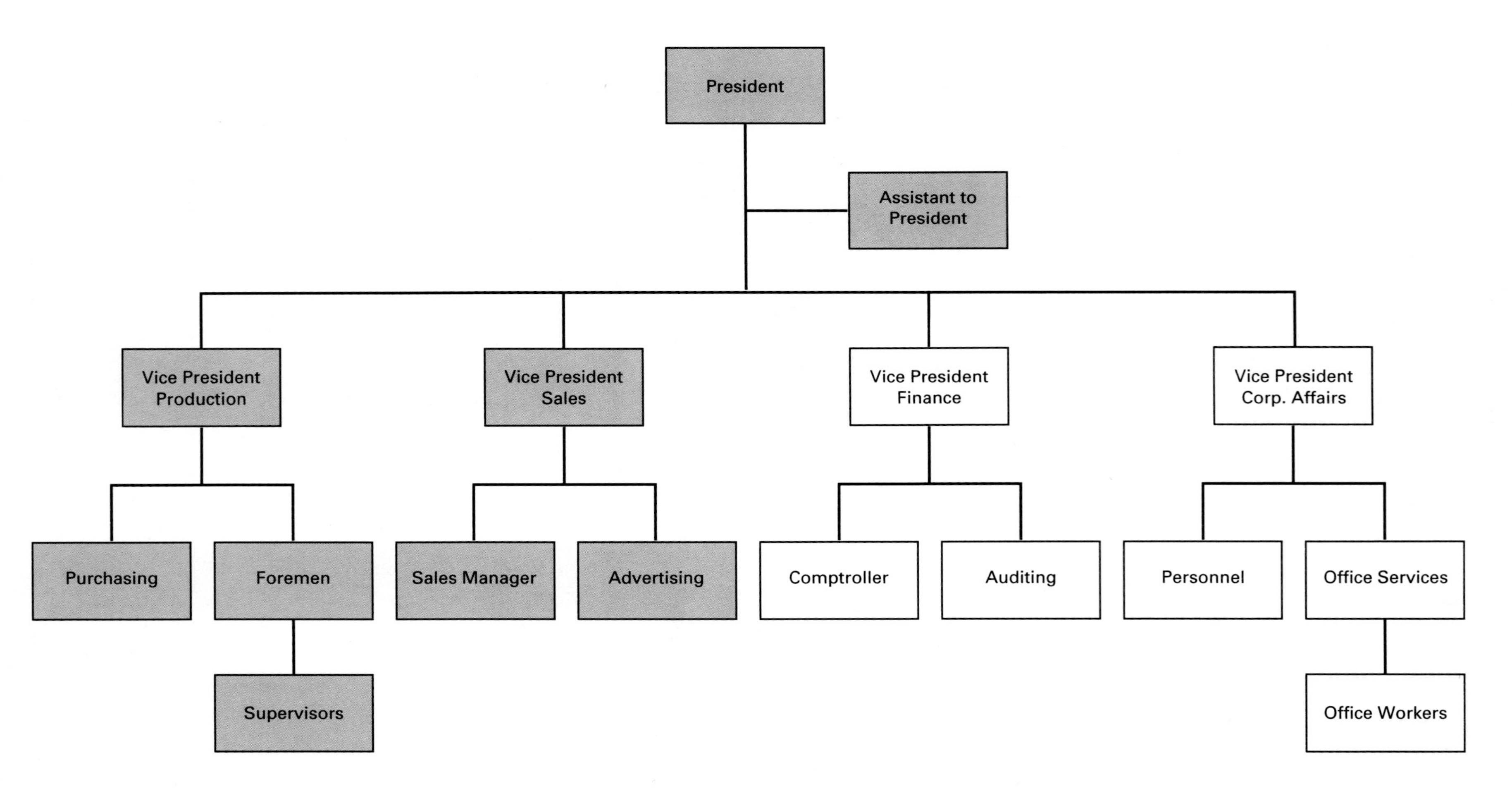

Figure 2-1 Partial organization chart depicting line and staff organization.

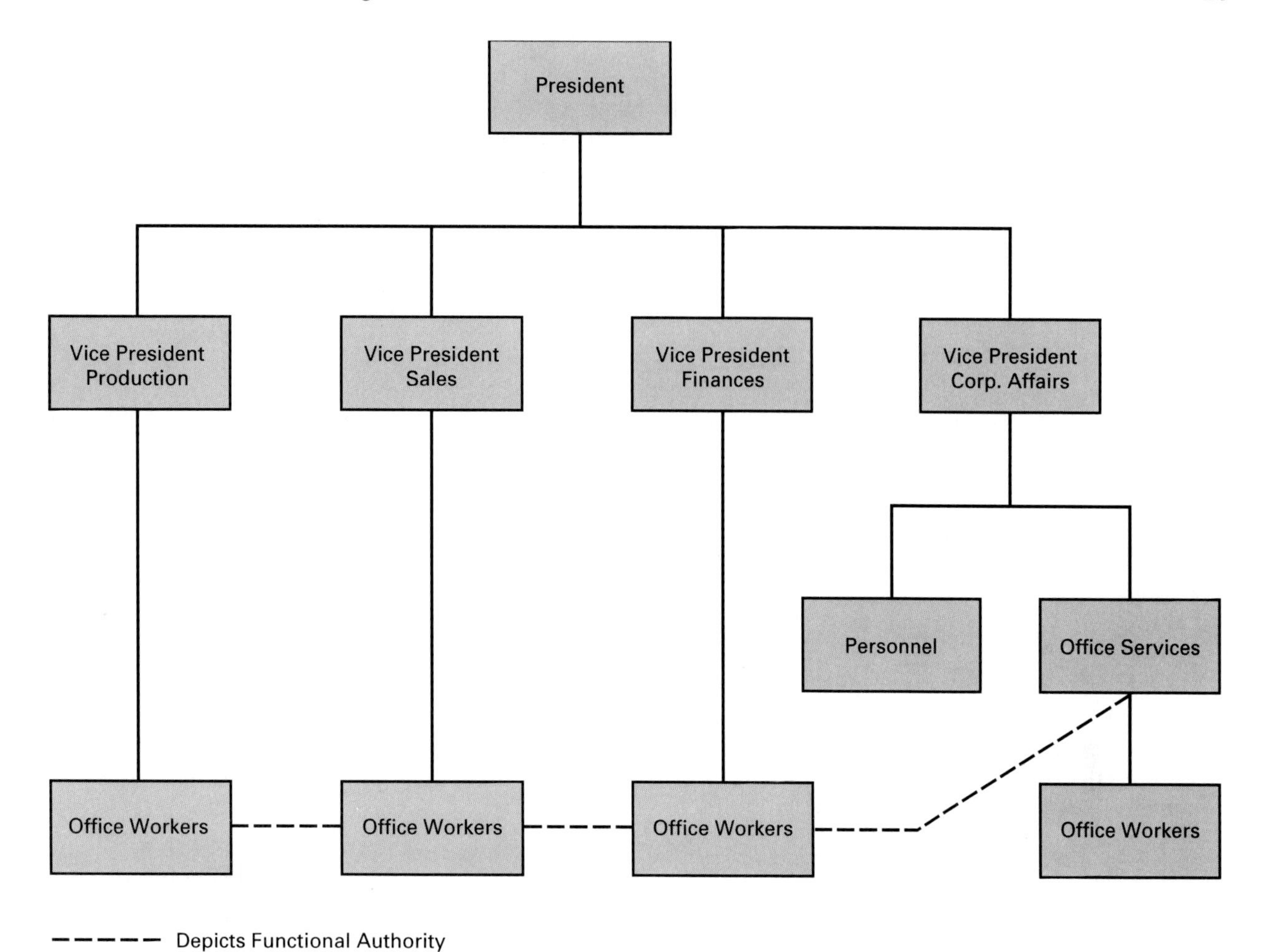

Figure 2-2 Partial organization chart depicting functional organization.

whom only functional authority exists, he or she generally has the right to issue orders and to make suggestions. With the functional structure, an employee may have two or more supervisors, a potential violation of the unity of command principle discussed earlier in this chapter.

Advantages of functional structure The most distinct advantage of using the functional organizational structure is the expertise provided by the functional specialists. Their expertise enables them to contribute significantly in solving complex problems that arise within their specialized areas. Unlike some of the others, the functional structure prevents employees from slighting certain specialized areas within the organization.

Disadvantages of functional structure The confusion that arises when an employee has two or more supervisors is a weakness of the functional structure. Another potential disadvantage is the tendency for some managers to evade areas in which they have functional authority, a situation that may impact negatively on the coordination of activities.

Product Structure

What is the essence of product structure?

When the **product structure** is used, a company's products provide the basis for its structure. Each major product is given division status, and a top-level official—perhaps a vice president or general manager—heads the unit. Line and staff organization is frequently used within each division. The product structure functions well when the various divisions of an organization are dispersed geographically from one another. Each division, by having its own functional areas, such as production, marketing, finance, personnel, and corporate affairs, operates as an autonomous unit.

The concept of product organization is presented in the partial chart in Figure 2-3. In the illustration, each of the major products is placed in separate divisions, with a vice president heading each unit. The vice presidents for finance and corporate affairs basically perform staff activities.

Advantages of product structure The product structure enables the various divisions to develop processes and procedures that best meet their needs. When an alternative structure is used—line and staff, for example—the processes and procedures are likely standardized throughout the organization. Furthermore, each division is able to coordinate its activities without undue constraint from headquarters.

Disadvantages of product structure The product structure allows each division to "go its own way," especially more so than some of the other structures. This may result in the failure of some divisions to work toward a common goal. Furthermore, the problems experienced by certain divisions may be felt throughout the entire organization.

Committee Structure

Although not everyone agrees that the **committee structure** should be viewed as an organizational structure, its use provides an important function in most organizations. Some committees perform important managerial functions, whereas others are simply advisory in nature. The purpose for which a particular committee is formed has a significant bearing on its perceived importance. This type of organizational structure is appropriately used in conjunction with any of the three types of organizational structures previously discussed. Although some committees within organizations have perpetual existence, others are dissolved after they fulfill their designated functions.

What are the advantages of committee structure?

Advantages of committee structure Recommendations made by a committee are often accepted more readily than are those made by one individual. In addition, the widely varying views of the committee members broaden the nature of their recommendations and increase their acceptance by others, seeming to increase the validity of the recommendations. The use of the committee structure also reduces the risk of making a wrong decision.

Disadvantages of committee structure Committees are often criticized for requiring considerable time to function properly. Not all committees are equally productive, especially those dominated by certain individuals.

Matrix Structure

The **matrix structure**, which is the newest of those presented in this chapter, is most frequently used by organizations undertaking a complex project. This structure integrates both vertical and horizontal relationships into a temporary new unit called a project. Figure 2-4 illustrates the matrix concept.

Matrix structure involves temporarily borrowing employees from vari-

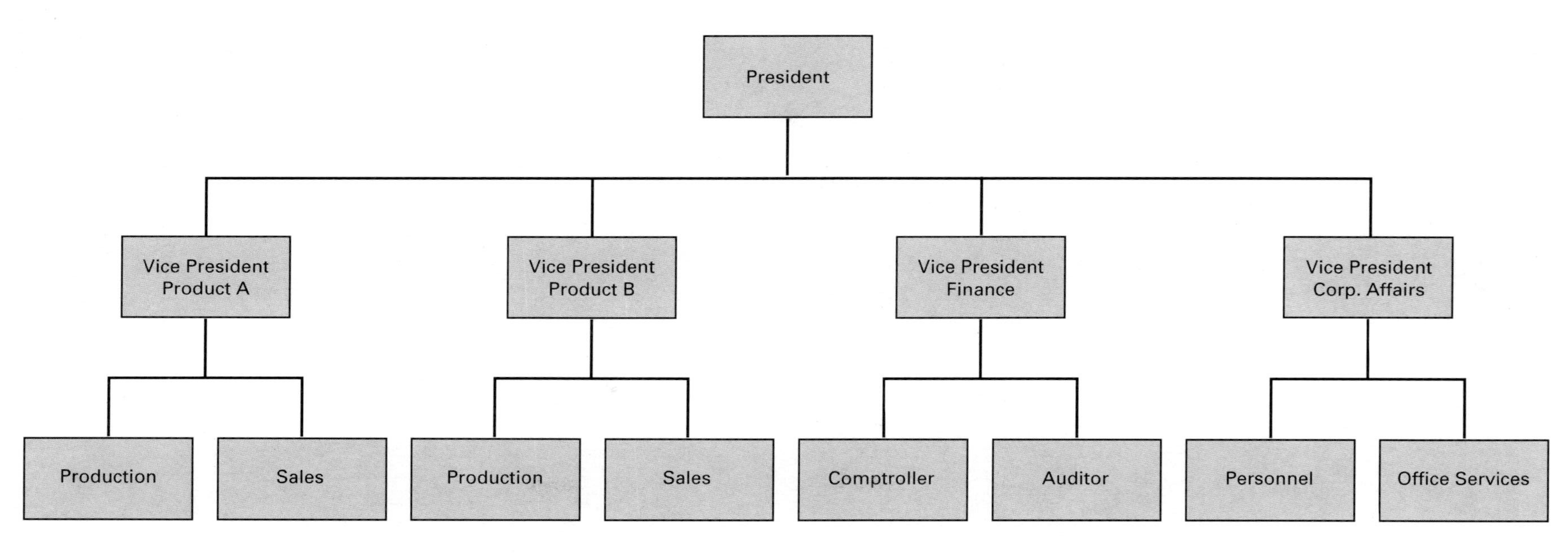

Figure 2-3 Partial organization chart depicting product organization.

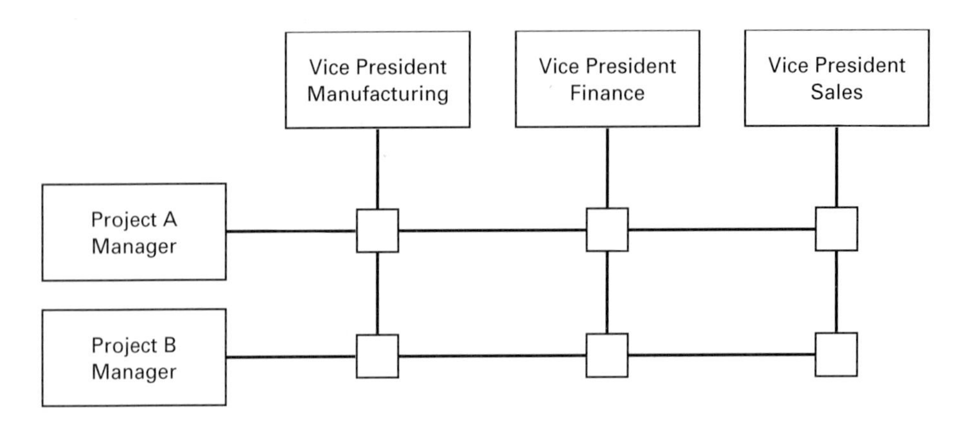

Figure 2-4 Matrix structure.

What are the characteristics of matrix structure?

ous functional areas—such as manufacturing, finance, and sales—and reassigning them to work part-time or full-time on a project. Those who are borrowed are likely to have expertise in various phases of the project. For example, if Project A involves developing, manufacturing, and marketing a new product, employees in these functional areas who have relevant expertise are the ones likely to be assigned to the project. Perhaps five employees from manufacturing, three from sales, and one from finance are temporarily reassigned. In the matrix structure, an employee can have his or her job split several ways—among several projects and the permanent position. Once the project is completed, employees generally return full time to their respective permanent units.

Advantages of matrix structure The use of the matrix structure enables organizations to assign employees with expertise in certain areas to work on complex projects, resulting in more efficient use of human resources. The alternative to this may result in the organization's having to hire employees with expertise in specialized areas to work on the project. But once the project is completed, employees either have to be terminated or integrated into a functional area, which may not be an easy task. The use of matrix structure also facilitates the involvement of employees from several functional areas. Its use facilitates the organization's adapting quickly to a given situation because employees with expertise in specialized areas can be readily reassigned to a project.

Disadvantages of matrix structure In an organization using the matrix structure, employees may have two supervisors—the manager of the functional area and the project manager. This situation violates the unity of command principle discussed earlier. Unity problems are more likely to occur when an employee works part time on the project and part time in a functional area. Also, some employees believe that the matrix structure creates job-related pressure. Managers may find greater difficulty in coordinating the activities of employees when they are temporarily assigned to a project than when they are permanently assigned to a functional area.

CENTRALIZATION VERSUS DECENTRALIZATION

Activities that were formerly decentralized in many organizations are now being centralized. **Centralization** involves placing related activities under the jurisdiction of one person. The activities may be performed centrally, or they may be performed in several locations. The former arrangement is known as centralized control over centralized operations; the latter is known as centralized control over decentralized operations. With **decentralization**, several individuals located throughout the organization have control or jurisdiction over related activities.

As an example, consider a centralized records management program. One individual within the organization is responsible for the program, and the records of the various functional areas are most likely stored in one central location. Conversely, if records management is decentralized, the managers of each unit are totally responsible for the maintenance of the records in their respective departments. In addition to records management, other office activities that may be centralized are mail services, reprographics, word processing, data processing, employee selection, and so forth.

Several degrees of centralization are found within the administrative office management area. The highest degree of centralization is the placement of all office activities under the jurisdiction of the administrative office manager, with the unit supervisors responsible for the day-to-day supervision of those employees who perform these activities.

Also quite widely used is the alternative that centralizes certain office activities, whereas other activities remain decentralized and under the jurisdiction of individual units or departments. The administrative office manager is responsible for the centralized office activities, whereas unit or department managers maintain responsibility for the decentralized office activities within their respective areas. In many cases, the managers of the other units or departments make use of the expertise of the administrative office manager in solving office-related problems found within their departments.

Computer technology facilitates the centralization of a variety of activities within the organization. One such example is data processing. On the other hand, some office activities, such as the organization's mail service, can be centralized without using computer facilities.

Factors that Determine the Feasibility of Centralization

What factors determine the feasibility of centralization?

Following is a discussion of several of the factors that determine the extent to which centralization of office activities is feasible or desirable.

Nature of organization The greater the volume of office work and paper processing activities found in the organization, the more desirable the centralization of office activities becomes. Two types of organizations—financial institutions and insurance companies—have centralized most of their office activities because of the vast amount of paperwork they process. Other types of organizations not as paper intensive may find centralization less crucial or desirable.

Size of organization As organizations become larger, the need for centralized control over certain operations increases. An example is the purchasing function. Without the coordination that results from centralized control, various activities may not be carried out efficiently.

Diversification of organization Organizations widely diversified in their products, processes, and personnel often find centralization to be somewhat awkward. Therefore, only a minimum number of office activities and perhaps even fewer other types of activities are likely to be centralized in widely diversified organizations.

Conformity to standardized processes Standardized procedures tend to be used in centralized activities. The extent to which standardization is possible determines the feasibility of centralization.

Quality of personnel Many organizations find that higher-quality employees are needed when office activities are decentralized than when they are centralized. When operations are centralized, activities are usually overseen by a specialist who is able to direct more closely the employees' activities. In decentralized operations, however, the unit or department manager may know little about specialized office activities. The employees, therefore, will have to assume greater responsibility for determining the proper ways to do their work.

Distribution of operations When the operations of an organization are distributed over a wide geographical area, physical centralization may be less feasible. An organization, however, may be able to centralize control over the activities even though they are carried out decentrally.

Attitude of personnel Regardless of the amount of time, effort, and planning expended in centralizing office activities, nothing will likely be gained as long as employees resist the change to centralization. In some instances, the process of overcoming employee resistance will consume more time than the actual planning of the change. Unless this resistance can be overcome, centralization may not be possible.

Advantages of Centralization

What are the advantages of centralization?

When compared with decentralization, centralization of office activities results in the following advantages:

1. Work methods and procedures are carried out more uniformly.
2. Duplication of effort and equipment occurs less frequently.
3. Duplicate copies of documents are not as likely to be stored.
4. Employees' skills are better used because workers can be assigned to their areas of specialization.
5. Work processes are standardized.
6. Peak workloads can be handled efficiently because all employees in the unit can be assigned to help with the peak work.
7. Absence of an employee does not disrupt the performance of a task or job.
8. Salaries are more equitable because management can easily determine which employees perform comparable jobs and therefore should receive comparable salaries.

Disadvantages of Centralization

The disadvantages of centralization include the following:

What are the disadvantages of centralization?

1. Centrally locating an activity may result in more employee time being consumed in transporting work to and from the unit.
2. Widely dispersed centralized activities may not be equally accessible to all personnel.
3. The technical nature of some work cannot be efficiently accommodated in a centralized unit.
4. The confidential status of materials cannot always be maintained when they are processed through a centralized unit.
5. Centralization does not always permit the assigning and completing of work according to its priority.

1. Hierarchical relationships should be determined to place individuals or departments of similar hierarchical importance on the same horizontal level.
2. Vertical and horizontal authority are identified by solid lines.
3. Functional authority is illustrated with dotted lines.
4. The titles illustrated on the chart should be complete.
5. The chart should include the name of the organization and the date of its preparation.

Figure 2-5 Guidelines for use in preparing organization charts.

ORGANIZATION CHART

The formal relationships between various individuals and the organizational structure are illustrated on an **organization chart**. The chart identifies lines of authority and responsibility, flow of work between individuals, and span of control. Although the chart illustrates who reports to whom, it does not illustrate informal relationships between individuals.

The organization chart illustrates hierarchical relationships; therefore, it is most logically constructed by starting at the top and working downward in a vertical arrangement. The primary functions of the organization and the subfunctions within each primary function must be identified. An alternative to the vertical arrangement is the horizontal arrangement in which the highest-ranking position is placed on the left and the lowest-ranking ones on the right.

What guidelines are useful in preparing organization charts?

Figure 2-5 identifies several guidelines helpful when preparing organization charts.

The organization chart, by identifying lines of authority, gives employees a better understanding of the formal structure of the organization. It also helps identify areas of overlapping responsibility that should be eliminated. Furthermore, the chart is used to identify promotional opportunities for job applicants and new employees, as well as to identify areas suitable for training and orientation.

The most significant disadvantage of the organization chart results from its failure to illustrate the informal interaction that is necessary between employees as they carry out their day-to-day activities. Another disadvantage is the impression the chart may give that all departments or units can be well defined and are distinguishable from one another, which may not always be the case.

INFORMAL ORGANIZATION

What is informal organization?

Formal organization—discussed earlier in this chapter—is planned organization established by formal authority. Many of the spontaneous personal and social relations that exist in an organization, however, are more appropriately classified as **informal organization**.

Informal groups and informal communication patterns are two important elements of informal organization. Informal groups tend to have a powerful influence on their members. Often, standards of conduct or performance are imposed on individuals by the work group to which employees belong. The behavior of the informal group can be either a help or a hindrance to the administrative office manager.

To illustrate how informal organization can be helpful, suppose a new procedure has been installed in a work unit. Also suppose the procedure, although efficient, is not popular among employees. If the manager can get the informal "leaders" in the work unit to accept the new procedure, they may also be able to convince others to accept the new procedure.

Informal organization can also be a hindrance to management. Suppose, for example, that an informal group loses confidence in the capability of the group's manager. The group can make life so miserable for the manager that he or she resigns. In some instances, the informal group may be able to pressure the manager's superior to force the manager's replacement.

IMPLICATIONS FOR THE ADMINISTRATIVE OFFICE MANAGER

The attention administrative office managers give to the organizing function contributes significantly to their success. Most managers agree that the more attention given to this function, the more readily able they are to stay abreast of activities for which they are responsible. Their management strategies can be more proactive and less reactive when they give the organizing function the attention it deserves and requires. When managers are in a proactive position, they are able to control their destinies; when they manage from a reactive position, the situation at hand essentially controls their destinies.

The organizing function helps administrative office managers in several ways, including the following: increases the efficiency with which they are able to carry out their job functions; promotes better working relations with subordinates and superiors; facilitates the development of effective work processes and procedures; enables them to maintain more effective control over their areas of responsibility; and helps in the coordination of various activities.

REVIEW QUESTIONS

1. What benefits result from giving adequate consideration to the organizing function?
2. Why should objectives be clearly defined?
3. What determines an adequate span of control for a supervisor?
4. Why should an employee be responsible to only one supervisor?
5. Why is the line structure not feasible in some organizations?
6. What are the basic differences between line structure and line and staff structure?
7. What basic concepts characterize functional structure?
8. What is meant by centralization and decentralization as the terms relate to the organizational process?
9. What is informal organization? Why cannot informal organization be depicted on an organization chart?
10. What guidelines are helpful when preparing organization charts?

DISCUSSION QUESTIONS

1. Identify the organization principles violated in the following situation:

   Supervisor A is responsible for the employees in her department in addition to three employees in another department and two employees in a third department. When any of these employees have a problem, they have been instructed to go immediately to the person to whom Supervisor A is responsible. Supervisor A is primarily responsible for enforcing the company's policies—but whenever an employee violates a policy, he/she is referred immediately to Supervisor A's superior.

2. When Joe Blewit was recently interviewed for the position of president of a company founded twenty-five years ago—a firm that presently has more than 200 employees—he made the following comments: "If I am hired, I will expect each manager to perform as a line manager. No room exists in this organization for staff managers. As far as I am concerned, staff managers are never able to pull their fair share." Discuss the fallacies in Blewit's thinking that caused him to lose the presidency.
3. Assume you are employed as an administrative office manager in a large company that manufactures electronic computer components. What can you do to convince line managers that your role is as vital as theirs—and not less vital, as some of them think?
4. Assume you have applied for an administrative office manager's position in a local insurance company. During the interview, you found out that the administrative office manager has functional authority for all office employees throughout the organization. Exactly what does this mean in terms of your relationship with the office employees? Does the functional authority relationship increase or decrease your desire for this position?
5. Kirk Schantz, founder and president of Schantz, Inc., a manufacturer of steel buildings, recently became so frustrated with certain company operations that he retained your services as a consultant. After Schantz had spent considerable time discussing his conception of the company's problems, you asked Schantz why managers at all levels failed to delegate appropriate authority to lower levels. Schantz, who went into a tirade, replied, "If a task can be delegated to a lower-level manager and that manager can perform the task satisfactorily, what am I paying these higher-level managers for? I want to get my money's worth from them. Besides, the lower-level managers probably aren't as competent as the higher-level managers to carry out many of these tasks—or else they would be holding a higher-level position." Discuss how you would respond to Schantz.
6. A recent issue of a professional magazine to which you subscribe had an article that discussed the centralization and decentralization of various office activities. A subsequent issue contained the following response to the article in the letter-to-the-editor section of the magazine:

   The article that appeared in the May issue of your magazine was informative, useful, and well written. Unfortunately, it did not mention that decentralization begets more problems than it is worth. As a manager, you can never be sure you will again be in control.

   Do you agree with the letter writer? Why or why not? How can control be maintained over decentralized operations?

STUDENT PROJECTS AND ACTIVITIES

1. Interview a manager in an organization that uses line and staff structure. What does this individual consider to be the most significant advantage of line and staff structure? The most significant disadvantage?
2. Discuss with an administrative office manager the nature of employee participation he or she uses in carrying out his or her job responsibilities.
3. Discuss with an office employee the nature of employee participation he or she experiences in his or her current job.
4. Discuss with a manager the nature of the informal organization found in his or her organization.
5. Examine an organization chart of an actual organization. Is functional authority/organization depicted on the chart? If so, how is it depicted?

MINICASE

You are an administrative office manager who works in the Department of Budget for the State of New York. At a recent meeting of the local management association, you were talking with Betty Brorsen, an administrative office manager in a medium-sized local insurance company. Betty was telling you about the problem they have been having with objectives in the company where she works. Betty indicated that each year objectives are formulated and approved—but at the end of the year, approximately 75 to 80 percent of the objectives have not been met. She also indicated that problems arise not so much from the process that is used to set the objectives but with the objectives themselves. She indicated the objectives handed down to her unit level from the higher levels of management are often vague and confusing.

Before you had an opportunity to provide Betty with some feedback regarding her concern about the situation she discussed with you, the program got underway and you didn't have an opportunity to visit with her later. Accordingly, you decide to send Betty a memo in which you

1. Identify the criteria the objectives should possess that higher-level management is handing down to lower-level management.
2. Identify ideas you have that will cause employees to work harder toward meeting the objectives, a problem she indicated existed in her company.

CASE

The Wilcox Company was founded fifteen years ago by two cousins, Sean Wilbur and David Cox. The company manufactures a variety of equipment and tools used in oil and gas drilling operations. For several years, the company's profits were marginal.

Because of a recent increase in well-drilling activity abroad, the company's sales have improved considerably. At the present time, the company employs only six individuals who have management responsibilities. The duties each of these individuals performs are not clearly defined, except that each of the six is involved either with production or marketing efforts.

The increased sales volume of the company is placing significant pressures on the six managers. They are no longer able to perform all their varied duties. The owners of the company decided that before any new managers are hired, the effectiveness of the organizational structure should be examined. Accordingly, they contracted with you, a consultant, to provide them with the feedback they need. You plan to present your impressions orally to Mr. Wilbur and Mr. Cox, along with presenting them a written report. Prepare the report (as a memorandum) in which you do the following:

1. Identify the organizational structure currently being used.
2. Make a recommendation regarding continuation of the current organizational structure or its replacement with another structure.
3. Present the factors that influenced your decision regarding the appropriate organizational structure for Wilcox Company.
4. Identify and discuss the significant problems the company will likely experience (a) if the present structure is continued or (b) if a new structure is implemented.

CHAPTER

3

THE COMMUNICATION PROCESS

CHAPTER AIM

After studying this chapter, you should be able to develop an appropriate philosophy regarding the important role communication plays in administrative office management.

CHAPTER OUTLINE

- Elements of Communication Process
- The Flow of Communication
  - Downward Communication
  - Upward Communication
  - Horizontal Communication
- Small-Group Communication
  - Reasons People Belong to Small Groups
  - Advantages and Disadvantages
- Large-Group Communication
- Nonverbal Communication
  - Impact of Nonverbal Cues on Communication Process
    - Confirming
    - Replacing
    - Contradicting
    - Emphasizing
  - Elements of Nonverbal Communication
    - Body Language
    - Paralanguage
    - Proxemics
    - Time
- Barriers to Effective Communication
- Development of Listening Skills
  - Elements of the Listening Process
    - Internal Elements
    - Contextual Elements
    - Relationship Elements
  - Suggestions for Improving Listening
- Application of Communication Process
  - Decision-making Process
    - Steps
    - Nominal Grouping Technique
  - Conflict Resolution
    - Sources of Conflict
    - Conflict Resolution Strategies
  - Implementation of Change
    - Steps
- Implications for the Administrative Office Manager

CHAPTER TERMS

Barriers
Body language
Communication process
Decision-making process
Downward communication
Gestures
Grapevine
Groupthink
Horizontal communication
Listening
Nominal grouping technique
Nonverbal communication

Paralanguage
Planned change
Proxemics
Reactive change
Small-group communication
Time
Upward communication

Administrative office managers spend a major part of each workday engaged in the common types of communication: reading, writing, speaking, and listening. In fact, in a typical workday, they will spend more time engaged in communicating than in any other activity. The vast majority of the tasks for which administrative office managers are responsible involves significant levels of communication. Many administrative office managers find that one of the keys to their success is their ability to communicate effectively.

Several variables affect the communication process. To illustrate, the nature of the message affects the process as does the background of the sender and receiver. Other variables include the following: environment in which communication occurs, the relationship between the sender and receiver, the time of day, and unusual mannerisms of those communicating. Time and effort are well spent by administrative office managers who try to improve their communicating effectiveness by minimizing the negative influence of any of these variables.

ELEMENTS OF COMMUNICATION PROCESS

What elements constitute the communication process?

The **communication process** comprises the following elements: sender, receiver, message, channel, feedback, and noise. Figure 3-1 presents a graphic illustration of the process.

Beginning the communication process is the sender's decision to communicate with the receiver. At this point, the sender forms a message either by creating a thought that he or she wishes to communicate or by selecting a bit of information to transmit. Before the message can be sent, it first has to be encoded, a process that involves translating the thoughts or information into words, signs, or symbols. This step enables the message to be transmitted to the receiver by means of a channel.

Using the message to express himself or herself, the sender typically uses one or more of the following formats: written words, spoken words, facial expressions, gestures, pictures, and so forth. In a face-to-face conversation, the nonverbal elements of the message often convey as much meaning as the spoken words—and in some cases even more meaning. In a written message, the way words are used often affects the outcome.

What is the purpose of the channel?

The message is transmitted to the receiver by means of the channel. The sender can use a variety of channels including face-to-face communication, written documents, telephone conversation, radio, television, and newspapers.

The receiver decodes the message upon receiving it. This process, which is essentially the opposite of encoding, occurs when the receiver interprets the message and gives it meaning from his or her own perspective.

Why is feedback important?

Feedback enables the sender to determine how much of the message was actually received and how accurately the receiver interpreted it. Only when the desired feedback is received can the sender be sure that he or she communicated accurately and effectively. Additional communication is likely to be needed when feedback indicates the receiver misinterpreted or misunderstood the message. Feedback can be in the form of a gesture or an expression that indicates understanding, a request for additional information, a re-

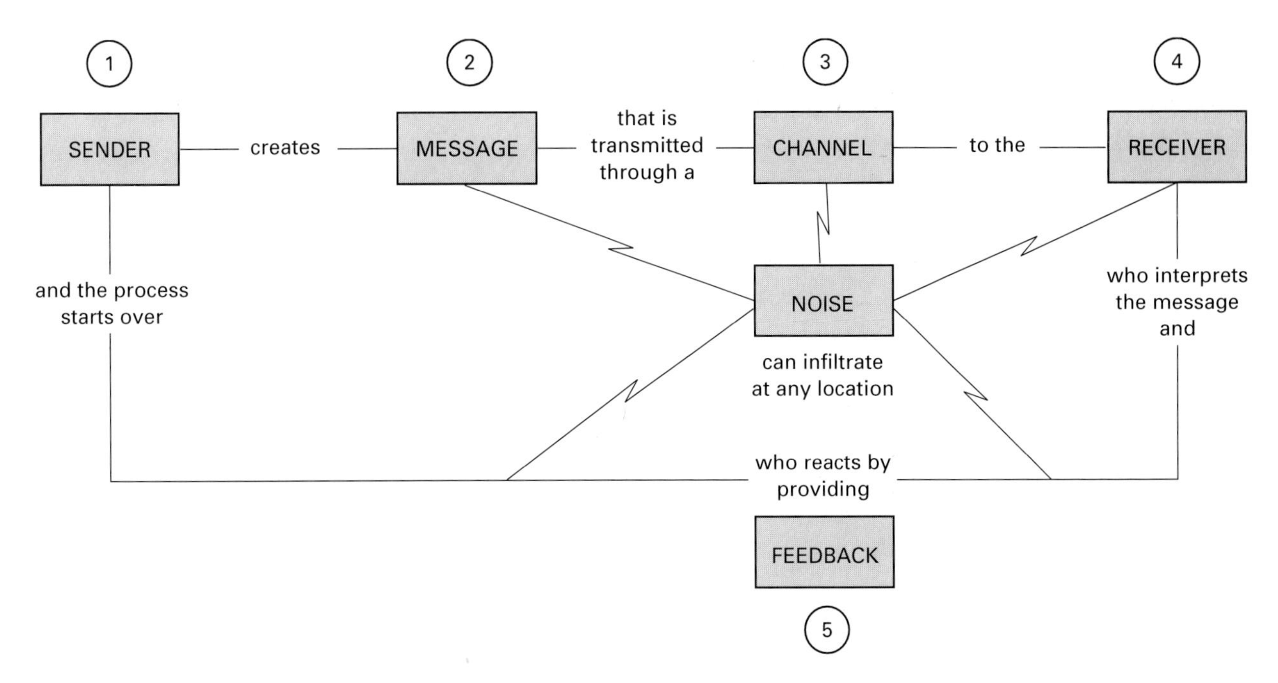

Figure 3-1 Model of the communication process.

quest for clarification, a facial expression, or even failure of the receiver to comply with the sender's request.

Noise, which can enter the communication process at each step, is a distraction or disruption in the communication process. Examples include physical noise, an inconsistency between what the speaker says and his or her facial expressions, and a garbled message.

THE FLOW OF COMMUNICATION

In what directions does communication flow in an organization?

In an organization, communication flows in three directions. Administrative office managers communicate in an upward direction with their superiors, downward with their subordinates, and horizontally with other managers. Most find that talking and listening activities consume more of their time than do reading and writing. Much of the content of this chapter is concerned with what occurs in talking and listening processes.

Downward Communication

What kinds of information are communicated through downward communications?

The success experienced by many administrative office managers is often determined by how well they communicate with their subordinates. Well-informed subordinates not only tend to be more productive, but also tend to derive greater satisfaction from their work. Administrative office managers use **downward communication** to keep their subordinates informed, give them job-related instructions, and provide them feedback regarding their performance.

Among the factors administrative office managers consider when deciding which medium to use in transmitting downward communication are the following:

1. Permanency of record. If an official written record needs to be kept, written communication rather than oral communication is used.

2. Immediacy. If the information needs to be communicated immediately, oral communication may be more appropriate than written communication.
3. Need for evidence of understanding or feedback. When evidence of understanding or feedback is needed, an oral conversation (either face to face or telephone) should be used.
4. Formality. If the communication situation is more formal than informal, then written communication needs to be used.

Employees need to be kept informed about a variety of items, including new policies, procedures, rules, benefits, and developments in the organization. The administrative office manager is responsible for keeping his or her subordinates informed unless someone above him or her does so. Both oral and written communication channels are used. Small-group meetings, manuals, and memorandums are three common techniques for keeping employees informed.

The communication of job instructions to employees has a twofold purpose: to inform them of their specific duties and to instruct them about how these duties are to be performed. A variety of techniques are used, including verbal orders and directions, written job descriptions and procedures statements, manuals, and handbooks. In situations involving complex duties, the use of two techniques (such as verbal directions and written procedures) may enhance subordinate understanding. In deciding which technique is appropriate for a given situation, the manager should consider the complexity of the task and the subordinate's background.

Employees interested in improving their work effectiveness as well as those who need reassurance that they are performing well desire feedback about their job performance. Performance appraisal, which is discussed in Chapter 11, is a formal procedure, whereas giving subordinates oral and written feedback about their performance is informal. Written feedback is considered to be more official than oral feedback.

Among the factors that affect the success of downward communication are the appropriateness of the communication channel that is used, the timing and clarity of the message, and the attitudes of those involved in the communication process. When the desired outcome of downward communication is to produce either an attitudinal or behavioral change in a subordinate, the manager has to be even more concerned about the factors that affect communication success.

In addition to the mediums already mentioned, others include house organs, bulletin boards, pamphlets, posters, annual reports, conferences, interviews, grapevine, public address, and speeches.

Upward Communication

The value of **upward communication** in organizations is more apparent today than ever before. Until the human relations movement emerged several decades ago, management solicited little if any input from subordinates, and minimal value was placed on the input it received.

Today, most employees have a strong desire to convey to supervisors and managers their feelings, ideas, aspirations, and attitudes. Employees rightfully believe they know better than their superiors what is best for themselves. Employees also believe supervisors and managers can and should consider and use their input.

Several types of information are transmitted upward from subordinates

What types of information are transmitted through upward communication?

to the administrative office manager. Although some of these communication encounters with the manager are optional, others are required. Examples of upward communication include information about one's job and work-related problems, organizational policies and procedures, and suggestions for improving existing practices. In most instances, upward communication enables subordinates to relate more closely to and identify with their superiors.

The factors considered in deciding which downward communication channel to use are the same ones considered when deciding which upward channel to use. Upward channels can be either written or oral.

Upward communication provides a useful feedback function, just as downward communication does. Management can use the input to assess the effectiveness of its practices. In addition, management often assesses the quality of subordinates' input in evaluating their promotability to higher-level positions.

The effectiveness of upward communication is influenced by such variables as the nature of the relationship between the subordinate and the manager; the quality of the subordinate's presentation of the message; the extent to which the content of the message is positive or negative; the timeliness of the message; and the extent to which the substance of the message is useful.

Examples of upward communication include suggestion systems, grievance procedures, face-to-face conversations, written and oral reports, and questionnaires.

Horizontal Communication

While upward and downward communication tend to have a more formal status, **horizontal communication** is more informal. Authority relationships that exist between senders and receivers in vertical communication do not exist in the horizontal communication that occurs between individuals of equal hierarchical ranks.

What is the function of horizontal communication?

Horizontal communication provides a useful function in the organization. In addition to helping employees fulfill certain socialization needs, it helps employees and departments coordinate their activities with one another. Horizontal communication enables others to understand better the nature of individual and departmental responsibilities. It is also used to help individuals solve their own problems before others have to become involved in these interpersonal entanglements.

The effectiveness of horizontal communication is influenced by the communication abilities and the interpersonal relations skills of the sender and the receiver. Common examples of horizontal communication are face-to-face conversation and small-group meetings.

What is the grapevine?

As a type of informal communication, the **grapevine** is an unofficial communication tool employees of the same hierarchical level use initially to share information with one another. Depending on the situation, the information may subsequently be shared with individuals in other hierarchical levels until it is transmitted throughout the entire organization. Sometimes the grapevine is activated because of the failure or absence of formal communication. The grapevine communication process, given its nature, is fast and surprisingly accurate. But in some cases, the information transmitted through the grapevine is nothing but an unfounded rumor.

Management can successfully use the grapevine to assess employee reaction to a proposed change. For example, suppose management is thinking about installing a cafeteria approach to fringe benefits. The grapevine can be used as a barometer to measure the level of employee acceptance of the cafeteria approach. If the level of acceptance is sufficiently high, the program can be installed; if not, the idea can be scrapped.

SMALL-GROUP COMMUNICATION

For administrative office managers, **small-group communication** has important implications because much of their oral communication occurs within groups of ten or fewer persons. In small groups, administrative office managers occupy three hierarchical levels. They can be the highest-ranking individual, be of equal rank with all the members, or be outranked by one or more of the members. Understanding the dynamics of small groups will help the manager more effectively maximize their use.

Small groups are more than just a mere assemblage of individuals who happen to be at the same place at the same time. Having a reason for existing, groups are structured so they can accomplish their tasks as efficiently as possible. They also typically operate according to guidelines or established procedures.

The administrative office manager's membership in some small groups is involuntary, especially within staff groups. A common example of such a group is one comprised of the administrative office manager and his or her subordinate supervisors. The administrative office manager usually presides over periodic group meetings in which problems are solved, decisions are made, and information is passed downward to the unit supervisors or upward to higher level managers.

Administrative office managers are also required to participate in staff groups comprised of their equals and presided over by their superior. Common functions of these groups are also problem solving, decision making, and information sharing.

Reasons People Belong to Small Groups.

Why do people belong to small groups?

People belong to groups for a variety of reasons. The extent to which group participation meets members' needs largely determines the amount of satisfaction they derive from their belonging.

Security, one of the reasons for which humans voluntarily join small groups, is one of the basic needs of humans. Employees who are either new to the organization or to their position often feel more secure when they belong to a small group that is relevant to their needs. In most cases, the employees who join small groups are all of equal rank, and the membership of the group may change fairly often.

Another reason employees sometimes voluntarily join small groups is for the power or strength that numbers can exert. The ideas and suggestions promoted by a group tend to be listened to and implemented more often than when the same ideas and suggestions are provided or supported by one person. This is especially true if management needs to be persuaded to take a particular action. Such groups tend to form as issues arise, and the group membership changes as issues change.

Some employees—managers especially—join small groups to have ready access to advice that others can provide. When managers have a specific problem to solve or desire feedback, a small group comprised of their equals is helpful, especially when they do not believe consulting their superior or subordinates is appropriate. Often these group members can provide the needed moral support. Although groups of this type operate rather informally, they can greatly enhance managerial effectiveness.

Advantages and Disadvantages.

The small-group process is characterized as having several advantages and disadvantages. A significant advantage results from the increased breadth and depth of information available within a group. In addition, groups are generally able to identify a greater number of approaches to problem solving than an individual can generate. Managers also find that involving employees as a group is an excellent way to increase their commitment to the solution of a problem.

What is groupthink?

One of the potential disadvantages that results from the small-group technique is the tendency for the process to produce conformity among its members. **Groupthink** considerably reduces a group's creativity because all members begin to think alike. Also of significance is the tendency for one or more persons to dominate the group, which may also reduce its effectiveness. In most instances, the group process is slower than the individual process; a group may become counterproductive once it begins to stray from its original mission.

LARGE-GROUP COMMUNICATION

The nature of large-group communication with which administrative office managers are concerned generally involves their planning or participating in meetings and conferences. The leadership capabilities of many administrative office managers enable them to play a critical role in planning a variety of large-group communication situations, including meetings and conferences.

1. Set date, time, and place of meeting or conference. If the meeting or conference is to be held off the premises, ample time will have to be allotted for locating a suitable facility where the event can be held. The greater the number of participants involved, the earlier the event will have to be scheduled.
2. Plan program or agenda. If the event is primarily designed to share information with the participants, the usual procedure is to plan a program with a variety of presenters or speakers. Ample time will have to be be allotted to ensure their availability to make the presentation and for them to prepare their presentation. The printed program needs to be distributed with the announcement of the meeting. If the event primarily has a decision-making focus, an agenda will likely be used. Parliamentary procedures or customs typically determine the order of the items on the agenda. The agenda needs to be distributed with the announcement of the meeting.
3. Arrange for supplementary materials and needed equipment. The individuals responsible for planning the meeting or conference are often responsible for the duplication of materials distributed by the presenters or speakers. Arrangements also have to be made for audiovisual equipment needed by those making presentations.
4. Arrange for dissemination of postmeeting communication. A variety of types of postmeeting communication is distributed to participants and others. Examples of such communication are proceedings, minutes, abstracts, reports, and so on. Those responsible for planning the event may also be responsible for the preparation or distribution of postmeeting communication.

Figure 3-2 Elements involved in planning meetings or conferences.

Although some of the meetings or conferences that administrative office managers help plan are job related, other events they help plan involve the professional and civic organizations to which they belong.

When planning meetings and conferences, several elements need to be considered including those presented in Figure 3-2.

NONVERBAL COMMUNICATION

The nonverbal element of the communication process speaks just as loudly as the verbal element—and at times even more so. Therefore, administrative office managers may learn just as much by assessing the nonverbal cues of those with whom they are communicating as they can by listening to the message being communicated. Managers not only should have an understanding of the significance of others' nonverbal cues but also should learn how to use these cues to maximize the effectiveness of their own communication.

Impact of Nonverbal Cues on Communication Process

Nonverbal cues can affect the communication process by

In what ways do nonverbal cues impact on the communication process?

Confirming These cues confirm a verbal message, such as when a person points to an object while mentioning it in a conversation.

Replacing These cues replace spoken words. An example is a negative nod replacing a verbal negative response.

Contradicting These cues, which contradict the verbal message, add an element of confusion to the communication process. In most cases, the nonverbal cues tend to be more reliable than the verbal message. An example is a person whose facial expressions indicate that he is in considerable pain but who says that he feels fine.

Emphasizing These cues support the verbal message by emphasizing certain aspects. For example, a speaker may emphasize an idea in a speech by slowing down and distinctly verbalizing key words as he pounds on the podium.

Elements of Nonverbal Communication

Nonverbal communication is expressed in several ways. The most common way is through **body language**; other ways are **paralanguage**, **proxemics**, and **time**.

What are the elements of body language?

Body language In the communication process, the human body speaks a language of its own. Gestures, posture, facial expressions, eye contact, and touch comprise the elements of body language.

When communicating, the **gestures** people use often provide cues about their emotional state, especially when gesturing occurs simultaneously with certain facial expressions. As people become more excited, their gestures tend to become more expansive. Anger and hostility are often signaled through clenched fists, whereas finger tapping and foot tapping indicate nervousness. Folding one's arms across the chest signals uneasiness or disinterest, whereas opened arms and hands show openness and receptivity.

Another common gesture that can either enhance or impede the communication process is head nodding. An affirmative nod from the listener shows agreement with the speaker's message and signals for the speaker to continue speaking. A negative nod signals disagreement—and often will cause the speaker to quit talking.

Posture often sends signals about an individual's mood. An upbeat, happy mood is generally signaled through an erect, upright posture, whereas a sad or unhappy mood often causes people to slouch.

Facial expressions play a large role in the communication process. Of all the parts of the human body involved in communicating, the face tends to be the most expressive. The muscular structure of the face enables several of its parts to communicate simultaneously. For example, certain simultaneous expressions of the jaw, lips, eyes, and forehead communicate anger. Happiness is communicated nonverbally through the lips and eyes, whereas disgust tends to be expressed through the lips, eyes, and forehead. Feelings of sadness and fear are communicated by the eyes and forehead.

People often use facial expressions to hide their true feelings in much the same way that individuals do not always verbalize their true feelings. Just as people learn to say the right things at the right time, they also learn to make the right facial expressions at the right time. Facial expressions inconsistent with the message add an element of confusion to the communication process. Therefore, the receiver does not know whether to believe the verbal message or the nonverbal message.

The communication between two people is also influenced by the nature of the eye contact between them. By maintaining direct eye contact with the speaker, the receiver signals that the communication channel is open and that he or she wishes to continue listening. Direct eye contact may also indicate solidarity, whereas a break in the contact may signal that the receiver desires to end the communication process. A break in eye contact may also indicate a feeling of tension, distrust, or uneasiness. Conversely, a cold stare signals a feeling of authority or domination.

Touching is often used in the communication process to support the verbal message that it accompanies. A handshake is a cordial nonverbal greeting that supports the verbal greeting. Even the firmness of the handshake is considered by many to carry a nonverbal message about one's assertiveness. A pat on the back during the verbal exchange indicates solidarity, approval, and support. The same feelings can be communicated by grabbing hold of someone's arm during the conversation.

What is paralanguage?

Paralanguage The way people express themselves—known as paralanguage—often communicates more meaning than their verbal messages. When voice quality is inconsistent with the verbalized message, the speaker's sincerity or credibility may be questioned. To be believed, people have to sound as though they mean what they say.

Among the voice elements that affect the communication process are range, rate of speaking, pitch, volume, pauses, and intrusions. The more variable the range of one's voice, the less monotonous it will be. Consistently speaking in a monotone conveys the impression of disinterest, whereas a more variable range conveys an impression of commitment and enthusiasm. A change in the rate of speaking is effectively used to emphasize the importance of certain ideas or thoughts.

Emotional feelings are conveyed by the pitch of the speaker's voice. A high-pitched voice signals excitement and enthusiasm, whereas a low-pitched voice signals seriousness. Importance is attached to key items by verbalizing them more loudly or softly. Pauses in speaking, which may indicate contemplation, are also effectively used to help recapture the listener's attention. Such intrusions as "ah" or "um" tend to signal tension, a feeling of pressure, or lack of certainty.

What is proxemics?

Proxemics Also having an impact on communication is the way people structure their territory and space, which is known as proxemics. When their space is inhibited, employees tend to become less comfortable and more inhibited.

The nature of the situation should be considered in determining an appropriate location to hold a communication encounter. For example, a manager who wishes to have a cordial discussion with a subordinate will find that a neutral location may enhance their discussion. An informal conversational area in the manager's office is more neutral than the space around the manager's desk. If the situation requires that the manager defend his or her position or negotiate with another person, territorial strength can be enhanced by remaining behind the desk, even though doing so creates a natural communication barrier. The amount of control one has over the communication process is greatly affected by the location of the encounter.

Humans continuously maintain "protective custody" of the space around themselves. This space moves with people as they move about. A distance ranging from 18 inches to 4 feet is reserved for visual and social encounters, whereas an area closer than 18 inches is reserved for intimacy. An inappropriate violation of one's space—regardless of the range—often creates a barrier in the communication process.

The ambience of the room in which the communication is occurring affects the communication process. Rooms that are warm and cheerful tend to create a more cordial communicating atmosphere, whereas a cold, unfriendly ambience may detract from the communication process. The nature of the seating arrangement also affects communication. People seated beside one another will find communication more difficult than will those who are seated across from one another.

The artifacts and objects in one's work area also communicate. Office furniture is an indicator of status. Wooden office furniture tends to communicate more status than metal furniture; optional pieces, such as credenzas and upholstered furniture, also communicate status. Artifacts, by providing a conversational topic, often enhance the communication process. Membership and award certificates provide clues about one's professional involvements, leadership, and expertise. Whereas they rarely stimulate the amount of conversation that artifacts do, certificates provide recognition for their beholder.

How does time communicate nonverbally?

Time The time of day that people communicate may provide insight into the importance of the message. For example, you would likely attach more importance to a request by your superior to see her "first thing in the morning" than to a request that you see her "tomorrow whenever it fits into your schedule." When you receive an after-work telephone call from your superior, the message likely will be interpreted as having more importance than if you received the identical message while you were at work.

When a caller arrives late for an appointment, the negative nonverbal message that is conveyed can be interpreted in several ways. Arriving late may signal that the caller is undependable, unreliable, or unorganized. It may also signal that the caller believes the person with whom he or she is meeting does not have sufficient importance or status to merit arriving on time.

How well people manage their time in meeting deadlines conveys a message about their work habits and organizational skills. Those who are habitually late are viewed as being disorganized and unable to manage their time well. The situation may be further compounded when people accept more responsibilities than they can effectively handle in the allotted time, which conveys the impression that they are inefficient in their work habits.

BARRIERS TO EFFECTIVE COMMUNICATION

What are the barriers to effective communication?

Regardless of our position in life, we continually need to work at becoming more effective communicators. Being aware of the **barriers** to effective communication is one way to improve communication abilities. Skilled communicators are able to minimize or neutralize the impact these barriers have on their communication activities.

A potential impediment to the communication process results from taking certain things or people for granted. For example, we may assume that a listener has the needed background information about a problem situation when in fact he has very little information. Or we may take for granted that the listener has almost no background information, and we provide several details about which he is already familiar.

In some instances, managers mistakenly believe that subordinates do not care to interact with their supervisor. In reality, subordinates often desire to have more opportunities to interact with management than are available. Incorrectly perceiving the amount of communication appropriate for a given situation can significantly hamper one's effectiveness.

Some of the characteristics of upward, downward, and horizontal communication also create barriers. For example, when downward communication makes no provision for feedback, management can never be certain how much of the message was received, understood, or interpreted correctly. In addition, management and subordinates often perceive downward communication differently. So what management believes is a reasonable rationale for a certain course of action, subordinates may interpret as an attempt to manipulate them. Because some subordinates are generally suspicious of their superiors, they question the validity of much of the downward communication they receive.

Upward communication is affected by certain barriers, just as downward communication is affected. When subordinates have an opportunity to communicate upward, they tend to transmit only the information that enhances their standing with their superiors. The message will likely become distorted if negative information is withheld. In other instances, subordinates provide the information they believe management wants to hear. A serious information void is created if subordinates misinterpret the type of information management desires or if they withhold information management badly needs.

Upward communication is also affected by management's reaction to the information it receives from subordinates. If management continually avoids making use of the information it solicits, subordinates will likely discontinue providing it. Unless management conveys the impression that it appreciates receiving information from employees in the lower levels of the organization, only minimum amounts of input are likely to be provided.

Semantics can also create a communication barrier. Because words mean different things to people, the manner in which individuals interpret the words can create a communication barrier. Consequently, if the speaker uses a word to which the listener attaches a different meaning, the opportunity for miscommunication is present.

A communication barrier can also be created by perception. We all have perceptions, often largely affected or influenced by our experiences. Miscommunication can occur when individuals who actually see the same phenomenon or hear the same message believe they saw or heard something else.

In addition, certain barriers affect horizontal communication, which is informal. Interpersonal rivalry between two individuals may cause one person to withhold information from another, primarily to put that person in a disadvantaged position. In other cases, a person may pass on preconceived notions as though they were true, which may cause some communication difficulties. As humans, we often tend to let our feelings about others affect our communication with them. Because actions tend to speak louder than words, disguising our true feelings may be difficult.

DEVELOPMENT OF LISTENING SKILLS

Although **listening** is the weakest communication skill of many administrative office managers, most, ironically, spend more time each day listening to others than reading, writing, or speaking. To improve their listening skills, managers may have to undertake their own development efforts because minimal time in formal education is devoted to these critical skills.

Elements of the Listening Process

The listening process is affected by internal elements, contextual elements, and relationship elements.

Internal elements If the listening process is to be effective, the listener not only has to hear the message but also has to be able to attach meaning to the words that constitute the message. The listening process breaks down when the listener either does not hear or does not understand the message.

Another internal element is the individual's capacity for listening. The length of time individuals are able to listen and the amount of information they are able to absorb in a given time varies considerably from person to person. An individual's listening capacity also varies from hour to hour and from day to day.

What are the contextual elements of the listening process?

Contextual elements The listening process is also affected by the context or environment in which communication occurs. Among the contextual elements are the presence of noise, the constraints of time, the accessibility of the sender and receiver to one another, and the communication channel that is used.

As managers move upward in the organization hierarchy, time pressures become more significant. Special care has to be taken to prevent these pressures from having a negative impact on managers' ability to listen. In addition, access to managers diminishes as they move upward, which may eliminate some opportunities for them to interact with others.

Also affecting the listening process is the type of communication channel being used. In some instances, individuals may be able to listen more effectively in a face-to-face conversation than in a telephone conversation. In other instances, the opposite will be true.

Relationship elements The nature of a relationship that develops between a sender and receiver as they communicate affects the listening process. A cordial relationship enhances listening; a strained relationship destroys listening.

1. Concentrate on what the sender says by clearing your mind of other thoughts and by giving the communication process your undivided attention.
2. Avoid doodling or playing with desk accessories of objects while interacting with others.
3. Accept senders for whom they are and not how they express themselves or how they appear.
4. Avoid "tuning out" senders whose conversation may not be intrinsically interesting to you because the content is dull, irrelevant, or difficult to understand.
5. Learn to "listen" to the nonverbal component of a message with your eyes as well as to the verbal component with your ears.
6. Keep your listening speed consistent with the sender's conversation rate.
7. Seek clarification of messages you do not understand.
8. Learn to listen more objectively by not allowing your preconceptions, biases, or prejudices to infiltrate the communication process.
9. Listen as intently to unimportant messages as you do to the important ones.
10. Avoid "listening between the lines" in oral communication in the same way that you avoid "reading between the lines" of a written message.

Figure 3-3 Suggestions for improving the effectiveness of listening skills.

When interacting with certain individuals, the desire to say the right thing at the right time may cause the listener to concentrate more on what he or she is going to say next rather than on listening to the message. Obviously, this destroys listening effectiveness.

For self-protection, the listener in other instances filters out the sender's negative comments. Adverse information is not allowed to penetrate the listener's mind and therefore will not be as "fully heard" as positive information.

Suggestions for Improving Listening

Managers who are effective listeners readily admit that these skills did not just happen; rather, they became better listeners as a result of their conscientious development efforts. Figure 3-3 presents several suggestions designed to help individuals improve their listening skills.

APPLICATION OF COMMUNICATION PROCESS

Administrative office managers extensively use the communication process as they make decisions, resolve conflict, and implement change. This section provides a discussion of these three important topics.

Decision-Making Process

One of the most important responsibilities of administrative office managers is decision making. The communication process is likely to be used actively before a decision is made. This is because administrative office managers often solicit information from others prior to making a decision. After the decision is made, it has to be communicated to others. Managers' effectiveness is often influenced by how well their decisions are communicated to those who are affected by the decisions.

What steps constitute the decision-making process?

Steps The **decision-making process** comprises the following steps:

1. Defining and limiting the problem (or situation).
2. Analyzing the problem (or situation).
3. Defining criteria to be used in evaluating various solutions.
4. Gathering the data/information.
5. Identifying and evaluating possible solutions.
6. Selecting the best solution.
7. Implementing the solution.

Within each step, various aspects of the participants' communication effectiveness can either enhance or impede the ultimate outcome of the decision. Too, the effort that is put into each step can affect the quality of the decision. The accuracy with which a problem/situation is defined at the outset often affects the outcome of the decision. During the entire decision-making process, considerable time and effort can be saved by working with a problem/situation that has been accurately defined. This is the time to ask a variety of questions about the problem/situation. In addition to focusing directly on the problem/situation, an examination of the peripheral circumstances may also be helpful. The more precisely the individuals involved in the decision-making process differentiate between a problem/situation and its symptoms, the more accurately the problem/situation can be defined.

The second step—identifying the circumstances or underlying factors that created the problem/situation—is facilitated by accurately defining the problem/situation. Examples are financial conditions, interpersonal problems between individuals, and poor management. Once the decision makers are aware of the causes of the problem/situation, its solution will be easier.

Those involved in making decisions generally are not given free rein but rather must act within certain constraints in solving a problem/situation; therefore, they need to be aware of their limits. In turn, these limits help when defining the criteria that are used in evaluating various solutions. Examples of criteria are financial considerations, procedural restrictions, human factors, time constraints, and policy restrictions. In some instances, individuals who rank higher than those responsible for making the decision define a portion or all of the criteria.

Once the decision makers are aware of their constraints, they are able to begin identifying possible solutions. The solutions that clearly exceed the limits of the criteria established in step 3 can be quickly eliminated from further consideration. This step will consume less time if the criteria are realistically defined at an early stage.

An effective way to evaluate possible solutions is to determine the impact that each solution will have on the desired outcome. Unless extenuating circumstances exist, the solution believed to provide the maximum positive effect is the one likely to be chosen. Once selected, the acceptability of the solution may be affected by the way in which others are informed of the decision. The more effectively the administrative office manager communicates the decision, the more likely he or she will be able to sell others on its merits.

Typically, communication is extensively involved in the implementation of decisions. Those affected by the decision have to be informed of the decision as well as about its impact on them. Implementation plans have to be developed, in addition to assigning responsibilities for various tasks. Depending on the nature of the decision, a fair amount of time and communication effort may have to be devoted to gaining its acceptance. Communication is a useful technique in diminishing individual resistance.

The nature of some decisions will require the use of certain control measures to help ensure that decisions are being properly implemented. These control devices may be in the form of progress reports, briefing sessions, or other types of follow-up techniques. When results show that corrective measures are needed, the administrative office manager will have to determine the appropriate measures.

What is the purpose of the nominal grouping technique?

Nominal grouping technique Group decision-making processes are becoming increasingly attractive to administrative office managers. The **nominal grouping technique**—a useful group decision-making process—is highly structured and minimizes the amount of personal interaction among the group members. This technique comprises the following five steps:

1. *Listing*. Working alone, each member of the group prepares a written list of ideas or suggestions for solving a given problem.
2. *Recording*. On a one-by-one basis, each member offers an idea from his or her list, and the group leader records each idea on a master list that everyone can see. The members continue to contribute their ideas, one by one, until all ideas are presented.
3. *Voting*. Each member selects the five best ideas on the master list and presents on a ballot his or her ideas in priority preference. The ideas are weighted (for example, the highest-priority idea receives five points).
4. *Discussing*. Each idea is discussed to help clarify any ambiguous points and to evaluate the worth of the various items.
5. *Final voting*. Each member votes a second time, again presenting the ideas in a priority order.

The nominal grouping technique is useful in situations in which members spend considerable time debating the worth of one another's suggestions. This technique enables individuals to spend more time in creative activity and less time in promoting their individual positions.

Conflict Resolution

Another task consuming an ever-increasing amount of managerial time is the resolution of conflict. Although conflict has always existed, managerial recognition of its presence is of rather recent origin. For many years, the prevailing belief seemed to be that if managers did not recognize conflict, then it did not exist, and, therefore, one need not have to deal with it.

A total absence of conflict within an organization is not necessarily a healthy situation. Properly managed conflict within a unit may increase its creativity. It may also increase the number of alternatives identified for solving a specific problem.

What are the sources of conflict?

Sources of conflict Conflict between individuals and within groups arises for several reasons. Most organizations have limited resources that individuals and groups must share. Conflict arises when individual employees or groups of employees believe they are not getting their "fair share" or that others are getting more than their fair share. Another source of conflict results from goal incompatibility. Although overall organizational goals are generally compatible with one another, conflict sometimes arises as a result of incompatibility between overall goals and individual or group goals.

Other sources of potential conflict are the various organizational reward systems. Examples of such reward systems are individual or unit incentive plans, merit salary increase plans, and so forth. When employees believe they have not been treated fairly in relation to others, conflict may result. Various changes in the organizational environment may also stimulate conflict. To illustrate, as the organization responds to a changing environment, the level of responsibility or importance of one unit may increase as the level of another unit decreases, giving rise to potential conflict between the two units.

Regardless of the nature of the conflict situation or the strategy selected for its resolution, the communication process is likely to be used extensively. A certain amount of conflict may have been avoidable had more extensive communication between individuals occurred. Therefore, communication is helpful in preventing a certain amount of conflict from arising and in forming resolution should problems arise.

Resolution strategies significantly determine the effectiveness and efficiency with which conflict is resolved. Before selecting a strategy, the astute manager will assess a variety of factors, including the following:

What factors should be considered in selecting a conflict resolution strategy?

1. *Background of the conflict situation*. Familiarity with the background of the situation helps the manager determine the amount of available flexibility in resolving the conflict. In some instances, almost no flexibility is apparent. The number of people involved in the conflict should be determined. Various issues that must be dealt with before the situation can be resolved also need to be determined.
2. *Background of those involved in the conflict*. Some employees do not find conflict all that unpleasant and, therefore, are likely to become involved more frequently and to a greater extent than other employees. These are the employees who often have a "cause," which results in their becoming preoccupied with the conflict situation. How managers deal with these individuals may be quite different from how they deal with those who are rarely involved in a conflict situation. In assessing the backgrounds of individuals involved in the conflict situation, such factors as their values, attitudes, and beliefs should be considered. The more a manager knows about the backgrounds of the conflicting parties, the more likely he or she will be able to select a strategy that ends a conflict rather than simply puts the conflict into remission.
3. *Relationship between conflicting parties*. The conflict between individuals may be of rather long duration. Even though the severity of the conflict may increase or decrease over time, it is always present. The strategy used to resolve this type of conflict may be quite different from the strategy that is used to resolve conflict between individuals who have never had difficulties with one another before. In addition, the way people feel toward each other may be a consideration in selecting a strategy.
4. *Benefits to be derived from resolving conflict*. In some instances, the conflicting parties may see almost no benefit from their settling differ-

ences with one another. When this happens, the manager may have to be somewhat more creative in his or her resolution efforts and use different strategies. In other instances, the manager may have to use his or her communication skills to convince the conflicting parties that settling their differences is not only desirable for the individuals but also for the work unit.

Conflict resolution strategies The strategies used to resolve conflict often enable some individuals to win and cause others to lose. Rarely will all of the parties involved in a conflict lose, and seldom can they all win.

The importance a person attaches to winning in a conflict situation is directly related to the importance he or she attaches to the issue. People naturally want to win in those situations they consider crucial—therefore, they exert more effort toward winning.

Employees will sometimes rationalize losing the "small ones." Because the odds are against their winning every conflict, they believe they can better their chances of winning the important situations if they lose the less important ones.

A person who has excellent persuasive communication skills tends to win more often than one whose skills are weak. Also, the power that a person can exert is a determinant as is the amount of support that can be mustered from others. The extent to which a person can compromise is also a factor. A small compromise may enable a person to win, perhaps to a lesser degree than he or she would like; however, the inability to make any compromise may result in total loss.

Implementation of Change

Increasingly, administrative office managers are finding themselves in the situation of having to respond to both internal and external forces that result in the need for change. One of the most effective managerial tools to implement change is communication.

Administrative office managers are confronted with two types of change: planned change and reactive change. **Planned change**, which is proactive, occurs as a result of careful planning, developing, and implementing. This type of change precedes the occurrence of events that necessitate change. **Reactive change**, conversely, is generally forced change, resulting from the occurrence of events that make change necessary. Of the types of change, planned change is generally considered to be superior to reactive change, primarily because those involved in implementing the change may have more flexibility at their disposal than when change is forced upon them.

Steps Among the steps involved in implementing change are the following:

What steps are involved in implementing change?

1. *Recognize need for change.* The need for change arises, either as planned change or reactive change, from internal forces, external forces, or a combination of the two. Communication is extensively involved in assessing the need for change.
2. *Plan the change.* Once the need for change arises, the planning process begins. During this step, several ideas are likely to be considered that have the potential for dealing with the various events necessitating the change. This step also involves extensive amounts of communication.

3. *Recommend a plan.* Generally, the recommendation of a plan for implementing the change is presented in a written proposal or report to the decision makers. The recommendation might be presented orally if the situation lacks complexity, however. The plan—whether it is presented in writing or orally—requires the effective use of communication skills.
4. *Decide about the plan.* After the decision makers have had an opportunity to consider the recommended plan, the next step involves making an implementation decision. The nature of the situation for which the plan is being proposed will likely determine who will make the final decision. Those charged with making a decision can range from the organization's board of directors to unit supervisors. Communication is used extensively in deciding whether or not to implement the plan.
5. *Implement the plan.* Once the plan has been approved, the next step involves making implementation plans, followed by the actual implementation. Included in this step is the commitment of various types of organization resources. This step makes extensive use of communication.

People have a natural tendency to resist change, resulting from such factors as fear of the unknown, self-interest, lack of trust in management, and lack of flexibility needed to adapt to change. Communication is one of the most effective tools management has at its disposal for overcoming resistance. Another effective tool is to allow those affected by the change to participate in the planning and implementing process. Supporting those affected by the change as they prepare for the change also helps reduce the amount of resistance.

IMPLICATIONS FOR THE ADMINISTRATIVE OFFICE MANAGER

The ability to communicate effectively is among the most crucial of the various background skills needed of the administrative office manager. No matter how well developed one's decision-making skills are or how well one manages a unit, an individual with weak communication skills will be limited in his or her managerial effectiveness.

Managers are more readily able to disguise weak reading skills than to disguise weaknesses in speaking, listening, or writing. Communication has become such an important criterion for managerial success that every attempt should be made to overcome any deficiencies. Self-study, formal courses, and seminars are three means available for use by managers to improve their skills.

The more effectively one's communication skills are developed, the more meaningful, satisfying, and relevant a person will find the communication process. For example, by learning to read nonverbal cues, the manager will find the verbal message has much more meaning. By being aware of potential communication barriers, the manager can more readily make adjustments to counteract the negative influence of any impediments. The best way to avoid the frustration that frequently accompanies conflict is to develop effective resolution skills.

Unfortunately, in some instances a manager takes the communication process for granted. The fact that an individual has communicated in one form or another since the moment of birth does not necessarily mean that his or her skills are well developed. Communication is spontaneously used many times during each day—and one's skills should be developed to a level where they help rather than hinder managerial effectiveness.

REVIEW QUESTIONS

1. What are the elements of the communication process, and what occurs within each?
2. Identify several specific differences between upward, downward, and horizontal communication.
3. Why do individuals join small groups?
4. In what ways do nonverbal cues affect the communication process?
5. What is paralanguage?
6. What is proxemics?
7. Identify several suggestions that will be helpful in improving one's listening skills.
8. What are the elements of the listening process?
9. What are the steps in the decision-making process?
10. What factors should a manager consider before he or she selects an appropriate strategy for resolving conflict?

DISCUSSION QUESTIONS

1. Assume you are an administrative office manager and that you are talking to an administrative office management class at the local university. One of the students asks you the following question: "What is the nature of the communication skills you use each day in your job?" How would you respond?
2. Because you are a supervisor in the company in which you work, you are concerned about how well and how quickly your new subordinates become "integrated" into the structure. You have observed that those who quickly identify with a small group tend to become acclimated sooner than those who don't. Identify possible reasons why your observation is true. Identify several ways that you might help a new employee become a member of a small group.
3. Do you believe the communication skills needed of today's administrative office manager are more important, equally important, or less important than the skills needed of a manager of forty years ago? Why?
4. Identify a communications weakness of a manager you know, and prepare a list of techniques this individual would find helpful in overcoming the weakness.
5. Some managers fail to recognize the importance of nonverbal communication in the communication process. In what ways is their communication effectiveness being hindered?
6. Assume the two finalists for the administrative office manager position in the company in which you work have been selected. While Applicant A's technical skills are better than B's technical skills, B's communication skills are better than A's skills. They are equal in all other respects. Which applicant do you recommend be hired and why?

STUDENT PROJECTS AND ACTIVITIES

1. Discuss with an administrative office manager the importance of effective communication skills to his or her job success.
2. Observe someone engaged in conversation. What nonverbal signals did you notice?
3. Discuss with a fellow student the reason(s) why he or she has joined one or more campus organizations.
4. Discuss with a supervisor the strategies he or she uses in resolving conflict within his or her work unit.
5. Discuss with a manager the process he or she has found most helpful in implementing change.

MINICASE

You are the administrative office manager in XYZ Manufacturing Company. The philosophy of the company president is to appoint a committee to deal with problems or issues when they arise rather than to bring in consultants. Consistent with this philosophy, he recently appointed you to chair a communications committee that is charged with the responsibility of developing an in-house seminar for employees who wish to improve their communication skills. The president has asked that you provide him with a memo in which you do the following:

1. Outline the methods you plan to use in determining the appropriate content for this seminar.
2. Identify topics or areas that you think should be included in the seminar.

CASE

John Lezenski, the administrative office manager of the L-H Paper Company located in Lincoln, Nebraska, recently attended a three-day management communication seminar. The brochure he received publicizing this seminar stated that it would present "practical, down-to-earth information" about ways managers can improve their communication skills. He was delighted to discover that the seminar did just that, because the following sessions were offered: improving listening skills, understanding the communication process, using nonverbal communication to one's benefit, and overcoming communication barriers.

Mr. Lezenski was also surprised to learn that communication was so important to job success. He was not aware before attending the seminar just how much he communicates on his job, nor was he aware of the extent that effective communication facilitates job performance.

During the seminar, participants were placed in small groups and given a two-part assignment in which they were to do the following:

1. Compose a list of questions a person can ask himself/herself that will be useful in determining the nature of any communication problems an individual might have. (Prepare questions that can be answered with a "yes" or "no" response.)

   After the group completed the list of questions, each participant in the group was asked to use the list to determine the nature of any communication problems he/she might have. Following this, the participants were asked to provide those within their group suggestions for overcoming any identified communication problems. John Galvano, a member of your group, indicated he has a problem with face-to-face communication encounters with his superior.
2. What suggestions can you offer him that will be useful in his overcoming this communication weakness?

OFFICE LAYOUT

CHAPTER AIMS

After studying this chapter, you should be able to design an efficient layout for a general office area.

CHAPTER OUTLINE

- The Preliminary Planning Stage
  - Work Flow
  - Organization Chart
  - Projection of Employees Needed in the Future
  - Communication Network
  - Departmental Organization
  - Private and General Offices
  - Space Requirements
  - Specialized Areas
    - Reception Area
    - Board or Conference Room
    - Computer Room
    - Mailroom
    - Printing and Duplicating Room
    - Central Records Area
  - Safety Considerations
  - Barrier-free Construction
  - Expansion
  - Environmental Conditions
  - Equipment and Furniture
- Costing of Office Space
- Open Office Concept
  - Modular Workstation Approach
  - Cluster Workstation Approach
  - Landscape Approach
- Principles of Effective Layout
- Preparing the Layout
  - Templates
  - Cutouts
  - Plastic Models
  - Magnetic Board
  - Computer-aided Design
- Implications for the Administrative Office Manager

CHAPTER TERMS

Barrier-free construction
Cluster workstation approach
Communication matrix
Communication network
Cybernetics
Modular workstation approach
Office landscaping
Open plan concept
Shared office
Space analysis
Work flow

An organization's productivity can be significantly affected—both positively and negatively—by the layout of its various work areas. From a cost-effectiveness standpoint, designing efficient work areas is critically important. Layout design requires consideration of the interrelationships between the following three components: equipment, flow of work, and employees. These interrelationships must be thoroughly studied and analyzed in the process of planning efficient employee work areas.

Office layout determines if space is used in an efficient and cost-effective manner as well as affects how much satisfaction employees derive from their jobs. Furthermore, layout has an impact on the impression people get of the work areas.

Efficient layout results in the following significant operational and economic benefits:

What are the operational and economic benefits of layout?

1. It provides effective allocation and use of floor space.
2. It creates a pleasant working environment for employees.
3. It has a positive impact on the organization's clients.
4. It facilitates efficient work flow.
5. It provides employees with efficient, productive work areas.
6. It facilitates future expansion when the need arises.
7. It facilitates employee supervision.

Extensive preliminary planning is essential when preparing the layout for a new facility or when making major renovations in an existing facility. Planning—the most important stage in the project—affects all other stages and will ultimately determine whether the final results are effective and efficient.

In addition to preliminary planning, which is discussed in detail in the next section, the undertaking of layout projects involves two other stages: preparing architectural and construction drawings, then constructing or renovating the premises.

Inadequate space planning is likely to result in reduced employee productivity, increased absenteeism, increased turnover, decreased physical comfort, and decreased employee morale. Among the commonest of the situations that result from inadequate space planning are the following:

1. Future growth that is not accurately anticipated.
2. Storage facilities and areas that are inadequate.
3. Office furniture that fails to meet the needs of its users.
4. Work flow patterns that are cumbersome and awkward.
5. Traffic patterns that are inefficient.

Organizations that have a facility manager will likely involve that person in workplace design, along with the administrative office manager. Although the facility manager and the administrative office manager have a differing set of responsibilities within the organization, they work cooperatively in a number of areas, including the design of each employee's workplace.

THE PRELIMINARY PLANNING STAGE

Preliminary planning of office layout is one of the areas in which administrative office managers are often and significantly involved. But once the preliminary work is completed, their involvement may decrease somewhat. Many of the activities of the planning stage focus on assessing the nature of the organization's needs. This information compiled from the assessment process is subsequently transformed into drawings and finally into the actual layout.

In some organizations, employees undertake the preliminary planning. Other organizations base their planning on the collaborative efforts of their employees and consultants.

The preliminary planning stage involves the consideration of several factors. Among the various factors that need to be considered are the following: work flow, organization chart, projection of employees needed in the future, communication network, departmental organization, private and general offices, and space requirements. Other factors include specialized areas, safety considerations, barrier-free construction, expansion, environmental conditions, and equipment and furniture.

Work Flow

What is involved in the flow of work in most departments?

Work flow refers to the movement of information either vertically (between superiors and subordinates) or horizontally (between employees of the same responsibility level). Accurate work flow analysis is critical in the designing of effective layout.

An efficient work flow places employees and equipment in a pattern that facilitates the straight-line flow of information, which helps eliminate backtracking and crisscrossing work patterns. To accomplish the straight-line flow, the duties, responsibilities, and activities of each employee must be thoroughly studied. Giving an inadequate amount of attention to work flow often results in delays in processing information, excessive handling of documents, and the need for personnel to exert more effort than would otherwise be necessary.

The flow of work in most departments usually involves major source documents, typically forms. For example, in a credit department, the major source document may be the credit application; in an accounts payable department, the payment voucher; and in a purchasing department, the purchase order. An effective means of studying the work flow is to follow the movement of the major source documents through the department. The movement may be traced in either of two ways: (1) by preparing and analyzing a flow chart (see Figure 18-7); or (2) by actually charting or diagraming the movement of the document through its work flow patterns (see Figure 18-8).

Because effective layout is based on the interrelationships among equipment, work flow, and employees, an analysis must be made of the effect the equipment component has on the flow of work between employees. More and more, the equipment component involves the use of computer or data processing devices or facilities.

Organization Chart

What does the organization chart depict?

Closely related to the study of work flow is the analysis of the organization chart. When the flow of work is primarily vertical (superior to subordinate or vice versa), the organization chart clearly depicts organizational lines of authority. The organization chart also identifies job relationships among employees of similar hierarchical rank, thus helping determine the appropriate location of employees and work units.

Projection of Employees Needed in the Future

Determining how much space will be needed in the years ahead requires a careful, accurate projection of employees needed in the future. The following should be considered in making the projection:

1. The likelihood of developing new products or services that will require large increases in the number of office employees.
2. The expected yearly growth rate of the firm as measured by profit.
3. The expected yearly increase in the number of employees.
4. The possible changes in office operations that will require new employees.

The absence of careful consideration of these factors may result in the planning of space that is inadequate to meet the organization's needs.

Communication Network

For what is a communication matrix used?

In addition to studying the flow of work between individuals and departments, an analysis of the nature of telephone and face-to-face contact between individuals and departments is essential. When the work flow, the organization chart, and the **communication network** indicate that certain individuals and departments have extensive contact and interaction, the individuals and departments are logically grouped near one another.

To summarize data about the frequency of telephone and face-to-face contacts, the preparation of a **communication matrix** similar to Figure 4-1 is useful.

This is a summary of tally sheets kept by each employee over a representative period (perhaps a two-week period that is void of any unusual fluctuations, such as those created by seasonally busy times of the year). For example, the data in Figure 4-1 indicate that forty telephone contacts were made between the president and assistant to the president, whereas sixty face-to-face contacts were made between these two individuals during the same time.

Departmental Organization

Most organizations continue to be organized by functions, specifically by departments or areas. Such technological developments as the computer, however, have brought about some changes in the structures found in many organizations. Deciding on the location of each department involves considering the flow of work between various departments.

Some departments, such as accounting and data processing, are closely related and should be placed near one another. Likewise, departments with frequent public contact, such as purchasing and personnel, should be located near the entrance or reception area of the building.

Noise-producing departments or areas—such as receiving or printing and duplicating, for example—should be located near one another and away from areas that require a noise-free environment. Areas that cut across all departments, such as central records and word processing, should be located as centrally as possible for reasons of convenience and accessibility. Individuals or departments with minimal public contact, such as the president and other executive officers, should be located in a less heavily traveled, fairly secluded, quiet area of the building.

	President	Assistant to President	Tax and Legal Advisor	V.P. Corporate Relations	V.P. Finances	V.P. Production	Administrative Officer Manager	Central Records Supervisor	Data Processing Supervisor	Sales Manager
President		40/60	10/17	18/10	20/7	10/12	3/0	0/0	3/0	1/0
Assistant to President			30/25	20/16	18/18	7/3	10/8	5/0	18/4	15/10
Tax and Legal Advisor				20/19	8/12	3/0	0/1	4/7	0/0	7/12
V.P. Corporate Relations					17/23	15/12	5/9	0/0	4/2	1/0
V.P. Finances						14/16	5/3	3/1	15/21	5/8
V.P. Production							5/3	4/1	10/5	18/23
Administrative Officer Manager								19/27	15/13	5/9
Central Records Supervisor									21/18	5/8
Data Processing Supervisor										15/18
Sales Manager										

The intersection of the rows and columns is coded as follows:
upper number - number of phone contacts between individuals
lower number - number of personal contacts between individuals

Figure 4-1 Communication matrix.

Private and General Offices

The use of more general offices and fewer private offices is emerging as a trend. In the past, private offices were used for reasons of prestige and status. They were also made available to employees who needed a quiet area for concentration and to those individuals whose jobs involved working with an abundance of confidential materials.

For what reasons are private offices being eliminated?

The following includes a list of reasons frequently cited for doing away with private offices: the cost of building private offices is considerably greater than providing a comparable amount of space in a general office; private offices complicate supervision of employees; the permanent walls surrounding private offices make layout changes difficult; the task of heating, cooling, and lighting private areas is more difficult than in open areas; and private offices impede communication.

Further reducing the need for private offices is the **open plan concept**, which is discussed in the "Open Office Concept" section later in this chapter.

Space Requirements

Several factors determine the minimum amount of space suitable for individual employees and various work areas. For example, employees who use equipment when performing their job functions will need more space than will employees whose jobs do not require the use of equipment. Other factors affecting the space allocation are nature and type of furniture, location of structural pillars and columns, windows, and nature of each employee's job responsibilities. For example, when an employee spends a significant portion of the work day communicating with one or more individuals in his or her office, more space will have to be allocated to accommodate this responsibility.

Minimum space requirements for various individuals and work areas are identified in Figure 4-2. The figures given in the illustration are helpful in approximating the total amount of space an organization requires.

Specialized Areas

A variety of specialized areas should be considered in planning office layout. The nature of the organization is a basic determinant of the areas that are needed or are useful.

Reception area The reception area affects one's first impression of the organization. Good first impressions impact positively on public relations and over the long run may result in increased profit for the organization.

What should be considered in planning the reception area?

The maximum number of individuals expected in the reception area at any one time is considered in determining the approximate size of the reception area. Thirty to 35 square feet of space is allocated for each individual. Therefore, if the maximum number of people anticipated at one time is ten, a space allocation of 300 to 350 square feet will be needed.

The flow of traffic through the area is also considered. The layout should facilitate the movement of people through reception without disturbing those seated in the area. Other important considerations include the choice of furniture, color scheme, lighting, and location of other rooms in relation to the reception area. Blocking the view of office areas from the reception area helps eliminate the possibility that visitors will distract employees.

Individual Room	*Space Requirements*
Top-level executives	425 square feet
Middle-level executives	350 square feet
Supervisors	200 square feet
Office employees	75–100 square feet
Modular workstation	100 square feet
Conference room	25 square feet per person
Reception room	35 square feet per person
Main corridor	6–8 feet wide
Secondary corridor	4–5 feet wide
Cross aisles (every 25–30 feet)	3–4 feet wide

Figure 4-2 Minimum space guidelines.

Some manufacturing organizations use the reception area to display company products, whereas others display a map identifying the location of branch offices. Still others provide short video presentations informing visitors about various organizational operations or activities.

Board or conference room Because the cost of office space is increasing, many organizations cannot afford the luxury of an infrequently used but elaborately appointed board room. Consequently, multipurpose board or conference rooms are often viewed as a desirable alternative. Such rooms are sufficiently elaborate to serve as the board room, yet functional enough to serve as a conference room, helping maximize the use of expensive office space. Depending on the size of the organization and the nature of its layout, additional smaller conference rooms may be located throughout the premises.

What special features might be found in the board or conference room?

Multipurpose board or conference rooms are typically designed with built-in soundproof dividers, which permits the area to be separated into two or three smaller rooms. This design makes possible the simultaneous use of these rooms.

The board or conference room is made more versatile by installing state-of-the art audiovisual and communications equipment. In large board rooms, microphones for voice amplification are sometimes installed in the ceiling; many rooms are equipped with telephones for making and receiving important telephone calls during meetings. Still others are equipped with network jacks that facilitate accessing the computer network. This jack permits the immediate accessing of data and information. In some instances, a teleconferencing system, which is discussed in Chapter 18, is installed in the board or conference room. Other commonly found devices are chalkboards, projector screens, and recording equipment. Limited kitchen facilities adjacent to the room are also common.

What needs to be remembered in planning the layout of the computer room?

Computer room Per square foot of space, the computer room is the most costly of all rooms in many organizations. No other room within an office building has a more restrictive environment. Computer manufacturers stress the importance of considerable preplanning in designing the computer room. Because computer hardware changes so rapidly, space needs to be accurately projected for several years hence. The physical specifications of the computer equipment also must be thoroughly analyzed and taken into consideration before determining the size of the room. Furthermore, provisions have to be made for computer and auxiliary devices located throughout the building to be interconnected to the equipment in the computer room.

In planning the computer room, a fundamental consideration is its location in a fireproof, noncombustible building. The walls, floors, and ceiling of the computer room also need to be constructed of noncombustible materials. Because water can severely damage computer installations, the fire extinguishing systems used in these rooms are gas-vapor based rather than water based.

Strict maintenance of temperature and humidity levels enhances the operation of computer equipment. A temperature of 75 degrees Fahrenheit and a relative humidity level of 50 percent are recommended. Most equipment manufacturers also suggest that the computer installation have its own air conditioning system independent of the building's system.

Typically, computer equipment is installed on a raised platform above the regular floor, a feature that permits future layout changes with a minimum of structural changes. The raised floor protects cables interconnecting the various devices. To conserve energy, some organizations in warmer climates use the air warmed by the equipment as an auxiliary heating system for the building. During the cooling season, the warm air created by the computer equipment is often vented from the room to reduce cooling requirements.

Extensive acoustical control is necessary because of the noise generated by some of the equipment in the computer room. Other factors to consider are providing suitable office space for the computer personnel (programmers, supervisors, and technicians) and suitable storage vaults for tapes, as well as space for the type and amount of auxiliary equipment needed.

Mailroom As a communication center, the mailroom has a significant impact on the efficiency with which information moves in and out of the organization. To a great extent, proper layout can enhance mailroom efficiency. The room should be located near the receiving area of the building and also be centrally located as much as possible. The following three areas are those found in mailrooms:

What areas are typically found in the mailroom?

1. Incoming area—where incoming mail is received and placed in dumping bins.
2. Sorting area—where mail is sorted and readied for distribution throughout the organization.
3. Outgoing area—where outgoing mail is stamped, sealed, and readied for mailing.

The flow of mail through the mailroom should be considered when deciding on the appropriate location of the various pieces of equipment. A more thorough coverage of the mailroom is presented in Chapter 24.

Printing and duplicating room The printing and duplicating room should be located where it is readily accessible to the majority of its users. This guideline often results in the location of the duplicating room near the physical center of the building. Special acoustical construction materials can control some of the noise that equipment makes. The room should also be properly ventilated because some materials found in printing and duplicating processes produce unpleasant fumes and generate a sizeable amount of heat. Other desirable special features are a darkroom, washing and storage facilities, and adequate counter space.

Central records area For maximum convenience, the central records area needs to be located centrally within the organization. Special provision may also need to be made for fire protection, proper atmospheric conditions, and security to prevent unauthorized entry of individuals. Because of the extreme weight of materials stored in the central records area, structural requirements may have to be considered in the construction process.

Safety Considerations

The design and layout of the office should facilitate the movement of employees from one area to another. Layout should enable employees to move easily through the aisles rather than having to take shortcuts through work areas. Aisles and corridors should not be obstructed by equipment or furniture nor should doors swing open into aisles. Stairwells and exits should conform with the guidelines established by the National Fire Protection Association Code No. 101.

Barrier-free Construction

In what buildings does barrier-free construction need to be provided?

The design of layout with **barrier-free construction** is another important factor to consider in planning layout. In 1973, Congress passed the Rehabilitation Act, which requires all new federal buildings and buildings of private organizations in which more than $2,500 of federal funds are used to be accessible to individuals with disabilities. Several states have passed companion legislation. As increasing numbers of organizations employ individuals with disabilities, making the facilities convenient and comfortable for them is essential. Architectural services are able to provide valuable assistance in designing and planning barrier-free work areas.

The 1990 Americans with Disabilities Act also has implications for planning office work areas. This act guarantees equal opportunity for individuals with disabilities in employment, public accommodations, transportation, state and local government services, and telecommunications. Employers are required to provide "reasonable accommodation" to individuals with disabilities, including job restructuring and modifying of equipment. Specifically, a work area or equipment that an employee with disabilities uses in performing his or her duties cannot be an impediment to job performance.

Of concern in planning layout are sufficiently wide aisles, corridors, and doors that facilitate wheelchair passage. Workstations large enough to accommodate wheelchairs require at least a 60- by 60-inch area to make a 180- or 360-degree turn.

Expansion

The possibility for expansion must be considered each time layout is changed. To maximize flexibility, many organizations prepare a yearly space analysis in much the same way that the yearly budget is prepared. A space analysis is usually made for each of the next five consecutive years, for the tenth year, and for the fifteenth year.

When undertaking a **space analysis**, the following categories of space are considered:

What categories of space are considered in undertaking a space analysis?

1. Space needed for employees at all hierarchical levels of the organization. To determine the amount of space for this category, the number of employees needed at various levels throughout the organization is calculated, by which the amount of space to be allocated each type of employee is multiplied.
2. Space needed for special areas including conference rooms, the computer room, and the mailroom. These areas generally contain furniture or equipment that consumes greater amounts of space than typical employee workstations. Therefore, a greater amount of space per employee has to be allocated for these areas than for areas that contain typical employee workstations (category 1).
3. Space needed for corridors and aisles. To accommodate future growth, sufficient space needs to be allocated for corridors and aisles.

Figure 4-3 presents a space analysis chart.

XYZ Company					
	Present needs		*Future needs*		
	No. of employees	*Sq. feet per person*	*No. of employees*	*Sq. feet per person*	*Total*
Corporate offices					
President					
Vice-Presidents					
Treasurer					
Middle managers					
Administrative Office Manager					
Systems and Procedures Manager					
Personnel Manager					
Open office area					
Accounting Department					
Sales Department					
Special areas					
Conference Room					
Computer Room					
Reception Area					
Word Processing Center					
Mailroom					
Copy Center					
Central Records Area					
Special purpose areas				Total (A)	
	No. required	*Sq. feet per item*	*No. required*	*Sq. feet per item*	*Total*
Filing cabinets					
Storage closets					
Corridors/aisles					
				Total (B)	
				Grand Total (A + B)	

Figure 4-3 Space analysis chart.

Environmental Conditions

Environmental conditions, including color, lighting, air conditioning, and noise control, are also important factors to consider in planning layout. Each of these is covered in Chapter 5.

Equipment and Furniture

Equipment and furniture, which have an effect on space requirements, decor, and noise, must also be considered in planning layout. The trend is to use systems furniture, which is comprised of a variety of modules enabling each employee to have the furniture configuration that best meets his or her needs. The topic of equipment and furniture is discussed in Chapter 6.

COSTING OF OFFICE SPACE

With organizations becoming increasingly concerned about the "bottom line," the cost of their office space is being closely scrutinized. In terms of cost, organizations' investment in physical facilities is generally exceeded only by their investment in human resources. A positive cost/benefit relationship is not only desirable, but required.

When an organization calculates the cost of its office space, a number of factors need to be considered. Included are such factors as rent or mortgage payments, utilities, maintenance, maintenance services, taxes, insurance, required environmental control equipment, special assessments, operating licenses and permits, and so forth.

Concern also has to be given to the potential cost of a variety of inefficiencies affecting layout. These include inefficient layout that impedes work flow, poor work space design that impedes maximizing employee productivity, and environmental elements that affect employee well being. Adequate planning early on helps minimize the negative effect of these problems.

In some organizations, the nature of certain employees' duties keeps them away from their work areas for extended periods of time. Examples of such employees are those involved with sales, auditing, and recruiting, as well as those who telecommute (includes employees who are able to work from their homes most of the time). Allocating a separate work area for each of these employees, a work area that is underutilized a significant portion of the time, has a negative impact on the cost/benefit return. For that reason, organizations are beginning to provide these employees with a **shared office**, which means they either share their assigned work area with others or they do not have an assigned work area but rather use any available work area in the shared office unit whenever they are on the premises. Using the shared office concept has enabled some organizations to put off for five to seven years the acquisition of additional office space.

OPEN OFFICE CONCEPT

A critical decision that will have to be made in designing office layout is whether to use conventional walled office layout or the open office concept. If the latter is selected, then a decision will have to be made about which one of various alternative approaches is best suited for the circumstances.

Many of the disadvantages inherent in conventional walled layout are overcome by the open office concept. The conventional approach, which uses many private offices with permanent walls, is based on the hierarchical structure of the organization. The open office concept, conversely, is based on the nature of the relationship between the employee and his or her job duties.

Approximately two out of three offices are presently being constructed or renovated with the open concept. Its popularity is increasing because it provides a cost-effective method of making layout changes. The open office concept is especially attractive in organizations that need to make rapid layout changes. The most frequently heard criticisms of the open office concept are the lack of privacy and noise that employees find distracting.

What is cybernetics?

Open office planning is based on the **cybernetics** of the organization, which means that information flows or processes are considered when designing layout. The information flow of the organization typically consists of paper flow, telephone communications, and personal visits. Open office planning is based on the simultaneously interacting relationships of the following factors: communication, workplace design, and the physical environment. For this reason, systems and procedures analysts and communications consultants should work closely with the architects and interior designers when using the open office concept.

Among the special features of the open office concept are the following:

What factors need to be considered in planning employee work areas in the open concept?

1. Open offices use only a minimum number of permanent walls. Large open areas with approximately 10,000 square feet of space are most desirable for developing the open office concept. By using a floor grid system (5 feet by 5 feet, for example) for electrical and telephone connections, individual workstations can be conveniently placed at any location and at any angle.
2. The location of each workstation affects the efficiency of work flow and helps prevent backlogs as well as crisscrossing and backtracking of work.
3. To provide a suitable work environment, special attention may have to be given to acoustics and noise control. The acoustical devices used in a conventional office may not be sufficient for large open office areas. Sound-absorbing walls, ceilings, panels, and carpeting may have to be used. Acoustical conditioning is sufficient when sounds are no longer disturbing at a distance of 15 feet from the source.
4. Uniform air conditioning and humidity control in large open areas is easily accomplished, although climatic systems appropriate for conventionally designed office areas may not be appropriate for large open areas.
5. Color schemes and furniture arrangements can provide a pleasant working environment for employees. The use of panels, modular furniture, and planters provides privacy while adding aesthetically to the area.
6. The furniture used in an open office facilitates worker efficiency. For example, if a portion of an individual's work is more easily performed in a standing position, the furniture can be designed to accommodate the employee in that position. The amount of storage space given each employee is determined by his or her storage needs. In most cases, conventional desks are replaced with function-oriented workstations.

Several benefits result from the use of the open office concept, including the following:

1. The cost of changing layout in an open space office is much less than changing conventional layout. Moving a square foot of open space costs approximately $1.10 compared with an approximate cost of $19.75 for moving a square foot of conventionally designed space.
2. The initial cost of installing an open office may be as much as 10 to 25 percent less than the cost of installing conventional space.
3. The elimination of permanent walls and private offices increases the amount of usable floor space by as much as 15 to 20 percent.
4. The open office concept improves office productivity by increasing the efficiency of work flow, improving communications, improving worker morale, increasing the feeling of worker involvement, and creating a more comfortable working environment.
5. The openness of open offices helps conserve energy because heating, ventilation, and air conditioning systems are not impeded by permanent walls.

Modular Workstation Approach

What are the characteristics of the modular workstation approach?

A characteristic of the **modular workstation approach** is the use of panel-hung furniture components to create individual work areas. Storage cabinets and files of adjustable height are placed adjacent to desks or tables. Modular units provide employees with a "total" office in terms of desk space, file space, storage space, and work-area lighting. These units, which can be specially designed to meet the specific needs of employees, are illustrated in Figure 4-4.

The modular approach, in certain circumstances, is preferred to either the cluster workstation approach or the landscape approach. The modular approach is especially suited for those situations that require considerable storage space. Also, when contrasted with conventional layout, the modular approach is highly advantageous because most permanent walls are eliminated, and the work area is designed around the specific needs of each user. Another distinct advantage is the ease and speed with which changes in layout can be made.

Cluster Workstation Approach

What are the characteristics of the cluster workstation approach?

The unique characteristic of the **cluster workstation approach** is the clustering of work areas around a common core, such as a set of panels that extend from a hub-like spokes in a wheel. Panels are used to define each employee's work area, which encompasses a writing surface, storage space, and filing space. Although exceptions exist, cluster workstations are not as elaborate as modular workstations nor work areas provided employees using the landscape approach. The cluster approach is well suited for work situations in which employees spend a portion of their work day away from their work area. Figure 4-5 illustrates the cluster workstation approach.

The cluster workstation approach provides the distinct advantage of considerable flexibility in changing layout and in redesigning individual work areas. In addition, this approach is seen as being more economical than either the modular or the landscape approach.

Figure 4-4 Modular work station unit. Courtesy: Steelcase, Inc.

Landscape Approach

What are the characteristics of the landscape approach?

Developed by the Quickboner Team in Germany, **office landscaping** was implemented in that country for the first time in 1960 and is now being used extensively in this country. To a certain extent, landscaping is a blend of the modular and cluster workstation approaches. In addition, it makes abundant use of plants and foliage in the decor. To partition off work areas, furniture is arranged in clusters and at various angles instead of in traditional rows. The landscape approach is illustrated in Figure 4-6.

What are the special features of landscaping?

In its "pure" form, landscaping uses no private offices. Increasingly, however, a "hybrid" landscape rather than the "pure" landscape is found. A ratio of 80 percent open area to 20 percent nonopen area is common in offices in which the "hybrid" version is found.

In conventional layout, having a private office is a status symbol. In landscaped offices, however, status is accorded employees through their work assignments, by the location and size of their work area, and from the type and amount of furniture they are given.

The panels used in modular, cluster, and landscape workstations are available in a variety of sizes and shapes and with several different types of outer surfaces including wood, metal, plastic, glass, and carpet. Panels can be prewired with telephone and electrical connections as well as constructed

Figure 4-5 Movable cluster workstation unit. Courtesy: Westinghouse Furniture Systems.

with special sound-absorbing materials. Some panels also incorporate heating, cooling, and air purification vents.

PRINCIPLES OF EFFECTIVE LAYOUT

Various principles of effective layout are useful in planning and designing office layout. Figure 4-7 shows several principles that can be used effectively as evaluative criteria.

PREPARING THE LAYOUT

The administrative office manager is likely to be largely responsible for planning and designing minor layout changes. In such instances, the information that follows will be helpful.

After completing the study and analyzing each of the important design and layout factors, a scaled model of the floor plan should be prepared. To facilitate its preparation, a construction blueprint that shows the location of support pillars, doors, windows, stairwells, and other structural features will be useful.

Figure 4-6 Office landscaping. Courtesy: Sheraton Worldwide Reservations, Raleigh, NC.

1. Interrelationships among equipment, information, and personnel in the flow of work should be analyzed.
2. Work flow should move in as straight a line as possible. Crisscrossing and backtracking should be avoided.
3. Work flow should revolve around major source documents.
4. Hierarchical and communication relationships between individuals should be considered in planning layout.
5. Individuals or work groups performing similar or related duties should be located near one another.
6. Individuals or work groups with frequent public contact should be located near the entrance to the premises.
7. Individuals or work groups whose tasks require considerable concentration should be placed in a low-traffic, quiet area of the building.
8. Space allocation should be based on the position of the individual, the nature of the work being performed, and the amount of special equipment required.
9. Groups or individuals providing specialized services should be located near those who use the specialized services.
10. Furniture and equipment should meet user needs.
11. Aisles should be sufficiently wide to accommodate the rapid, efficient movement of employees.
12. Safety considerations should be given high priority in planning layout.
13. Large open areas are more efficient than are smaller enclosed areas.
14. Adequate provisions have to be made for lighting, decor, air conditioning, humidity control, and noise control.
15. Concern for future expansion is important.
16. Work should come to the employee, not vice versa.

Figure 4-7 Principles of effective office layout.

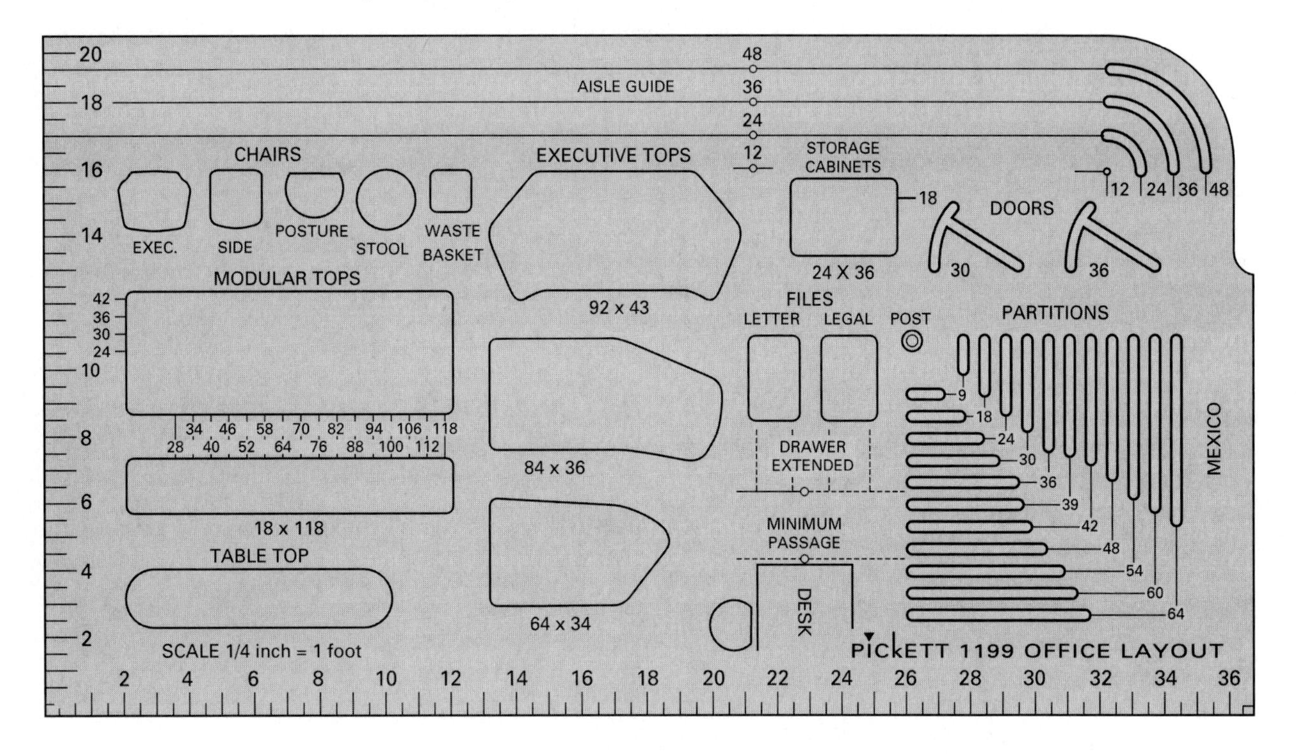

Figure 4-8 Office layout template. Courtesy: Pickett Industries.

What tools are used in planning layout?

Once the floor area has been scaled, the exact location of each piece of furniture and equipment should be determined. Tools available for preparing the layout are templates, cutouts, plastic models, magnetic models, and computer-aided design. To ensure accurate spatial relationships, the floor drawing and the furniture and equipment drawings must use the same scale.

Templates

Consisting of scaled versions of furniture and equipment, templates are typically constructed of cardboard or plastic. The template, which is used in tracing the various items on the layout, is illustrated in Figure 4-8.

Cutouts

Cutouts are purchased in sheets. To use, individual furniture or equipment drawings are simply cut from the sheet. Two types of cutouts are available: paper and self-adhering Mylar. Figure 4-9 illustrates paper cutouts.

Plastic Models

Plastic models are scaled versions of various pieces of office furniture and equipment. The ease with which these models can be repositioned on the floor plan facilitates experimentation with various layout possibilities. Figure 4-10 illustrates plastic models positioned on a layout board.

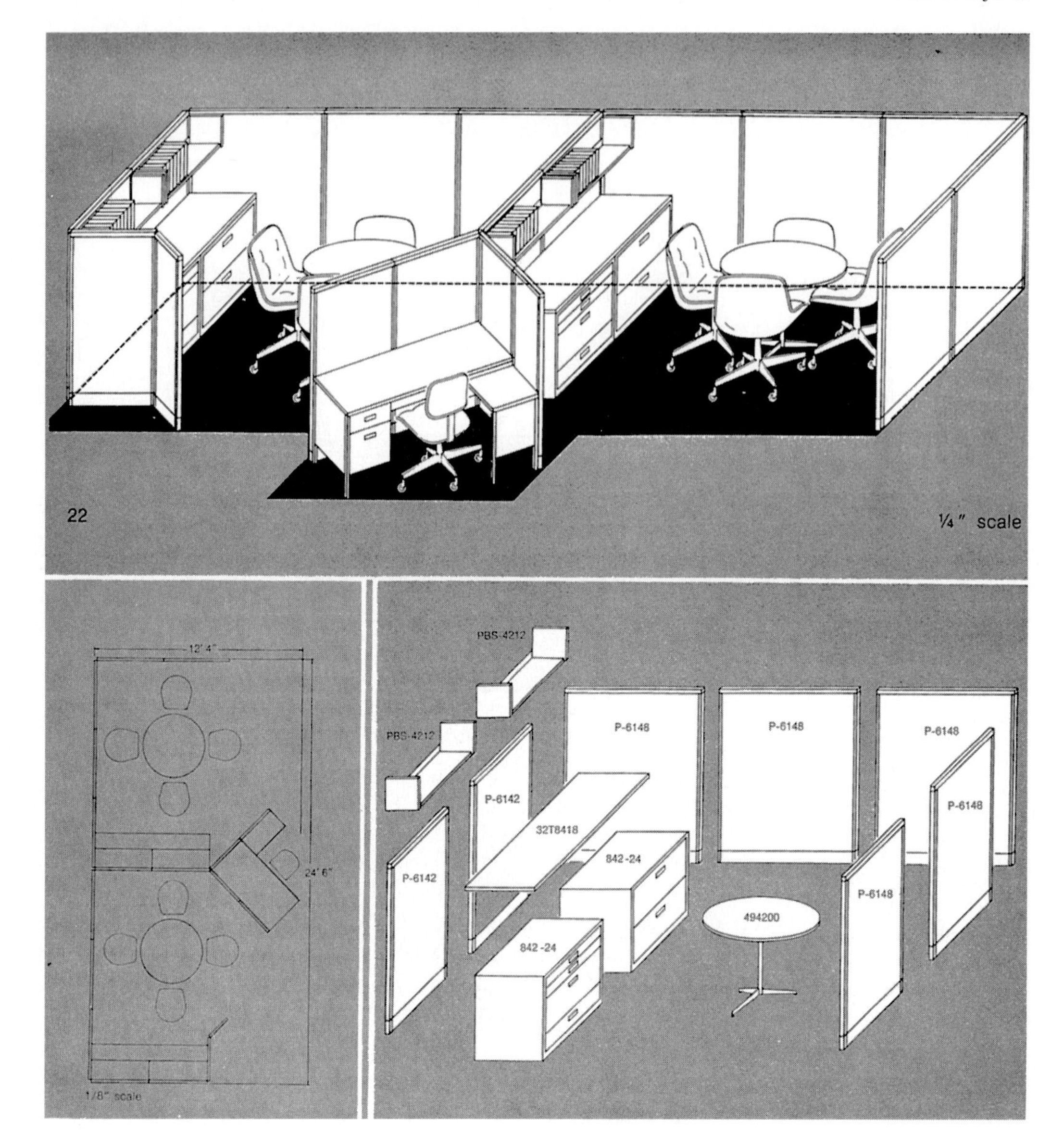

Figure 4-9 Paper cutouts. Courtesy: Steelcase, Inc., Grand Rapids, MI.

Magnetic Board

Magnetized models of furniture and equipment are another frequently used method for preparing office layouts. Although magnetism readily adheres the models to the board, they can be easily repositioned. A layout using a magnetic board is illustrated in Figure 4-11.

Computer-aided Design

Computer-aided design (CAD) uses computer technology and the appropriate program to assist in the designing of effective layout. Several affordable microcomputer software packages are now available that facilitate an easy and efficient layout design process.

Some CAD programs provide an optimum design of the layout after inputting such important variables as area dimensions, size and number of workstations, and aisles and corridors. Others require that the user "draw" the

Figure 4-10 Plastic models. Courtesy: A.D.S. Company, Indianola, PA 15051.

area dimensions and workstation configurations on the video display terminal (VDT) screen. Any items on the screen, such as a wall or piece of equipment or furniture, can be easily relocated using a light pen. Most CAD systems also facilitate the preparation of a printed copy of any screen configuration.

IMPLICATIONS FOR THE ADMINISTRATIVE OFFICE MANAGER

In many organizations, the administrative office manager has the distinction of possessing greater expertise than any other employee in planning and designing layout. The reason for this distinction is apparent: He or she is more familiar than anyone else with many of the factors that have to be considered in the planning and designing process. No other employee is likely to be as familiar with organizationwide work flow patterns or communication processes. Unless the organization employs a full-time space planner, no one else is likely to be more knowledgeable about new developments in layout than the administrative office manager.

A layout project involves more than simply placing furniture and equipment in a given area. Organizations that undertake layout projects by merely rearranging furniture and equipment soon discover that the outcome is not as

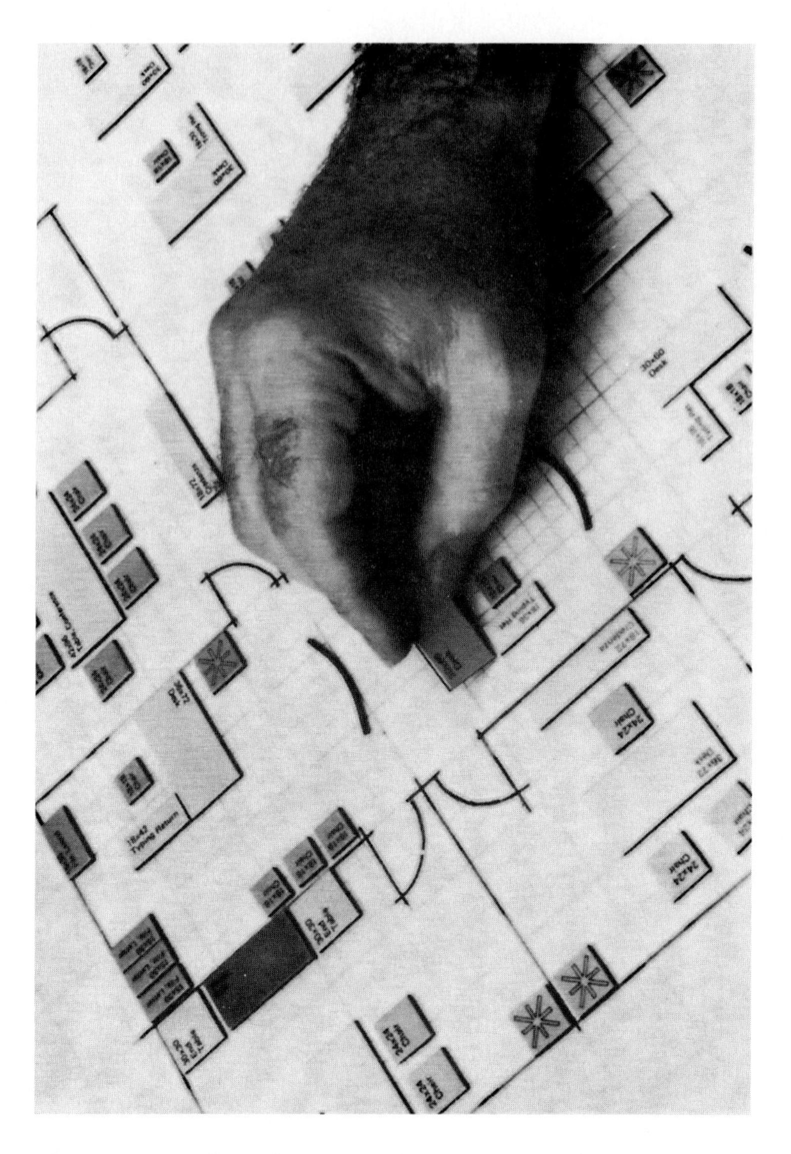

Figure 4-11 Magnetic board. Courtesy: Magna Visual, Inc.

substantial as anticipated. The only way to salvage projects undertaken in this manner is to assess carefully other important factors that impact on office layout and then to make the necessary changes.

Unless the administrative office manager has had in-depth training in designing layout, he or she is well advised to consult individuals who have the needed expertise. The consulting costs will likely be offset many times by having an efficient, effective layout from the beginning, especially if the alternative is a layout developed through a hit-or-miss process.

REVIEW QUESTIONS

1. How does the layout of an office impact on its efficiency and productivity?
2. What do you consider to be the five most important factors that have to be dealt with during the prelimi-

nary planning stage of a layout project? Be prepared to discuss the factors you identify.
3. When planning layout, why is the study of the work flow important? How might the work flow be studied?
4. What reasons are responsible for decreased use of private offices in office buildings?
5. What factors determine the appropriate amount of space to allocate to each individual within the organization?
6. What factors should an organization consider in determining the cost of its office space?
7. What are the characteristics of open planning?
8. What are the characteristics of office landscaping, and what are its benefits?
9. Discuss five principles of effective layout and give or cite examples where you have seen these principles violated.
10. What tools are available for use in preparing office layout diagrams?
11. What is CAD?

DISCUSSION QUESTIONS

1. During a recent conversation with a friend of yours, you mentioned that you had just been appointed the task of studying layout in your department and that your input will be used in making necessary changes. Your friend indicated he felt this was an unwise use of your time. He said he felt the best way to arrange work space was to set desks in "nice, neat rows." Explain why your friend's thinking is not valid.
2. You are a member of an office layout planning committee. You volunteered to be responsible for designing a form to be used in determining the nature and amount of communication that takes place between employees. What types of information do you plan to gather on the form? What uses do you anticipate for this information?
3. The company in which you work is getting ready to move to a different facility. No immediate remodeling of the new facility is planned; and because most of the offices are private, a system will have to be designed for assigning specific individuals to specific offices. What factors should be considered in making specific office assignments?
4. The architects who are presently designing the new headquarters building for the organization in which you work have been told to use the open plan concept. The present layout makes extensive use of private offices. When the employees heard about the use of open space planning, many expressed negative feelings about the concept. You, as an administrative office manager, know well the success of open planning may be jeopardized if these negative feelings continue to prevail. Yet, the extensive use of private offices in the new building is out of the question. What can you do to reduce employee resistance to the open plan concept?
5. You were recently asked, as the assistant to the administrative office manager, to prepare a scaled model of the floor plan of a large open area in which thirty-five to forty employees will soon be relocated. In preparing the model, you simply drew "little boxes" to represent the furniture and equipment of each employee. The boxes you drew did not necessarily reflect the shape or size of the items they depicted. When you gave the drawing to your boss, she rejected it, indicating that you had wasted your time. Why would the type of drawing you prepared be impossible to use in designing layout?
6. You recently attended the monthly meeting of a professional organization to which you belong. The speaker's topic was concerned with office environment. During the question-answer period that followed the presentation, the speaker was asked to identify the differences between the open plan concept and office landscaping. He replied that virtually no differences existed between the two concepts and that if you are familiar with one concept, you are familiar with the other as well. Do you agree with the speaker? Why, or why not?

STUDENT PROJECTS AND ACTIVITIES

1. Talk with an office space designer regarding the specific tasks he or she is concerned with in planning office space.
2. Talk with an architect about the specific requirements he or she must be concerned with in designing barrier-free office areas.
3. Tour an office that uses the modular plan and one that uses the cluster approach. What are their similarities? What are their differences?
4. Tour an office that uses open space planning. In what specific ways is employee privacy provided?
5. Talk with an administrative office manager who is responsible for space planning in the organization in which he or she works. How does this individual keep abreast of the need for greater amounts of employee work space?

MINICASE

When the Donovan Insurance Company built its new building seventeen years ago, conventional office layout was used. Many private offices with almost no open space were used. The board of directors recently approved an extensive remodeling project, resulting in the updating of the facilities. Before any decisions are made about the new layout, the vice president in charge of coordinating the renovation project has requested you, the administrative office manager, to determine whether or not landscaping is feasible. Prepare the report for the vice president in which you

1. Identify the factors that should be considered in determining whether or not landscaping is feasible.
2. Present the advantages that would result from the use of landscaping if it were used in designing the new layout.

CASE

Tom Gaffey and Peter Finney, partners in a law practice, are adding a third partner, Richard DeFrain, to their practice. This necessitates moving to a new location. They have purchased a building that contains approximately 2,000 square feet. Except for the restrooms, a small galley-type kitchen, and the mechanical room, the area is open.

You, an office designer, have been hired by the law firm to design the layout of its new facility. Except for the permanent walls that already exist, the attorneys have specified that no others are to be added except for their offices and the conference room. Movable partitions are to be used to achieve privacy in the other areas. The following personnel are to be planned for in designing the layout:

3 attorneys
2 legal secretaries
2 clerk typists
1 receptionist
1 law clerk (this individual compiles briefs for the attorneys and is responsible for the law library)

The equipment and furniture consists of the following items:

9 desks and desk chairs
16 four-drawer file cabinets
6 credenzas (one for each attorney, one for each legal secretary, and one for the law clerk)
10 four-shelf bookcases (one for each attorney and the remainder are to be placed in the law library)
4 sofas (one for each attorney and one in the reception area)
12 straight-back chairs (four for each attorney's office)
3 small round conference tables (one for each attorney)
1 conference table

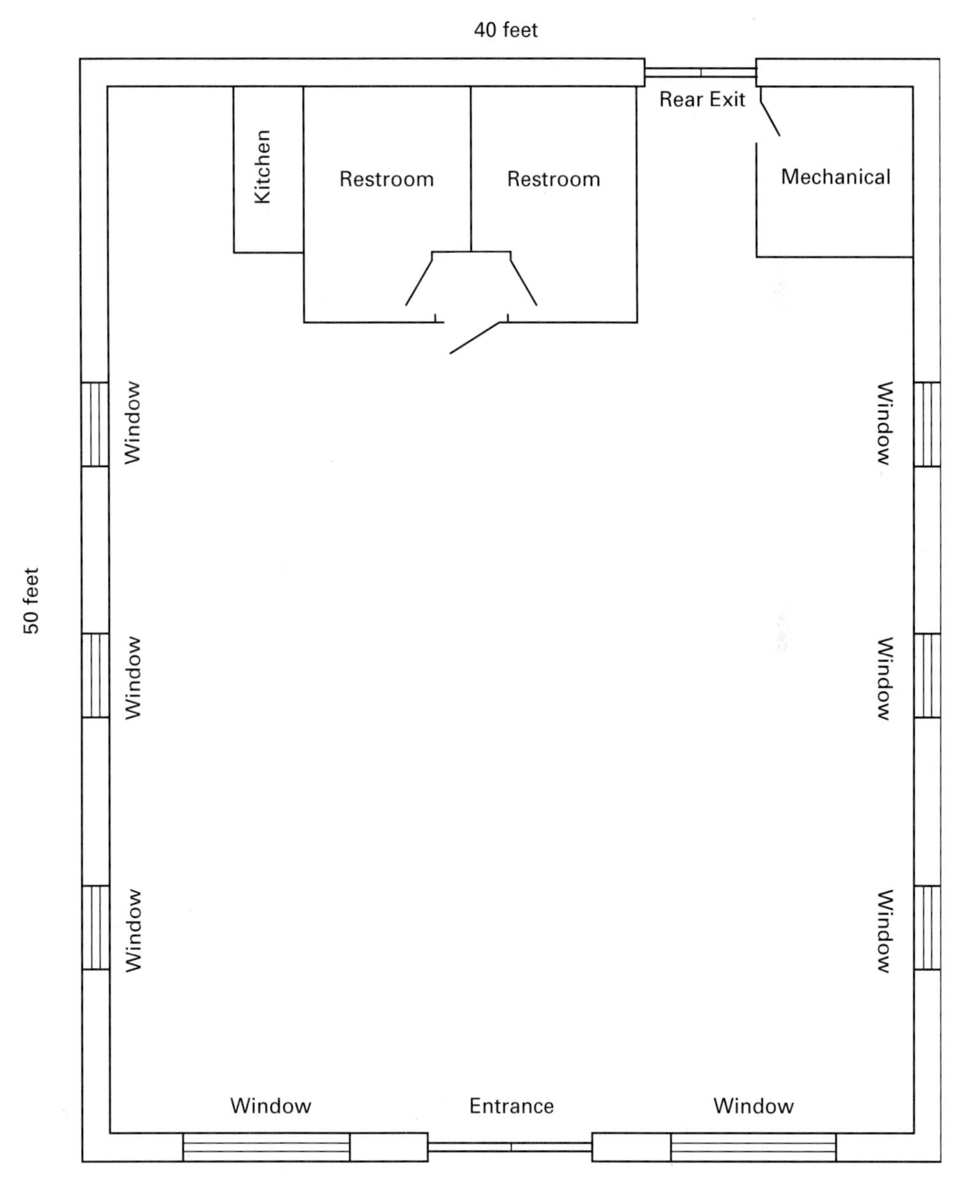

Figure 4-12 Layout.

10 conference chairs

8 chairs (four each in the law library and reception area)

5 computers and tables (used by the legal secretaries, clerk typists, and receptionist primarily for performing word processing functions)

Using an enlargement of the diagram, prepare a layout showing the location of permanent walls, the location of each piece of furniture and equipment, and the location of the movable partitions (Figure 4-12). (Note: Your instructor will provide you with paper cutouts of the various pieces of furniture and equipment that are to be placed on the layout.)

CHAPTER

OFFICE ENVIRONMENT

CHAPTER AIM

After studying this chapter, you should be able to design an effective environment for a general office area.

CHAPTER OUTLINE

CHAPTER TERMS

Decibel
Direct lighting
Equivalent Spherical Illumination (ESI)
Ergonomics
General diffuse lighting
Indirect lighting
Masking-sound system
Office environment
Primary colors
Secondary colors
Semidirect lighting
Semi-indirect lighting
Smart office
Task/ambient lighting
Task Illumination (TI)
Tertiary colors
Visual Comfort Probability (VCP)

The physical environment of the area in which employees work can have a significant effect on their productivity as well as their job satisfaction. Consequently, a number of the elements of the **office environment** can affect the financial well-being of the organization either positively or negatively. Whenever making environmental changes, the potential financial impact of these elements should be calculated. In some instances, decreased employee productivity rapidly erodes monetary gains.

A number of the environmental elements, especially lighting, heating, cooling, and energy conservation, increasingly are becoming computerized. This practice results in what is often referred to as a **smart office**. Several technologies are likely to be either partially or fully integrated in the smart office, including data communications, data processing, environmental control, office automation, security, and fire/life protection systems. Among the more common features of a smart office are the following:

What is a smart office?

1. Small-zone lighting, heating, and air conditioning. These systems light, heat, and cool small areas rather than entire floors. Consequently, employees who work after hours or on weekends have their area accommodated without having to light or heat/cool the entire floor. While the lights might be activated by motion or body heat sensors, the heating/cooling system is likely activated by means of a telephone.
2. "Smart-wired" telecommunications systems. Included in many new office buildings is a "smart-wired" telecommunications system in which a telephone is used to perform a number of functions, including voice and data communication, electronic mail and messaging, energy management, fire protection, and life/safety systems. The keypad on the telephone is typically used to activate and/or control several of the systems, while others, such as fire protection, operate automatically. A growing number of developers of office buildings are installing telecommunications systems for their tenants who simply lease the telephone system and needed phone lines from the developer. A shared system enables tenants to have a more sophisticated system at a lower cost than they might otherwise be able to afford.

The environment of the office is multifaceted. A number of factors, including lighting, color scheme, acoustics, and condition of the air, affect the environment. Each of these topics is discussed in this chapter. Layout, which was discussed in Chapter 4, and furniture and equipment, which are discussed in Chapter 6, also affect the environment. Some of the environmental elements impact significantly on an organization's energy consumption. A discussion of energy conservation programs is also included in this chapter.

THE IMPACT OF THE OFFICE ENVIRONMENT ON EMPLOYEES

What is ergonomics?

Each of the elements of the office environment can affect office employees physically and psychologically. **Ergonomics**, the study of the relationship of employees to their physical environment, is helpful in designing a suitable environment. Thus, ergonomics helps assure that the task, the tools and equipment, and the environment in which the employee works match his or her needs. Special effort should be directed toward modifying those ergonomic factors or elements that impact negatively on employees.

Ergonomics, by integrating several disciplines—including psychology, physiology, sociology, and communication theories—provides useful guidelines for designing an effective environment. The integration of the various disciplines helps assure the employees' well-being and the ability to maximize their productivity. The use of ergonomics means employees' work areas are based on their needs, and the methods they use to carry out their job tasks are based on their capabilities.

Evidence of the failure to consider the environment of the office may be noticed in several ways. An unsatisfactory environment often results in decreased levels of productivity and employee morale. Absenteeism and tardiness are apt to increase, as are the number of errors made by employees. In extreme cases, the employees' physical well-being may even be jeopardized.

THE HEALTHY OFFICE ENVIRONMENT

One of the office environment concerns receiving an increased amount of attention is how to provide a healthy workplace for the employees. No longer can employers assume that a healthful environment "just happens." Rather, it must be planned.

The sick-building syndrome that results from unfavorable environmental conditions is a phenomenon of the last two decades. This syndrome manifests itself among employees in the following ways: headaches, dizziness, abnormal tiredness, nausea, breathing difficulties, sore throats, upper-respiratory infections, coughing, skin rashes, and so forth. The syndrome is considered to exist in a particular building when at least 20 percent of the employees complain of similar symptoms that tend to disappear after they leave the premises.

Among the most common of the specific environmental conditions that cause the sick-building syndrome are indoor air pollution, noise pollution, and lighting glare. The syndrome is most commonly found in office buildings constructed after the late 1960s and early 1970s that have permanently sealed windows.

What conditions detract from a healthy environment?

Included in the growing list of concerns that detract from a healthful environment are the following:

1. Repetitive motion injuries are occurring among employees who perform repetitive tasks without interruption for long periods of time. For office employees, the most prevalent repetitive motion injury is called carpal tunnel syndrome, resulting from the long-term irritation of the tendons connecting one's hand and arm. Among the ways to overcome this situation is to place the employees' keyboards and screens at the

appropriate height, require that they take frequent breaks away from their work areas (short, frequent breaks are more beneficial than longer, less-frequent breaks), and provide them with wrist rests, adjustable chairs and moveable keyboards. Stretching exercises involving the back, arms, wrists, and fingers are also helpful. Taking the action necessary to reduce the incidence of repetitive motion injuries is not that costly, especially when compared with the benefits received. In the United States, medical costs and lost wages resulting from repetitive motion injuries consume between $20 and $30 billion a year.

2. Electromagnetic radiation emanating from video display terminals is the cause, according to some researchers, of higher-than-average rates of miscarriage, cancer, birth defects, and heart disease. Among the ways to diminish this concern are the following: Install a radiation screen on the face of the display unit, use an MPR II-certified low-frequency monitor, or use a liquid-crystal-display (LED) unit commonly found on laptop computers. Having employees distance themselves a minimum of 28 inches from their VDTs and 40 inches from other VDTs is also a viable recommendation.
3. Indoor air pollution is a result of improperly designed building ventilation systems; unclean ventilation systems; and outdated heating, ventilating, furnishings (especially carpeting and items made with pressed wood), cleaning solvents, tobacco smoke, and air conditioning systems. Some types of office equipment, most specifically electrostatic copiers and laser printers, produce an ozone that is also a source of indoor air pollution. Some ventilation problems occur when an organization remodels office areas without giving consideration to the ventilation needs of the new premises. The ventilation system appropriate for the original premises may not be appropriate for a remodeled area. Those responsible for equipment maintenance also need to make sure that the ozones produced by the equipment are properly filtered. In some instances, additional air purification and filtration devices may need to be installed.
4. Noise pollution is another contributor to the sick-building syndrome. This phenomenon results from the occurrence of high levels of unwanted sound originating from conversation, machines and equipment, telephones, and various noise-producing building systems. Several ways to diminish noise pollution are discussed in a subsequent section of this chapter.
5. Lighting systems can also diminish the healthiness of an office environment. The goal of light is to provide employees with the proper type of light for the tasks they perform. One of the most significant lighting problems in offices is glare, which is light reflected from the surface of an object. Of particular concern is the glare on video display terminals. Such glare is likely to manifest itself in the following ways: eyestrain, fatigue, and headaches. Equipping video display terminals with an anti-glare screen is an effective way to eliminate problems caused by screen glare, as is the prevention of light directly hitting the screen.

LIGHTING

Affecting employees both physically and psychologically, lighting is one of the most important aspects of the office environment. Physically, inadequate

How does the lighting system affect office employees?

lighting increases employees' fatigue as a result of excessive eye strain. Psychologically, inadequate lighting results in loss of morale and eventually causes a decrease in the quantity and quality of employee performance. Effective lighting takes into consideration the quantity and quality of illumination best suited for the employees, their work styles, their tasks, and the space involved.

In addition to being concerned about providing employees with satisfactory lighting, organizations are increasingly concerned about another lighting dimension: its cost. In 1991, the Environmental Protection Agency (EPA) initiated the Green Light Program that encourages organizations to use energy-efficient lighting. Because lighting accounts for approximately 25 percent of the nation's energy consumption, the Green Light Program helps organizations rid themselves of energy-inefficient lighting. To help organizations install energy-efficient lighting, the EPA provides low-cost loans and advice about designing new, efficient lighting systems.

Characteristics of Lighting Systems

Lighting systems should possess certain well-defined characteristics. Several changes in the way these characteristics are used have taken place in the last few years. To illustrate, for many years, the foot-candle[1] and the foot-lambert[2] were the two commonly used measures of lighting systems. Now, **Equivalent Spherical Illumination (ESI)**, **Visual Comfort Probability (VCP)**, and **Task Illumination (TI)** are also used to describe these characteristics.

What is Equivalent Spherical Illumination?

Equivalent Spherical Illumination ESI is used to measure the effectiveness of lighting systems. The task being performed at the work surface determines the appropriate ESI value for a given area. The value is influenced negatively by glares and reflections on the work surface and is affected by the degree of contrast between the work surface and the materials with which the employee works. An ESI value of 40 or higher is recommended for most work surfaces.

ESI is also used to provide a measure of the uniformity of the lighting system. If the minimum ESI of the work surface is at least two-thirds of the maximum ESI, the lighting of the work area is considered adequately uniform. Thus, if the maximum ESI is 60, the minimum ESI will have to be at least 40.

What does Visual Comfort Probability measure?

Visual Comfort Probability Visual Comfort Probability is a direct-brightness ratio and should be at least .70. A VCP of .80 means that 80 percent of the employees seated in the least desirable locations of an office are not bothered by glares created by the lighting system or by veiling reflections when working on flat surfaces directly beneath the lighting fixture. While employees whose tasks are primarily paper oriented should work in areas in which the VCP is at least .70, those whose tasks involve frequent use of a terminal screen should be provided a VCP of .90.

Sources of bright light visible to the naked eye or visible reflectors that are bright can cause a poor VCP ratio. When fixtures are selected, their design should be evaluated to make sure neither of the preceding conditions exist.

[1]The foot-candle, which describes the quantity of light, is the amount of light a distance of 1 foot from a standard candle. One watt of light per square foot produces approximately 15 foot-candles.

[2]The foot-lambert measures the brightness of light and is approximately equal to 1 foot-candle of either directed or reflected light.

What is the unit of measure of Task Illumination?

Task Illumination Expressed in raw foot-candles, Task Illumination measures the quantity of light at the work surface. It does not measure quality or visibility. A high TI value does not necessarily ensure high visibility in a work area, especially if glares and reflections are present. Most office work areas require a TI of 100 to 150 foot-candles.

Types of Lighting Systems

Lighting systems consist of the following types: **direct**, **semidirect**, **indirect**, **semi-indirect**, and **general diffuse**.

How do direct and semidirect lighting systems differ?

Direct This type of lighting system, by directing approximately 90 to 100 percent of the illumination downward to the work surface, is likely to create bothersome glares and reflections. Shadows are created because only a minimal amount of light is diffused. Unless the light fixtures are quite close together, the working areas most likely will not be uniformly lit.

Semidirect With semidirect lighting, 60 to 90 percent of the light is directed downward. The remainder of the light is directed upward and then reflected back downward. Semidirect systems eliminate some of the shadows that are characteristic of the direct lighting system.

Indirect Indirect lighting is the system recommended for most types of office tasks. With indirect lighting, 90 to 100 percent of the light is first directed upward. The light then becomes diffused and is reflected downward to the work area. The diffusion of the light eliminates most shadows and glares.

Semi-indirect With semi-indirect lighting, 60 to 90 percent of the light is directed upward and then reflected downward. The remainder of the light is immediately directed downward. Although the semi-indirect lighting system may produce a greater amount of light for the same wattage level than the indirect system, shadows and glare are also likely to be a greater problem with semi-indirect lighting.

General diffuse This lighting system directs 40 to 60 percent of the light directly to the work surface, with the remainder of the light reflected downward. Although this system produces more light for the same wattage than does the semi-indirect system, shadows and glare are also more noticeable than when using semi-indirect lighting.

Task/ambient Lighting

What are the differences between task lighting and ambient lighting?

The newest concept in office lighting is known as **task/ambient lighting**, which uses fixtures mounted in the furniture. Task lighting illuminates the work surface, while ambient lighting illuminates the area surrounding the work surface. Task lighting is frequently downward-directed lighting; ambient lighting is generally directed upward. By replacing the ceiling light fixtures with fixtures installed a short distance (perhaps 3 feet) above the work surface, task/ambient lighting results in an efficient, economical use of energy. Less wattage is required because light has to travel shorter distances to the work surface. In some instances, task lighting uses 40 percent less wattage per square foot than ceiling-mounted fluorescent fixtures. An illustration of task lighting is presented in Figure 5-1.

Figure 5-1 Task/ambient lighting. Courtesy: Steelcase, Inc., Grand Rapids, MI.

Accent lighting is often incorporated into task/ambient systems. This type of lighting, which is directional, acts as a stimulant by drawing attention to a horizontal or vertical surface. Properly done, accent lighting also provides a sense of dimension.

Figure 5-2 identifies the advantages of task/ambient lighting.

Kinds of Lighting

The four most commonly used kinds of office lighting are natural daylight, fluorescent, incandescent, and high-intensity discharge lighting.

Natural light Although natural light is an efficient lighting system, its lack of dependability requires the use of alternative lighting systems. In addition to its efficiency, natural light often provides psychological advantages for employees. However, natural light is not capable of penetrating very far into work areas. On extremely bright days, the intensity of natural light may result in its having to be controlled.

Many newer office buildings are constructed with a glass-enclosed courtyard at the center of the building, a feature that increases the number of working areas with windows. Consequently, a greater number of employees can take advantage of natural light.

Employees whose work areas utilize natural light should be situated so that light comes over their left shoulders if they are right-handed but over their right shoulders if they are left-handed. Under no circumstances should employees face windows in their normal working positions.

When an abundance of natural light is used to illuminate a work area, additional consideration will have to be given to the effect that the light has

1. Task lighting, unlike ceiling systems, is not permanent, which facilitates the rearrangement of workstations in an office area.
2. Areas are illuminated in a nonuniform pattern, which provides a greater sense of dimension than is possible with systems that provide uniform lighting.
3. The acoustical system is easier to develop because of the limited number of lighting fixtures that are used.
4. Task lighting eliminates glare and reflections.
5. Because task lighting requires less wattage, less energy is consumed.
6. Installation costs are significantly reduced.
7. Because fewer fixtures are used, fewer bulbs have to be replaced.
8. The amount of space needed between the ceiling and the floor above it is reduced, which increases the amount of usable vertical space in a building.
9. Because the fixtures are considered to be part of the furniture, a tax advantage may result.
10. Renovation of work areas is easily accomplished.
11. The absence of light fixtures in the ceiling helps improve the fire rating of the facility because of the unbroken nature of the ceiling.

Figure 5-2 Advantages of task/ambient lighting.

on air temperature. Because natural light is heat-producing, additional air-cooling measures may have to be taken—especially during the summer months—to moderate the effect of the heat.

What are the advantages of fluorescent lighting?

Fluorescent lighting The use of fluorescent lighting continues as the most common type of light source found in office buildings. The illumination fluorescent lighting produces closely resembles natural light. Although fluorescent lighting is more expensive to install than incandescent lighting, fluorescent lighting offers the following advantages over incandescent lighting: (1) it produces less heat and glare, (2) fluorescent tubes last ten times longer than incandescent bulbs, (3) it consumes less electricity, (4) the illumination it provides is more evenly distributed, and (5) fluorescent lighting is approximately five times more efficient than incandescent lighting.

Many buildings have been constructed with luminous ceilings similar to the one illustrated in Figure 5-3. A significant advantage of this ceiling is the extent to which shadows and glares on the work surfaces are eliminated. Because of the uniformity of light produced by the luminous ceiling, several techniques are used to produce lighting variation in office areas. One such device is the small, strategically placed spotlight.

Incandescent lighting Using filament bulbs, incandescent lighting is the type most commonly found in homes. It can also be used effectively in offices, although fluorescent lighting is generally regarded as more efficient. Incandescent lighting is often used to break up the monotony of lighting panels, as well as effectively used to create attention for certain areas. Compared with other kinds of lighting, incandescent lighting is the least cost effective in terms of the amount of light produced in relation to the energy consumed.

The cost of installing incandescent lighting is less than the cost of in-

Figure 5-3 Illuminated ceiling. Courtesy: Armstrong Cork Company.

stalling fluorescent lighting. Among the disadvantages of incandescent lighting when compared with fluorescent lighting are the following: an incandescent bulb does not last as long, colors appear less natural, it consumes more electricity, and it is apt to produce a greater amount of glare and shadowing.

In some instances, the heat generated by incandescent bulbs is used as an auxiliary heating source. This technique is discussed in the "Conditioning the Air" section of this chapter.

High-intensity discharge lamps The use of high-intensity discharge lamps for illuminating office areas is fairly new. These lamps, which were first used for street and stadium lighting, provide an extremely efficient lighting system. The greatest disadvantage of these bulbs is their effect on color as they sometimes make more difficult the ability to distinguish between various colors of objects in offices.

Automatic Light Control Systems

Automatic light control systems are now being installed in many office buildings. These systems have a positive impact on energy conservation, which enables the organization to recoup purchase outlay in a relatively short time.

One type of automatic light control system uses a photocell to measure the amount of illumination in a given area. With an electronic feedback mechanism, the control system is able to maintain the desired preset lighting level. As lamps age and accumulate dirt, they produce less light. To compensate, the control system increases the amount of light to maintain the desired preset illumination level. For areas near windows and skylights, the control system adjusts the quantity of artificial light in relation to the amount of natural light that is available. The primary advantage of this type of control system is the lighting consistency it facilitates.

Another type of automatic light control system senses the presence of people in a given area. Automatic light control systems use two types of sensors: ultrasonic wave sensors that detect movement and infrared occupancy sensors that detect body heat. The sensors function by automatically activating the lighting system when people are detected. Automatic light control systems de-activate the lighting system a specified amount of time (perhaps ten minutes) after the presence of people is no longer detected by the sensors. In addition to conserving energy, this system also has a residual benefit of providing security.

Some automatic light control systems utilize computer technology. At predetermined times, lights are automatically turned on and off. Certain devices, most commonly the telephone, are used to override the system should it be necessary to do so.

Lighting Maintenance

Over time, lamps used to produce artificial light begin to provide less output for the same amount of energy. The output depreciation begins after approximately 100 hours of usage. At some point during the life of each type of lamp, replacing old ones, even though they haven't totally burned out, is cost effective. Increasingly, organizations are implementing lamp replacement programs that result in the regular replacement of all lamps in a given work area. Replacement schedules take into consideration the average rated life of the lamps being replaced. From a labor standpoint, total replacement is also more cost effective than waiting until lamps burn out to replace them.

A regular fixture cleaning program is another important aspect of lighting maintenance. As fixtures gather dust and grime, their light-reflection surfaces are not as effective, thus reducing illumination effectiveness. Dirt and grime buildup on fixtures, coupled with aging lamps, deplete output by as much as 50 percent during the life of the lamp.

Lighting and Video Display Terminals

Adding to the complexity of designing efficient lighting systems is the presence of video display terminals found in many offices. Failure to given adequate attention to proper lighting in areas where the terminals are found may result in a significant number of employee concerns and/or problems.

Among the suggestions for helping design a lighting system for use in an area that contains terminals are the following:

1. Eliminate glare by reducing the amount of artificial or natural light hitting the terminals.
2. Use tiltable terminals to help reduce the amount of lighting glare.
3. Adjust either or both the contrast and brightness controls on the terminals to minimize the amount of glare.
4. Consider the use of screens to reduce the amount of glare on the terminals.
5. Minimize the amount of downward-directed light and maximize the amount of indirect lighting in the VDT work area.

COLOR

Color is another of the elements of the office environment that impacts significantly on humans. While most employees are aware of the physical impact of color, many are not aware of its psychological impact—both positive and negative—on their productivity, fatigue, morale, attitudes, and tension. Therefore, color in an office provides not only an aesthetic value, but also a functional value.

Color Considerations

What color considerations are important?

Among the important factors that should be considered in developing a desirable color scheme are color combination, effect of light on color, reflectance value of color, and impact of color. Each factor is discussed in the following sections.

What is the composition of tertiary colors?

Color combination Combining the **primary colors**—yellow, red, and blue—produces **secondary colors**. For example, mixing red and yellow makes orange, yellow and blue makes green, and blue and red makes violet. **Tertiary colors** are made by combining two parts of one primary color and one part of another primary color. This concept is illustrated in Figure 5-4. Tertiary colors are yellow-orange, yellow-green, blue-violet, and so forth. The twelve colors in Figure 5-4 provide the foundation for color coordination because the colors for a scheme are selected according to their position on the color chart. Some acceptable color coordination schemes are

1. Complementary colors—opposite each other on the color chart. For example, red-green, violet-yellow, and blue-orange.
2. Split-complementary colors—the colors on either side of a complementary color. For example, blue-violet and blue-green are the split complementary colors of orange.
3. Triad colors—the three colors equally distant from one another on the color chart. Triad colors are orange, green, violet, or yellow-orange, blue-green, and red-violet.

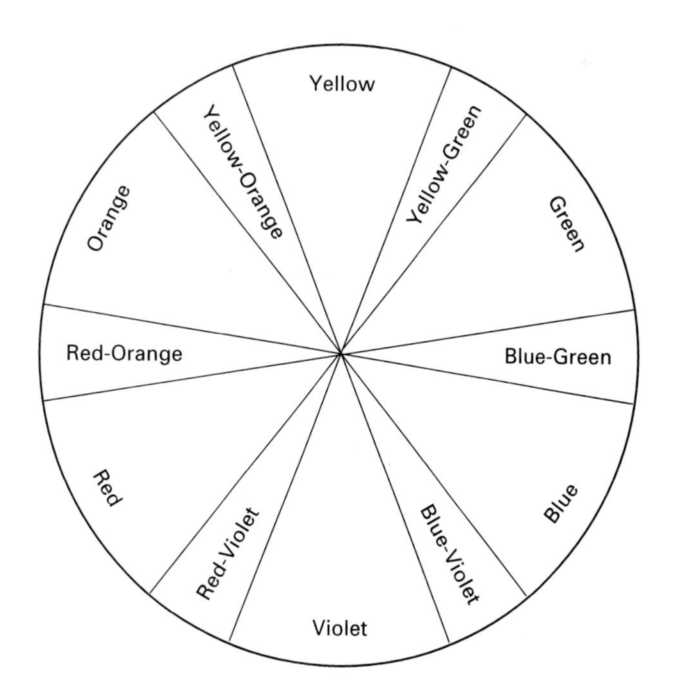

Figure 5-4 Color Chart.

Effect of light on color Because various types of artificial light have different color spectrums, the lighting system used in an office may also have a significant effect on the color scheme. The light source will enhance only those colors that fall within the spectrum of the light source. To illustrate, fluorescent lighting generally will not enhance reds and oranges because most fluorescent tubes are void of these two colors. Incandescent lighting will not enhance purple-blue color schemes, although fluorescent systems may. When compared with either fluorescent or incandescent lights, high-intensity lamps have a rather insignificant impact on color enhancement.

Reflectance value of color Various colors possess different reflectance values. For example, lighter colors reflect a greater percentage of light than do the darker colors. Certain areas of the office require colors with higher reflectance values than others do. The ceiling, for example, requires a color with a higher reflectance value than does the floor. A light-colored ceiling helps reflect light downward, which reduces glare and shadows on work surfaces. In areas in which natural light is minimal, light-colored walls will help reduce the amount of artificial light that must be provided to achieve lighting adequacy, thus helping conserve energy consumption as well.

Figure 5-5 illustrates the reflectance value for various colors.

Impact of colors Colors tend to create moods. Cool colors—blue, green, and violet—create calm and retiring moods. Warm colors—red, orange, and yellow—on the other hand, create warm and cheerful moods. The natural tints, including beige, buff, peach, and off-white, are mildly stimulating, while deep purple and pale violet often create depressing moods. Gray tends to create a sleep-inducing effect.

Guiding Principles

What principles must be considered in designing a color scheme?

Illustrated in Figure 5-6 are a number of guidelines useful in developing a color scheme. Those responsible for developing a color scheme in an office should be thoroughly familiar with the principles before beginning the planning process.

Color	*Reflectance value (percent)*
White	86
Light green	67
Light yellow	64
Light blue	58
Light gray	54
Medium yellow	47
Orange	35
Medium red	23
Dark blue	17
Dark red	13
Dark green	10

Figure 5-5 Reflectance values of colors.

1. Color cannot be considered by itself; rather, its impact on the total office environment must be considered.
2. Black and white influence other colors. Black makes other colors appear lighter and more distinctive. White makes other colors appear darker.
3. Any color used against a darker color will appear lighter than it actually is, whereas any color used against a lighter one will appear darker.
4. Colors lose their brilliance and "wash out" in bright light, and darken and lose their intensity in dim light.
5. Warm colors are considered to advance, whereas cool colors recede.
6. The use of two sharply contrasting colors tends to tire the eyes rather quickly.
7. Small areas of bright, secondary colors that are balanced with the colors used in large areas are often attractive.
8. Light colors will make a small room look larger.
9. A narrow area can be made to appear wider by using a color on the end walls that is brighter than the color used on the side walls.
10. Of the deep colors appropriate for office use, brown is the most preferred.
11. A low ceiling can be made to appear higher by painting it a lighter color than the walls.
12. In working areas, floors should be darker than walls, and the walls should be darker than the ceiling.
13. Because of excessive contrast, dark colors should not be used on walls with windows.
14. When natural light enters a work area from the north or east, a warm color should be used on the wall opposite the window; however, when the natural light is from the south or west, a cool color should be used on the wall opposite the window.
15. Window coverings, such as drapes and other kinds of shades, should be functional as well as aesthetic.

Figure 5-6 Color scheme guidelines.

Floor Coverings

The color of walls and ceilings is just one aspect of the color scheme in an office. The color of the floor covering is also important. Although tile and other floor finishes are still widely found, carpeted office work areas are more prevalent. Coordination is quite simple because of the almost infinite number of carpet colors that can be coordinated with other aspects of the color scheme.

Among the advantages of using carpet as the floor covering are

What advantages result from the use of carpeting as a floor covering?

1. Carpet is useful for noise control.
2. Carpet is often less costly to maintain than other types of floor coverings.
3. Carpet, when compared with other types of floor coverings, is more comfortable and less tiring for employees who stand a substantial portion of each day.

When carpeting creates electrostatic charges, special provisions may have to be made to prevent these charges from interfering with the operation of sensitive electronic office equipment. The fire-retardant rating of the carpet is also a concern that cannot be ignored, especially if local restrictions/regulations are in existence.

Wall Coverings

Carpeting has become a popular wall covering because of its aesthetic value and its ability to absorb noise. The carpeting used on walls must have a high fire-retardant value. Carpet with a foam backing is not recommended as a wall covering because of the dense smoke it creates when it burns.

A variety of other types of wall coverings are used frequently in offices, including vinyl, cloth, cork, and paper. Interior designers are helpful in selecting an appropriate covering for a given wall.

Color of Furniture

When planning an appropriate color coordination scheme for an office, consideration must also be given to furniture color. Most furniture outlasts wall colors; therefore, alternative color schemes should be considered at the time the initial color scheme is planned. Flexibility is destroyed when floor and furniture colors allow the use of only one or two wall colors.

An emerging trend is to select furniture colors that contrast with wall colors. This practice not only provides greater flexibility in designing a color scheme, but also helps eliminate some of the monotony of having similar colors. An example is a scheme built around gray walls and upholstered furniture in deep blues and greens.

When selecting furniture, the contrast value and the reflectance value of the working surface should be considered. If these values are excessive, undue eyestrain will occur. Shiny and highly polished surfaces on furniture should also be avoided if the lighting system produces an appreciable amount of either direct or reflected glare.

NOISE CONTROL

The noise level in an office is another of the environmental factors that must be considered. When noise reaches an undesirable level, various physical and psychological conditions occur. For example, continued high noise levels can result in either temporary or permanent hearing loss. High noise levels produce fatigue and hamper productivity, as well as cause nervous conditions, tension, and irritability. In addition, high noise levels can increase one's blood pressure and metabolic rate, both of which can create serious health problems.

What is a decibel?

The **decibel**, the unit measure of sound, is the smallest change in sound detectable by the human ear. The faintest sound that the human ear can detect is zero decibels. Therefore, other sounds with greater intensity have decibel values higher than the zero value. Figure 5-7 illustrates the decibel values for several common office sounds. Because the decibel scale is logarithmic, a small increase in a decibel value doubles the actual sound level. The maximum decibel level in an office should be 90, while a decibel level of 50 is preferred. Sustained decibel levels of 120 or higher may result in hearing loss.

The goal of a noise control system is to produce speech privacy. Confi-

Office area	*Decibels*
Loud office machines room	90
Noisy office	70
Average office	50
Quiet office	30
Soundproof office	10

Figure 5-7 Decibel levels of office sounds.

dential privacy is achieved when no more than 5 percent of the words are understood in an adjacent area. Normal privacy is achieved when no more than 20 percent of the words in a conversation can be understood in an adjacent area.

Today, noise control in many organizations is handled through a systems approach, integrating such components as a sound-absorbing ceiling; effective sound barriers, such as sound-absorbing panels, window coverings, and floor coverings; and a noise-masking system. While none of the components by themselves is effective, when integrated into a system, they produce the desired results.

Control of Office Noise

Several techniques are available for controlling the noise in an office, including proper construction, use of sound-absorbing materials and devices, and installation of a **masking-sound system** designed to make noise levels less noticeable.

What is structural sound?

Proper construction Significant amounts of office noise can be controlled by using effective building construction techniques. Sound travels either through the air (called airborne sounds) or through structural facilities (structural sound) prior to its becoming airborne. Examples of airborne sound are conversation and the sound generated by various pieces of equipment. An example of structural sound is equipment vibration; before becoming airborne, vibration sounds travel through a structural device in the work area.

The following construction techniques are recommended as ways of eliminating undesirable structural sounds:

1. Attach a network of feeder ducts to the main ducts in the heating/cooling system. A system using only main ducts allows considerable noise to be carried through the ducts.
2. Use windows and doors that seal properly.
3. Build dead airspace into the structural features, which helps decrease the amount of noise that travels from one feature to another.
4. Use construction materials that prohibit vibration noises from occurring.

Sound-absorbing materials Available today are many types of sound-absorbing materials suitable for office use. Most of the materials, which include ceiling-, wall-, window-, and floor-covering materials, have a functional as well as an aesthetic value.

Sound absorption is measured using a noise reduction coefficient (NRC). Most materials carry a rating of .50 to .95. A rating of .50 means that 50 percent of the sound is absorbed by the materials. For the purpose of controlling noise, materials with a NRC of less than .75 are ineffective.

Of the noise-controlling wall-covering materials that are available, soft, porous materials, such as cork and carpeting, are most desirable. In addition, several companies manufacture permanent, full-length sound-absorbing wall panels.

If the ceiling and floor coverings are adequate to control noise, special wall coverings probably are not needed. In offices in which a high concentration of noise exists, special ceiling, wall, and floor materials may be needed.

The most efficient sound-absorbing floor covering is carpet. Because static can affect office equipment, special consideration may have to be given to the installation of static-free carpet. Static can also be controlled by placing a grid of copper grounding wires beneath the carpet.

For maximum benefit, materials used for noise control should possess three characteristics or qualities:

What characteristics should sound-absorbing materials possess?

1. Absorption—the degree to which noise is absorbed within the material. Absorption is measured by the Noise Reduction Coefficient discussed earlier.
2. Reflection—the degree to which sound is not absorbed by various materials but is reflected back into space.
3. Isolation—the degree to which materials prevent sounds from passing through them.

A proper balance between reflection and absorption is needed to help eliminate work areas with a "dead" sound. As noise levels increase, absorption needs to be increased and reflection decreased. Materials with hard surfaces—metal, glass, and plastic—reflect a greater amount of noise than surfaces with soft finishes—draperies, porous ceiling tiles, and the like. Isolation of noise is affected by such characteristics as airtightness, weight, and stiffness of materials.

Sound-absorbing devices Several sound-absorbing devices are frequently used as a means of controlling office noise. Sound-absorbing materials can be placed under certain kinds of office machines—for example, the typewriter or dot-matrix printer. Another device used in many offices is a sound-absorbing cover placed over a noise-generating machine, such as a typewriter or printer. Figure 5-8 displays a sound-absorbing cover.

In addition to being used for privacy, movable panels, such as those illustrated in Figure 4-5, are also used to absorb sound.

Masking Another noise-controlling method is the masking technique that involves blending office noise with low-level, nondisturbing background sounds. Also known as white noise, masking noise is similar to the sound heard when air passes through a duct or tunnel. Public address systems are frequently used to transmit masking sound throughout the work areas.

Control of Noise in Offices Using Open Space Planning

Open space planning provides special challenges for noise control. Greater amounts of sound-absorbing materials may have to be used because most permanent walls are eliminated when open space planning is used. In addi-

Figure 5-8 Sound-absorbing cover. Courtesy: Gates Co., Santa Rosa, CA.

tion, noise-masking devices may also have to be used. If the office area continues to be too noisy after all the noise control techniques are used, greater space between workstations may have to be provided to achieve the desired level of speech privacy.

In the near future, domes of silence will be commercially available. These devices, at the push of a button, will "enclose" or acoustically isolate a specific area. Voices will not penetrate through the dome and therefore cannot be heard outside the dome.

CONDITIONING THE AIR

The air in which employees work also impacts on their physical and psychological well-being. In fact, with employees spending 90 percent of their waking hours indoors (approximately 2,000 hours per year), air quality is a major concern. In many of today's office buildings, the air contains more chemical irritants and biological matter than the outside air contains. Air-quality factors involve temperature, humidity, ventilation, and air cleanliness. Major contributors to the indoor air pollution found in many of today's buildings are excessive levels of moisture, inadequate mechanical ventilation, and tobacco smoke.

Most new office buildings located in areas with varied climates are constructed with a year-round, integrated air conditioning system. Therefore, the atmospheric condition of the office is constant day after day.

In most instances, the benefits of installing systems designed to condition the air properly in an office exceed their cost. For example, if the comfort of the employees is improved, greater levels of productivity and efficiency can be expected. Absenteeism and tardiness are reduced; and in some cases, employees' health is improved. Furthermore, cleaning and redecorating costs can be reduced by using an integrated air conditioning system.

What new devices help reduce heating costs?

Several technological advances are now available that help organizations reduce their heating costs. These new devices use reclaimed heat to warm work areas. For example, the heat created by lights, office equipment, and even humans is collected through special vents and redistributed throughout the premises. This reclaimed heat can also be used to heat water. During the summer, reclaimed heat is removed from the premises to reduce air cooling needs.

Several new computerized heat control systems are used in office buildings. Temperature sensors continually provide a computer with temperature data from each area of the building. The computer then makes needed temperature adjustments. During nonworking hours, temperatures are automatically adjusted to conserve energy.

Temperature of Air

When the humidity level is within the proper range, the ideal working temperature in an office is 68 degrees Fahrenheit. To conserve energy, the temperature should be lowered a few degrees in winter and raised a few degrees in summer.

In the future, solar energy will undoubtedly be a primary heating source in office buildings. Depending on the geographical location of the building, solar energy may be able to provide all the heat that is needed.

Two types of air-cooling units are available: central units similar to those found in most new office buildings and self-contained units that are often installed in buildings that were not designed to accommodate central systems. One way to determine whether or not installing an air-cooling system is cost-worthy is to determine its impact on increased worker efficiency. The use of professional consultants is recommended when the installation of an air-cooling system is being considered.

Humidity Level of Air

For maximum comfort, the humidity level of an office should range somewhere between 40 and 60 percent, with the optimum humidity level around 50 percent. A year-round air conditioning system humidifies the air in the winter and dehumidifies it in the summer.

How does humidity affect the comfort of various temperature levels?

The humidity level has an impact on the temperature level. If the humidity level is within the recommended range, the actual temperature of an office can be lowered in the winter and raised in the summer and still be comfortable. If the humidity level is less than the recommended range, the temperature will have to be either raised or lowered to achieve the same degree of comfort.

Circulation of Air

The air in working areas, especially those in which equipment produces heat buildup, must be properly circulated if its quality is to be maintained. Without air circulation, the temperature of the air that surrounds an individual tends to increase, which results in a certain amount of discomfort. An adequate air exchange rate is 25 cubic feet of air per minute per person. Therefore, a "block" of air measuring approximately 4 feet by 3 feet by 2 feet will have to be replaced each minute for each employee in a given area. An acceptable standard for air circulation is approximately 50 feet per minute. Hence, a "block" of air that moves 50 feet in one minute is acceptable. Air circulated at too fast a rate creates a draft. Greater air circulation will have to be provided if smoking is allowed in the work area.

Cleanliness of Air

Devices designed to cleanse the air are now being installed in many office buildings. These devices cleanse the air of germs, dust, and dirt. Air cleanliness is becoming a greater concern as buildings become more airtight and energy efficient, two features that entrap unclean, stagnate, stale air within the confines of work areas. While ultraviolet lights are useful for killing germ-laden bacteria, mechanical filters are used to remove dust and other foreign particles. Because of the sensitivity of computer equipment, a dust-free atmosphere is essential in the data processing center. Of significant concern are such air pollutants as cigarette/cigar/pipe smoke and toxic substances, including asbestos and carbon monoxide. Eventually, the presence of tobacco smoke will be a nonconcern as organizations are rapidly moving toward a smoke-free work environment.

MUSIC

A music system produces several beneficial results. Music in an office helps increase job satisfaction and productivity by eliminating job boredom and monotony. Music also has the general effect of relieving mental and physical fatigue and reducing nervous tension and strain. The type of music being played affects the productivity of employees. In addition, music has a positive effect on employees' attitudes, often resulting in their making fewer errors and their being absent and tardy less often.

Several alternatives are possible for developing a music system. Music can be obtained from a service vendor that specializes in programming music for offices. One such vendor is Muzak. Service vendors typically charge according to the number of employees in the organization.

A local radio station can also be used as the music source. Special equipment is available that shuts the system down during the broadcast of commercials and news so that only music is heard. Some organizations provide their own music source, such as tapes and CDs. In most cases, conventional public address systems satisfactorily accommodate each of the alternatives just discussed.

The success of a music system is significantly affected by the nature of the music programming. The kind of work being performed should be considered in determining the types of music—show tunes, classical numbers, semi-classical numbers, and popular tunes—that should be played. Employees whose work requires a high degree of concentration should be subjected to only the most subdued types of music.

The time of the workday that music is played in relation to its intended impact on the employees should also be considered in programming. Playing more stimulating music is psychologically advantageous when employees' efficiency is below par as a result of fatigue or boredom. Fatigue is generally most noticeable midway through the morning and afternoon work periods and just before the lunch hour and quitting time.

What impact does continuously played music have on employees?

Research has also shown that continuously played music loses its full impact because employees are no longer conscious of its presence. Therefore, short breaks in the music program create awareness. An on-for-fifteen-minutes, off-for-fifteen-minutes cycle provides the necessary breaks.

CONSERVATION OF ENERGY IN OFFICES

One of the realities of life is the growing need to conserve energy. An increasing portion of the administrative office manager's job is devoted to this important task. No longer can conservation be taken for granted; rather, it has to be a formally planned and coordinated activity. The development of a proper attitude toward energy conservation has to start at the top of the organizational management structure.

The Energy Conservation Program

An energy conservation program is comprised of several components, including an energy conservation committee, an energy efficiency study, and the development of goals for conserving energy.

What are the responsibilities of the energy conservation committee?

Energy conservation committee Appointment to the energy conservation committee is often made by the organization's president, which helps signal organizational commitment to this important activity. The members of the committee, who generally have expertise in energy conservation, oversee the total energy program. Important activities include undertaking the energy efficiency study and formulating goals. The committee can also provide a valuable public relations function. To perform effectively, the committee must have the authority to ensure compliance with its recommendations.

In some instances, the administrative office manager will chair the committee. In other instances, the committee will be chaired by a full-time energy advisor. In extremely large organizations, the energy advisor will likely be supported by a full-time staff.

Energy efficiency study Before a conservation plan can be devised, an energy conservation study of the facility must be undertaken. The purpose of this study is to identify areas where excessive energy is being used, as well as to determine areas where energy conservation techniques might be implemented. Special emphasis should be placed on those areas where the greatest energy conservation can be realized. The results of the study provide the basis for the development of the conservation goals, another vital component of the energy conservation program.

Development of energy conservation goals Once the energy efficiency study has been completed, conservation goals are developed. After their approval, every effort should be made to ensure their attainment. A periodic follow-up should be undertaken to determine the amount of progress toward reaching the goals. Those areas in which progress is not sufficient should be closely scrutinized. Successful goal attainment should be well publicized throughout the organization.

Techniques for Conserving Energy

With concerted effort, many organizations have been able to reduce their energy consumption by at least 10 to 15 percent. Because of its potential financial impact, energy conservation has to be a top-priority activity in most organizations.

Following is a discussion of several techniques for conserving energy.

Conserving energy in the lighting system Because the lighting system may well consume as much as 25 percent of the total energy outlay, special attention should be focused on the system. The following suggestions outline energy conservation techniques in terms of the lighting system:

1. Use the appropriate amount of light—but not more than is needed—for the task being performed. Lighting systems that provide the same amount of light in all areas of the premises tend to waste energy.
2. Provide sufficient light needed in a given area; providing more light than needed may require additional air cooling, which adds to energy consumption.
3. Develop a practice of turning off lights when not needed.
4. Use task lighting or high-intensity discharge lamps where possible. Each of these uses less energy than alternative types of lighting.
5. Consider installing automatic light control systems to help conserve energy. The pay-back period for these systems is typically quite short.
6. Clean bulbs and tubes regularly. Dirty light bulbs and tubes reduce the amount of light output they provide.
7. Use light colors that reflect more light. Dark colors tend to absorb light and therefore are more wasteful of energy.
8. Reduce outside lighting except where needed for safety and security.
9. Engage the services (usually free) of the local utility company to conduct an energy audit, the purpose of which is to determine where additional savings from the lighting system can be attained.

Conserving energy in the heating/cooling system The energy used for heating/cooling also consumes a large part of the total energy allocation. Some suggestions for conserving energy are listed below.

1. Conserve energy by reducing the temperature to 65 degrees Fahrenheit in the winter and increasing the temperature to 78 degrees Fahrenheit in the summer.
2. Make sure windows and doors seal properly.
3. Use reclaimed heat where possible, such as that produced by office equipment.
4. Adjust the temperature of work areas when they are not being used.
5. Reduce ventilation during nonworking hours.
6. Consider the installation of an automatic control device that ensures the efficient utilization of energy. The cost of the equipment is likely to be offset quickly by energy savings.
7. Make sure heating and cooling equipment is properly maintained to ensure proper functioning.
8. Maintain proper humidity levels as a means of enhancing human comfort.

Other conservation measures The following is a list of other conservation measures:

1. Install an adequate amount of insulation.
2. Incorporate energy conservation devices and techniques, including solar devices, when designing and constructing new buildings.
3. Purchase equipment that has a high energy-efficiency level.
4. Use one temperature of water (around 95 degrees Fahrenheit) in the

restroom lavatories to avoid having to mix hot and cold water to attain a comfortable hand-washing temperature.

5. Replace old faucet aerators with reduced-flow aerators, and reduce water levels in toilet tanks.
6. Encourage employees to conserve energy whenever and wherever they can.
7. Encourage employees to adjust their attire to compensate for warmer work area temperatures in the summer and cooler work area temperatures in the winter.

OFFICE SECURITY

Office security is becoming an area of significant concern in many organizations. Security has two dimensions: protection of the organization's physical property (such as equipment, machines, and furniture) and protection of the organization's vital information (data and records) that if stolen or lost would have dire consequences on the organization's ability to continue to function. In some cases, vital information that becomes available to competitors, perhaps because of a lack of proper security, seriously erodes the organization's ability to remain competitive within the marketplace.

Among the factors that should be examined to determine the need for and extent of security are the following: office equipment and machines, computer terminals, data files (including both hard and soft copy), and office furniture. The more valuable an item is to the organization, the more securely it will need to be maintained.

What types of security devices are commonly used?

Limiting access to vital areas is a common means of providing a secure environment. Among the devices used to restrict access are photo IDs, push-button locks, card-lock systems, and physical attribute systems (most commonly fingerprint- and eye-oriented systems).

Another level of security is provided by the automatic light control systems that are activated by either motion or body heat sensors. These systems, when activated, can be designed to summon police units automatically unless they are overridden by an employee with the proper authorization to do so. Also used are intrusion-alarm and sound-alarm systems that also automatically summon police units. In addition to these devices, many organizations use closed-circuit television to provide security for an area. Security guards are also commonly used in many organizations.

A common means of securing vital data stored within a computer system is to require the use of passwords to access the data. To maximize security, passwords can be changed frequently. In some instances, a system is used that requires two or more employees to enter passwords before data can be accessed. The level of security provided for the organization's data/information is usually determined by the importance of the data/information. A system that uses a combination of passwords and the security devices discussed earlier provides maximum security.

IMPLICATIONS FOR THE ADMINISTRATIVE OFFICE MANAGER

The nature of his or her background and training makes the administrative office manager well qualified to guide organizational efforts in designing an effective office environment. No employee in the organization is likely to be more familiar with the basic components of an effective environment.

In most instances, the environment in which employees work will affect them more than the layout of their work area. Except for a few fundamental management practices, office environment is likely to impact more extensively on employees than any other factor.

An effective environment is balanced in an integrative way. Improving one element of the environment while other elements are unsatisfactory is useless. Rather, a more logical approach is to improve all unsatisfactory elements as much as possible.

The administrative office manager will find an understanding of the physical and psychological needs of employees helpful in planning an effective environment. Each element of the environment affects employees physically and/or psychologically.

REVIEW QUESTIONS

1. How does the environment of an office impact on employees?
2. What causes the sick-building syndrome?
3. What do Equivalent Spherical Illumination, Visual Comfort Probability, and Task Illumination measure?
4. What are the advantages and disadvantages of each of the five kinds of ceiling lighting systems discussed in this chapter?
5. What advantages result from the use of task lighting?
6. In what ways do task lighting and ambient lighting differ from one another?
7. What suggestions are helpful in designing a lighting system in areas where terminals are used?
8. How are complementary colors, split-complementary colors, and triad colors used in developing a color scheme?
9. What is the average decibel noise level found in most offices?
10. What characteristics should sound-absorbing materials possess?
11. What temperature, humidity, and circulation standards should exist for most offices?
12. What is the principal factor used to determine the nature of the music that is most appropriate for different times of the day?
13. What are the components of an energy conservation program?

DISCUSSION QUESTIONS

1. Comment on the validity of the following statement that was recently heard during a conversation between two individuals who were discussing the topic of office environment:

   Why pay much attention to the office environment? Humans have an amazing capacity to be dissatisfied, so regardless of what is provided, some employees will never be satisfied. For example, some will find a work area too hot, while others will find it too cold. In the final analysis, ignoring the environment will result in approximately the same amount of satisfaction as will trying to maximize the environment.

2. Most of the illuminating of your work surface comes from a desk lamp that uses an incandescent bulb. Now that the winter season is approaching and the number of cloudy days is increasing, you are finding the quality of light to be inadequate. When you mentioned this problem to your supervisor, she indicated that the problem could be easily resolved by putting a larger bulb in the lamp. Although her suggestion may result in more light, discuss other types of lighting problems that may either be

intensified or sustained by this action. Explain how the problem you identify might be resolved.

3. When you were discussing the task lighting concept recently with a coworker who is near retirement age, she commented that task lighting is not new. She said that when she first started working in an office many years earlier, each desk had its own desk lamp. In what ways do you think the lighting system found in offices many years ago differs from today's task lighting concept? In what ways is today's task lighting concept likely to be more effective than the desk lamp concept of yesterday?
4. An increasing number of the employees in the organization in which you work seem to be complaining about eye fatigue at the end of the work day. You decide to investigate the situation. In your study efforts, what do you plan to examine as possible contributory factors to the eye fatigue complaint?
5. To conserve energy, the temperature of the work areas in the organization in which you work will be increased in the summer and decreased in the winter. You have been asked to prepare a list of "things" that can be done within the environment to offset the effect of temperature adjustment. Identify the "things" you plan to put on your list.
6. You are the coordinator of the energy conservation committee in the organization in which you work. At the first meeting of the committee, one of the members said he thought this committee was a waste of time because "very little can be done to conserve energy unless we start with an energy-efficient building." Obviously, as chairperson of this committee, you do not agree with this individual. Defend your committee by identifying some of the significant things that can be done to conserve energy in a building that was constructed before the widespread use of energy-efficient construction techniques.

STUDENT PROJECTS AND ACTIVITIES

1. Tour the office area of an organization to learn what special kinds of noise control techniques are used.
2. Discuss with an organization's facilities manager the special energy conservation techniques that are used.
3. Discuss with an office space designer the illusions he or she has created with various colors.
4. Talk with an office employee who uses a video display terminal a significant portion of each day. What special concerns does this individual have about these terminals?
5. Tour an office area to examine its lighting system. What type of lighting was used?

MINICASE

The Rich-Lu Company has hired you, a consultant in office environment systems, to assess the feasibility of a new task/ambient lighting system for its building. The present ceiling lighting system is costly in terms of energy consumption. The furniture used in the open work areas could be easily modified to accommodate task/ambient lighting.

Prepare a report for Rich-Lu in which you

1. Identify the special benefits a task/ambient lighting system would provide.
2. Identify the problems Rich-Lu may encounter in installing a task/ambient lighting system at this point.

CASE

The Graff Pharmaceutical Company is located in Omaha, NE. Graff, which is one of the largest suppliers of prescription drugs in the Midwest, was founded in 1922 by Karl and Heinz Graff. It has become a leader in developing certain kinds of drugs, especially those for use in treating cardiovascular ailments.

The original part of the building the company presently occupies was built in 1958. Because of its rapid growth in the late 1960s, the company built an adjoining structure in 1971. Space needs have been fairly stable since that time.

One of the reasons attributed to the financial success of Graff is its prudent management practices. The firm's profitability has always exceeded the industry average.

A recent analysis of last year's organizational goals indicates the company's voluntary energy conservation efforts have not been successful. The company decided to try a two-year voluntary program consisting primarily of public relations activities. At that time, the decision was made that the voluntary program would be abandoned in favor of a formal energy conservation program if the voluntary one was not successful.

You, a specialist in energy conservation, have been contacted by Graff regarding working with it to help achieve the conservation goals. After your recent tour of Graff's facilities, you decide to prepare a report to submit to its management.

1. In the report, what are you going to recommend as the common elements of a formal energy conservation program?
2. What are the specific functions of each of these elements?
3. In accordance with a request by Graff's vice president, you decide to include in your report a list of what you consider to be the ten most important energy conservation techniques. What techniques comprise your list?

CHAPTER

OFFICE EQUIPMENT AND FURNITURE

CHAPTER AIM

After studying this chapter, you should be able to select appropriate equipment and furniture for a general office area.

CHAPTER OUTLINE

- Office Equipment
  - Planning Considerations
  - Use of Comparative Analysis Form
  - Obtaining Office Equipment
    - Leasing Considerations
    - Purchasing Considerations
    - Making the Decision
  - Equipment Maintenance Considerations
    - Service Contract
    - Call Basis
    - In-house Service
  - Replacement Considerations
  - Inventory Control Considerations
- Office Furniture
  - New Developments in Office Furniture
    - Modular Design
    - Portable Design
    - Functional Design
    - Ergonomics Design
  - Use of Safety and Performance Standards
- Implications for the Administrative Office Manager

CHAPTER TERMS

Break-even analysis
Business and Institutional Furniture Manufacturers Association (BIFMA)
Buyers Laboratory, Inc.
Ergonomics design
Functional design
Lease with option to purchase
Modular design
Payback period
Portable design
Sale-leaseback
Systems furniture
True lease

More so than ever before, those responsible for selecting office equipment and furniture are exercising greater care in the selection process. Attributable reasons are the following: (1) equipment and furniture represent a significant investment for the organization; (2) a greater number of equipment and furniture sources now exists than ever before, thus providing a far greater number of options; (3) the specialized nature of much of the equipment and furniture requires considerable care in the selection process; and (4) the increased need for employees to be as productive as possible requires use of equipment and furniture that enhances their productivity.

What problems are likely to arise when equipment and furniture are not carefully selected?

Among problems likely to result when the equipment and furniture selection process is not given the care it deserves are the following:

1. The equipment and furniture, although adequate at the present time, will not meet future needs.
2. The equipment and furniture are not sufficiently functional, thus having a detrimental effect on employee productivity.
3. The organization is unable to achieve a desirable return on its equipment and furniture investment.

OFFICE EQUIPMENT

Often a time-consuming process, the selection of office equipment is especially involved when a large amount and a variety of equipment is needed. The information in the following sections will be helpful to those undertaking this important task.

Planning Considerations

Several factors need to be considered when selecting new office equipment. The number of factors and their importance are likely to be determined by the type of equipment needed and the functions for which the equipment will be used. Although only a few factors have to be considered in selecting some types of equipment, all of the factors should be considered in selecting other types.

What is the purpose of the comparative analysis?

A comparative analysis of the various brands of equipment being considered is often helpful in selecting office equipment. Each brand is evaluated on the basis of the functions it is capable of performing, its manufacturer, and its vendor.

The following is a discussion of the factors that should be considered in selecting new office equipment. Each factor is classified as an equipment consideration, a vendor consideration, or a maintenance consideration.

Equipment considerations include the following:

1. *Needs of the equipment*. Before selecting new equipment, its needs must be determined. This can be either partially or wholly determined by the work the equipment will be used to process. Too often, organizations either purchase or lease equipment that is more sophisticated than is needed. Equipment functions that are never used increase the cost of the equipment and lower the organization's return on its investment. If an operating system is to use the new equipment, have someone who is familiar with the system determine equipment needs. Equipment that fails to meet the needs for which it was obtained often results from an inaccurate assessment of how it will be used.

2. *Determination of appropriate equipment.* After the equipment needs have been assessed, determining which brands of equipment will most appropriately meet these needs is possible. Because equipment needs often can be adequately met by several brands of equipment, a fairly comprehensive equipment search should be undertaken. One of the most commonly used means of identifying the appropriate equipment is to provide vendors with detailed descriptions of the way in which the equipment will be used. The vendors can then determine which equipment is appropriate. This step is generally less important with low-cost, nonspecialized equipment than it is with high-cost, specialized equipment.

How can equipment dependability be determined?

3. *Dependability of equipment.* Once the various brands of equipment appropriate for the situation have been identified, then the dependability of the equipment is assessed. Although some equipment manufacturers have reputations for producing dependable office equipment, others do not enjoy the same reputation.

   Equipment dependability can be assessed in several ways. One way is to contact the administrative office manager in other organizations that use the same type of equipment. Although most equipment vendors willingly provide the names of their most satisfied customers, other users of the same equipment should also be contacted when possible. The names of other equipment users can usually be obtained quite readily.

   The dependability of the equipment can also be determined by reading equipment reports compiled by such independent organizations as **Buyers Laboratory, Inc.**, a New Jersey-based testing firm. A final way to assess equipment dependability, although not always totally reliable, is to assess the dependability of other equipment of the same brand used within the organization.

4. *Specifications of the equipment.* For certain types of equipment, specifications have to be determined. In this chapter, specifications refer to such factors as equipment size, electrical requirements, installation requirements, and special structural requirements. Some equipment, although suitable in all other respects, has to be eliminated from consideration because of inappropriate specifications. Now that devices are being interlinked to one another, especially computer peripheral equipment, the compatibility of these devices with one another is also important.

5. *Cost of the equipment.* The cost of equipment has a significant impact on the organization's return on its investment. Although cost is important, some organizations place too much emphasis on this factor. Consequently, less expensive equipment is selected. If it fails to perform as well as other equipment or is less efficient than other equipment that was considered, however, the organization will not be able to maximize the return on its investment.

6. *Operational processes of the equipment.* Some types of office equipment require the use of specialized supplies, especially certain photocopying and printing equipment. The necessity of such specialized supplies should be determined as well as the possibility of using these supplies on other brands of equipment.

7. *Safety features.* Also to be considered are the safety features of office equipment. Although most routine office equipment is not haz-

ardous, certain types of equipment used in printing and duplicating processes can be, especially when employees misuse the equipment.

How is equipment flexibility determined?

8. *Flexibility of equipment.* Increasingly, equipment is becoming available that can be modified with additional components or attachments as the need arises. Although these attachments may not be needed at the time of purchase, consideration should be given to the possibility of future need. Another dimension of equipment flexibility is its possible use for a variety of work processes. Because some equipment is more suitable than other equipment for a wider variety of work processes, its flexibility should be thoroughly evaluated.
9. *Ease of equipment operation.* Also to be considered is the ease with which the equipment is operated; as office devices are not equally user friendly. One of the more efficient ways of determining operating ease is to seek input from individuals who will operate the equipment being considered. To make a comparative analysis, having the vendors outline in detail how the equipment can be used to perform several specific procedures may be desirable.
10. *Speed of equipment operation.* In some instances, the operational speed of the equipment is an important consideration. If this is the case and if the speeds are quite variable, the operational speeds of the different pieces of equipment should be assessed.
11. *Cost of equipment operation.* The per unit cost of producing work is especially important when selecting equipment to be used in high-volume operations. Although operating costs may be quite similar for various devices being considered, differences in costs may be significant over time. Cost comparison is especially important when selecting printing, duplicating, and photocopying equipment. Because the various operating processes are quite variable, the per unit cost may vary considerably.
12. *Equipment operator input.* Employees who will be responsible for operating the equipment are often given an opportunity to provide input into deciding which piece of equipment to select. This practice not only improves the opportunity for selecting equipment that employees find suitable, but also gives them a feeling of involvement. Unless employees are satisfied with the operation of a particular piece of equipment, its efficient use cannot always be guaranteed.

What advantages result from standardizing equipment brands?

13. *Standardization of equipment.* The use of only a few different brands of equipment, resulting in standardization, is found desirable by most organizations. This practice may enable the organization to take advantage of quantity purchasing as well as reduce its service costs because fewer brands of equipment have to be maintained. Another advantage is the ease with which employees can learn to operate similar pieces of equipment.

Vendor considerations include the following:

1. *Reputation of the equipment vendor.* An important consideration when selecting office equipment is the reputation of the equipment vendor. Factors that affect the vendor's reputation are age of the vendor firm, size of the firm, services provided by the firm, financial stability of the firm, range of equipment sold by the firm, and the vendor firm's reputation in the community. Most organizations are more concerned about the reputation of the vendor when purchasing specialized,

costly equipment than when purchasing low-cost, nonspecialized equipment.

Why should the nature of training provided by manufacturers or vendors be determined?

2. *Training provided by the manufacturer or equipment vendor.* Because of the specialized nature of some new types of office equipment, employees may need to be trained before they are able to use the equipment effectively. The quality of training experiences the various manufacturers or vendors provide is quite variable. Some vendors provide training only at the time the equipment is installed, whereas others provide training whenever a new operator uses the equipment. Thus, if the original equipment operator leaves the organization, the vendor will train the replacement operator. When specialized equipment is being considered, an investigation should be made of the nature of the training experiences provided by the manufacturer or vendor.

   Fewer manufacturers and vendors are providing training now than before. The trend is to provide the purchaser with quality training materials that enable users to self-train. In such cases, the quality of the training materials should be evaluated during the selection process.
3. *Purchasing option.* Some vendors only sell certain types of equipment, whereas others lease as well as sell equipment. If an organization is interested in only one of the two options, but not both, this factor needs to be considered early in the selection process. The advantages and disadvantages of purchasing and leasing are discussed in the "Obtaining Office Equipment" section of this chapter.
4. *Delivery of the new equipment.* The timing of equipment purchase or replacement cannot always be planned. Because of circumstances beyond the organization's control, the immediate delivery of new equipment may be important. Vendors unable to guarantee a delivery date may have to be eliminated from consideration.

Maintenance considerations include the following:

1. *Servicing the equipment.* The ability to obtain fast, reliable service on the equipment is another factor that should be considered in selecting equipment. This is especially true in situations where no backup equipment is available to perform crucial work processes. Some equipment vendors do not provide the same quality of equipment servicing as others; therefore, this factor should be carefully weighed, especially when purchasing expensive, intricate or specialized equipment. In addition, the geographical location of the vendor may be important. Vendors who are located a considerable distance from the organization may not be able to provide rapid service.
2. *Equipment maintenance.* Another factor to be considered is the nature of the routine maintenance required by the equipment. This factor is important because some brands of equipment require more routine maintenance than other brands. The nature of equipment maintenance is especially important when purchasing printing, duplicating, and photocopying equipment, because the amount of maintenance required varies considerably from brand to brand of equipment.

Use of Comparative Analysis Form

When several brands of equipment are being considered, the equipment has to be compared on a systematic, objective basis. As the number of brands under consideration increases, the task of comparing the equipment becomes more difficult. To facilitate the comparison, the use of a form such as the one illustrated in Figure 6-1 is helpful. The form ensures the comparison of the equipment on a consistent, objective basis.

Obtaining Office Equipment

What two alternatives are available for obtaining office equipment?

Basically, organizations have two alternatives for obtaining office equipment: leasing and purchasing. Before making a final decision, the advantages and disadvantages of using both alternatives for the procurement of specific pieces of equipment should be considered.

Leasing considerations Some organizations find equipment leasing to be a more desirable alternative than purchasing. Of all the various types of office equipment leased, computers are the most common, followed by office copiers.

What is the difference between true leases and leases with the option to purchase?

Two basic types of office equipment leases are available: **true leases** and **leases with the option to purchase**. A true lease is one in which the lessee never intends to purchase the equipment. True leases may be obtained either for a short time or for a longer time with an option to renew. Short-term leases are frequently used for obtaining equipment when an organization has a short-term heavy workload or is concerned about the equipment's becoming technologically obsolete in a relatively short time. This enables the lessee to avoid having to pay on a lease for a long time, having to purchase additional equipment, or having to use obsolete equipment.

The long-term lease with an option to renew is used for leasing equipment that will be needed for several years. At the end of the initial lease period, some lessors lower the cost on renewal of the lease.

A lease with the option to purchase is also used for obtaining office equipment. At the end of the lease period, or at any time the lease is in effect, the lessee has the option of purchasing the equipment. The amount that the lessee has paid on the lease is usually applied toward the purchase price. Some organizations use this alternative to determine how well the equipment will meet its needs before making a purchasing decision.

What is sale-leaseback?

Another alternative, although one that is not too commonly used for obtaining office equipment, is **sale-leaseback**. The organization purchases the equipment, which is then sold to a lessor, who then gives the organization a lease on the equipment. This alternative is desirable for organizations that have to obtain capital rather quickly.

To help determine which of the various leasing alternatives to use, answers to the following questions will be helpful:

1. What will the organization want to do with the equipment at the end of the lease period? (Exercising the right to purchase equipment likely to become technologically obsolete in a relatively short time is generally an unwise decision.)
2. What is the status of the organization's cash flow situation? (The longer a cash flow concern is likely to exist, the more desirable a longer-term lease becomes.)

Name of Manufacturer	Model No.	Pitch	Price	Correction Buffer Size (Characters)	Text Memory Size (in K)	Memory Protection	Visual Display Size (Characters)	Automatic Error Correction	Automatic Underlining	Automatic Word Wraparound	Automatic Centering	Automatic Relocate	Automatic Line Spacing	Playback Speed	Hyphenation	Column Layout	Search-Replace
1																	
2																	
3																	
4																	
5																	
6																	
7																	

Figure 6-1 Comparative analysis form.

3. What is the organization's tax liability situation? (The greater the need to lease equipment for a tax advantage, the more desirable is a true lease rather than a lease with the option to purchase, which has no tax advantage.)
4. What length of time will the organization likely want to use the equipment? (True leases provide greater flexibility in terms of lease length.)

What are the advantages of leasing?

Leasing office equipment results in several advantages:

1. Leasing conserves capital that may be needed for other purposes. The working capital that might otherwise have been used for equipment purchase is now available for other uses, such as expansion, market development, or construction.
2. The organization is able to obtain up-to-date equipment. The financial cost of exchanging obsolete leased equipment is less than the cost of purchasing new equipment and trying to sell or trade in old equipment. A related advantage is the ease with which the organization can keep replacing currently used equipment with the technologically latest equipment.
3. True lease payments are tax deductible. A lease with an option to purchase is considered as a conditional sales contract and, therefore, is not deductible.
4. Leasing equipment enables an organization to use its financial resources more efficiently. A short-term lease is advantageous for obtaining equipment needed for only a short time each year. An organization that purchases equipment for such purposes is unable to maximize the return on its investment.

Although leasing office equipment is desirable for several reasons, the following distinct disadvantages also result:

What are the disadvantages of leasing?

1. Leased office equipment is frequently more costly than is purchased equipment. The total lease payments frequently exceed the purchase price of the equipment.
2. The lease may stipulate that the lessee is responsible for equipment maintenance and repairs. Equipment leased under these terms can be quite costly if its service needs are higher than average.
3. Most leases stipulate that the lessee keep detailed records on the leased equipment. If this is the case and if the organization leases a considerable amount of equipment, the paperwork may become quite burdensome.
4. If the lease gives the lessee an opportunity to purchase the equipment, the lease payments are not tax deductible. Only payments made on true leases are deductible.

A fairly new development in office equipment leasing is the emergence of leasing companies. Rather than lease equipment from an equipment vendor or manufacturer, the equipment is obtained from a leasing company. The leasing company—by purchasing the desired equipment from the manufacturer and then leasing the equipment to the lessee—acts as a third party between the lessee and the manufacturer. One desirable characteristic of leasing companies is the flexibility of the leasing arrangements they provide.

Equipment leasing and rental differ from one another in the following ways: Leasing frequently involves a contract that clearly stipulates the length of time the lease is in effect. Rental, conversely, may not require that the lessee use the equipment for a specified period. At any time, the equipment can be returned with no further obligations to its owner.

What are the advantages of purchasing?

Purchasing considerations Many organizations prefer to purchase their office equipment because it is considered an asset and it can be used in whatever manner the organization wishes. Some leasing arrangements put restrictions on the use of leased equipment. Purchased equipment can also be disposed of by selling, which to some individuals makes the purchasing alternative preferable to the leasing alternative.

Purchased equipment provides the organization with financial advantages that are not available when equipment is leased. To illustrate, purchased equipment can be depreciated, which helps reduce the organization's income tax obligation.

Some equipment manufacturers provide their customers with financial assistance. To illustrate, some manufacturers sell their equipment on an interest-free credit basis. For example, a six-months-same-as-cash arrangement is a common offer many manufacturers provide. In other instances, the organization is able to obtain a loan through the manufacturer that has a lower interest rate than a loan obtained from a commercial lending institution.

Making the decision Among the various factors that should be considered when deciding whether to lease or to purchase office equipment are the following:

1. *How rapidly are new technological developments occurring in the type of equipment being considered?* If the equipment is undergoing frequent technological change, leasing may be more desirable. Thus, the organization is able to update its equipment regularly.
2. *What is the purchase cost of the equipment?* Some of the more expensive equipment is leased rather than purchased. When equipment is obtained in this way, capital is available for more urgent needs.
3. *What leasing arrangements are equipment vendors willing to provide?* Although most equipment vendors in a given geographical area are quite competitive in terms of the leasing arrangements, some vendors may provide conditions that make leasing more desirable than purchasing. In such cases, leasing should be given serious consideration.
4. *What special provisions become available when leasing equipment?* In some instances, the lessor is responsible for equipment maintenance. Some organizations find this to be a significant reason for leasing rather than purchasing.
5. *How stable are the various work processes for which the equipment is needed?* If the work processes are expected to change significantly during the life of the equipment, leasing should be given serious consideration. Consequently, the organization is not burdened with having to sell an unneeded piece of equipment or burdened with a device that does not adequately meet its work processing requirements.
6. *What is the per unit cost of work when leasing equipment and when purchasing equipment?* When the equipment is to be used for high-volume operations, the per unit cost of each of the two alternatives should be determined. If the leasing alternative is considerably less costly over time, leasing may be a more desirable option.
7. *What are the results of a break-even analysis?* Often helpful in making a decision about leasing or purchasing equipment is a **break-even analysis**. Such an analysis is calculated for both the leasing and the purchasing alternatives. The break-even point occurs when the income from the units produced by the equipment equals the aggregate expenses incurred in producing the units. Stated another way, the point occurs when the organization experiences neither income nor loss in terms of the number of units produced. If the organization an-

What is break-even analysis?

ticipates that it will use the equipment to produce more than the minimum number of units needed to achieve the break-even point, the procurement of the equipment is likely to be financially feasible. If the break-even point is not likely to be reached in terms of the volume produced, then the financial feasibility of the equipment is questionable. To calculate the break-even point, the following data are needed: fixed costs, variable costs, and anticipated production volume.

8. *What is the length of the payback period?* Also helpful in making a decision about which procurement alternative to use is the calculation of the **payback period**. This calculation will enable the organization to determine how long it must use the equipment to recover an amount of cash equal to the procurement cost. Depending on the type of equipment, the payback period may be so long that the use of the equipment cannot be financially justified. In some cases, the payback period for purchasing and leasing is similar; in other instances, one of the two alternatives is clearly advantageous. If the purchase alternative has a long payback period and if the equipment has a chance of becoming obsolete within a short time, the leasing alternative becomes much more attractive.

What is meant by the payback period?

Equipment Maintenance Considerations

Maintenance of office equipment is important not only because of problems arising from improperly maintained equipment, but also because of the cost of repairs resulting from inadequate maintenance. The life of office equipment can be affected by the quality of its maintenance. Day-to-day operator maintenance is also helpful in increasing the useful life of equipment and for decreasing the number of needed equipment repairs.

The maintenance of equipment is typically provided by one or more of the following three methods: service contract with a representative of the equipment manufacturer or service agency; service provided on a call basis by a representative of the equipment manufacturer or service agency; and an in-house service department. Some organizations put a portion of their equipment on a service contract, and the remainder is maintained on a call basis. Each of the three methods is explained in the following paragraphs.

What are the benefits of using the service contract method of equipment maintenance?

Service Contract This method of equipment maintenance involves a service contract with a representative of the manufacturer or with a service agency. Most contracts are valid for increments of one year. During the term of the contract, the representatives of the equipment manufacturer or service agency generally are responsible not only for equipment repairs, but also for routine maintenance, such as cleaning and lubrication.

Some service contracts specify that equipment will receive a thorough cleaning and lubrication once a year, in addition to a specified number of routine inspections during the year. Preventive maintenance is a distinct characteristic of this method. Depending on the nature of the contract, the cost of minor replacement parts may be covered, whereas the owner of the equipment may be responsible for the cost of major replacement parts.

Service contracts provide several important benefits. Perhaps most important is the preventive maintenance benefit. Another advantage is the reduced amount of paperwork that is involved. If maintenance is provided on a call basis, over time the amount of paperwork involved in preparing vouchers and checks can be quite extensive. When a service contract is used, the paperwork is processed only once a year. Another advantage of the service contract is the fairly quick response time that it provides.

Perhaps the most significant disadvantage of service contracts is their cost. Depending on the provisions and the type of equipment covered, the cost may range from one hundred dollars to several hundred dollars a year per device. Therefore, equipment needing no repairs will cost as much to maintain as equipment needing frequent repairs. Although service contracts may be quite expensive, their cost can be partially offset in a variety of ways, making their use more feasible. Equipment may last longer, which helps offset the cost of the contract. The cost can also be partially offset by the reduced amount of paperwork.

Before an organization purchases a service contract, the following provisions in the contract need to be carefully assessed:

What factors about a service contract need to be considered before signing the contract?

1. Nature of the coverage of service calls, parts, and labor.
2. Minimum number of inspections during contract period.
3. Provisions or restrictions for on-site and shop work.
4. Renewal conditions.
5. Availability of loaner equipment when needed.
6. Mileage for service technician.
7. Nature of exclusions.
8. Specific machines covered by the equipment.
9. Dates of coverage.
10. Cost of contract.

Call basis When equipment is maintained on a call basis, the representative of the equipment manufacturer or service agency is called each time the equipment needs to be repaired. Unless special provisions are made, the equipment does not receive the yearly cleaning and lubrication customarily included with service contracts. The owner of the equipment, therefore, pays only for services performed.

In comparison to a service contract, this method of equipment maintenance appears on the surface to be less costly. But when the cost of preparing payment invoices and checks and the lack of preventive maintenance are considered, the call basis may be more expensive over the long run than having a service contract on the equipment. Furthermore, the call basis typically does not produce as fast repair time as the service contract basis provides.

In-house service Large organizations sometimes have their own in-house service departments. The organization employs individuals trained to service the equipment. Because of frequent changes in equipment technology, these employees periodically have to undergo training to update their knowledge. In addition to the salaries of these individuals, the organization must also consider the cost of fringe benefits as well as the cost of retraining. For these reasons, this maintenance method is generally feasible only for larger organizations. When an organization has its own in-house service, the number of brands of equipment is frequently kept to a minimum. This may prevent the organization from achieving the flexibility that is possible when a greater number of brands of equipment is used.

The use of an in-house service department often results in more rapid repair of equipment than is possible with either of the other two methods. This has a significant impact on equipment downtime. When the service de-

What factors should be considered in deciding which method of equipment maintenance to use?

1. Cost and provisions of a service contract.
2. Frequency of equipment repair.
3. Impact of preventive maintenance on increasing the life of equipment.
4. Availability of and expense incurred in employing trained service personnel.
5. Number of different brands of office equipment owned by the organization.
6. Type of equipment to be maintained.
7. Cost of paperwork associated with equipment maintenance.
8. Speed with which the equipment must be repaired.

Figure 6-2 Factors to consider when deciding on equipment maintenance method.

partment is not busy with equipment repair, preventive maintenance on equipment can be performed. In addition to the cost of staffing the in-house service department, equipment parts and tools must be considered.

When deciding which of the three methods of equipment maintenance to use, Figure 6-2 identifies several factors to consider.

Replacement Considerations

The administrative office manager also has to be concerned about equipment replacement. The useful life of office equipment is often determined by the nature of the equipment and by the amount of its usage. Equipment that receives considerable use or that tends to become obsolete quite rapidly may be depreciated over a shorter time than other types of equipment. For example, a typewriter used most of each workday may be depreciated over a five-year period, whereas an adding machine that is seldom used may be depreciated over a ten-year period. At the end of the depreciation period, the equipment is traded for new equipment.

Keeping office equipment for the length of time that it is being depreciated is not always financially feasible. Changes in technology or work processes may make the present equipment inefficient, or perhaps a particular piece of equipment requires frequent repair. In those instances, the organization may consider accelerating the trade-in time. Some equipment has a good repair record at the time it is to be traded in, however, and the decision may be made to keep the equipment longer.

Inventory Control Considerations

The administrative office manager is also frequently given the responsibility for equipment inventory. The absence of accurate inventory control records makes maintaining control over equipment more difficult. Inventory control involves keeping detailed records on each piece of equipment, includingsuch information as the following:

1. Serial number of each piece of equipment the organization owns, leases, or rents.
2. Date the organization purchased, leased, or rented the equipment.
3. Purchase cost of the equipment.

What information about each piece of equipment needs to be kept for inventory control?

4. Life of the equipment (either actual life or lease life).
5. Yearly depreciation of the equipment.
6. Book value of the equipment.
7. Location of each piece of equipment.
8. Inventory control number assigned to the device.
9. Costs involved in servicing the equipment.

Keeping the inventory control records up-to-date is critical. Otherwise, little will be gained by maintaining an inventory of the equipment. Most organizations undertake a detailed inventory on a yearly basis to determine whether or not equipment is located where the record indicates it is.

OFFICE FURNITURE

The selection of office furniture should receive the same careful attention received by the selection of office equipment. The effect of improperly selected office furniture may be felt for a long time because the disposal of pre-owned furniture, which is typically purchased rather than leased, is often quite difficult. The useful life of office furniture is generally quite long, making its proper selection even more critical.

Several factors guide the selection of office furniture. The impact of these factors should be thoroughly assessed before the furniture is selected.

What factors need to be assessed in selecting office furniture?

1. *Intended use of the furniture*. Before furniture is selected, its intended use must be thoroughly analyzed. To select furniture without first considering this factor often results in inappropriately selected furniture. The users of the furniture should be considered when analyzing furniture use.
2. *Appropriateness of furniture in relation to decor of office*. The coordination of the office furniture with the decor is desirable. Because most offices are redecorated several times during the life of the furniture, its versatility for use in other color schemes should be considered. To select office furniture appropriate only for the present decor is a questionable practice.
3. *Suitability of furniture for its users*. Much employee fatigue can be prevented by adjusting furniture to meet user requirements. Most chairs and some desks are adjustable to compensate for the variability of employees' physical characteristics. Floor-mounted furniture components, such as the desk, are easier to adjust than are panel-mounted furniture components.

   Of special concern are furniture components suitable for long-term users of VDTs. The nature of their jobs typically puts them in a stationary position for longer periods than any other category of office employees. Consequently, these employees can experience considerable discomfort unless the furniture is adjustable to meet their specific physical characteristics.

   The work area on which the terminal sits should be adjustable, making it possible for the employee to be able to look slightly downward at the display. The center of the terminal display should be 30 to 45 inches above the floor, and the keyboard should be at a height that enables the employee to keep his or her arms nearly level. The employee's chair should provide back support and promote upright posture, and the chair height should put the employee's knees slightly higher than his or her hips.

4. *Versatility of furniture.* Some types of office furniture have more than one function. An example is a desk that can also function as a drafting table. Therefore, investigating furniture versatility is advisable.
5. *Durability of furniture.* The durability of the furniture is determined by manufacturing techniques and the materials of which it is constructed. For example, metal furniture is generally more durable than wooden furniture.
6. *Hierarchical level of furniture user.* Because certain types of office furniture have more prestigious characteristics than other types, most organizations match the prestige of the furniture with the hierarchical level of the user. Employees at higher levels are generally given more prestigious furniture than those at lower levels. Furniture characteristics that determine prestige are the materials used in the construction process, the size of the furniture, and the special design characteristics of the furniture.
7. *Size of furniture in relation to room or area size.* When selecting new office furniture, the size of the area or room in which the furniture is to be placed must be considered. Selecting furniture too large for its area causes a variety of problems, including aesthetics.
8. *Fire-retardant value of furniture.* Upholstered office furniture must be constructed of fire-retardant materials that will have a positive impact on eliminating some of the dense smoke created in a fire.

New Developments in Office Furniture

New developments in office furniture use the systems approach. Comprised of a number of furniture components designed to accommodate the user and the tasks he or she performs, **systems furniture** is replacing traditional office furniture in many offices. Systems furniture possesses the following characteristics: **modular design**, **portable design**, **functional design**, and **ergonomics design.** Each of these characteristics is discussed in the following sections.

When compared with traditional office furniture, systems furniture enjoys several distinct advantages. Systems furniture requires less floor space. It also provides a wide range of finishes (both wood and non-wood); a variety of heights, shapes, and color; and a response to user needs. Systems furniture is also more adaptable to existing space than is traditional furniture, and it can be readily modified to accommodate changes in work flow, employees' tasks, and workforce needs.

What are the characteristics of modular design?

Modular design This characteristic refers to the design of office furniture that facilitates the use of different components and variations in the way the components are arranged. A modular unit may consist of such components as a desk or working space, storage space, file space, and shelf space.

The employee's job responsibilities are considered when determining the components needed in a modular unit. Those employees whose jobs require greater amounts of working space and less storage space can be easily accommodated. In many cases, modular design results in a self-contained workstation, such as the one illustrated in Figure 6-3. These stations, in addition to containing the necessary working and storage space areas, also contain electrical and telephone connections.

Portable design The increasing use of open space planning in office layout has increased the need for the portability of office furniture. One of the

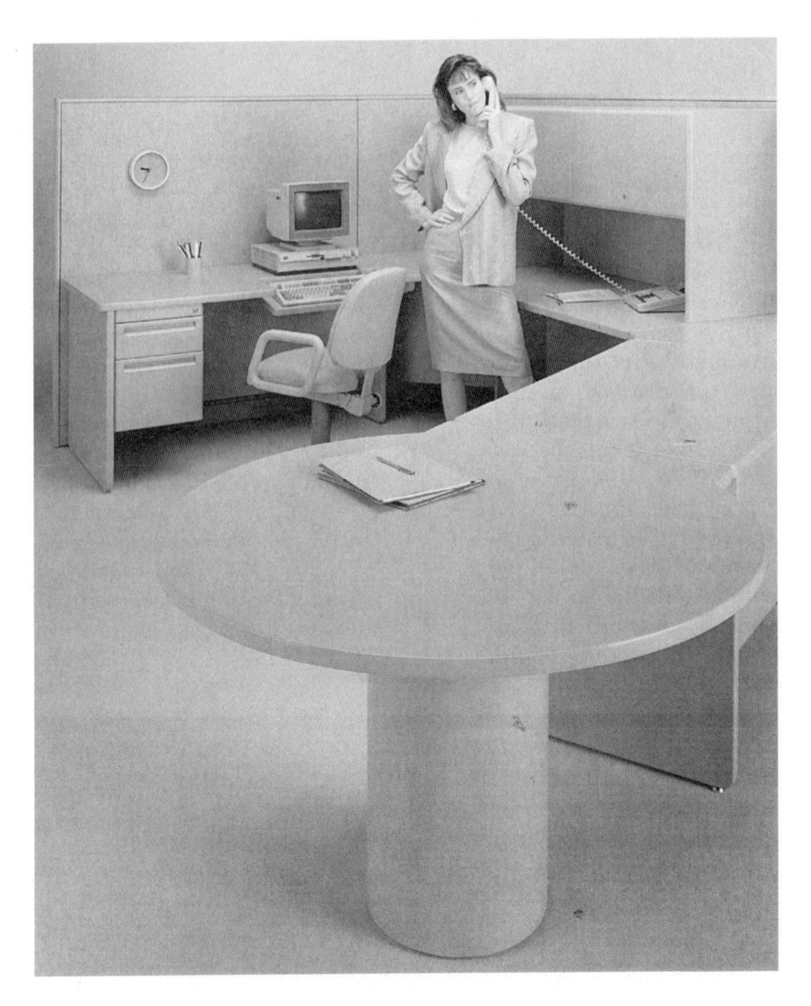

Figure 6-3 Modularly designed workstation. Courtesy: TAB Products Co.

characteristics of open space planning is the ease with which office areas can be arranged. Movable panels and screens, such as those illustrated in Figure 6-4, are examples of portable office furniture. Movable panels, which are used to accomplish the same purposes as permanent walls, are desirable because extensive remodeling is not required when rearranging office space.

What are the characteristics of portable design?

What are the characteristics of functional design?

Functional design Basing the design of office furniture on individual needs results in functional design. Much of the new office furniture has a research base resulting from an analysis of work processes and employees' effort in the performance of their jobs. This information is subsequently used in designing furniture components and their appropriate configuration in the work area.

To illustrate, if the employee is able to perform job duties more effectively by standing rather than by sitting, the functionally designed furniture can readily accommodate the user. In fact, a number of the office furniture manufacturers have added to their product line an upscale desk, costing several thousands of dollars, that enables the user to adjust it easily to accommodate work in the normal sitting position, a standing position, or tilting the desk top for document display. Another feature in these desks is a regular beep to remind users to change their position, a technique that helps relieve fatigue and boredom.

Figure 6-4 Portable furniture components. Courtesy: The Knoll Group.

In addition, increasing numbers of manufacturers are becoming more sensitive to the needs of individuals with disabilities. Most people with disabilities find a 28-inch desk more comfortable than the standard 29-inch desk. Office chairs should be equipped with arms to enable people with disabilities to lift themselves more easily. The Americans with Disabilities Act passed in 1990 has important implications for the accommodation of individuals with disabilities in the workplace.

Ergonomics design Growing numbers of furniture manufacturers are taking ergonomics into consideration when designing office furniture. Ergonomics is the scientific study of the relationship between employees and their physical environment.

The science of ergonomics can be applied most directly to the chairs employees use. An ergonomically designed chair is adjustable to accommodate variations in the sizes and shapes of human bodies. More chairs are becoming readily adjusted to accommodate the various work styles of the user. For example, if the user is working at his or her desk, a locked position to support the back is likely preferred. When the user is in conference, however, being able to lean back is desirable. A truly ergonomic chair readily accommodates the following adjustments: back height, seat height, arm height, back tilt, seat tilt, and arm width. Ergonomic chairs are now available with such a variety of adjustments that each individual user needs a "fitting" when the chair is put into use, especially the height, the lumbar support, and backrest position.

What are the characteristics of ergonomics design?

Ergonomically designed office furniture is more comfortable, less fatiguing and mentally exhausting, and provides better support for the human body. Employees who use ergonomically designed furniture are often able to produce more work at a higher quality than are those who use standard furniture.

Figure 6-5 illustrates the design characteristics of new developments in office furniture.

Figure 6-5 Drawing showing new developments in office furniture. Courtesy: School Arts Magazine, Davis Publications, Inc.

Use of Safety and Performance Standards

The **Business and Institutional Furniture Manufacturers Association (BIFMA)** provides an important service to administrative office managers involved in selecting office furniture. The BIFMA, by being concerned with safety and performance standards in office furniture, benefits the purchaser. Any office product carrying a BIFMA rating has been subjected to certain testing and evaluation procedures that certify its safety and performance level.

IMPLICATIONS FOR THE ADMINISTRATIVE OFFICE MANAGER

The administrative office manager plays a significant role in the process of selecting office equipment and furniture. Areas in which the manager has expertise are the following: determining equipment needs and evaluating how well various devices actually meet these needs. Often, the amount and variety of equipment now available enable the organization to maximize the match between needs and functions.

In most organizations, the administrative office manager is the individual who determines which alternative—leasing or purchasing—should be exercised in obtaining office equipment. This may involve calculating per unit cost of work, which is affected by the volume of the work processed by the device. Generally, as volume increases, the per unit cost decreases.

The process of selecting furniture is often as involved as selecting equipment. The functionality of the furniture has to be evaluated, in addition to its appropriateness for the work areas in which it will be used. Its suitability for the overall decor also has to be assessed. Unless careful attention is paid to important details, some of the attractiveness of the environment can be destroyed once the furniture is in place. Now that furniture is available in so many exciting, vibrant colors, even greater care has to be exercised in selecting furniture.

The background and training of the administrative office manager enables him or her to direct the process of selecting office equipment and furniture. No other individual is likely to have as broad an understanding of what is involved or as much knowledge about the process.

REVIEW QUESTIONS

1. In what ways can the dependability of equipment be determined?
2. When selecting new equipment, why should the ability to obtain fast, reliable equipment service be considered?
3. When selecting new equipment, why is its flexibility an important consideration?
4. When a particular line of equipment is experiencing rapid technological advancements, is purchasing or leasing generally more desirable? Why or why not?
5. How do equipment leasing and rental differ from one another?
6. What are the advantages and disadvantages of equipment leasing?
7. What types of services are provided by equipment leasing companies?
8. When determining which alternative—service contracts, call basis, or in-house maintenance—would be most desirable, what factors should be considered?
9. In what ways do functional design and modular design of office furniture differ from one another?
10. What is meant by ergonomic ~~design~~ in office furniture?

DISCUSSION QUESTIONS

1. The company in which you work always purchases the same brand of such office equipment as typewriters, computer printers, copiers, and faxes. No other brand of equipment is ever considered. Discuss the implications of this situation.
2. You were recently discussing with your supervisor the pending requisition of some new office equipment. In the course of this conversation, your supervisor said that the most important factor to consider is how efficiently the equipment performs the functions for which it will be used. Do you agree that this is the most important consideration? Justify your response.
3. As the newly appointed department manager in a large bank, one of your first duties was to make plans to obtain additional office equipment. You suggested to the bank's director of purchasing that the equipment be leased. He replied that the bank has a policy requiring the purchase of all office equipment. Discuss the implications of this policy.
4. In the past, the organization for which you work has purchased all of its office equipment. For several reasons, the organization's executive committee now believes leasing some of its equipment may be a wise move. You have been given the responsibility of devising a list of criteria that could be used to help determine whether equipment should be purchased or leased. State the criteria as questions that require a yes or no response. The greater the number of yes responses, the more desirable the leasing option is.
5. You are the newly appointed administrative office manager in the corporate headquarters of an automobile manufacturer. The vice president to whom you are responsible asked you to prepare, as one of your first tasks, some standard guidelines for use in the replacement of office equipment. Each department now handles its own replacement, which results in little uniformity in the way equipment is replaced. Identify the guidelines that will help standardize the procedures used in equipment replacement.
6. The organization in which you work makes extensive use of modular workstations in its open office areas. You were surprised to learn recently that your request for additional shelf space could not be fulfilled because the shelving that was available couldn't be attached to your workstation panels. When you asked about this situation, you learned that all of the components of these workstations are obtained on a bid basis, which explains the reasons for several brands of components that are not compatible. Discuss the implications of the use of bids to obtain these components.

STUDENT PROJECTS AND ACTIVITIES

1. Using a comparative analysis form, evaluate two comparable brands of a specific type of office equipment.
2. Discuss with an office equipment sales representative the leasing versus purchasing of a piece of office equipment.
3. Compare the various features found on two chairs suitable for use in an executive office.
4. Discuss with an administrative office manager the procedures found in the organization in which he or she works that are used to determine appropriate office furniture for various types of employees.
5. Discuss with an administrative office manager the specific procedures used in maintaining the inventory of office equipment and furniture.

MINICASE

The management of the Randolph Corporation, a manufacturer of shop tools, recently decided to move to another building that better meets its space needs. One of the objectives of the move is to modernize its facilities. Much of the furniture presently used was purchased about twenty-five years ago. As the administrative office manager, you have been asked by the executive vice president to provide her with information about some of the new developments in office furniture that should be considered in making purchasing decisions. In the written report you plan to transmit to the executive vice president,

1. Identify and discuss the characteristics of new developments in office furniture.
2. Identify several characteristics you believe the company should consider when purchasing office furniture.

CASE

The Sunlight Manufacturing Company, which is located in Tulsa, Oklahoma, is a manufacturer of oil-drilling equipment. For a number of years, the company experienced a fairly slow but steady growth pattern. During the decade of the 1970s, the company estimated it had about 30 percent of the market in the oil-producing states in the Southwest region of the United States.

During the last several years, the company has experienced a phenomenal rate of growth. Many oil-drilling companies are now replacing older, less efficient equipment with newer, more efficient equipment, a situation that has produced a significant demand for Sunlight's oil rigs and other equipment it manufactures.

Increases in demand for the company's products have also increased the amount of office equipment needed for the company to function efficiently. The company also realizes that sooner or later the supply will catch up with the demand for its products, which will likely result in the need for less equipment. However, a possibility exists that the additional office equipment will be needed for several years, which may make its purchase more costly than leasing it would be.

As the administrative office manager for the company, you have been asked by its president to write a position paper in which you do the following:

1. Identify and discuss the guidelines to be used when determining whether ownership or leasing the equipment is preferable.
2. Identify the advantages of each alternative.
3. Explain how the company can determine if the guidelines you are presenting are realistic.

CHAPTER

7

SELECTING OFFICE EMPLOYEES

CHAPTER AIM

After studying this chapter, you should be able to design an effective program for selecting office employees for any type of organization.

CHAPTER OUTLINE

- Sources of Potential Office Employees
  - Internal Sources
    - Employee Referral
    - Employee Promotion
    - Data Banks
  - External Sources
    - Unsolicited Applications
    - Advertising
    - Educational Institution Placement Services
    - Professional Organizations
    - Employee Leasing
    - Public Employment Agencies
    - Private Employment Agencies
    - Temporary Help Agencies
    - Resume Banks
- Outsourcing
- Hiring People with Disabilities
- Selection Process
  - Employee Requisition Blank
  - Job Descriptions and Job Specifications
  - Screening Interview
  - Application Blank
  - Biographical Information Blank
  - Employee Testing
  - Background and Reference Investigation
  - Selection Interview
  - Medical Exam
  - Payroll Change Notice
  - Employee File
- Testing Program
  - Test Reliability and Validity
  - Legal Considerations
  - Types of Testing
    - Performance or Achievement Tests
    - Aptitude Tests
    - Intelligence Tests
    - Personality Tests
- Interviewing Process
  - Patterned Interview
  - Direct Interview
  - Indirect Interview
  - Functional Interview
- Affirmative Action Program
- Federal Legislation
  - Civil Rights Act of 1964
  - Age Discrimination in Employment Act of 1967
  - Equal Employment Opportunity Act of 1972

- Executive Orders
- Vocational Rehabilitation Act of 1973
- Vietnam Era Veterans' Readjustment Assistance Act of 1974
- Pregnancy Discrimination Act of 1978
- Americans with Disabilities Act of 1990
- Civil Rights Act of 1991

Making the Decision
- Single-predictor Approach
- Multiple-predictor Approach

Monitoring Selection Process

Implications for the Administrative Office Manager

CHAPTER TERMS

Aptitude tests
Biodata tests
Biographical information blank
Bona fide occupational qualifications (BFOQ)
Career fairs
Construct validity
Content validity
Criterion-related validity
Differential validity
Direct interview
Employee leasing
Employee requisition blank
Functional interview
Indirect interview
Intelligence tests
Job descriptions
Job specifications
Offer-to-hire ratio
Outsourcing
Patterned interview
Performance (achievement) tests
Resume banks
Personality tests
Selection ratio
Test reliability
Test validity
Unsolicited application
United States Employment Service (USES)

The success of many organizations is enhanced because of the quality of their workforce, which is directly related to their employee selection process. Each time a hiring decision is made, the ability of the organization to achieve its goals is to a certain extent influenced either positively or negatively. An effective selection program helps reduce employee training time, absenteeism, and turnover and helps increase overall employee productivity.

The organization's workforce requirements have to be determined before the process of selecting employees begins. Selection is comprised of several steps, beginning with employee recruitment and ending with job placement.

The cost of hiring one office employee earning an average salary is now approximately $3,500. An effective selection process is advantageous for a number of reasons, one of which is the cost reduction attributable to hiring activities.

An increasing number of organizations are now hiring individuals with disabilities, and the results are positive. A section on hiring people with disabilities is included later in this chapter.

SOURCES OF POTENTIAL OFFICE EMPLOYEES

What internal and external sources of potential office employees exist?

The recruitment of office employees can be done either internally or externally. Internal sources consist of employee referral, promotion from within, and data banks, whereas external sources are more varied and consist of the following: unsolicited applications, advertising, educational institution placement services, professional organizations, employee leasing, public employment agencies, private employment agencies, temporary help agencies, and resume data banks.

Employee recruiting can be enhanced in several ways. Among these are using a sufficient number of recruiting sources, using appropriate recruiting sources for the position being filled, and identifying clearly the requirements of the vacant position. Furthermore, recruiting from a sufficiently wide geographical area may also enhance the quality of the applicant pool.

Internal Sources

The use of internal sources in some respects is more desirable than external sources. If a new supervisor is needed in a certain department and one of the present employees meets the stated requirements, promoting that individual to the supervisory position may be a wiser move than hiring from outside.

Employee referral When the referral method is used, employees recommend individuals for open positions within the organization. Although referral may give employees a feeling of recognition and importance, it may also create some problems. For instance, an employee may experience considerable embarrassment if the individual he or she recommended does not perform satisfactorily. Some organizations consider this recruiting source to be so valuable that bonuses are given to employees if the individuals they recommend stay with the organization a specified length of time.

Why is the use of employee promotion desirable?

Employee promotion A second internal source is promoting employees to higher-level positions. Promotion is desirable for several reasons. Employees are apt to perform better when they know promotions are available. Furthermore, morale is likely to increase and turnover decrease when employees can be promoted. Perhaps the greatest disadvantage of filling open positions through promotion is that new ideas are not brought in from the outside.

Data banks Numerous organizations, especially larger ones, are maintaining their employees' job qualifications in a computerized data bank. Thus, the entire workforce can be easily and quickly screened to determine which employees are presently qualified for an open position. Those who possess the qualifications are then further screened to determine suitability for the open position. The information stored in data banks is also helpful in preparing a variety of employment reports. To maintain a high level of validity, the information in data banks must be continually updated.

External Sources

The use of an external source may be preferable to an internal source. An external source should be considered if none of the present employees is qualified for or interested in the open position.

What is an unsolicited application?

Unsolicited applications An **unsolicited application** is used by an employee who applies for a position without knowing if an opening actually exists. Individuals using this method may apply either in person or by a mailed-in application.

To a certain extent, unsolicited applications are viewed negatively in some organizations, although a percentage of the individuals who use unsolicited applications have excellent qualifications. An organization should not totally discount the value of all unsolicited applications simply because this recruiting source may not yield a high number of acceptable applicants.

Advertising As a recruiting source, advertising includes classified newspaper advertisements, magazine and journal advertisements, and radio and television notices. The newest form of advertising open positions is on electronic bulletin boards found on the Internet. Because advertising reaches a wide audience in a short time, many individuals may apply for only a few openings. Using this source of recruiting may result in many marginally qualified or even unqualified applicants. Consequently, the screening process may be considerably more time consuming. The use of advertising may be desirable, however, when many employees are needed in a short time, such as when a new facility opens.

What services are provided by educational institution placement services?

Educational institution placement services Use of the placement services of educational institutions to recruit potential employees is common in large organizations and a growing number of smaller organizations. Educational institution placement services provide important services to both the employer and the job seeker. For example, the placement service usually develops interview schedules and provides recruiters with copies of references. A potential disadvantage is the tendency for some organizations to recruit only at a limited number of colleges or universities. In time, because of a lack of diversity in the backgrounds of employees, an organization may find its managerial philosophy has narrowed.

Increasingly, educational institutions are holding periodic job or **career fairs** that are designed to bring together at one time a number of potential employers and potential employees. Although the fairs are primarily designed for graduating students, persons who are a year or two from graduation are often invited to attend as a means of obtaining career- or employer-related information. Students actively seeking employment may either be interviewed at the fair or invited to interview at a later date.

Professional organizations As a benefit to their members, a growing number of professional organizations are developing and operating placement services. These professional organizations often provide job placement services at their conventions or meetings. In addition, many of these organizations also list openings in their journals and other publications. Because the members of professional organizations tend to be homogeneous, screening of applicants to identify those who are not qualified is not of much concern.

What is employee leasing?

Employee leasing Another means of obtaining employees is through **employee leasing**, which is also known as contract staffing. In this arrangement, workers who are employees of the leasing company are "leased" to various employers in the community. The leasing company and the employer enter into a contract whereby the employer's permanent workers are provided by the leasing company. As with any contractual arrangement, organizations that lease employees need to be sure what their rights and responsibilities are as well as the rights and responsibilities of the leasing company.

In many cases, when an organization enters into an employee-leasing arrangement, its employees are terminated at the end of one work day and return the next as employees of the leasing company. Thus, operational continuity can be easily maintained. When new employees are needed in the organization, the leasing company screens applicants; but the organization generally has final approval over which applicants are hired.

The employee-leasing concept is similar in many respects to the temporary help agency concept that is discussed below. The main difference is in the length of employment. In the temporary arrangement, the employee works for a short time; in the leasing arrangement, the employee works for the employer on a permanent basis.

The leasing arrangement is particularly attractive to employers who have only a handful of employees. These employers may not be able to provide the same number or level of fringe benefits as larger employers—and thus are not as competitive in terms of hiring top-quality employees. The leasing company is able to provide its leased employees a greater number of benefits because of economy of scale.

Some employers also enter into an employee-leasing arrangement because of its positive impact on reduction of personnel administration costs and associated costs, such as administrative paperwork. Because the leasing company is responsible for all facets of personnel administration, the employer is able to eliminate a variety of related costs. In addition, the leased employees are provided with a more extensive fringe benefits package, resulting in improving morale and lessening turnover among employees. For small companies, employee leasing also enables them to avoid having to comply with certain federal and state regulations that pertain to employers with ten to twenty-five employees.

Public employment agencies Although the **United States Employment Service (USES)** has control over public employment agencies, each state is responsible for operating its own agencies. Public employment agencies are found in nearly all metropolitan areas and in several smaller cities in every state. Some of the services these agencies provide are the following: helping employers design testing programs, assisting with wage surveys, and helping with job analysis and evaluation.

By law, an individual who receives unemployment compensation must be registered with the state's public employment agency. The law also requires that an individual who receives unemployment compensation be willing to accept any suitable employment offer. Neither an employer nor the employee is charged for the use of services provided by public employment agencies.

USES will eventually provide a nationwide service that will enable individuals in one state to learn of job openings in another state. At the present, USES distributes a monthly publication, *Occupations in Demand*, to help job seekers become more aware of employment opportunities in other regions.

Who typically pays the fee for the use of the services of a private employment agency?

Private employment agencies Unlike public employment agencies, private agencies charge for the services they provide. The amount of the fee private agencies charge largely depends on the nature of the open position (higher fees are usually charged for higher-level positions), the location of the agency, and the reputation of the agency. Fees may range anywhere from a few days' salary to a percentage of the annual salary outlay of the position being filled.

In many instances, the employer pays either a portion or all of the fee the employment agency charges. Generally, the higher the agency fee, the greater the likelihood that the employer will pay for most or all of it.

Certain factors should be considered when selecting a private employment agency. The reputation of a private agency can be determined to a certain extent if it is a subscribing member of the National Employment Association. Employees and individuals might also contact the agency's former clients to determine how well others are satisfied with its services. Another factor to consider is the agency's ability to provide the quality of employee sought by the organization.

Temporary help agencies Numerous organizations use temporary help agencies to obtain office workers for a short time—from one day to as long as

For what situations are temporary help agencies typically used?

two months. Temporary help agencies are frequently used to obtain employees during seasonally busy times as well as to obtain substitutes for ill or vacationing employees.

The services of the temporary help agency are monetarily attractive, especially for short-term projects. The organization pays the temporary agency for the service rendered, and the agency pays the individual. Consequently, the organization is relieved of the responsibility of having to pay Social Security benefits, payroll taxes, unemployment compensation, insurance benefits, or any of the other fringe benefits the organization provides its full-time employees.

In many instances, an organization will find the cost of a temporary employee to be less than the cost incurred when hiring a full-time employee. Another advantage is the decrease in the amount of time consumed by recruiting applicants and filling the job. Furthermore, many organizations find the use of temporary employees is an excellent way to obtain employees with specialized skills, especially skills in data entry, word processing, and so forth. Finally, the use of temporary employees provides greater staffing flexibility than does the hiring of permanent employees. Kelly Services and Manpower, Inc., are two of the better known temporary agencies for office employees.

Resume banks A relatively new external source of job applicants are **resume banks**, similar to the data banks discussed earlier, with one exception. The data bank is an internal source that maintains the job qualifications of only its own employees. Resume banks, on the other hand, maintain the resumes of any individual, regardless of where he or she works, who wishes to pay the fee to have his or her resume scanned and stored—usually a fee of $50 or less. Organizations wishing to use the services of the resume bank firm by having it do a search for a particular type of individual to fill an open position will also pay a fee, perhaps ranging between $350 and $500.

The search is conducted using job-related terms and phrases. Because terminology is critical, resume bank firms generally work with individuals in selecting appropriate terminology to use in their resume and with their clients in identifying appropriate terminology to use in conducting a useful search. After the computer search is completed, a manual screening is made of the resumes of the individuals identified as possible applicants. The manual screening helps ensure a closer match between an applicant's qualifications and an organization's needs. The client firm then contacts these individuals about interviewing for the open position.

OUTSOURCING

What is outsourcing?

Although not a new means of obtaining employees to staff various work units, **outsourcing** is receiving considerably more attention today than ever before. When using outsourcing, the organization turns over certain of its functions to an outside agency that has the specialization necessary to perform those functions well. The outside agency is responsible for the following: providing employees (including supervisors and management), supplies, and equipment to perform the function. Some of the more common functions performed by outsourcing are the following: office services, food service, janitorial, security, payroll processing, mail room, records management, copying and duplicating, computer processing, and health and wellness services. Generally, any function can be outsourced that is not central to the organization's primary operations.

The use of outsourcing results in several advantages, perhaps most significant of which is cost reduction. Often outsourcing firms that specialize in certain functions are able to perform the functions less expensively (because of economy of scale) than the organization is able to perform that function itself. Because the outsourcing agency is responsible for their employees' salaries and fringe benefits, as well as the equipment it uses, the organization is able to reduce some of its recurring costs. Too, overstaffing is more often found in an in-house staffed work unit than it is when outsourcing is used.

Another distinct advantage of outsourcing is the quality of work processes it provides. Because the outsourcing agency likely provides the same services in a number of other organizations, it is able to use quality work processes that it has refined over the years. The more efficient and cost effective the outsourcing agency is, the more profitable it will become.

A third distinct advantage is the organization's elimination of the need to supervise or manage the outsourced functions, thus saving on administrative overhead. These are the responsibilities of the outsourcing agency. While the organization has to be concerned about advancement opportunities and/or promotions and the periodic appraisal of the work performance of its own employees, it is not concerned about these personnel matters for the outsourced employees.

HIRING PEOPLE WITH DISABILITIES

The impetus for hiring people with disabilities stems from the passage of the Vocational Rehabilitation Act in 1973 and its 1980 amendments. The law requires federal contractors or subcontractors that have a federal contract exceeding $2,500 to take affirmative action to hire, advance, and treat qualified employees with disabilities in a nondiscriminatory way. Those contractors with a contract ranging from $2,500 to $500,000 must submit to the Department of Labor an affirmative action program that outlines their procedures for hiring people with disabilities. The Office of Federal Contract Compliance (OFCC) is the agency that enforces the provisions of the law. The Vocational Rehabilitation Act is also concerned with training, promotion, transfer, and termination practices.

Also well known is the Americans with Disabilities Act that was passed in 1990. This act covers both private and public employers engaged in an industry affecting commerce and who have fifteen or more employees for each working day in each of twenty or more calendar weeks in the current or preceding calendar year. Employers cannot discriminate against an individual with a disability as long as the person is otherwise qualified for the job. During the hiring process, employers can ask about one's ability to perform a job but cannot inquire if an applicant has a disability nor subject the applicant to tests designed to eliminate him or her from further consideration. Furthermore, employers need to provide "reasonable accommodation" in the employment and placement of individuals with disabilities on the job, including—but not limited to—job structuring, restructuring, and equipment modification.

The two primary reasons that organizations have been reluctant to hire people with disabilities are (1) the fear that the employer's insurance costs will increase and (2) the belief that people with disabilities do not perform as well as people without disabilities. Research has proved the fallacy of these two claims.

The following advantages result from employing people with disabilities:

1. Insurance costs do not increase.
2. Job performance of many persons with disabilities equals and often exceeds the performance of able-bodied persons.

What advantages result from the employment of people with disabilities?

3. Absenteeism and tardiness rates of people with disabilities tend to be lower than those of people without disabilities.
4. The accident rates of people with disabilities tend to be lower than those of people without disabilities.

Several sources are available for use in locating people with disabilities seeking employment, including Social Security divisions, hospitals, vocational rehabilitation agencies, and physicians. In addition, the President's Committee on the Employment of the Handicapped has published the *Directory of Organizations Interested in the Handicapped*, a document that identifies 225 organizations that assist employers in locating qualified people with disabilities.

THE SELECTION PROCESS

The selection process begins when a position becomes vacant or a new position is created. The following is a detailed discussion of the various steps involved in a comprehensive selection program.

Employee Requisition Blank

For what is an employee requisition blank used?

In a well-developed employee selection process, the first step is to notify the personnel department that an opening exists. In many instances, the manager or supervisor of the unit that has an opening completes an **employee requisition blank**. This authorizes the personnel department to begin recruiting potential employees to fill the open position. Some employee requisition blanks contain limited information including date, name of department, and the title of the open position. Other employee requisition blanks are more comprehensive and include a description of job duties and requirements of the job holder.

The employee requisition blank lists a number of qualifications, which must have a direct, obvious relationship to successful job performance. The absence of such a relationship may violate federal legislation. The "Federal Legislation" section of this chapter provides a discussion of pertinent legislation.

The employee requisition blank is useful for those organizations that maintain an applicant waiting list. By using the information contained on the requisition, an employer can quickly identify the individuals on the waiting list who are well qualified for the vacant position. Individuals who have the needed qualifications can then be contacted and invited to interview for the position if they are still available.

Job Descriptions and Job Specifications

How do job descriptions and job specifications differ?

Job descriptions and **job specifications**, which are discussed in detail in Chapter 12, should play an integral role in employee selection. Job descriptions identify the duties and responsibilities of a particular job, whereas job specifications outline the requirements of the job. Applicants who are shown the job description and specification for a particular job can readily determine if they are qualified for and interested in the position. This step can provide an important screening function because individuals who decide they lack qualifications or interest in the job can terminate the application process at this point. Those who wish to continue do so by participating next in the screening interview.

Screening Interview

Although not a part of the selection process of all organizations, the screening interview is used to screen job applicants further. Skillful interviewers are frequently able to determine which applicants are obviously not qualified. An effective screening interview process conserves time and effort for the interviewer and the applicant.

Applicants in some organizations fill out only a portion of the application blank before they participate in a screening interview. In other organizations, applicants will have filled out the entire application blank before the interview. In still other organizations, applicants will be given the application blank to complete after the screening interview.

The screening interview is usually fairly short, and the interviewer should make every effort to develop good rapport with the applicant. Subsequent interviews with applicants will then probably be more realistic, and the information provided by the applicants will be more valid. Most questions asked during a screening interview are of a direct nature and are designed to assess the applicant's qualifications.

The interviewer conducting a screening or selection interview has the potential for creating a legal liability for himself or herself and the employer if questions are asked of the interviewee about the following topics: children, age, disabilities, physical characteristics, citizenship, maiden name, arrest record, smoking habits, AIDS and HIV positive test, and sexual orientation.

Application Blank

An applicant who is qualified for a position typically is required to complete an application blank, which continues to be the form that is most widely used in the selection process.

For what is an application blank used?

The application blank is useful for collecting from all applicants the same categories of information. Therefore, the blank is helpful when comparing the background of one applicant with another's background. The application is also used by some organizations to provide a record of each individual's employment history. Depending on the questions or items included on the blank, the psychological impact of certain applicant responses may also be determined. All the information found on the application blank is a potentially significant indicator of an applicant's interests, motivation, personality, and employment qualifications.

The content of application blanks must be closely scrutinized because federal legislation prohibits the inclusion of any items that might result in unfair discrimination against any job applicant. Content sections frequently found are personal data, educational background, employment history, and references. The information asked for on the blank has to be directly related to job performance.

Following is a partial list of topics or areas that cannot be included on the application blank:

1. Applicant's citizenship.
2. Applicant's arrest record.
3. Applicant's marital status or spouse's employment status.
4. Nature and number of dependents the applicant has.
5. Applicant's arrangements for child care.
6. Nature of the applicant's military discharge.

7. Applicant's race or color of hair, skin, or eyes.
8. Applicant's gender.
9. Applicant's religious preference including holidays observed.
10. Applicant's club, organization, society, and lodge affiliation.
11. Applicant's height, weight, or nature of disabilities that do not have a bearing on the ability to perform the job for which he or she is applying.
12. Nature of the applicant's pregnancy record.
13. Nature of any changes in the applicant's name.

Figure 7-1 illustrates a typical application blank.

Increasingly, organizations are designing application blanks that incorporate numerical scoring scales. A score can be obtained for each applicant, and those whose scores fall below a minimum cutoff point are automatically eliminated from further consideration.

The individuals who are still considered to be viable applicants at this point may be asked to take one or more of a variety of tests.

Biographical Information Blank

As a supplement to the application blank, the **biographical information blank** is being used in an increasing number of organizations. The biographical information blank provides the applicant an opportunity to provide information about his or her preference for working alone, being transferred, being a member of a rotating pool, working overtime and on weekends as the need may arise, and so forth. The items included on the biographical information blank are determined by the nature of the job being filled. Essentially, the questions are tailored to the specific job. Biographical information blanks, over the long run, help reduce job turnover resulting from various employment conditions.

Employee Testing

Common in many organizations is the use of tests in selecting office employees. Although numerous standardized tests are available, some organizations have developed their own.

The use of well-designed tests is desirable for the following reasons: (1) test results can be objectively obtained, which eliminates some of the effect of human bias that may develop during an interview; (2) depending on the nature of the test, unknown talents or skills of applicants may be uncovered.

A more detailed discussion of employee testing is presented in the "Testing Program" section later in this chapter. Care must be taken to ensure that the testing program conforms with the Equal Employment Opportunity Act of 1972, which is discussed later in the "Federal Legislation" section.

Background and Reference Investigation

What are the uses of the background and reference investigation?

Individuals who remain viable candidates after test results have been analyzed may be subjected to a background and reference investigation. These investigations are used (1) to verify information provided by the applicants, (2) to obtain additional information about the applicants' backgrounds, and (3) to obtain information about the applicants' performance while employed elsewhere.

Application For Employment

Applicants are considered for all positions without regard to race, color, religion, sex, national origin, age, marital or veteran status, or the presence of a non-job-related medical condition or handicap.

(PLEASE PRINT)

Date of Application ______

Position(s) Applied For ______

Referral Source: ☐ Advertisement ☐ Friend ☐ Relative ☐ Walk-In ☐ Employment Agency ☐ Other ______

Name ______
LAST FIRST MIDDLE

Address ______
NUMBER STREET CITY STATE ZIP CODE

Telephone ( ) ______ Social Security Number ______
AREA CODE

If employed and you are under 18, can you furnish a work permit? ☐ Yes ☐ No

Have you filed an application here before? ☐ Yes ☐ No If Yes, give date ______

Have you ever been employed here before? ☐ Yes ☐ No If Yes, give date ______

Are you employed now? ☐ Yes ☐ No May we contact your present employer? ☐ Yes ☐ No

Are you prevented from lawfully becoming employed in this country because of Visa or Immigration Status? ☐ Yes ☐ No
(Proof of citizenship or immigration status may be required upon employment)

On what date would you be available for work? ______

Are you available to work ☐ Full Time ☐ Part-Time ☐ Shift Work ☐ Temporary

Are you on a lay-off and subject to recall? ☐ Yes ☐ No

Can you travel if a job requires it? ☐ Yes ☐ No

Have you been convicted of a felony within the last 7 years? ☐ Yes ☐ No

If Yes, please explain ______

AN EQUAL OPPORTUNITY EMPLOYER M/F/V/H

Veteran of the U.S. military service? ☐ Yes ☐ No If Yes, Branch ______

Do you have any physical, mental or medical impairment or disability that would limit your job performance for the position for which you are applying? ☐ Yes ☐ No

If Yes, please explain ______

Are there workplace accommodations which would assure better job placement and/or enable you to perform your job to your maximum capability? ☐ Yes ☐ No

If Yes, please indicate: ______

Indicate what foreign lanuages you speak, read, and/or write.

	FLUENTLY	GOOD	FAIR
SPEAK			
READ			
WRITE			

List professional, trade, business or civic activities and offices held.
(Exclude those which indicate race, color, religion, sex or national origin): ______

Give name, address and telephone number of three references who are not related to you and are not previous employers.

Special Employment Notice to Disabled Veterans, Vietnam Era Veterans, and Individuals with Physical or Mental Handicaps.

Government contractors are subject to Section 402 of the Vietnam Era Veterans Readjustment Act of 1974 which requires that they take affirmative action to employ and advance in employment qualified disabled veterans and veterans of the Vietnam Era, and Section 503 of the Rehabilitation Act of 1973, as amended, which requires government contractors to take affirmative action to employ and advance in employment qualified handicaped individuals.

If you are a disabled veteran, or have a physical or mental handicap, you are invited to volunteer this information. The purpose is to provide information regarding proper placement and appropriate accommodation to enable you to perform the job in a proper and safe manner. This information will be treated as confidential. Failure to provide this information will not jeopardize or adversely affect any consideration you may receive for employment.

If you wish to be indentified, please sign below.

☐ Handicapped Indiviudal ☐ Disabled Veteran ☐ Vietnam Era Veteran

Signed ______

Employment Experience

Start with your present or last job. Include military service assignments and volunteer activities. Exclude organization names which indicate race, color, religion, sex or national origin.

#		Dates Employed		Work Performed
		From	To	
1	Employer			
	Address			
	Job Title	Hourly Rate/Salary		
		Starting	Final	
	Supervisor			
	Reason for Leaving			
2	Employer	Dates Employed		Work Performed
		From	To	
	Address			
	Job Title	Hourly Rate/Salary		
		Starting	Final	
	Supervisor			
	Reason for Leaving			
3	Employer	Dates Employed		Work Performed
		From	To	
	Address			
	Job Title	Hourly Rate/Salary		
		Starting	Final	
	Supervisor			
	Reason for Leaving			
4	Employer	Dates Employed		Work Performed
		From	To	
	Address			
	Job Title	Hourly Rate/Salary		
		Starting	Final	
	Supervisor			
	Reason for Leaving			

If you need additional space, please continue on a separate sheet of paper.

Special Skills and Qualifications
Summarize special skills and qualifications acquired from employment or other experience ____________

Education

	Elementary	High	College/University	Graduate/ Professional
School Name				
Years Completed: (Circle)	4 5 6 7 8	9 10 11 12	1 2 3 4	1 2 3 4
Diploma/Degree				
Describe Course of Study:				
Describe Specialized Training, Apprenticeship, Skills and Extra-Curricular Activities				

Honors Received:

State any additional information you feel may be helpful to us in considering your application.

Agreement

I certify that answers given herein are true and complete to the best of my knowledge.

I authorize investigation of all statements contained in this application for employment as may be necessary in arriving at an employment decision.

In the event of employment, I understand that false or misleading information given in my application or interview(s) may result in discharge. I understand, also, that I am required to abide by all rules and regulations of the Company.

Signature of Applicant ____________ Date ____________

For Personnel Department Use Only

Arrange Interview ☐ Yes ☐ No

Remarks ____________

INTERVIEWER DATE

Employed ☐ Yes ☐ No Date of Employment ____________

Job Title ____________ Hourly Rate/ Salary ____________ Department ____________

By ____________ ____________

NAME AND TITLE DATE

Figure 7-1 Application blank. Courtesy: Amsterdam Printing and Litho Corporation.

Several legislative acts have been enacted that restrict the type of information employers are able to obtain when checking background information about applicants. This legislation includes the Privacy Act, the Fair Credit Reporting Act, the Family Education Rights and Privacy Act, the Freedom of Information Act, and the Privacy Protection Act.

Among the guidelines that should be considered when requesting background information about applicants are the following:

1. Request only job-related information.
2. Obtain written releases from applicants before requesting information from others.
3. Disregard the use of subjective information obtained from others when evaluating and assessing the applicants.

The validity of written letters of recommendation has been challenged recently by many organizations because applicants normally ask for letters of recommendation only from those individuals who are certain to provide positive information. Therefore, the information in letters of recommendation may be somewhat distorted. For this reason, many organizations place more emphasis on information obtained from former employers than on the information provided in letters of recommendation.

During the background check, increasing numbers of present or former employers are providing potential employers with less information about an applicant. Employers are reluctant to provide potential employers with information that could hurt the employee's opportunity to be hired, primarily because of the fear of being sued for defamation. Consequently, some employers are providing information limited to the following areas: the applicant's last job title, his or her last salary, and dates of employment.

Selection Interview

Who typically conducts the selection interview?

At this point in the selection process, the two or more applicants thought to have the greatest potential for succeeding will have been identified. These applicants are usually interviewed by the department manager or supervisor of the department in which the opening exists. The selection interview should provide information that enables the manager or supervisor to identify the candidate who is best qualified. Interviewing will be discussed in greater detail in the "Interviewing Process" section of this chapter.

Medical Exam

With the passage of the Americans with Disabilities Act, requiring applicants to undergo a medical exam before a job is offered is prohibited. Therefore, no longer can an organization screen out an applicant who has an increased risk of an on-the-job injury or a medical condition that could be worsened by the demands of the job being sought by the applicant. However, an organization can require the applicant to satisfactorily pass a medical exam as a condition of the employment offer. The exam results cannot be used to withdraw the offer unless they show that the individual is not able to perform the tasks required by the position.

Payroll Change Notice

After the applicant who is offered the position accepts it, a payroll change notice is completed. This notice authorizes the payroll department to begin paying the new employee. A payroll change notice is illustrated in Figure 7-2.

TO: PAYROLL DEPARTMENT

Please Enter the Following Change(s) in Your Records to Take

Effect ______________________
(Date and Time)

Employee ______________________

Social Security No. ______________________ Clock No. ______________

THE CHANGE(S)

✓ Check all Applicable Boxes	From	To
☐ Department		
☐ Job		
☐ Shift		
☐ Rate		
☐		

REASON FOR THE CHANGE(S)

☐ Hired
☐ Re-Hired
☐ Promotion
☐ Demotion
☐ Transfer
☐ Merit Increase
☐ Union Scale

☐ Probationary Period Completed
☐ Length of Service Increase
☐ Re-evaluation of Existing Job
☐ Resignation
☐ Retirement
☐ Layoff
☐ Discharge

☐ Leave of Absence From ______________ (Date) Until ______________ (Date)

☐ Other (Explain) ______________________

Change Authorized by ______________________ Date ______________

Change Approved by ______________________ Date ______________

Form # 08320 Amsterdam Printing and Litho Corp. Amsterdam, N.Y. 12010

Figure 7-2 Payroll change form. Courtesy: Amsterdam Printing and Litho Corporation.

Employee File

Although not an official part of the selection process, once an applicant has accepted a job offer, an employee file will have to be created. The file contains a variety of employment-related information, including an employment history form, a data sheet, absences, vacation days used, and salary increases. The information in the file is continuously updated.

The information in the employee file has a variety of functions including use in appraising employee performance, validating procedures, and preparing various statistical reports required by government agencies.

TESTING PROGRAM

The administration of selection tests and the interpretation of their results requires the exercising of care on the part of those involved. Some organizations now employ individuals who have specialized training in testing and evaluation procedures. Other organizations have eliminated completely the testing element of the selection process. Reasons attributed to this are the belief that testing is risky and that validation requirements are too laborious. Still other organizations contract with professional test designers to prepare valid and reliable selection tests.

Test Reliability and Validity

How do test reliability and validity differ?

Before using a test as a measurement tool, its **reliability** and **validity** must be determined. A test is considered reliable if it produces consistent results. If the same test is given to matched sets of people or if the same group of people takes a slightly different version of the test, it is reliable when approximately equal scores are obtained on several different test administrations.

Test validity refers to the predictive value of the test. In other words, to be valid the test must predict the performance that it is intended to predict. A valid selection test will predict those likely to succeed and those likely to fail in a particular job or in a particular skill or task.

Several types of test validation procedures are used. Included are criterion-related validity, construct validity, content validity, and differential validity.

Criterion-related validity is the process of statistically relating measures of job performance, such as training time and work proficiency, to test scores. A valid test predicts how well the applicant will be able to perform his or her job duties. These criteria must be critical to the job for which the test is designed. Criterion-related validity studies are carried out in two ways. Concurrent studies use present employees to gather data on both test scores and employee performance. Longitudinal studies compare the prehiring test scores of individuals with their performance data after they have been on the job for a period of time.

Construct validity provides a measure of specific theoretical constructs, such as aptitude and intelligence, that are crucial to job performance.

Content validity measures the relationship between test items and job tasks.

Differential validity provides test results for each cultural subgroup as a means of predicting job success for the members of the various subgroups.

If tests are properly used and if the results are properly interpreted, many available standardized tests are both reliable and valid. Reliability and validity cannot be guaranteed when tests are used improperly, however.

A commonly used test in the selection of office workers is a five-minute timed typing or keyboarding test. Although the test is reliable (applicants will be fairly consistent in their typing or keyboarding rates), the test lacks validity. A five-minute timed test does very little to predict a typist's performance when typing or keyboarding letters, statistical tables, reports, and so forth. A much more valid test could be developed to include typing or keyboarding tasks that applicants will actually experience on the job.

Legal Considerations

What legal aspects must be considered when developing the testing program?

To avoid discriminating against any ethnic or cultural group, special attention should be focused on the legal considerations of the testing program. Section 703(h), Title VII of the Civil Rights Act, which includes the Tower Amendment, states that a test will not be considered discriminatory as long as it does not by design, intent, or use discriminate on the basis of race, color, religion, gender, or national origin.

Special attention also needs to be focused on the culturally disadvantaged. A test may be considered discriminatory if the members of a culturally disadvantaged group obtain significantly lower test results than their counterparts, provided both groups are equally successful on the job.

Biodata tests are being used to eliminate the adverse impact that standardized tests tend to have on certain cultural groups. Questions asked on biodata tests are related to the examinee's academic achievement, attitudes toward work, perception of self, physical orientation, and so forth. These tests generally reduce by at least 50 percent the differences in scores received by whites and minorities on traditional intelligence or aptitude tests.

The Equal Employment Opportunity Act of 1972, which is discussed later in this chapter, prohibits the use of a selection test that unfairly discriminates against any applicant.

Some organizations have routinely administered polygraph (lie detector) tests to job applicants. The passage of the Employee Polygraph Protection Act in 1988, however, restricts the use of the polygraph in preemployment screening. Among the types of employers that can continue to use the polygraph in preemployment screening are private security firms and drug companies.

Types of Testing

Several types of tests are used in screening applicants. Among the more common are **performance** or **achievement tests**, **aptitude tests**, **intelligence tests**, and **personality tests**.

Performance or achievement tests The proficiency of an applicant for an office job is measured effectively by performance or achievement tests. These tests help determine how well an applicant can perform those tasks for which he or she is being considered. For example, applicants' transcription skills can be accurately measured by giving them realistic dictation to transcribe. Applicants for clerk-typist positions might be asked to type or keyboard a series of letters as well as code and file a set of documents. For jobs that require considerable decision making, the applicants might be asked to react to several situations that require realistic decision making.

What is an aptitude test?

Aptitude tests An individual's potential to learn either the tasks for which he or she is being considered or the tasks he or she might be expected to perform in the future is measured by aptitude tests. Therefore, if an applicant is being considered for a position in which job holders frequently move up to a higher-level position, an aptitude test may be administered.

Intelligence tests When mental and reasoning abilities are crucial to the success of a job holder, an intelligence test most likely will be administered to each applicant. The specialized interpretation processes these tests require have resulted in some organizations abandoning the use of intelligence tests, especially if none of the employees is qualified to interpret the results. The use of intelligence tests has been criticized recently because such tests tend to favor applicants who have had considerable verbal and numerical experience. Therefore, applicants who have limited verbal and numerical experiences are to a certain extent discriminated against.

What do personality tests measure?

Personality tests Although personality tests are used less frequently in the selection process than they once were, organizations still administer these tests to individuals applying for jobs that require certain personality traits or characteristics. Some of the factors personality tests measure are interpersonal relations, motivation, ability to handle pressure, self-concept, interests, and individual needs. One of the reasons these tests are no longer used as frequently as they were in the past stems from the fact that individuals are able to determine which test responses are the most desirable. This may result in an unrealistic response that could affect test validity.

INTERVIEWING PROCESS

Considered by many to be the most crucial step in the hiring process, the selection interview serves a variety of functions:

1. The interviewer can ask questions to clarify any ambiguous areas about the applicant's background.
2. The interviewer can emphasize areas of particular concern to the organization.
3. The applicant's self-expression, confidence, poise, and appearance can be readily assessed.
4. The applicant can ask additional questions about the job and the organization.
5. The applicant can emphasize certain areas about his or her background that might be helpful in making an employment decision.

Anyone who has experienced a job interview knows it can be either a frustrating or a rewarding experience. The interviewer can do much to enhance the success of the interview. Among the ways to make interviews more successful is for the interviewer to try immediately to put the applicant at ease, to develop rapport with the applicant, and to avoid asking personal questions that are not relevant to the position of interest to the applicant.

Many organizations use specialists in the testing aspect of the selection process, although fewer organizations use employees who are professionally trained to conduct interviews. Increasingly, organizations are beginning to discover the crucial role of the interview and are realizing the necessity for using adequately trained interviewers.

Several types of interviews are used in selecting office employees. Interviews are categorized by the amount of control the interviewer is able to exert during the interview. In some instances, the interviewer will exert considerable control, whereas in other instances, the interviewer will give the applicant much leeway.

The most common types of interviews used for selecting office employees are **patterned**, **direct**, **indirect**, and **functional**.

Patterned Interview

What are the characteristics of the patterned interview?

The patterned interview generally requires the use of a form similar to the one illustrated in Figure 7-3. The form provides a list of the questions the interviewer will ask. Sufficient space is also provided on the form for the interviewer to record the interviewee's responses.

Under certain circumstances, the use of the patterned interview is especially desirable. For example, when many people are applying for the same position, the form facilitates comparing the backgrounds of the various applicants. Furthermore, if an organization makes a practice of inviting former applicants to apply for an open position, the patterned interview form helps determine which former applicants will be invited to reapply.

Perhaps the most significant advantage of using the patterned interview, provided the interviewer follows the form, is that all crucial areas are covered. The patterned interview also ensures that the interviewee will have ample opportunity to provide information about his or her background. Too often, interviewers spend excessive time discussing the organization or job, leaving too little time to get sufficient information from applicants. This practice is virtually eliminated when the patterned interview technique is used.

Direct Interview

What are the characteristics of the direct interview?

The direct interview is characterized as being conducted rather quickly because the interviewer asks only those questions directly related to the interviewee's background and the qualifications he or she has for a particular job. The direct interview is also characterized as being somewhat limited in the amount of information that can be collected.

The nature of the direct interview limits its use primarily to lower-level office jobs or as an initial screening device. The direct interview, which is not feasible for exploring needs, attitudes, and feelings of applicants, is most useful when a limited amount of information must be gathered rather quickly. To use this interview for any other purpose is a questionable practice.

Indirect Interview

What are the characteristics of the indirect interview?

As its name implies, the indirect interview covers a much broader range of topics than the direct interview does. The indirect interview is unstructured in format, which gives the applicant considerable freedom in selecting discussion areas. Many interviewers believe that the primary use of the indirect interview is to stimulate the interviewee to talk about himself or herself—to discuss needs, attitudes, and feelings.

Because of its unstructured format, the indirect interview is difficult for many interviewers to conduct. Although the interviewer is responsible for "keeping the interview on target," he or she has to be a good listener and should interrupt only when the applicant appears reluctant to provide important information or when the interviewer is asked specific questions.

PATTERNED INTERVIEW
(Short Form)

Name ______________________ **Date of Birth** __________ **Soc. Sec. No.** __________

The age discrimination in the employment act and relevant FEP Acts prohibit discrimination with respect to individuals who are at least 40 but less than 65 years of age.

Address ______________________

SUMMARY

Rating: 1 2 3 4 **Comments:** ______________________
In making final rating, be sure to consider applicant's stability, industry, perseverance, loyalty, ability to get along with others, self-reliance, leadership, maturity, motivation; also domestic situation and health.

Interviewer: __________ **Job Considered for:** __________ **Date** __________

If you were hired, how long would it take you to get to work? __________ How would you get to work? __________
Is there anything undesirable here?

WORK EXPERIENCE. Cover all positions. This information is very important. Interviewer should record last position first. Every month since leaving school should be accounted for. Note military service in work record in continuity with jobs held since that time (in New Jersey exclude Military questions).

	LAST OR PRESENT POSITION	**NEXT TO LAST POSITION**	**SECOND FROM LAST POSITION**
Name of Company			
Address			
Dates of employment	From To	From To	From To
Nature of work		Do these dates check with application?	
		Will applicant's previous experience be helpful on this job?	
Starting salary			
Salary at leaving			
What was especially liked about the job?	Has applicant made good work progress?		General or merit increases?
		Has applicant been happy and contented in his/her work?	
What was especially disliked?	Were applicant's dislikes justified?		Is applicant chronically dissatisfied?
Reasons for leaving		Are applicant's reasons for leaving reasonable and consistent?	

OTHER POSITIONS

Name of Company	Type of Work	Salary	Date Started	Date Left	Reasons for Leaving
	Has applicant stayed in one line of work for the most part?				
	Has applicant gotten along well on his/her jobs?				
	Are applicant's attitudes toward his/her employers loyal?				
	Was applicant interested in creative work? In work requiring activity?				
	Has applicant improved self and position?				

Form No. OP-202

Figure 7-3 Patterned interview form. Courtesy: The Dartnell Corporation, Chicago, IL.

How many times did you draw unemployment compensation? ______ When? ______ Why? ______

Does applicant depend on self?

How many weeks have you been unemployed in the past five years? ______ How did you spend this time? ______

Did conditions in applicant's occupation justify this time? Did applicant use time profitably?

What accidents have you had in recent years? ______

Is applicant "accident-prone"? Any disabilities which will interfere with work?

SCHOOLING

How far did you go in school? Grade: 1 2 3 4 5 6 7 8 High School: 1 2 3 4 College: 1 2 3 4 Date of leaving school ______

Is applicant's schooling adequate for the job?

If you did not graduate from high school or college, why not? ______

Are applicant's reasons for not finishing sound?

What special training have you taken? ______

Will this be helpful? Indication of perseverance? Industry?

Extracurricular activities. (Please omit any organizations which reflect race, color, sex, national origin or religion.) ______

Did applicant get along well with others?

What offices did you hold in these groups? ______

Indications of leadership?

FAMILY BACKGROUND	PERSONAL SITUATION
Leisure time activities ______ Habits of industry?	When did you have last drink? ______ Sensbile?
Summer vacations ______ Did applicant keep busy?	What types of people rub you the wrong way? ______ Bias?
Group activities ______ See note after Extracurricular activities.	Ever convicted of a felony? ______
Position of leadership ______ Leader?	Charges ______ Immaturity? (This does not constitute an automatic bar to employment)

HEALTH

What serious illnesses, operations, or accidents did you have as a child? ______

Has applicant retained any infantile personality traits due to childhood illnesses?

What illnesses, operations, or accidents have you had in recent years? ______

Are applicant's illnesses legitimate rather than indicating a desire to "enjoy ill health"?

How much time have you lost from work because of illness during past year? ______

Will aplicant be able to do the job?

How are your teeth? ______

Does anyone in your home suffer ill health? ______

Are spouse, children, or family relatively healthy?

Do you suffer from:

- ☐ Poor Eyesight
- ☐ Poor Hearing
- ☐ Rupture
- ☐ Rheumatism
- ☐ Asthma
- ☐ Heart Trouble
- ☐ Diabetes
- ☐ Ulcers
- ☐ Hay Fever
- ☐ Flat Feet
- ☐ Nervousness

ADDITIONAL INFORMATION: ______

Figure 7-3 Continued.

Functional Interview

What are the characteristics of the functional interview?

The functional interview is comprised of a series of job-related questions accompanied by predetermined answers. All applicants being interviewed for a particular job respond to the same questions.

The following four types of questions are generally used in the functional interview:

1. What-if questions. These questions, which are generally in an oral format, involve hypothetical job-related situations. The interviewer responds to each question by stating what he or she would do with the situation or how he or she would handle the situation.
2. Job knowledge questions. These questions, which can be either in oral or written format, are designed to assess the interviewee's knowledge about the technical aspects of a job or the basic knowledge required to learn the job.
3. Job sample questions. These questions typically are performance oriented because interviewees are asked to perform a sample job task. The more closely the sample tasks match the actual job, the more effective these questions will be. In some instances, the task performance will have to be in a simulated environment.
4. Attitude questions. These questions are often used to assess the interviewee's willingness to do such job-related tasks as repetitive physical work, travel, work in certain environmental conditions, and so on. The content of these questions should be restricted to actual characteristics or duties of the job.

A distinct characteristic of the functional interview is the use of an interview committee. Two of the committee's responsibilities are evaluating the worth of the interviewee's responses and preparing the interview questions and desired predetermined answers. The relative worth of each answer is predetermined. For example, good answers may carry a value of 5; average or marginal answers, a value of 3; and poor answers, a value of 1. The sample answers should be realistic and be based on present job requirements.

The most significant advantages of the functional interview are its reliability and accuracy. It minimizes the subjectivity and inconsistency often present in other types of interviews.

Regardless of the type of interview being conducted, only those questions proved to relate to a **bona fide occupational qualification (BFOQ)** can be asked. A bona fide occupational qualification is a legitimate qualification—one the job holder needs to possess in order to have a satisfactory job performance. Unless the following topics have occupational relevance, they cannot be legally asked during an interview:

What types of questions cannot be legally asked during an employment interview?

1. Arrest record of the applicant.
2. Pregnancy history of the applicant.
3. Spouse, spouse's employment, or number of children the applicant has.
4. Marital status of the applicant.
5. Home ownership of the applicant.
6. Military status of the applicant.
7. Health status of the applicant.

8. Age or date of birth of the applicant.
9. Race, religion, or national origin of the applicant.

AFFIRMATIVE ACTION PROGRAM

The process of employee selection has two crucial elements. One element is the process that enables the organization to hire the best possible individual for each opening. The other element is the use of selection procedures consistent with federal or state equal employment opportunity laws.

Executive Order 11246 mandates that any organization with a federal contract exceeding $50,000 and with fifty or more employees is required to submit an affirmative action program for each of its facilities, such as a plant or field office. The plans, which must be submitted within 120 days of receiving the contract, are filed with the Office of Federal Contract Compliance Programs.

Organizations with federal contracts that range from $2,500 to $50,000 are mandated to include in their contracts an affirmative action clause, but they do not have to file a written affirmative action plan. Those with federal contracts less than $2,500 are not covered by the provisions of the Executive Order 11246.

Affirmative action programs contain several elements including utilization analysis, statistical analysis, goals, and timetables. The utilization analysis determines the number of women and minorities employed within an organization. Availability analysis, conversely, provides information about the number of women and minorities who are available to work in an organization.

To assess the adequacy of the affirmative action program, a variety of questions can be asked. Nontechnical questions dealing with employee selection include the following:

What types of nontechnical questions are to be included in written affirmative action programs?

1. Does the recruiting phase of the program attract a balance of applicants in terms of race or gender?
2. Are all jobs open to women and minorities?
3. Is a concerted effort made to place women and minorities in top-level positions?
4. Do managers and supervisors attempt to achieve a balance of applicants by race and gender? Some organizations find less effort is exerted by managers and supervisors to achieve balance than is exerted by the personnel department. In such instances, the personnel department may have to take a more active role in employee selection.
5. Does the system have the necessary machinery and procedures to effectively monitor the affirmative action program?
6. Does management regularly communicate the importance of establishing, reviewing, and updating affirmative action goals?

Other questions dealing with other personnel aspects are the following:

1. Are job standards realistic?
2. Are all employees offered the same training opportunities, or are some given greater preference?
3. Do employees receive equal pay for equal work?

4. Do all employees have an equal chance of being identified as a high-potential employee?
5. Are disciplinary policies equal for all employees, and are they uniformly administered?
6. Are personnel decisions made on the basis of factors other than age?

An important aspect of affirmative action is upward mobility. Compliance with affirmative action legislation mandates promoting to higher-level positions those employees for whom the legislation exists.

Persons with major responsibilities for employee selection will find the *Uniform Guidelines on Employee Selection Procedures* useful. The *Guidelines* document, which supersedes EEOC and OFCCP Guidelines as of September 25, 1978, specifies that an employer must be able to verify the predictive validity of its employee selection process. The *Guidelines* further require that knowledge, skills, abilities, and other worker characteristics assessed in the selection process must be necessary prerequisites for performance of critical tasks.

What is meant by adverse impact?

The *Guidelines* stipulate that the selection procedures the organization uses must not have an adverse impact on any protected group. If an organization's selection rate for any group protected by virtue of gender, race, or ethnic origin is less than 80 percent of the selection rate for the group with the highest selection rate, adverse impact may be present. To illustrate how the concept works, consider the following facts:

> In the current year, XYZ Company hired sixty of the one hundred white applicants who applied; therefore, the white hiring rate is 60 percent.
>
> In the current year, XYZ Company hired twenty of the forty Asian applicants who applied; therefore, the Asian hiring rate is 50 percent.
>
> In the current year, XYZ Company hired thirty of the sixty African-American applicants who applied; therefore, the African-American hiring rate is 50 percent.

The white group had the highest hiring rate of 60 percent. If the hiring rate of the two protected groups was at least 80 percent of the white hiring rate, adverse impact is not present. The following shows the calculation of these rates:

Asian: 50/60 = 83.33 percent (no adverse impact).

African-American: 50/60 = 83.33 percent (no adverse impact).

Had the hiring rate for either of the two protected groups been 40 percent rather than 50 percent, adverse impact would be present because a 66.66 percent rate (40/60) would have resulted.

If adverse impact is found, the organization is compelled to determine the reasons for the impact. Among the reasons that might be investigated are the following: insufficient number of members of protected groups apply, selection tools unfairly eliminate members of protected groups from further consideration, and bias or prejudice against members of protected groups is present.

How do disparate impact and disparate treatment differ from one another?

When a suit is filed against an employer for alleged discrimination, either disparate impact or disparate treatment will be the focus of the suit. Disparate impact refers to discrimination against a protected group of individuals. The 80 percent rule discussed earlier is used in determining the presence or existence of disparate impact.

Disparate treatment, conversely, refers to discrimination against a protected individual. This type of discrimination occurs when a protected individual, although qualified, is rejected—after which the employer continues seeking applicants who have the same qualifications as the one who was rejected.

FEDERAL LEGISLATION

Any individual in an organization involved with employee selection should be thoroughly aware of the federal legislation that might have an impact on the selection process. Specific legislation prohibits discrimination on the basis of age, race, national origin, and religion. Once an individual is hired, other legislation prohibits the use of an individual's gender as a salary determinant.

Civil Rights Act of 1964

Title VII of the Civil Rights Act has significant implications for the hiring process by requiring that employers or unions with twenty-five or more workers treat all persons equally, regardless of their gender, race, color, national origin, or religion. An exception to this provision allows an employer to use gender, national origin, or religion as a selection factor if justifiable as a bona fide occupational qualification. Groups protected by Title VII are women, African-Americans, Native Americans, Hispanics, and Asian-Pacific Islanders.

Age Discrimination in Employment Act of 1967

What are the important provisions of the Age Discrimination in Employment Act of 1967?

This act, which was amended in 1978 and 1986, prohibits employers with twenty or more persons from using age to discriminate against employees and applicants who are more than forty years old. In 1986, the age cap, which had been set at 70, was lifted for most occupations. Federal employees and most private-sector employees are allowed to work beyond the age of seventy if they are able to perform their job effectively. The act forbids an employer's using a protected applicant's age as a basis for refusing to hire, for determining compensation, for discharging an employee, or for forcing retirement. Approximately one-third of the states have also passed companion legislation.

Equal Employment Opportunity Act of 1972

This act significantly amended Title VII of the Civil Rights Act of 1964. The Equal Employment Opportunity Act of 1972 has several significant implications for hiring, transferring, training, or retraining employees. This act amended the 1964 act by defining the employer as a person engaged in industry affecting interstate commerce and having fifteen or more workers. Both public and private employers are covered by the act. The Equal Employment Opportunity Commission, which is the regulatory agency of the act, originally issued guidelines for the implementation of validation procedures. These guidelines are now incorporated into the *Uniform Guidelines on Employment Selection Procedures*.

Although test validation is feasible for large organizations, smaller ones have more difficulty because they have fewer employees to use in the validation process. In certain instances, when an insufficient number of employees are available, the results of validity studies conducted by other organizations, such as those cited in test manuals, may be considered acceptable if the jobs and the individuals in the two organizations are similar. This regulation has resulted in some employers abandoning the use of tests in the selection process.

Other selection devices, such as application blanks and interview sheets, that discriminate against a class of people protected by Title VII or that are discriminatory in nature are prohibited under the provisions of the Equal Employment Opportunity Act of 1972. When challenged, the employer is responsible for proving that a test or selection device is not discriminatory.

Executive Orders

What are the provisions of the executive orders?

Executive Order 11246 (amended by Executive Order 11375) and Revised Order No. 4 are both designed to prohibit discrimination in selecting employees. Some organizations that are excluded from abiding by the provisions of the Civil Rights Act are required to abide by the regulations of either or both of these executive orders.

Executive Order 11246 pertains to government contractors and subcontractors with a federal construction contract. The executive order forbids the following: advertising for employees by gender classifications, basing seniority lists on gender, or making personnel decisions on the basis of one's marital status. Revised Order No. 4 requires that nonconstruction organizations with one hundred or more employees and federal contracts of $100,000 or larger have an affirmative action program.

Vocational Rehabilitation Act of 1973

Designed to provide equal employment opportunities for qualified people with physical and mental disabilities, the Vocational Rehabilitation Act of 1973, which was amended in 1980, has resulted in progress being made in hiring people with disabilities. Organizations with a federal contract exceeding $2,500 must include an affirmative action clause in the contract. This clause must state that people with disabilities will be given due consideration and will not be discriminated against either in the selection process or after they have been hired.

Vietnam Era Veterans' Readjustment Assistance Act of 1974

Vietnam Era Veterans' Readjustment Assistance Act pertains to government contractors whose federal contracts exceed $10,000. The provisions of the act state that such employers are required to hire and promote qualified Vietnam era veterans and veterans with disabilities. In addition, such employers are required to list vacancies with local employment services. The veterans covered by the provisions of the act are to be given referral priority.

Pregnancy Discrimination Act of 1978

As an amendment to the Civil Rights Act, employers cannot discriminate against pregnant women by firing or refusing to hire them because they are pregnant. In addition, the same benefits to which nonpregnant employees are entitled must be available to pregnant employees.

Americans with Disabilities Act of 1990

This act, which is essentially a bill of rights for individuals with physical and mental disabilities, has important implications for the selection process. Essentially, the act forbids discriminating against an individual with a disability who is otherwise qualified for the job. The act also forbids the use of selection devices that "screen out" individuals with disabilities by virtue of their disability. Furthermore, employers are required by law to make a "reasonable accommodation" to hire and place on the job individuals who have disabilities. ADA makes illegal the refusing to hire or firing of a person because of a disability except when the impairment prevents the individual from performing the stated basic job functions. The act covers employers with fifteen or more employees.

Some employers have tried to determine a disabled person's suitability for employment by asking him or her to provide a list of the compensation claims he or she has filed over the years. Asking for such information is illegal until a conditional job offer is made—and then it is suitable only to determine whether a disabled person's prior injury/disability may prevent him or her from carrying out the stated job duties.

Civil Rights Act of 1991

With the passage and signing into law of the Civil Rights Act of 1991, employers need to exercise even more care in the hiring, promoting, and firing of employees. The act provides the right to a jury trial, in addition to punitive (the larger the number of employees in the organization, the greater the punitive damages that can be received) and expanded compensatory damages to persons who have been intentionally discriminated against. The act amends Title VII of the 1964 Civil Rights Act.

The need has become critical for organizations to have in place policies that identify how they will conform with various elements of this act (and other relevant acts) regarding the hiring, promoting, and firing of employees. The presence of these policies should be well publicized, and the policies should be readily available for employee use. Another important aspect of the policy is that employees who file charges, regardless of the outcome, will not be subjected to retaliatory actions in the future because they filed charges. To do so is also a violation of the act.

MAKING THE DECISION

Administrative office managers use two approaches in deciding which applicant will be offered the position: the single-predictor approach and the multiple-predictor approach. The type and level of position being filled often determines the approach.

Single-predictor Approach

How does the single-predictor approach differ from the multiple-predictor approach?

When the single-predictor approach is used, one device, such as an interview or a test, will be the primary determinant in making a selection decision. To use the single-predictor approach, those responsible for hiring will want rather substantial evidence that one device provides results just as valid as the results provided by multiple devices. The single-predictor approach is typically restricted for use in filling positions that possess repetitive, routine tasks.

Multiple-predictor Approach

The use of the multiple-predictor approach results in the consideration of data and information gathered from several devices (tests, interviews, background checks, references, and so on) commonly used in the selection process. Some organizations require that for an applicant to be considered as a finalist for the position, he or she must possess minimum scores on all predictors. Therefore, a score that falls below the minimum will disqualify an applicant from further consideration. The use of the minimum score technique is acceptable as long as none of its components results in adverse impact.

Other organizations using the multiple-predictor approach opt for the compensatory technique. In this situation, a good score received by the applicant on one device will compensate for poor score on another. As a result, a greater number of applicants, including those in protected groups, will likely be able to continue longer in the selection process.

Still other organizations use a combined approach that uses a single predictor in addition to multiple predictors. To be considered for a position, an applicant must meet a minimum requirement in a single predictor (net words per minute keyboarding rate, for example). Those who meet the minimum requirement in the single predictor are then further evaluated in terms of certain multiple predictors.

In selecting an approach, the following factors should be considered:

1. Quality of the results it provides.
2. Ease with which the approach is used.
3. Degree to which the approach meets all of the requirements of federal and state legislation regarding employee selection.
4. Objectivity of the approach.
5. Degree to which the approach provides a satisfactory number of applicants from which to choose.

MONITORING SELECTION PROCESS

The employee selection process should be monitored continually. The results of the monitoring process will provide a quantity of information useful in improving the quality of the process. Two quality indicators are the following:

1. **Selection ratio**, which is calculated by dividing the number of applicants by the number of individuals hired. A 3:1 or 4:1 ratio should be attained. A ratio less than 3:1 may indicate that more recruiting is needed; a ratio higher than 4:1 may indicate that initial screening is not sufficiently refined.
2. **Offer-to-hire ratio**, which is calculated by dividing the number of offers made by the number of individuals hired. The ratio should be close to 1:1. Ratios above 1:1 or 1:0 are unacceptable and may indicate that the organization either has an image problem or that the job requirements are too strenuous for employment conditions.

IMPLICATIONS FOR THE ADMINISTRATIVE OFFICE MANAGER

The responsibility of the administrative office manager for selecting office employees varies from organization to organization. In some instances, the manager will become involved at the end of the process when it is time to select the best applicant from a list of the three or four top candidates. In other instances, the manager will become involved at the beginning of the selection process.

Regardless of the step in the process at which the administrative office manager becomes involved, he or she needs to be knowledgeable about all the elements of the process. The manager also needs to be familiar with provisions of relevant federal and state legislation that will help him or her avoid actions prohibited by law.

The use of effective selection procedures is more crucial now than ever. This is true for the following fundamental reason: Poor hiring decisions are costly to the organization in a variety of ways. Not only are average or below-average employees less productive over the long run, but also they may lack incentive to try to improve. Employees whose attrition rates are higher than average cause the organization to incur additional recruiting and hiring expenses. Average or below-average employees may need to be given training in certain areas, which also can be costly. Furthermore, terminating employees whose performance is substandard is becoming increasingly difficult.

One of the most effective ways for the organization to improve the overall quality of its operations is to improve the quality of its workforce. Employee selection is a good place to begin the process of improving workforce quality.

REVIEW QUESTIONS

1. What is the most significant disadvantage of the employee referral method of employee selection?
2. If an organization needs to hire many employees in a short time, which recruiting source is most likely to yield the greatest number of applicants?
3. In addition to assisting organizations in employee recruitment, what other types of assistance does the USES provide?
4. What are the advantages of using temporary help agencies to obtain additional employees?
5. What are the primary functions of the employee requisition blank?
6. In what ways are job descriptions and job specifications of value in the selection process?
7. What are the advantages of employee testing?
8. What impact does the Employee Polygraph Protection Act of 1989 have on employee selection?
9. In what ways do criterion validity, construct validity, content validity, and differential validity differ from one another?
10. What are the special advantages resulting from the use of patterned interviews?
11. In what ways do the Civil Rights Act of 1964, the Age Discrimination in Employment Act of 1967, the Equal Employment Opportunity Act of 1972, the Vocational Rehabilitation Act of 1973, the Vietnam Era Veterans' Readjustment Assistance Act of 1974, the Pregnancy Discrimination Act of 1978, the Americans with Disabilities Act of 1990, and the Civil Rights Act of 1991 impact on employee selection?

DISCUSSION QUESTIONS

1. You have just become aware that one of the employees you recently hired falsified his educational qualifications on his job application. By providing false information, this individual was able to meet the minimum educational requirements for the job. Although this employee has been on the job for only three weeks, you are quite impressed with his performance. In fact, you believe he probably has the greatest potential of all the employees you supervise. Discuss what you plan to do about this situation, and provide a rationale to support the course of action you plan to take.
2. Applicants for an opening in a de-

partment in which you are the supervisor were asked to provide three letters of recommendation. Two favorable letters were received immediately on behalf of the applicant you felt was the best qualified for the position. After two weeks passed and you hadn't received a letter from the third reference, you decided to call this individual to get a verbal recommendation. Because this individual was out of the country and would not be returning for another five weeks, you decided to hire the applicant on the basis of her two favorable recommendations. You just received the third letter of recommendation, which contains some discouraging information. The individual who wrote the letter indicated that he could not recommend this applicant. In fact, had she not quit a few weeks ago, she probably would have been terminated because he has fairly good evidence that she embezzled several hundred dollars during the three years she worked for that company. You are now quite concerned because this new employee will also be handling large sums of money in your company. Explain what you plan to do about this situation. Be prepared to defend your plan of action.

3. You recently discovered that one of the supervisors for whom you are responsible lists unusually heavy lifting requirements on employee requisition blanks. It appears these requirements are aimed at disqualifying women for any of the openings. How can you verify the likelihood this supervisor is listing unusually heavy lifting requirements? Assuming you find your discovery to be true, outline what you plan to say to the supervisor about this practice.
4. When you were recently interviewed for a position in an insurance company, you asked to see a copy of the description of the job for which you were being interviewed. You could tell by the tone of the supervisor's verbal reaction to your request that you brought up a sore point. You decided not to pursue your request any further during the interview. Now that you have been on the job for several weeks, you again tell the supervisor you would like to see a description of your job. At this point, the supervisor gives you his philosophy about job descriptions. The following summarizes the main points of his conversation: (1) He threw the job descriptions away about three years ago because they were outdated; (2) Job descriptions are more damaging than they are worth because employees can use them to their advantage to avoid performing unpleasant tasks; (3) They destroy managers' flexibility in assigning work; (4) They are outdated about as soon as they are prepared; (5) If employees can't determine which tasks comprise their jobs without looking at a job description, then it is questionable if they are qualified. Discuss the nature of the flawed thinking this supervisor exhibits.
5. You are an employee in a department that has a fairly high turnover rate. The head of this department administers the tests used in employee selection. In discussing the applicant-testing situation with your coworkers, you discover that some were given tests during the application process and others were not. One day you asked the department head to explain why some employees had to take tests and others did not. He replied that he sees no value in testing employees he knows he wants to hire; but when he is uncertain about a particular individual, he administers a test. He also said that no two applicants will likely be given the same test because he likes to tailor each test to each applicant. Comment on the implications of the testing procedures your department head uses.
6. The company in which you work has a fairly high turnover rate among employees during the first three years they work for the company. A number of managers are blaming this phenomenon on the employee selection process. You have been asked to prepare a list of criteria to be used in judging the effectiveness of the program. The criteria are to be stated in the form of questions that can be answered with a yes or no response.

STUDENT PROJECTS AND ACTIVITIES

1. Talk with a personnel manager to learn about the sources most commonly used when recruiting office employees in the organization in which he or she works.
2. Talk with an administrative office manager to determine what types of tests are used in screening office employees in the organization in which he or she works.
3. Obtain the application blanks for two organizations. How do they compare in terms of the content found within each?
4. Talk with a personnel manager to determine what kinds of information he or she provides about former employees whose background is being investigated as part of their job-seeking efforts.
5. Talk with a personnel manager to determine what kinds of interviews are used for various types of applicants who are seeking employment in the organization in which he or she works.

MINICASE

The Tri-State Corporation, which is located in Cleveland, Ohio, is in the process of redesigning its applicant testing program. The company has always used tests in the selection of office employees, and the personnel manager believes the practice should be continued. You have been asked to serve on an advisory committee that is to prepare a report which answers the following two questions.

1. Should different types of tests (aptitude, intelligence, and so on) be used for different levels of office employees? Why or why not?
2. What one type of test does the advisory committee recommend for testing junior-level secretaries? For testing executive secretaries? Justify each recommendation.

CASE

Located in Chicago, Illinois, the Zebat Corporation is the largest chain manufacturer in the state. The company manufactures a variety of chains, ranging from those used on bicycles to those used on ship anchors.

The company is reputed throughout the Chicago area as being one of the better companies in which to work. Because of its favorable reputation, the company has been able to use only walk-ins and unsolicited applications as recruiting sources. The personnel manager has believed until recently that walk-ins and unsolicited applications yielded results comparable to other recruiting sources. An increasing number of department heads are now complaining that they have had to hire individuals whose qualifications do not exactly match the position requirements.

As a consultant whose services were hired by Zebat Corporation, you have been asked to prepare a report in which you respond to several questions, including the following:

1. Is the exclusive use of walk-ins and unsolicited applicants likely to be responsible for producing the situation about which the department heads complain? (Explain your response.)
2. What are the negative aspects of using only walk-ins and unsolicited applications?
3. What other recruiting sources might the company investigate?
4. How can the company assess the effectiveness of the other recruiting sources it might decide to try?

CHAPTER

DEVELOPING OFFICE EMPLOYEES

CHAPTER AIM

After studying this chapter, you should be able to design an effective orientation and training program for an organization, based on its needs.

CHAPTER OUTLINE

CHAPTER TERMS

Active learning
Audio cassette training
Business games
Case method
Civil Rights Act of 1964
Closed-circuit television
College-level refresher courses
Computer-assisted instruction
Conference method
Counseling
Distance learning
Education-employer cooperative training
Employee attitude survey
Employee development
Employee performance analysis
In-basket
Incident method
Individual differences
Information distribution techniques
Interactive video instruction
Job content analysis
Job rotation
Laboratory education
Learning by doing
Lecture method
Motion pictures and slide presentations
On-the-job coaching
On-the-job techniques
Orientation
Orientation kits
Passive learning
Population needs analysis
Principles of learning
Programmed instruction
Role playing
Sensitivity training
Simulation techniques
Training
Vestibule training
Video training
Vocational Rehabilitation Act of 1973

By helping ensure the maximum use of human potential, **employee development** is seen as a continuous process that lasts for the duration of an employee's working for an organization. Beginning with employee orientation, the employee development process continues with the training, counseling, appraising, and motivating of employees.

In what ways do the organization and its employees benefit from employee development?

Both the organization and its employees benefit from employee development. The organization benefits because employees are more readily able to achieve important organizational goals, such as those relating to productivity. Employees benefit because they are able to achieve their potential more quickly and easily, which has a positive impact on the amount of satisfaction they derive from their work.

The new technology used in the office has substantially increased the need for providing training experiences for office employees. This chapter provides a discussion of several training techniques, in addition to information about employee orientation and counseling. Motivation and performance appraisal, two other important components of employee development, are covered in later chapters.

ORIENTATION

Enabling employees to adjust more readily to their new jobs and to the organization, **orientation** has a positive impact on employee productivity. As a result of the orientation process, employees are likely to make fewer costly and time-wasting mistakes. Quality orientation also enables employees to experience greater job satisfaction.

Effective orientation helps employees feel more "at home" and enhances their understanding of the nature of their job duties. Although the content of the program will vary from organization to organization, some of the topics commonly included are the items found in the orientation checklist in Figure 8-1.

What is the "buddy" system?

One way some organizations help their new employees adjust more quickly to their job and the organization in which they work is to use a "buddy" system. Experienced employees help new employees by answering their questions. Psychologically, this system has significant advantages for new employees. Occasionally, new employees may hesitate to ask questions of their supervisors, although they are comfortable asking questions of their fellow employees. When an experienced employee is unable to answer the questions, either the new employee is referred to someone else, or the experienced employee can attempt to obtain answers from another person.

Several orientation delivery systems are used including ones that have verbal, written, and audiovisual components. Verbal orientation involves a

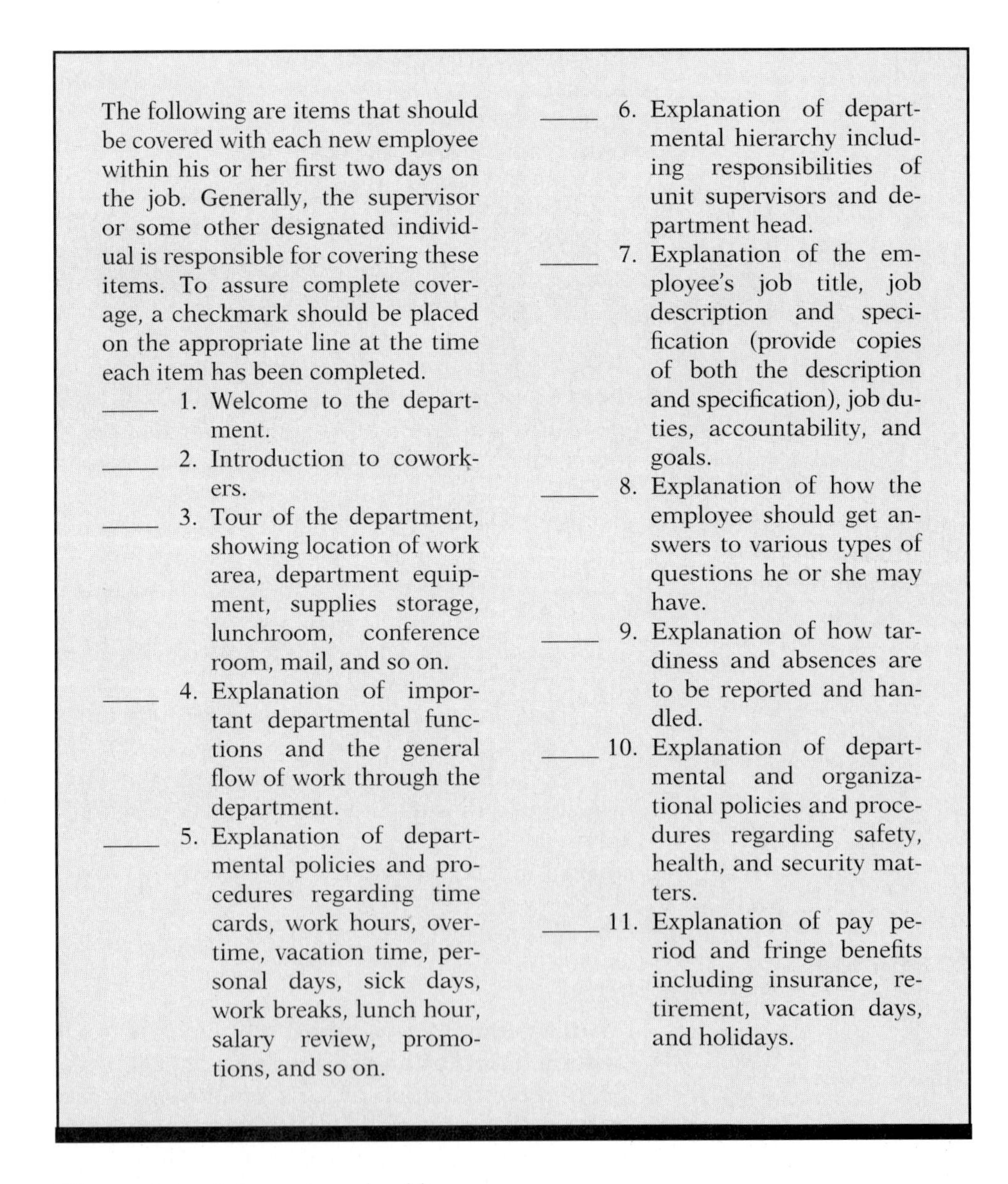

The following are items that should be covered with each new employee within his or her first two days on the job. Generally, the supervisor or some other designated individual is responsible for covering these items. To assure complete coverage, a checkmark should be placed on the appropriate line at the time each item has been completed.

____ 1. Welcome to the department.

____ 2. Introduction to coworkers.

____ 3. Tour of the department, showing location of work area, department equipment, supplies storage, lunchroom, conference room, mail, and so on.

____ 4. Explanation of important departmental functions and the general flow of work through the department.

____ 5. Explanation of departmental policies and procedures regarding time cards, work hours, overtime, vacation time, personal days, sick days, work breaks, lunch hour, salary review, promotions, and so on.

____ 6. Explanation of departmental hierarchy including responsibilities of unit supervisors and department head.

____ 7. Explanation of the employee's job title, job description and specification (provide copies of both the description and specification), job duties, accountability, and goals.

____ 8. Explanation of how the employee should get answers to various types of questions he or she may have.

____ 9. Explanation of how tardiness and absences are to be reported and handled.

____ 10. Explanation of departmental and organizational policies and procedures regarding safety, health, and security matters.

____ 11. Explanation of pay period and fringe benefits including insurance, retirement, vacation days, and holidays.

Figure 8-1 Orientation checklist.

one-on-one or a group situation. Written orientation typically involves the use of handbooks or manuals. Audiovisual presentations consist of movies or video cassette recorder tapes, slide-tape presentations, closed-circuit television and computer-driven multimedia presentations.

As a way to ensure the exposure of all new employees to each element of the orientation process, many organizations use a checklist to keep a record of the topics each employee has covered. The checklist is especially useful when the orientation process lasts for more than a day and when more than one person is involved with the orientation of the new employee. A representative checklist is illustrated in Figure 8-1.

Orientation Kit

An increasing number of companies are developing **orientation kits** that supplement the employees' formal orientation experiences. Although the materials in the kit will vary, some of the commonly included items are the following:

What information is included in an orientation kit?

1. Organization chart
2. Map of the premises (if the premises is large)
3. Copy of the employee handbook
4. Copy of the union contract (if the organization is unionized)
5. List of fringe benefits
6. Copy of insurance plans
7. Copy of performance appraisal form and outline of appraisal procedures
8. Copy of emergency and evacuation procedures
9. List of names and telephone numbers of key organizational employees and units

TRAINING

Providing employees with directed experiences that enable them to perform their job tasks more effectively, **training** is a vital function. Well-designed training experiences will bring about changes in employees' attitudes, work habits, and performance levels. Among the advantages of effective training are the following: employee morale is improved, turnover is lessened, errors are reduced, employee self-confidence is increased, productivity is increased, employees adjust more readily to their jobs, and less supervision is required.

Development of Training Programs

The development of training programs consists of the following well-defined steps:

Step 1: Determine need for training program Several factors are helpful in determining the need for a training program. The degree to which new employees are qualified for their jobs is a primary consideration. If a significant number of employees are marginally qualified, training experiences are needed. Employee attitudes about the development of a training program might also be considered. In addition, supervisory feedback is often useful when determining program need, as are the results of employee performance appraisals. Areas in which performance is generally regarded as weak or deficient are typically considered as being suitable for training.

To also help determine the need for a training program, answers to the following questions will be helpful:

1. What are employees not doing that they should be doing?
2. What are employees doing that they should not be doing?
3. What key expectations are the employees not achieving?
4. What are the nature of customer complaints that are employee related?
5. Are employees fully apprised about their job expectations?
6. Do employees get regular feedback regarding their expectations?
7. How far is the organization deviating from key measurable aspects of employee performance, including such aspects as error rates, manufacturing standards, employee turnover rate, operating expenses, and so forth?

Several specific types of analyses are also useful in determining the need for employee training. Included in these analyses are job content analysis, employee performance analysis, employee attitude surveys, and population needs analysis.

The **job content analysis** examines the content of present and anticipated openings. This analysis provides information about the tasks to be performed by employees, the skills employees need to perform these tasks, and the minimum acceptable employee performance standards.

For what is employee performance analysis used?

The **employee performance analysis** determines if a discrepancy exists between the employees' actual performance and the minimum acceptable performance standards determined in the process of analyzing job content. This analysis is generally performed on each specific job dimension.

For what is an employee attitude survey used?

The **employee attitude survey** is useful for determining the attitudes of employees regarding their perceived need for training. A strongly perceived need for a training program will likely need to be addressed. The organization's failure to address the training issue will likely result in diminished employee morale, increased turnover, decreased productivity, and so forth. Although some employee attitude surveys are quite general, others solicit information about specific job dimensions.

The **population needs analysis** is used to determine specific training needs of specific populations of workers. To illustrate, an organization that hires many new high school graduates may need to offer specific training experiences in areas in which this segment of its employee population is deficient. Different employee populations often have different training needs that have to be addressed.

Step 2: Define objectives of training program Before determining the nature of training experiences to provide employees, the objectives of the program have to be defined. While some training programs are designed to provide job-entry experiences, others provide retraining experiences designed to help employees improve their effectiveness.

Step 3: Determine type of training program On the basis of the perceived need for a training program and the stated objectives, determining the type of training program needed is quite simple. The following are the common types of training programs provided office employees:

What are the common types of training programs provided office employees?

1. Basic knowledge: Training experiences of this type are designed to help new employees qualify for the positions for which they have been hired. In many instances, employees who are exposed to such training programs have very little, if any, knowledge about the activities that constitute their jobs.
2. Job exposure: This type of training program is also frequently used for new employees. Individuals who are offered job exposure training programs typically have basic knowledge about their jobs but need training in certain areas. Such programs frequently involve training employees to perform certain job activities.
3. Refresher training: This is designed to help employees maintain a desirable level of effectiveness in performing their jobs. Changes in procedures, new technology, or in jobs make refresher training desirable—and perhaps fairly often. In some instances, refresher training is used to upgrade employees.

Another type of training, which is discussed in Chapter 9, is supervisory training.

Step 4: Determine appropriate training techniques Once the need for training programs has been established and the areas suitable for training have been determined, the training techniques should be selected. Important principles of learning should be considered in selecting the appropriate training technique for the material/information being presented.

Step 5: Provide training experiences After the training technique has been devised, the next step is to offer the training experiences. In some cases, these experiences might be provided by an employee of the organization, whereas in other situations they are provided by an outside agency through a contractual arrangement. Depending on the training techniques that are used, provisions may have to be made for frequent assessment of employee progress. In addition, achievement levels will have to be determined, as well as an appropriate method for measuring achievement. Without this information, the success of the training program cannot be fully realized.

Why do training follow-up studies need to be conducted?

Step 6: Conduct follow-up studies Upon completion of their training experiences and return to their jobs, follow-up studies of the learners' performance should be conducted, perhaps at six-month intervals. This type of feedback is a direct indicator of the program's success. The effect of the training experience on each learner's performance should be assessed as well as his or her attitude toward the training experience. Subjecting employees to training experiences that fail to meet their expectations will have a negative impact on the program's overall effectiveness.

Additional information about the following, which are indirect indicators of program success, will be helpful in assessing whether the organization's training efforts were successful:

1. Feedback from managers and staff involved with the training program.
2. Determination of how well the stated learning objectives were fulfilled.
3. Determination of the training program's impact on the measurable aspects mentioned in Step 1.
4. Calculation of the cost-benefit ratio.

Responsibility for Training

Although the personnel department in most organizations is responsible for the overall coordination of the training program, the administrative office manager or designated subordinates are often responsible for other specific aspects of training office employees. This is especially true when job exposure and refresher training experiences are provided. In many organizations, each department is responsible for its own specialized training of new employees and for training designed to upgrade employees.

PRINCIPLES OF LEARNING

Several **principles of learning** should guide the development of training programs. Program effectiveness can be maximized only when the structure of training techniques is consistent with these principles.

Learning by Doing

Why is active learning more efficient than passive learning?

Learning by doing actively involves the trainees in the learning process. In contrast to **passive learning**, **active learning** is a fast, efficient process for acquiring knowledge. The greater the number of senses involved in the learning process, the more active the learner is and the better the outcome is likely to be. Trainees subjected to passive learning methods are less likely to assimilate the material being presented because they are not required to give their total attention to the situation.

Motivation

For learning to be effective, trainees must want to improve their job performance, which, in turn, will enable them to be promoted and to advance. Learners who want to be promoted will experience greater satisfaction from their involvement in a training program than those who are involved out of fear of being dismissed because of poor job performance. Greater satisfaction, in turn, provides greater motivation to succeed. Individuals responsible for the training experiences must provide an atmosphere that encourages trainees to want to learn and improve.

Knowledge of Results

Why do learners need knowledge of results?

Having access to learning results provides many trainees with the reinforcement they need. Knowledge about how closely their behavior or responses match expected behavior or responses is found helpful by many trainees. Knowledge of results enables trainees to continue to make correct responses or to modify incorrect responses. Correct responses should be reinforced in order that the trainee will continue to make them. To be most effective, feedback should be offered as soon as possible after the response has been made.

Individual Differences

Trainees vary considerably in their ability to learn as well as in their attitudes, motivation, initiative, prior knowledge, and commitment. Therefore, **individual differences** must be recognized in training endeavors. Some trainees learn more rapidly than others, some need greater amounts of practice than

tant issues unless the training sessions are highly structured; and (3) it is restricted to small groups.

Programmed instruction Used to train office employees in certain areas, **programmed instruction** is currently receiving a fair amount of attention. When preparing programmed instruction materials, learning objectives have to be clearly defined. After the material is divided into component parts, the instructional unit is prepared. Careful attention must be given to the ordering of the component parts; otherwise, improper sequencing is confusing to the user. Also, the information needs to be presented in small segments or units.

What two formats are used in presenting programmed instructional units?

The instructional unit may present the material to the learner in textbook format or in teaching machine format. After presenting small units of information, the learner answers questions by making a response (textbook format) or by pushing a button (teaching machine format). If the learner's response is correct, the learner is then instructed to proceed to the next unit of information. If an incorrect response is made, the learner is given additional material on the same unit of information. Another question is subsequently presented to evaluate the learner's mastery of the review material.

The programmed instruction training technique has three distinct advantages: the learner obtains immediate knowledge of results, progresses through the instructional unit at an individualized pace, and takes an active role in the learning process. Among the disadvantages are high initial cost and the time consumed in developing the instructional units. Furthermore, some learners, unless they receive adequate direction from a trainer, find pacing themselves through the material to be somewhat difficult.

What are the characteristics of sensitivity training?

Sensitivity training Like the conference method, **sensitivity training** also uses small groups and individual participation. This technique, which was originally developed to train individuals to use democratic rather than autocratic decision-making processes, differs from the conference method in terms of the nature of the material discussed. Although the material covered in the conference method frequently helps individuals develop problem-solving abilities and decision-making skills, the sensitivity training technique uses the behavior of the participants as a base for discussion.

Sensitivity training is designed to help individuals become more sensitive to the characteristics of working groups. Individuals discuss the reasons for their comments and their reactions to others' comments. Consequently, they are concerned with their ability to communicate, with the self-defenses they develop to protect their egos, and with the reasons why certain individuals verbally attack or reinforce others.

The success of sensitivity training is dependent on the willingness of group members to honestly and freely communicate their feelings about the group members. Through sensitivity training, learners develop an awareness of the influence they have on others as well as of the ways they may unconsciously hinder the process.

Sensitivity training often produces frustration and conflict when individuals attempt to use their previously established behavior patterns. The members of the sensitivity training group are likely to question some of these behavior patterns—for example, why an individual is trying to protect his or her self-image, why he or she becomes defensive, or why he or she is critical of others in the sensitivity group.

The role of the group trainer in sensitivity training is crucial. This individual typically serves as a resource person or as a behavior model for the other group members. The trainer openly and honestly communicates his or her feelings but does not become defensive or withdraw because of criticism. In some instances, the trainer may follow a nondirective approach, which permits the group to determine the direction it follows. In still other instances, the trainer—by offering more guidance—informs the group about what is happening and interprets for the members what they are actually saying to one another.

The negative impact that sensitivity training may have on learners should be considered when an organization is evaluating its use as a training method. Learners who become upset may need special help in dealing with the personal distress caused by the criticism leveled against them.

As a training technique, sensitivity training frequently is concerned with solving a specific problem. Group members examine the interpersonal skills they use in developing a solution to the problem. Sensitivity training often enables learners to understand their actions toward one another and the ways in which each learner's behavior affects other learners. It can provide an understanding of why other individuals act as they do, as well as promote an increased tolerance of and appreciation for others' behavior. In addition, sensitivity training can provide individuals with the opportunity to experiment with new ways of interacting with others.

As a technique for training office workers, sensitivity training is considered by many to be less useful than some of the other techniques. Much of the problem solving that office employees have to do is not learned as effectively through sensitivity training as through some of the other training techniques. In addition, many organizations do not employ individuals who have the background needed to conduct sensitivity training sessions.

What is laboratory education?

Laboratory education As a training technique, **laboratory education** uses sensitivity training as a primary element but also uses other training techniques, including short lectures and role playing. A laboratory design, which specifies the content of the training sessions, the duration of the sessions, the participants in the training sessions, and their sequence, is developed for each training experience. The diversity of the laboratory design facilitates the development of many different training variations. This type of training technique can be individualized because the training needs of the learner and the characteristics of the situation are considered in developing the structure of the training experience.

Closed-circuit television Another frequently used information distribution technique—**closed-circuit television**—enables an organization to develop its own videotapes of various procedures, processes, or methods. The learners then view the videotapes as often as needed to master the subject matter. This technique is useful for initial learning as well as a refresher course. Videotapes custom designed for the organization enable the learner to identify more closely with the material being presented.

Compared with lectures, closed-circuit television offers certain advantages. For example, individuals with excellent presentational skills can be used as presenters. The same may not be true of a lecturer. Furthermore, close-ups of procedures or processes can be presented on closed-circuit television, which is not always possible with the lecture method.

Motion pictures and slide presentations Although not as flexible as closed-circuit television, **motion pictures and slide presentations** are two other techniques used to train office employees. Closed-circuit television is more flexible because videotapes can be erased and reused, an impossibility with motion pictures and slide presentations. The use and end results of motion pictures, slide presentations, and closed-circuit television are all comparable.

Distance learning As a new training technique, **distance learning** involves taking the material to be taught to the employees' worksite rather than having the employees come to the location of the trainer. More often than not, distance learning will be expedited by two-way compressed video. The trainer stays at his or her worksite, and the material he or she is covering is transmitted as television images through telephone lines. Being compressed, it is an economical type of training. At the receiving end, the trainees will see the trainer's motions on a television screen, but the trainer's motions will be slower than "real time," meaning they are compressed. The fact that it is two-way, the trainees can see the trainer when he or she is talking, and the trainer can see the trainees when they ask questions. The images can be recorded on videotape as they are being transmitted, thus enabling the tapes to be replayed at a later time.

This technique works well in a large organization with distributed employees and facilities. Rather than incurring the expense of having the individuals being trained come to the trainer's location—or vice versa—the material being taught is economically transmitted over the telephone lines.

College-level refresher courses Some organizations either sponsor employees or reimburse them for a percentage of the tuition cost of enrolling in **college-level refresher courses**. These courses, which cover a variety of topics, are sometimes taught at an educational institution; in other instances they are taught within the organization. An example of a commonly taught refresher course is a review class designed for individuals wishing to take the Certified Professional Secretary examination.

Simulation Techniques

Placing the learners in an artificial representation of a real-life situation, simulation techniques require learners to react as if the situation were real. Simulation training is also known as **vestibule training**, which has the following characteristics: the training usually occurs on the organization's premises away from the workstation, and it uses actual equipment and procedures.

How is role playing used as a training technique?

Role playing When **role playing** is used as a training technique, learners assume the roles of the individuals involved in a given situation. For example, to train employees to deal with certain human relations situations, the trainer might assume the role of an angry client, whereas a learner assumes the role of the employee dealing with the client. The observers who are not involved in the role-playing situation have an opportunity to evaluate the correctness or incorrectness of the actions of the role player. At the conclusion of role playing, the observers and the trainer have the opportunity to discuss the learner's handling of the situation.

Role playing is especially useful as a training technique in areas such as human relations. Its disadvantages are as follows: it is time-consuming; only a few individuals have an active role at a given time; and because human relations situations involve so many variables, the chances are slight that the learner will often experience an identical situation on the job.

Case method When the **case method** is used, learners are given a description of certain organizational conditions involving either a hypothetical organization or the organization for which the learner works. The participants in the case are typically required to identify problems, to develop solutions, or to make recommendations, all of which put emphasis on the employee participation process.

The amount of information presented to the learner varies from case to case. In some instances, the information is so brief that the learner has to make realistic assumptions in arriving at a solution. In other instances, irrelevant information is presented in the case, which makes the learner responsible for sorting the important from the unimportant material.

The case method is advantageous for the following reasons: The learners who actively participate are able to obtain feedback on their suggestions and recommendations, and the technique often provides transfer from the case situation to the real-life situation. The case method has been criticized because it does not allow for the teaching of general principles, nor are the learners generally given all the information they need for problem solving that they will have in a real-life situation.

What are the characteristics of the incident method of training?

Incident method Another simulation technique—the **incident method**—is closely related to the case method. In the incident method, learners are given a few of the details about a specific situation. To obtain sufficient background information for developing a solution, learners ask questions of the trainer. When the learners believe they have sufficient information to make a decision, the questioning process is concluded, and the learners prepare a solution to the problem being considered. After the learners have presented their solution, the trainer discloses any additional information the learners failed to obtain through the questioning phase of the problem. The trainer also typically provides a solution based on all the important facts, not just those that were made accessible to the learners.

Business games As a training technique, **business games** are useful for increasing learner understanding of the economic aspects of an industry, an organization, or a subunit of an organization. Games incorporate a set of rules developed from economic theory or from the financial operations of an industry or organization. These rules determine how input variables (raw materials, capital, equipment, and personnel), along with certain mediating variables (wages, finished product prices, and advertising expenditures), affect the output variables (quantity sold, amount of profit, and net worth).

Learners have to decide what product prices to charge, how much money to allocate for advertising, what new equipment to purchase, how many additional employees to hire, and so forth. A primary advantage of business games is their realistic nature. To provide additional realism, computer usage is incorporated into many of today's business games. One of the criticisms leveled against business games is their use of "gadgetry," which tends to detract from the purpose for which the game was developed. The time-consuming nature of some games is also a disadvantage.

Games are especially well suited to help employees acquire an understanding of the various interrelations within the organization and the degree to which these interrelations affect the success of the organization's operations. Although business games are perhaps more suitable for training managers than for training office employees, the technique can be effectively modified for use in training office employees.

What are the characteristics of the in-basket method of training?

In-basket Used as a technique for training office employees, the **in-basket** is especially suited for such areas as decision making and problem solving. An in-basket contains the types of materials that would accumulate over time (perhaps two weeks) in the in-basket on one's desk. It consists of internal and external communications, customer or client complaints, reports, and other items that typically accumulate.

The learner is required to do two things with each situation: determine the priority in which each situation is to be considered and devise a solution or recommendation for expediting the situation. After each learner completes the in-basket situation, the trainer and learners discuss various solutions and recommendations.

The in-basket technique can be made more realistic by using actual organizational situations rather than contrived situations. Although the technique does very little in teaching general principles, it is useful for developing the learners' decision-making skills.

Computer-assisted instruction Two computer functions—memory and storage—make possible the storage of a variety of training materials in a computer. Training activities that readily lend themselves to **computer-assisted instruction** are certain kinds of drill and practice exercises, simulations, and problem solving. The same format used in programmed instruction materials is often used in presenting computer-assisted instructional materials.

Among the advantages of computer-assisted instruction are its low cost, simplicity, and flexibility in accommodating a wide variety of situations and skill levels of learners. Furthermore, it provides an excellent opportunity for employees to become familiar with computer usage.

Perhaps the most significant disadvantage of computer-assisted instruction is the lack of discipline among some employees to complete the instructional process.

Audio cassette training As increasing numbers of **audio cassette training** systems are becoming available, audio cassette training is becoming a more prominent training technique. Cassette systems typically include one or more tapes and a textbook manual. In training systems designed to teach a computer software package, a diskette is also generally included. Cassette systems take from three or four hours to complete to as many as forty hours. Although cassette systems cover a number of topics, those involving computer operations and a variety of software packages are among the most plentiful.

Three significant advantages result from the use of audio cassette training. It accommodates those learners who learn best from an auditory approach, it is economical, and it can be used by learners anywhere and any time they have access to a tape player, including in a car or plane. Two of the most significant disadvantages are the inclusion in the package of some material that may not be relevant to all learners and the cost of the training package.

Video training As a technique designed to train employees, the use of video has become common. Included in **video training** systems are the tapes (or laser video disks) and the learner manual or guidebook. Systems concerned with topics involving computers and software packages also typically include diskettes. As a training system, the use of videos enables the trainee to see the concept being taught, hear about the concept, and finally perform the concept.

Among the advantages of video training are its convenience, the fast learning results it provides, and its availability for future use. Cost is seen as a disadvantage of video training.

Interactive video instruction Of the various employee training techniques, **interactive video instruction** is among the newest. Interactive video training generally involves the use of a computer, although the topic may not be computer related. The trainee carries on a dialogue with the computer, which he or she uses to ask himself or herself questions, to review material, and to provide responses by either touching the screen or using the keyboard. Although computer-assisted training and interactive video instruction are similar in some respects, interactive video is a more sophisticated training technique.

What are the advantages of interactive video instruction?

Considering the advantages of interactive video instruction, the following are found: It results in fast learning time and learners are able to master more and retain more than when using some of the other training techniques. The most significant disadvantage of this training technique is the cost of equipment and materials.

On-the-job Techniques

Training programs consisting of on-the-job techniques are popular for training office employees. On-the-job training experiences are often combined with the performance of actual job tasks. These techniques readily enable employees to transfer their training experiences to their jobs.

Education-employer cooperative training The **education-employer cooperative training technique** combines formal classes with on-the-job experiences. Cooperative training, which is most often found at the high school and college levels, enables learners to be enrolled in school while being employed part time in a related job.

What are the characteristics of the education-employer cooperative training technique?

The students learn in their school experiences how various office tasks are performed. In their part-time jobs, they have the opportunity to put their knowledge into practice. The students receive direction from both their employers and a specially trained employee of the school, commonly known as a co-op coordinator. Because organizations frequently offer full-time jobs to the students on completion of their educational experiences, this training technique is considered by some organizations to provide a valuable source of employees.

On-the-job coaching When **on-the-job coaching** is used, the learner's supervisor is the trainer. Therefore, the supervisor-subordinate relationship is also a trainer-trainee relationship. Although few would disagree with the practice of making the supervisor responsible for training subordinates in certain areas, the critics of this technique point out that being a good supervisor or manager may conflict with being a good trainer. Unless this conflict can be kept to a minimum, the individual who has dual supervisory and training responsibilities may find this technique to be somewhat disconcerting.

Figure 8-3 presents a list of suggestions designed to improve the effectiveness of employee coaching.

How is job rotation used as a training technique?

Job rotation Although **job rotation** is useful in training certain individuals, it is not used often as a technique for training office employees. The length of time over which the job rotation spans as well as the fairly high cost of using the technique are two disadvantages of the job rotation training tech-

1. Recognize that individuals have varying needs and that they respond differently to work pressure, challenge, and change.
2. Make sure employee is *fully* aware of his or her job responsibilities.
3. Make sure that the employee's strengths are matched with his or her job responsibilities.
4. Provide the employee with clearly defined objectives and priorities.
5. Open up communication lines with the employee by asking open-ended questions.
6. Explore with the employee what he or she and you (the supervisor) can do to make his or her job easier and more satisfying to perform.
7. Replace criticism with clarification, explanation, encouragement, suggestions, and discussions.
8. Maintain as much as possible on-the-spot accessibility.

Figure 8-3 Suggestions for improving the effectiveness of employee coaching.

nique. Learners rotate from one area to another, giving them an opportunity to become familiar with the activities of several functional areas. The extent to which learners perform duties in the various functional areas depends on the organization. Learners are sometimes allowed to perform tasks in each of the areas; in other instances, they simply observe.

LEGAL CONSIDERATIONS IN TRAINING

Several federal laws impact on organizational training programs. Denying training to individuals in protected classes—a denial that may ultimately hamper their promotion to higher-level positions—is illegal. Affirmative action, which requires that all employees be given equal opportunity for advancement, also requires equality in the availability of training opportunities. The **Civil Rights Act of 1964** assures the equality of training experiences for all employees.

The **Vocational Rehabilitation Act of 1973** outlines the nature of affirmative action for individuals with disabilities. When a contract or subcontract exceeds $50,000, a detailed plan is required in which the following topics are covered: hiring, advancement, discharge, as well as other employment practices.

COUNSELING

Another important component of the development process is employee **counseling**. In some organizations, employee counseling is carried out in a rather haphazard manner. The prevailing philosophy in some organizations is that once employees are hired, then all of their needs are satisfied, they enjoy their work, and they find their jobs challenging.

Although predicting the times when employees will need conferences with their supervisors is difficult, a routine conference schedule can be developed. Supervisor-subordinate conferences may be held after employment of one month, three months, six months, and twelve months. Because of unpredictable situations, the opportunity must be made available for additional conferences when the need arises.

How can employee conferences be made more effective?

The effectiveness of conferences can be improved if they are conducted away from the employee's workstation, perhaps in the privacy of the supervisor's office or in a conference room. The supervisor is responsible for setting the stage for the conference, the effectiveness of which will be diminished if the employee feels uncomfortable with the situation. The supervisor must also be willing to listen to the employee as well as to provide suggestions and advice when sought. Both the supervisor and the employee must have respect for one another and must have an appreciation for each other's viewpoints. In addition, the supervisor must display a willingness to be helpful, a sense of fairness, and a general concern for the employee.

Many supervisors prefer to use the nondirective counseling approach, which gives subordinates the opportunity to determine the scope of the session. The supervisor listens to the subordinate but does not evaluate the substance of the subordinate's comments. A goal of the nondirective approach is to get employees to express their feelings without fear of retribution or criticism.

The subordinate's freedom of expression in the nondirective approach tends to reduce tension, anxiety, and frustration. In addition, the openness of the approach often helps the subordinates more clearly see the various dimensions of the situation.

IMPLICATIONS FOR THE ADMINISTRATIVE OFFICE MANAGER

Familiarity with the various elements of employee development is becoming more important as the administrative office manager is assuming greater responsibility for certain specialized areas of the development process. Although overall responsibility in most organizations continues to be centralized within the personnel or training department, unit managers are often given responsibility for providing certain aspects of the process.

Providing quality development experiences is especially crucial to new employees. More often than not, their initial impression of the organization—which may ultimately become their prevailing impression—is affected by the quality of their early development experiences.

Managers sometimes wrongly assume that recently hired employees are adjusting well to their new situation, especially when they do not ask questions. Obviously, this assumption is incorrect because some employees are not comfortable questioning their supervisors and therefore refrain from doing so.

The philosophy that prevailed in many organizations a few years ago was that development existed only for new employees. Now, most organizations are committed to a lifelong employee development process. When managers discovered that employees' development needs increase as various situations arise—regardless of how long they have worked for the organization—the new philosophy began to prevail.

REVIEW QUESTIONS

1. What components of employee development are commonly found?
2. What is typically found in an orientation kit?
3. What advantages result from employee training?
4. In what ways can the need for an employee training program be determined?
5. What types of training programs are used, and how do they differ from one another?

6. Why is knowledge of results important to trainees?
7. When determining which training techniques to use, what factors should be considered?
8. How do the lecture method and the conference method differ from one another?
9. Provide a comparison and contrast of the sensitivity training and laboratory education methods of training.
10. What are the advantages of computer-assisted instruction as a training technique?
11. Why is employee counseling an important part of employee development?

DISCUSSION QUESTIONS

1. On several occasions during the first few weeks that you worked for your present employer, you asked your supervisor for help in solving some problems you were having with several of your assigned tasks. Your supervisor, in a firm but polite tone, said that he felt you would remember more by solving these problems yourself and that you may come up with some creative ways on your own to perform these tasks. Discuss the implications of this situation.
2. You work in a department that has a fair amount of employee dissention, which has resulted in the development of employee factions. It has resulted in an uncooperative attitude among employees, which makes the supervisory process even more difficult. Other than the negative attitude the supervisor frequently displays, no other causes for this dissention can be identified. When the supervisor was recently approached about implementing a "buddy" system for helping new employees adjust more rapidly, he quickly rejected the proposal, saying "I don't want a new employee contaminated early by an experienced employee." Is the buddy system likely to create a contamination of new employees in this situation? Explain the reasons for your belief. Do you think the buddy system should be used under the present circumstances? Why?
3. The personnel manager in the organization in which you are a supervisor is proposing the personnel department be totally responsible for orienting new employees. At the present time, each supervisor is responsible for orienting new employees their first day on the job. The personnel manager apparently is attempting to "build an empire" by trying to assume greater control over certain functions. As a supervisor, you believe you can provide excellent orientation for your new employees. How can you convince the executive vice president, the person to whom the personnel manager reports, that the present system for orienting new employees should be maintained?
4. Each new employee in the organization in which you work is given an employee handbook that contains a variety of valuable information. As a supervisor, you find that employees seem to be making less use of their handbooks because they are asking you an increasing number of questions about things covered in their books. You believe employees should use their handbooks whenever possible rather than bother you. What reasons may account for the failure of employees to use their books? What suggestions do you have for handling this frustration?
5. The organization in which you work provides a variety of training situations for its new employees. Until two years ago, the training program was considered by top management to be one of the more effective areas in the company. During the last two years, the results of the training efforts have not been as remarkable. The reasons for the deterioration are difficult to identify because no significant changes have been made in program structure, personnel, or training methodology. What reasons might account for the gradual erosion of the program's earlier success? What changes do you recommend be made to eliminate the negative effect of the reasons you identified?

6. The organization in which you work offers what is known as a "selective training process." This means employees are chosen by their supervisor to participate in a training program. Often those who have the best rapport with their supervisor are the ones who are chosen instead of those who actually need the training. Discuss the implications of this situation.

STUDENT PROJECTS AND ACTIVITIES

1. Talk with the personnel director of an organization about the nature of its orientation program. Who is in charge of orientation, and how long does the orientation program last?
2. Talk with the director of training in an organization. How does he or she determine the nature of training needs?
3. Talk with an individual who has just completed an organization's training program. What did this individual like most? Like least?
4. Talk with an individual who is responsible for counseling employees. Have this individual identify five key points for being a successful counselor.
5. Talk with an individual who has been trained using the computer-assisted instructional technique. Ask this individual to assess the effectiveness of this training technique.

MINICASE

The Jackman Electric Company is currently revamping certain aspects of its training program. One of the more important changes that will likely occur is the type of training techniques that will be implemented. In the present program, the lecture method is widely used. On-the-job coaching has been strongly endorsed by several supervisors, although no final decision has been made yet.

You were recently appointed by the company's president to chair a committee examining the effectiveness of the current program and to make recommendations regarding needed changes. While the final decision about the training techniques to be used is the responsibility of top management, you decide to include in a written report the following information:

1. How your committee assessed the desirability of the various training techniques it considered as possibilities.
2. A presentation of the advantages and disadvantages of the on-the-job coaching method, especially in comparison with the lecture method.

CASE

You are a consultant who has considerable expertise in the area of training programs. You just finished spending several days assessing the training program in Chicago-based Barracks Corporation, a large manufacturer of equipment used in bowling alleys. After spending several days in Barracks, you conclude that its program has several serious shortcomings.

Approximately 95 percent of the training experiences Barracks offers were developed primarily because of trainer interest in specific areas rather than because of trainee need. Management did not discourage this practice because of its belief that "something was better than nothing." For this reason, some training experiences have little value.

You also found out that the lecture method was widely used because of its relatively low per-trainee cost. Furthermore, you found that no employee follow-up is conducted after employees have been trained because "we really don't know what to expect of employees after they have completed their training experiences."

In the consultant's report you prepare for the company, you decide to include the following:

1. A discussion of the problems found in this company with respect to its training program. Discuss the implications of each of these problems.
2. A detailed discussion of your recommendations for eliminating the problems that are identified.

SUPERVISING OFFICE EMPLOYEES

CHAPTER AIM

After studying this chapter, you should be able to develop effective strategies for supervising subordinates.

CHAPTER OUTLINE

- Leadership Role
  - Behavioral Theories
    - Leadership Styles
    - Leadership Orientation
  - Situational Theory
- Functions of Supervision
  - Planning
  - Organizing
  - Staffing
  - Directing
  - Controlling
- Characteristics of Effective Supervisors
  - Getting Others to Cooperate
  - Listening to Others
  - Delegating Responsibilities
  - Understanding Subordinates
  - Treating Others Fairly
  - Building Teams
- Special Skills of Supervisors
  - Conceptual Skills
  - Human Skills
  - Technical Skills
  - Teaching Skills
  - Coaching Skills
  - Counseling Skills
  - Communication Skills
- Supervisory Training
- Special Responsibilities of Supervisors
  - Career Goal Planning
  - Ethical Behavior
  - Tardiness
  - Absenteeism
  - Alcoholism and Drug Abuse
  - Stress and Burnout
  - Sexual Harassment
  - Multicultural Issues
- Disciplining Employees
- Terminating Employees
- Working with a Union
  - Duration of Agreement
  - Union Security
  - Management Prerogatives
  - Wages and Hours
  - Promotion, Layoff, and Recall
  - Discipline of Members
  - Grievances
  - Strike Clauses
- Implications for the Administrative Office Manager

CHAPTER TERMS

Achievement-oriented supervision
Agency shop
Autocratic approach
Behavioral theories

Boss-centered leadership	Management by objectives (MBO)
Democratic approach	Management prerogatives
Dues checkoff	Outplacement services
Escalator clauses	Participative management
Grievance	Situational theory
Labor agreement	Subordinate-centered leadership
Laissez-faire approach	Subordinate-oriented supervision
Maintenance-of-membership shop	Union shop

A common responsibility of administrative office managers—indeed one of the most common—is the supervision of subordinates. Supervision is comprised of several activities including those of a planning, organizing, staffing, directing, and controlling nature. Many managers claim that their supervisory responsibilities are one of the more rewarding aspects of their job.

What factors determine the amount of leadership ability required of a supervisor?

The amount of leadership ability and skill the manager possesses affects his or her supervisory effectiveness. Some supervisory positions require greater leadership skills than other positions. The amount of leadership ability required of a supervisor is affected by several factors: the hierarchical level of the supervisor, the number of individuals for whom the supervisor is responsible, the nature of the work performed by the subordinates, the background of the subordinates, and the stability of the work unit.

To appreciate fully the importance of leadership in the supervisory process, an understanding of the leadership role is needed, which is discussed in the following section.

LEADERSHIP ROLE

The role of leadership in the supervisory process can be examined by studying **behavioral theories** of leadership and the **situational theory** of leadership.

Behavioral Theories

Two behavioral theories of leadership exist—leadership styles and leadership orientation. Each theory has distinct characteristics.

Leadership styles Although leadership styles vary between an **autocratic approach** and a **democratic approach**, several degrees between these two approaches can also be found. Although some supervisors can be classified as being autocratic and others democratic, most use an approach somewhere in between the two extremes. The following illustrates the autocratic-democratic leadership continuum:

Autocratic————————Democratic

What are the characteristics of autocratic supervisors?

Supervisors using the autocratic approach make decisions without seeking the ideas, suggestions, and recommendations of subordinates. Those who use this approach tend to exert extensive control over the behavior and actions of their subordinates. For example, subordinates may be disciplined before an attempt is made to determine the reasons responsible for their misconduct. Too, autocratic supervisors rarely deviate from the norm or from the expected course of action; and they tend to be inflexible, often the cause of subordinate resentment.

Democratic supervisors make extensive use of the ideas, suggestions, and recommendations of their subordinates. When the impact of a decision affects subordinates, they are likely to be invited to participate in the decision-making process—even though the supervisor is the one who is ultimately responsible for the decision. This management technique is officially known as **participative management**. In addition to using subordinate participation, the democratic approach is also more flexible than the autocratic approach. Those who use the democratic alternative are more likely to investigate the reasons for subordinate error or misconduct before they decide whether disciplinary action is appropriate.

The **management-by-objectives (MBO)** technique makes extensive use of democratic processes. With MBO, employees and their supervisors jointly establish objectives regarding the tasks performed by employees. At periodic intervals, the supervisors evaluate their subordinates' performance to determine progress toward goal achievement.

What are the characteristics of laissez-faire supervisors?

A third leadership approach that differs from either the autocratic or democratic processes is the **laissez-faire approach**. Supervisors who use the laissez-faire approach generally give subordinates considerable freedom and provide very little, if any, assistance. Some supervisors who use this approach are not concerned about their subordinates. Others use it because they believe they will be more popular with their subordinates if they give them considerable freedom.

Each of the three approaches is useful in certain situations. For example, when subordinates are poorly trained, when they are basically undisciplined, or when an emergency or crisis situation exists, the autocratic approach may be most desirable. Conversely, if subordinates are trained, highly motivated, or need to work together as a team, a more democratic approach may be appropriate. In technical groups in which creativity is needed, the laissez-faire approach may be most useful. In many office situations, a democratic approach is generally considered as the most desirable of the three approaches.

Leadership orientation The leadership role can also be studied by examining the nature of the supervisor's orientation toward subordinates. Supervisors who are only concerned with the achievements of their subordinates use **achievement-oriented supervision** practices. When supervisors are greatly concerned about the welfare of their subordinates, they use **subordinate-oriented supervision**.

What are the characteristics of achievement-oriented supervisors?

Achievement-oriented supervisors expect their subordinates to maintain a high output level regardless of the impact of productivity expectations on the employees. The subordinate-oriented supervisor is also concerned with output—but to a lesser degree than the achievement-oriented individual. The subordinate-oriented supervisor is committed to the belief that if subordinates' needs are fulfilled, they will perform at a satisfactory level.

Situational Theory

What is meant by the situational theory of leadership?

A growing number of individuals believe the situational theory of leadership is more realistic than the behavioral theories. The situational theory is based on the belief that the amount of leadership a supervisor should exert will vary from situation to situation. Although some situations require extensive amounts of leadership, others require considerably less.

Figure 9-1 illustrates the situational theory on a continuum. As the amount of authority used by the supervisor increases, leadership becomes more boss centered. Conversely, as the amount of subordinate freedom increases, leadership becomes more subordinate centered. **Boss-centered**

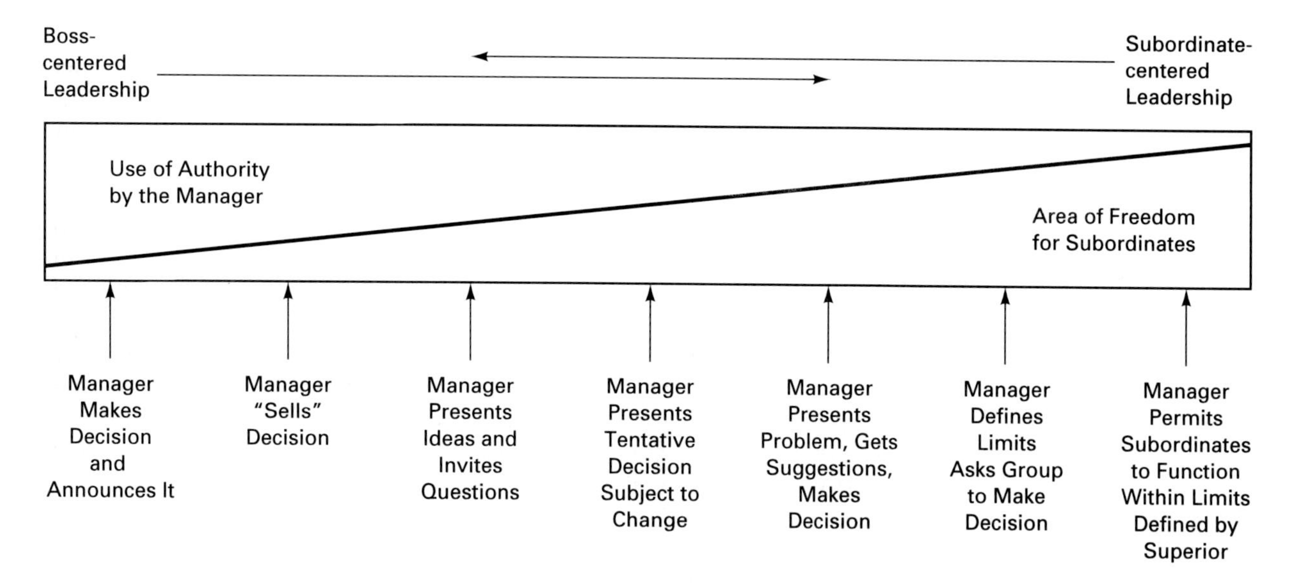

Figure 9-1 Leadership continuum. Copyright (c) 1958 by the President and Fellows of Harvard College. All rights reserved. Reprinted by permission of the *Harvard Business Review*. "How to Choose a Leadership Pattern," by Robert Tannenbaum and Warren H. Schmidt, March-April, 1958.

leadership is autocratic, whereas **subordinate-centered leadership** is democratic. Any given situation will determine how much supervisory authority or subordinate freedom is appropriate for the circumstances.

An effective supervisor is readily able to determine how much subordinate participation is appropriate for each situation. Extensive participation is appropriate in some instances; little or no subordinate participation is appropriate in other situations.

FUNCTIONS OF SUPERVISION

What are the five functions of the process of supervision?

Supervision involves five functions: planning, organizing, staffing, directing, and controlling.

Planning

The amount of time that the supervisor's job is consumed by the planning process is often directly related to the hierarchical level of his or her position. Higher-level supervisors spend more time in the planning function than lower-level supervisors. Furthermore, the plans developed by lower-level supervisors are usually for a shorter duration than those developed by higher-level supervisors. This is because the planning activities of the lower-level supervisors frequently involve implementing the goals and objectives developed by higher-level managers.

Organizing

The organizing function involves determining which of the subordinates in the work unit are best qualified for a particular job that has to be done and then assigning that job to the appropriate individuals. Consequently, organizing involves developing a staff system that facilitates the accomplishment of established plans. Another dimension of the organizing function is the development of an environment in which subordinates can be productive and efficient. The supervisor is also responsible for developing effective work processes and procedures.

Staffing

In some instances, the supervisor's staffing activities are quite extensive; in other instances, however, they are quite limited. Higher-level supervisors frequently have considerable control over selecting new employees for their respective work units. Lower-level supervisors, especially first-level supervisors, may not have as much control.

Other staffing activities of a supervisory nature involve orienting new employees, training new employees, retraining employees, and counseling employees. Supervisors find their jobs easier when their subordinates are efficient and well trained. When they are not, supervisors will most likely have to be more concerned with the activities involved in the planning, organizing, directing, and controlling functions.

Directing

What is meant by the directing function?

Some of the activities involved in the directing function include leading, motivating, developing, and recognizing the efforts of subordinates. The directing function is concerned with the manner in which the supervisor relates to a subordinate on a person-to-person basis or to a group of subordinates on a person-to-group basis. To maximize the directing efforts, a supervisor must not only be concerned with the goals and objectives of the organization, but also with how well the needs of each subordinate are related to the organization's goals and objectives. Although the activities in the directing function are important to lower-level supervisors, they are generally not as important to the higher-level supervisors.

Controlling

Why is the controlling function necessary?

The controlling function involves comparing actual results with anticipated results. The activities in this function are likely to consume a considerable portion of the supervisor's time, especially when actual results are less than what was anticipated. The supervisor is responsible for taking corrective action to remedy these situations.

The absence of standards against which to compare actual results diminishes the value of controlling efforts. The supervisor is also responsible for determining the validity of the standards that are used in the comparison process.

CHARACTERISTICS OF EFFECTIVE SUPERVISORS

Over the years, several characteristics of effective supervisors have been identified. The following is a discussion of five of these characteristics: getting others to cooperate, listening to others, delegating responsibilities, understanding subordinates, and treating others fairly.

Getting Others to Cooperate

One of the most important characteristics of effective supervisors is their ability to gain the cooperation of others. Supervisors find their jobs are exceedingly more difficult when their subordinates are uncooperative.

How can a supervisor gain subordinates' cooperation?

An effective way to gain subordinates' cooperation is to make them aware that higher-level management is dependent on them for their ideas and suggestions. In many instances, the employees who work most closely with a given work procedure are able to provide valuable contributions when changes have to be made. Managerial acceptance of their ideas enhances subordinate cooperation.

When employees are able to see rather quickly that their ideas are accepted and used, their cooperation is likely to increase. Accepting but not using employees' ideas may be more destructive in the long run than if their ideas and suggestions were not accepted in the first place.

Supervisors can also gain cooperation by providing as much variety as possible in the daily routine. Subordinates tend to become rather complacent and soon lose interest when their jobs lack variety.

The inability of a supervisor to justify the existence of certain policies and procedures also has a destructive impact on employee cooperation. An effective supervisor is able to answer subordinates' questions; if the answer is not known, the supervisor should make every attempt to obtain the answer. Much cooperation is lost by telling subordinates that something "has to be done a certain way because that is the way it has always been done."

Listening to Others

Another characteristic of a good supervisor is the willingness to listen to subordinates. Some supervisors have difficulty hearing out their subordinates, especially those for whom negative feelings exist. But unless subordinates are convinced their supervisors are willing to listen, the development of an effective interpersonal relationship may be difficult.

Some supervisors are guilty of not listening to a subordinate who wishes to discuss a situation about which the supervisor and subordinate disagree. The supervisor gives the impression that the subordinate is not in a position to question or discuss the incident. Another fault some supervisors have is making decisions or judgments about a situation even before the subordinate has finished talking. Such a habit reflects negatively on the supervisor because subordinates are likely to get the impression that the supervisor has little concern for them or their ideas.

Another undesirable listening habit of some supervisors is the injection of their comments or feelings about the situation before they are aware of all the relevant facts. The supervisor who does this is likely to "force" the subordinate to have the same beliefs as he or she does.

Listening to a subordinate is not enough. The supervisor also must pay attention to or concentrate on what the subordinate has to say. Although the supervisor may have difficulty concentrating totally on what the subordinate is saying, concentration is crucial.

The mark of a good listener is the ability to hear what the subordinate is actually saying—and not just what the supervisor wants to hear. Supervisors who hear only what they want to hear cannot be completely objective when having to make decisions.

Delegating Responsibilities

One of the most important characteristics of good supervisors is their ability to delegate meaningful tasks to subordinates. Unless supervisors make use of delegation, they either have to do much of the work themselves, or they have to depend on others to assume the responsibility for undertaking a number of their tasks. Effective delegation helps extend the supervisors' capabilities, encourages team work, and results in higher productivity. When delegating, the supervisor must remember the need for commensurate authority and responsibility. To make a subordinate responsible for a certain task without giving him or her the necessary authority to carry out the task is futile.

Some supervisors are hesitant to delegate, either because they do not know how to delegate effectively or because they are afraid to delegate. Supervisors are sometimes reluctant to delegate for one or more of the following reasons: They believe they can perform certain tasks more effectively than those to whom they might delegate; they find they can perform the tasks more easily themselves than teach someone else; or they want the tasks done their way, which might be different from the way the subordinates might choose to do the tasks.

What guidelines enhance the effectiveness of the delegation process?

Adherence to several guidelines improves the effectiveness of the delegation process.

1. *Select the appropriate person to whom a task is to be delegated.* Because all subordinates are not equally able to perform the tasks with the same level of quality, the supervisor needs to be selective in making assignments. Much of one's success in delegating can be attributed to choosing the appropriate person for each task.
2. *Select tasks that can be delegated.* A good supervisor is selective in delegating tasks. Although some tasks cannot be delegated, others should be selectively delegated. Generally, those tasks that can be delegated are routine in nature, they may involve minimal amounts of judgment, and the task steps can be easily identified.
3. *Help the person to whom tasks have been delegated.* Effective supervisors help subordinates to whom they delegate tasks. Some supervisors have the mistaken notion that if a subordinate is qualified to undertake a task, no assistance or help should be needed. Therefore, the subordinate is left alone to do the assigned tasks. Most subordinates are able to do many tasks without supervisory help, but help should be available when needed.
4. *Make sure that work assignments are fully understood.* An effective supervisor is patient with subordinates who have been delegated a task for the first time. Even though subordinates may think they fully understand their assignment, questions often arise once they begin.

A supervisor who delegates tasks to subordinates is usually held responsible for task completion. Subordinates to whom tasks are assigned should have commensurate authority and responsibility to ensure task completion.

In delegating tasks to subordinates, many supervisors have difficulty accepting the fact that often more than one desirable or effective way may exist to do a particular task. No matter how much a supervisor would like to have a subordinate do a task his or her way, the relationship may be jeopardized if the supervisor requires the subordinate to follow certain procedures when others are just as effective.

Understanding Subordinates

How can supervisors develop a better understanding of their subordinates?

Because the supervisor is responsible for motivating subordinates, a thorough understanding of their needs, drives, interests, and attitudes is important. Without this background knowledge, a supervisor may have difficulty inspiring each subordinate to perform to the best of his or her ability.

Familiarity with several aspects of each subordinate's background is desirable, including the following:

1. *Ability to think*. To understand a subordinate fully, the supervisor must be aware of the subordinate's thinking capability. The ability to sort the important from the unimportant and to organize important thoughts in a logical way is also helpful.
2. *Social traits*. For a supervisor to understand subordinates fully, an awareness of the social traits of each subordinate is needed. The supervisor needs to know which subordinates have a tendency to become aggressive, withdraw, dominate the situation, and put others at ease.
3. *Personality traits*. To have an effective working relationship with subordinates, the supervisor should have a fairly comprehensive understanding of each subordinate's personality. Without this knowledge, a supervisor has difficulty knowing how to respond to or how to supervise subordinates. An understanding of personality traits can also be used to assess the emotional needs of subordinates.
4. *Character*. Also needed is an awareness of each subordinate's character; otherwise, the supervisor can only guess the degree to which subordinates can be trusted. Because subordinates do not all have the same amount of integrity, the supervisor may have to place greater trust in some subordinates than in others.
5. *Work habits*. A knowledge of subordinates' work habits is also needed by supervisors, including an awareness of who is a self-starter, who needs some direction, and who needs considerable direction. Work habits of subordinates are a significant determinant of the degree of supervision they require.
6. *Relations with others*. To understand subordinates, the supervisor must be aware of how they relate to others. This understanding is important in deciding which subordinates are able to work together on a given project, which subordinates have good public relations skills, and so forth.

Supervisors who know and understand their subordinates well can assign them tasks they are sure to enjoy. Happy, satisfied subordinates make the supervisor's job much easier. Knowing and understanding subordinates also enables the supervisor to respond more effectively to their individual needs.

Treating Others Fairly

The last characteristic of effective supervisors to be discussed in this chapter is the fair treatment of others. The relationships between many supervisors and their subordinates have been damaged because of a lack of fairness on the part of the supervisor. A perceived lack of fairness is often as damaging to the relationship as is a real lack of fairness.

When the supervisor's personal feelings about subordinates sways the making of decisions, supervisors often have difficulty treating their subordinates fairly. Those subordinates for whom the supervisor has strong positive feelings are likely to receive favored treatment, whereas those about whom the supervisor feels negatively are likely to be treated unfairly.

Effective supervisors treat all subordinates in a consistent manner in similar situations. Policies that exist for one subordinate should exist for all subordinates.

In some instances, when a subordinate is involved in a situation of a serious nature, the immediate supervisor perhaps should not be the only one involved in deciding upon an appropriate course of action. For example, if a subordinate's conduct or actions are serious enough that dismissal is a possibility, the final decision regarding the subordinate should be made in consultation with higher-level individuals. The subordinate, therefore, cannot claim that the supervisor was unfair because of prior bias or negative feelings toward him or her.

Building Teams

Research findings clearly illustrate the value of building an effective teamwork attitude among employees. Included as benefits of team building are the following: Employees have greater control over their jobs, it encourages individual creativity and the use of creativity in solving a variety of work-related problems, and it gives employees the feeling that they have a more significant role in what happens in the organization.

When employees work together as integral members of a team, productivity increases, quality of work improves, and employees feel they play a more significant role within the organization. The end result is a happier, more satisfied workforce. The supervisor is responsible for building teamwork, either by teaching his or her subordinates how to become a better team player or by arranging for others to provide work-team indoctrination. Once a work group is committed to the work-team attitude, the orientation/instruction does not end. Rather, the orientation/instruction continues virtually for the life of the work group. At some point, instruction will change its focus from "how to" to refinement of the team-building concept.

SPECIAL SKILLS OF SUPERVISORS

In addition to possessing the characteristics discussed in the preceding section, supervisors need certain skills. These include such skills as conceptual, human, and technical skills, as well as skills in teaching, coaching, counseling, and communicating. These skills are often developed through supervisory training experiences made available to new supervisors or to supervisors who need or desire refresher training.

Conceptual Skills

What is the nature of the conceptual skills needed by supervisors?

Critical to the success of the supervisor is the possession of conceptual skills. This vital attribute enables the supervisor to perceive quickly how one phenomenon may impact on another phenomenon. Specifically, conceptual skills help the supervisor determine the full impact of a change or a variety of changes. Supervisors with well-developed conceptual skills are often able to avert or eliminate situations that may later develop into problems. Possessing conceptual skills is seen by some supervisors as a "fifth" sense in dealing with organizational matters. As supervisors move higher in the organizational hierarchy, their use of conceptual skills increases.

Although conceptual skills are generally learned through experiences and the educational process, some conceptual skills are intuitive. Skills of an intuitive nature often enable the supervisor to make the correct decision simply because it seems to be the correct decision.

Human Skills

Why must a supervisor possess effective human skills?

Also critical to the success of the supervisor are skills in working effectively with others including subordinates, peers, and superiors. Without effective human skills, the supervisor is likely to alienate others with whom he or she must work. Once the working relationship is damaged, especially in dealing with subordinates, the supervisor will likely have difficulty maximizing the cooperation of subordinates, motivating them, or maintaining their loyalty. The use of effective human skills greatly diminishes the occurrence of such problems.

An understanding of human skills will give the supervisor greater insight into working effectively with each subordinate in each situation. Because personalities and situations vary so much, the supervisor must be able to maintain the proper amount of closeness or distance, whichever is appropriate for the situation. Supervisors who remain distant in every situation or who tend to have close relationships with their subordinates soon find they are considered to be either uncooperative individuals or that they can be taken advantage of quite easily. In either case, the subordinates will likely lose respect for their supervisors.

Human skills can be learned either through on-the-job training or through courses designed to help individuals improve their supervisory skills. Some supervisors also complete college-level courses to acquire more effective skills in working with others.

The importance of human skills to supervisory success remains rather stable at all levels of the organizational hierarchy. Therefore, supervisors at the lower levels of the hierarchy and those at the upper level have comparable needs with regard to human skills.

Technical Skills

The possession of technical skills is often one of the most important criteria considered in selecting an individual for his or her first supervisory position. The supervisor needs technical skills to understand certain operations or tasks.

What determines the nature of the technical skills needed by a supervisor?

The nature of technical skills the supervisor needs is determined by his or her areas of responsibility. The ever-increasing technological nature of office functions increases the technical skills office supervisors need. As a person moves higher in the organizational hierarchy, however, the technical skills the supervisor needs diminishes somewhat.

Technical skills are typically acquired by means of the various training techniques discussed in Chapter 8. Some of the training techniques discussed in the chapter, however, are better suited for the acquisition of technical skills than are other techniques.

Teaching Skills

Supervisors responsible for teaching or training subordinates need special teaching skills. Although most supervisors could probably teach subordinates without prior training in this area, a more effective job is likely to result when supervisors have been appropriately trained.

Two important elements of teaching in which a supervisor should be skilled are demonstrating and explaining. In addition, skill in evaluating subordinates' performance is needed. Supervisory teaching skills are effectively learned through college and university courses and through supervisory training experiences provided by the organization.

Coaching Skills

What types of coaching skills are needed by supervisors?

The ability to coach subordinates is another of the skills needed by effective supervisors. Coaching involves a concerted effort by the supervisor to develop a subordinate. The development process is concerned with the subordinate's job and the problems related to that job. The objective of coaching is to improve job skills and to increase the subordinate's understanding of the technical aspects of the job.

A distinct difference exists between on-the-job training and coaching. On-the-job training involves teaching the subordinates about the techniques of job performance, but coaching is more comprehensive. As an example, coaching might involve helping a subordinate develop managerial skills, especially if these skills are needed by an employee about to be promoted to a managerial position.

Coaching skills are effectively learned through organization-sponsored supervisory training programs.

Counseling Skills

Over the years, supervisors have counseled subordinates in a variety of areas, some of which are generally considered to fall within the domain of the supervisor-subordinate relationship. Other areas are clearly outside the scope of the relationship.

Most supervisors do not have time to provide counseling in all the areas in which their subordinates experience problems. Although the supervisor must listen to some of the subordinates' problems to maintain an effective relationship, the supervisor must also use good judgment in selecting the areas in which to become involved.

Increasingly, employee assistance programs (EAPs) are being installed in larger organizations. The rationale behind this practice is that supervisors do not have the time or the qualifications to counsel subordinates in certain areas, such as substance abuse. EAPs are discussed in detail in Chapter 16.

What is the nondirective approach to counseling?

Several counseling techniques are used, ranging from a nondirective approach in which the subordinate does most of the talking, to a technique in which the supervisor is responsible for directing the process. What is appropriate for one individual and one set of circumstances may be totally inappropriate for another individual and another set of circumstances.

Counseling skills can be learned through college and university training as well as through organization-sponsored training programs.

Communication Skills

The effectiveness of the supervisor-subordinate relationship is heavily dependent on communication. Therefore, well-developed communication skills are needed if the supervisor-subordinate relationship is to be maximized.

An effective supervisor is aware of the forces that impede the communication process, namely, the following:

What forces impede the communication process?

1. *Lack of knowledge or background information*. A lack of knowledge or background information on the part of the receiver or sender will impede the communication process. Absence of knowledge often results from lack of education, intelligence, or exposure to the topic being discussed.
2. *Inappropriate vocabulary usage*. Not everyone has the same level of vocabulary understanding. To use words that are not understood by the receiver injects a barrier into the communication process.

3. *Presence of bias or prejudice*. Showing bias or prejudice is another force that impedes the communication process. A prejudiced comment leveled against an individual impedes effective communication.
4. *Impact of filtering*. As messages pass from one individual to another, the original intent of the message may become distorted or changed in meaning. This process is called filtering.

Effective communication, which depends so heavily on trust, also involves the ability to show empathy and concern for others. The communication between two individuals is often hampered because either or both of these factors are absent.

Another way the supervisor can make the communication process more effective is to avoid developing a defensive attitude. When an open, trusting relationship between the supervisor and subordinate exists, the supervisor may at times be criticized by the subordinate. The supervisor, by becoming defensive, will create a communication barrier.

The supervisor can further strengthen the communication process by using a direct approach when it is appropriate and an indirect approach when it is appropriate. When dealing with a sensitive situation, the supervisor may wisely use an indirect approach when communicating with a subordinate.

Courses designed to help individuals develop effective communication skills are taught at colleges and universities as well as in supervisory training programs. Because most individuals spend considerable time each day communicating, they may believe they already possess effective communication skills. Although this may be true in certain instances, many supervisors can and do profit from formal training in the communication area.

As increasing numbers of employees are working off-site (free-lance employees, telecommuting employees, and employees who work in satellite offices, primarily), maintaining effective communication with them becomes especially crucial. An especially important recommendation is to guard against an "out-of-sight, out-of-mind attitude" toward those employees. Although the supervisor (in some cases known as a facilitator in these situations) will likely not have as much contact with these subordinates, he or she needs to keep abreast of the projects on which they are working, offer assistance when needed, refer the employees to others in the organization who may be able to provide assistance, and so forth. Generally, the employees who work off-site will feel more a part of the team if they are invited to attend department meetings.

SUPERVISORY TRAINING

Because most individuals are promoted to supervisory positions from production-oriented jobs, many can profit from supervisory training experiences. Although most have the necessary technical competence, they need to be trained in other areas. A variety of techniques, many of which are discussed in Chapter 8, are used in training supervisors.

One of the most important factors in designing training programs for supervisors is determining the areas in which they need training. Largely, these areas are determined by the nature of the organization in which supervisors are employed and the duties they are expected to perform. Because supervisors do not all need training in the same areas, some discretion should be used in selecting appropriate experiences for each individual. Topics frequently covered include the following:

What topics are frequently covered in supervisory training programs?

1. Delegating work.
2. Disciplining employees.
3. Training employees.
4. Hiring, orienting, and promoting employees.
5. Handling grievances.
6. Scheduling work.
7. Designing effective work procedures.
8. Developing effective human relations skills.
9. Developing effective communication skills.
10. Developing effective counseling skills.
11. Acquiring a working knowledge of the important aspects of relevant federal and state legislation.

Some supervisory training programs are intensive and conducted over a short time. Others are less intensive and continue for a longer time. The effectiveness of the trainer often determines the success of the training program.

SPECIAL RESPONSIBILITIES OF SUPERVISORS

The extent to which the supervisor helps his or her subordinates attain certain career goals and then progress toward the attainment of other goals affects his or her supervisory image. Supervisors who are concerned about their subordinates consider career goal planning to be an important responsibility.

Increased absenteeism and tardiness of some employees is often the result of supervisory laxness. Individuals who know they can be late to work or absent from work with little or no penalty tend to be late or absent more often. The supervisor is responsible for making sure that employees do not violate the organization's tardiness or absenteeism policies.

Because supervisors are in close contact with their subordinates, many organizations are now asking their supervisors to be more aware of employees who may have problems with alcohol or drug abuse. Organizations are more commonly taking a paternalistic view toward substance abuse by attempting to help employees who may not only seek help, who also may benefit from the help.

Supervisors also have a responsibility for helping employees cope with stress and burnout. Although these two topics are covered in detail in Chapter 16, they are covered briefly in this section.

Career Goal Planning

Why do supervisors need to become involved in the career goal planning activities of their subordinates?

Employees who perceive that they are making progress in the attainment of their career goals are often more productive and satisfied than those lacking such a perception. Effective supervisors think of themselves as having an important responsibility in helping subordinates attain their career goals. For those subordinates without clear-cut career goals, the supervisor plays a vital role in helping them in their career-planning efforts. Supervisors who are perceived by their subordinates as an impediment to the attainment of important career goals most likely will not be able to maximize the development of an effective supervisor-subordinate relationship.

For those subordinates who have clear-cut goals, the supervisor often helps them (1) assess their strengths and weaknesses, (2) develop strategic plans to attain their goals, and (3) put their plans into action. For those individuals who lack clear-cut career goals, supervisors can often enhance the satisfaction their subordinates derive from their jobs. By helping subordinates assess their strengths and weaknesses, the supervisor is able to identify possible areas of career interest. Therefore, supervisory familiarity with the specific characteristics of various careers is helpful. Once subordinates have identified their career goal preferences, supervisors can help their subordinates develop strategic plans and then put the plans into action.

Ethical Behavior

How is ethical behavior among employees developed?

The supervisor can make a significant impact on how ethically his or her subordinates behave. The presence of unethical behavior may also indicate the presence of illegal behavior. For example, employee theft is illegal as well as unethical. Conversely, the making of personal long-distance telephone calls from an office telephone—in violation of company policy—is not illegal but is unethical. Basically, ethics are rules or codes of conduct.

Some employees will engage in unethical behavior when they believe that such behavior will not be detected. Other employees will avoid unethical behavior even when the chance of having this behavior detected is minimal to nonexistent. For most employees, as the opportunity for detection of unethical behavior increases, their willingness to engage in unethical behavior decreases.

One of the most effective ways to increase ethical behavior among employees is for the managers and supervisors throughout the organization to display ethical behavior themselves through their actions and words. A manager who tells his or her subordinates that ethical behavior is important but then engages in unethical behavior is not likely to have a significant impact on stimulating his or her subordinates to behave more ethically.

Another effective way to increase the ethical behavior of employees is to implement a code of ethics by which all employees are expected to live—regardless of job title or hierarchical level. Depending on the situation and the employees, ethical behavior might also be included as a topic in employee training programs. In some organizations, an ethics review committee is formed to determine what constitutes ethical behavior in given situations. Because the supervisor is the link between the subordinate and the next higher level in the chain of command, the supervisor is a key player in determining the extent to which employees behave in an ethical manner. Finally, rewarding ethical behavior and taking punitive action against unethical behavior is also an effective way to promote ethical behavior among employees.

The lack of ethical behavior among employees is frequently seen in such activities as the use of the organization's WATS line for making personal calls and taking organizational supplies for personal use. Some organizations have implemented a practice of allowing employees to use the WATS line for making personal calls after work hours. If the organization has a lower long-distance toll rate than employees have at home, allowing employees to make personal calls—but requiring reimbursement for such calls—is another alternative.

Closely related to the misuse of long-distance services and organizational supplies is the personal use of the organization's facsimile and copying devices. This situation can be virtually eliminated by making certain individuals responsible for operating these devices. Employees are less likely to use the organization's fax and copying devices for personal use when a designated individual is responsible for their operation.

Illegal copying of the organization's software is another common type of unethical behavior. Increasing numbers of organizations are obtaining site licenses that allow the use of the software on a specific number of machines.

This practice does not allow the use of the software on the employee's home computer, however. Stressing the need to avoid illegal copying of software is perhaps the most effective way of dealing with this situation.

Tardiness

How should a supervisor deal with employee tardiness?

Over time, tardiness can be quite costly to an organization. The supervisor is responsible for determining the legitimacy of tardiness-producing situations over which subordinates have no control. Examples are traffic jams, automobile malfunctions, mass transportation problems, and the like.

The supervisor can deal with the actions of employees that result in their being tardy in a variety of ways. Most supervisors believe that as the problem becomes more severe, the discipline leveled against the employee should also become more harsh. Employees may first receive an oral or written reprimand. If this does not help, the next course of action may be a pay reduction. If the problem continues, the employee may be given a week's layoff without pay. Finally, the last course of action is to discharge the employee.

Some organizations have found that the best way to eliminate tardiness is to reward employees for being punctual. The reward system may be on an individual or group basis, such as a work unit or department. Examples of rewards are time off, monetary bonus, public recognition, faster promotion, and larger salary increases.

By setting a good example, supervisors themselves can do much to help eliminate employee tardiness. Requiring an employee to be punctual when the supervisor is not punctual is difficult to justify.

The organization's cost of tardiness can be easily calculated. Assume that the employees in a given work unit during a month's time were tardy 480 minutes. If a standard 8-hour workday (480 minutes) exists, the equivalent of one employee's workday is lost because of tardiness during the month. If the average yearly salary of the employees in the work unit is $20,000, $83.35 (the average daily salary) is lost in a month's time because of employee tardiness ($20,000/12 = a monthly salary of $1,667 or a daily salary of $83.35).

To help control absenteeism, tardiness rates should be monitored by calculating a monthly tardiness ratio. Assuming that fifteen employees were tardy 480 minutes in a month's time, the average employee tardiness rate is 32 minutes (480/15). Tracking this figure over several months enables the supervisor to determine when tardiness is becoming a significant problem. Interwork unit figures can also be compared.

Absenteeism

How should a supervisor deal with employee absenteeism?

The employee absenteeism rate is a concern in many organizations. Absenteeism is costly not only in terms of salaries, but also in terms of lost productivity. The cost of absenteeism can range up to $500 or more per employee per year.

In many instances, 10 to 20 percent of an organization's workforce is responsible for 75 to 80 percent of the absences. By paying particular attention to these percentages, the supervisor may be able to find more effective ways to control absenteeism.

Some absences are unavoidable, such as those caused by illness, job-related injuries, illness of a family member, and death of family members or close friends. Although these situations create legitimate absences, some employees use these situations as excuses for being absent. The supervisor must therefore attempt to determine when an employee's stated reason for being absent is legitimate and when it is not.

A common reason for employee absenteeism is a lack of job satisfaction. Although the employee will generally offer some other reason for being absent, the real reason may be a lack of job interest. In such situations, the supervisor may take one of the following courses of action: Determine ways in which the job can be made more interesting and challenging; determine if the job requirements are considerably less than the employee's capability; determine the reasons for the employee's taking the job in the first place, besides the need for money; and determine if the working conditions are satisfactory.

Supervisors can handle absenteeism in the same way that they handle tardiness. The following courses of action are frequently used in dealing with employees whose absenteeism is a problem: oral or written reprimand, pay deduction, temporary layoff, and discharge.

In many organizations, providing employees with personal days has considerably reducedabsenteeism. In these organizations, employees are typically given two personal days per year. One restriction often found is the requirement that the taking of personal days be approved several days in advance. Being able to plan for the employee's absence is less likely to be disruptive to the work process.

Organizations have experimented with the following ways to reward employees who have good attendance records:

1. Adding an extra day or two to an employee's yearly vacation time.
2. Giving an employee a monetary bonus.
3. Recognizing each employee who has a good attendance record.
4. Making available a "pool" in which an employee's chances of winning are increased each day the employee is at work.
5. Giving an employee higher salary increases and faster promotions.

How can the cost of employee absenteeism be calculated?

The cost of employee absenteeism can also be calculated by using the same process as that used for determining the cost of employee tardiness. Assume that a work unit comprises fifteen employees who have an absenteeism rate of twelve days per month. Using the same average daily salary figure of $83.35, the monthly cost to the organization is $1,000. If this average existed each month for a year's time, the cost to the organization is $12,000 ($1,000 x 12). If additional help is hired to compensate for this rate of absenteeism, an employee earning a yearly salary of $20,000 would have to work 7.2 months ($12,000/$1,667) to make up the work deficiency of the employees who are absent.

The monthly work unit absenteeism rate can be calculated by dividing the number of workdays employees were absent by the average number of employees in the work unit. This absenteeism average can then be compared with rates of the same work unit in other months or with the rates of other work units.

Alcoholism and Drug Abuse

Another of the special responsibilities of many supervisors is the detection of employees who have a substance-abuse condition. In the past, many organizations discharged employees addicted to alcohol. Because of a growing awareness about alcoholism, many organizations have developed rather sophisticated programs designed to help their addicted employees. Most of these programs have been quite successful in helping employees once again become fully productive, wage-earning members of society. Important aspects of the organization's program are the following:

What are the important aspects of organizational alcoholism and drug-abuse programs?

1. The organization's treatment of alcoholism as a health condition that requires medical attention.
2. The organization's willingness to provide assistance to alcoholic employees.
3. The organization's commitment to the employee as long as improvement is made and/or maintained.
4. The organization's thorough communication of program elements to all employees.

Alcoholic employees cost American business and industry billions of dollars each year. Data compiled by the National Council on Alcoholism indicate that alcoholic employees are absent nearly three times more often than nonalcoholic employees. Job-related accident rates are two to four times higher than the rates of nonalcoholic employees. Off-the-job accident rates of alcoholic employees are four to six times higher, and accident and sickness benefits paid out are three times higher for alcoholic employees.

The National Council on Alcoholism has been helpful in getting alcoholism considered as a disease. Alcoholics are more readily accepted when their addiction is considered as a treatable disease rather than a personal weakness or character flaw. Being accepted by coworkers enables alcoholic employees to respond to treatment more quickly. The National Council on Alcoholism has also done an outstanding job of educating the general public about the abuses of alcoholism.

What is the nature of the supervisor's responsibilities in alcoholism programs?

Organizations that have installed programs to help alcoholics generally depend heavily on the supervisor, who is in an excellent position to detect the signs of alcoholism. Supervisors are given training to detect these signs, which include deteriorating job performance, withdrawal, increased tardiness, increased absenteeism, and so on. Because most supervisors are not in a position to help employees overcome alcoholism, the usual course of action is to refer them to the appropriate individuals, such as physicians or counselors.

The recovery rate of alcoholic employees is approximately 50 to 75 percent. With this level of success, one has difficulty trying to understand why executives in some organizations do not believe in the establishment of such worthwhile programs.

The use of drugs by employees is a fairly new problem for many organizations. This explains why many organizations have been slow to develop programs designed to help employees with drug addiction problems. Most organizations, however, have provided their employees with information about drug abuse. This information can be developed in-house or obtained from such agencies as the Bureau of Narcotics and Dangerous Drugs and the U.S. Public Health Service. In addition, many local police departments have narcotics divisions that make drug-abuse information readily available to organizations.

What is the nature of the supervisor's responsibilities in drug-abuse programs?

Supervisors in many organizations are responsible for detecting employees with a drug-addiction condition. The symptoms of drug abuse are typically not as noticeable as those for alcohol abuse. Some signs of drug abuse, although not foolproof, include frequent absenteeism, industrial accidents of an unexplained nature, long lunch breaks, the wearing of dark glasses to hide dilated pupils, and high pilferage rates. The supervisor must be especially careful not to accuse someone of drug addiction without the presence of substantial evidence. Supervisors who do so wrongly may be putting themselves and their employer in a precarious legal situation.

When evidence of drug addiction is available, the supervisor generally refers the individual to a professional capable of providing the needed assistance. Once the individual agrees to rehabilitation, most organizations will continue employment as long as rehabilitation progress continues.

Stress and Burnout

As the personal lives of individuals become more hectic, they begin to experience increased levels of stress. More often than not, personal stress and job stress eventually become interrelated to the point that making distinctions between the two becomes difficult. Supervisory intervention may occasionally be needed.

Some of the more common causes of stress and burnout are the following: having too much to do in too short a time, not having clearly defined goals, not being involved, not being challenged, and having personal problems.

The earlier the supervisor tries to help subordinates cope with stress, the less significant stress levels are likely to become. When stress becomes excessive, employees may need to seek professional assistance.

Among the ways that employees are able to cope with stress are the following:

1. Develop an appropriate attitude toward work and life in general.
2. Take an unpaid leave of absence as a means of "relaxing" and "regrouping."
3. Transfer to a less stressful position.
4. Join a therapy group.
5. Seek professional counseling.
6. Take advantage of opportunities for physical activity.
7. Take advantage of vacation time.

Burnout and stress are often related. When stress becomes excessive, employees may begin to experience burnout. Symptoms of burnout are lack of concern for the job, poor-quality work, failure to meet deadlines, frequent absenteeism and tardiness, frequent fatigue, hostile attitude, and negative feelings about work and life in general.

Sexual Harassment

Supervisors also are responsible for avoiding the sexual harassment of their subordinates and for stressing that their subordinates avoid sexually harassing one another. Sexual harassment is most often seen in unwelcomed sexual advances, in requesting sexual favors (in exchange for a salary increase, a promotion, and so forth), and in dialogue of a sexual nature. Not only is sexual harassment illegal because it violates Title VII of the Civil Rights Act, but also it creates numerous interpersonal problems. The Civil Rights Act of 1991 allows punitive damages and emotional-distress awards for plaintiffs who win sexual-harassment lawsuits. The 1991 law also gives an individual the right to a jury trial for cases involving sexual harassment.

Supervisors are responsible for knowing what constitutes sexual harassment and for helping their subordinates become familiar with what constitutes sexual harassment. Proper education and the implementation of an organization-wide policy that prohibits sexual harassment are two effective ways of dealing with the situation.

Multicultural Issues

Organizations increasingly are becoming multicultural in terms of their workforce. As a result, supervisors—typically the ones who work on a daily basis with individuals of diverse cultures—are obligated to accept the diversity and deal with it in a professional, responsible manner. Failure on the part of the supervisor to accept the diversity renders him or her a less-effective supervisor.

Some individuals of other cultures differ in fairly significant ways from the typical individual who grew up in a mainstream America culture. Differences are likely to be found in various beliefs, attitudes, mores, work habits, ethics, and so forth. Not only must supervisors be tolerant of and sensitive to the differences, but also they need to work with their subordinates as a means of getting them to accept the differences. In some cases, the process of getting others to accept the differences is as easy as creating greater awareness among all subordinates about the nature of the cultural differences. In other cases, the process is more difficult, with the supervisors' having to help certain subordinates "deprogram" themselves where they have to overcome long-standing biases, stereotyped notions, and attitudinal differences. When supervisors are able to get all their subordinates—regardless of their cultural background—to accept one another for whom they are, they are dealing effectively with multicultural diversity.

How can a supervisor learn to deal with multicultural diversity?

Supervisors can learn to deal with multicultural diversity in a number of ways, including the following: attending seminars and workshops dealing with multicultural diversity, engaging in self-study, enrolling in courses dealing with multicultural diversity, and discussing various multicultural issues with others. In most instances, supervisors take advantage of more than one of these alternatives.

DISCIPLINING EMPLOYEES

Because subordinates do not always perform as expected or behave in acceptable ways, they may have to be disciplined, which is another common responsibility of the supervisor. Effectively done, disciplining a subordinate will not cause irreparable damage to the supervisor-subordinate relationship. Discipline should teach at the same time it corrects.

Before a supervisor disciplines an employee, a thorough understanding of the situation is crucial. Discipline leveled against an employee who is unaware of the nature of his or her problem will be different from the discipline taken against an employee who is aware of the consequences of his or her actions.

Several suggestions for improving the effectiveness of the discipline process can be offered:

How can the disciplining process be made more effective?

1. If at all possible, discipline should be immediate.
2. Discipline should be administered fairly and consistently to all guilty subordinates.
3. The severity of the discipline should match the severity of the situation.
4. The employee should know exactly what is required of him or her to prevent the situation from occurring again.
5. The employee should be made aware of how to correct the situation so it will not occur again.

6. The discipline should be restricted to the problem at hand—and not to a variety of earlier problems that have or have not been dealt with.
7. A follow-up of the situation should be made at a specified time; and the supervisor needs to be sure he or she follows through as discussed during the interview.

An increasing number of organizations are incorporating disciplinary interviews into the employee discipline process. The use of interviews is primarily limited to the more serious situations and to repeated occurrences of the same situation. Disciplinary interviews have the following fivefold purpose:

1. To provide an appropriate environment in which to discuss the situation.
2. To give the supervisor and subordinate the opportunity to hear both sides of the situation.
3. To give the supervisor an opportunity to outline the nature of the disciplinary action that will be taken against the employee.
4. To provide formal, official documentation of the situation should later discharge become necessary.
5. To help teach the employee how and why he or she should avoid repeating the situation in the future.

To help make the disciplinary interview more effective, the following suggestions are offered:

1. Prepare a written document that contains the supervisor's comments. Record on this document the employee's comments made during the interview, as well as the disciplinary action that is to be taken. Both the supervisor and employee should sign and date the document.
2. Remain unemotional and rational during the interview; don't attack the subordinate or threaten.
3. Conduct the interview in privacy so that neither party's comments can be overheard by others.
4. Discuss only the situation at hand.
5. Mention only relevant, objective facts.
6. Criticize the work; not the worker.
7. Offer growth opportunities.
8. Listen to the employee's side of the story.

TERMINATING EMPLOYEES

Chances are, the supervisor will eventually be confronted with the task of recommending the termination of a subordinate. Most supervisors consider termination to be a last resort and, therefore, may try one or more of the following alternative actions before terminating: transferring the employee to another position, demoting the employee, making a leave of absence available to the employee, suspending the employee, retraining the employee, or giving the employee an opportunity to resign or take early retirement (if that is feasible). If the ultimate action is termination, the supervisor needs to exercise as much care—and perhaps even more—as he or she exercises in hiring new employees.

Before a supervisor decides to recommend termination, he or she needs to understand the condition under which the employee was hired. Some employees have a written contract of employment, whereas others (namely, employees of federal, state, and local governments) are protected by civil service regulations. Still others are covered by collective bargaining agreements.

Another category of hiring is at-will, which means that the employee is hired to work for an indefinite length of time and that the employee has no employment rights specified in an employment contract, civil service regulations, or a collective bargaining agreement. Employee handbooks, policy statements, and oral commitments at the time of hiring may constitute an implied contract. In the past, employees covered by contract, civil service regulations, or collective bargaining agreements had greater protection against termination than the at-will employees had. Because of significant abuse in terminating at-will employees, legislation and court decisions are now affecting this area.

Essentially, the at-will termination of employees has been replaced with just-cause termination, a process that necessitates undertaking alternative actions to avoid discharging the employee. Termination is seen as the only remaining viable alternative. The just-cause process requires upholding the following standards:

What standards must the just-cause termination process uphold?

1. The employee's termination involves a job-related or work-performance problem.
2. The employee is forewarned of the possible disciplinary consequences of his or her actions.
3. The organization's expectations and requirements of the employee are reasonable.
4. Before recommending dismissal, the supervisor makes a reasonable attempt to ascertain the extent to which the employee's performance is either satisfactory or unsatisfactory.
5. The employee is given ample opportunity to tell his or her view of the situation.
6. Any investigation that is undertaken is done so in an objective, unbiased, and fair manner.
7. The investigation provides ample evidence of wrongdoing or guilt to warrant dismissal.
8. The organization has treated similarly all other employees who are guilty of the same offense.
9. The penalty fits the offense, considering the employee's past record.
10. The penalty is carried out within a reasonable time.

If any of the standards is missing, the employee may be able to prove in a court that he or she was discharged for reasons other than just cause. When this happens, the organization may be confronted with a costly settlement.

Among the suggestions for improving the effectiveness of the termination process are the following:

1. *Use termination as the last and only remaining viable alternative*. If another alternative is available, its use should be considered.

2. *Have a written record of previous offenses, subsequent warnings, and disciplinary actions taken*. Increasingly, courts are requiring written evidence that the employee has had ample warning regarding his or her performance. The written records should also be signed by the employee as proof that he or she was made aware of the possible consequences of his or her actions. Recent court rulings also indicate that the reason given the employee has to be the actual reason.
3. *Follow precisely all organization-approved terminations policies and procedures*. One's failure to follow approved policies and procedures may result in a court's overturning of the termination decision should the employee decide to file a lawsuit.
4. *Prepare a record of the termination conversation*. In some organizations, the termination conversation has to be witnessed by another employee. Even if a witness isn't required by organizational policy, having a witness present is an excellent decision. An alternative may be to have the actual termination carried out by the unit manager, and the employee's supervisor serves as a witness to the conversation. In other cases, the termination conversation is recorded, obviously with the employee's knowledge. Written notes of the conversation that transpired should also be prepared. Ultimately, a word-for-word transcript should be prepared from the recording.
5. *Provide new managers during their orientation and training with information about employee termination*. Ignorance about acceptable procedures in termination of employees is not a defensible excuse for making mistakes.
6. *Require that an upper-level manager or a representative of the personnel department be consulted before an employee is terminated*. An investigation of the situation may indicate that sufficient grounds for termination do not exist. To continue with the process of terminating the employee might incur legal liability.

Because of the legalistic nature of termination and because of new court decisions, the organization's legal counsel should be consulted before making a termination. Most supervisors do not have time to keep abreast of recent developments in employee termination procedures.[1]

Some organizations make **outplacement services** available to their employees who are terminated. The objective of outplacement is to help individuals become reemployed as quickly and easily as possible, thus minimizing the amount of disruption in the employees' lives. Also, the more quickly a person is reemployed, the less likely he or she will continue to create a public relations problem for the organization. Consultants or consulting firms with specialization in providing outplacement are often used to provide the outplacement services.

Among some of the services provided by outplacement specialists are the following: counseling designed to help alleviate anger and frustration resulting from being terminated, coaching in how to find contacts who might be aware of suitable openings, preparation of a suitable letter of application and resume, preparing for the job interview, secretarial support, and ways to handle salary negotiation. Because some individuals who are terminated decide to leave permanently the field in which they were working, interest assessment is also a function provided by outplacement services. In some instances, retraining may also be provided or arrangements made for retraining.

WORKING WITH A UNION

What are the important provisions of the labor agreement?

In addition to understanding the basic structure and functioning of unions, the administrative office manager needs to be familiar with the **labor agreement**, a document that contains the proposals accepted by both parties during the negotiation process. Although the content of labor agreements varies from situation to situation, the trend is to develop longer, more detailed agreements than in the past. The advantage of this is the lessened opportunity for misunderstandings, which likely reduces the number of grievances filed by employees against management. The labor agreement must also contain certain clauses required by the Taft-Hartley Act and the Fair Labor Standards Act.

Some of the more essential provisions of the labor agreement are the following:

Duration of Agreement

This specifies the length of time the agreement is in force. Periods ranging from one to five years are common, with two- and three-year agreements being most common.

Union Security

This outlines the extent to which the union is responsible for the disciplinary control of its members. Also commonly included in this section is the identification of the type of union security found, including union shop, maintenance-of-membership shop, agency shop, and dues checkoff.

The **union shop** is the most common form of union security. This means the employee must be a member or become a member of the union within a specified time. An individual who refuses to do so can have his or her employment terminated.

The **maintenance-of-membership shop** form of union security, which occurs only infrequently, requires that employees who voluntarily join a union must remain in good standing during the life of the agreement. The **agency shop** conversely stipulates that employees have to pay dues because the union serves as their bargaining agent, although they do not have to join the union. The agency shop is often found in states with right-to-work laws that forbid mandatory union membership. **Dues checkoff** is a written agreement between the employer and the employee that allows the employer to withhold the employees' union dues from their paychecks.

Management Prerogatives

The clause of the labor agreement that specifies the rights or prerogatives retained by management is known as **management prerogatives**. Generally, anything that is not contained in the labor agreement or restricted by law remains with the employer as a management prerogative.

Wages and Hours

Law requires that labor agreements contain a section on wages and hours. Included in this section are methods of payment, rates of pay, commissions, bonuses, and incentive pay plans. **Escalator clauses**, which provide for cost-of-living increases (commonly referred to as COLA), are also common in many labor agreements today. The Fair Labor Standards Act and the Taft-Hartley Act specify the nature of information about wages and hours that must be included in the agreement.

Promotion, Layoff, and Recall

Also commonly included in labor agreements are clauses about the promotion, layoff, and recall of members.

Discipline of Members

Identified in labor agreements are the situations for which employees may be disciplined, as well as the type of discipline that may be leveled for various rule infractions. Actions for which employees might be disciplined are the following: intoxication, fighting, insubordination, dishonesty, and violation of company rules.

Grievances

Also outlined in most labor agreements are the procedures for filing a **grievance**, a process used when an employee charges the employer with unfair treatment. The clauses in the agreement should be carefully worded to avoid misinterpretation, which will subsequently reduce the number of grievances.

The manner in which grievances are handled is likely to bear significantly on the cordiality of relations between the employer and employees. Even though the two parties carefully negotiated the agreement in good faith, grievances are often inevitable, especially when employees believe they have been treated unfairly and inconsistently. Generally, the more quickly complaints are resolved, the better.

Most well-developed labor agreements contain a section that outlines how grievances are to be handled. The procedures should be followed carefully and exactly, which will help prevent the supervisor's becoming entangled in more problems with the union.

Strike Clauses

Some labor agreements contain clauses that prohibit striking or walking out by employees during the time that the current agreement is in force. Increasingly, unions are becoming reluctant to allow a no-strike clause to be included in a labor agreement because of the possibility of its being used in the event of a wildcat strike.

IMPLICATIONS FOR THE ADMINISTRATIVE OFFICE MANAGER

One of the most common duties of administrative office managers is their supervisory responsibilities. The number of individuals for whom managers are responsible varies quite extensively from organization to organization.

The quality of managers' supervisory ability often affects the success of their goal-achievement efforts. Employees who respect their supervisors are generally willing to put forth more effort to achieve organizational goals than are those who have little or no respect for their supervisor.

The amount of natural supervisory talent of administrative office managers is quite variable. Although some perform excellently with little or no training, others need extensive training. In most organizations, the value put on training new supervisors is reflected in the number of supervisory training experiences that are offered.

In addition to the value of participating in a variety of training opportunities, many administrative office managers also stress the value of work experience in becoming a more effective supervisor. The more extensive their supervisory experiences, the more likely they are to develop their own personal supervisory styles.

Supervisors soon learn that the strategies they use have to be adaptable because the techniques they use in a situation one day may not be equally effective in a similar situation another time. Much supervisory success is dependent on properly assessing the situation variables and then selecting the appropriate strategies for the situation.

NOTE

1. A portion of the material in the "Disciplining Employees" section and most of the material in the "Terminating Employees" section of this chapter was adapted from Zane K. Quible, *How to Select and Retain Valuable Employees*, Trevose, PA: Administrative Management Society, 1985.

REVIEW QUESTIONS

1. How do the characteristics of autocratic, democratic, and laissez-faire leadership styles differ from one another?
2. How do achievement-oriented supervisors and subordinate-oriented supervisors differ from one another?
3. How do boss-centered leaders and subordinate-centered leaders differ from one another?
4. What is the nature of the supervisory duties in the directing function?
5. How might a supervisor gain the cooperation of subordinates?
6. How do on-the-job training and coaching differ from one another?
7. What is meant by conceptual skills, an attribute possessed by effective supervisors?
8. What kinds of topics are frequently involved in supervisory training programs?
9. What is the nature of the supervisor's responsibility for employee absenteeism and tardiness and for alcoholism and drug-abuse detection?
10. What are the differences between at-will and just-cause termination?
11. What suggestions can you offer to help a supervisor improve the effectiveness of the discipline process?

DISCUSSION QUESTIONS

1. You have just begun working in the application processing department of an insurance company. Your supervisor explained the nature of your job duties to you the first day you were on the job and then immediately began to assign you work. A few minutes ago when you ran into a problem with an application that you didn't know how to handle, you asked your supervisor for help. He responded by saying that he would like you to solve the problem yourself because in the long run, you will benefit more by this approach than if he helped you. He also asked that you discuss your solution with him as soon as you figured it out. Discuss

the implications of handling the situation in this way.

2. You are a supervisor in the company in which you work. During a recent conversation with another supervisor, you were both sharing your philosophies about supervision. You said that you tend to be a subordinate-oriented supervisor because you believe that subordinates will put forth their greatest effort when the supervisor treats them this way. The supervisor with whom you were talking said that he puts more emphasis on subordinate output because, after all, if they weren't productive, their jobs may be jeopardized. Justify your use of the subordinate-centered approach.
3. The company in which you work places full responsibility for staffing on its supervisors. The personnel department does little more than maintain personnel records. Supervisors are responsible for taking applications, screening candidates, administering tests, and so forth. The rationale for using this approach is that the unit supervisors know better than anyone else the nature of their needs. Discuss the implications of having the supervisor totally responsible for staffing.
4. You recently received the formal evaluation of your performance as an office supervisor. Your supervisor gave you high marks in each area, with the exception of "controlling." You are troubled by this because you believe you do a good job of ensuring conformity. What are the reasons that may account for an apparent laxness in the controlling function of your job? How might you correct this apparent dilemma?
5. As a newly appointed supervisor, you recently attended a training session concerned with substance abuse. From what you learned during the session, you believe one of your subordinates has an alcohol dependency condition. Outline how you plan to handle the situation and what you plan to say to the individual when you first approach him.
6. As supervisor, you are responsible for disciplining subordinates. Lately, it seems that whenever you discipline your subordinates, they, in effect, say to you, "Why do you pick on me when there are others who have done the same thing and they didn't get reprimanded? It just doesn't seem fair." Outline a strategy for overcoming this problem.

STUDENT PROJECTS AND ACTIVITIES

1. Discuss with an office supervisor the techniques he or she uses to get employees to cooperate with one another and with the supervisor.
2. Discuss with an office supervisor the nature of his or her experiences (other than education) that have been invaluable in the supervisor's acquiring the necessary skills to be an effective supervisor.
3. Discuss with a manager the process he or she uses in disciplining subordinates.
4. Discuss with a manager who has the right to terminate employees the specific steps he or she must follow in terminating an employee.
5. Discuss with a manager the techniques used in the organization in which he or she works that are designed to keep employees from using organizational property or services for their own personal use.

MINICASE

You are the chair of a committee responsible for interviewing for a supervisor in the payroll department in the City Electric Company. When Dennis Garfield was being interviewed for this position, he was asked to explain his philosophy of supervision. He responded by saying that he believes subordinates should for the most part be "left alone" to do their work and that the supervisor generally should not get involved unless sought out by a subordinate.

As chair of the committee, you are to write a report that will be submitted to a committee of vice presidents who will interview the finalists. In writing your report, you want to address the following:

1. The leadership approach you believe Garfield advocates.
2. Why you believe this approach is the best one (or not the best one) for the situation. Explain.

CASE

Last night, you, a local management consultant, and David Brock, the new administrative office manager in the Prime Insurance Company, which is located in Philadelphia, attended the Greater Philadelphia Management Association monthly meeting. At the meeting, he told you about his new position, asking for advice. However, before you were able to provide him with advice, the speaker began his presentation; and you were unable to visit with him after the meeting. Accordingly, you decide to send him a memo that contains suggestions for overcoming the problems he mentioned.

David's predecessor, Sam Worthington, was fired when he failed to comply with certain management directives. Specifically, he was asked to be more strict in supervising his subordinates so they would more fully comply with certain policies. In addition, management was greatly concerned about the continuing deterioration of the unit's productivity during Worthington's tenure and had even established certain productivity goals for his unit that were never met. Worthington's subordinates did not especially care for him as a person—but they did appreciate his letting them "do their own thing."

When Brock was interviewed for the position, he was intrigued by the challenges this situation would provide him; therefore, when a job offer was extended, he readily accepted it. Now he is beginning to have second thoughts about the wisdom of his decision.

Brock's first day on the job was a frustrating experience. He met with all of his subordinates in small groups of five or fewer employees. During these sessions, he outlined the nature of his expectations and discussed the changes he planned to implement. More than one-half of these small groups bluntly told him that most of the changes he planned would not work. When he questioned these groups about the reasons for their beliefs, they indicated that the employees simply would not cooperate enough to make the changes work. Evidence is now available of a conspiracy to undermine Brock's authority since the first day that he was on the job.

In the memo, you decide to address the following:

1. Suggestions regarding how Brock should go about eliciting subordinate cooperation in this department.
2. A way he might have handled his first day on the job rather than the way he actually handled it.
3. A way that Brock might deal with the apparent conspiracy against him.

MOTIVATING OFFICE EMPLOYEES

CHAPTER AIMS

After studying this chapter, you should be able to design an effective employee motivation program.

CHAPTER OUTLINE

CHAPTER TERMS

Ability
Aggression
Anxiety
Aptitude
Behavior modification
Disequilibrium
Emotions
Equilibrium
Equity theory
Expectancy theory
Frustration
Goals
Interests
Job dissatisfiers
Job satisfiers
Motivation-hygiene theory
Need-hierarchy theory
Needs
Needs theory
Perceptions
Personality
Reinforcement theory
Self-concept
Stimuli
Values

An important responsibility of the administrative office manager is that of motivating the employees for whom he or she is responsible. The motivation of employees is maximized when they are able to use their abilities and realize their potential. Ultimately, motivation stimulates employees to perform more effectively than they otherwise would.

Employees who lack motivation cost organizations millions of dollars each year. They tend to be absent and tardy more frequently than their motivated counterparts. Furthermore, their turnover rates are likely to be higher, they are less productive, their work is of poorer quality, and they are less loyal to the organization. In addition, they are likely to derive less satisfaction from their jobs, and they are more difficult to supervise than their motivated counterparts.

Several basic human traits that affect motivation are discussed in this chapter, as are several popular theories of motivation. Also included is a discussion of the nature of changes in values that affect employee motivation.

BASIC HUMAN TRAITS

Several basic human traits affect employees' job-related behavior and performance. These human traits include ability, aptitude, perceptions, self-concept, values, interests, emotions, needs, and personality.

Ability

Varying considerably from person to person, employees' abilities determine how capable they are of carrying out their jobs. The amount of **ability** employees use in their jobs is affected by how highly motivated they are.

To help individuals fully realize their potential, the administrative office manager needs an accurate assessment of the amount of ability each subordinate has. Several tests are available to measure individual ability.

Aptitude

What is aptitude?

The extent to which employees are motivated is also affected by their **aptitude**, which is a measure of their potential. Employees whose job duties are not closely matched with their aptitudes are often more difficult to motivate.

For a variety of reasons, the aptitudes and job duties of many employees do not complement one another, a situation that is detrimental to both the employees and their employer.

Perceptions

Employees bring to the workplace their own views of the world. These **perceptions**, which are influenced by the employees' personal experiences, affect their motivation.

Self-Concept

An employee's **self-concept** is basically shaped by his or her perception of self. The better one's self-concept is, the more motivated the person is likely to be. Employees who perceive themselves to be high performers are generally willing to accept new responsibilities.

Values

Employees' **values** affect their behavior on the job as well as their level of motivation. Values are significantly influenced by the environment in which employees live and work. During the last few years, several changes have occurred in the perceived importance that employees attach to certain values. These changes are discussed in greater detail in another section of this chapter.

Interests

Individual **interests** vary significantly from person to person. Some employees lack motivation because they are not interested in their jobs. Perhaps the best way to eliminate motivation problems resulting from a lack of employee interest is to match the employee's qualifications with the requirements of his or her job. Careful screening of individuals during the hiring and promotion processes generally helps minimize the amount of mismatching.

Emotions

Employees' **emotions** or feelings affect much of what they do or say at any given moment. The way supervisors deal with employees' emotions and feelings may significantly affect their motivation level.

Needs

In what way do employees' needs affect the motivation process?

Employees' **needs** also affect their motivation because their goals often originate from unsatisfied or unmet needs. Motivation provides employees with the "fuel" they need to attain their goals. The motivation of an employee to achieve a goal is related to (1) the importance of the goal to the individual and (2) the extent to which the need has not been met. Therefore, motivation is higher when the goal is important to the employee and when the need is largely unfilled.

Personality

Basic **personality** characteristics of employees also affect their motivation. Some of the important personality characteristics are the introverted or ex-

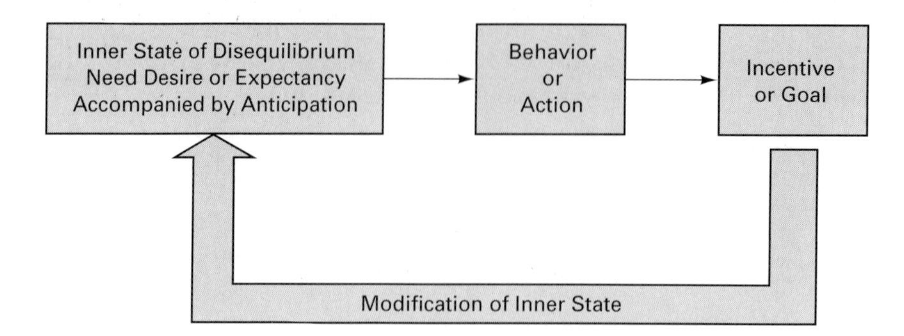

Figure 10-1 Motivation model. Source: M. D. Dunnette and W. K. Kirchner, *Psychology Applied to Industry,* (c) 1965, p. 125. Reprinted by permission of Prentice-Hall, Inc., Englewood Cliffs, NJ.

troverted nature of employees, their aggressive or passive nature, whether they are tolerant or impatient, and whether they are cooperative or uncooperative.

Each of the basic human traits affects the behavior of employees as well as their level of motivation. The more familiar a supervisor is with the basic traits of each subordinate, the more effective the superior-subordinate relationship will be. Supervisors who are familiar with their subordinates' traits will also find the task of motivating them less challenging.

MOTIVATIONAL PROCESS

What impact does disequilibrium have on the motivation process?

A model of the motivational process is illustrated in Figure 10-1. The model indicates that a person's behavior is a response to **stimuli** associated with an inner state of **disequilibrium** resulting from a need, desire, or expectancy. The disequilibrium state, which is accompanied by anticipation, produces behavior or actions that are directed toward goal attainment. The individual anticipates that goal achievement will be a satisfying experience and that a state of **equilibrium** will be restored. Therefore, goal achievement will result in the modification of the individual's inner state.

THEORIES OF MOTIVATION

Administrative office managers who understand various theories of motivation will be able to work more effectively with their subordinates. Two broad categories of motivation theory exist: external (extrinsic) and internal (intrinsic). The external theory is based on the external consequences of a person's behavior, whereas the internal theories are based on a person's internal feelings.

What are the characteristics of behavior modification?

A well-known external theory of motivation is **behavior modification**, a theory developed by B. F. Skinner. The proponents of behavior modification indicate that a person's behavior is determined by external consequences. Therefore, a person's behavior is a result of the consequences or rewards associated with that behavior. If the reward is positive, the behavior will continue to be repeated. Conversely, if the behavior is unacceptable, rewards will be withheld until the behavior is modified sufficiently to be worthy of receiving a reward. Although most employees are motivated by rewarded behavior, some are motivated as a consequence of unrewarded behavior.

Among the internal theories of motivation examined are the need-hierarchy theory, motivation-hygiene theory, needs theory, equity theory, expectancy theory, and reinforcement theory.

Need-Hierarchy Theory

Human behavior is influenced by one's desire to have his or her needs fulfilled. Supervisors or managers who fail to realize this psychological fact often find the behavior of their employees puzzling or bewildering. The supervisory process is more enjoyable and rewarding when supervisors clearly understand the needs of each of their subordinates.

What are the characteristics of the need-hierarchy theory?

Several schemes for classifying human needs have been developed over the years. One of the most widely used is the **need-hierarchy theory** developed by the late A. H. Maslow.

Human needs, according to Maslow, exist at five basic levels. The categories are in a hierarchical order; therefore, the higher-level needs are not important to the motivation process until most of the lower-level needs have been satisfied. As a need becomes either mostly or totally satisfied, it is no longer a motivator. Maslow's model specifies the following needs:

1. Physiological needs
2. Safety needs
3. Belonging and love needs
4. Esteem needs
5. Self-actualization needs[1]

According to Maslow, until an individual's physiological and safety needs are satisfied, his or her belonging and love needs are not important nor are esteem and self-actualization needs. The primary needs (physiological and safety) are important for survival. The secondary needs (belonging and love, esteem, and self-actualization) help individuals improve the quality of their lives.

Physiological needs For humans to survive, their physiological needs must be satisfied. Included in this category are such needs as food, water, oxygen, rest, muscular activity, and freedom from extreme temperatures. Because these needs are basic or primary, higher-level needs are not important until the lower-level needs are mostly satisfied. For most individuals in an industrialized society, physiological needs are fairly well satisfied. Employees' salaries and wages assist them in satisfying some of these needs.

What is the nature of safety needs?

Safety needs After one's physiological needs are satisfied, the safety needs, which include both physical and psychological elements, become important. The safety needs of a physical nature include such items as clothing, shelter, and freedom from physical danger. Like the physiological needs, the safety needs of a physical nature can be at least minimally satisfied by the salaries or wages employees receive.

The safety needs of a psychological nature include job security and a wide variety of fringe benefits. Supplemental unemployment benefits, retirement benefits, and disability pay provide financial and emotional security and therefore are classified as safety needs of a psychological nature. The absence of these benefits may result in significant psychological insecurity.

Jobs and the environments in which they are performed satisfy the safety needs for many employees as they become quite secure in their positions. Uncertainty is created when jobs are changed or when the environment in which the jobs are performed is changed. Because many employees resist change, managers and supervisors must often help employees adjust to new situations.

Belonging and love needs Once the physiological and safety needs are satisfied, belonging and love needs become important. Included in this category are the need for belonging to a group, the need for companionship, the need for love or affection, and the need for socializing.

More so than ever before, employees view the environment in which they work as an important means of satisfying these needs, especially their socializing needs. When barriers within the working environment prevent the satisfaction of these needs, people tend to react by becoming frustrated.

The manager or supervisor who believes that employees must use their nonworking environments to satisfy all of their belonging needs does not fully understand the important role the working environment plays in need satisfaction. Employees want to feel they are accepted by the other members of their work group and by their supervisor. An understanding of supervisor-subordinate relations as well as an understanding of group relations is helpful to supervisors concerned about the belonging needs of their subordinates.

Although money is used to purchase the things that satisfy many of the physiological and safety needs, it cannot be used to purchase the things that satisfy belonging and love needs. Although physiological and safety needs can be satisfied by physical and tangible objects, the belonging and love needs are of a more intangible nature.

What are esteem needs?

Esteem needs Once physiological, safety, and belonging and love needs are satisfied, esteem needs become important in the motivation process. Two types of esteem needs exist: self-esteem and esteem of others. Self-esteem needs include the desire for achievement, self-respect, confidence, and mastery. The esteem of others includes such needs as recognition, attention, prestige, and status. The self-esteem needs originate within the individual, whereas esteem of others requires the recognition and attention of others.

When individuals believe their esteem needs are being satisfied, they have a feeling of worth, importance, and confidence. When these needs are not satisfied, however, employees are likely to feel dejected, incompetent, and useless. These feelings can ultimately lead to behavior of a neurotic or hostile nature.

Some of the most long-lasting, useful techniques for motivating employees capitalize on satisfying esteem needs. For example, some employees receive the recognition they desire from having the opportunity to participate in organizational decision making.

What are self-actualization needs?

Self-actualization needs The highest-level needs in the hierarchy—self-actualization needs—are the most difficult level for a majority of employees to satisfy. Before self-actualization needs become important in the motivation process, the other needs in the hierarchy must be largely satisfied. Self-actualization refers to one's desire to achieve maximum potential—or to become what one is capable of becoming.

Many different situations thwart individuals in the satisfaction of their self-actualization needs. One common situation is the job itself. Another situation is the presence of a seniority system. In such instances, employees generally have to work their way through the ranks; and until individuals with the greatest amount of seniority either resign or retire, employees with less seniority are unable to reach their aspired levels. Another situation that thwarts some individuals is their aspiration for positions that require greater ability than they have. These employees will never be able to fully satisfy their self-actualization needs.

Some employees find that although their jobs only minimally satisfy their self-actualization needs, other aspects of their self-actualization needs are quite well satisfied by their personal lives. Success in one area most likely stimulates employees to put forth more effort in the other area.

Summary Employee motivational programs based on Maslow's hierarchy of needs are more successful than are those that fail to consider the impact of human needs on motivation. A motivated employee—one whose needs are for the most part being satisfied—is likely to be a more productive employee.

Some of the lower-level needs are satisfied largely through the acquisition of money that is used to purchase such objects as food, clothing, and shelter. Therefore, most employees work to earn money for use in satisfying their lower-level needs. Money, on the other hand, cannot be used to satisfy the higher-level needs in the hierarchy. These needs are primarily satisfied by the individual's relationship with others and by the degree to which he or she is successful in the organization.

Although some of the basic physiological functions of people occur without the individual's being motivated, most conscious behavior is motivated or caused. Managers, therefore, should stimulate employees to work toward successful task completion.

Whereas lower-level needs pertain to the physical body, the higher-level needs are related to the mind and spirit. And lower-level needs are finite for the most part while higher-level needs are essentially infinite.

What is the primary value of Maslow's theory?

The primary value of Maslow's theory appears to lie in the premise that the most effective way to motivate employees is to appeal to their needs. Therefore, a supervisor who focuses on individual needs is often more successful in motivating employees to perform at desired levels than is a supervisor who ignores individual needs.

Motivation-Hygiene Theory

What are the characteristics of the motivation-hygiene theory?

A well-known study of employee job satisfaction, conducted by Frederick Herzberg, involved interviewing two hundred engineers and accountants in nine different companies in several different geographical locations. The outgrowth of this study is the **motivation-hygiene theory** developed by Herzberg and his associates.[2]

Interviews were conducted to determine which job aspects satisfied and which ones dissatisfied the engineers and accountants. The respondents were asked to identify those critical incidents about their work that caused them to feel exceptionally good or exceptionally bad. The researchers also probed into the reasons that caused these feelings.

The research conducted by Herzberg and his colleagues found that employees' job experiences that produced *positive attitudes* were associated with the *content* of the job. Conversely, the job experiences producing *negative attitudes* were associated with the *environment* in which the employees performed their jobs. They also found that experiences leading to *positive attitudes* were related to the *psychological needs* of employees but that experiences leading to *negative attitudes* were related to the *basic needs* of employees. Herzberg labeled those experiences leading to positive attitudes as **job satisfiers** or *motivators*. The experiences leading to negative attitudes are labeled as **job dissatisfiers** or *hygiene factors*.

What are Herzberg's motivators?

Motivators Among the factors responsible for producing positive attitudes or job satisfaction are the following:

1. *Achievement*. Opportunity for task completion, for seeing results of effort, and for solving problems independently.
2. *Recognition*. Positive acknowledgment of task completion and of individual achievement.
3. *Work itself*. Tasks that a job comprises.
4. *Responsibility*. Opportunity to be accountable and responsible for task completion and for individual performance and for being able to decide how and when tasks are to be completed.
5. *Advancement*. Advancement or promotion to higher-level job or position.
6. *Growth*. Opportunity for growth and for new experiences.

What are Herzberg's hygiene factors?

Hygiene factors Although the motivators (satisfiers) are concerned with job content, the hygiene factors (dissatisfiers) are concerned with the environment in which the job is performed. The hygiene factors include the following:

1. *Company policy and administration*. Effectiveness of the organization and the way in which its policies are administered.
2. *Supervisors and relationships with supervisors*. Technological expertise of the supervisor as well as the fairness with which the supervisor deals with subordinates.
3. *Working conditions*. Environment of the place of work and the adequacy of equipment and supplies.
4. *Salary*. All types of compensation.[3]
5. *Interpersonal relations*. Relationship between an employee and his or her own peers.
6. *Personal life*. Impact that an individual's personal life may have on job performance and vice versa.
7. *Relationship with subordinates*. The success with which the supervisor relates to subordinates.
8. *Status*. Amount of status the job provides.
9. *Security*. Amount of security provided by the job.

An illustration of Herzberg's motivation-hygiene theory is shown in Figure 10-2.

On the basis of his research, Herzberg concluded that the absence of various job conditions is dissatisfying to employees. When present, however, these job conditions do not act as significant employee motivators (or satisfiers). Conversely, another set of job conditions, when present, produce employee satisfaction (or motivation). The absence of such conditions does not result in employee dissatisfaction, however. Thus, according to Herzberg, the various motivators (satisfiers) and hygiene factors (dissatisfiers) are not opposite ends of a continuum, but rather the factors are separate and distinct. In other words, the opposite of employee satisfaction is not employee dissatisfaction.

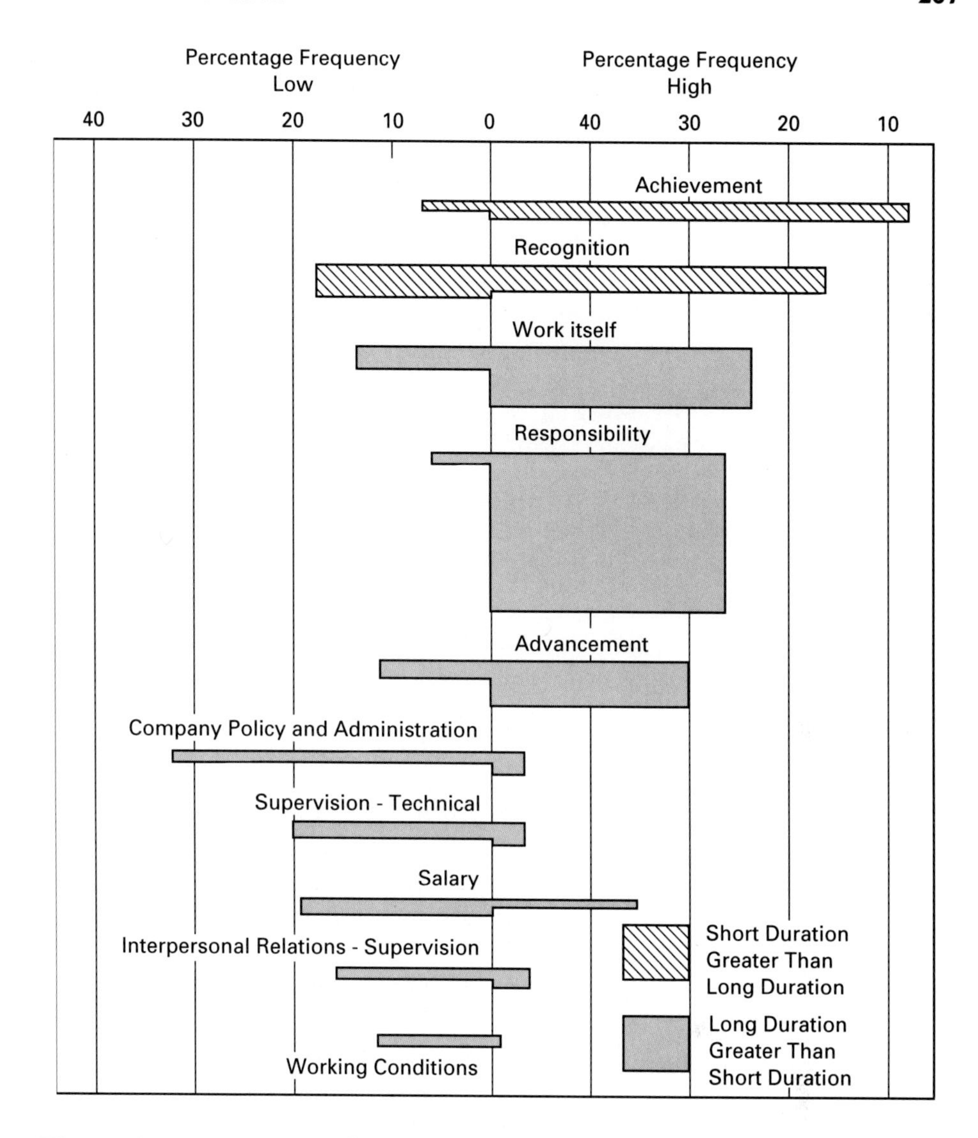

Figure 10-2 Motivation-hygiene theory. Source: *The Motivation to Work*, by Herzberg, Mausner, & Snyderman. Copyright (c) 1959. Reprinted by permission of John Wiley & Sons, Inc.

A major impact of Herzberg's theory focuses on the design of jobs. His theory supports the belief that jobs should be enriched by making work more meaningful and by providing greater opportunities for achievement, recognition, responsibility, and advancement.

Figure 10-3 presents a comparison of Maslow's hierarchy of needs model and Herzberg's motivation-hygiene model. An examination of the illustration reveals that various factors included in Maslow's hierarchy are the same factors that Herzberg has identified on his model.

Needs Theory

What are the characteristics of the needs theory?

David McClelland, the individual who developed the **needs theory** of motivation, was more concerned with the secondary motives than the primary motives of behavior.[4] He believed that the primary motives have a physiological base and therefore are not acquired. The secondary motives, which are

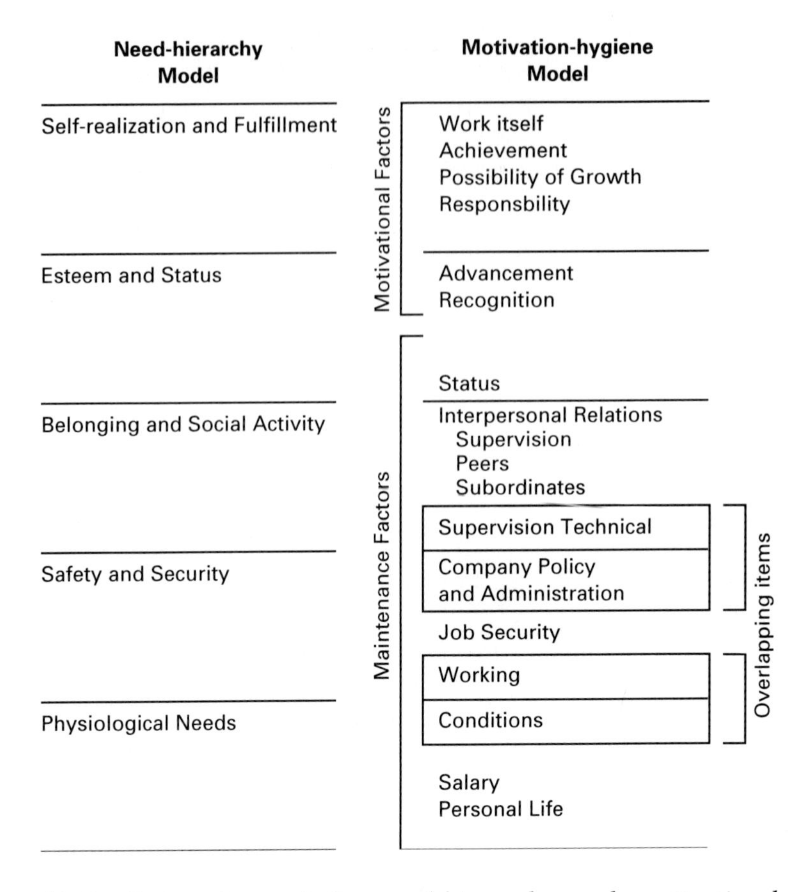

Figure 10-3 Comparison of the need-hierarchy and motivation-hygiene models. Source: Keith Davis, *Human Relations at Work,* 1972, McGraw-Hill Book Company. Reproduced by permission.

learned, have a powerful impact on one's behavior and are generally acquired from one's culture. According to McClelland, three secondary motives are of considerable importance: need for achievement, need for power, and need for affiliation.

Need for achievement Individuals with high needs for achievement willingly accept personal responsibility for their work and actions, and they have a strong desire for immediate feedback regarding the worth or value of their actions. Furthermore, they have a strong need to advance and to face head-on those challenges that block their advancement. They also tend to be task oriented. Individuals with a high need for achievement often have difficulty delegating authority or responsibility to others. Although these individuals thrive on challenges, they tend to set only moderate goals.

Need for power Individuals with a high need for power desire to control other people and have a strong influence on the behavior of others. Furthermore, they desire to be responsible for others. As a rule, individuals with a need for power seek out situations that are competitive and status oriented. Generally, they are more concerned about their self-image than about the quality of their task performance. Compared with those individuals who have a strong need for achievement, those with a strong need for power are higher risk takers.

Need for affiliation Individuals with a high need for affiliation tend to be socially interactive. Of great importance to them is the quality of their personal relationships, especially being liked by others. The quality of their relationships is more important than the quality of their task performance. Those with a high need for affiliation sometimes find decision making an unpleasant experience because of the priority they place on their relationships with others.

One way to maximize employee performance is to place individuals into positions that will allow them to have their needs fulfilled. To illustrate, an employee with a strong need for achievement will find greater satisfaction and consequently will likely perform better in a position that is task oriented. An employee with a strong desire for affiliation needs to be placed in a position that allows him or her to have considerable human interaction.

Equity Theory

What are the characteristics of the equity theory?

According to the **equity theory**, motivation results from an individual's desire to reduce feelings of inequity that result when he or she finds (1) an imbalance in the ratio between his or her input and outcome or (2) an imbalance when comparing his or her input-outcome ratio with the ratio of others. If the individual believes his or her input is greater than the outcome (represented by pay, promotion, and so on), a feeling of inequity will occur. The individual then becomes motivated to reduce input-outcome inequity. The strength of the employee's motivation is directly related to the magnitude of the input-outcome imbalance.

Employees react to the inequity in the following ways:

1. They alter their input level.
2. They alter their outcome expectation.
3. They change the base of their input-outcome comparison.

Expectancy Theory

According to Victor Vroom[5], the individual credited with developing the **expectancy theory**, the stronger the perceived relationship between effort and outcome, the higher employee motivation will be. If, for example, employees have reason to expect a good pay raise as a result of their hard work, they will be motivated to put forth the extra effort required to obtain the desired outcome.

What are the conditions on which the expectancy theory is based?

According to the expectancy theory, employee motivation will occur when the following three conditions are present:

1. The employee believes that additional effort will be worthwhile.
2. The employee believes that higher performance will result in greater outcomes or rewards.
3. The employee places a high value on the outcomes or rewards.

Reinforcement Theory

What are the characteristics of the reinforcement theory?

Motivation is a function of the consequences of behavior, according to the **reinforcement theory**. Therefore, behavior that is reinforced tends to be repeated, whereas nonreinforced behavior tends not to be repeated.

A primary strategy of this theory is positive reinforcement, which is designed to increase the strength or frequency of desired behavior by positively reinforcing each occurrence of desired behavior. Reinforcement theory also uses negative reinforcement to increase the strength or frequency of desired behavior. Therefore, undesirable consequences that result from undesirable behavior tend to motivate employees to behave in a desirable manner. To illustrate, employees will improve the effectiveness of their performance to avoid being reprimanded by their supervisor.

GOAL SETTING

Goals are an important component of the process of motivating employees. In fact, employees who are without goals often lack motivation; as a result, their productivity level is often substandard. Employees who have unmet goals tend to be motivated toward the fulfillment of those goals; however, the goals cease being motivational once they have been met.

Goals have several important attributes, including the following:

What are the important attributes of goals?

1. *Concreteness of goals.* A direct correlation exists between the concreteness of goals and the effort employees are willing to expend in their attainment. General goals usually have minimal impact on maximizing employee motivation. Goals that can be quantified are more powerful than those that cannot be quantified.
2. *Feedback on progress toward attainment of goals.* Employees who receive regular feedback—especially individuals who have high needs for achievement—are likely to be more highly motivated than are those who receive ineffective or minimal amounts of feedback. One of the characteristics of effective supervisors is providing subordinates with quality and timely feedback about their performance.
3. *Probability of succeeding in the attainment of goals.* The more feasible the attainment of a goal is, the more likely the employee will work toward its fulfillment. Goals with little probability of being attained result in the expenditure of little if any effort toward their attainment. Just as overly difficult goals result in the expenditure of minimal effort, so do goals that are overly easy to attain.
4. *Participation in the setting of goals.* Employees who have an opportunity to participate in the setting of their goals are much more likely to work toward their attainment than are employees who have their goals thrust on them by their supervisor or higher-level managers. Participation in goal setting increases the employee's acceptance and understanding of the goal. Because employees differ from one another regarding the amount of participation in goal setting they desire, some will find this a more important attribute than will others.
5. *Amount of dedication to the attainment of goals.* Employees who are dedicated to the attainment of goals are motivated to work harder toward their fulfillment than those who lack dedication. The amount of dedication employees have to the attainment of their goals is influenced by each of the four attributes presented previously, in addition to a host of personal characteristics. For example, an employee who plans to retire shortly is likely to be less dedicated to the attainment of a particular goal than is an employee just beginning his or her career.

ATTITUDE OF MANAGEMENT

Managerial attitude toward employees plays a significant role in employee motivation. Some managers or supervisors view employees simply as human robots whose sole function is to produce. The relationship between the supervisor and the subordinate is based primarily on units of input and output. In most instances, the only human need that concerns these managers or supervisors is helping employees satisfy the need to be productive.

Other managers or supervisors use a paternalistic approach. These supervisors believe they know what programs, benefits, and so forth, are best for their subordinates. As a result, employees have very little control over their welfare. This attitude also increases the difficulty some employees have in satisfying some of their needs.

Still other managers or supervisors use a noninvolvement approach. The belief is that managers should not be involved in helping employees satisfy their needs and that the employees themselves are responsible for the satisfaction of their higher-level needs. Using this approach also prevents the full satisfaction of certain employee needs.

The humanistic approach is generally considered by managers and supervisors as the most appropriate. Managers and supervisors recognize that they can help employees satisfy certain needs, whereas other needs can only be satisfied by the employees themselves. This approach also recognizes individual differences among employees. Managers and subordinates work as a cooperative team in the satisfaction of employee needs.

CHANGING EMPLOYEE VALUES

Of all the dimensions of motivation, changes in employee values seem to be having the greatest impact on the motivational process. To illustrate, the following values were considered important by most employees as recently as the early 1970s:

What values are changing among employees?

1. Good salary.
2. High status.
3. Fast promotions.
4. Secure and stable job.
5. Strong organizational loyalty.
6. Close identification with work roles.

Employees who believed in the importance of these values were more loyal because the organizations for which they worked sponsored much of their training and skill development.

Today, organizations do not play as important a role in the training and skill development of their employees. The contemporary employee tends not to be as loyal as earlier employees because job skills and knowledges are often acquired independently of the organization.

The following list identifies new trends in the value system the contemporary employee finds important:

1. Greater desire to have achievement recognized by the organization.
2. Greater desire for more leisure time.

3. Greater desire for having rewards related to job performance.
4. Greater desire for work that is challenging and worthwhile.
5. Greater desire to participate in decisions about things that affect him or her.
6. Greater desire for effective communication from management.
7. Greater desire for job-related growth opportunities.
8. Greater desire for increased job creativity.
9. Less concern for organizational loyalty.

When designing strategies and programs to enhance employee motivation, the administrative office manager should consider the new values that are important to the contemporary worker. What may have been motivational to employees fifteen to twenty years ago may no longer be as motivational.

EMPLOYEE MOTIVATION TECHNIQUES AND STRATEGIES

Several techniques and strategies are useful for motivating employees. Following is a brief description of several of these techniques or strategies. Included in Chapter 16 is a more thorough discussion of each technique or strategy. Their use can have a significant impact on increasing the productivity of office employees.

1. Job enrichment: Motivational strategy that enables employees to assume greater levels of responsibility for and control over their jobs while increasing their job planning opportunities.
2. Employee participation: Management technique that gives employees an opportunity to participate in decisions that directly affect them.
3. Management by objectives: Program in which an employee and his or her supervisor jointly determine the employee's objectives that are to be achieved within a specified time.
4. Flextime: Strategy that enables employees to select the starting time of their workday.
5. Incentives: Motivational technique that rewards employees for increasing their productivity.
6. Job sharing: Management technique that allows two employees to share one position.
7. Team building: Strategy that stresses the need for employees to work closely together as a means of increasing their productivity.
8. Self-managed work teams: Management strategy in which supervisors coach subordinates and help them assume greater responsibility for their own production improvement and problem solving.
9. Gain sharing: Strategy that provides employees with a monetary bonus equaling the dollar amount of cash savings that results when their productivity increases above a certain level.
10. Telecommuting: Strategy that enables employees to work at home or at a satellite office part or all of the time.

DO'S AND DON'TS OF MOTIVATION

Managers and supervisors, when creating conditions to maximize employee motivation, should remember several factors. These are presented in Figure 10-4 as do's and don'ts of motivation.

Do's

1. Do keep in mind the amount of ability each subordinate has.
2. Do try to help subordinates achieve their maximum potential.
3. Do keep in mind the values subordinates consider to be important.
4. Do become familiar with the needs of each subordinate.
5. Do remember that money can help subordinates satisfy some—but not all—of their needs.
6. Do remember that subordinates' lower-level needs are finite for the most part but their higher-level needs are essentially infinite.
7. Do remember that job satisfaction originates from the content of the job but job dissatisfaction originates from the environment in which the job is performed.
8. Do remember that a feeling of inequity resulting from an input-outcome imbalance may motivate some employees to engage in certain types of behavior as a means of overcoming the imbalance.
9. Do remember that the motivation of certain employees will be higher when they have reason to expect a greater reward for desired performance.
10. Do remember that the work-related values employees consider to be important change from time to time.
11. Do know how to deal with subordinate frustration that results from lack of success in goal achievement or need satisfaction.

Don'ts

1. Don't forget that perceptions affect subordinate motivation.
2. Don't forget that interests vary from subordinate to subordinate.
3. Don't overlook the importance of the display of subordinates' emotions and feelings.
4. Don't forget that subordinates prioritize their needs, so that higher-level needs are not important until lower-level needs have been satisfied.
5. Don't overlook the fact that what is motivational for one subordinate will not necessarily be motivational to others.
6. Don't forget that techniques for motivating subordinates that take their needs into consideration are more successful than the techniques that do not.
7. Don't forget that subordinates' higher-level needs are largely satisfied through their interrelationships with others and by their level of success in the organization.
8. Don't forget that subordinates' positive attitudes about their job are associated with job content but that negative attitudes are associated with the environment in which the job is performed.
9. Don't forget that the opposite of job satisfaction is not job dissatisfaction.
10. Don't forget that reinforced behavior tends to be repeated while nonreinforced behavior tends not to be repeated.
11. Don't forget that managers' or supervisors' attitudes toward subordinates play a significant role in employee motivation.

Figure 10-4 Do's and don'ts of motivation.

HANDLING EMPLOYEE FRUSTRATION

Managers and supervisors are well aware that employees are not always successful in achieving their goals or satisfying their needs. Some supervisors are unaware of ways to deal with the **frustration** employees experience when they are not successful in goal attainment. The greater the employees' motivation to achieve a goal or satisfy a need, the greater is the level of frustration that results from their lack of success. Managers and supervisors must be concerned about employee frustration, especially when it interferes with the employee's job performance.

Frustration occurs when a barrier prevents the achievement of a goal or the satisfaction of a need. The barrier may have either an internal or external origin. Examples of internal barriers are lack of ability, aptitude, interest, or judgment. External barriers result from boring work, inadequate supervision, restrictive company policies, or poorly designed work procedures.

Manifestation of Frustration

How does frustration manifest itself?

The presence of frustration is likely to manifest itself in the display of several types of behavior. Employees may select an alternative goal, become aggressive, experience anxiety, use a defense mechanism, or take corrective action. Managers or supervisors who understand the ways in which frustration manifests itself will be more effective in dealing with it.

Alternative goals When employees become frustrated because of their inability to achieve a goal, they may respond by selecting an achievable alternative goal. The motivation to achieve the new goal may be just as high as it was with the original goal, and its achievement may be just as satisfying as the achievement of the original goal would have been.

Aggression Lack of success in achieving a goal or satisfying a need results in frustration, perhaps manifesting itself in employee **aggression**. The employee may respond by verbally or physically abusing the person who is accused of preventing goal achievement or need satisfaction. Employees who respond to frustration in this way present special challenges to their manager or supervisor.

Anxiety In some employees, frustration manifests itself in a feeling of **anxiety**. As the level of anxiety increases, so does the amount of tension experienced by the employee. In extreme cases, anxiety can cause a variety of medical problems.

Defense mechanism Frustration may also manifest itself in some employees by their building a defense mechanism to protect their egos from psychological damage. The defense mechanism may take the form of fantasizing, rationalizing, withdrawing, or developing a negative attitude.

Corrective action Some employees respond to frustration by correcting the situation that produced the frustration. Employees modify or change the situations that are responsible for their lack of success. Of all the ways in which employees respond to frustration, this is generally the most mature, rational approach. Over the long run, this approach also produces positive rather than negative results.

Effective managers and supervisors are concerned about the problems that result when barriers prevent their subordinates from achieving their goals or satisfying their needs. They also need to work with their subordinates who experience frustration.

IMPLICATIONS FOR THE ADMINISTRATIVE OFFICE MANAGER

For the following reasons, administrative office managers should be concerned about the level of their subordinates' motivation: motivated employees tend to be more satisfied with the jobs and with life in general than are those who lack motivation, and unit goals and objectives can be more readily achieved when employees are motivated than when they are not. Consequently, the level of motivation impacts not only on the organization as a whole but also on the employees themselves.

Even though the elements of motivation are basic to human life, the motivational process is complex. These elements—ability, aptitude, interests, and so on—are themselves complex; and when they interact with one another, the motivational process becomes even more complex.

The increasing managerial concern for the human element in the organization has had a positive impact on employee motivation. The human relations era that emerged several decades ago continues to provide ample proof that managers or supervisors who make the subordinates responsible for self-motivation are doing an injustice to both the employer and the employees. Nowadays, managers and supervisors are more willing to assume their fair share of the responsibility for motivating subordinates than they once were.

In many instances, the strategies that are used to motivate subordinates are virtually cost free and consume little time. The failure to motivate employees is likely to create a number of serious problems for the organization, its managers, and its employees.

NOTES

1. Data are based on the Hierarchy of Needs in "A Theory of Human Motivation" in MOTIVATION AND PERSONALITY, 2nd Edition, by Abraham H. Maslow. Copyright © 1970 by Abraham H. Maslow. Reprinted by permission of Harper & Row, Publishers, Inc.
2. F. Herzberg, B. Mausner, and B. Synderman, *The Motivation to Work*, © 1959. Reprinted by permission of John Wiley and Sons, Inc.
3. New evidence indicates that salary is increasingly becoming a satisfier rather than the dissatisfier that it was a few years ago.
4. David C. McClelland, *The Achievement Motive*, Appleton-Century-Crofts, 1953. Reprinted with permission.
5. Victor Vroom, *Work and Motivation*, © 1953. Reprinted with permission of John Wiley and Sons, Inc.

REVIEW QUESTIONS

1. How do employees' needs and drives affect their motivation?
2. What is the essence of the behavior modification theory?
3. What are the elements of safety needs in Maslow's theory?
4. According to Maslow, when do belonging and love needs become important to an individual?
5. What is meant by self-actualization?
6. What are the basic differences be-

tween what Herzberg identifies as job satisfiers and job dissatisfiers?
7. What is the origin of motivation in the equity theory?
8. According to the expectancy theory, what conditions must be present for motivation to occur?
9. According to the reinforcement theory, of what is motivation a consequence?
10. What are the important attributes of goals?
11. In what ways can frustration manifest itself in employees?

DISCUSSION QUESTIONS

1. At a meeting you recently attended, you overheard a conversation between two individuals. One said to the other that the best way to motivate employees is to pay them what they feel they are worth. Do you agree with this statement? Explain your answer.
2. You are a new supervisor of a unit that has ten employees. You notice the level of employee motivation changes from day to day. Employees who are highly motivated some days are quite "unmotivated" other days. What factors are likely to affect the level of motivation from day to day?
3. Assume you are a supervisor, and you can assess only two human traits that affect the motivation of those individuals who apply for jobs in your department. Identify the two traits you would like to assess, and explain why you selected these two.
4. You are becoming increasingly aware that identical situations do not always have the same impact on the motivation of employees. For example, some employees tell you that they would find participation in certain decision-making processes motivational while other employees claim they don't want to be bothered with having to participate. How can you explain the fact that the same things affect the motivation of employees differently?
5. Consider the equity, expectancy, and reinforcement theories of motivation. Which theory seems to be the one that guides your behavior most of the time? Explain why you chose the theory you did, and cite recent situations in which your behavior was guided by this theory.
6. As a supervisor, you often have to deal with subordinate frustration. You know that effectively managed and controlled frustration can actually benefit a subordinate. Suggest strategies you can use to turn subordinate frustration from a liability to an asset.

STUDENT PROJECTS AND ACTIVITIES

1. Discuss with an administrative office manager the aspects of his or her job that he or she finds most motivational. Discuss with an office employee for whom the administrative office manager is responsible the aspects of his or her job that he or she finds most motivational. Did the items they identified differ from one another?
2. Discuss with an office employee the various ways he or she handles job-related frustration.
3. Discuss with an administrative office manager the perceived responsibility for helping subordinates with goal setting.
4. Discuss with an employee who has had several years of work experience the nature of changes in values he or she has experienced over the years.
5. Discuss with an office employee the elements of equity theory. Ask the employee if his or her motivational patterns correlate well with the equity theory.

MINICASE

Many of the managers in the Babcock Corporation are concerned about the declining level of employee motivation. The absence of motivated employees is reflected in several ways including lower output, higher absenteeism, greater waste, and so forth. Some of the managers blame the company's salary administration program for these problems. Employees all receive an across-the-board increase each year. Therefore, little incentive exists for an employee to work harder than others because the additional effort will not be reflected in higher salary through a merit increase.

As a consultant hired by Babcock to examine the employee motivation concern, write a report in which you

1. Comment on the implications of this situation on employee motivation.
2. Discuss the theory of motivation most clearly violated by this situation.
3. Discuss changes you recommend be made in the salary administration program so it is consistent with the theory you identified in question 2 above.

CASE

Emanuel Garcia is the new administrative office manager in the Gateway Corporation, a furniture manufacturer located in Albany, New York. Of the twenty-three applicants for the position, Garcia was selected primarily because of his reputation for working well with subordinates. Each of Garcia's previous employers mentioned his ability to motivate subordinates and to get them to put forth their best efforts. Garcia's predecessor had a reputation for being quite ineffective in dealing with subordinates.

When Garcia first arrived on the job, he asked each subordinate to schedule an appointment with him so they could get to know one another better. Although the "interviews" were quite unstructured, Garcia attempted to obtain the same information from each one. For example, he asked questions designed (1) to help him learn about the aspirations of each subordinate, (2) to find out what each subordinate liked and disliked about his or her job, and (3) to help him assess the self-concept of each subordinate.

Although some of the subordinates willingly provided answers to his questions, others were a bit more reluctant to answer, perhaps because of the fear that they did not want to say anything that could later be held against them.

Several of the employees did mention that the company provided few opportunities for promotion and that they may have to seek employment elsewhere if they expected to further their careers.

You are Garcia's supervisor. You and Garcia recently met to discuss what Garcia learned from his subordinates. At the end of the conversation, Garcia asked that you provide him with written feedback regarding the following items:

1. Whether or not you believe Garcia overstepped his authority when he tried to extract information from each subordinate during their interviews. Explain your belief.
2. The human need(s) being unfulfilled if employees are being denied the opportunity for promotion to higher-level jobs.
3. Your suggestions for Garcia that will be useful in increasing the motivation of his subordinates.

APPRAISING PERFORMANCE OF OFFICE EMPLOYEES

CHAPTER AIM

After studying this chapter, you should be able to design an effective program for appraising the performance of office employees.

CHAPTER OUTLINE

Uses of Performance Appraisal
Characteristics of Performance Appraisal Programs
Establishment of Performance Standards
Methods of Performance Appraisal
- Traditional Appraisal Methods
  - Graphic Rating Scale
  - Paired Comparison Appraisal
  - Checklists
  - Simple Ranking
- New Appraisal Methods
  - Forced Choice
  - Critical Incidents
  - Peer Rating
  - Group Rating
  - Self-Appraisal
  - Narrative Appraisal
  - Field Staff Review
  - Results-Oriented Appraisal
  - Behaviorally Anchored Rating Scales Appraisal (BARS)
  - Mixed Standard Scales

Rating Errors
- Halo-Horns Effect
- Influence of Recent Performance
- Bias
- Central Tendency

Analysis of Appraisals
Appraisal Interviews
Employee Promotion
Implications for the Administrative Office Manager

CHAPTER TERMS

Appraisal interview
Behaviorally anchored rating scales appraisal (BARS)
Bias
Central tendency rating
Checklists
Critical incidents appraisal
Employee promotion
Field staff review
Forced-choice appraisal
Graphic rating scale appraisal
Group rating appraisal
Halo-horns effect
Mixed standard scales
Narrative appraisal
Paired comparison appraisal

Peer rating appraisal
Performance standards
Results-oriented appraisal
Self-appraisal
Simple ranking appraisal

Influencing work-unit productivity directly, performance appraisal is one of the more important responsibilities of the administrative office manager. An effective appraisal system helps the organization increase its productivity as well as helps employees satisfy their desire to know how well they are performing. The absence of feedback about their job performance will likely cause employees to experience frustration, anxiety, and job-related insecurity.

USES OF PERFORMANCE APPRAISAL

What are the purposes of performance appraisal?

Performance appraisal was originally designed to help supervisors identify who should be promoted and/or who should receive salary increases. Several additional uses now exist. Supervisors frequently use the appraisal process as a means of helping to identify their subordinates' strengths and weaknesses. Appraisal results are used when making decisions about salary increases, promotions, and employee transfers, as well as when developing strategies for increasing the value of the employees to the organization.

Providing an objective basis for evaluating employees, performance appraisal helps eliminate charges of favoritism and bias. Too, the program motivates individuals to work harder as a way of obtaining higher salary increases and faster promotions.

Performance appraisal results are often used in workforce planning because appraisal data help to identify the positions that will likely become vacant soon as a result of employees' promotion. The results of the appraisal process are also used to determine areas suitable for employee training because the appraisal data clearly identify areas in which employees' performance is weak.

The performance appraisal process also helps strengthen the communication between supervisors and subordinates. By discussing the appraisal results, communication lines between the supervisor and subordinate are established. Another by-product of the appraisal process is improved quality of supervision. Typically, supervisors who have performance appraisal responsibilities are apt to be more aware of their subordinates' strengths and weaknesses. Performance appraisal also has a positive impact on the career growth and development of employees, thus enabling them to realize their potential more quickly.

The results of performance appraisal are often used in making decisions about promoting and rewarding employees. Civil rights legislation and several court cases indicate that performance appraisal results cannot be used to discriminate unfairly against protected classes.

CHARACTERISTICS OF PERFORMANCE APPRAISAL PROGRAMS

Effective performance appraisal programs possess the following identifiable characteristics:

What characteristics should performance appraisal programs possess?

1. The program must elicit a change in the behavior of employees. When they are aware of their weaknesses, employees are able to modify their behavior.

2. The program must provide a basis for making compensation decisions. An effective program helps identify those employees whose contribution to the organization warrants a higher level of compensation.
3. The program must provide information used as a basis for making promotion, transfer, or termination decisions. Any program that fails to provide appropriate job-change information is ineffective.
4. The program must motivate employees to work harder. If the program fails to identify those employees whose contribution to the organization is considerably above average, its value is questionable.
5. The program must provide feedback for use in validating various phases of the personnel program. The results, for example, of the program are useful in helping determine the effectiveness of the personnel selection program.
6. The program must facilitate supervisor-subordinate communication. A program's effectiveness is reduced when employees are not informed of their appraisal results.
7. The program must use the appropriate evaluation base in relation to the intended use of the appraisal results. Three bases are used: (a) evaluating an employee by comparing his or her performance with the performance of others, (b) evaluating an employee by comparing his or her performance against individually determined performance objectives, and (c) evaluating an employee by comparing his or her performance against generally accepted **performance standards**.

ESTABLISHMENT OF PERFORMANCE STANDARDS

How are performance standards used in performance appraisal programs?

The basis against which employees are to be evaluated has to be predetermined. These evaluation standards or criteria should be made available to each individual at the time of initial employment. Otherwise, a match between an employee's actual performance and his or her expected performance may simply be a coincidence.

To be considered when selecting the appraisal criteria is the use that will be made of the information gathered during the appraisal process. For example, the criteria used to determine who should be promoted are different from the criteria used to determine whether or not the employee should be discharged.

Performance standards should exist for all positions, but they are especially important in nonproduction jobs (those jobs that involve more than a quantity or quality output). In nonproduction jobs, such factors as human relations, ability to work with others, initiative, judgment, and so on, are more important.

The appraisal process used to evaluate unionized employees often has a different emphasis than the process used to appraise nonunionized employees. Seniority often plays an important part in determining who will be promoted in unionized organizations.

METHODS OF PERFORMANCE APPRAISAL

Some of the methods for appraising the performance of employees have been in existence for many years while others are quite new. Several methods in each of the two broad categories—traditional and new—are discussed.

Traditional Appraisal Methods

Performance traits are often the basis of the traditional appraisal methods. Unless these traits are observable, fairly standard for similar jobs within an organization, and capable of objective measurement, the effectiveness of using a traditional rating method may be hampered. Traits measured by subjective means may create legal and morale problems for organizations.

Among the traditional appraisal methods are graphic rating scales, paired comparison appraisal, checklists, and simple ranking.

What are the characteristics of the graphic rating scale technique of performance appraisal?

Graphic rating scale The **graphic rating scale**, which continues to be the most widely used performance appraisal method, requires a scale similar to the one illustrated in Figure 11-1. In completing the scale, the rater indicates the degree to which the individual being appraised possesses each specific characteristic or trait.

Three methods are commonly used in constructing the evaluation section of the graphic rating scale: (1) descriptive phrases, (2) descriptive words, and (3) numerical scales.

The use of descriptive phrases provides more rating objectivity than either of the other two methods. For the trait *job knowledge*, the descriptive phrases might be "thoroughly understands the job," "more than adequately understands the job," "has sufficient knowledge of the job," and so forth. Some appraisal forms using descriptive phrases provide space for written comments about each trait.

When descriptive words are used, such as "outstanding," "excellent," "above average," "average," "below average," and "poor," raters may not be consistent with one another in their interpretation and application of these words. Consequently, what is "outstanding" to one rater may only be "above average" to another. Appraisal forms using descriptive words also frequently provide space for written comments as well as a definition of each trait, as illustrated in Figure 11-2.

Numerical scales involve a series of numbers (perhaps 1 to 6, with 1 being low and 6 being high) for appraising the performance of each individual on each trait. Assuming that all traits are weighted equally, the numerical values can be added to get a composite score for each individual. To make this method as objective as possible, the numerical values and each trait should be defined. Numerical scales can also be designed with space so the rater can provide written comments about the various traits being assessed.

The traits used in appraising the performance of employees must be measurable. Traits dealing with employee behavior or performance results are more measurable than are those traits dealing specifically with the personality of employees. Rating forms that contain irrelevant traits or that omit important traits generally result in unsatisfactory appraisal instruments.

Greater objectivity can be achieved by placing the scale values in a random order on the form. Rather than placing the highest value for each trait at the left and the lowest value at the right, the values should be reordered from one trait to the next. Therefore, the rater has to exert more care appraising employee performance, which should result in a more thorough, objective evaluation.

Also commonly included on graphic rating scales is a summary section consisting of two subsections: one for general comments about the individual being rated and the other to provide an overall rating of the individual (superior, above average, average, and so on).

Although the graphic rating scale is a fairly simple and quick appraisal method, it does possess several serious shortcomings, including the following:

Name ______ Social Security number ______ Present salary ______

Present position ______ Date employed ______ Date of last promotion ______

QUALITY OF WORK Refers to neatness, accuracy, completeness of work	X Quality of work is considered above average and only rarely does any have to be redone	X Quality of work is superior and none ever has to be redone	X Quality of work is improving but is still substandard	X Much work has to be redone	X Quality of work is average and only some of it has to be redone
Comment:					
QUANTITY OF WORK Refers to volume of output	X Normally works at above average rate and wastes little time	X Works at a consistently high level with very little wasted time	X Is not able to produce at acceptable level	X Produces at an average rate but is steady and wastes little time	X Output is frequently below expected level. Wastes time
Comment:					
INITIATIVE Refers to ability to develop ideas and to ability to get things done	X Is capable of working without being told what to do	X Because of lack of initiative, always has to be told what to do	X Self starter. Never has to be told to do something	X Rarely does anything without first being told	X Develops new ways of doing things. Is resourceful
Comment:					
RELATIONS WITH OTHERS Refers to ability to get along with others	X Is respected by everyone, is helpful, and is looked upon by others as a "leader"	X Is disagreeable and does not get along well with others. Has few friends. Is a troublemaker	X Has a good attitude toward others and is liked and respected by others	X Is friendly and gets along well with others	X Is not friendly and is generally disliked by others
Comment:					
DEPENDABILITY Refers to trustworthiness and amount of supervision required	X Is always dependable, is completely trust worthy, and requires very little if any supervision	X Is not always dependable, cannot be trusted in all respects, and requires frequent supervision	X Is very trustworthy, is always dependable, and requires very little supervision	X Cannot be trusted, is not dependable, and requires constant supervision	X Can be trusted most of the time, is dependable, and requires only an average amount of supervision
Comment:					
JOB KNOWLEDGE Refers to the knowledge the individual has about the job	X Has average knowledge about job	X Knows about everything there is to know about the job	X Is very knowledgeable about the job	X Lacks job knowledge and is generally unwilling to learn	X Lacks job knowledge but is willing to learn
Comment:					

Summary Comments:

Overall rating: ______ Outstanding; ______ Above average; ______ Average; ______ Below average; ______ Poor

Today's date ______

Employee's signature ______

Appraiser's signature ______

Figure 11-1 Graphic rating scale.

Simple ranking The **simple ranking appraisal** method ranks employees from the best to the poorest. The method is fairly simple and can be used for appraising a fairly large number of employees. To use the method, each employee's name is put on an index card, and the cards are arranged and rearranged until the proper ranking is achieved.

The advantages of this method are readily offset by its lack of specificity and usefulness to the individual being rated. Only when the rater identifies problem or weak areas for the employees do they know the reasons for a poor rating. Unless the rater uses an objective basis for appraising the individuals, bias and subjectivity may be present in the evaluation process.

New Appraisal Methods

Although the traditional methods of performance appraisal are still frequently used in organizations, some newer appraisal methods are becoming increasingly popular. Among the newer appraisal methods are forced choice, critical incidents, peer rating, group rating, self-appraisal, narrative, field staff review, results oriented, behaviorally anchored rating scales (BARS), and mixed standard scales.

What are the characteristics of the forced-choice appraisal technique?

Forced choice The **forced-choice appraisal** method consists of twenty-five to forty sets of statements. From each set, the rater chooses the statement *most* descriptive and the statement *least* descriptive of the person being appraised. Figure 11-5 is an example of two sets of such statements.

Because the rater does not know which statement in each set is viewed as favorable and which is viewed as unfavorable for the individual being rated, bias and subjectivity can be almost totally eliminated. Only two statements within each set affect the person being appraised (the most and the least favorable statements), whereas the other three are treated as neutral statements. The selection of neutral statements will not affect the individual being rated. But when the rater chooses the favorable statement, the individual's appraisal is affected positively; and when the rater chooses the unfavorable statement, the individual's appraisal is negatively affected.

The use of this appraisal method has significant advantages over the use of some of the other methods (eliminates bias and subjectivity); however, its use also has some serious limitations. The method is costly to develop and in-

Most	*Least*	
1	1	Wants to do things his or her own way.
2	2	Is valuable in a new operation.
3	3	Does not go outside area of authority.
4	4	Is viewed by peers as a leader.
5	5	Realizes capabilities of others.
Most	*Least*	
1	1	Needs complete information about a situation before willing to make a decision.
2	2	Would be easy to replace.
3	3	Is sensitive to needs of others.
4	4	Stands up well under pressure.
5	5	Has gone about as far as his capabilities will permit

Figure 11-5 Forced-choice statement sets.

stall because the statements generally have to be designed for specific job categories. The results of the appraisal are also difficult to use as a basis for employee counseling and development.

What are the characteristics of the critical incidents appraisal technique?

Critical incidents The **critical incidents appraisal** method involves formulating a list of critical job requirements for each position. To illustrate, the critical incidents for a secretary might include the ability to work with others, the ability to meet deadlines, and the ability to perform at a quality level.

After the critical requirements have been identified, the office supervisor observes each subordinate for favorable or unfavorable displays of these requirements. The examples or incidents are immediately recorded on the appraisal form as a means of building an appraisal record for each subordinate. The favorable incidents are listed on one side, whereas the unfavorable incidents are listed on the other side. Figure 11-6 is an example.

A distinct advantage of this method is basing the appraisal on objective facts and evidence rather than on traits that are rated subjectively. Furthermore, the rater is also required to list specific incidents in appraising subordinates. The method also provides the opportunity for supervisors to discuss immediately with subordinates the favorable and unfavorable incidents.

A potential disadvantage of this method is the impression among subordinates that the supervisor keeps a "little black book" in which unfavorable incidents are recorded. This belief may create resentment among some subordinates.

Peer rating The **peer rating appraisal** method uses coworkers to evaluate the performance of an individual. Peers, who often see a different type of behavior than what the supervisor sees, are given an opportunity to evaluate that behavior. The technique is useful in identifying the members of a work group whose characteristics may be best suited for assuming leadership positions within an organization.

What are the characteristics of the group rating appraisal technique?

Group rating When the **group rating appraisal** method is used, a group of individuals who are familiar with the person being rated does the appraisal collectively rather than individually. The group generally consists of the individual's immediate supervisor, the supervisor's superior, and other persons who are familiar with the individual being appraised. The objectivity of the appraisal efforts is probably increased because more than one individual is involved in the appraisal process. This method is also effectively used in organizations in which individuals have responsibilities in two departments or work units.

Ability to Work With Others

10/16—Mary stayed after hours to help Pat finish a project. 10/17—When several office workers were ill today, Mary helped reorganize work so deadlines could be met.	12/3—Mary asked to not be assigned to work on a particular project with Carol (for personal reasons).

Figure 11-6 Critical incidents record.

Self-appraisal The **self-appraisal** method typically uses a rating form, such as a graphic rating scale. Both the employee being rated and the employee's supervisor complete the form. During the appraisal interview, the responses of the employee and the supervisor are compared, trait by trait. When a discrepancy occurs, an average of the two ratings is often calculated to determine the official rating.

The most distinct advantage of the self-appraisal method is the active role the employee takes in the appraisal process. Performance appraisal is for the benefit of employees; when they take an active part in the process, they are able to get a more realistic picture of their overall performance. This method also results in greater employee acceptance of the rating process.

Narrative appraisal Some organizations prefer to use the **narrative appraisal** method in which the supervisor prepares a written report about the employee's performance. The most distinct advantage of this method is that it provides detailed coverage about certain phases of the employee's job-related performance. Identified strengths and weaknesses can be covered in sufficient detail to eliminate ambiguities or incomplete information.

Making a comparison of the appraisal results of various supervisors is not possible with narrative appraisal. Because the method does not lend itself to standardization, comparing employees with one another on the basis of the written reports prepared by the raters is generally impossible. Also, the method is limited by the ability of the supervisors to prepare well-written reports.

What are the steps in field staff review?

Field staff review Of the various appraisal methods discussed in this chapter, the **field staff review** method is the only one that uses an objective outside appraiser in the evaluation process. The employee being evaluated and the employee's supervisor are questioned orally by the appraiser, who is generally from the organization's personnel department. The responses of the employee and the supervisor are generally recorded on a form.

An advantage of the field staff review technique is the objective, uniform, and thorough results it provides. A potential disadvantage is the inability to provide appraisals as often as they should be provided, especially when an insufficient number of appraisers is available.

Results-oriented appraisal A significant trend in performance appraisal nowadays is the use of **results-oriented appraisal**. The philosophical foundation of this appraisal method lies within the management by objectives concept, which is discussed in detail in Chapter 16. The method generally involves the following steps:

What are the steps in results-oriented appraisal?

1. Employee performance goals that are measurable are set jointly by the supervisor and the subordinate.
2. Specific courses of action are agreed on as a means of accomplishing these goals.
3. The supervisor and subordinate, at interim intervals, discuss the progress that has been made toward accomplishing these goals.
4. The supervisor and subordinate, at the conclusion of the time period (perhaps six months to a year), officially evaluate the degree to which the specified goals were accomplished.
5. Goals for the next evaluation period are set.

Many organizations that have installed a results-oriented appraisal program use it in conjunction with another appraisal method, such as the graphic rating scale, to identify employee strengths and weaknesses. The performance goals are aimed at helping the employee overcome identified weaknesses.

Results-oriented appraisal can be used in organizations that do not use management by objectives. In many organizations where MBO is used, results-oriented appraisal is linked to the objectives specified by the goal-setting process of MBO. For example, if the organization has a specific goal of increasing profit, many employees in the organization are apt to have waste-reduction goals as part of their results-oriented appraisal program. Individual objectives should be developed around the following guidelines:

1. Only measurable objectives should be used. For the most part, personality traits are not suitable because they cannot be measured.
2. The number of individual objectives should be determined by the nature of the employee's performance.
3. The objectives should be achievable within a relatively short time, although they do not all have to be achieved at the same time.
4. The objectives should consist of three elements: (1) the desired results, (2) the quantity or amount of change, and (3) the time frame in which each objective is to be achieved.

Advantages of using results-oriented appraisal are the following:

What are the advantages of results-oriented appraisal?

1. The appraisal method emphasizes the future (over which the employee has some control) rather than the past (over which the employee no longer has any control).
2. The method emphasizes performance rather than personality traits.
3. The method helps identify areas suitable for training.
4. Subordinates are compared against their own progress rather than competing with their peers.
5. The method tends to strengthen superior-subordinate cooperation because the superior is in a prime position to help subordinates achieve their specified goals.
6. Employees tend to work harder when they have a specific goal they are trying to achieve.
7. The appraisal is tailor-made for each employee.
8. Employees are motivated to work harder for the attainment of major organizational objectives.

The following are seen as disadvantages of the results-oriented appraisal method:

1. Subordinates may set their goals too high or too low.
2. The work performed by some employees cannot be quantified or measured.
3. The use of this appraisal method may require certain managers to adjust their managerial style. In some instances, managers cannot or will not make the necessary adjustments to make the method work.

4. Some supervisors believe no need exists to counsel their subordinates because they can readily determine how well they are achieving their goals.
5. The method leads employees to work only for measurable goals and not unmeasurable goals (morale, for example).

What are the characteristics of the behaviorally anchored rating scales appraisal technique?

Behaviorally anchored rating scales appraisal An appraisal method being used in an increasing number of organizations is the **behaviorally anchored rating scales (BARS)** technique. This method uses a series of five to ten scales in the appraisal of employee performance. Each important job dimension has a separate scale. Among the job dimensions that might be used are the following: job knowledge, quality of work, quantity of work, initiative, dependability, and so forth. An example of one such scale is shown in Figure 11-7.

Each scale has a set of seven anchors that reflect varying degrees of job performance. The anchors are arranged in order from excellent to unacceptable. To appraise an individual's performance, the rater reads through the anchors to find the one that best reflects the quality of the individual's performance.

The BARS method produces objective and consistent results. In addition, the scales that are used for various jobs can be tailored to reflect specific job attributes. The most significant disadvantage is the amount of time consumed in developing the various scales.

Mixed standard scales Similar to a number of the other performance appraisal methods discussed earlier, the **mixed standard scales** technique is also tailored to specific positions. The rating scale used in conjunction with this method contains a list of statements the rater considers in appraising the employee. The following three qualitative values are used:

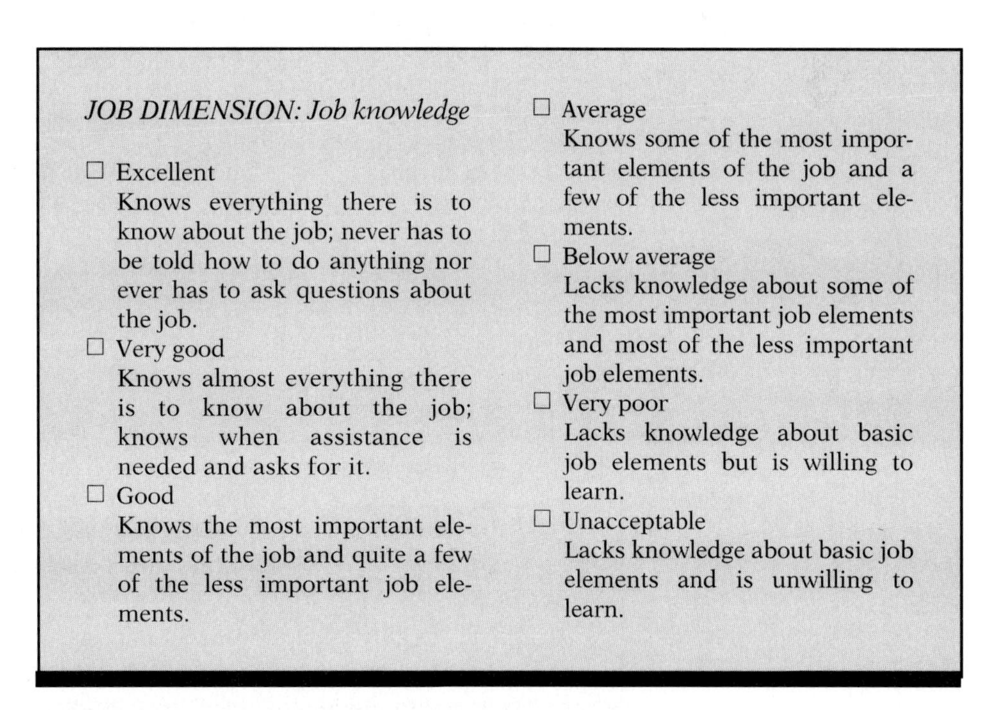

JOB DIMENSION: Job knowledge

☐ Excellent
Knows everything there is to know about the job; never has to be told how to do anything nor ever has to ask questions about the job.

☐ Very good
Knows almost everything there is to know about the job; knows when assistance is needed and asks for it.

☐ Good
Knows the most important elements of the job and quite a few of the less important job elements.

☐ Average
Knows some of the most important elements of the job and a few of the less important elements.

☐ Below average
Lacks knowledge about some of the most important job elements and most of the less important job elements.

☐ Very poor
Lacks knowledge about basic job elements but is willing to learn.

☐ Unacceptable
Lacks knowledge about basic job elements and is unwilling to learn.

Figure 11-7 Behaviorally anchored rating scale.

\+ indicates that the person being rated performs better than the performance level contained in the statement.

0 indicates that the person being rated performs exactly like the performance level contained in the statement.

− indicates that the person being rated performs worse than the performance level contained in the statement.

What are the advantages of the mixed standard scales technique?

The individual doing the appraisal places one of the three values on the appropriate line beside each performance statement. The various performance statements, which are arranged in a random order, contain positive as well as negative attributes. Once the employee has been rated, the results are analyzed to determine an overall qualitative assessment of the employee's performance. The rating scales designed for some jobs contain as many as twenty-five to thirty performance standards.

Two of the most distinctive advantages of the mixed standard scales method are that the performance statements can be tailored to specific positions, and the rater only has to work with three qualitative values. Therefore, the rater does not have to decide whether the employee's performance in a certain area is *excellent* or whether it deserves a rating of a *7* or a *6*. The second advantage listed earlier for the mixed standard scales method also becomes its primary disadvantage: The employee being rated is unable to determine how much better or how much worse his or her performance is than what is expected. The employee can only determine that his or her performance is better or worse than expected.

A portion of a mixed standard scale is found in Figure 11-8.

Name__________ Supervisor__________

Department__________ Date__________

Rate each of the statements listed below, using the following values:

"+": Indicates that the person being rated performs better than the performance level contained in the statement.

"o": Indicates that the person being rated performs exactly like the performance level contained in the statement.

"−": Indicates that the person being rated performs worse than the performance level contained in the statement.

____ 1. Always arrives at work on time.

____ 2. Carries out work on a reasonable and timely basis.

____ 3. Idles the time away when he or she has nothing to do.

____ 4. Greets office callers cheerfully.

____ 5. Has difficulty coping with job pressures.

____ 6. Could be more meticulous in handling the details of the job.

____ 7. Is sometimes discourteous to coworkers.

____ 8. Returns from breaks on time.

____ 9. Sometimes asks questions rather than trying to find answer on own.

____ 10. Occasional carelessness sometimes results in the waste of office supplies.

____ 11. Does not participate in "office gossip."

____ 12. Rarely volunteers to help others.

Figure 11-8 Mixed standard scale for a secretary.

RATING ERRORS

The various appraisal methods that use scoring scales (whether the scale involves descriptive phrases, words, or numerical values) are subject to human rating errors that often distort appraisal results. The rating errors usually involve judgment and occur when traits cannot be quantified or measured on an objective basis. The impact of many rating errors can be minimized with the proper training of supervisors.

Halo-Horns Effect

What is a halo effect?

The **halo-horns effect** results when the rating on one trait influences the rating an employee receives on other traits. For example, if undue emphasis is placed on attitude, the halo effect occurs when those employees whose attitudes are judged to be above average are rated excessively high on all other traits. The horns effect is present when an employee whose attitude is judged to be below average is rated excessively low on other traits. The halo-horns effect can be minimized if raters consider each trait individually and do not allow the rating on one trait to influence the rating on other traits.

Influence of Recent Performance

The recent performance of a subordinate is also likely to have an impact on the appraisal process. Employees whose recent performance is considerably above average (even though their earlier performance may have been below average) are likely to be rated unduly high. Likewise, employees whose performance decreases immediately before the appraisal process occurs may receive a rating that does not truly reflect the quality of their performance. The critical incidents method, which provides an ongoing appraisal of each employee, is not subject to this type of rating error.

Bias

Overcoming unconscious **bias** or prejudices is difficult for some supervisors. The appraisals of subordinates are likely to be affected by this bias, especially when their preferences are not consistent with the supervisor's preferences. Assuming that the bias is short-lived, a technique that will minimize the effect of bias involves having the supervisor appraise each subordinate two different times—perhaps two weeks apart. The results of the two appraisals are compared, and any differences are resolved.

Central Tendency

What is a central tendency error?

The **central tendency rating** error occurs when the ratings of subordinates all fall within a narrow range. Regardless of individual employee performance, all employees are rated at average or above-average levels. The presence of the central tendency rating error diminishes the usefulness of the appraisal of employee performance.

ANALYSIS OF APPRAISALS

Even though quality appraisal forms may be used in the appraisal process, the reliability and validity of the appraisal results should be determined. This analysis is especially important when the graphic rating scale and forced-choice appraisal methods are used.

How can the reliability of appraisal results be assessed?

To determine the reliability of results, employee ratings in different work units or in different jobs should be analyzed. If significant differences are found, an adjustment may be necessary. For example, some raters believe that individuals who hold more important jobs should receive a higher rating than those whose jobs they consider to be of lesser importance. Raters should always be cognizant of the fact that appraisals are concerned with how well employees perform their jobs rather than how important the jobs are within the organization.

One way to determine the validity of appraisal results is to make an analysis of the strictness or leniency with which each rater appraises his or her subordinates. Ratings made by overly strict or lenient supervisors cannot be fairly compared with supervisors whose ratings tend to fall between these two extremes. An adjustment factor may have to be used to assure the comparability of results.

Ratings can be made more reliable by determining the importance of each trait within the position. Because traits are rarely equally important, results will be more reliable if each category is assigned a specific weight in relation to its importance.

Another means of assessing the quality of the appraisal process is to follow up employees who have been promoted to high-level positions primarily because they received high evaluations in the appraisal process. The effectiveness of the appraisal process can be verified to a certain extent if employees who received high ratings while holding one position continue to receive high ratings while holding a higher-level position.

APPRAISAL INTERVIEWS

The success of the performance appraisal program is greatly dependent upon the appraisal form, on the elimination of rating errors, and on the analysis of appraisal results. The program will not be totally successful, however, unless employees are informed of the evaluation results. The **appraisal interview** is designed to inform employees of the results of their appraisal.

What is the purpose of the appraisal interview?

In many organizations, before the time of the appraisal interview with the employee, the supervisor completes the appraisal, which is then given to the supervisor's immediate supervisor for his or her approval. This practice results in several advantages: (1) if the superior does not agree with the supervisor's rating, he or she can make suggestions for modifying the rating; (2) the superior can determine areas suitable for training; and (3) the superior can become more familiar with the employees for whom he or she is responsible. After the superior approves the supervisor's rating, the evaluation form is shown to the subordinate. Following this, the supervisor and the subordinate discuss the evaluation results during the appraisal interview.

The advantages of conducting appraisal interviews are (1) the present performance of the subordinates can be discussed as well as the areas in which improvement is desirable; (2) the interview provides an opportunity for the supervisor and subordinate to become more familiar with one another's goals, aspirations, feelings, and attitudes; and (3) the interview tends to strengthen lines of communication between the supervisor and subordinate.

The disadvantages of the appraisal interview are (1) supervisors who are not comfortable with the interviewing process are reluctant to conduct the interviews unless so required; (2) poorly conducted interviews are likely to

1. Start the interview by having the employee evaluate his or her performance.
2. Try to put the employee at ease immediately.
3. Emphasize strengths before discussing weaknesses.
4. Point out any strengths not identified by the employee.
5. Let the employee decide, if at all possible, how the weaknesses will be overcome.
6. Limit the areas of employee improvement to those that can be overcome within a reasonable length of time.
7. Substantiate ratings with specific examples of performance.
8. "Hear out" the individual being appraised.
9. Minimize authoritarian behavior.
10. Allow extensive two-way communication.
11. Try not to bring up topics that threaten the self-esteem of the employee.
12. Try not to cover too much material in one interview.
13. Let the employee read the written appraisal before the interview.

Figure 11-9 Suggestions for improving the effectiveness of appraisal interviews.

cause resentment and hostility between the supervisor and subordinate; (3) some supervisors believe that conducting appraisal interviews is a low-priority responsibility and, therefore, they either hurry through the interview or they fail to conduct it altogether; and (4) subordinates become defensive when criticized.

Illustrated in Figure 11-9 is a list of suggestions that will result in the conducting of more effective appraisal interviews.

EMPLOYEE PROMOTION

Employee promotion is viewed by most employees as a means of helping them achieve their needs, especially the esteem and self-actualization needs identified earlier in Maslow's Need-Hierarchy Theory (see Chapter 10). Promotion (or advancement) was also identified as a motivator in Herzberg's Motivation-Hygiene Theory (also see Chapter 10). Consequently, the absence of promotional possibilities is likely to result in decreased employee satisfaction.

What is the basic difference between a major and a minor promotion?

Organizations generally make two types of promotions: major and minor. A major promotion results when an employee is given a new job title, most likely in conjunction with a variety of new job responsibilities. Such a promotion results, for example, when the supervisor of records management is promoted to the position of administrative office manager. A minor promotion, conversely, results when an employee keeps his or her present job title but moves from one level to another. An example is the executive secretary, level III, who is promoted to senior executive secretary.

In some organizations that have a low turnover rate, which often reduces substantially the opportunities for promotions, moving employees laterally is an option. The primary reason for using lateral moves is to motivate employees and to reduce the opportunities for their burnout. Perhaps an employee realizes that the opportunities for promotion in his or her present work unit are quite poor but that if he or she were to make a lateral move to another work unit, the eventual promotional opportunities would be more abundant and would likely occur more rapidly.

The lateral-move technique is also frequently used in organizations that undertake a major restructuring of their work processes, resulting in a significant change in the nature of employees' jobs. When the changes are significant, some organizations terminate all their affected employees and ask them to reapply for the new positions (with a guarantee that each employee who reapplies will have a job and no one will experience a pay cut).

Decisions about employee promotion generally take into consideration both objective and subjective factors. Among the objective factors are length of time the employee has worked for the organization and has held his or her present position, nature of previous work experience, and education. Among the subjective factors are the quality of his or her work performance, the ability of the employee to perform the next higher job, and interview ratings.

Just as hiring practices must be nondiscriminatory, so do promotion practices. An organization that uses different promotion standards for different groups among its workforce is committing an illegal act. Therefore, groups of workers protected by various provisions of federal laws (Civil Rights Act, Age Discrimination Act, and so forth) must be promoted using guidelines free of bias or discrimination. The promotional standards and/or criteria that are used must be applied uniformly throughout the organization, regardless of who is being promoted. The following suggestions help assure bias-free, nondiscriminatory promotion practices:

What suggestions help assure a bias-free nondiscriminatory promotion practice?

1. Allow employees to bid on job openings communicated to all employees throughout the organization.
2. Base the written performance appraisal on written job-related performance standards with which the employee is familiar.
3. Discuss the written performance appraisal with the employee at which time he or she is asked to sign the written appraisal. (This document is likely to be a critical one should an employee either file a discrimination charge against the supervisor and/or organization or sue the organization because of its promotional practices.)
4. Track the promotions of employees categorized as a member of a protected group as identified in the federal and state legislation.
5. Have supervisors keep a log of subordinates' work performance—both desirable and undesirable—and attendance and tardiness.

Although the employee expects the organization to use fair, uniform, and consistent procedures in promoting employees, the employee also has a number of responsibilities related to its promotion practices. Among these are the following: an understanding of the lines or channels of promotion, expectations of his or her present position, duties and responsibilities of the next higher position, and qualifications needed by employees in the next higher position.

Increasingly, organizations are maintaining computerized data banks that contain information useful in making promotion decisions. These banks, which are used as an internal recruiting source of employees, are accessed to determine which of the present employees possess the qualifications needed for the position that is vacant. From the list of qualified employees, those who are considered as deserving of a promotion are then further assessed to determine their suitability for the vacant position.

IMPLICATIONS FOR THE ADMINISTRATIVE OFFICE MANAGER

Performance appraisal is one of the most useful tools available to administrative office managers who wish to improve the operating efficiency of their units. Employees who overcome the weaknesses identified by the appraisal process are often able to perform at higher levels than previously.

Well-designed performance appraisal programs are psychologically worthwhile to employees. The absence of job-performance feedback denies employees the opportunity to satisfy the need of knowing how well they are performing.

Administrative office managers are vitally involved in designing many organizational performance appraisal programs. For example, they commonly serve on advisory committees that provide input into program development. The background, training, and performance appraisal experiences of these individuals provide them with the necessary qualifications for making a significant contribution to this area.

At the unit level, managers must be especially careful to avoid using subjective appraisal practices. Regardless of how well designed an organization's program is, much of its success will be destroyed by managers who are not objective in their appraisal efforts. Imagined subjectivity is often as damaging to the appraisal process as actual subjectivity.

REVIEW QUESTIONS

1. What are the various uses made of performance appraisal?
2. What are the characteristics of effective performance appraisal programs?
3. What suggestions can you offer that will be useful in designing an objective graphic rating scale?
4. What are the advantages and disadvantages of the paired comparison, checklists, and simple ranking methods of performance appraisal?
5. What is the nature of the opposition of employees to the critical incidents method of performance appraisal?
6. What is the unique characteristic of the field staff review appraisal technique?
7. What guidelines should be followed when establishing the goals for the results-oriented appraisal method?
8. What kinds of rating errors are likely to occur when appraising employees' performance? Give examples of each type of error.
9. How can reliability and validity of an appraisal rating form be determined?
10. What suggestions can you provide for improving the effectiveness of performance appraisal interviews?
11. What is the basic difference between a major and a minor promotion?

DISCUSSION QUESTIONS

1. Effective performance appraisal programs are designed to eliminate charges of favoritism and bias in the rating of employees. Yet, many employees complain that their performance is not fairly evaluated. Identify and discuss several of the reasons that may prevent the fair, unbiased appraisal of an employees' performance.
2. Your supervisor has given you the responsibility for designing a new graphic rating scale for use in appraising employee performance. After your supervisor had an opportunity to examine the form you designed, she indicated that she liked it with one exception: It didn't allow for the rating of employee attitude.

She also indicated that she felt the rating of employee attitude was important because of the significant impact of attitude on employee performance. You purposely left this trait off the form because it is so difficult to quantify. Build the defense you plan to use for not including attitude as a rating factor on the form.

3. Your supervisor approved the appraisal form you developed for the situation in question 2, but still insisted that a rating of employee attitude be included. She also asked you to provide for her a list of items supervisors should consider when assessing employee attitude. Each of the items on your list can either positively or negatively affect employee attitude. What items do you plan to include on the list?
4. The organization in which you are a supervisor uses an appraisal method that rates employees on the basis of their past performance. One of your subordinates recently challenged you about the use of a rating method based on past performance. He contends that it is too late for him to do anything about improving his performance once he is made aware of his deficiencies during the appraisal interview. Prepare a response that you will use in justifying to him the continued use of a method based on past performance.
5. You have an apparent "personality conflict" with one of your subordinates. In fact, this individual has told you several times during the last few months to "get off his back." This employee just received his lowest-ever performance rating from you, a rating that you are convinced was deserved. Explain the procedures you used to ensure your objectivity in rating the employee's performance, especially in light of the fact that you readily admit that he sometimes "irks" you.
6. You have been asked by your supervisor to prepare for her a list of reasons why she should either support or not support a proposal that your employer change from the graphic rating appraisal method to the field staff review method. Commit yourself to one of these two alternatives and prepare a defense outlining the reasons for your commitment to that alternative.

STUDENT PROJECTS AND ACTIVITIES

1. Obtain from two different organizations their employee appraisal forms. What are the similarities in the content found on the two forms? The differences?
2. Talk with an administrative office manager to learn how he or she diminishes the impact of rating errors when appraising the performance of employees.
3. Discuss with a personnel manager how the organization in which he or she works established the performance standards used in appraising the performance of employees.
4. Talk with an office employee who recently participated in an appraisal interview. What did this employee like best about the interview? The least?
5. Discuss with an administrative office manager the employee promotion process used in the organization in which he or she works. How has the process changed over the years?

MINICASE

The Rudman Corporation manufactures a variety of lawn-care tools and equipment. Several years ago, many of the management functions were decentralized, which gave unit managers almost total autonomy in managing their units. The new president has decided that because the organization is growing rapidly, certain management functions should be centralized. He hopes that will provide better, more effective coordination of the various functions. One of the first functions to be centralized is employee performance appraisal. At last count, twelve different appraisal techniques were being used in the various units. As the president's assistant, you are asked to prepare a report to be transmitted to each unit manager/supervisor in which you do the following:

1. Discuss the desirability of having a centralized performance appraisal program.
2. Discuss why the present decentralized process that uses at least 12 different appraisal techniques is not effective.

CASE

During the last year, the First American Bank in Tulsa, Oklahoma, has had a 20 percent increase in its workforce. If the volume of business increases as much this year as last, the bank projects its workforce will have to increase an additional thirty to thirty-five individuals this year. Although most of the new employees who have been hired are office employees, a few have been hired at the management level. The same ratio between management and office employees is expected to be needed among new employees this year as in recent years.

The rapidly increasing number of employees is "straining" several of the bank's management functions including its performance appraisal program.

At the present time, a graphic scale is used to appraise employee performance. The form was originally developed for an insurance company nearly fifteen years ago and has not been changed during the fourteen years the bank has used it.

The executive vice president has asked you, the administrative office manager, to prepare a report for her in which information about the results-oriented performance appraisal approach is presented. Accordingly, you decide to include the following items:

1. An overview of the results-oriented performance appraisal program.
2. Techniques the bank could use to sell its employees on the use of the results-oriented approach after the graphic rating scale approach has been used for so long.
3. Suggestions to help ensure the success of the results-oriented appraisal approach, assuming it is the one that is selected.

CHAPTER

12

ANALYZING JOBS OF OFFICE EMPLOYEES

CHAPTER AIM

After reading this chapter, you should be able to design an effective program for analyzing the jobs of office employees.

CHAPTER OUTLINE

The Nature of Job Analysis
Uses of Job Analysis
- Job Analysis Program
- Methods of Collecting Job Information
  - Questionnaire Method
  - Interview Method
  - Observation Method
  - Combination of Methods

Describing the Job
- Job Description
- Job Specification
- Uses of Job Descriptions and Job Specifications

Implications for the Administrative Office Manager

CHAPTER TERMS

Critical incidents technique
Interview method
Job analysis
Job description
Job information worksheet
Job specification
Observation method
Questionnaire method
Time and motion study
U.S. Employment Service

As managers and supervisors become less familiar with the various duties their subordinates perform, the more important job analysis becomes. Generally, managers and supervisors are not as familiar as they were in the past with various aspects of their subordinates' jobs. This is because a decreasing number have actually held all the positions for which they have managerial or supervisory responsibility. In addition to providing input useful in job structuring, analysis also results in better control and coordination of employee output.

THE NATURE OF JOB ANALYSIS

How do job descriptions and job specifications differ from one another?

Job analysis is the formal process of collecting information about the components a job comprises. The information collected through job analysis is used to prepare job descriptions and job specifications. A **job description** is the written document that outlines the duties and responsibilities of a job. A **job specification**, conversely, refers to the written document that outlines the personal qualifications an employee must possess to perform the duties and responsibilities of a particular job. The description pertains to the job, whereas the specification pertains to the job holder.

USES OF JOB ANALYSIS

What are the uses of job analyses?

As an important administrative management function, job analysis has several uses. The information collected in job analysis is ultimately used in recruiting, selecting, and placing employees in positions that match their qualifications. Job analysis is used to help determine qualifications of employees, and it facilitates employee performance appraisal, promotion, and transfer. Furthermore, job analysis is used to identify areas in which new or existing employees may need training.

Job analysis is also used to standardize the same job performed by several employees. Control over employee production is improved because standardization improves the efficiency with which employee output is measured. As a result, employees have greater assurance their work load is consistent with normal expectations. Because it improves the quality and quantity of job-related information shared with employees, job analysis also provides an important human relations function. Last, job analysis, by providing data about the relative difficulty of the various job tasks, is used in the development of equitable salary scales.

Although the job analysis process may identify inefficient use of time and motion in office procedures, it should not be confused with time and motion study. By providing data relating to specific jobs, **time and motion study** is primarily an industrial engineering function. Job analysis, conversely, is an administrative management function. The basic purpose of time and motion study is to identify waste and inefficiency, whereas the basic purpose of job analysis is to identify job duties and responsibilities. Jobs that contain wasteful motions and that are inefficient should be subjected to time and motion study before they are analyzed. Otherwise, the analyzed results will be based on nonproductive functions, making the analysis process invalid.

Job Analysis Program

An effective job analysis program requires important preparatory work, including a clear identification of program objectives, program purposes, and

What must be considered before beginning a job analysis program?

procedures to be followed in collecting data. Before starting the analysis procedures, the following four items must be considered: (1) the jobs that will be included in the analysis, (2) the order in which the jobs will be analyzed, (3) the nature of the information to be collected, and (4) the method to be used in collecting the information. To minimize their resistance to the program, detailed information about the objectives, purposes, and benefits of the program must be communicated to employees.

The cooperation and support of employees will be obtained more quickly when they are made aware of the following benefits of job analysis:

1. Job analysis provides an objective basis for determining the importance of each job, determining the rate of pay for each job, and appraising the performance of each employee.
2. Job analysis enables each employee better to understand job duties and responsibilities that his or her position comprises.
3. Job analysis facilitates making more equitable employee work load assignments.
4. Job analysis assists employees in areas where self-improvement is appropriate.
5. Job analysis aids supervising employees because each job is clearly defined.

Methods of Collecting Job Information

To a large extent, the success of the job analysis program is affected by the reliability of the collected information. Three methods are frequently used to collect information: **questionnaire**, **interview**, and **observation**. In some instances, a combination of two or more methods may be appropriate.

Questionnaire method Employees who are most familiar with the job being analyzed generally complete the data-gathering questionnaire, which typically consists of a series of short-answer questions. The success of this method depends on the employee's ability to make a correct interpretation of the questionnaire items and to provide accurate and easy-to-classify answers.

Questionnaires used to collect information from employees are typically designed in the following ways: by the administrative office manager, by the organization's job analyst, and by a consultant. Regardless of who prepares the questionnaire, its design will have a significant impact on the success of the program.

The design of the questionnaire is determined by the number of employees who are expected to complete it. In organizations with a small workforce, a simplified questionnaire that includes the following items may be sufficient.

Title of job
Description of job
Tasks performed daily, weekly, monthly, quarterly, and annually
Special requirements (skills, experience, knowledge) for the job
Special work performance for the job

A questionnaire with more detail may be needed when the number of employees expected to complete it increases. An example of such a questionnaire is illustrated in Figure 12-1.

Your Name ______	Supervisor's Name ______
Title of Job ______	Today's Date ______
Level of Job ______	D.O.T. Number ______ (To be filled in by analyst)
Department ______	

A. *Description of Duties:* Please describe the duties and responsibilities of your job as you understand the situation. In your description, please be as specific as you can in telling what your job consists of, the importance of each duty and responsibilty, and the frequency with which each is performed. The following suggestions may facilitate your response:

1. Divide your job into specific duties and steps.
2. In describing each step, indicate from whom the work is obtained, explain the nature of the operation, indicate to whom the finished work is given, and indicate the frequency of the operation.

   (If the space provided below is not sufficient, please continue on the reverse side of this page.)

B. *Educational Requirements:* Please place a check mark (✓) beside the amount of education required for the job you hold.

No education requirement ______	College degree ______
High school diploma ______	Years of college work required ______
Some college work ______	Other ______ (Please specify)

C. *Skills Required*: Please indicate the nature of any skill requirements for the job you hold, including the level of skills required.

Nature of skills	*Level required*

D. *Experience Requirements:* Please indicate the nature of any job experience requirements for the job you hold, including the number of years required.

Nature of experience	*Years of required experience*

E. *Job Knowledge Requirements*: Please indicate the nature of any job knowledge (specific or general) for the job you hold, including the appropriate sources for obtaining the required knowledge.

Job knowledge requirements	*Source of gaining knowledge*

F. *Equipment/Tools Used:* Please list the equipment and tools used in the discharge of your job, including the frequency of usage and the amount of skill required in using the equipment and tools.

Equipment/Tools	*Frequency of use*	*Skills required*

Figure 12-1 Job analysis questionnaire.

The analysis of some jobs is facilitated by studying the special methods, forms, and reports the employees use, especially when the items are used extensively in a particular job. Failure to analyze these items adequately may result in the preparation of unrealistic job descriptions and specifications.

G. *Materials and Forms Used:* Please list the materials and forms used in the discharge of your job, including the frequency of use.

Materials and forms used	*Frequency of use*

H. *Source of Supervision:* Please identify, by title only, the individual(s) responsible for supervising your work, including the degree to which you are supervised.

Supervisor's title	*Degree of supervision*

I. *Contact with Others:* Please indicate with whom (outside your own department) you come in contact, the nature or purpose of the contact, and the medium through which the contact is made (phone, person, etc.). Include only company employees.

Contact with	*Nature of contact*	*Medium of contact*

J. *Working Conditions:* Please indicate to what extent your work is performed in undesirable or hazardous conditions. Consider such items as noise, temperature, air, lighting.

K. *Physical Requirements:* Please indicate the nature of any physical requirements for the job you hold.

L. *Responsibility Requirements:* Please indicate the nature of any responsbility you have for exercise of judgments, direction of others, and public relations.

M. *Physical Effort Requirements:* Please place a check mark (✓) in the appropriate columns.

	Very Frequently	*Frequently*	*Sometimes*	*Seldom*	*Never*
Walking	______	______	______	______	______
Sitting	______	______	______	______	______
Lifting	______	______	______	______	______
Reaching	______	______	______	______	______
Stooping	______	______	______	______	______
Standing	______	______	______	______	______
Other ______________	______	______	______	______	______
Other ______________	______	______	______	______	______

N. *Other Considerations:*

1. How long does it take to become familiar with this job?
2. What is the next job in the promotion channel?
3. What is the present salary for this job? (Give range)
4. Please provide any other information you care to that would assist in analyzing this job.

Figure 12-1 Continued.

A successful job analysis program requires the gathering of accurate and complete information. Situations to guard against are omission of important facts, inclusion of inaccurate information, or statements that misrepresent the importance of certain job attributes.

Situations for which the questionnaire method is especially appropriate are the following:

For what situations is the questionnaire method used?

1. When the job being analyzed can be described quite easily.
2. When the job being analyzed consists mostly of physical activities rather than human relations or personality factors. (Employees often have difficulty assessing the importance of job-related human relations or personality factors.)
3. When a considerable number of jobs are to be analyzed.
4. When the questionnaire can be precisely and clearly worded.
5. When job information has to be obtained quickly.

An alternative to developing a questionnaire for use in job analysis is the use of a standardized questionnaire. Among the more common standardized job analysis questionnaires are the Position Analysis Questionnaire (PAQ), the Task Abilities Scale, and the Management Position Description Questionnaire. The instruments used in each of these techniques are research based, and their use helps increase the reliability and validity of the survey results.

What are the characteristics of the Position Analysis Questionnaire?

The PAQ contains 194 elements in six major areas that include the following: information input, mental processes, work output, relationship with other persons, job context, and other job characteristics. Employees respond to each of the 194 elements, using a scale with six choices: *Does not apply, nominal/very infrequent, occasional, moderate, considerable,* and *very substantial.* The PAQ helps identify the behaviors involved in the performance of job tasks, duties, and responsibilities.

The questionnaire method facilitates the rapid collection of a large amount of information. Some organizations, however, supplement the questionnaire method with a combination of interviews and observations to ensure the collection of accurate information.

A potential disadvantage of the questionnaire method is the construction of an instrument that is too complex, confusing, or long to be effective. These conditions may result in the collection of inaccurate information. Another disadvantage of the questionnaire method is the tendency for some employees to overestimate or underestimate the importance of the jobs they perform. Finally, the information gathered on the questionnaire has to be collated and synthesized, which tends to be a time-consuming process.

Interview method The interview method involves questioning employees—either at their workstations or in the interviewer's office—about their job duties and responsibilities. Interviews conducted at the workstation enable the interviewer to observe the job during the interview process, which, in effect, combines the interview and observation methods of gathering job information.

In the same way that a printed questionnaire facilitates the questionnaire method, a **job information worksheet** facilitates the interview method. The items included on the job information worksheet are similar to the items included on the questionnaire. Accuracy and completeness of information can be increased by reading employees' responses back to them. Some organizations also have supervisors confirm the accuracy of the information their subordinates provide.

For what situations is the interview method used?

The interview method of gathering job information is appropriate in the following situations:

1. When the number of employees whose jobs are to be analyzed is quite small.
2. When the job being analyzed is quite complicated. (This method en-

ables the interviewer to ask questions of the employees until he or she sufficiently understands the job duties and responsibilities.)

3. When the interviewer's data-collection efforts are enhanced by observing the employee at work while talking with him or her about job tasks.
4. When the job being analyzed is largely comprised of human relations and personality factors.

The primary advantage of using the interview method is the ability of the interviewer to collect all the desired facts about a particular job. The occurrence of incomplete or omitted information, conditions sometimes found in the questionnaire method, is rare when using the interview method.

A disadvantage of the interview method is the time-consuming task of talking with each employee. The data-collection process is much slower than when using the questionnaire method. Furthermore, unless rapport is readily established between the interviewer and the employee, the completeness and accuracy of the employee's responses may be affected.

Observation method A third method of gathering job information involves observing the employee at work. Observations can take place either at the employee's workstation or at the various locations where the employee works. The analyst records the observations on a job observation sheet, which includes many of the same items found on a job questionnaire or the job information worksheet.

The observation method is appropriately used in the following instances:

For what situations is the observation method used?

1. When the nature of the job prohibits the employee's absence from his or her workstation.
2. When, because of the complexity of the job, the analyst has difficulty analyzing the job on the basis of the information gathered through a questionnaire or interview.
3. When the number of jobs to be analyzed is small.

The primary advantage of the observation method is the accuracy of the information the analyst can gather. In addition, the analyst is able to observe the employee for the needed length of time without interrupting the work flow.

A disadvantage of this method results from the time-consuming process of gathering information. Another possible disadvantage is the uncomfortable feeling some employees experience while being observed. Furthermore, some employees change their work patterns when they know they are being observed, which has the potential for distorting the results.

Combination of methods To obtain information about a particular job, two or more of the previously described methods can be combined. Using a combination of methods usually ensures accurate and complete input because of the ease with which information collected by one method can be verified by the second method. Therefore, details omitted while using one method will usually be obtained through the use of a second method. Having more accurate, complete information available may offset the disadvantages of using a more time-consuming, costly process.

An adaptation of the combination method is the **critical incidents tech-**

What are the characteristics of the critical incidents technique?

nique, which involves obtaining records of behavior (incidents) that led to either effective or ineffective job performance. These incidents are collected in a variety of ways including the use of questionnaires and interviews from both supervisors and employees. After the incidents are available, they are then grouped and placed into several categories. The list of critical incidents identifies the behaviors that employees in various positions need for successful job performance.

DESCRIBING THE JOB

One of the important outcomes of the job analysis program is the identification of duties and responsibilities comprising a particular job. When employees' duties are not formally determined or are not put into writing, management has less control over employee performance. In some cases, an employee might perform only those duties he or she is willing to perform. Formal written descriptions of jobs help to ensure that employees are performing their assigned duties. Descriptions also prevent job holders from gradually changing the nature of the job. Furthermore, descriptions help prevent misunderstandings between employees and their supervisors about specific job duties. The job needs to be described as it presently exists and not as the preparer of the description wishes it to exist.

Job descriptions and specifications can be combined into one document, or they may be maintained as two separate documents. Presenting them separately is advantageous when the information in the description and specification is used for different purposes, as is commonly the case.

Job Description

How can a job description be made more effective?

The use of clear, concise statements is crucial in preparing job descriptions. The following are offered as suggestions for writing effective job descriptions:

1. A simple, direct sentence structure should be used.
2. A functional verb in the present tense should be used to begin each sentence. Examples of such verbs are *plans*, *prepares*, and *originates*.
3. Conciseness can be achieved by eliminating all unnecessary words and phrases.
4. The description should focus on the skills involved in performing the job as well as on the tools and equipment used.
5. Job titles that appear in the description should be printed in all capital letters.
6. The content in the description should accurately reflect the nature of job duties.
7. The job description should be as thorough as possible.

Job titles in job descriptions should compare closely with the listings in the *Dictionary of Occupational Titles* (D.O.T.), a document prepared by the **U.S. Employment Service** in the U.S. Department of Labor. The latest edition of the D.O.T., which was published in 1991, contains data on approximately twenty thousand jobs.

The D.O.T. descriptions help standardize organizational job titles and descriptions. Standardized information is useful in reporting a variety of statistical information. In selecting the D.O.T. number to place on the job description, the number in the D.O.T. description that most closely matches the organization's description is used.

Figure 12-2 illustrates the D.O.T. job description for a clerical position.

Although job descriptions are not presented in a standard format, they typically consist of the following sections:

What sections are typically found in job descriptions?

1. *Job identification*. This section includes the title of the job, the level of the job, the department in which the job is found, the comparable D.O.T. number, and the date on which the job description was approved and adopted.
2. *Summary of job*. This section is a brief summary of the job. Sufficient information should be included in the summary so one can clearly differentiate between the job being described and other similar jobs.
3. *Duties of job*. This section clearly describes the primary duties and responsibilities of the job. The statements should identify the duties and responsibilities and their frequency of occurrence. To prevent ambiguities and possible misunderstanding, uncommon duties and responsibilities should be explained in sufficient detail and with sufficient justification. Although the following items may be included in other sections of the job description, they may also be included as part of this section: (a) identification of the tools and equipment, forms, and materials used in carrying out the job; (b) title of the indi-

203.362-022 WORD PROCESSING-MACHINE OPERATOR (clerical) word processor.
Operates word processing equipment to record, edit, store, and revise correspondence, reports, statistical tables, forms, and other materials, utilizing clerical skills and knowledge of word processing functions. Reads instructions to determine procedures to be followed regarding material to be prepared or revised and required format for finished copy. Depresses keys on word processing equipment to adjust controls for spacing, margins, and tabulation, and places tape cassette, diskette, or other magnetic recording medium in holder. Keyboards (types) original material into machine memory, typing from printed copy, machine dictation, or related sources. Reads proof copy of material entered into machine memory, and depresses keys to correct typographical errors, print out final copy, and record material onto magnetic medium. Locates medium in file when revisions are required, places medium in holder and presses keys to insert (type), delete, correct, reposition, or reformat designated material. May operate equipment that extends word processing capabilities, such as cathode ray tube (CRT) displays, single or multiple printers, or optical character recognition (OCR). Important variations are kinds (trade names) of word processing equipment operated. May operate electronic typewriters with limited editing capabilities. GOE 07.06. 02 PD S 08 09 10 12 13 15 M1 L3 SVP 4 SOC 4624

Figure 12-2 D.O.T. job description. *Dictionary of Occupational Titles.*

vidual responsible for supervising the job holder and the degree of supervision received; and (c) relationship of the work flow, transfer, and promotion characteristics between the job being described and other similar jobs.

A description is illustrated in Figure 12-3.

Title of Job	Secretary	D.O.T. Number	201.368
Level of Job	Level III	Date Approved	11/30/XX
Department	Office Services		

SUMMARY OF JOB: The individual holding this job performs secretarial duties for the manager of the department. Since the job involves relieving the manager of some of his or her administrative duties, a considerable amount of the work is administrative in nature. The individual also supervises other office employees.

DUTIES OF JOB:

Most Frequent Duties: (Comprising at least 70 percent of work day)

1. Taking dictation and transcribing materials
2. Keeping manager's appointments calendar
3. Supervising other office employees
4. Working with office budget
5. Answering correspondence
6. Protecting confidentiality of materials
7. Acting as RECEPTIONIST for manager's callers
8. Answering telephone
9. Preparing weekly salary data
10. Allocating work among others

Least Frequent Duties: (Comprising not more than 30 percent of work day)

1. Filing documents and materials
2. Preparing reports
3. Designing interoffice forms
4. Evaluating subordinates
5. Duplicating materials
6. Maintaining petty cash

TOOLS AND EQUIPMENT USED:

Typewriter, computer, calculator, copy machine, dictation equipment

FORMS AND REPORTS USED ON JOB:

Departmental budget, payroll forms, personnel evaluation forms, petty cash disbursements, and other office reports as called for

SUPERVISED BY: DEPARTMENT MANAGER

RELATION TO OTHER JOBS:

This position is related to all other secretarial and clerical jobs in the department, since the individual is responsible for assigning work to other employees.

Since this position is the highest secretarial position in the department, promotion possibilities include a secretarial position in the central offices or as an ADMINISTRATIVE ASSISTANT.

Figure 12-3 Job description.

Job Specification

Like the material in the job description, the content of the job specification is not presented in a standard format. The writing guidelines given for presenting job descriptions are also appropriate for presenting job specifications.

Job specifications typically consist of some or all of the following parts:

What sections are typically found in job specifications?

1. *Job identification*. This section includes the title of the job, the level of the job, the point value of the job (if appropriate), the department in which the job is found, the comparable D.O.T. number, and the date on which the job specification was approved and adopted. In addition, a column may be provided on the right side of the specification for the purpose of recording the number of points assigned each factor during the job evaluation process.
2. *Experience requirements*. This section is used to specify the minimum experience requirements. In addition to specifying the nature of the requirements, the statement should include the required number of years of experience.
3. *Educational requirements*. Identified in this section are the minimum educational requirements for the job holder. Any required courses or technical training should also be listed.
4. *Human relations requirements*. This section specifies human relations and personality factors required of the job holder. Although the nature of these factors is difficult to assess, many times they are critically important in the performance of a particular job. Typically included are personality traits, initiative, ambition, resourcefulness, and cooperation.
5. *Job knowledge requirements*. This section identifies any job knowledge requirements not covered in the experience and educational sections. Typically included are such items as tools, equipment, and materials.
6. *Responsibility requirements*. This section provides a description of the areas of responsibility for the job being described. The extent of the responsibility should also be included in the description. Possible areas of responsibility are safety, equipment and materials, other employees, work of others, quality of work, and cost reduction.
7. *Skill requirements*. Provided in this section is a list of the skills required to perform the job. If different skill levels exist, the level of skill required should also be identified. Examples of skill levels are variable typing or keyboarding rates and machine operation rates.
8. *Physical effort requirements*. This section of the job specification describes the nature of the physical effort requirements including such factors as walking, sitting, lifting, reaching, stooping, and standing. The specification should stipulate the amount of physical effort required and the amount of time consumed by each type of physical effort.
9. *Environmental conditions*. Described in this section are the conditions and surroundings under which the job is performed. Factors to be included are lighting, air, temperature, and noise levels.

A representative job specification is illustrated in Figure 12-4.

Only justifiable personal requirements should be included in a job specification. Sometimes specifications are prepared that include requirements more strenuous than may be necessary. Trying to justify a keyboarding rate of seventy words a minute is difficult when a fifty words-per-minute rate is adequate for the demands of the job.

Title of Job	Secretary	D.O.T. Number	201.368
Level of Job	Level III	Date Approved	11/30/XX
Department	Office Services	Point Value	270

	RATING Points
EXPERIENCE REQUIREMENTS: A minimum of 3 years' previous experience is required.	40
EDUCATIONAL REQUIREMENTS: A high school diploma is required and some college work is desirable.	30
HUMAN RELATIONS REQUIREMENTS: Ability to get along well with people, to meet people, to be creative, and to cope with stress stiuations.	40
JOB KNOWLEDGE REQUIREMENTS: Ability to perform bookkeeping functions and to use calculating equipment, in addition to regular secretarial requirements.	50
RESPONSIBILITY REQUIREMENTS: Responsibility for assuring the quality of work of others, as well as being responsible for assuring the maintenance of equipment.	50
SKILL REQUIREMENTS: Ability to type 60 words a minute and ability to take shorthand at 100 words a minute.	50
PHYSICAL REQUIREMENTS: Must be able to sit for long periods of time.	10

Figure 12-4 Job specification.

State and federal laws prevent the use of age, sex, race, religion, and color as a basis for identifying job requirements. Job specifications should be reviewed periodically to determine if any requirements are discriminatory or ambiguous.

Uses of Job Descriptions and Job Specifications

The value of job descriptions and specifications is determined by how they are used. Both documents should be readily available to job holders and their supervisors.

What uses are made of job descriptions and job specifications?

Appropriate uses of job descriptions are the following:

1. To inform the job holder about the duties and responsibilities of his or her job.
2. To assist the job holder in improving his or her job performance.
3. To assist the job holder in preparing for promotion or transfer.
4. To facilitate orientation and training of new employees.
5. To assist in the arbitration of employee grievances.

The uses of job specifications are the following:

1. To facilitate recruitment and selection of employees, especially in screening job applicants.
2. To facilitate the job evaluation process.

IMPLICATIONS FOR THE ADMINISTRATIVE OFFICE MANAGER

The administrative office manager has important responsibilities in job analysis activities. In many organizations, the administrative office manager serves as a key member of the job analysis advisory committee. In addition, managers are often responsible for communicating information to their subordinates about key aspects of job analysis activities including benefits and uses. The manager is also responsible for motivating his or her subordinates to provide accurate responses in job information collection efforts.

The absence of job analysis information can be a serious impediment to the effective management of organizational functions and to employee supervision. For example, when job information is unavailable, managers cannot be sure that positions are properly designed or that employees have equitable workloads. Nor can they be sure that employees' salaries are properly related to the importance of job duties.

The absence of job analysis information unnecessarily compounds the employee selection process. Job descriptions and job specifications that are prepared on the basis of job analysis information are integral components of the employee selection process. The absence of job descriptions also compounds the difficulty of employee supervision because neither the supervisor nor the employee can be certain of the official duties that a job comprises. Lack of certainty about appropriate job duties often creates disagreements, which may impede the development of effective supervisor-subordinate relations.

REVIEW QUESTIONS

1. How do job analysis, job descriptions, and job specifications differ from one another?
2. Are job analysis and time and motion study related to one another? Explain.
3. Identify the benefits of job analysis.
4. In what situations is the questionnaire method of job analysis especially suitable?
5. In what situations is the interview method of job analysis especially suitable?
6. In what situations is the observation method of job analysis especially suitable?
7. What suggestions can you offer for writing effective job descriptions?
8. In what ways are job descriptions and job specifications used?

DISCUSSION QUESTIONS

1. The speaker at a meeting you recently attended was asked a question about the appropriate uses made of information collected in job analysis. The speaker replied by saying, "There is only one legitimate use of information collected during job analysis and that is to provide input for preparing job descriptions and job specifications. The use of this information for any other purposes cannot be justified." Do you agree or disagree with the speaker's comment about what constitutes a proper use of job analysis information? Justify your response.
2. You are on a committee recently formed to provide input for use in undertaking a thorough analysis of the jobs in the organization in which you work. When committee members were discussing the design of an employee questionnaire, one member said that he felt employees should not be given questionnaires to complete because they won't provide accurate responses. He indicated he felt the supervisors should complete

these questionnaires on behalf of their subordinates because they have a "better idea of what is going on." Do you believe this employee's comment about not having employees complete job analysis questionnaires is valid? Discuss the implications of this situation.

3. One of the benefits of job analysis that was identified in this chapter is that it "enables each employee to better understand job duties and responsibilities." Explain why this is a true statement.
4. An article pertaining to job analysis that you read recently advocated using only one technique to gather information from employees about their jobs. The writer of this article mentioned the necessity to curtail costs—and using a combination of methods increases the cost of the program. The writer concluded by saying that if employees are subjected to two methods, they may conclude that management does not trust them and that the second method is used only to "spy" on employees. Do you agree with the writer of this article? Defend your response.
5. You work in a small company currently developing a job analysis questionnaire to be completed by its employees. When you recently asked the person who is in charge of job analysis the reason for choosing the questionnaire technique, he replied, "That is the only method that anyone in our company knows how to use. To use any other method would require our bringing in an expensive consultant that we simply cannot afford." Discuss the implications of the way this company is undertaking its job analysis efforts.
6. At a recent staff meeting, the supervisor of your unit announced that some of the employees in the unit will be observed soon to gather information for use in analyzing jobs. One of the workers in this unit continually tries to undermine the supervisor. Just as soon as the meeting was over, this worker went around to other employees and suggested that all of them sabotage their work performance to "throw off" the validity of the data. He also told the employees that this information will eventually work against their best interests. What are some of the implications of this worker's suggestion that they sabotage their work performance? What suggestions can be made to help prevent this from occurring?

STUDENT PROJECTS AND ACTIVITIES

1. Obtain a job analysis questionnaire used in analyzing the jobs of office employees. How does its content compare with the content of the job analysis questionnaire found in this chapter?
2. Obtain the job descriptions for two comparable jobs. What are the similarities in the identified tasks? The differences?
3. Obtain the job specifications for two comparable jobs. What are the similarities in the identified qualifications? The differences?
4. Talk with an office employee to obtain his or her perception of the value of job analysis.
5. Obtain from the D.O.T. the description for an administrative office manager's (or office manager's) position.

MINICASE

The Rebecca Company, a cosmetics manufacturer, recently undertook an extensive job analysis program. The data have all been collected, and a committee has been organized to revise job descriptions and job specifications for the office positions in the organization. One committee member suggested at a recent meeting that skills requirements be stated at a high level, primarily to screen out "undesirables." This individual also indicated that the high skill requirements could be waived when an applicant was found whom the company wanted to hire.

1. Discuss the implications of the suggestion made by the committee member who advocated putting high skill requirements on the job specification.
2. How can an organization ensure that the requirements presented on the job specification are realistic?

CASE

A few years ago, Dartmouth Industries, a toy manufacturer in Buffalo, New York, undertook a thorough analysis of its jobs. For a variety of reasons, this endeavor was generally regarded as having created several problems, some of which continue to prevail. A large share of the problems that resulted can be attributed to the personnel manager who was in charge of the job analysis efforts.

The personnel manager, according to many sources, was using job analysis to "get even" with the employees because of their entering into collective bargaining. The sources believed that because the personnel manager was indeed the one who "lost" on collective bargaining, he would "win" on job analysis.

Even though this personnel manager continues to work for Dartmouth, some of the negative sentiment toward job analysis has subsided. Obviously, no one wants the same mistake to be repeated during the pending job analysis efforts.

1. Outline the committee's charge regarding its undertaking an organization-wide analysis of all nonmanagement jobs found within Dartmouth.
2. Explain the need for the committee to be reasonable, fair, and nonjudgmental in its efforts, thus helping avoid the problems that plagued the earlier job evaluation efforts.
3. Outline steps you would like the committee to use during the upcoming job analysis, thus preventing a recurrence of the problems with the earlier job analysis efforts.

CHAPTER

13

EVALUATING JOBS OF OFFICE EMPLOYEES

CHAPTER AIM

After studying this chapter, you should be able to design an effective program for evaluating the jobs of office employees.

CHAPTER OUTLINE

CHAPTER TERMS

Factor comparison
Job classification
Job evaluation
Job grading
Key jobs
Monetary comparison scale
Nonkey jobs
Nonquantitative method
Point evaluation
Quantitative method
Ranking
Standard job description

Organizations use **job evaluation** to provide information about the relative worth of jobs, which, in turn, helps determine their monetary worth. The process of evaluating jobs uses the information collected through job analysis, the topic of Chapter 12.

What are the benefits of a formally established job evaluation program?

A formal job evaluation program is beneficial for several reasons. Job evaluation is used to provide an objective determination of the value of each job. Determining job worth by any other means is apt to produce subjective results. In addition, employees are more likely to accept the relative values of their positions when job evaluation is the process used to determine job worth. Job evaluation gives employees a greater appreciation for and understanding of the relationship between the demands of their jobs and their compensation. It also helps reduce the number of employee complaints about wage inequities.

Another benefit of job evaluation is its use in identifying lines of authority and patterns of advancement within an organization. It can also be used to identify areas appropriate for new employee orientation and training as well as to facilitate employee transfer.

JOB EVALUATION METHODS

How do the nonquantitative and quantitative methods of job evaluation differ from one another?

Two types of job evaluation methods are used: nonquantitative and quantitative. A **nonquantitative method** of job evaluation involves evaluating a job as a whole job rather than evaluating it on the basis of its parts. When job parts or job factors provide the evaluation basis, however, a **quantitative method** is being used. The two most popular nonquantitative methods of job evaluation are ranking and job grading. Of the quantitative methods, factor comparison and point evaluation are the most popular.

Ranking

What are the characteristics of the ranking method?

Of the various job evaluation methods, the simplest and oldest method is the **ranking** or order-of-merit system. The job description and specification for each job are used in the evaluation process. After the relative importance of all the jobs being evaluated is determined, then each job is assigned to a specific job level. The individual or the committee doing the evaluating is responsible for determining the number of job levels.

Three steps constitute the ranking method: (1) the number of different levels to be used in the job evaluation process is determined, (2) by means of a ranking device, the various jobs are ranked from the most important to the least important; and (3) each job is assigned to one of the predetermined job levels.

Illustrated in Figure 13-1 are two aspects of the ranking method of job evaluation: (1) the rank of each job, from the least important to the most important, and (2) the level to which each job is assigned. After the jobs are ranked, the next step involves determining the range of pay for each of the job levels. For an organization to remain competitive, it has to provide salaries comparable to those paid by other organizations in the community. Methods of gathering information about salary rates in other organizations in the community are covered in Chapter 14.

Figure 13-2 illustrates the range of pay for each job level included in Figure 13-1. For example, job level 6, which includes the administrative secretary I and the correspondence secretary II positions, was found to have an average monthly salary of $2,100 in other organizations in the community. In the or-

Job title	*Job level*
Messenger	1
Mail Clerk	2
Requisitions Clerk	2
File Clerk	3
Data Entry Operator I	3
Micrographics Clerk	4
Data Entry Operator II	5
Correspondence Secretary I	5
Administrative Secretary I	6
Correspondence Secretary II	6
Administrative Secretary II	7
Correspondence Secretary III	7
Computer Programmer	7
Administrative Secretary III	8
Executive Secretary	8
Administrative Assistant	9
Systems Analyst	9

Figure 13-1 Ranking method of job evaluation.

Job level	*Average salary paid for job level in other organizations*	*Salary range*		
		Minimum	*Midpoint*	*Maximum*
1	$1,270	$1,180	$1,260	$1,340
2	1,200	1,200	1,300	1,400
3	1,350	1,230	1,340	1,450
4	1,510	1,380	1,500	1,620
5	1,840	1,720	1,850	1,980
6	2,100	1,940	2,080	2,220
7	2,350	2,180	2,330	2,480
8	2,590	2,440	2,600	2,760
9	3,210	2,940	3,200	3,460

Figure 13-2 Salary ranges.

ganization for which this salary scale was prepared, job level 6 has a monthly salary range of $1,940 to $2,220 with $2,080 per month as the midpoint salary. Creating a salary range for each job enables an organization to compensate employees on the basis of their performance and longevity with the organization.

The ranking of jobs is frequently done by means of index cards. The title of each job is placed on a separate card, and the cards are then arranged and rearranged until they are sorted in the order of job importance.

The ranking method is frequently limited to situations in which a minimum number of jobs is to be evaluated. The method becomes too cumbersome when more than twenty-five to thirty jobs are being considered. Because the ranking method is a fairly quick and inexpensive evaluation method, it is also appropriately used when time and financial cost are important considerations.

The use of the ranking method results in several advantages: It is readily understood by employees, it is a fairly quick and simple method to use, and it is fairly inexpensive to install.

What are the disadvantages of the ranking method?

The use of the ranking method also results in several disadvantages. It does not provide a highly refined index of job worth because comparisons are made on the basis of the job as a whole job and not on the basis of its parts or factors. The importance of the job may be influenced by the job holder. In addition, job ranking may be influenced by the going wage and salary rates rather than by actual importance.

Job Grading

The **job grading** method (also known as **job classification**) is another of the nonquantitative methods of job evaluation. The job grading method is used in the federal civil service system.

What are the characteristics of the job grading method?

The grading method involves evaluating jobs on the basis of a number of predetermined classes or grades. Several factors affect the number of classes or grades used including the nature of job duties, responsibilities, skills, and knowledges. Once the predetermined classes have been set, standard job descriptions are prepared. More objectivity can be achieved if an organization compares its **standard job descriptions** with those of similar organizations. The competitive salary ranges are developed in much the same way as the ranges are developed for the ranking method. Each job is then compared with the standard job description to determine the level of best fit.

What is a standard job description?

Generally, different standard job descriptions have to be developed for each of the family groups found in an organization. These groups typically include clerical, stenographic, sales, accounting, and data processing categories.

Figure 13-3 illustrates a standard job description for clerical positions.

To summarize, the job grading method comprises the following four steps:

1. The predetermined classes of jobs are designated.
2. A standard job description is prepared for each of the predetermined classes.
3. The jobs are placed into the various predetermined classes.
4. Each job is compared with the various levels outlined on the standard job description to determine the level into which the job should be placed.

When is the job grading method typically used?

Figure 13-4 illustrates the job grading method of evaluating clerical, stenographic, and data processing jobs. For example, the lowest level clerical job is assigned level 1, while the lowest level stenographic and data processing positions are assigned to levels 3 and 2, respectively. The highest-ranked data processing position (systems analyst) is considered more important than the highest-ranked clerical and stenographic positions. The file clerk position, for example, is most comparable with level 3 on the standard job description. For this reason, the file clerk has been graded as level 3.

The job grading method is appropriately used in the following three situations: (1) when the organization has too many jobs for the ranking method to be used effectively; (2) when the organization consists of several different family groupings of jobs (clerical, stenographic, data processing, accounting, for example); and (3) when time and cost are of some consideration.

The job grading method is rather inexpensive to use. It is an easy method to explain to employees, and employees tend to accept the evaluation results quite readily.

Level 1

Job duties include mail sorting, simple typing, some filing. There is almost no responsibility for decision making and use of judgment. The job requires no special equipment or special skills or knowledges.

Level 2

Job duties include working with records (other than indexing or coding) and typing. There is very little responsibility for decision making and use of judgment. No specialized equipment is used, nor are any special skills or knowledge required.

Level 3

Job duties include indexing and coding records and filing records, as well as typing. There is some responsibility for decision making and judgment, some specialized equipment is used, and a knowledge of indexing and coding rules is required.

Level 4

Job duties include typing, machine calculations, filing. There is an average amount of responsibility for decision making and use of judgment. This level requires the use of various calculating machines.

Level 5

Job duties include complex typing, machine calculations, and filing. There is an above-average responsibility for decision making and use of judgment. A knowledge of calculating machines is required.

Level 6

Job duties include typing and transcription. There is a considerable amount of responsibility for decision making and use of judgment. This level also requires the use of dictation-transcription equipment, and special skills and knowledge required include ability to operate word processing equipment and ability to proofread and use punctuation and grammar properly.

Level 7

Job duties include typing and complex transcription. There is extensive responsibility for decision making and use of judgment. The use of dictation-transcription equipment is required as is the ability to proofread and to use punctuation and grammar properly.

Figure 13-3 Standard job description.

Level	*Clerical*	*Stenographic*	*Data processing*
1	Mail Clerk		
2	Requisitions Clerk		Data Entry Operator I
3	File Clerk	Secretary I	
4	Clerk Typist I		Data Entry Operator II
5	Clerk Typist II	Secretary II	
6	Word Processing Typist I		
7	Word Processing Typist II	Executive Secretary	Computer Programmer
8			
9		Admin. Assistant	Computer Technician
10			
11			Systems Analyst

Figure 13-4 Job grading method of job evaluation.

A disadvantage of the job grading method results when overlap occurs between two of the levels in the standard job descriptions. The whole job is evaluated without regard for the proportionate importance of specific job parts or factors. Also, the importance of a particular job may be somewhat biased by current rates of pay or by certain job holders.

Factor Comparison

As a quantitative method of job evaluation, **factor comparison** determines the relative worth of jobs on the basis of their parts rather than on the basis of whole jobs. Although the factors vary from organization to organization, the five factors that seem to be most frequently used are the following:

What factors are typically included in the factor comparison method of job evaluation?

1. Skill requirements
2. Mental requirements
3. Physical requirements
4. Responsibility requirements
5. Environmental requirements

The factor comparison method consists of six well-defined steps:

Step 1. **Key jobs** are identified.

Step 2. Key jobs are ranked factor by factor.

Step 3. Salary is apportioned among each factor, and key jobs are ranked accordingly.

Step 4. Factor ranking of each job is compared with its monetary ranking.

Step 5. **Monetary comparison scale** is developed.

Step 6. **Nonkey jobs** are evaluated using the monetary comparison scale as a basis.

What steps constitute the factor comparison method of job evaluation?

Step 1 For this step, fifteen to twenty key jobs are usually considered a sufficient number. The key jobs should be somewhat standard, they should vary in difficulty and importance, and salary rates for the key jobs should be internally and externally consistent.

Step 2 This step consists of ranking the key jobs, factor by factor, using job importance as a basis for the ranking. The ranking technique discussed previously is also suitable for ranking jobs when using this method. To ensure greater consistency of results among rates when a committee is responsible for the ranking process, common definitions should be developed for each of the factors. For example, the common definition of skill might be as follows: a technical proficiency (usually physical or manual) developed either through education or actual experience or by a combination of both. The factor ranking (FR) of jobs can be facilitated by preparing a chart similar to that in Figure 13-5. (For expediency, fewer than the normal number of jobs will be used to illustrate this method.)

Illustrated in Figure 13-5 is the factor ranking of each of the five key jobs. For example, although the skill requirements are the most extensive for the executive secretary, they are the least extensive for the messenger.

Step 3 This step consists of apportioning the monetary worth of the key jobs among each of the factors. The importance of each factor to each key job is the basis of the apportionment. The job evaluation committee determines the relative importance of each job factor, and the more important job

	Factor ranking				
	Skill	*Mental*	*Physical*	*Responsibility*	*Environment*
Exec. Secretary	1	1	4	1	4
File Clerk	4	4	2	3	3
Data Entry Operator	3	3	3	4	1
Messenger	5	5	1	5	2
Secretary I	2	2	5	2	5

Figure 13-5 Factor ranking of key jobs.

factors will receive a greater proportion of the total salary. For example, Figure 13-6 indicates that skill is the most important factor in the executive secretary position because it receives a greater proportion of the total salary. As illustrated, the executive secretary position pays an average monthly salary of \$1,865. Of the total monthly salary, \$485 is paid for skill requirements; \$375 for mental requirements; \$315 for physical requirements; \$405 for responsibility requirements; and \$285 for environmental conditions.

Following the apportionment of the total monthly salary among each of the factors, they are then ranked according to their salary components. These results are illustrated in Figure 13-6 under the monetary ranking (MR) columns. As an example, the executive secretary position with a \$485 allocation for skill ranks first among the key jobs, whereas the messenger with a \$265 allocation ranks last.

Step 4 This step involves comparing the factor ranking of key jobs with the monetary ranking of key jobs. A chart similar to the one illustrated in Figure 13-7 facilitates the comparison. The figures in the factor ranking column come from Figure 13-5; the figures in the monetary ranking column come from Figure 13-6.

When a disagreement exists between the factor rankings and the monetary rankings, adjustments are made to bring the rankings into agreement with one another. The job evaluation committee must decide whether to adjust the factor ranking or to change the salary apportionment, which will affect the monetary ranking. In Figure 13-7, the rankings for mental requirements of the file clerk and the data entry operator illustrate a situation in which the rankings did not agree during the preliminary evaluation procedures. The numbers in the parentheses represent the new rankings. For example, the original factor ranking for mental requirements for the file clerk was ranked as 4, and the data entry operator was ranked as 3. To bring the

	Average Monthly Salary	*Skill*		*Mental*		*Physical*		*Responsibility*		*Environmental*	
		Prop.	*MR*	*Prop.*	*MR*	*Prop.*	*MR*	*Prop.*	*MR*	*Prop.*	*MR*
Executive Secretary	\$1,865	\$485	1	\$375	1	\$315	4	\$405	1	\$285	4
File Clerk	1,635	315	4	305	3	345	2	335	3	335	3
Data Entry Operator	1,685	365	3	295	4	335	3	325	4	365	1
Messenger	1,545	265	5	275	5	365	1	285	5	355	2
Secretary I	1,745	465	2	335	2	305	5	365	2	275	5

Figure 13-6 Proportion and monetary rank of each factor.

	Skill		*Mental*		*Physical*		*Responsibility*		*Environment*	
	FR	*MR*	*FR*	*MR*	*FR*	*MR*	*FR*	*MR*	*FR*	*MR*
Exec. Secretary	1	1	1	1	4	4	1	1	4	4
File Clerk	4	4	4	3	2	2	3	3	3	3
Data Entry Operator	3	3	3	4	3	3	4	4	1	1
Messenger	5	5	5	5	1	1	5	5	2	2
Secretary I	2	2	2	2	5	5	2	2	5	5

Figure 13-7 Comparison of factor ranking and monetary ranking of key jobs.

rankings into agreement, the factor rankings of the two positions were reevaluated, and the numbers in the parentheses represent the final rankings.

For what is a monetary comparison scale used?

Step 5 The fifth step in the factor comparison method is the development of a monetary comparison scale similar to the one shown in Figure 13-8. This scale facilitates determining the worth of each nonkey job. The monetary worth of each of the five factors constituting each key job is then placed on the scale. This information is obtained from the proportion column in Figure 13-6.

Salary	*Skill*	*Mental*	*Physical*	*Responsibility*	*Environmental*
$545					
535					
525					
515					
505					
495					
485	Exec. Sec.				
475					
465	Sec. I				
455					
445					
435					
425					
415					
405				Exec. Sec.	
395					
385					
375		Exec. Sec.			
365	Dt. Ent. Op.		Messenger	Sec. I	Dt. Ent. Op.
355					Messenger
345			File Clerk		
335		Sec. I	Dt. Ent. Op.	File Clerk	File Clerk
325				Dt. Ent. Op.	
315	File Clerk		Exec. Sec.		
305		File Clerk	Sec. I		
295		Dt. Ent. Op.			
285				Messenger	Exec. Sec.
275		Messenger			Sec. I
265	Messenger				
255					

Figure 13-8 Monetary comparison scale.

Step 6 The final step consists of evaluating each of the nonkey jobs, using the monetary comparison scale as a reference point. The position of each key job on the monetary comparison scale serves as a guide for evaluating the nonkey jobs. As each nonkey job is evaluated, factor by factor, the monetary value of each factor is entered on the scale. Evaluation is facilitated by examining the relationship between the job being evaluated and the jobs already entered on the scale. The monetary worth of each nonkey job is determined by totaling the monetary values assigned to each factor.

The factor comparison method of job evaluation is primarily used when job factors vary too much to use one of the whole-job evaluation methods. It is appropriately used in organizations with a large variety of jobs to be evaluated.

The following are advantages of the factor comparison method:

What are the advantages of the factor comparison method?

1. It provides more accurate results than either the ranking or job grading methods of job evaluation because it compares factors against factors.
2. Because different evaluative factors may be selected, factor comparison can be designed to meet the specific needs of the organization.
3. The actual worth of each factor is easily determined.
4. The evaluation of nonkey jobs is simplified greatly by using a device such as the monetary comparison scale.

Disadvantages of the factor comparison method are the following:

1. Periodic adjustment of salary rates may result in the development of inequities in the organization's salary structure.
2. Inequities in salary rates of key jobs will affect the evaluated worth of nonkey jobs.
3. A wrong interpretation of the importance of any one of the factors can cause a serious error in the evaluated worth of a job.
4. Because of the complicated nature of the method, explaining the system to employees is sometimes difficult, and employees sometimes have difficulty understanding the system.

Point Evaluation

What are the characteristics of the point evaluation method of job evaluation?

The most commonly used evaluation technique is the **point evaluation** method in which jobs are evaluated on the basis of such factors as job skills, effort, responsibilities, and working conditions. The factors are divided into degrees, and each degree is assigned a specific number of points.

Figure 13-9, as an example, illustrates (1) the four typical job factors, (2) the subfactors that constitute each of the factors, (3) the degrees for each of the subfactors, and (4) the number of points allocated to each of the degrees. The percentages found beside each of the four primary job factors indicate the importance of each factor to the whole job.

A reasonable amount of judgment must be exercised in selecting factors and subfactors used in point evaluation. In large, complex organizations, several plans may have to be developed, because what is appropriate for evaluating office jobs, for example, is not appropriate for evaluating factory jobs. The factors and subfactors that are chosen must be appropriate for the needs of the organization as well as representative of the jobs. Generally, eight to sixteen subfactors are sufficient for this method.

Factors	*First degree*	*Second degree*	*Third degree*	*Fourth degree*	*Fifth degree*
Skill (30%)					
1. Education	10	20	30	40	50
2. Experience	10	20	30	40	50
3. Job knowledge	15	30	45	60	75
4. Manual dexterity	5	10	15	20	25
Effort (25%)					
5. Physical	10	20	30	40	50
6. Mental	10	20	30	40	50
7. Visual	5	10	15	20	25
Responsibility (30%)					
8. Equipment/tools	8	16	24	32	40
9. Materials/products	10	20	30	40	50
10. Work of others	5	10	15	20	25
Job conditions (15%)					
11. Surroundings	10	20	30	40	50
12. Hazards	5	10	15	20	25
13. Safety of others	5	10	15	20	25

Figure 13-9 Allocation of points for job factors.

What information is found in the point manual?

Point manual The point evaluation method requires the preparation of a manual that describes each of the degrees into which the subfactors have been divided. The manual also lists the number of points allocated to each of the degrees.

Care should be taken to select only subfactors that are pertinent to the jobs being evaluated. Likewise, care should be taken to eliminate subfactors that tend to overlap with others, that cannot be clearly defined, or that tend to evaluate personal rather than job factors.

When selecting the appropriate number of degrees, two conditions should be considered: the relative importance assigned to each subfactor and the ease with which individual degrees can be defined. Although Figure 13-9 shows five degrees for each subfactor, in some instances, subfactors are divided into as few as 3 degrees, whereas others are divided into as many as 8 degrees.

Two methods are generally used to assign the number of points to each degree: (1) the straight arithmetic method by which the points increase by a constant amount (for example, 10, 20, 30, 40 or 8, 16, 24); and (2) the geometric progression method by which the points increase by a constant percentage (such as 3, 6, 12, 24). Figure 13-10 illustrates a partial point manual with descriptions for office jobs.

A variety of trade associations, management consulting firms, and companies have developed point manuals. Among the more widely used manuals are those prepared by the National Metal Trades Association and the National Electrical Manufacturers Association. When one of the prepared manuals is adopted, care must be taken to ensure that the manual meets the specific needs of the organization in which it is being used.

Evaluating the jobs The last step involves evaluating each job. The job specification is compared subfactor by subfactor with the degree or level descriptions in the point manual. When the appropriate degree is determined, the actual job factor is then assigned the corresponding number of points. Each

EDUCATION: This subfactor is concerned with the nature of the educational experience of the employee. High school equivalency certificates will be accepted in lieu of a high school diploma. As far as college work is concerned, community college and business and/or technical school attendance is accepted. Work taken in adult education programs does not count as college-level work.

Degree	*Points*	*Description*
1st	10	Less than high school diploma
2nd	20	High school diploma but no college work
3rd	30	High school diploma and not more than 2 years (60 semester hours) of college work.
4th	40	High school diploma, at least 2 years (60 semester hours) of college work, but no college degree
5th	50	College graduate

EXPERIENCE: This subfactor is concerned with the amount of time that it takes an employee to obtain and develop skills necessary to perform a particular job. It is assumed that the individual already possesses the required job knowledge before starting the time element involved in the experience factor. Any previously obtained experience, either inside or outside the organization, is recognized.

Degree	*Points*	*Description*
1st	10	Up to and including three months' experience
2nd	20	Over three months' but less than one year of experience
3rd	30	Over one year but less than two years' experience
4th	40	Over two years' but less than four years' experience
5th	50	Over four years of experience

PHYSICAL: This subfactor is concerned with the amount of physical effort expended in carrying out the duties of the job. In determining the appropriate level to which a particular job is to be assigned, "normal" efficiency in carrying out the duties should be used as a guidline.

Degree	*Points*	*Description*
1st	10	This level involves a balance of physical effort: sitting, standing, or walking. Included in this level are those office jobs with a normal amount of physical effort.
2nd	20	This level involves expending a considerable amount of physical effort through the job holder's moving around a considerable amount.
3rd	30	This level involves expending physical effort through one continuous activity, such as sitting, typing, machine operation, etc. Some lifting may be involved; the job holder typically works for a long period in one position.
4th	40	This level involves a considerable amount of walking or standing, especially for long periods
5th	50	This level involves continuous standing in one place or a considerable amount of walking or lifting for long periods.

Figure 13-10 Point manual (office jobs).

point value is also entered on the job specification. After each factor has been evaluated, the relative worth of the job is determined by adding the total number of points assigned to the various factors. The total points value for each job is subsequently converted into salary rates, as illustrated in Figure 13-11.

Total Points	*Midpoint*	*Minimum*	*Maximum*
0–300	$1,700	$1,600	$1,800
301–320	1,750	1,640	1,860
321–340	1,800	1,680	1,920
341–360	1,840	1,720	1,960
361–380	1,870	1,740	2,000
381–400	1,920	1,770	2,070
401–420	2,000	1,840	2,160

Figure 13-11 Salary range: point evaluation.

What steps constitute the point method of job evaluation?

To recap, the point method of job evaluation involves five steps. First, the factors and their relative worth are determined. Second, the factors are then divided into subfactors. Third, the point manual is developed, specifying the number of points assigned to each degree for the various subfactors. Fourth, the job specification of each job is compared subfactor by subfactor with the degree descriptions in the point manual as a means of determining the appropriate number of points to assign each subfactor. Finally, the points assigned to each subfactor are added to determine the worth of the job. The higher the number of points a job receives, the greater is its importance.

The point evaluation method is appropriately used in organizations that have a considerable number of diversified jobs. When intraorganizational problems require the use of a sophisticated job evaluation method, this one is appropriate.

The advantages of using the point evaluation method are the following:

What are the advantages of the point evaluation method?

1. Of all the methods, it is the most difficult to manipulate; and only minimal opportunity exists for pressure to be exerted on the individual or committee doing the evaluating.
2. The method has a high degree of objectivity and consistency of results.
3. Salary increases can be given that do not affect the evaluated jobs because the point values of the jobs stay the same until the components of the job are changed.
4. Because of the flexibility in selecting subfactors, degrees, and points, developing a system tailor-made for the organization is possible.

The disadvantages are the following:

What are the disadvantages of the point evaluation method?

1. Developing a point manual can be a difficult, time-consuming task.
2. Hiring specially trained personnel to install the system may be necessary.
3. Selecting and writing definitions of degrees is not an easy task.
4. Allocating points among each of the subfactors may be somewhat arbitrary.

ADOPTING JOB EVALUATION METHOD

A variety of organizations have developed job evaluation programs that others can adopt. Adopting a program without first making certain it meets the organization's needs is not recommended, however. A program that is quite successful in one organization may be just as unsuccessful in another organization unless certain modifications are made. The following should be closely examined when modifying an existing program:

1. The nature—specific and general—of the jobs in the organization.
2. The duties and responsibilities that constitute the jobs in the organization.
3. The procedures used to determine salary rates.
4. The philosophy of the organization's management regarding the job evaluation program.

JOB EVALUATION COMMITTEE

What are the advantages of using job evaluation committees?

The nature of job evaluation makes desirable the use of a committee that is typically responsible for designing the program and subsequently revising it when the need arises. The use of a committee adds credibility to the program because of the common perception that programs developed by a committee have a broader base than those developed by only a few individuals. The committee is also generally responsible for monitoring the program to ensure compliance with various operating policies.

When evaluating job worth, many organizations prefer that committee members work independently of one another. The results of their evaluation efforts are then reviewed collectively by the various committee members before developing the final results. Although each committee member has considerable input, committee decisions override individual decisions.

The advantages of using a committee are that (1) the results of the program tend to be more objective, (2) the employees are more likely to accept a program developed by broad-based representation, and (3) the results tend to be more accurate.

IMPLICATIONS FOR THE ADMINISTRATIVE OFFICE MANAGER

The administrative office manager often has important job evaluation responsibilities, which include serving on both the organization's advisory committee and the job evaluation committee. The advisory committee is ongoing and is generally headed by the individual who has overall responsibility for job evaluation efforts, most likely someone in the personnel department. The job evaluation committee, conversely, is not ongoing but rather functions periodically for the purpose of engaging in job evaluation efforts.

Administrative office managers can eliminate some undesirable situations by assuring comparability of the relative value and the monetary value of the jobs for which they have responsibility. When discrepancies between these two values exist, employees' morale may shrink; they may begin to restrict their output; and turnover, absenteeism, and tardiness levels tend to be higher.

Administrative office managers are well qualified to take an active role in organizational job evaluation activities. Their background and training provide them with the knowledge they need to accept important responsibilities and to assume crucial leadership roles in this area.

REVIEW QUESTIONS

1. Identify the benefits provided by a job evaluation program.
2. Explain why the job ranking method is considered a nonquantitative method, whereas the factor comparison method is considered quantitative.
3. Compare and contrast the job evaluation techniques discussed in this chapter in terms of the following:
   a. Number of jobs for which each method is suitable.
   b. Any special apparatus required by each method.
   c. Special characteristics of each method.
   d. Validity of results of each method.
   e. Special conditions for which the use of each method is appropriate.
4. Why is the use of a committee advantageous in undertaking a job evaluation project?

DISCUSSION QUESTIONS

1. A few days ago, you and a friend were discussing the evaluation of jobs. You indicated that job evaluation helps determine the relative worth of specific jobs. Your friend said that he was under the impression that salaries determined job worth because there always seems to be a direct correlation between the importance of a job and the salary paid the job holder. Explain why the salary paid a job holder cannot be used as a process to determine job worth.
2. A number of the individuals with whom you work complain frequently that their salaries are lower than those of other employees in the organization who have less responsible jobs. According to these individuals, some employees get paid more than they are worth, while these individuals with whom you work believe they get paid less than they are worth. These individuals also contend that the situation seems to have gotten worse since their new jobs were evaluated last year. Even though the jobs were recently evaluated, what factors may be responsible for the lack of consistency between job worth and salaries paid job holders?
3. At a recent unit staff meeting, the supervisor mentioned that she would soon be undertaking an evaluation of the jobs in your unit. The supervisor also indicated that because there were only a few jobs to be evaluated, she would be doing the evaluation herself. Discuss the implications of this situation.
4. You recently accepted a supervisory position in a company that was started by its current president. You are one of several supervisors who signed a memo requesting that the president implement a job evaluation program. He replied by saying, "We've survived this long without job evaluation. I don't need a sophisticated process to tell me what jobs are worth. When you've been at it as long as I have, my intuition tells me what jobs are worth." Discuss the implications of the president's view about job evaluation.
5. The company in which you work recently completed a thorough evaluation of all its nonmanagement jobs. The evaluation was done by a local management consulting firm. The relative worth of approximately 25 percent of the jobs was upgraded, approximately 10 percent were downgraded, and the relative worth of the remaining jobs remained unchanged. Those whose jobs were downgraded are furious because of the rumor that their salaries will be lowered to reflect job worth. What helpful suggestions can you offer to those who have to deal with this situation?
6. You were recently appointed to serve on a job evaluation committee in the organization in which you work. The chairperson of the committee announced that the ranking method

would be used to evaluate the worth of the fifty-three jobs that are to be assessed. He said that he decided to use the ranking method because it is the easiest to use and because the results do not have to be all that precise because management will likely never do anything with the results. Discuss the implications of this situation.

STUDENT PROJECTS AND ACTIVITIES

1. Discuss with an office employee the value he or she perceives of job evaluation.
2. Discuss with an administrative office manager the value he or she perceives of job evaluation.
3. Obtain from an organization a portion of its point manual used in the point evaluation method of job evaluation. What kinds of factors are included in the evaluation process?
4. Obtain from two different organizations the evaluated worth of two comparable office positions. How comparable is the evaluated worth?
5. Discuss with an administrative office manager his or her preferred job evaluation method. Why is this particular method preferred?

MINICASE

You and several supervisors in Jaminez Import Company, which is located in San Diego, believe that an evaluation of all office jobs should be undertaken. These supervisors also know that management will likely not approve your request unless factual evidence is available to support their belief that a job evaluation project is necessary. You have been asked to prepare the memo to send to the executive vice president in which you request the evaluation of all office jobs. In the memo, you decide to

1. Identify several signals the executive vice president might use as evidence to support your belief that the evaluation of office jobs is necessary at this time.
2. An identification of the job evaluation method you believe should be used if the decision is made to evaluate the office jobs, as well as the reasons why you believe this particular method should be used.

CASE

The Briarwood Dairy Company, which is located in Milwaukee, Wisconsin, is one of the largest dairy processors in the Midwest. Approximately ten years ago, the company undertook a thorough job evaluation project. Employer-employee relations before the undertaking of the job evaluation were not especially cordial, and the relations have been less cordial since. In fact, on several occasions, the employees have been on the verge of unionizing. In many instances, management has "backed off," which undoubtedly diminished temporarily the amount of employee interest in unionizing.

It now appears that a thorough job evaluation again needs to be undertaken. Management knows that if it does not proceed with caution, the employees most likely will unionize. As the assistant to the president of Briarwood you have been asked to prepare a memo that will be shared with other members of the executive committee in which you

1. Discuss suggestions that will be helpful to management in undertaking a job evaluation project that these employees will accept.
2. Discuss suggestions for management to use to get employees to accept the job evaluation results once they are implemented.
3. Discuss ways management can evaluate the effectiveness of the job evaluation results once they have been implemented.

ADMINISTERING SALARIES OF OFFICE EMPLOYEES

CHAPTER AIM

After studying this chapter, you should be able to design an effective program to administer the salaries of office employees.

CHAPTER OUTLINE

- Federal Legislation
  - Fair Labor Standards Act
  - Equal Pay Act
  - Walsh-Healey Act
  - Davis-Bacon Act
  - Pregnancy Discrimination Act
  - Pension Reform Act
  - Age Discrimination in Employment Act
  - Economic Recovery Tax Act
  - Deficit Reduction Act
  - Consolidated Omnibus Budget Reconciliation Act
  - Family and Medical Leave Act of 1993
- Implications for the Administrative Office Manager

CHAPTER TERMS

Ability to pay
Age Discrimination in Employment Act
Collective bargaining
Consolidated Omnibus Budget Reconciliation Act
Cost-of-living index
Davis-Bacon Act
Deficit Reduction Act
Economic Recovery Tax Act
Equal Pay Act
Fair Labor Standards Act
Family and Medical Leave Act of 1993
Fringe benefits
Gain sharing
Going rates
Individual incentive
Key contributor program
Legislation
Merit pay
Pension Reform Act
Piecework plan
Pregnancy Discrimination Act
Relative worth of the job
Reimbursement account programs
Salary scattergram
Time-off bank
Walsh-Healey Act
Wellness programs

Employee compensation in many organizations consumes as much as 80 percent of the operating budget. While the need to control compensation expenditures is obvious, providing employees with salaries sufficiently high to maintain morale is also paramount.

Job evaluation provides the input for developing effective salary programs. Once the relative worth of jobs has been determined, a salary administration program helps ensure employees receive equitable compensation. Inequities are likely to result when salary decisions are made by a process other than a formal salary administration program.

Equitable, fair compensation is important to employees for several of the following reasons.

Why is equitable, fair compensation important to employees?

1. It is a basic determinant of their worth to the organization.
2. It provides a measure of status and recognition.
3. It directly affects their standard of living.
4. It is a reward for the time and effort they contribute to the organization.

When employees believe the relationship between the compensation they receive and the services they provide the organization is out of balance, one or more of the following will likely occur: Their productivity will decrease, their morale will deteriorate, and their turnover rates will increase.

SALARY ADMINISTRATION PROGRAM

Being able to assure employees that they are receiving an equitable salary has a positive impact on their output and morale. The salary administration program, which is responsible for determining equitable compensation, is helpful in recruiting, selecting, and retaining capable employees. As the quality of employees improves, so does the organization's ability to produce higher quality goods or services at lower prices.

Goals of Salary Administration Program

Efficient, effective salary administration programs operate within the framework of several well-defined goals, namely the following:

What are the common goals of salary administration programs?

1. *To provide a systematic determination of equitable compensation for employees.* Effective programs provide a sound foundation for determining equitable employee compensation. Such programs also help reduce the number of salary-related grievances filed by employees.
2. *To help the organization conform with existing legislation pertaining to employee compensation.* Legislation affecting employee compensation is frequently enacted, and existing legislation is periodically amended. Fewer violations of this legislation will occur when the director of the salary administration program is responsible for ensuring program compliance.
3. *To help the organization control its salary costs.* A well-designed salary administration program benefits the organization by helping it control its salary costs. The program helps provide balance between the worth of each job and the salary paid for that job. Therefore, salary programs help organizations more readily operate within their salary budgets.
4. *To help reduce employee turnover.* When an organization's salary structure is neither internally equitable nor externally competitive, employee turnover greatly increases. A salary administration program helps minimize problems of this nature.
5. *To motivate employees to perform at an optimum level.* Providing employees with various financial or nonfinancial incentives motivates them to become more efficient and productive. The guidelines, procedures, and policies used to reward deserving employees are important components of the salary administration program.
6. *To promote good employer-employee relations.* When employer-employee relations are cordial and pleasant, employees tend to be more cooperative and supportive. Management-union disagreements often originate in the organization's compensation process. A sound salary administration program minimizes disagreements; however, when they arise, an effective program helps resolve problems quickly without having to resort to arbitration. Effective programs also ensure that employees receive a fair day's salary for a fair day's work.

Policies and Procedures of Salary Administration Program

Decision making in well-designed salary administration programs is guided by policies and procedures that result in consistent and fair actions. The policies are also useful to management by providing it with the necessary authority to achieve desired goals and objectives.

Many organizations adopt a salary structure that uses a range for each job grade or level. To ensure the equal, fair treatment of all employees, policies and procedures must be developed to help determine where a newly hired employee or a recently promoted employee should be placed within the salary range. Policies outlining the advancement of employees from one salary range to another should also be available.

Other policies and procedures should exist that specify the organization's plans for periodic review of its salary structure, in addition to its plans for periodic review of its various job classifications. Also needed is a policy that identifies the appropriate steps to be used when filing a compensation-related grievance.

What is the result of an absence of clearly defined policies and procedures to guide the salary administration program?

The absence of clearly defined policies and procedures may result in the use of factors other than individual performance as a basis for making merit increases. The policies and procedures by which these decisions are made must be thoroughly communicated to employees.

The policies and procedures regarding salary increases also need to be clearly defined. Salary increases usually consist of either (1) a flat increase of a certain number of cents per hour or (2) a percentage-of-salary increase.

The use of the flat rate enables the employees with the lower salaries to get a larger percentage increase than those employees with higher salaries. In time, unless adjustments are made, the salary differential between the lower- and higher-paid employees will diminish, resulting in salary compression or even inversion. Some claim that when the salary differentials diminish significantly, employees will no longer have as much incentive to prepare themselves for the higher-paying jobs or for those jobs that typically require higher skill levels. This situation will eventually result in a scarcity of skilled employees.

Fringe benefits, another function of the salary administration program, must also be guided by well-defined policies and procedures. For example, in some organizations, paid holidays are considered a fringe benefit. When an employee is absent from work the day before or after the paid holiday, policies should specify the conditions under which the employee will or will not be paid for the day of absence.

Policies regulating shift or overtime pay should also be developed. Federal legislation specifies minimum rates for overtime pay, but some organizations pay more than the minimum rate in certain situations. If, for example, an organization has a salary differential for day and night shifts, regulating policies should be clearly defined.

In a unionized organization, many of the policies regulating various phases of employee compensation are written into the union-management contract. Fewer misinterpretations will result when these policies are clearly and specifically worded.

Also needed are policies that guide the incentive pay programs or performance-based programs. Many organizations, for example, provide employees with a variety of bonuses. To determine the actual amount of the bonus payment, a formula based either on a percentage of total profit or a percentage of total profit in excess of a specified amount is commonly used.

Responsibility for Salary Administration Program

Salary administration programs that operate with centralized control are administered uniformly. The hierarchical placement, duties, and responsibilities of the director of the salary administration program are largely determined by three factors: the size of the organization, the nature of goods or services produced by the organization, and the types of jobs for which the director is responsible.

Even though responsibility for the salary administration program in many organizations rests with the personnel department, the administrative office manager is often extensively involved. The manager frequently serves on the advisory committee that assists the director of the salary administration program. The members of advisory committees often have a broad understanding of the technical aspects of certain jobs and are therefore able to supply the program's director with information regarding important job requirements and compensation rates.

In small organizations, the personnel director is frequently responsible for the salary administration program, in addition to other personnel functions. In larger organizations, the salary administration program is headed by a full-time director. In some organizations, the director of the salary administration program reports to the personnel director, while in others, the personnel director and the director of the salary administration program are co-equals.

DETERMINING SALARY STRUCTURE

Determining an appropriate salary structure, which is a fairly complex process, begins with an examination of the various factors that impact on the salary program.

Factors Affecting Salary Structure

What factors affect the salary structure?

The following provides a discussion of the significant factors affecting the salary structure that must be considered. Included in the discussion are such factors as the relative worth of the job, going rates, cost-of-living index, legislation, collective bargaining, organization's ability to pay, and level of productivity.

Relative worth of job Employees rightfully expect their salaries be properly related to the demands of their jobs and to the salaries paid to employees performing other jobs in the organization. If not, salary inequities are likely to occur, a situation that most likely will impact negatively on employee attitudes. The **relative worth of the job** is determined by means of job evaluation procedures.

Going rates When **going rates** are used to determine the salary structure, employees consider themselves to be treated more fairly, and they accept the results more readily. Occasionally, the going rates for comparable jobs can be obtained from prepared salary surveys. The unavailability of these surveys may mean that the organization will have to conduct its own salary survey.

The following discussion provides important information about several prepared salary surveys.

The *National Survey of Professional, Administrative, Technical, and Clerical Pay*, conducted annually since 1961 by the Bureau of Labor Statistics, provides salary data for eighty-one different occupational work levels. The survey includes nationwide data for each of the eighty-one positions, in addition to presenting data on clerical positions for several metropolitan areas throughout the country. The survey also includes information on a variety of fringe benefits and provides brief descriptions of jobs.

What is an exempt employee?

Edward N. Hay and Associates compiles *Compensation Comparisons—Industrial and Financial Management,* which is an annual update of salary trends for exempt executive, management, and technical employees. The information for the survey is gathered from a comprehensive sample of national and international firms. Differences between exempt and nonexempt positions are discussed in the "Federal Legislation" section of this chapter. Persons in these positions are "exempt" from receiving extra compensation for overtime work.

The Administrative Management Society annually updates its *Directory of Office Salaries,* which includes twenty commonly found office and data processing positions. The survey includes weekly salary data for the twenty jobs in cities in which Administrative Management Society chapters are found, in addition to including regional average salaries and nationwide averages for each of these positions.

In 1973 the Administrative Management Society conducted its first annual management survey, the *AMS Guide to Management Compensation.* This survey, which is now conducted by the Administrative Management Society Foundation, provides salary data on twenty key exempt middle-management positions as well as information on fringe benefits, length of workweek, paid vacations, holidays, and pension plans.

Numerous local chambers of commerce and trade associations compile salary data for jobs found in their localities. Using the results of these surveys, when they are available, will save many organizations considerable time, effort, and money.

The absence of published salary data may result in an organization's having to conduct its own survey. Without this vital salary information, the organization has no way of knowing whether its salaries are competitive with other organizations in the community.

When designing a salary survey, the following guidelines will be helpful:

What guidelines are helpful in designing a salary survey?

1. If only a portion of the total number of organizations in a community is to be surveyed, special provision must be made to ensure the random selection of those that are to be included.
2. The number of organizations to be surveyed must be large enough to be representative of the lot from which the sample is drawn.
3. For best results, the organizations to be surveyed should be of the same classification and approximate size as the organization conducting the survey. For example, banks should survey other banks, manufacturing organizations should survey other manufacturing organizations, and so forth.
4. The questionnaire must be designed to gather the desired information. Frequently included in salary surveys are the following:
   a. Number of employees in the firm.
   b. Number of employees in each job category on which the salary data are based.
   c. Salary range for each job category.
   d. Number of hours per week for each job included in the survey.
   e. The pay policy for employees who work on holidays.
   f. The type and monetary worth of supplemental pay (includes bonuses, profit sharing, stock options, and pension plans).
   g. The holidays for which employees receive pay.
   h. The organization's policy regarding vacations with pay, sick leave,

insurance, salary increases, overtime, incentive pay, and shift differential pay.

5. To provide some assurance that jobs are comparable, the job descriptions should be obtained from the organizations being surveyed. Even though jobs in several organizations have comparable titles, they may differ significantly in terms of duties and responsibilities.

After collecting the relevant job information, a median or average salary for each job can be computed. The organization is then able to decide how competitive its salary structure is in comparison with the salary structures of other organizations.

Cost-of-living index During inflationary times, the **cost-of-living index**, which is calculated by the federal government, is frequently used by an organization in developing its salary structures. The use of the cost-of-living index as a salary determinant results in a periodic upward adjustment of salaries, which enables employees to maintain their purchasing power. Therefore, employees' salaries increase by the same amount as the increase of the cost-of-living index.

In unionized organizations, the salary structure may be mathematically tied to the cost-of-living index by an escalator clause written into the union-management contract. For example, some contracts stipulate that when the cost-of-living index increases by a certain percentage, employees' salaries will automatically increase by a specified amount. Although the cost-of-living index is popularly used as a salary determinant during inflationary times, it is generally not popular with unions during times of economic stability.

Legislation Another determinant of the organization's salary structure is the compensation-related **legislation** enacted at both national and state levels. Provisions of this legislation affect minimum salary rates, overtime pay, child labor, fringe benefits, and so on.

What legislation impacts on salary administration programs?

Some of the more significant acts—including the Fair Labor Standards Act, the Equal Pay Act, the Walsh-Healey Act, the Davis-Bacon Act, and the Pension Reform Act—are discussed in the "Federal Legislation" section of this chapter.

Collective bargaining When the employees of an organization belong to a union, their salaries are determined by a **collective bargaining** process. Although going rates, cost-of-living increases, and job worth most likely will be considered in the bargaining process, the salary rates agreed on will reflect the degree of "give and take" between the two parties. Organizations with unionized employees frequently set salary trends that nonunionized organizations follow as a means of maintaining a competitive salary structure.

Organization's ability to pay Also affecting the organization's salary structure is its **ability to pay** salaries and wages. Generally, this ability is affected by such factors as competition and the overall profitability of the industry. The more keen an organization's competition is, the less able it is to pay top salaries and wages. Likewise, as the industry with which the organization is associated experiences declining profits, the ability to pay top salaries and wages becomes more prohibitive.

Level of productivity An organization's level of productivity affects the amount of money available to pay employees. As an organization's productivity increases, so does the amount of money potentially available for increasing wages and salaries. Directly linking the amount of salary increase to productivity improvement often motivates employees to improve their performance. Salary increases paralleling comparable increases in productivity will not increase an organization's labor costs. When salaries increase faster than productivity increases, however, the organization's labor costs will consume a larger percentage of the total operating budget.

Developing Wage Curve

After the relative worth of each job has been determined by one of the job evaluation methods discussed in Chapter 13, the monetary worth of the job can be determined. For example, when the job ranking method of job evaluation is used, the relative importance of each job influences the predetermined level into which each job is placed. By using the procedures presented in this chapter, the monetary worth for each of the levels is determined. The job grading method uses the same basic procedures to determine the monetary worth of jobs.

When the factor comparison method is used, the monetary worth of each key job is first determined. This information provides a basis for determining the monetary worth of the nonkey jobs. When the point evaluation method is used, the point value of each job determines its monetary worth. Because point evaluation is the most frequently used method of job evaluation, it will be used to illustrate the salary determination process.

What is the function of a salary scattergram?

Salary scattergram Determining the monetary worth of each job begins by preparing the **salary scattergram**, such as the one illustrated in Figure 14-1. The scattergram shows the relationship between the relative worth and the monetary worth of each job. The horizontal axis of the scattergram identifies the points value or relative worth of the jobs, whereas the vertical axis identifies the monetary worth.

The relative worth (point value) and monetary worth (salary) of each job are plotted on the scattergram. For example, if a two-hundred-point job pays a salary of $900, a dot is placed on the scattergram at the intersection of these two values. After all the jobs are plotted, a correlation line is drawn on the scattergram where an approximately equal number of dots appear above and below the line. The scattergram clearly identifies the relationship between the relative importance of various jobs and their monetary worth.

The external competitiveness of an organization's salary structure is assessed by comparing its correlation line with the correlation line of a composite of several other organizations in the same community. If the organization's salary structure is lower than the composite line, the organization will need to make adjustments in its salary program if it is to remain competitive. Such an adjustment is illustrated in Figure 14-2.

How is the salary range established?

Establishing salary range Once the correlation line has been officially established, the next step involves setting for each pay grade the upper and lower limits of the salary range. This is easily done by placing a line a fixed percentage amount (10 percent, for example) above the correlation line and another line the same percentage amount below the correlation line.

Figure 14-3 illustrates the upper and lower limits of each pay grade, using a salary range of 10 percent on either side of the midpoint (correlation) line. At the lowest and highest ends of the midpoint line, base points 10 percent above and 10 percent below are placed on the chart. The upper and

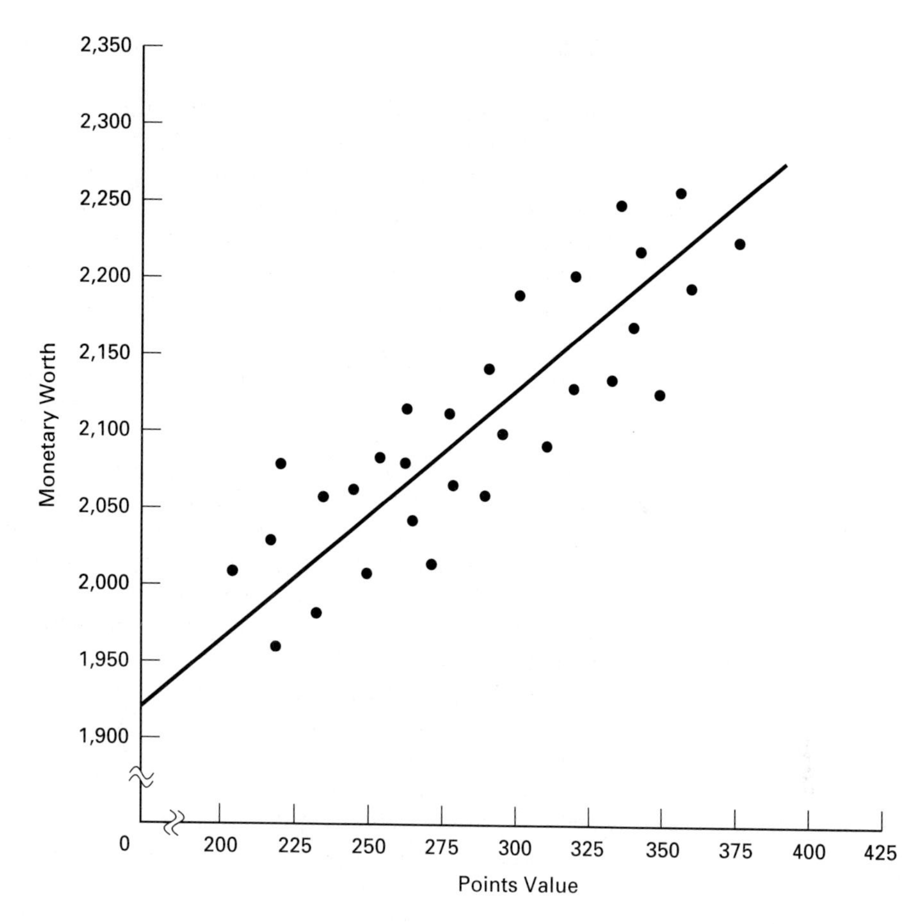

Figure 14-1 Scattergram.

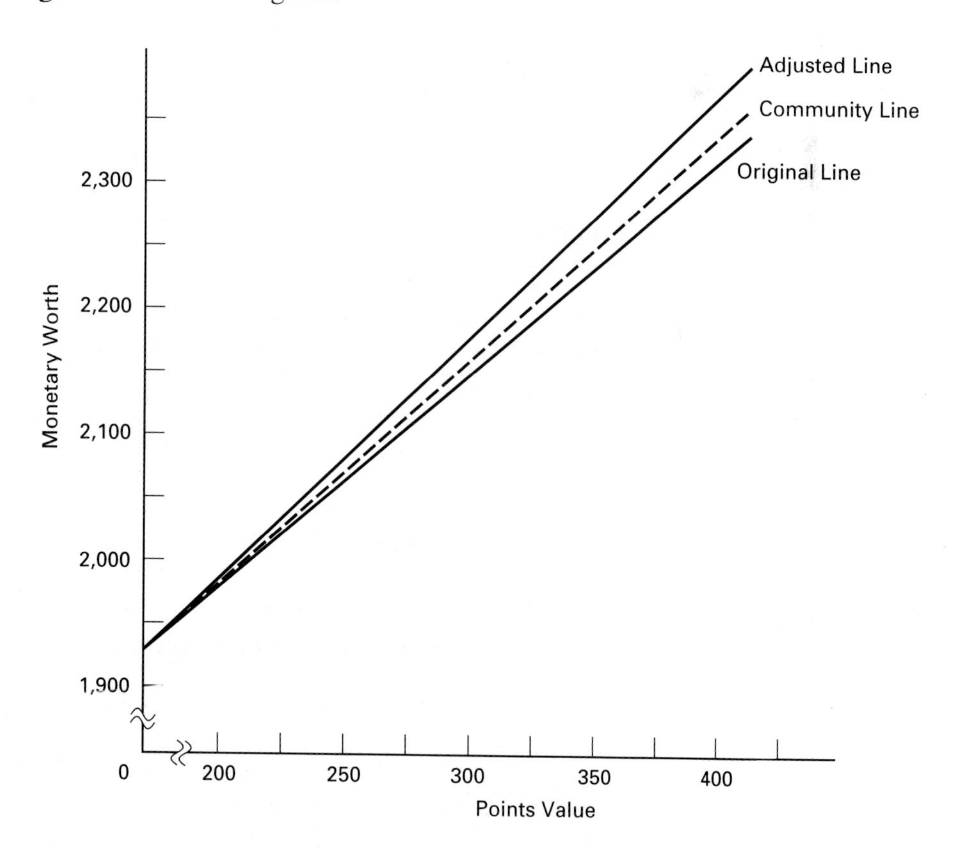

Figure 14-2 Salary comparison and adjustment.

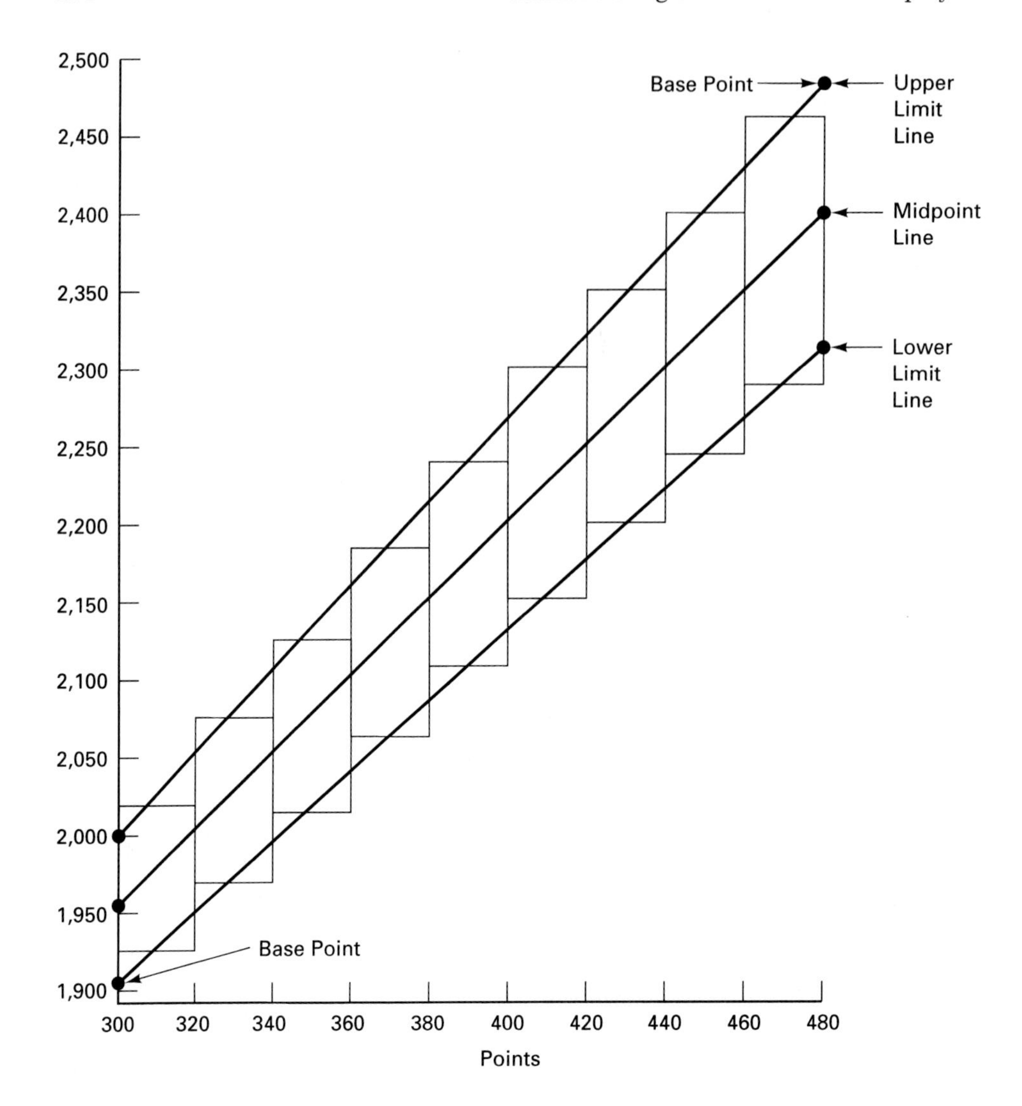

Figure 14-3 Salary ranges.

lower limits of the salary range can then easily be determined by connecting the two base points above and the two below the midpoint line. For each points category, rectangular-shaped boxes that intersect the upper- and lower-limit lines are then drawn on the figure. Once this is done, the rectangular-shaped boxes readily identify the upper and lower limits of each salary range.

Most salary structures are designed with overlapping rates for adjoining job categories. This concept is illustrated in Figure 14-3. The jobs in the 300-to-320-point category receive a salary of $1,925 to $2,080. The salary range for the adjoining category (321 to 340 points) is $1,970 to $2,135. These two ranges overlap by $110. The use of salary structures with overlapping rates enables employees with considerable experience to be paid an amount equal to or higher than a relatively inexperienced employee in the next higher category.

When an organization undertakes a thorough job evaluation and adjusts its salary structure, the suggested compensation for some employees will fall outside the recommended limits. The salaries of the employees earning less than the suggested minimum are generally adjusted upward. Several techniques are used to deal with employees who earn more than the maximum allows. Sometimes they are trained and promoted to higher-level jobs more commensurate with their present salaries. In other instances, the employees are promoted as quickly as circumstances allow, which will help achieve parity between their job responsibilities and salaries. Some organizations will award smaller and less frequent salary increases to these employees until their salaries fall into the recommended range for their job responsibilities.

How are employees' salaries typically increased?

Planning for salary increases Procedures for increasing employees' salaries have to be built into the organization's salary administration program. Salary progression enables employees to move upward within their range and facilitates increasing their salaries when they are promoted from one job level to another. Keeping employees informed about procedures for increasing their salaries is essential.

Employees' salaries are usually increased in three ways: at specific time intervals, by merit, or by a combination of both specific time intervals and merit. The use of time intervals enables employees whose performance is satisfactory to receive automatic salary increases at regular intervals, most likely once or twice a year.

Also used frequently to increase employees' salaries is the merit method that ties the quality of an employees' performance to the amount of his or her increase. Thus, employees whose work is distinctly superior receive a larger salary increase than those employees whose work is considered above average.

The use of the combination method results in the increase of salaries at specific time intervals until employees reach the midpoint or average salary for their respective salary ranges. For an employee to reach the upper limit of the range, his or her performance must be outstanding. Therefore, salary increases are automatic from the lower limit to the midpoint of the range, but merit increases are necessary for an employee to receive the salary at the top of the range.

An increasing number of organizations that use the combination approach increase the salaries of all employees a fixed percentage—4 percent, for example—and the remainder of their salary increase is comprised of **merit pay**. Employees tend to be more highly motivated to improve their performance when their merit pay is directly related to job performance. One way to link job performance and merit pay is to give those employees whose performance is outstanding an 8 percent merit increase added to their fixed amount increase; those whose performance is rated above average, a 6 percent merit increase; and so forth. Employees whose job performance is rated average or below generally are not eligible for merit increases.

INCENTIVE PAY

What are the characteristics of typical effective incentive pay plans?

An increasing number of organizations are presently installing employee incentive pay plans that take into consideration the employees' performance in relation to work standards established through work measurement procedures. Properly designed incentive pay programs benefit both the organization and its employees. The organization's productivity is increased, which improves its profitability; and the employees are able to increase their compensation.

The following characteristics are typical of effective incentive pay plans:

1. Employees are convinced that a direct correlation exists between their level of performance and the amount of incentive pay they receive.

2. Employees are aware of the precise level at which they must perform to be eligible to receive incentive pay.
3. Management thoroughly communicates its expectations to employees.
4. Incentive pay is given only to those employees who increase their effectiveness.
5. Employees are fully convinced that they will benefit substantially as a result of improved performance.

When incentive pay plans are put in place, quality and quantity of output improve, costs decrease, and employee morale improves.

Types of Incentive Pay Plans

Two broad types of incentive pay plans are found: individual and group. Individual plans are more common than group plans.

Individual incentive plans A common type of individual plan is the **individual incentive** that involves measuring each employee's output; individual rewards are based on that output. Although individual incentive plans are not as readily available to office workers as they are to workers in other types of industry (textile, steel, and clothing, for example), an increasing number of organizations are installing incentive plans for their office employees.

How do partial plans differ from whole plans?

Some individual incentive pay plans are partial plans, whereas others are whole plans. The determining factor is how much of the employee's total compensation is based on his or her output. With partial plans, a portion of the amount of an employee's paycheck is based on his or her output that exceeds the minimum threshold amount. With whole plans, the entire paycheck is based on the amount of the employee's output. A common type of whole plan is a piecework plan.

The **piecework plan**, a type of individual incentive, was common during the early decades of this century and is regaining its popularity in some industries. The piecework plan pays employees a standard rate for each unit of output. Some piecework plans use a differential system that enables higher-producing employees to receive a higher rate than the lower-producing employees.

How are compensation rates determined in incentive plans?

Two types of rate determination are used in individual incentive plans: (1) units of production and (2) time required to complete a unit. The rate determination method that uses units of production is commonly used for office employees, especially for those whose jobs primarily involve data entry (either numerical or alphabetical). The computer system they use automatically counts their keystrokes, which serve as the basis of their incentive pay.

Incentive plans based on the amount of time required to complete a unit are typically used for longer-cycle jobs with mental or creative task components. Some of the more successful individual incentive plans reward employees by paying one amount for a given level of production but increase the amount after the individual's output exceeds that level. For example, employees whose output exceeds the minimum level might be paid an additional 25 cents for every two hundred keystrokes up to ten thousand keystrokes, but 27 cents for every two hundred keystrokes above ten thousand.

Group incentive plans The growing interdependence of employees' jobs makes group incentive plans more desirable in some organizations than individual incentive plans. These plans are often based either on the amount of profit earned by the organization or on the amount of cost reduction it realizes.

Group incentive plans based on the profit earned by the organization tend to motivate employees to increase their productivity, either by increasing their output or by decreasing their inefficiency. A percentage of the increased profit is returned to deserving employees as a reward for helping their employer increase its profitability. The employees who receive the reward are generally the members of a work unit whose output exceeds the minimum threshold for incentive pay.

When group incentive pay is based on cost reduction, the members of a work unit whose output costs are less than the threshold amount are entitled to a reward. Although most of the amount saved is divided among the employees, most employers retain a portion of the savings to help pay for other programs that ultimately benefit the employees.

PERFORMANCE-BASED PAY

How do performance-based pay plans differ from incentive pay plans?

A basic difference between the incentive plans discussed earlier and performance-based pay plans is that the latter tend to place greater emphasis on key employees than do the incentive plans. Another distinction is that the performance-based plans reward total performance rather than just one component of an employee's job, such as output. Some performance-based plans are better suited for rewarding employees who have a management status than are the typical incentive plans.

One type of performance-based pay plan is the **key contributor program**. This program is designed to retain key employees, often those with management status, whose special skills and contributions to the organization have a significant impact on the its overall performance. Among the types of rewards made to the key contributors are a hiring bonus, cash benefits, stock option plan, and increased salary, perhaps as high as 140 to 160 percent of the normal salary. Although a sizable portion of the organization's employees might be rewarded under an incentive pay plan, only a handful are likely to benefit from the key contributor plan.

What is gain sharing?

Gain sharing, another of the performance-based plans, is a goal-based, organization-wide plan that involves employees extensively in the plan's operation. The plan is generally based on employee-generated costs in relation to company sales. Whenever the employee-generated costs are less than the threshold amount, the difference is divided among the employees. Results are reported frequently—perhaps weekly—with rewards distributed monthly.

With gain sharing, production-oriented employees know that if they increase the efficiency of their output and sales-oriented employees know that if they increase sales volume, then they all will be able to share the "gain." Although an incentive plan sometimes entices employees to increase the quantity of their output without regard to the quality of output, performance-based plans focus on the quality of output. If production increases at the expense of quality, sales will decrease, thus reducing the amount of "gain" to be shared among the employees.

LEGALLY REQUIRED BENEFITS

What benefits are legally required?

Employers are required by federal and state law to provide certain benefits for their employees. Among these benefits are Social Security, workers' compensation, and unemployment compensation. In addition, several states have enacted a mandatory disability insurance program.

Social Security

Officially known as the Old-Age, Survivors, Disability, and Health Insurance program, the Social Security program taxes most employers and employees. The Federal Insurance Contributions Act, which initiated the Social Security program, has been amended to include Medicare, a health insurance program for the elderly and disabled.

Qualifying recipients of Social Security receive their payments monthly. Now that the program is tied to the cost-of-living index, recipients' payments increase as living costs increase. The tax levied on employers and employees also increases periodically.

Workers' Compensation

The workers' compensation program is designed to protect employees and their dependents against losses resulting from job-related injury or death. This tax is levied only against employers in all states except Oregon, where the program is supported by both the employer and employee.

Unemployment Compensation

Another of the legally required programs is unemployment compensation. This program provides a stipend for unemployed persons. In some states, employers make the full contribution, whereas in other states, both employers and employees contribute to the program.

Disability Insurance

An increasing number of states require participation in the disability insurance program. The cost of this program is generally borne by both the employer and employee. The program provides payments to employees who become disabled as a result of a job-related injury.

FRINGE BENEFITS

Fringe benefits are supplemental compensation in excess of the direct compensation employees receive for performing a specific job. The amount of fringe benefits paid employees has increased rapidly over the years. According to the *Employee Benefits* survey conducted in 1991 by the U.S. Chamber of Commerce, the average amount paid by all organizations (manufacturing and nonmanufacturing) for fringe benefits was 39.2 percent of the total payroll, and the average benefits per employee per year amounted to $13,126.

What advantages result from the availability of fringe benefits?

Fringe benefits availability has a positive impact on employees' morale and their loyalty to the organization. Employees are more satisfied with their jobs, and their productivity is increased as a result of receiving fringe benefits. Furthermore, benefits provide an element of job security. To help sustain employees' positive feelings about fringe benefits, an increasing number of organizations are providing frequent and detailed information about the benefits they provide their employees.

An increasing number of organizations give employees an opportunity to select the ones that best meet their needs from those benefits that are available. This cafeteria approach, as it is called, gives each employee a lump sum of money, and he or she selects the benefits that will best meet individual needs. With the increased number of families in which both husband and wife work, this approach is highly desirable. Rather than having duplicate fringe benefits, such as medical insurance coverage, the husband and wife can each decide which benefits to receive from each employer.

Some of the most frequently found fringe benefits provided employees are discussed in the paragraphs that follow.

Paid Holidays

Organizations commonly pay employees for national holidays that fall on working days. For example, many employees are compensated for New Year's Day, Memorial Day, Independence Day, Labor Day, Thanksgiving, and Christmas. In many organizations, employees are paid for Fridays when holidays fall on Saturday and for Mondays when holidays fall on Sunday. Some organizations also pay employees for the following holidays: Washington's Birthday, Lincoln's Birthday, Martin Luther King Jr.'s Birthday, and Veteran's Day. In addition, some organizations observe special state holidays.

Paid Vacations

Many organizations also pay their employees while they are on vacation. In most instances, the length of the paid vacation is determined by the employee's longevity with the organization. Exempt employees frequently receive longer paid vacations than nonexempt employees because exempt employees are not eligible to receive overtime pay. Some organizations also give employees a paid vacation day on their birthdays.

Sick Leave

Another fringe benefit frequently provided employees is sick leave. Most organizations provide a specified number of days of sick leave per year. In some organizations, employees are permitted to accumulate sick days from one year to the next. In other instances, employees can extend their paid vacations by adding their unused days to their vacation time. In still other instances, when employees retire, they are paid for unused sick days accumulated over the years. A trend is emerging to reward employees for not using their sick days. Unless closely controlled, some employees have the tendency to abuse sick-leave benefits.

Paid Personal Days

An increasing number of organizations are giving employees a certain number of paid personal days that can be used as they wish. Employees given paid personal days are less apt to use sick days for reasons other than illness. When an employee has no more personal days, his or her wages are likely to be reduced for absences that exceed the maximum allowed.

Educational Assistance

Many organizations pay a portion or all of the tuition costs incurred by employees who attend school part time. Of these, most also help pay for the cost

What is the nature of the educational assistance fringe benefit?

of books and supplies. Some stipulations that are frequently part of the employer-employee educational assistance agreement are (1) the course must be directly related to the employee's job or to a higher-level job for which the employee is trying to qualify; (2) the employee must successfully complete the course; (3) the course must be taken at an institution approved by the organization; and (4) the employee, after completing the course, must continue working for the organization for a specified length of time, perhaps a year or two.

Life Insurance Programs

Another common benefit employees receive is life insurance paid either partially or wholly by the employer. In many instances, the amount of life insurance provided each employee is related to his or her salary. In addition to death benefits, many life insurance programs also provide dismemberment or accidental death benefits.

Health Care Insurance

Group medical, surgical, and dental insurance benefits are also paid either partially or wholly by many employers. Although some provide coverage for all the members of an employee's immediate family, others provide dependent coverage for a nominal cost. An increasing number of organizations are making major medical insurance available to their employees. Major medical coverage is used when the limits of health insurance coverage have been reached. Other types of medical insurance provide coverage for vision care and prescriptions.

Disability Insurance

Disability insurance is also provided by some organizations. This coverage provides payments to employees who become disabled by a job-related accident or by a sickness that prevents their continuing to work.

Health Maintenance Organizations

What is the function of a health maintenance organization?

As an alternative to group health care insurance benefits, an increasing number of employees have an opportunity to enroll in health maintenance organization (HMO) plans. HMOs, which stress preventive medicine, provide free office calls for their subscribers. Hospital coverage is also provide by the HMO. Those who opt to use the services of the HMO are no longer under the care of their private health care professionals.

Medical and Fitness Facilities

A growing number of organizations are providing medical and fitness facilities. A portion of the cost of each of these facilities may have to be borne by the users. Some medical facilities provide only first aid, whereas others provide a sick-room service. In some organizations, the medical facility is operated by nurses; in others, by a full medical staff.

The fitness facility provides employees an opportunity to participate in fitness programs as well as to participate in health-related seminars. In other instances, the organization may pay for a portion of the cost incurred when employees participate in off-premise fitness programs. This benefit is receiving an increasing amount of attention because organizations have discovered that healthy, fit employees are able to attain higher productivity, they are absent less often, and their medical costs are lower than their counterparts. As a result, any investment in such programs is usually offset by employees' increased productivity.

Maternity Leave

Many organizations provide their employees with maternity leave, even though they do not come under the provisions of the Family and Medical Leave Act of 1993. In some cases, the leave can be paid up to the limits of the employee's accumulated sick leave or vacation leave. An increasing number of organizations are providing paternity leave for their male employees. These employees may also be able to use their sick leave or vacation days in order to receive a paid leave. Some firms also provide their employees adoption leave for use when adopting a child. A growing number of organizations are reimbursing their employees for a portion or all of the cost incurred in child adoption.

Under the provisions of the **Family and Medical Leave Act of 1993**, which affects all U.S. businesses with fifty or more employees, employers have to provide their employees—both males and females—with twelve weeks of unpaid leave per year in certain situations. Among the situations are the following: having a child, adopting a child, assuming responsibility for a foster child, caring for an ill child, spouse, or parent, or the employee's having a serious illness. Furthermore, the employee is guaranteed that he or she will be able to return to an equivalent job upon returning to work.

Employee Assistance Programs

What is the function of employee assistance programs?

Many organizations of sufficient size to have full-time attorneys and accountants permit their employees to use their services on a limited basis. For personal situations of a complicated nature, employees will most likely be referred to professionals outside the organization.

Included as part of some employee assistance programs is a counseling and referral service. These programs are commonly used by employees who have an addiction to alcohol or drugs and by those with emotional problems.

Pension Plans

Another common fringe benefit provided employees is a pension plan. Important regulations are provided by the Pension Reform Act, which is discussed in greater detail later in this chapter.

Profit Sharing

An increasing number of organizations are installing profit-sharing plans that enable employees to share a specified amount of yearly profits. A portion of the increased profits is usually retained by the organization for use in supporting various operations. In some instances, employees receive a cash payment, whereas in other instances they receive stock in the organization. The latter is known as an employee stock option plan.

Child Care Services

To accommodate working mothers, many organizations provide child care centers for the children of their employees. Certain restrictions—for example, age and health status of the child—are frequently imposed by the organization.

Car Pools

A growing number of organizations are making employees' participation in car pools increasingly attractive. Some organizations provide choice parking places to employees who belong to car pools, whereas other organizations provide free parking for those who participate in a pool. Still other organizations use van pooling, which involves giving employees a ride to and from work in an organization-owned vehicle.

Cafeteria Services

Eating facilities are provided by organizations, primarily for the convenience of their employees. In some instances, these cafeterias operate on a break-even basis, resulting in reduced meal costs for employees. From the cafeterias in some organizations, employees are able to obtain on a take-out basis the food for their evening meal.

Company Discounts

As a benefit for their employees, some organizations make their products or services available at reduced costs. The discount may range anywhere from 10 percent to being able to purchase the product or service at cost.

Wellness Programs

Either as a stand-alone program or as a supplement to their fitness facilities, **wellness programs** are being installed in an increasing number of organizations. These programs are geared toward the employee's maintaining a total health program. In some of these programs, routine physicals are an important component, as is dietary and health maintenance counseling.

In some organizations, the eradication of smoking is an important aspect of wellness programs. Accordingly, an increasing number of organizations (1) permit smoking only in designated areas or (2) ban smoking on organizational premises. Some organizations are also paying bonuses to employees who quit smoking, whereas others are paying for the employees to attend seminars aimed at helping attendees quit smoking.

Eldercare

An increasing number of organizations are becoming cognizant of the rapidly growing number of elderly in the United States, many of whom are dependent on their offspring for varying amounts of their care. To accommodate as much as possible those employees with dependent elderly parents, some organizations implement flextime programs that enable employees to delay the starting time of their workday. Thus, an employee is able to provide whatever parental needs may be necessary before going to work. Other organizations allow employees to establish a flexible spending account (a provision of the

Deficit Reduction Act discussed in the "Federal Legislation" section of this chapter) in which a given percentage of pretax dollars can be deducted from their paychecks to provide care for either dependent children or dependent elderly parents.

Reimbursement Account Programs

What are reimbursement accounts?

An ever-increasing number of organizations are installing **reimbursement account programs** that are financially advantageous both to the employees and the employer. Employees have deducted from each paycheck a predetermined amount. Because the amount deducted is not considered as taxable income, employees' tax obligation is reduced. For example, for every $1,000 an employee at the 28 percent income tax bracket puts into a reimbursement account, his or her tax obligation is reduced $280. In addition, the employee and the employer both save on Social Security taxes.

When the employee has either a medical expense not covered by his or her insurance coverage or a dependent-care expense, the reimbursement account is used to reimburse the employee for the amount of these expenses. Reimbursement can be obtained for deductibles, co-pay, and such non-insured expenses as dental care, eye care, or prescription drugs.

Time-Off Bank

One of the newest fringe benefits made available to employees is the **time-off bank**. Rather than giving employees a specified number of vacation days, they are given hours in their time-off bank that they can use for vacation, personal time, illness, or additional holiday time. In most cases, the hours in the time-off bank are a composite of vacation days, personal days, and paid sick-leave days. The number of hours an employee is eligible to have put in his or her time-off bank is often determined by the hierarchical level of the job and the employee's longevity with the organization.

In most organizations, employees are permitted to spend their accrued time in hours, days, or even weeks if their time accrual is sufficient. Generally, employees are also able to move all or a portion of their unspent hours forward into the next year. Some organizations also pay employees for their unspent hours at the end of each year or upon their retirement or when they terminate their employment.

FEDERAL LEGISLATION

The provisions of federal legislation are also important considerations in developing a salary administration program. Among the more important acts are the Fair Labor Standards Act and its amended act, the Equal Pay Act; the Walsh-Healey Act; the Davis-Bacon Act; the Pregnancy Discrimination Act; and the Pension Reform Act. The important provisions of these acts that impact on the salary administration program are discussed in this section.

Fair Labor Standards Act

How does the Fair Labor Standards Act impact salary administration?

According to the **Fair Labor Standards Act**, employees who are covered by the act must be paid at least the legal minimum wage. The act also contains specific provisions for overtime pay, equal pay for equal work, and minimum ages of children who can be hired.

The act as originally passed by Congress applied only to companies involved with interstate commerce. With a number of amendments passed over the years, the act now encompasses almost all firms in the United States.

An important provision of the act is its distinction between exempt and nonexempt employees. A common misconception is that all salaried employees are exempt from minimum wages and overtime pay, while nonexempt employees (employees paid by the hour) are covered by the minimum wages and overtime pay provisions of the act. The act identifies four exempt job categories: executive, administrative, outside sales, and professional. In these categories, other criteria—which vary among the categories—must be present to make an employee fully exempt. For example, in the executive category, the additional criteria that need to be present to classify an employee as exempt are the following: have management responsibilities, supervise employees, have authority to hire and fire or to make recommendations to hire and fire, devote certain percentage of work time to managerial duties, and receive a minimum weekly salary. Even though an employee may be salaried, to be exempt, he or she must also possess these additional criteria.

Equal Pay Act

The **Equal Pay Act** of 1963, which amended the Fair Labor Standards Act (FLA), applies to the same employers as the FLA. Under the provisions of the Equal Pay Act, an employer cannot have unequal pay policies or fringe benefits for men and women who perform equal jobs that require equal skill, effort, and responsibility and that are performed under similar working conditions. The Equal Pay Act also makes it illegal for an employer to reduce the salary rates of employees of one gender as a means of eliminating salary differentials.

Walsh-Healey Act

The **Walsh-Healey Act** covers employees working on government contracts that use materials and equipment in excess of $10,000. The act stipulates that employees must receive at least the minimum wage, that they must receive overtime pay, and that child labor must not be used.

Davis-Bacon Act

The **Davis-Bacon Act**, passed in 1931, is also known as the Prevailing Wage Law. The act sets minimum wages for persons employed on public works projects worth more than $2,000. The minimum wage rate is established at the prevailing level of pay for other similar jobs in the area.

Pregnancy Discrimination Act

Passed in 1978, the **Pregnancy Discrimination Act** forbids employers from mandating that pregnant employees take a maternity leave at a prescribed time during their pregnancy, regardless of their ability to carry out their job duties. The act also gives employees the right to return to their jobs after giving birth, and their retirement benefits and seniority must remain intact.

Pension Reform Act

The **Pension Reform Act**, officially known as the Employee Retirement Income Security Act of 1974, has a significant impact on organizations' pension

How does the Pension Reform Act impact salary administration?

plans. The act does not require an organization to have a pension plan; however, if it does, the plan must meet the requirements outlined in the act. Organizations that offer a pension plan are required to meet a minimum funding standard, which means they must contribute at least a minimum amount to a qualified defined benefit or money purchase pension or to an annuity plan.

An organization can have an exempt, fully insured plan if certain requirements are met during the plan year. One such requirement is that the plan be funded exclusively with individual insurance or annuity contracts. Another requirement is that the contracts must provide for the payment of level annual (or more frequent) premiums from the time an employee becomes a participant in the plan until the employee reaches retirement age or until the employee ceases participation in the plan.

If the organization has a plan that is subject to the provisions of the act, all employees who have reached the age of twenty-five and who have worked for the organization for one year (one thousand hours in industries of an intermittent or seasonal employment nature) are covered.

The following outlines some of the more important provisions of the act. Pension plans must be vested, which means that employees are entitled to the amount they contribute to their pension plans, in addition to a share of their employer's contribution, under one of the following options: (1) fully vested after ten years of continuous service; (2) partially vested after a time (for example, after five years of service, 25 percent vested; after ten years, 50 percent vested; and after fifteen years, 100 percent vested); (3) vesting under the "forty-five rule," which means that after five years of service, the employee is entitled to 50 percent vesting when the sum of the employee's age and years of service exceeds forty-five, with added vesting for additional years of service until the employee is entitled to 100 percent vesting (for example, an employee who has ten years of service and whose age and service equal or exceed fifty-five is entitled to 100 percent vesting).

In most cases, employees who are hired after a mandatory retirement age are also covered by the act. Employees changing jobs can take their vested benefits with them. If the new employer approves, the vested benefits can be transferred to the new employer's retirement program, although such transfers are limited to once every three years. The annual benefit payable to any employee covered by the act may not be greater than the lesser of $75,000 or 100 percent of the employee's average compensation for the three consecutive calendar years in which the employee received his or her highest salary.

The benefits of the plan must be communicated to the employees in a summary plan description that contains the following:

What information about benefits must be communicated to employees in a summary plan description?

1. The name of the plan; the common name of the plan; the employer and address; the type of plan; how the plan is administered; the administrator's name and address; the date of the plan's fiscal year; the employer identification number; the name and address of the person responsible for the legal services of the organization; and the names, titles, and addresses of the plan's trustees.
2. Requirements for participation and the benefits; description of joint and survivor benefits; service requirements for accruing full benefits; how benefits are prorated for less than a year's service; and who pays for the plan.
3. Identity of any organization that maintains the plan's funds or provides benefits; the manner in which claims are to be filed; the procedure to follow when a claim is denied; and whether or not the plan is insured under the Pension Benefit Guaranty Corporation.

Age Discrimination in Employment Act

According to the provisions of the 1986 amendments to the **Age Discrimination in Employment Act**, neither male nor female employees who work for a private business with at least twenty employees can be forced to retire. An exception is top-level executives who can be retired at seventy years of age.

Economic Recovery Tax Act

Passed in 1981, the **Economic Recovery Tax Act** allows employees, depending on their yearly income and filing status, to contribute up to $2,000, tax deductible, to an employer-sponsored pension, profit-sharing, or savings account or to an individual retirement account.

Deficit Reduction Act

The **Deficit Reduction Act** that was passed in 1984 taxes some benefits, especially flexible spending plans. In return for reduced pay, however, one type of flexible spending plan gives employees the choice between several nontaxable benefits.

Consolidated Omnibus Budget Reconciliation Act

An important provision of the **Consolidated Omnibus Budget Reconciliation Act** passed in 1985 gives terminated or laid-off employees the right to maintain health insurance by paying their own premiums for up to eighteen months. Coverage is extended to employees with reduced work hours, a situation that might otherwise make them ineligible for coverage.

What does the Family and Medical Leave Act of 1993 provide employees?

Family and Medical Leave Act of 1993

The Family and Medical Leave Act of 1993, which covers employers with fifty or more employees, is primarily used by employees to take an unpaid leave upon the birth of a child, when they adopt a child, or when they have an ill child, spouse, or parent who needs their assistance. It guarantees twelve weeks of unpaid leave during a year's time for employees who have worked for their current employer a minimum of twelve months and who have worked a minimum of 1,250 hours during the year before the leave begins. In some instances, an employer can require that an employee use any available paid leave as part of the twelve-week leave if any is available.

IMPLICATIONS FOR THE ADMINISTRATIVE OFFICE MANAGER

The degree to which employees are satisfied with their salaries often affects the interest they take in their jobs. Dissatisfaction can result in increased turnover, higher levels of absenteeism and tardiness, and reduced productivity. Unfortunately, when problems do arise in the salary administration program, rebuilding employee confidence can take a long time to accomplish.

The administrative office manager in many organizations, especially in larger ones, plays an important advisory role in the salary administration program. In some of these organizations, the administrative office manager also has certain functional responsibilities for the program, which may include conducting salary surveys and helping determine new salary schedules.

In some organizations, the administrative office manager determines the amount of merit increase for each employee for whom he or she has either direct or indirect responsibility. In other instances, the manager determines the amount of merit increase for those subordinates for whom direct responsibility exists and merely approves the merit increase for those employees for whom he or she is indirectly responsible. The amount of increase for these employees is determined by their immediate supervisor.

REVIEW QUESTIONS

1. What is the nature of the relationship between job evaluation and salary administration?
2. How does a salary administration program help employees perform at an optimum level?
3. What types of policies should be developed to improve the efficiency of the operation of the salary administration program?
4. In a large organization, who is generally responsible for salary administration? In a small organization?
5. Which of the prepared salary surveys are suitable for determining going rates for the following:
   a. Office or clerical employees?
   b. Middle management?
   c. Exempt employees?
   d. Data processing employees?
6. How can the salary range for specific jobs be determined?
7. How can an organization be sure that its salaries are competitive with salaries paid by other organizations in the community?
8. What characteristics are typically found in effective incentive pay plans?
9. Why do organizations make fringe benefits available to employees?
10. Which provisions of the Fair Labor Standards Act have special significance for salary administration?
11. What workers are covered by the Walsh-Healey Act? By the Pension Reform Act?

DISCUSSION QUESTIONS

1. You have just been appointed to serve on the salary administration committee in the organization in which you work. For the last several years, the organization has used the flat-increase method of adjusting employee salaries. The chairperson of the salary administration committee indicated at a recent meeting that he now favors using the percentage of salary increase method to adjust salaries. Explain the reasons the committee chairperson now probably favors the percentage-of-salary increase method for making salary adjustments.
2. You are a supervisor in a small company. The personnel manager is responsible for salary administration. During a recent conversation with her, you mentioned that perhaps the company should undertake a job evaluation project since the worth of the jobs has never been formally established. She reacted negatively to your comment. When you asked her how she determined an equitable salary range for each job, she replied, "I primarily use intuition and perception. It must work because I've never had any complaints." Discuss the adequacy of the method that is used to determine equitable salary ranges in the company in which you work.
3. At a recent salary administration committee meeting in the organization in which you work, several committee members indicated that the average of next year's salary increase for the organization should not exceed 8 percent. The individuals who argued this point said that since the organization's productivity increased 8 percent, the amount of salary increase should not exceed that amount. Explain the philosophy behind this reasoning.
4. The director of the salary administration program in the organization in which you work recently made a comparison of your organization's salary levels and those of competing organizations. When he discovered that your organization's salary levels

were the highest of any organization, he undertook a campaign to hold the line on salary increases. He indicated that the organization is justified in giving smaller salary increases because of its present salary levels. Discuss the implications of the action recommended by the director of the salary administration program.

5. The organization in which you work recently implemented an incentive pay program. Your supervisor, who frequently confides in you, told you this morning that he has not noticed any appreciable difference in employee performance. You explained that this may be resulting from the attitude among employees that they will all receive incentive pay regardless of their performance. Employees obviously do not understand the functioning of an incentive pay plan. What information about the program should be communicated to them to correct the mistaken ideas they presently have?
6. During the last few weeks, the pending development and implementation of a productivity improvement program in your organization has been widely discussed. You, as supervisor, notice that employee opposition to a program has been increasing with each passing week. Employee opposition seems to be centered around the fear that fewer employees will be needed if they become more productive. The employees are interpreting this to mean that some of them will be laid off because of an eventual work force surplus. Outline the discussion you plan to have with your subordinates in which you attempt to diminish the level of their fears. Obviously, you will want to convey to them that management does not intend for such a program to result in the layoff of even one employee.

STUDENT PROJECTS AND ACTIVITIES

1. Obtain from two organizations in your community (perhaps a large organization and a small organization) a list of the fringe benefits they provide their employees. What are the similarities in the benefits that are provided?
2. Discuss with an administrative office manager the nature of the incentive pay program offered the employees in the organization in which he or she works.
3. Discuss with an office employee who receives incentive pay his or her perception of the value of the program.
4. Discuss with a personnel manager the procedure he or she uses each year in setting new salary ranges.
5. Using whatever printed salary surveys you can obtain, compare the salaries for a comparable job found on the East Coast, the Midwest, and the West Coast. Which location paid the most? The least?

M I N I C A S E

The Kirkendall Glass Company, which is located in Lincoln, Nebraska, has recently discovered that the salary scale for some of its lower-level jobs is no longer competitive, although the scale for the higher-level jobs still seems to be competitive. The lack of competitive salaries seems to be having a negative impact on the organization's ability to hire well-qualified employees at salaries currently being offered. You are on the salary administration committee and have been "elected" by your peers to send the company's president a memo in which you discuss this situation. In the memo, you decide to

1. Provide other evidence the company should collect to determine whether or not its salaries lack competitiveness.
2. Outline the process the organization should use to determine what constitutes competitive salaries.

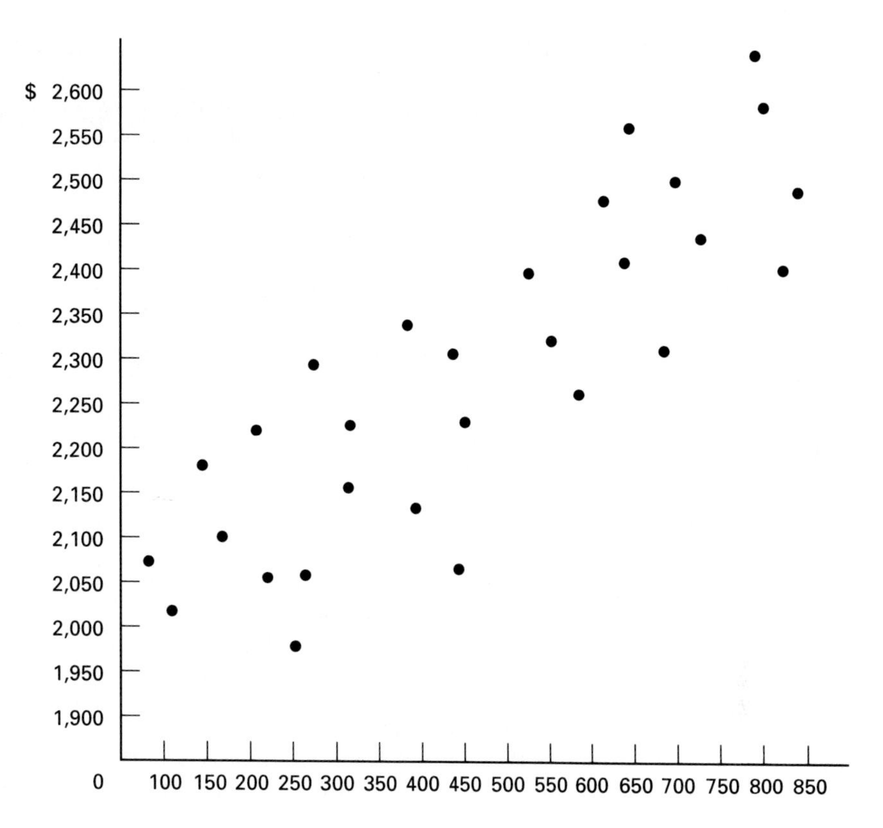

Figure 14-4 Relationship between salaries and evaluated worth for each job in Mandez Bakery.

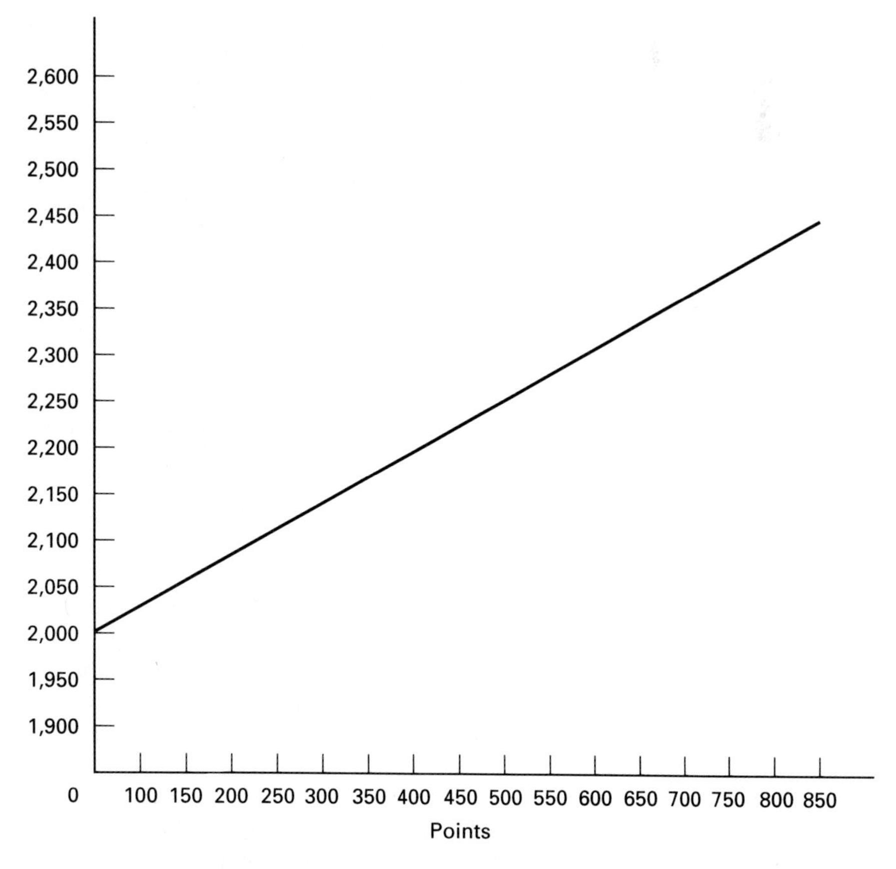

Figure 14-5 Correlation line for comparable jobs in community.

CASE

The salary administration program at Mandez Bakery, Inc., was formally established about ten years ago. You were recently appointed to a committee responsible for determining a new salary structure. The project has progressed to the point that the salaries for comparable jobs in the community have been determined. Figure 14-4 is the salary scattergram depicting the relationship between the salaries and evaluated worth for each job in the Mandez Corporation. Figure 14-5 depicts the correlation line for comparable jobs in the community. The company strives to pay salaries above the community average, which are depicted by the line in Figure 14-5.

1. Determine what you believe would be an appropriate correlation line (midpoint) for salaries in the Mandez Corporation.
2. On the basis of the new midpoint line, prepare a salary range at 10 percent above and below the midpoint. Prepare a salary range chart to depict this information.

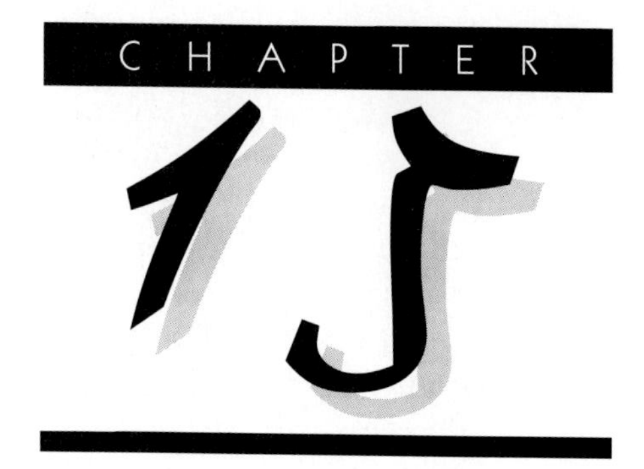

MEASURING OUTPUT OF OFFICE EMPLOYEES

CHAPTER AIM

After studying this chapter, you should be able to design an effective strategy for measuring the output of office employees.

CHAPTER OUTLINE

- Nature of Work Measurement
  - Objectives of Work Measurement
  - Advantages
  - Characteristics of Measurable Office Activities
- Work Measurement Program
- Work Measurement Techniques
  - Production Records
  - Work Sampling
    - Determining Sample Size
    - Advantages and Disadvantages of Work Sampling
  - Time Study
  - Micromotion Study
  - Predetermined Standard Time Data
- Performance Leveling
- Work Standards
  - Advantages of Work Standards
  - Types of Standards
    - Quantity Standards
    - Quality Standards
    - Descriptive Standards
- Implications for the Administrative Office Manager

CHAPTER TERMS

Continuous timing
Descriptive standards
Lapsed timing
Microchrometer
Micromotion study
Performance leveling
Predetermined standard time data
Production records
Quality standards
Quantity standards
Random observations
Stopwatch study
Time log
Time study
Time study sheet
Work measurement
Work sampling
Work standards

Work measurement is used to help determine what constitutes a fair day's work from both the employer's and the employee's standpoint. Employers need evidence that employees are producing at an acceptable level, and employees need assurance that they are being compensated equitably in relation to their output.

What is the function of work standards?

Used in setting work standards, the information collected through the work measurement process specifies expected quantities of output within a given amount of time. Such information enables an organization to compare actual productivity of its employees with expected productivity.

Several methods are used for measuring work. Some office activities are measured by counting the number of units employees produce or process. Others require more sophisticated measures, such as those presented in this chapter.

NATURE OF WORK MEASUREMENT

Because an increasing number of administrative office managers are becoming more concerned about work efficiency and productivity, the measurement of office activities is receiving greater attention than in the past. Greater control over office operations can be exercised when work standards are used for comparing actual results with anticipated results. Although standards can be developed to measure the effectiveness of most office activities, developing standards for nonmeasurable activities is not possible.

Objectives of Work Measurement

What are the objectives of work measurement?

By determining a reasonable level of productivity, work measurement is especially useful in assessing how well an employee's actual output compares with expected output. Work standards are used to express expected output or production levels.

Another use of work measurement is to aid the planning and scheduling of work. By using work standards, the administrative office manager is able to determine a realistic amount of time to complete a given job. The standards can also be used to determine the number of employees who will be needed to complete a project within the allotted time. Work measurement provides the basis for determining if additional employees are needed for the timely completion of a project.

Another objective of work measurement is to help determine the efficiency of work methods and processes. The task of determining whether the employee is overproducing or underproducing is made easy by comparing an employee's output level with generally accepted standards. If employees consistently produce less than expected, an attempt should be made to determine the reasons for the low production levels. If the reason can be attributed to employee inefficiency, the need for an employee training program might be investigated.

Additionally, work measurement helps determine the cost of office operations. Unit cost is calculated by dividing total cost by the number of units produced. Unit output costs are used in two ways: to facilitate the comparison of an organization's performance data with comparable data of other organizations and to aid the budget-preparation process. The amount that should be budgeted for each activity or work process is easily estimated by projecting the total units of output that will be produced during the budget period and then multiplying this projection by the unit output cost.

Finally, work measurement helps determine equitable employee workloads. By using standards to determine load, greater equity in assigning work can be ensured. Equally important is a greater employee understanding of expected performance, which has a positive impact on morale.

Advantages

What are the advantages of work measurement?

A work measurement program results in several significant advantages. Greater control over work processes and methods is possible. Work measurement helps determine the appropriateness of the number of employees assigned to a work unit, as well as the efficiency with which individuals produce. Greater efficiency in planning work is possible, and backlogs can be avoided by using the results of work measurement in scheduling work. Finally, the results of work measurement can be used to help simplify work processes.

Characteristics of Measurable Office Activities

What are the characteristics of measurable office activities?

The measurement of office activities requires tasks that can be isolated and counted. Thus, the tasks constituting specific office jobs must be identifiable. To ensure accurate results, office tasks must be fairly consistent from one measurement to another because fluctuations can readily destroy the measurement results. Office tasks should also be of sufficient quantity to justify the cost of measurement. Typically unjustifiable is the measurement of low-volume office tasks that are expensive to measure.

Activities that require considerable amounts of judgment and decision making are typically unmeasurable. Because the time consumed in performing these tasks varies so widely, measurement results may not be sufficiently reliable to develop accurate standards. Although office tasks involving considerable creativity are difficult to measure, methods have been devised for use in developing standards for such nonroutine creative jobs as drafting and editing.

WORK MEASUREMENT PROGRAM

The installation of a work measurement program involves considerable planning and a thorough investigation of various available alternatives. The number of options available enables organizations to develop programs tailored to specific needs.

Selling a work measurement program to employees and gaining their support are critical to the program's success. Without employee acceptance, program success will be diminished, sometimes quite significantly.

A variety of techniques is successfully used in selling work measurement programs. Employees desire information about the nature of job-related changes they may have to make. Employees desire to learn whether the work measurement results will be used by the organization in assessing the need to retain or eliminate their positions. Assuring employees that the results of work measurement will not cause anyone to be terminated is often critical to employee acceptance of the program. Attrition can often be used to make any needed staffing adjustments.

Among the other techniques used to gain employee support are group meetings in which the group discusses the merits of a work measurement program, case studies about other organizations that have successful work measurement programs, and detailed information about the installation of the work measurement program. Once the decision has been made to install the program, employees should receive from a top-level executive a memo or letter in which information about the program is clearly outlined.

The following is a step-by-step plan for installing a work measurement program:

What steps are involved in installing a work measurement program?

1. *Preliminary plans.* The objectives of the program should be outlined, the work measurement techniques should be selected, and the timetable for installing the program should be determined. If consultants are needed to help install the program, contracting for such services should be considered at this point.
2. *Hire employees.* The duties and responsibilities of the individuals who are responsible for the program should be determined before their selection.
3. *Gain acceptance of and support for the program.* The individuals involved with the installation and operation of the program should be used extensively in gaining acceptance of and support for the program.
4. *Collect important data.* If the work measurement technique that is selected requires gathering data from various work units, the individuals responsible for data collection should be familiarized with the mechanics of the technique.
5. *Analyze collected data and develop standards.* Once the necessary data have been collected, they should be analyzed, and standards should be developed accordingly. If the work measurement program uses predetermined standards purchased from an outside source, the appropriate standards for the various office activities should be developed during this step.
6. *Train supervisors and managers.* Each supervisor and manager in the organization who is directly or indirectly responsible for an employee whose job is affected by work measurement should receive training on the use of work measurement and the implementation of standards.
7. *Instruct employees.* Once supervisors have received training in the implementation and use of standards, they should inform their subordinates of expected levels of production.
8. *Follow up.* Successful work measurement programs are evaluated periodically, with the follow-up occurring more frequently during the early stages of the program. Management needs to know how actual results compare with expected results. When actual results do not compare favorably, the reasons for the discrepancy should be determined, and the program should be modified accordingly.

WORK MEASUREMENT TECHNIQUES

Several work measurement techniques are used to develop work standards. When selecting an appropriate technique to use, the following criteria should be considered:

1. The intended use of the standards.
2. The degree of accuracy required of the standards.

What criteria should be considered in selecting an appropriate work measurement program?

3. The cost the organization is willing to assume in developing the standards.
4. The nature of the work for which standards are desired.
5. The degree to which individuals responsible for the program understand the elements of work measurement and work standards.

Among the work measurement techniques available are production records, work sampling, time study, micromotion study, and predetermined standard time data.

Production Records

As a work measurement technique, the use of **production records** is rather simple and quick. It uses employee production records to determine the amount of time needed to complete a particular job.

What is the function of a time log?

Figure 15-1 illustrates a **time log** that is helpful when using the production records technique. The log enables each employee to keep a record of the work he or she produces and the amount of time taken to produce the work. Each task the employee performs is entered in coded form on the time log (column 1). The number of units produced (column 2) and the amount of time taken to produce the units (column 3) are also entered on the time log. The time increments are usually expressed in units of five or ten minutes.

Each employee should keep a time log for as long as needed to smooth

Activity 1	Units Produced 2	Time 3
D	1	8:00 8:10
A	15	8:20 8:30 8:40
C	2	8:50 9:00
D	1	9:10
F	15	9:20 9:30 9:40
		9:50 10:00 10:10 | | | 12:00

Figure 15-1 Time log.

out or balance any unusual fluctuations. In most instances, a period of two weeks is considered a minimum amount of time to record data.

On accumulating the production records of all the employees, a calculation is made of the total units they produce and the total amount of time taken to produce the units. By dividing the total units produced by the total time taken to produce the units, a unit output standard can be determined. In some instances, the standard will be adjusted either upward or downward as a means of pacing an employee's performance against the average standard. This is done by a leveling process discussed in detail in the "Performance Leveling" section of this chapter.

When the various tasks in a work process change or when the conditions under which work is performed change, the standards most likely will have to be adjusted. This is the reason for routinely investigating the validity of the standards determined by this technique.

Sometimes, department production records kept over a period of time are also used to determine work standards. For example, the log regularly maintained in most word processing centers might be sufficient to set work standards. These logs are frequently used to keep track of the time taken to transcribe the contents of a magnetic dictation belt or tape. By approximating the number of words on a belt or tape and by knowing how much time the transcription process takes, a words-per-minute typing standard can be developed. Allowances have to be made, however, for variations in the dictator's speed of dictation, the complexity of the material, and so forth. The greater the number of uncontrolled variables, the less accurate this technique is likely to be.

What are the advantages of the production records technique?

Among the advantages of the production records technique are the following: The technique is simple, easily understood, and inexpensive to use. Therefore, it is the only technique financially feasible for many organizations. In addition, standards can be quickly developed and implemented without the need for specially trained individuals.

A disadvantage of using the production records technique is the possibility that it may contribute to setting inaccurate standards when employees fail to maintain accurate time logs. Also, the standards developed by this technique are readily affected by changes in work processes. Therefore, employees may have to keep time logs quite regularly for use as input in adjusting standards. Furthermore, because it determines "what is" rather than "what should be," adjustments may have to be made.

Work Sampling

What are the characteristics of the work sampling technique?

Using a statistical base, the **work sampling** technique requires **random observations** to determine the amount of time consumed by each element of an office procedure. This statistical base incorporates the following law of probability: If a procedure is observed randomly a sufficient number of times, the results will be as reliable as when the procedure is observed continuously over a period of time. An important aspect of the work sampling technique is the accurate identification of the type of activity being performed by an employee at the time of each random observation.

Observations are considered random if the employee or employees being observed are randomly chosen and if the time of the observations is randomly determined. These random observations are used to determine what percentage of the total process each activity consumes.

The filing of insurance applications is used to illustrate the work sampling method. The filing process involves five distinct activities. A total of one hundred random observations was determined to be a sufficient quantity. Random observations are made to determine the percentage of the process that each activity consumes. Figure 15-2 illustrates this relationship. For example, of the one hundred random observations, activity A was observed twenty times; activity B, ten times; activity C, forty times; and so forth. The total filing process consumed 500 minutes. Therefore, if activity A constitutes 20 percent of the total process in terms of the number of observations, activity A should also constitute 20 percent or 100 minutes of the total time consumed by the filing process. (This is determined by multiplying 500 by .20.)

Records also have to be examined to determine the number of units produced during each activity. This is illustrated in column E of Figure 15-2. During the 500 minutes consumed by the filing process, 250 units were produced during activity A, 100 units during activity B, and so forth. To determine the standard for activity A, the amount of time (100 minutes) is divided by the number of units produced (250). Therefore, a standard of .4 is derived for activity A. Consequently, one unit is produced during each .4 of a minute or every 24 seconds.

The random selection of the employees and the times they are to be observed can be greatly expedited by using a table of random numbers. These tables and directions for their use can be found in statistics books.

What factors are considered in determining appropriate sample size?

Determining sample size The appropriate sample size is critical to the success of the work sampling technique. The appropriate number is dependent on the following: (1) the portion of time the smallest activity consumes in the total work process; (2) the degree of tolerance required; and (3) the reliability of results required.

The smaller the portion of time consumed by the smallest activity in the total work process, the greater the need for a larger sample. This is because a sufficient number of observations need to be made to ensure the reliability of results; an insufficient number of observations will likely result in insufficient reliability. Generally, the activity that is selected should consume a minimum of 5 percent of the total time. Any activity consuming less than 5 percent is sometimes eliminated from consideration.

Referring to the degree of accuracy required, tolerance is another of the critical elements to be considered when determining appropriate sample size. As the need for a higher tolerance increases, so does the number of observations that have to be made. Conversely, a lower tolerance results in the need for a smaller number of observations.

The degree of reliability required also affects the number of observations that need to be made. Situations that require greater reliability will require a higher number of observations.

A Activity	*B Observations*	*C Percent*	*D Time (min)*	*E Units Produced*	*F Standard (D ÷ E)*
A	20	20	100	250	.4
B	10	10	50	100	.5
C	40	40	200	200	1.0
D	20	20	100	50	2.0
E	10	10	50	125	.4
Totals	100	100	500	725	

Figure 15-2 Illustration of work sampling method.

The following illustrates the impact of variances among three factors that need to be considered in determining the appropriate sample size. If the smallest activity in the work process consumes 25 percent of the total process and if 90 percent accuracy and 80 percent reliability of results are required, 510 observations will be needed. On the other hand, if the smallest activity consumes 5 percent of the total process and if 95 percent accuracy and 80 percent reliability are desired, 12,840 observations will be needed. These numbers are obtainable from appropriate tables in statistics books.

Advantages and disadvantages of work sampling The advantages of the work sampling technique are as follows:

What are the advantages of the work sampling technique?

1. The results are highly accurate, provided that random observations are made.
2. The technique does not require the services of a highly trained analyst.
3. The technique is fairly reasonable in terms of its installation cost.
4. The results can be gathered rather quickly.
5. Work sampling is well suited for long-cycle work processes.

Among the disadvantages of the work sampling technique are the following:

1. Some employees have a tendency to perform differently if they know they are being observed. If unusual performance occurs frequently, the results of work measurement could be affected significantly.
2. Procedures consisting of numerous minute activities are not suitable for work sampling.
3. To set standards, production records have to be used to determine units of output. Such output records are not always readily accessible.
4. The use of work sampling is sufficiently complex that a trained analyst is needed.
5. Various elements of the process are somewhat difficult for employees to understand. As a result, employees may not fully support the program.

Time Study

Also known as **stopwatch study** or stopwatch time study, **time study** uses a stopwatch in the data-gathering process. To improve the effectiveness of this technique, all wasted motions should be eliminated before the work process is analyzed. Standards based on inefficient work processes are of little value.

The time study technique involves the following three steps:

What steps are involved in the time study technique?

1. Break the job down into its basic elements.
2. Record on a **time study sheet** the amount of time consumed by each element of the work process. This step is repeated for several cycles of the work process.
3. Determine the appropriate standards on the basis of the time consumed by each element of the work process.

Figure 15-3, which outlines the process for calculating payroll, illustrates a time study sheet used in conjunction with the time study technique.

Work Process Calculating Payroll
Date: September 3, 19xx

Analyst's Name: L. Davis
Worker's Name: Sandy Evans

	Cycle																	
	1		2		3		4		5		6		7		8			
Elements	T	R	T	R	T	R	T	R	T	R	T	R	T	R	T	R	Standard	Notes
Determine Total Hours Worked	15	00 15	16	126	15	234	14	342	15	451							15	
Multiply Hours Worked by Base Rate of Pay to Arrive at Gross Pay	22	37	21	147	21	255	22	364	* 26	* 457							22	*Put wrong value in machine – had to start over (lost 4 seconds)
Calculate Deductions	55	92	53	200	55	310	54	418	54	511							54	
Subtract Deductions to Get Net Pay	18	110	19	219	18	328	18	436	18	529							18	

Figure 15-3 Time study sheet.

The time study sheet is completed by entering into the appropriate columns the amount of time consumed by each of the elements of the work process. Five cycles of the process were timed, according to the information on Figure 15-3. In an actual situation, more than five cycles may be needed.

What is the difference between continuous timing and lapsed timing?

The time study technique uses two timing techniques: either the **continuous timing** of the entire process or **lapsed timing** for each element of the entire process. When the continuous technique is used, the analyst simply records in the "R" (reading) column of cycle 1 the stopwatch reading at the conclusion of each element of the process. For example, in cycle 1, the first element was completed when the stopwatch showed 15 seconds; the second element, 37 seconds; the third element, 92 seconds; and the fourth, 110 seconds. The amount of time consumed by each element is then entered in the "T" (time) column. The first element consumes 15 seconds; the second, 22 seconds (37 minus 15); and so forth. The timing of the work process is repeated a sufficient number of cycles to compensate for erratic performance.

The use of the lapsed time technique requires that the analyst reset the stopwatch to "0" at the completion of each element of the process. These figures are immediately recorded in the "T" column. Unlike the continuous method, no subtraction is required when the lapsed time technique is used.

The validity of standards is directly affected by the performance of the employees whose output is being timed. In some organizations, the employees who are most respected by their coworkers are the ones timed because of the assumption that the standards will have greater credibility among all employees. If the employees who are timed are also the most skilled workers, the standards most likely will have to be leveled to accommodate the less skilled employees. The leveling process is discussed in the "Performance Leveling" section later this chapter.

Another important characteristic to consider when selecting employees to participate in the timing process is the consistency with which they perform their jobs. An erratic performance is apt to have a negative impact on the reliability of the standards. If the procedure being measured lacks efficiency, the inefficiency should be eliminated before subjecting the procedure to time study. Otherwise, the time study data will not be accurate.

What advantages result from the use of time study?

Time study has the following advantages: (1) It results in the development of accurate standards; (2) it produces more accurate results when measuring work processes comprised of minute elements than either the production records technique or the work sampling technique; and (3) it results in the development of standards that can be readily used for assessing the performance of employees.

Among the disadvantages of time study are the following: (1) The measurement process often requires the use of a trained analyst, which adds to the cost of the work measurement program; (2) office employees tend to have a negative reaction to standards determined by the stopwatch technique; and (3) the technique is not useful for measuring time-consuming elements of a work process.

Micromotion Study

Of the various work measurement techniques, **micromotion study** is the only one that uses a visual recording (either a motion picture or a video tape) of the work process being analyzed. This technique is especially appropriate for work processes that involve both people and machines. An analysis of the visual recording reveals inefficiency in task performance as well as task elements that need to be simplified.

When the primary purpose of micromotion study is to provide data for setting standards, the visual recording is analyzed to determine the amount of time consumed by each element of the work process. Multiplying the number of frames on which an element appears by the speed of the film as it advances through the camera provides the amount of time each element consumes. This result becomes the standard for the element. To illustrate, if two thousand frames advance through the camera per minute and if a particular element of the process appears on two hundred frames, the standard would be one-tenth of a minute (six seconds).

What is a microchrometer?

The use of a **microchrometer** may be needed when the elements of the work process are minute. The microchrometer, which is a special timing device attached to the camera, enables the unit of time to be photographed on each frame of the motion picture. The standard for each element is determined by subtracting from the time that appears on the first frame of a particular element the time that appears on the last frame of the element.

The tendency for micromotion to be an expensive work measurement technique often restricts its use to high-volume, costly work processes. Many believe its use cannot be justified except for processes that possess the volume and cost characteristics mentioned earlier.

The advantages of micromotion study are as follows: (1) It is extremely accurate; (2) it is well suited for analyzing the most minute elements of a work process; and (3) it can also be used to simplify work processes because wasted motions appear on the recording.

The micromotion study technique also possesses several disadvantages. The technique is more costly than some of the other work measurement techniques. Its use is limited to high-volume, costly work processes. It also requires the services of a trained analyst, which precludes some organizations from selecting micromotion study as a work measurement technique.

Predetermined Standard Time Data

From where are predetermined standard time data obtained?

The **predetermined standard time data** technique is the only one discussed in this chapter that typically uses data obtained from external sources. Predetermined standard time data are generally purchased from management consulting firms or from work measurement associations. The purchased data are used as a base for setting the organization's work standards. In rare instances, an organization may develop its own predetermined standard time data, a process that requires the use of individuals who have extensive training in work measurement.

The predetermined standard time data technique is based on the following premise: When motions are performed under identical conditions, the time values of the motions will be constant from one situation to another. Therefore, an organization can use predetermined standard time data to set standards for basic motions, provided the motions are performed under the same conditions as when the predetermined standard times were set.

When using predetermined standard time data, the analyst uses the following steps:

What steps constitute the predetermined standard time data technique?

1. The work process is broken down into its most minute elements.
2. Each element is analyzed in terms of the motion involved.

TABLE II - MOVE - M

Distance Moved Inches	Time TMU				Wt. Allowance			CASE AND DESCRIPTION
	A	B	C	Hand In Monitor B	Wt. (lb.) Up to	Dynamic Factor	Static Constant TMU	
3/4 or less	2.0	2.0	2.0	1.7				
1	2.5	2.9	3.4	2.3	2.5	1.00	0	
2	3.6	4.6	5.2	2.9				A Move object to other hand or against stop.
3	4.9	5.7	6.7	3.6	7.5	1.06	2.2	
4	6.1	6.9	8.0	4.3				
5	7.3	8.0	9.2	5.0	12.5	1.11	3.9	
6	8.1	8.9	10.3	5.7				
7	8.9	9.7	11.1	6.5	17.5	1.17	5.6	
8	9.7	10.6	11.8	7.2				
9	10.5	11.5	12.7	7.9	22.5	1.22	7.4	B Move object to approximate or indefinite location.
10	11.3	12.2	13.5	8.6				
12	12.9	13.4	15.2	10.0	27.5	1.28	9.1	
14	14.4	14.6	16.9	11.4				
16	16.0	15.8	18.7	12.8	32.5	1.33	10.8	
18	17.6	17.0	20.4	14.2				
20	19.2	18.2	22.1	15.6	37.5	1.39	12.5	
22	20.8	19.4	23.8	17.0				
24	22.4	20.6	25.5	18.4	42.5	1.44	14.3	C Move object to exact location.
26	24.0	21.8	27.3	19.8				
28	25.5	23.1	29.0	21.2	47.5	1.50	16.0	
30	27.1	24.3	30.7	22.7				
Additonal	0.8	0.6	0.85		TMU per inch over 30 inches			

Figure 15-4 Predetermined standard time data.

TYPICAL MCD–MOD–I ELEMENTS

A ARRANGE PAPERS		
COLLATE		
TWO SHEETS	ACT	42
ADD'L. SHEETS	ACA	27
SORT		
GROUPS	ASG	47
PIGEONHOLES	ASP	69
ALPHABETICALLY		
0 THRU 19	ASA01	72
20 THRU 29	ASA02	79
OVER 30	ASA03	85

G GET AND ASIDE		
GET ONLY		
BATCH OF PAPERS (Loose)	GGB	31
JUMBLED OBJECT	GGJ	27
MEDIUM OBJECT	GGM	18
SHEET OF PAPER	GGS	21
ASIDE ONLY		
TO FIXTURE	GAF	23
TO OTHER HAND	GAH	20
TO PILE	GAP	32
TO TABLE	GAT	15
COMBINED GET & ASIDE		
BATCH TO FIXTURE	GBF	54
BATCH TO PILE	GBP	63
BATCH TO TABLE	GBT	46
JUMBLED TO FIXTURE	GJF	50
JUMBLED TO OTHER HAND	GJH	47
JUMBLED TO TABLE	GJT	42
MEDIUM TO FIXTURE	GMF	41
MEDIUM TO OTHER HAND	GMH	38
MEDIUM TO TABLE	GMT	33
SHEET TO FIXTURE	GSF	44
SHEET TO OTHER HAND	GSH	41
SHEET TO PILE	GSP	53
SHEET TO TABLE	GST	36

B BODY ELEMENTS		
ARISE and SIT	BAS	208
SEATED TURN	BST	122
BEND and ARISE	BBA	61
WALK PER STEP	BWS	17

M MAILING		
FOLD		
INSERT		
NO-SEAL		
REGULAR ENVELOPE	MFIN01	195
MANILA ENVELOPE	MFIN02	240
STRINGED ENVELOPE	MFIN03	226
SEAL		
REGULAR ENVELOPE	MFIS01	275
MANILA ENVELOPE	MFIS02	340
IDENTIFY		
LABEL/STICKER		
DRY	MIL01	49
WET	MIL02	85
STAMP		
NORMAL PER TIME	MIS01	13
SELF-INKING	MIS02	56
DATE SET	MIS03	49
OPEN		
SEALED		
FOLDED		
REGULAR ENVELOPE	MOSF01	192
MANILA ENVELOPE	MOSF02	199
UNFOLDED		
REGULAR ENVELOPE	MOSU01	132
MANILA ENVELOPE	MOSU02	169
UNSEALED		
FOLDED		
REGULAR ENVELOPE	MOUF01	101
MANILA ENVELOPE	MOUF02	110
STRINGED ENVELOPE	MOUF03	148
UNFOLDED		
REGULAR ENVELOPE	MOUU01	41
MANILA ENVELOPE	MOUU02	80
STRINGED ENVELOPE	MOUU03	118
UNFOLDED		
INSERT		
SEAL		
REGULAR ENVELOPE	MUIS01	130
MANILA ENVELOPE	MUIS02	258
NO-SEAL		
REGULAR ENVELOPE	MUIN01	50
MANILA ENVELOPE	MUIN02	158
STRINGED ENVELOPE	MUIN03	145

F FASTEN/UNFASTEN		
BINDER		
DUO-TANG		
FASTEN	FBDF	125
UNFASTEN	FBDU	77
THREE RING		
OPEN	FBTO	31
CLOSE	FBTC	31
CLIP		
PAPER		
PLACE	FCPP	75
REMOVE	FCPR	43
RUBBER BAND		
PLACE	FRP	129
REMOVE	FRR	16
STAPLE		
HAND		
FIRST	FSHF	77
ADDITIONAL	FSHA	35
TABLE		
FIRST	FSTF	37
ADDITIONAL	FSTA	20
REMOVE		
FIRST	FSRF	84
ADDITIONAL	FSRA	52

H HANDLE PAPER		
JOG		
CARDS		
UP TO 1" THICK	HJC01	5
OVER 1" THICK	HJC02	9
SHEETS		
UP TO 1" THICK	HJS01	8
OVER 1" THICK	HJS02	12
PUNCH		
THREE HOLE	HPT	30
SHIFT		
FLIP OR TURN	HSF	23
GENERAL	HSG	27
TEAR		
CARE	HTC	32
NO-CARE	HTN	23

O OPEN AND CLOSE		
BINDER		
COVER		
8 1/2 X 11	OBC01	48
DRAWERS and DOORS		
DESK DRAWER	ODD	62
FILE DRAWER	ODF	78
TOPS		
FLAPS	OTF	95
HINGED LID	OTH	35
LOOSE LID	OTL	71

Figure 15-5 Master clerical data. Courtesy: Serge A. Birn Company.

3. To determine the appropriate standard, each motion of the work process is compared with the purchased predetermined standard time data. This step is repeated for each element. Figure 15-4 illustrates one of the tables found in one system.
4. The standard for the entire process is found by adding the standard times for each of the motions.

Internally and externally developed predetermined standard time data are generally developed by either stopwatch time studies or by micromotion study. The use of either of these techniques provides accurate data.

Several predetermined standard time data systems are available. Included are such systems as Motion-Time Analysis, Methods Time Measurement (MTM), Basic Motion Time Study, Universal Maintenance Standards, and Master Clerical Data. Although the same basic principles were originally used in developing each of the systems, certain elements of the various systems differ significantly.

The data illustrated in Figure 15-4 represent one of the thirteen tables found in the MTM system. The time measurement unit (TMU) used in MTM is one hundred-thousandth of an hour. Because the time units are so minute, MTM is not well suited for many common office work processes. For example, grasping and putting a sheet of paper into working position can involve three or four different MTM motions.

Master Clerical Data, which is an adaptation of MTM, classifies clerical work into thirteen distinct elemental categories. The data in the categories are used to provide input for determining standard times for various elements of clerical work processes. Figure 15-5 illustrates the standards for a portion of the MCD system.

The use of predetermined standard time data results in several advantages. The technique results in accurate standards. Once the predetermined data are available, additional work measurement analyses do not have to be completed when a work process is changed or when a new work process is developed, even though new standards have to be calculated. Because of the specificity with which the standards are developed, employees accept the results more readily than when some of the other less sophisticated techniques are used. Finally, the application of the technique is fairly rapid.

Several disadvantages also exist. The technique is costly because of the necessity of using highly trained analysts and expensive predetermined standard time data. Certain office operations, primarily those of long cycle, are not adaptable to the predetermined standard time data technique. Also, when predetermined standard time data are developed internally, the technique is time consuming and is likely to be a costly process.

PERFORMANCE LEVELING

Why is performance leveling sometimes necessary?

Designed to determine what constitutes a fair day's work, the results of work measurement are used by both the employer and the employee. To accomplish this purpose, standards may have to be adjusted by using a process known as **performance leveling**. Adjusting standards will help ensure that they are reasonable.

Because most work measurement techniques gather data on continuously performed work processes, the techniques may not take into consideration the individual differences between employees, the effect of fatigue on employees, interruptions, coffee breaks, rest periods, and so forth. To make standards as reasonable as possible, they may have to be leveled to compensate for these conditions.

Full attainment of standards is desirable, although rarely can that goal be achieved even under the best of conditions. When standards are set too high for all employees to reach, including the most productive employees, the results of the work measurement program will likely be negligible. This situation makes performance leveling desirable.

The use of trained analysts for performance leveling is advantageous. The knowledge and experience of these individuals adds considerably to the accuracy of the leveling process. If trained analysts are not available (for example, when the production records technique is used), the individuals in charge of the work measurement program may have to adjust the standards several times until they are appropriate for the circumstances.

The following illustrates how the leveling process is used. Assume that a standard for filing documents was set at forty per hour. This standard was set using predetermined standards. Because none of the presently employed file clerks are able to attain that standard, the rate was leveled to thirty-five units per hour. Now, 80 percent of the file clerks regularly attain that rate.

WORK STANDARDS

A primary objective of work measurement is to collect data for use in setting standards for office work. Unless care is exercised in performing work measurement activities, the reliability of the resulting standards is likely to be affected. Not recommended is the use of input in some form other than that derived from accurate work measurement.

Work standards should not be set at a level that only the most efficient, productive employee can attain. Nor should they be set at such a low level that each employee is capable of effortlessly attaining the standards. Rather, they should be set at a level that provides a sufficient incentive for the employee to perform well but also at a level where the average employee can be reasonably successful. If the standards are to be used effectively, they must be acceptable to the employees. In many instances, the most difficult and time-consuming task in developing standards involves gaining employee acceptance.

Advantages of Work Standards

The use of work standards provides several important benefits.

What advantages result from the use of work standards?

1. Standards help increase the efficiency with which employees perform their jobs.
2. Standards help inform employees of their expected production levels.
3. Standards assist managers in making personnel decisions, because the employees who are performing beyond expected levels of production can be readily identified.
4. Because employees are aware of the procedures for performing their jobs, less supervision is needed and greater control over the work process is possible.
5. Standards provide the basis for incentive wage systems.
6. Standards help improve employee morale by making employees aware of what is expected of them.

Types of Standards

Among the types of standards used in offices are quantity, quality, and descriptive standards. Although work measurement is used only to develop quantity standards, the others are important for various kinds of office work or functions.

Quantity standards **Quantity standards** are expressed as units of output per unit of time. For longer work cycles, the unit of time is usually expressed in hours. For shorter work cycles, the unit of time may be expressed in minutes or even seconds.

Two types of quantity standards exist: subjective and engineered. Subjective standards are based on an educated guess or supposition. Therefore, no scientific or research processes are used in their calculation, which sometimes causes their accuracy to be challenged. Engineered standards, conversely, are much more precise because they are based on the results of work measurement. Although subjective standards are more arbitrary, engineered standards are more accurate, reliable, and acceptable.

Quality standards Although not determined by work measurement, **quality standards** are crucial in an office. They are used to measure the accuracy and acceptability of work. For example, quality standards are helpful in determining the suitability of typewritten or keyboarded work and the accuracy of filing, arithmetical calculations, and data entry. Although adherence to strict quality standards will result in the redoing of some work, the enforcement of the standards will likely be cost-effective in the long run.

What are descriptive standards?

Descriptive standards Like quality standards, **descriptive standards** are not determined by work measurement. These standards are used to identify acceptable descriptive characteristics of areas or objects within an office. For example, descriptive standards are used to determine the appropriate amount of office space for the different categories of employees. To illustrate, a vice president is entitled to more square feet of floor space than a clerk-typist.

Some organizations also use descriptive standards to identify the size and type of working areas or desks to which the various categories of employees are entitled. They are also used in purchasing office supplies, equipment, and items that may have an effect on the working environment—for example, the lighting in the office.

IMPLICATIONS FOR THE ADMINISTRATIVE OFFICE MANAGER

The availability of a work measurement program and realistic work standards help administrative office managers supervise their subordinates. When standards are available, concern for what constitutes a fair day's work can be greatly diminished.

Employees have assurance that their expected production rates do not exceed their level of responsibility and compensation rates. The employer has assurance that it is getting its "money's worth" from the employees. In essence, work measurement and standards remove much uncertainty in the organization's production processes.

For the administrative office manager, getting employees to accept the work measurement program and standards is generally the most significant problem. Employee acceptance is fundamental to program success. Much of the time and effort the administrative office manager devotes to the program, especially in the preliminary development stages, is concerned with obtaining employee acceptance. If employees are made aware of the program benefits and are convinced that they will be treated more fairly, many of their concerns can be eliminated.

REVIEW QUESTIONS

1. How can work measurement be used to determine the efficiency of work methods and procedures?
2. How can work measurement be used to provide a greater amount of control over work processes and methods?
3. How is work measurement useful in determining equitable workloads?
4. How do the production records technique and the work sampling technique of work measurement differ from one another?
5. What is the difference between continuous and lapsed time methods of timing work for the time study method of work measurement?
6. Because predetermined standard time data frequently use data purchased from an outside source, how can one justify their use in other organizations?
7. Why is performance leveling necessary?
8. Discuss the various uses of work standards.
9. What are descriptive standards?

DISCUSSION QUESTIONS

1. The organization in which you are employed recently implemented a work standards program. The employees enthusiastically supported the program at the beginning because they felt they would finally know what was expected of them. They are not as enthusiastic about the program now because the standards were set so high that virtually no one can reach them. When the individual who set the standards was questioned about this situation, he said, "I did it this way so that even the best employees would be challenged." Discuss your reaction to this situation.
2. You are a supervisor in an organization that uses work standards. Quite often the employees in your unit fail to reach these standards. When you asked several employees about their lack of concern for the standards, the majority indicated that they could reach them but that they didn't want to because "there wasn't anything in it for them when they did." When you asked them what they desired in return for reaching the standards, the common response was "a monetary bonus," but you know that a bonus of any kind is not realistic at this time. What strategies do you plan to use to motivate the employees to attain their standards?
3. You recently read an article about work standards that appeared in a professional journal to which you subscribe. The main theme of the article seemed to be that a happy medium needs to be reached in setting standards—they should be high enough to challenge and motivate employees but not so high that they cause employees to get discouraged. What suggestions can you provide that will be helpful in developing standards that strike a happy medium?
4. When the management of the organization in which you work began to express interest in implementing a work standards program, the employees became quite alarmed. They indicated that they were afraid the implementation of work standards was just one more way for management to manipulate them. Identify

several situations relating to work standards that might cause employees to develop a negative attitude about standards. Explain how each of the situations can be eliminated.

5. Most of the employees in the organization in which you work are opposed to the use of work standards. Management was not surprised when it recently received from employees an overwhelmingly negative response to a vice president's suggestion that a work standards program be installed. What should management do to get employees to accept a work standards program?
6. A few months ago, the organization in which you work used the production records method to provide input in setting work standards. Some of the standards that resulted from the use of the production records technique were not very accurate. The organization now plans to use the predetermined standard time data method to back up the results of the production records method. When both are compared with one another, what are the advantages of the predetermined standard time data technique? Why is it likely to provide more accurate standards?

STUDENT PROJECTS AND ACTIVITIES

1. Discuss with an administrative office manager the process used in setting work standards in the organization in which he or she works.
2. Discuss with an office employee who has participated in work measurement processes the value he or she perceives for work measurement.
3. Obtain from two organizations their work standards for a comparable office task. How similar are the standards? What work measurement techniques were used to set the standards?
4. Discuss with an administrative office manager the success his or her employees have in reaching set work standards. What percentage of the employees generally meet the standards?
5. Examine an organization's descriptive standards. To what do the items pertain?

MINICASE

The Blevins Bakery Company, which is located in Deerfield, Illinois, has grown quite rapidly the last few years. Several management practices and programs found in most firms of a comparable size are not found in Blevins. Perhaps the fact that most of management's effort has been devoted to expansion rather than operations improvement explains the reason why a work measurement program has never been implemented. As a new administrative office manager, you decide to prepare a memo for the executive vice president in which you

1. Discuss the advantages that would result from the implementation of a work measurement program
2. The components that you recommend be included in such a program.

CASE

The Taylor Rubber Corporation, a manufacturer of vehicle tires, belts, and hoses, is located in Cleveland, Ohio. Except for the performance of four of its administrative units, management is quite satisfied with the organization's overall accomplishments. The performance of the office employees in these four units contrasts sharply with the performance of the office employees in the other units. The employees in these four units are not as productive as their counterparts in the other units. They work at a slower pace, their work contains errors, and some of their work has to be redone.

Several of the managers believe that the installation of a work standards program in these four units would be beneficial. These same managers acknowledge that installing work standards in only these four units may cause these employees to believe that they are being "picked on." These managers also acknowledge that if the standards were installed throughout the organization, the employees in the other units may become resentful, which would adversely affect their performance. As the administrative office manager for the company, you have been asked by the executive vice president to provide her with a report in which you

1. Recommend the installation of a work standards program in either the four problem units or company wide. (Justify your recommendation.)
2. If the decision is made to install standards throughout the company, explain how management can justify this action to those employees whose performance is adequate.
3. If the decision is made to install standards in only the four units, explain how management can justify this action without alienating the affected employees.

CHAPTER

IMPROVING PRODUCTIVITY OF OFFICE EMPLOYEES

CHAPTER AIM

After studying this chapter, you should be able to design a program that helps employees maximize their productivity.

CHAPTER OUTLINE

CHAPTER TERMS

- Alternative workweek
- Burnout
- Communication
- Cost-benefit ratio
- Employee assistance programs (EAP)
- Employee participation
- Flextime
- Horizontal loading
- Incentives
- Job design
- Job enrichment
- Job rotation
- Job security
- Job sharing
- Job simplification
- Management by Objectives (MBO)
- Measurement data
- Mental and emotional stress
- Per unit cost
- Problem solving
- Productivity improvement program
- Productivity manager
- Quality circles
- Quality of work life (QWL)
- Task force
- Team building
- Time management
- Total Quality Management (TQM)
- Vertical loading

One of the primarily responsibilities of administrative office managers is maximizing the productivity of their employees. To do this, a well-designed, structured program is needed. A formal approach to productivity improvement generally ensures a favorable return on the investment of organizational resources in the program.

The familiarity of administrative office managers with the new technology that helps increase employee output enables them to play a vital role in the development of productivity improvement programs. They are also familiar with the various management practices that have a favorable impact on productivity. In some organizations, the administrative office manager coordinates the productivity improvement program. In other organizations, the administrative office manager serves on the productivity **task force** that is coordinated by the **productivity manager**.

By definition, productivity is the result obtained from dividing output by input. Consequently, the more output an organization obtains from constant levels of input, the better its productivity.

Included in this chapter is a discussion of several topics, including various elements of productivity improvement programs. Later chapters contain information about the technology that has a positive impact on office productivity.

THE PRODUCTIVITY DILEMMA

Awareness about the productivity dilemma increased significantly during the mid- and late-1970s and early-1980s when productivity in the United States began to stagnate. The productivity dilemma in this country received even more attention when most industrialized countries continued to increase their productivity during the years that U.S. productivity declined. An overall deterioration in productivity levels is particularly troublesome because of its negative impact on the country's economic vitality.

Responsible for the stagnation of productivity in the United States are the following situations:

What conditions are responsible for the stagnation of productivity in the United States?

1. Constraining nature of government regulations, actions, and policies.
2. Declining work ethic.
3. Declining research and development expenditures.
4. Declining capital investment.
5. Increasing number of service workers.
6. Changing characteristics of workforce.
7. Constraining practices, policies, and attitudes of management.

An administrative office manager who is interested in improving office productivity will find that reducing the constraining practices, policies, and attitudes of management is the one area among those listed above about which he or she can do something.

THE PRODUCTIVITY IMPROVEMENT PROGRAM

Establishment of a formal **productivity improvement program** is an effective way for an organization to increase its productivity. The use of an informal approach will likely result in fewer desirable outcomes.

Included in this section is a discussion of the following program elements: characteristics of successful programs, steps in developing programs, and measuring office productivity.

Characteristics of Successful Programs

Successful productivity improvement programs possess several common characteristics, including

What are the characteristics of successful productivity improvement programs?

1. *Top-management support.* Without the endorsement and support of top management, any effort expended in improving productivity will likely result in less than maximum results. Top-management support is a most crucial program characteristic. In addition to endorsing the changes that must be made to improve productivity, top management must also be willing to allocate the necessary financial resources to the program.
2. *Employee commitment.* Employees who are committed to improving their productivity are an important ingredient of successful productivity improvement programs. Once the program begins functioning, employees have a large impact on its success or failure. The greater the level of employee commitment at the beginning, the better the chances for program success.
3. *Top-priority status.* Another hallmark of effective productivity improvement programs is their top-priority status. High-priority programs generally attain faster, more significant results than programs carrying lesser status.

4. *Productivity goals*. Successful productivity improvement programs possess measurable productivity goals that are reasonable and attainable. While the organization has broad goals, employee goals must also be formulated. Employees who are aware of their expected performance are generally found to be more highly motivated to achieve predetermined goals.
5. *Employee participation*. One of the most effective ways to increase employees' desire to improve their productivity is to involve them in the process of program design. Participation generally increases program success. In addition, employees are often able to contribute excellent ideas about ways they can increase their productivity. Once the program is functional, employees should be continually encouraged to contribute their ideas for increasing their productivity.
6. *Employee rewards*. Productivity improvement programs that reward employees for increasing their productivity are more successful than those that provide no rewards. Faster promotions, incentive pay, profit sharing, and recognition are among the types of rewards successfully used. The availability of rewards is perceived by many employees to be just as important as the type of rewards they receive.
7. *Program leadership*. Overall authority and responsibility for the coordination of a productivity improvement program are generally assigned to one individual. Many organizations also use a task force that serves in an advisory capacity to the individual responsible for the program.
8. *Program communication*. Successful productivity improvement programs have extensive amounts of communication between management and employees. Lack of information often produces employee anxiety about the need for establishing a program. Communication will help diminish the concern of employees that they are being manipulated by management. In addition, communication between employees and management is useful when modifying the program. Employees should be given ample feedback about all program accomplishments, including those that fall short of expectations.
9. *Measurement techniques/devices*. Another characteristic of successful productivity improvement techniques is the use of appropriate measurement techniques/devices. While some of the work performed in offices is easily measured or counted, other activities (such as creative effort) are difficult to measure. Determining the success of productivity improvement efforts is more difficult when activities cannot be accurately measured.

Steps in Developing a Productivity Improvement Program

The development of a formal productivity improvement program should proceed through several logical, well-defined steps:

What steps are involved in developing a productivity program?

Step 1. Carry out preliminary planning Careful planning during this first step will help ensure successful results once the program becomes operational. In fact, unless a solid foundation is laid at this stage of program development, designing a quality program is difficult. Once top management approves the development of a program and appoints the productivity manager, various activities within this step can be undertaken.

An important activity is the identification of the program's objectives. Although top management may provide some broad objectives, additional specific objectives should be formulated by the task force. The nature of the general and specific objectives will be affected by the amount of financial resources that management commits to the program. The specific objectives should be expressed in quantitative, measurable terms, which will facilitate the eventual assessment of program accomplishments.

Also important in preliminary planning is determining the program's scope, which will identify the departments or units that are to be included in the improvement efforts. The scope will be affected by the availability of financial resources and need. To determine which units will benefit most from productivity improvement, the following techniques are often used: surveys, observations, and work analyses.

The individuals who will be involved extensively in the productivity improvement program should also be identified at an early stage in the developmental process. Besides the administrative office manager, others who can make significant contributions to the task force are individuals with expertise in data processing, systems design, and human resources utilization.

Providing input and direction into the development and operation of the program are two responsibilities of the task force. It may also be responsible for developing or carrying out certain tasks. Common responsibilities of the task force are formulating specific program objectives and productivity goals, monitoring program results, approving productivity improvement suggestions initiated at lower organizational levels, and developing control procedures that help ensure the success of the program.

In some organizations, input is obtained from committees within those departments or work units extensively involved in productivity improvement efforts. Common responsibilities of these groups include the following: providing pertinent data and information to the task force, identifying areas/activities in need of improved productivity, developing productivity improvement initiatives, and communicating with all unit employees about productivity improvement efforts.

Keeping employees abreast of developments will increase their acceptance of the program. Managerial communication should begin during this stage and continue throughout the duration of the program.

Why does the current situation have to be assessed?

Step 2. Assess current situation Before an organization can make any changes to improve its productivity, the current situation has to be assessed. This process involves measuring the present productivity performance of department functions and employee activities. In addition to helping reveal areas/activities in need of change, preliminary **measurement data** can also be used as a benchmark to evaluate program results after the changes have been implemented. The pre- and postcomparison of data will help determine if efforts to improve productivity are successful.

Assessing the current situation involves identifying and analyzing the nature of the various departmental work processes and procedures. Also important is the analysis of the efficiency of the interrelationships between employees, equipment and machines, and work processes. Examining the nature of these interrelationships helps identify which elements may be responsible for restricting productivity. Those areas or activities creating problems should be included in the productivity improvement program.

The department or unit manager is often responsible for coordinating the assessment of the activities under his or her control. Before undertaking the assessment, though, the program's staff should thoroughly orient the manager about proper procedures to be followed. Having the manager rather than the productivity unit staff conduct the assessment is recommended because the manager is more likely to better understand the internal functions of his or her department than an outsider. Involving department employees as much as possible in the assessment process is also helpful.

In addition to assessing department functions, assessing the way in which employees perform their assigned duties is important. Special attention will be focused on those activities that impede employee productivity. In some instances, employees simply lack the motivation to increase their productivity; in other instances, various elements of their work processes impede their output. Effort should be made to eliminate the negative effect of either of these two situations on employee productivity.

The next major section provides more detailed information about the process of measuring office productivity.

At the conclusion of this step, a fairly comprehensive list of areas and activities potentially targeted for inclusion in the productivity improvement program will have been formulated.

Step 3. Select areas/activities From the comprehensive list of areas/activities identified in step 2, those in greatest need of improvement are selected. The amount of financial resources allocated to the productivity improvement program may also have to be considered in determining the feasibility of including various areas/activities. Conceivably, the cost of improving the productivity of certain areas or activities may exceed the availability of financial resources.

What factors can be used to prioritize the areas and activities being considered for productivity improvement efforts?

When the inclusion of all the areas on the comprehensive list is not possible, objective criteria should be used to prioritize those being considered. The criteria that are used in the prioritizing process include (1) the extent to which the area/activity encompasses the entire organization; (2) the projected amount of improvement that is possible; (3) the cost-benefit ratio of each improved area/activity; and (4) the quantity of work in the area that is being considered for change or the frequency with which various activities occur.

At the conclusion of this step, a new list is compiled of the areas/activities to be included in the productivity improvement program.

Step 4. Develop alternative solutions Generally, several alternatives will be available to help increase the productivity of the various areas/activities that were selected in the previous step. As the number of alternatives identified increases, so does the amount of planning flexibility that is available.

The task force and the various internal unit committees play a key role in identifying the alternative solutions. The more expertise the group members have in both the technological and human resource areas, the more useful their input will be.

What is the function of the cost-benefit ratio?

An assessment should be made of the potential impact of each of the alternative solutions on related areas/activities. Those alternatives with a potentially negative impact should be eliminated from consideration. The calculation of a **cost-benefit ratio** for each of the alternatives will be useful in weighing their relative advantages and disadvantages.

After each alternative is carefully assessed and evaluated, the one identified as having the greatest potential for productivity improvement is chosen. The task force plays a key role in identifying the best alternative for improving the productivity of the various areas/activities.

Step 5. Design the solution Once the alternative solution is selected, the next step involves designing the solution. In some instances, the design process is fairly simple and takes little time and effort. In other instances, the design process is rather complex and time consuming.

When the chosen solution requires new equipment and/or extensive changes in work procedures, the design process will be more complex. Involving equipment vendors and systems specialists in the design process may be worthwhile. In some instances, involving individuals who have expertise in areas other than the affected areas is also useful.

Often required by top management is its approval of certain solutions before the design process gets underway, especially when solutions require significant amounts of new equipment or extensive changes in existing procedures. For less involved solutions, middle management approval may be sufficient.

Step 6. Develop an implementation plan and implement the solution Occasionally, the development of a plan for implementing a solution will consume nearly as much time and effort and will be nearly as involved as the design process. The more thought and planning that go into the development of the implementation plan, the more easily the solution can be implemented. The complexity of the implementation plan varies directly with the complexity of the situation.

The success of a new solution is often affected by the level of commitment unit managers and employees have for its succeeding. Therefore, they are often involved in the development of the implementation schedule. Their input may make a significant difference in determining whether or not the solution is successful.

Other important aspects of this step involve installing the new equipment, training or retraining of employees, "debugging" the new system, obtaining software, and so forth. Also important is determining the dates by which various activities should be completed as well as identifying the individual(s) responsible for carrying out these activities.

The last part of this step is the implementation of the solution, a process made easier when the previous steps are carried out as suggested.

Step 7. Conduct follow-up of solution Once the solution has been in operation for a few months, it should be evaluated to determine how well its actual performance compares with expected performance. Pre- and postmeasurements can be compared to determine if objectives are being attained. When actual results are less than what was expected, the reasons for the discrepancy should be determined before any modifications are made.

Measuring Office Productivity

Several techniques are available for use in measuring the tasks performed by office employees. While several techniques have existed for a number of years, others are fairly new. A number of measurement techniques are discussed in detail in Chapter 15.

Measuring the productivity of various office activities is a crucial element of step 2 (assess current situation) when designing a productivity improvement program. The productivity status of an area or activity has to be assessed before any recommendations for improvement can be made. Making changes on the basis of a perceived need rather than a carefully measured need is not recommended.

What types of office activities can be easily measured?

Several characteristics of specific office tasks determine the ease with which they are measured. An easily measured task possesses the following characteristics: the task can be isolated, which helps determine the point at which it begins and ends; the amount of effort involved in performing the task and the amount of time consumed in completing it are fairly uniform from one undertaking to another; and the task is easily countable.

Two types of office tasks are not as readily measured as tasks with a manual or physical nature: those that involve a fair amount of creativity and those that use considerable amounts of judgment. The tasks that require greater levels of creativity and judgment are those for which some of the newer measurement techniques have been developed.

Several types of data can be obtained through the measurement process. One type of data is quantitative in nature, which is calculated by dividing the amount of time consumed in producing the units by the total units of output produced. When both a quantity and quality measure of office productivity are desired, the productivity rate will have to be adjusted to reflect the amount of poor-quality work that has to be redone.

In some instances, the availability of cost data is helpful. This is calculated by using the **per unit cost** of materials and pro-rating the cost of labor, equipment, and overhead. Computing the per unit cost is necessary when calculating cost-benefit ratios of either existing procedures or various alternative procedures being considered.

Suggestions for increasing the effectiveness of productivity measurement follow:

How can the effectiveness of productivity measurement be determined?

1. Determine the measurement objective (quantity, quantity and quality, or cost) before selecting the measurement technique.
2. Consider the characteristics of the area/activity being measured and select the simplest, easiest-to-use technique that circumstances will allow.
3. Teach those who are responsible for measurement the proper use of the various techniques.
4. Use a sufficiently long measurement period to compensate for any abnormal fluctuations in the workload.

Data gathered during the measurement process are used in several ways. One important use is to help identify those areas/activities in need of improved productivity. The data are also used to provide a benchmark to make comparisons of office productivity before and after the various solutions have been implemented. Furthermore, the data are used to help identify viable solutions for increasing productivity.

When the measured results indicate a need to improve the productivity of an area/activity, the following four broad options are available:

Office automation The productivity of office employees can often be increased when they use the new automated equipment that enables them to perform their tasks faster and with less effort. Office automation is covered in detail in Chapter 22.

Work processes and procedures Office employees can improve their productivity by using efficient work processes and procedures. Several of the chapters in this text contain sections concerned with improving the efficiency of various work processes and procedures.

Working environment The environment in which employees work can be designed to stimulate their desire to become more productive. Information about designing an effective working environment is also covered in several chapters in this text.

Personnel Employees who have positive attitudes about their jobs and the organizations for which they work tend to be more productive than those with negative attitudes. The following section provides a discussion of several techniques that help improve employee attitudes about their jobs and their employers.

PRODUCTIVITY IMPROVEMENT TECHNIQUES

Office productivity can be enhanced by increasing the output of office employees. Frequently, the performance of employees either impedes or enhances the productivity of the office function, regardless of the effectiveness of the automated technology they use, the efficiency of the work processes that comprise their jobs, or the environment in which they work.

Included in this section is a discussion of the following productivity improvement techniques: job design, flextime, job sharing, Management by Objectives (MBO), job security, employee participation, quality circles, quality of work life, employee assistance programs, communication, burnout reduction, incentives, mental and emotional stress reduction, team building, problem solving, time management, and alternative workweek.

Job Design

Job design clearly affects the amount of satisfaction employees derive from their work and the level of productivity they attain in performing their job functions. Employees generally want their jobs to possess several characteristics, including task variety, importance, and autonomy. Furthermore, they want to be able to identify with their job as well as to receive feedback regarding their job performance. Designing jobs with these characteristics will have a positive impact on employee productivity.

Several job-related approaches are successfully used to help employees improve their productivity. Included among these approaches are the following:

In what way can job rotation be used to improve employee productivity?

Job rotation The use of **job rotation** as a technique for improving productivity enables employees periodically to exchange their work assignments with others. This technique enables the organization to maximize the opportunities for employee growth and development. Not only does the job satisfaction of employees improve, but also their productivity increases. Furthermore, employees benefit from the additional training they are likely to receive. Another advantage results from a reduction in the monotony employees experience with their jobs when they perform the same tasks for an extended time.

Psychologically, job rotation has a positive impact on the productivity improvement efforts of many employees who use it as a way of temporarily exploring other jobs. Those who enjoy the jobs they rotate into frequently apply for these positions when they become open. The employer also benefits from having employees who are cross-trained.

Job simplification Another aspect of job design having a positive impact on productivity improvement efforts is **job simplification**. This technique involves removing repetitive, dull tasks from jobs as well as removing such impediments as awkward work flow and communication barriers. Much of the new office technology is capable of handling the repetitive, mundane tasks employees used to perform manually.

What is job enrichment?

Job enrichment Of the various job-design approaches useful for improving productivity, **job enrichment** may provide the best long-term results. Enrichment enables employees to assume greater levels of responsibility for and control over their jobs while increasing their job planning opportunities. Essentially, job enrichment humanizes employees' jobs by giving them greater opportunities to experience achievement, recognition, and job growth.

Job enrichment and job enlargement are different from each other. Whereas job enlargement provides employees with a broader range of job duties without corresponding increases in responsibility and control, job enrichment provides a broader range of duties with corresponding increases in responsibility and control. Job enlargement has little impact on improving employee productivity.

Horizontal loading, similar to job enlargement, gives the employee more duties with identical or similar types of task characteristics. **Vertical loading**, which is similar to job enrichment, provides the employee with a job comprised of duties having varied characteristics. From a psychological standpoint, vertical loading has a more beneficial impact on employee productivity than horizontal loading.

The enrichment of jobs is successful for several fundamental reasons. Employees become motivated because of increased opportunities for achievement, responsibility, recognition, and so forth. Furthermore, jobs that are enriched have greater variety, which has a positive impact on the employees' job satisfaction. When jobs are enriched, their intrinsic rewards increase. Overall job enrichment results in higher productivity, lower error rates, greater job satisfaction, and improved worker-management cooperation.

Job enrichment is most successful in situations in which the following conditions are found: Jobs consist of natural units of work; the employee can be given control over his or her job tasks; the employee can be rewarded for assuming increased responsibility; the employee is not satisfied with his or her present job; jobs consist of fragmented tasks that can be combined; and the employee believes his or her job makes a meaningful contribution to society.

The process of enriching jobs consists of three steps. The first step is to identify the natural units of work. If employees' jobs enable them to complete these natural units, they will most likely have a feeling of greater control and responsibility for task completion.

The second step in the enrichment process involves training employees to complete the natural units of their work. In some instances, employees can be trained to assume the entire work process immediately. In other instances, employees will assume the new work process gradually. The supervisor determines the pace with which employees are able to assume responsibility and control for their enriched jobs.

The third step is to gather feedback about the success of the job enrichment efforts once the employees begin performing their newly designed positions. This feedback is useful when changes have to be made.

Flextime

What are the characteristics of flextime?

Also having a positive impact on employee productivity is a technique known as **flextime**. This technique enables employees to select their starting times, usually within a two- to three-hour period. Consequently, employees are able to begin working as early as 6 A.M. or as late as 9 or 10 A.M. Even though the employees' starting times are flexible, most programs require employees to work a required number of hours per day, known as core hours. A few programs allow employees to accumulate excess hours that can be used later when they need to be absent from work.

Most companies that use flextime adopt certain well-defined guidelines to help employees decide when to begin their workday. For example, most organizations require that their employees be on the job during certain core hours of the day—spanning perhaps the hours of 10 A.M. and 3 P.M. Most flextime programs also specify the time span within which employees are to report to work.

Scheduling is simplified when employees are required to report to work at the same time each day for a week's duration. Some organizations also have policies prohibiting participation of employees whose output provides input for other employees. This policy is especially prevalent in situations in which productivity of the work unit might be hampered because of the variability of employee starting times.

Flextime provides some rather distinct advantages:

1. It significantly decreases the rate of absenteeism and almost totally eliminates tardiness.
2. Production increases because employees are responsible for a full working day regardless of when they arrive on the job.
3. Employees experience greater job satisfaction because flextime helps them fulfill some of their human needs.
4. Employees experience less frustration in going to and from work because public transportation facilities and highways may be less congested during travel time.
5. Employees whose leisure activities require several hours of daylight are able to plan their work schedules around their leisure-time schedules.
6. Employees can use their own time for scheduling appointments with doctors, dentists, lawyers, accountants, and so forth.
7. Flextime reduces employee tension levels caused by the pressure of meeting strict work schedules.

Among the disadvantages are the following:

1. An employee whose output becomes another employee's input may not be permitted to participate in the flextime program. In some instances, larger inventories of processed work are maintained so productivity is not hampered when employees take advantage of variable starting hours.
2. Planning employees' work schedules may become cumbersome, especially in organizations that use multiple shifts.

Job Sharing

What are the characteristics of job sharing?

Increasing numbers of organizations are using **job sharing** to help employees increase their productivity. Job sharing is a technique in which two people share what was originally a full-time job. Individual salaries and fringe benefits are pro-rated according to the amount of each employee's contribution of effort. Job sharing is especially attractive to those individuals who want to or have to combine employment with raising a family. Increasingly, older employees who want to continue to work but not on a full-time basis find the job-sharing technique attractive.

Job sharing results in several advantages. It reduces absenteeism and tardiness because employees can often work around those situations that keep them from going to work or keep them from their arriving on time when they have a full-time position. If a job characteristically has certain times when the presence of both part-time employees would be advantageous, such arrangements can often be made. In addition, one employee may be able to work a full day to accommodate the work partner's personal schedule.

Many organizations have found that the combined output of two individuals sharing one job exceeds the output level expected of one full-time employee. When working a portion of a day, employees may be able to sustain higher productivity levels because they are not likely to experience the same level of fatigue experienced by those who work a full day.

Job sharing also has some disadvantages. The amount of employer paper work increases, as does the number of records that must be maintained. Perhaps the most significant problem is the splitting of fringe benefits. By dividing some benefits between two employees, such as insurance, for example, the amount of coverage may not be sufficient. To obtain adequate coverage, the employees may have to pay for a portion of the cost of the fringe benefit, whereas full-time employees are likely to have the full cost of their coverage paid for by the employer. The division of benefits is to a certain extent simplified in organizations that use the cafeteria approach to fringe benefits. The coordinating of tasks performed by each employee may also create some difficulties.

Management by Objectives (MBO)

What are the characteristics of Management by Objectives?

Another successful technique in helping employees improve their productivity is **Management by Objectives (MBO)**. The supervisor and employee jointly determine the employee's objectives that are to be achieved within a specified time period. The supervisor and employee also determine the strategies for achieving the objectives and the criteria that will be used to measure the employee's achievements.

Generally, the objective-setting process should be a joint effort between the employee and the supervisor. Although the supervisor may not always participate in the objective-setting process, he or she must review and approve subordinates' objectives.

On a regular basis, perhaps every three to six months, the employee and the supervisor will discuss the employee's success in attaining the previously defined objectives. The elapsed time between the review sessions should be long enough that the employee can see progress but sufficiently short that he or she does not lose sight of the objectives. If the employee has been successful, a new objective may be defined. Two common ways of dealing with objectives that are not attained by a specified date include the following: They are continued during the next evaluation period, or they are modified after considering the employee's current performance.

Employees find MBO desirable because it gives them the chance to become involved in the decision-making process. Having an opportunity to participate motivates employees to exert greater effort toward the attainment of their objectives.

What are the advantages of Management by Objectives?

The use of MBO results in several advantages:

1. It satisfies human needs, thus providing employees with the necessary motivation to achieve their objectives.

2. It helps employees become more involved within the organization because they believe their jobs take on added importance.
3. It provides employees with definite objectives toward which they should work, thus eliminating ambiguous work assignments.
4. It helps employees take considerably greater interest in performing their jobs because they have an opportunity to participate in defining their objectives, they are given the latitude to achieve their objectives, and they know their performance will be measured against how successful they are in achieving their objectives.

Among the disadvantages of MBO are the following:

1. The objective-setting process is time consuming.
2. The desired results are sometimes not reached because of lack of supervisory involvement in working with employees.
3. The absence of a definite reward system prevents some employees from making a positive response to the technique.

Job Security

Some individuals are reluctant to increase their productivity because they fear fewer employees will be needed as a consequence. Although many of these employees readily admit that they could be more productive, the absence of **job security** often keeps them from increasing their output. Productivity improvement efforts most likely will not be successful if employees always have to be concerned about the impact of their increased output on the stability of their employment.

Within a typical organization, the office function is one in which employees can be reasonably assured that their employment will not be terminated if they increase their output. The large number of office employees throughout the organization and their characteristically high attrition rates facilitate making staffing adjustments when the need arises.

Employees will more likely accept a variety of other changes designed to improve organizational productivity if they do not have to be concerned about the effect of these changes on their employment status. Not only does job security stimulate greater employee productivity, but also it improves employee morale and attitudes.

Employee Participation

Another effective way to help employees improve their productivity is to involve them in decision-making processes, a technique officially known as **employee participation**. Nowadays, employees want to be involved in decisions that directly affect them. In many instances, they can make a significant contribution because they are more knowledgeable and much better informed about certain job aspects than their supervisors who have ultimate responsibility for making decisions.

Furthermore, when employees' input is sought, they are less likely to resist pending changes. Too, employee input is helpful in enlisting their cooperation. Participation also gives employees greater control over their jobs and enables them to express themselves more creatively.

What prerequisites must be present for successful employee participation?

For employee participation to be successful, two prerequisites must be present. First, management, although not bound by employees' suggestions, must consider their input in making decisions. Second, employees must be convinced that management wants the benefit of their input in the decision-making process.

Generally, employees tend to accomplish what they want to accomplish. Employee participation often gives employees the motivation to accomplish more than they might otherwise want to accomplish. Furthermore, the ideas, suggestions, and recommendations generated by the employees who will be affected by the input often stand a better chance of being implemented than when management imposes ideas, suggestions, or recommendations.

Quality Circles

Of the various techniques that have been used successfully in improving employee productivity, **quality circles** are one of the newest. A circle is a voluntary group of eight to twelve employees who perform similar or related work. The members of the circle meet on a regular basis to identify, analyze, and develop solutions to a variety of their work-related problems. The meetings, which are generally held on company time, are often scheduled weekly for approximately an hour. The success of quality circles is affected by the way they are organized and operated. Before employees become involved with a circle, they should thoroughly understand the purpose, composition, and benefits of the concept.

The quality circle leader, who is responsible for conducting the weekly circle meetings, is typically the supervisor of a work unit. By having a good grasp of the nature of the problems brought before the group, the leader will help the members define, analyze, and solve work-related problems. During the meetings, the leader should disassociate himself or herself as a work unit supervisor, which enables him or her to function as a group member at the circle meetings rather than as a manager or supervisor.

Most organizations that use quality circles appoint a facilitator, who is responsible for working with circles and for coordinating the activities involved in using the technique. The facilitator is also responsible for providing training experiences for circle leaders as well as for preparing a variety of written materials for use in improving the effectiveness of the technique.

The following advantages result from the use of quality circles:

1. They help employees become more productive.
2. They increase the opportunities for employees to grow and develop.
3. They are economical to use.
4. They help increase employee job satisfaction.
5. They improve the communication between management and employees.

Quality of Work Life

What is meant by quality of work life?

As a management process, the **quality of work life (QWL)** concept impacts on the following elements of an employee's position: working conditions, economic rewards and benefits, interpersonal relations, and a variety of organization contributions. The outcome of the QWL technique is the improvement of employees' attitudes and morale, which will impact positively on their productivity. When their quality of work life is improved, employees have more positive feelings toward their jobs and the organization for which they work.

Through the usage of the QWL technique, an organization is able to improve its operating effectiveness in many ways, including the following: reducing production costs; improving employee productivity; reducing absenteeism, tardiness, and turnover; and improving quality of work.

Organizations that use the QWL technique often appoint a joint management-labor committee responsible for providing important program direction. The committee may also be responsible for identifying areas that need improvement, for identifying strategies that will help improve the quality of work life for employees, and for providing periodic evaluations of the technique.

Some of the strategies that are used to improve the quality of employee work life are flextime, MBO, job enrichment, job security, job rotation, Total Quality Management (TQM), and employee participation.

Employee Assistance Programs

One of the values of **employee assistance programs (EAP)** is their impact on employee productivity. These programs provide counseling to employees whose personal problems have a negative impact on their job performance. The counseling is provided by individuals with the necessary specialized training.

Among the types of situations for which employees receive assistance are substance abuse (alcohol and drugs), nervous disorders, emotional problems, mental health problems, family relations problems, marital problems, physical health conditions, care for children and aging dependents, and legal concerns. Nearly any type of personal problem that prevents employees from performing at their maximum can be included in the program. In some cases, primary problems (marital problems, for example) give rise to secondary problems (substance abuse, for example).

While employee assistance programs require a specially trained staff, most organizations find that the savings resulting from increased productivity more than offsets staffing costs. A favorable cost-benefit ratio helps justify the implementation of an EAP.

Communication

Another effective technique for improving employee productivity is increasing the quantity and quality of **communication** between management and employees. An important part of the communication process is feedback.

Employee productivity is often impeded because management fails to communicate its expectations to employees. In most cases, management doesn't purposely withhold information from employees. Rather, management either takes for granted that employees are aware of its productivity expectations or it miscalculates the amount of information employees desire.

Feedback provides a vital function in productivity improvement efforts. It helps reinforce the productive behavior of employees, and it is useful in correcting undesirable behavior that hampers employee productivity.

Burnout Reduction

Employees experiencing **burnout** are generally unable to perform at their maximum capacity. Burnout, which results from physical and mental fatigue that is stress related, can be experienced by any employee at any stage of his or her career. However, certain personality types—specifically those with high energy levels and strong self-actualization needs—tend to be more susceptible.

Some of the causes of burnout result in its perpetuation. For example, stress and anxiety, two common causes, tend to fuel burnout. A reduction of stress and anxiety often helps an employee eliminate his or her burnout condition. Symptoms of burnout include fatigue, forgetfulness, physical problems (headaches, stomach problems, and backaches), job boredom, and poor attitude.

How can burnout be reduced?

Several cures are available for burnout, stress, and anxiety reduction, including professional counseling, a leave of absence, rotation or promotion into another position in the organization, and reduction in the number of assigned job duties.

Incentives

The more employees are rewarded for increasing their productivity, the more likely they will try to improve their performance. Several types of **incentives** have been developed to reward employees for increasing their productivity. While some plans are based on group performance, others are based on individual performance. In plans based on group performance, all members of the group share the rewards for increasing the group's productivity. An individual-based plan rewards the individuals who increase their productivity.

Following are several guidelines that will be helpful when implementing an incentive pay plan:

1. The reward system must be easily understood.
2. The rewards should be distributed after predetermined levels of employee productivity have been attained.
3. The rewards should increase in proportion to increases in productivity.
4. The rewards should be sufficiently large to motivate improved performance.
5. The rewards should be distributed fairly often.

To help keep employees continually aware of the benefits of improving their productivity once the program begins functioning, they should receive frequent communication about the incentive pay program. The absence of such communication may diminish employee interest in the program.

Mental and Emotional Stress Reduction

Employees with unusual levels of **mental and emotional stress** typically are unable to maximize their productivity. A number of causes of mental and emotional stress can be identified: unsatisfactory interpersonal relations, low self-esteem, tension, stress, worry, job boredom, job isolation, job insecurity, and unpleasant work conditions. One of the most effective ways to reduce mental and emotional stress is to eliminate the source or cause of the problem. Stress also leads to burnout conditions.

When employees experience severe levels of mental and emotional stress, they may need professional help, such as that made available by counselors in employee assistance programs, by psychologists and psychiatrists in the community, and by self-help groups. Another technique for reducing stress is the use of accurate job descriptions so employees are fully aware of the duties and responsibilities of their job before they accept it. Another technique is to ensure the adequacy of the physical environment, including lighting, seating, and noise control.

Flexible work schedules and rotation of work assignments are also successfully used by some organizations to reduce employee stress. Providing employees with the opportunity to attend stress-reduction programs, seminars, and meetings is another useful technique.

Supervisors play a key role in identifying their subordinates who are experiencing mental and emotional stress. Among the symptoms are reduced job performance, increased absenteeism, moodiness, and inability to concentrate. Before referring the subordinate to specialists who can provide professional help, the supervisor should have ample evidence that the stress condition actually exists.

Team Building

When the members of a work group wish to become more productive, the team-building technique is effective. **Team building** enables a work group to identify, diagnose, and solve its own problems.

Team building helps a work group increase its productivity in one or more of the following ways: by improving the performance of individual members of the work group, by improving the interpersonal relations among the members of the work group, and by improving the effectiveness of work procedures as a means of attaining group goals.

Crucial to the success of the team-building technique is a consultant, most likely an outsider but who can be an internal resource person. The consultant plays several important roles, including those of facilitator, change agent, resource person, trainer, and analyst. The consultant should avoid prescribing solutions because this denies the members a valuable opportunity to grow and develop. Rather, the consultant should identify several alternative solutions and then let the group select the one which it believes is best for the circumstances.

Also crucial to the success of the team-building technique are (1) a team leader who is committed to the team-building concept; (2) the support of top management; (3) the involvement of each team member; (4) a feeling of personal security of each team member; and (4) adequate time for the process to work.

The team-building technique provides several advantages:

What are the advantages of team building?

1. Eliminates those situations that impede employee productivity.
2. Sensitizes team members to the impact of their behavior on the performance of the group.
3. Develops a team spirit that motivates members to perform as effectively as possible so the group can achieve its goals.

The most significant disadvantages result from the time-consuming nature of the process and the expense of bringing in an outside consultant.

An adaptation of the team-building technique is the self-managed work-team concept. These teams, which are given a high degree of autonomy, are often able to set their own production goals (which are based on centralized volume goals), set their own work hours, choose the members of their teams, initiate transfers and discharges, and so forth. The self-managed team concept produces among employees the belief that they own their jobs—which results in their wanting to perform as productively as possible.

The use of self-managed work teams has lessened the need for authoritarian control when dealing with subordinates. This approach gives the supervisor an opportunity to focus on productivity improvement and problem solving rather than on punitive or disciplinary actions.

Problem Solving

Another technique employees find helpful for improving their productivity is effective **problem solving**. The use of such an approach is especially important when dealing with complex situations.

What steps are involved in problem solving?

An effective problem-solving approach begins by identifying the problem. Those involved with the situation must be able to differentiate between the problem and its symptoms, as the two are often confused. While solving the problem will usually eliminate the symptoms, treating the symptoms rather than solving the problem may be counterproductive. Once the problem is identified, then it can be defined, which involves identifying the main issues involved in the situation.

After problem identification and definition, the next step involves collecting information about the problem. The more complete this information is, the more effectively the problem is likely to be solved. Information is collected by several means: examining records, interviewing others, and observing others. Before undertaking a subsequent step in the problem-solving process, every effort needs to be made to ensure that this step is complete.

After the information has been collected, the next step involves analyzing the information. This is often the most time-consuming step in the process. An attempt is made to determine how each bit of information affects the problem, i.e., how the parts affect the whole. Maintaining a sense of objectivity during this phase will enable those involved with the situation to maximize their efforts. Analysis involves looking at relationships and interrelationships, comparisons and contrasts, and similarities and differences.

Before the information is analyzed, the criteria that will be used to evaluate the effectiveness of the various solutions need to be identified. The absence of these criteria will make it difficult—perhaps impossible—to compare one solution with another.

After completing the analysis of information and the identification of the criteria steps, those involved with the problem are able to begin identifying solutions to the problem. Depending on the situation, this step may be carried out by several individuals. The various solutions to the problem might be identified by means of the brainstorming technique. After the various alternatives have been identified, the next step involves selecting the best alternative for solving the problem. The criteria that were identified earlier are used in selecting the best solution.

Once the best solution has been identified, it is implemented. After a period of time has passed, an evaluation is made of the effectiveness of the solution. The results of the "solved" problem are compared against the criteria that were identified earlier. This will help determine the effectiveness of the solution. This step may also identify the need for fine tuning or making some minor adjustments in the solution.

Time Management

How can an individual become a better manager of his or her time?

The extent to which an individual is an effective manager of time is a significant determinant of his or her productivity level. One key to effective **time management** is being able to estimate accurately how long the completion of various tasks will take. For routine tasks, this is easily done by keeping track of the amount of time a specific task takes to complete. By timing task completion several times and calculating an average of the results, a realistic assessment can be made.

Another key to effective time management is proper daily planning. A daily task list should be prepared, either at the end of the previous day or as the first undertaking of the current day. The task list identifies which tasks the individual needs to complete during the day. Also included on the list is the priority for getting each task completed that day. An "A-B-C" priority scheme is often used. A task assigned an "A" priority must be completed that day, while a "C" task carries the least critical priority. The unfinished tasks on the current day's task list are placed on the next day's list, along with the current priority or a new priority.

By being aware of how much time a particular task takes to complete, the individual is able to use his or her task list to schedule the timely completion of the task. This helps the individual more effectively meet deadlines and due dates, which will have a positive impact on how well he or she manages time. The individual will also experience less job-related stress if he or she is aware of the amount of time typically taken to complete a task.

Some specific suggestions for the effective management of time are the following:

1. Complete the most difficult tasks first.
2. Develop a daily routine during which time similar tasks are completed, such as making phone calls or answering correspondence.
3. Delegate work to others when and where appropriate.
4. Maintain a project calendar that identifies deadlines/due dates for major projects or tasks.
5. Simplify work flow.
6. Use "waiting" or idle time effectively.

Alternative Workweek

Some organizations are instituting workweeks other than the traditional 8-hour, 5-day workweek. Most common is the 4-day, 36- or 40-hour workweek. An **alternative workweek** of 36 hours results in a 9-hour day while a workweek of 40 hours results in a 10-hour day. For those employees who value a 3-day weekend, the alternative workweek is desirable. Increased employee productivity results from the decreased absenteeism or tardiness of employees who have to use part of their normal workday for taking care of their personal matters.

From a management perspective, an alternative workweek may increase problems associated with work scheduling and employee supervision. To deal with this situation, some organizations are open only 4 days a week, which helps reduce overhead costs. Perhaps only a skeleton workforce is present on the day that the organization's offices are closed.

Total Quality Management (TQM)

Although the primary outcome of **Total Quality Management (TQM)** is not necessarily to help employees become more productive, several of its ingredients have the residual outcome of productivity enhancement. Overall, TQM is designed to help an organization improve the quality of its products and/or services as well as everything the organization does to get its products and/or services into the hands of its customers.

What are the two critical ingredients of TQM?

Two critical ingredients of TQM, teamwork and empowerment, have a positive impact on employee productivity. The importance of teamwork was discussed in an earlier section of this chapter. Employee empowerment gives the employees the right to recommend changes that will have a positive impact on their output. Once management accepts the recommended changes, employees are then given the responsibility to determine how they should be implemented. Over the long run, employees are responsible for determining the success of the recommended changes and fine-tuning them to ensure their success. By empowering employees in this manner, which does not result in managerial abdication, they are more extensively committed to ensuring the success of the recommendations they implement. Because management does not have to be as greatly concerned about day-to-day operations (this is now an enhanced responsibility of the employees), it can spend more time focusing on planning for the future.

IMPLICATIONS FOR THE ADMINISTRATIVE OFFICE MANAGER

The amount of responsibility administrative office managers have for productivity improvement varies from organization to organization. Some are responsible only for coordinating the productivity improvement efforts within their own units. Others have organization-wide responsibility through their involvement as a member of the task force that advises the productivity manager. And some administrative office managers serve as the coordinator of the productivity improvement programs within their organizations.

The contributions of administrative office managers to the improvement of organizational productivity are unmistakable. Their familiarity with the new technology that impacts significantly on productivity improvement and their awareness of the variety of strategies used in managing employees enable them to perform a vital function.

A number of alternatives are available for increasing organizational productivity, especially in the process of managing employees. The majority of the managerial techniques that facilitate increasing employee productivity are quite economical because they don't require large cash outlays. The primary cost is in the expenditure of time and effort.

Organizations generally find that when a high priority is placed on productivity improvement, attained results are well worthwhile. In fact, most organizations can no longer afford to ignore their productivity performance, because over the long run, the impact of productivity on profitability can be substantial.

REVIEW QUESTIONS

1. What is productivity?
2. What reasons are responsible for the stagnation of productivity in the United States?
3. What are the characteristics of effective productivity improvement programs?
4. Why is the use of employee participation desirable in the development of a productivity improvement program?
5. What important activities comprise the preliminary planning phase of the development of a productivity improvement program?
6. What broad options are available for improving the productivity of an area or activity?
7. What are the advantages and disadvantages of the flextime concept?
8. In what way can job security have a positive impact on productivity improvement?
9. How do quality circles function?
10. What is the purpose of employee assistance programs (EAP)?

11. Why does team building work as a technique for improving employee productivity?
12. What two ingredients of TQM have a positive impact on employee productivity?

DISCUSSION QUESTIONS

1. Why do the "constraining practices, policies, and attitudes of management" have a negative impact on productivity in the United States?
2. The company in which you work is presently installing a productivity improvement program. Many of the employees believe that management's desire to install the program stems from the notion that regardless of how productive employees are, room for improvement always exists. The employees believe that they are considerably above average in their productivity. Therefore, management must have some ulterior motive for installing the program—such as increasing its profitability—at the expense of the employees. What can be done to help mobilize the employees behind the implementation of a productivity improvement program?
3. You work in a company that implemented a successful productivity improvement program several years ago. At the time the program was installed, management did not make any promises about sharing the increased productivity with the employees. Management's response was, "Let's wait and see." For the last three years, the firm has been more productive than ever before. Increasingly, the employees are asking for a share of the increased profit resulting from increased productivity—and management keeps putting the employees off. Analyze this situation from an employee's viewpoint and management's viewpoint and discuss how you think the issue should be resolved.
4. You recently read an article in a professional journal that outlined the desirability of decentralizing an organization's productivity improvement efforts. The author of the article claims that unit managers—more than anyone else in the organization—have a better awareness about the most effective ways to increase unit productivity. The author suggests making each unit manager responsible for developing the productivity improvement program in his or her unit and then coordinating the program once it is operable. You do not agree with the author of this article because you believe that a centralized approach produces more effective results. Explain why you believe a decentralized approach is not as effective as a centralized approach.
5. You are an office supervisor in a medium-sized insurance company. You and several other supervisors in your company believe that the development and implementation of a productivity improvement program would be highly desirable. During a recent informal conversation with the executive vice president, you brought up the topic of productivity improvement programs. The executive vice president's support for such an undertaking is crucial, but his reaction to your idea seemed rather cool. You are of the opinion, however, that if the supervisors who believe a productivity improvement program should be implemented were to build a strong case for a program, then you might be able to increase its receptivity. Explain how you plan to build a strong case for the development and implementation of a productivity improvement program in this company.
6. During the last few weeks, the pending development and implementation of a productivity improvement program in your organization has been widely discussed. You, as supervisor, notice that employee opposition to a program has been increasing with each passing week. Employee opposition seems to be centered around the fear that fewer employees will be needed if they be-

come more productive. The employees are interpreting this to mean that some of them will be laid off because of an eventual workforce surplus. Outline the discussion you plan to have with your subordinates in which you attempt to diminish the level of their fears. Obviously, you will want to convey to them that management does not intend for such a program to result in the layoff of even one employee.

STUDENT PROJECTS AND ACTIVITIES

1. Assemble a list of five of the techniques designed to improve employee productivity. Show the list to an office employee and ask him or her to rate these techniques in terms of how effective each is in enticing the employee to increase his or her productivity.
2. Talk with an employee in an organization that uses the flextime concept. What does the employee like best about the concept? Like least?
3. Interview a high-level manager in a company regarding the process he or she uses in solving problems. Compare the process the manager uses with the process outlined in this chapter.
4. Talk with the director of an organization's employee assistance program. Ask questions about the program's successes and failures. Determine what percentage of the program's clients are successful in dealing with the condition that caused them to use the program's services.
5. Talk with two individuals involved in job sharing. What do they like best about the concept? The least?

MINICASE

Donald O'Mallary, one of five vice presidents in the Swift Telephone Company, is responsible for appointing employees to serve on the company's productivity task force. He is well aware of the significant contribution this task force can make in ensuring the success of the company's productivity improvement program.

1. What qualifications should be possessed by the individuals O'Mallary appoints to the task force?
2. When he invites these individuals to serve on the task force, what should he tell them about the importance of the productivity improvement program that will help convince them to accept this invitation?

CASE

Mary Lemincz was recently appointed coordinator of the productivity improvement program in the Bonnick Corporation, which is located in Dallas. Bonnick is one of the largest U. S. manufacturers of oil drilling equipment.

Lemincz enthusiastically accepted the appointment as productivity coordinator. She has had tremendous support from many employees thus far. In fact, because of this support and the extra effort these employees have put into the development of the program, the project is actually ahead of schedule.

At its last meeting, Lemincz mentioned that the task force will soon begin thinking about developing productivity measurement techniques. She acknowledged to the members of the task force that this will not be easy because of the nature of the measurement process.

1. What suggestions can you offer Lemincz that will help her to develop the measurement process of the productivity improvement program?
2. Why is productivity measurement crucial during the program development phase and also once the program is operable?
3. What uses are made of the measurement data?

SYSTEMS ANALYSIS

CHAPTER AIM

After studying this chapter, you should be able to evaluate the effectiveness of an office system.

CHAPTER OUTLINE

The Systems and Procedures
- Concept
- Definitions
- Objectives
- Advantages and Disadvantages
- Characteristics of Systems
- Elements of Systems
  - Input
  - Processing
  - Output
  - Feedback
  - Controlling
  - A Purchasing Subsystem: An Illustration

The Systems and Procedures Staff
Designing or Modifying Systems
Systems and Procedures Tools
- Workload chart
- Flow Process Chart
- Office Layout Chart
- Right- and Left-Hand Chart
- Operator-Machine Process Chart
- Horizontal Flow Process Chart
- EDP Block Diagram

Implications for the Administrative Office Manager

CHAPTER TERMS

EDP block diagram
Flow process chart
Horizontal flow process chart
Integrated systems
Methods
Office layout chart
Operator-machine process chart
Procedures
Right- and left-hand chart
Subsystem
System
Workload chart

The use of **integrated systems** has enabled many organizations to control their rapidly increasing office costs as well as improve their operating efficiency. Among the functional or operational areas typically incorporated into the integrated system are sales, production, marketing, purchasing, and finance. With the inclusion of these areas in an integrated system, the areas become interrelated, which generally results in the improvement of the organization's operating efficiency.

Integrated systems are often comprised of several subsystems, which are commonly the organization's functional areas. In a manufacturing-oriented organization, these subsystems often include sales, marketing, and purchasing. When the operating functions are not interrelated but are maintained as separate entities, each function operates as a system rather than as a subsystem. Most systems—whether integrated or not—make extensive use of computer technology.

THE SYSTEMS AND PROCEDURES CONCEPT

What components comprise functional systems and subsystems?

Several components—including employees, equipment, and forms or materials—are incorporated into functional systems and subsystems. Through systems analysis, the interrelationships of the components are studied in an attempt to simplify work processes and to provide a solid foundation for managerial decision making.

In many organizations, the systems concept encompasses a broad range of activities. For example, in large organizations, finding the following activities either directly or indirectly related to the systems function is common:

Administrative auditing	Quality control
Budgeting	Records management
Forms management	Standardization of operating processes
Job standards	Systems design
Manpower planning	Time and motion study
Office layout and design	Work measurement
Operations research	Work sampling
Procedures analysis	Work simplification
Promotion and training	

Definitions

What is a method?

A **system** refers to a series of **subsystems** comprised of interrelated **procedures** that help achieve a well-defined goal. While procedures consist of related **methods** necessary to complete various work processes, methods consist of specific clerical or mechanical operations or activities. Figure 17-1 graphically illustrates the relationships between a system and its subsystems, procedures, and methods.

Objectives

The objectives for developing and using systems vary from organization to organization. The following, however, identify the major objectives for using the systems concept:

1. To maximize the efficient utilization of the organizational resources.
2. To control operating costs.
3. To improve operating efficiency.

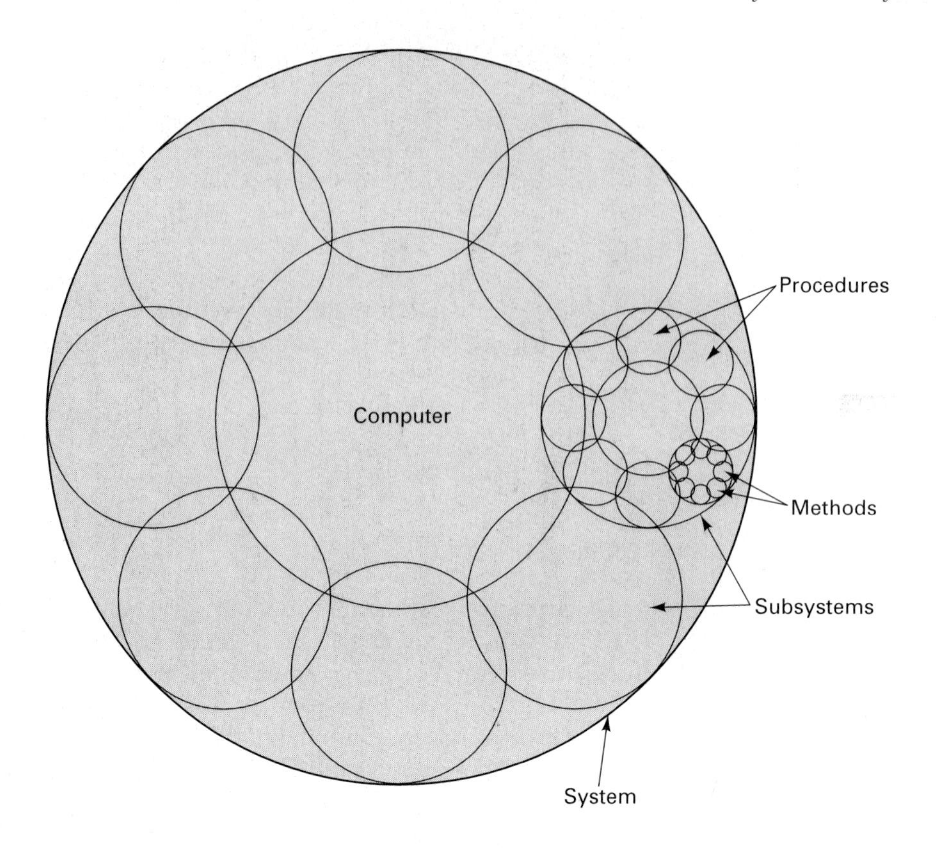

Figure 17-1 Design of a system.

4. To help achieve the objectives of the organization.
5. To help carry out the various functions of the organization.

Advantages and Disadvantages

What advantages result from systems utilization?

Several advantages result from using the systems concept, including the following: (1) the various functions of the organization are better coordinated; (2) the use of systems helps eliminate wasteful, unproductive, and uneconomical activities; (3) the use of systems helps improve the operating efficiency of the organization; and (4) more effective control can be exerted over various activities and functions.

Among the potential disadvantages of systems usage are (1) a certain amount of operating flexibility may be destroyed when using the systems concept; (2) any inefficiency that is built into the system likely will disproportionately increase as work flows through the system; and (3) a totally integrated system may be affected somewhat when changes are made in one of its subsystems.

Characteristics of Systems

Well-designed systems possess several characteristics, including the following:

What characteristics do well-designed systems possess?

1. *Flexible*. Although an effective system is structured, it should be sufficiently flexible to accommodate special or unusual circumstances.
2. *Adaptable*. If a system is well designed, changes in the system can be made without destroying or hindering its functioning.

3. *Systematic*. An effective system is systematic and logical.
4. *Functional*. For a system to be effective, it must serve the purpose for which it was intended.
5. *Simple*. A system should be as simple as circumstances will allow.
6. *Resourceful*. A well-designed system makes appropriate use of organizational resources.

Elements of Systems

Systems are comprised of several elements: input, processing, and output, as well as two related elements—feedback and controlling. Each element plays an integral role in moving work through the system.

Input The flow of work through a system begins with the input of some type of resource. In the office area, common types of input are data, information, and materials. Included as part of input are the requisite employee skills and knowledges, as well as the equipment they need to carry out the various methods and procedures comprising the system. In many instances, the output of one system becomes the input for another system.

Processing The transformation of the input into desired output takes place during the processing element. Processing involves the methods and procedures that comprise the system. Common processing activities involve counting, computing, sorting, classifying, and retrieving data/information.

Output Interaction between the input and processing elements produces output, commonly in the form of either paper or an "electronic" document. Output is often the data/information that employees use in carrying out their job responsibilities. The quality of the output is likely to have a significant impact on the overall efficiency and profitability of the organization. This output is often the input of another system.

Feedback During the time that data/information are being processed through the system, feedback enables the system to determine whether results are meeting expectations. For example, if unit costs exceed the acceptable standards, then additional controls may have to be invoked, which is another element of the process. Feedback enables the system to evaluate the effectiveness with which input is being processed prior to preparing the output. The amount of needed feedback varies from system to system. The more crucial the system is to organizational survival, the more critical feedback becomes.

Controlling Another of the vital elements of some systems is controlling, an element that has both internal and external dimensions. The internal dimensions are the organizational policies and procedures to which the system must adhere. The external dimensions, on the other hand, involve local, state, and federal rules and regulations that impact on the system, as well as ethical and moral considerations. As a rule, the more effort that goes into systems design, the less important feedback and controlling elements are because they have been planned for during the development of the system.

A purchasing subsystem: An illustration A system designed for purchasing office supplies is presented to illustrate the systems concept. Shown in Figure 17-2 are the various procedures and methods that constitute a purchasing

Procedure 1:	Requisition supplies
Methods:	A. Fill out purchase requisition
	B. Obtain necessary authorization
Procedure 2:	Obtain quotations from possible vendors
Methods:	A. Fill out quotation forms
	B. Send forms to prospective vendors
	C. Catalog respective bid quotations on receipt
Procedure 3:	Order supplies
Methods:	A. Fill out purchase order
	B. Send purchase order to vendor
Procedure 4:	Receive order
Methods:	A. Check order to verify quantities and acceptability
	B. Deliver supplies to appropriate department
	C. Notify accounts payable of receipt of order
Procedure 5:	Pay vendor
Methods:	A. Prepare payment voucher
	B. Prepare check
	C. Send check to vendor

Figure 17-2 Purchasing subsystem.

system. Each of the system's components—employees, forms, equipment—is found in this system.

THE SYSTEMS AND PROCEDURES STAFF

What factors govern the selection of the most appropriate staffing alternative for systems analysis and design?

Several alternatives are available for staffing the systems and procedures function within an organization. To a large extent, the most appropriate staffing alternative is governed by

1. The size of the organization.
2. The type (manufacturing, service, etc.) of the organization.
3. The organization's commitment to the total or integrated systems approach.
4. The philosophy of top management toward the systems and procedures function.

Alternatives for staffing the systems and procedures function include (1) use of outside consultants (includes individuals employed in firms specializing in the design of systems as well as consultants employed as service representatives by office equipment or supplies vendors); (2) use of a full-time systems staff; and (3) use of a part-time systems staff.

When organizations use outside consultants, they are frequently hired on a retainer basis in much the same way that the organization's lawyer might be retained. Consultants generally provide recommendations but leave the final decision to management.

Use of outside consultants results in several advantages. Most significant is the expertise consultants are able to provide. Because consultants are outsiders, they can be objective in making recommendations. And when retained over a period of years, outside consultants are able to keep their clients' systems up-to-date. The most significant disadvantage of using outside consultants is the high cost of their services. Another disadvantage may result from their unavailability at needed times.

Some organizations choose to use their own full-time systems staff, which, for them, is likely the most advantageous of the alternatives. A full-time staff enables the organization to develop and improve on a continual basis all of its systems and work processes—not just the most important ones. A full-time staff is also advantageous when problems arise and immediate assistance is needed. But for some organizations, the cost of employing a full-time staff is not economically feasible. The conflict that may arise between line managers and the systems staff is considered by some to be another potentially significant disadvantage.

The individuals who belong to a full-time staff are known as systems analysts. The following identify some of the qualifications they must have: understanding of data/information processing and work flow; familiarity with analysis, design, and installation of systems; knowledgeable about departmental functions and operating processes; and ability to conduct research.

When an organization is too small to warrant the use of outside consultants or a full-time staff, the systems function is often assigned to an individual who functions in some other capacity. Most likely this individual is the administrative office manager. The primary advantage of this alternative—its economy—is sometimes overshadowed by the inability of the individual to carry out the assignment effectively because of insufficient time or expertise.

DESIGNING OR MODIFYING SYSTEMS

The development of a new system or the modification of an existing system is enhanced by following a series of well-designed, sequential steps. While the development of new systems uses only steps 1, 4, and 5, steps 1 through 5 are appropriate for the modification of an existing system.

What steps are involved in systems design?

1. *Define clearly the process to be studied*. A clear definition and delineation of the process results in an analysis suitable for the situation being studied. Studies are often conducted because of one or more of the following problem situations: bottlenecks in work flow, crisscrossing or backtracking work flow, inefficient work flow, inefficient use of organizational resources (both human and non-human), and duplication of effort. In some cases, the study of work processes has to be restricted to repetitive, high-volume tasks.
2. *Outline the details of the present process*. Before the system can be modified, the present process has to be clearly outlined. The process can be outlined in narrative form or by using one of the charts described in the next section of this chapter. Outlining the present process on the appropriate form requires that each step be identified and broken down into its minute parts. The completeness of the step can be ensured when the following questions can be answered: who, what, when, where, why, and how.
3. *Analyze the present process*. The next step involves analyzing the process. Questioning the necessity of each step helps identify those that can be simplified, eliminated, or combined with others. When work processes consist of complex steps, simplification becomes a

primary focus. And sometimes when one step can be eliminated, subsequent steps can also be eliminated.

4. *Outline the improved process.* After the present process has been thoroughly analyzed, then the improved process is clearly outlined, generally on the same type of form or chart used to outline the present process. As much as possible, care should be taken to simplify the design of the improved process. In many cases, the improvement can be tried during a "trial run" before it is officially adopted. Modifications can be made, and determining the degree to which the proposed process is an improvement over the present process is possible.
5. *Install the new process.* After a decision has been made to implement the new process, it is ready for installation. Some employees may need to be convinced that the new process is actually an improvement over the old, which is typically the responsibility of the supervisor. The new process should be subjected to periodic follow-up and review. Doing so will facilitate making any needed modifications in the various elements of the process.

In some instances, problem solving is used to design or modify systems. The problem-solving steps outlined in Chapter 16 are appropriate for use.

SYSTEMS AND PROCEDURES TOOLS

A number of tools are available for use in modifying existing systems or for developing new systems. When selecting a tool for either purpose, care should be taken to ensure its appropriate use.

Workload Chart

What information do workload charts provide?

Also referred to as a work distribution chart, the **workload chart** is a useful tool for developing efficient systems and for simplifying work processes. A workload chart will identify the following:

1. The major activities performed by a given work unit.
2. The amount of time the work unit as a whole spends on each activity.
3. The activities performed by each employee and the amount of time he/she spends performing the activities.

Answers to the following questions should be sought when analyzing the information provided by the workload chart:

1. Is the work unit performing the work it is intended to perform?
2. Are employees performing too many duplicate operations?
3. Are the tasks that each employee performs of a related nature?
4. Are the special skills and talents of the employees being used to the fullest extent?
5. Are the major functions of the work unit actually consuming the greatest amount of work time and effort?
6. Are the employees' workloads evenly distributed?
7. Are the employees productive?
8. Is the flow of work efficient?

Employee's Name Esther Jones		Department Purchasing
Employee's Title Clerk - Typist		Today's Date 9/23/xx
Clock Time	**Time Consumed**	**Activities**
8:00 - 8:30	30 minutes	Type report
8:30 - 8:45	15 minutes	Type quotations
8:45 - 9:15	30 minutes	Type Purchase orders
9:15 -10:15	60 minutes	Type letters (follow-up)
10:15-10:30	—	Take break
10:30-12:00	90 minutes	Compile data for report

Figure 17-3 Daily log.

The workload chart helps identify areas of inefficiency that should be corrected prior to developing a system. A basic purpose for using the systems concept is violated if inefficient procedures or methods are allowed to be built into the new system.

Information needed to complete the workload chart should be collected over a typical work period, perhaps one to two weeks. Each employee records on a daily log sheet, such as the one illustrated in Figure 17-3, the activities he or she performs. At the end of the information-collecting period, a summary log, such as the one illustrated in Figure 17-4, is prepared.

What is the relationship between the workload chart, a summary log, and an activity list?

Following each employee's completion of the summary log, an activity list is compiled. The purpose of the activity list is to identify the activities performed by the entire work unit. A partial activity list is illustrated in Figure 17-5.

Illustrated in Figure 17-6 is a workload chart prepared from the information presented in the summary log and the activity list. Each activity is as-

Employee's Name Esther Jones / Employee's Title Clerk - Typist	Department Purchasing / For Period Ended 9/27/xx	
Activities	**Hours**	**Minutes**
Type quotations	5	
Type Purchase orders	21	30
Type letters (follow-up)	6	15
Compile data	1	30
Receive callers	2	
Type reports	3	
Keep vendor interview appointments	1	30
Answer phone	1	30

Figure 17-4 Summary log.

Department Purchasing *For period ended* 9/27/XX

Number of employees 5

Activities performed	*Activity code*
File	A,B,C,D,E,F
Type follow-up letters	D
Review receipt of orders	C
Answer telephone	F
Compile data	F
Prepare payroll	F
Type reports	F
Type purchase orders	B
Type quotations	E
Duplicate materials	F
Review purchase requisitions	B
Approve purchase requisitions	B
Handle personnel matters	F

Figure 17-5 Activity list.

signed a code, and the activities are then entered in coded form in the "activity number code column" at the far left of the chart. The activity column provides a brief description of the activity, and the "hours column" lists the total amount of time consumed by the various activities. Each employee in the work unit is provided a separate column that lists the activities he or she performs and the amount of time each activity consumes.

Examining the activity column in Figure 17-6 reveals that activities are listed in descending order of decreasing time consumption. In the employees' section of the chart, the individuals with the highest level of job importance are listed at the left, and those with the least amount of importance are listed at the right.

Flow Process Chart

What information do flow process charts provide?

Also frequently used to analyze and simplify work is the **flow process chart**, a tool especially helpful for identifying each step in a specific work process. The various steps in the process are categorized and identified by one of the following symbols:

Operation: changing the physical or chemical characteristics of an object. Examples of operations are erasing, stapling pages together, typing, keyboarding, underlining, and circling words.

Transportation: the movement of an object from one location to another. An example of transportation is giving to the word originator a letter to be signed.

Inspection: verifying data or checking an object. A common example is proofreading.

Delay: situations that cause the next step in the process to be delayed. A letter awaiting signature is an example.

Storage: storing and/or protecting an object. Filing is a typical example of storage.

Activity Code	Activity	Hours	Susan Brown Purchasing Agent	Hours	Jack Adams Buyer	Hours	Ralph Anders Audit Clerk	Hours	Esther Jones Clerk-Typist	Hours	Mary Green File Clerk	Hours
A	Interview vendors	49	Interview vendors	12	Interview vendors	25			Receive vendors Keep interview appointment sheets	2 1	File literature	9
B	Review requisitions Approve requisition Prepare purchase orders	44	Review requisitions and proposals Approve requisitions Dictate memos explaining disapproval	7 2 5	Approve purchase orders	1			Type purchase orders	21	File approved requisitions File purchase orders	4 4
C	Verify receipt of orders, audit invoices, approve invoices	42			Review receipt of orders	1	Compare invoice with receipt of order forms and note discrepancies Audit invoices Approve invoices for payment	15 15 3			File receipt of order forms File invoices	4 4
D	Follow-up	12	Review major discrepancies	1	Dictate follow-up letters and review of discrepancies	3			Type follow-up letters	6	File follow-up letters	2
E	Obtain quotations	11			Request quotations	1	Maintain quotation forms	3	Type quotations	5	File quotations	2
F	Miscellaneous	42	Appointments Reading brochures Preparing reports Personnel matters Preparing payroll	2 3 5 2 1	Reading brochures Compiling data	8 1	Compiling data	4	Compiling data Typing reports Answering phone	1 3 1	Miscellaneous filing Duplication material	2 9
TOTALS		200		40		40		40		40		40

Figure 17-6 Workload chart.

Each of the operation steps in a particular work process can also be classified as a *get ready, do,* or *put away* step. Special attention should be focused on the *do* steps: By eliminating these, the *get ready* and *put away* steps are also eliminated. The justification for a step can be determined by assessing it in terms of who, why, where, how, and when. Those steps that cannot be substantially justified should either be eliminated or combined with other steps.

Why should special attention be focused on "do" steps?

The flow process chart briefly describes the nature of each step in the process, identifies the distance that objects are transported, and provides the amount of time consumed by each delay step. To facilitate the analysis, the symbols representing each step are connected with a line, and those symbols depicting *do* operations are darkened. After the work process is outlined on the chart, the process is analyzed to determine where simplification may be appropriate. Each step should be subjected to several questions. Is the step necessary? If so, why? Can the step be eliminated, simplified, or combined with another step? Is each step properly sequenced within the total process?

After the process has been analyzed, the right-hand part of the flow process chart is prepared to outline the proposed work process. The present and proposed processes are then summarized in the upper-left corner, as Figure 17-7 illustrates.

Office Layout Chart

What information do office layout charts provide?

Frequently used in conjunction with the flow process chart, the **office layout chart** is well suited for visualizing work flow. The layout chart clearly identifies backtracking, crisscrossing, and inefficient work flow patterns.

The layout chart is actually a scale drawing of the present office layout, and the flow of work is depicted by using lines to connect the various workstations. When the layout and the flow process charts are used in conjunction with one another, layout charts should also be prepared for the proposed work flow.

Figure 17-8 illustrates layout charts for the present and proposed work flow that was outlined in Figure 17-7.

Right- and Left-Hand Chart

What information do right- and left-hand charts provide?

The **right- and left-hand chart** is used to identify hand movements in a particular work process. Similar to the flow process chart, hand movements are classified into various categories, namely:

Operation: the movement of the hand at one location, such as grasping an object, stapling, writing, keyboarding, or using a calculator.

Transportation: the movement of the hand when transporting an object from one location to another. Examples include inserting a form in a typewriter and placing an object in an out-basket.

Hold: the holding of an object while the other hand is used to do something to the object. An example is holding several sheets of paper with one hand while using the other hand to operate a stapler.

Delay: the situation of an idle hand while the other hand is in motion. An example would be a motionless hand while the other hand holds a letter being proofread.

The right- and left-hand chart consists of four distinct sections. The upper-left corner is the layout section, which is used to illustrate the arrange-

	Present	Proposed	Difference
○ No. of Operations	8	7	1
⇨ No. of Transportations	4	2	2
□ No. of Inspections	3	1	2
D No. of Delays	1	1	–
▽ No. of Storages	1	1	–
Distance Traveled	149	117	32

Job: Processing Credit Applications
Forms Used: –
Charted by: L. Davis
Department: Office Services
Date: 11/30/xx

Present Method	Operation / Transportation / Inspection / Delay / Storage	Distance in Feet	Time in Minutes	Present Method	Operation / Transportation / Inspection / Delay / Storage	Distance in Feet	Time in Minutes
Credit applications opened by mail clerk	● ⇨ □ D ▽			Credit applications opened by mail clerk	● ⇨ □ D ▽		
Credit applications alphabetized	● ⇨ □ D ▽			Mail clerk scans applications for completeness	○ ⇨ ☒ D ▽		
Credit applications transported to credit clerk	○ ⇨(x) □ D ▽	17ft.		Credit applications alphabetized by mail clerk	● ⇨ □ D ▽		
Credit clerk scans applications for completeness	○ ⇨ ☒ D ▽			Credit applications transported to credit clerk	○ ⇨(x) □ D ▽	17ft.	
Credit clerk contacts references	● ⇨ □ D ▽			Credit clerk contacts references	● ⇨ □ D ▽		
Credit clerk waits for references	○ ⇨ □ D(x) ▽		1 week average	Credit clerk waits for references	○ ⇨ □ D(x) ▽		1 week
Information provided by reference entered on application	● ⇨ □ D ▽			Information provided by reference entered on application	● ⇨ □ D ▽		
Applications transported to supervisor	○ ⇨(x) □ D ▽	15ft.		On routine applications, credit clerk decides on desirability and limit	● ⇨ □ D ▽		
Supervisor inspects applications	○ ⇨ ☒ D ▽			Application sent to data Processing	○ ⇨(x) □ D ▽	100 ft.	
Supervisor decides on desirability of applicant	● ⇨ □ D ▽			Information keypunched on card	● ⇨ □ D ▽		
Supervisor assigns credit limit	● ⇨ □ D ▽			Application stored	○ ⇨ □ D ▽(x)		
Applications transported back to credit clerk	○ ⇨(x) □ D ▽	17ft.		Credit card prepared	● ⇨ □ D ▽		
Credit clerk inspects application	○ ⇨ ☒ D ▽				○ ⇨ □ D ▽		
Application transported to data processing	○ ⇨(x) □ D ▽	100 ft.			○ ⇨ □ D ▽		
Information keypunched on card	● ⇨ □ D ▽				○ ⇨ □ D ▽		
Application stored	○ ⇨ □ D ▽(x)				○ ⇨ □ D ▽		
Credit card prepared	● ⇨ □ D ▽				○ ⇨ □ D ▽		

Figure 17-7 Flow process chart.

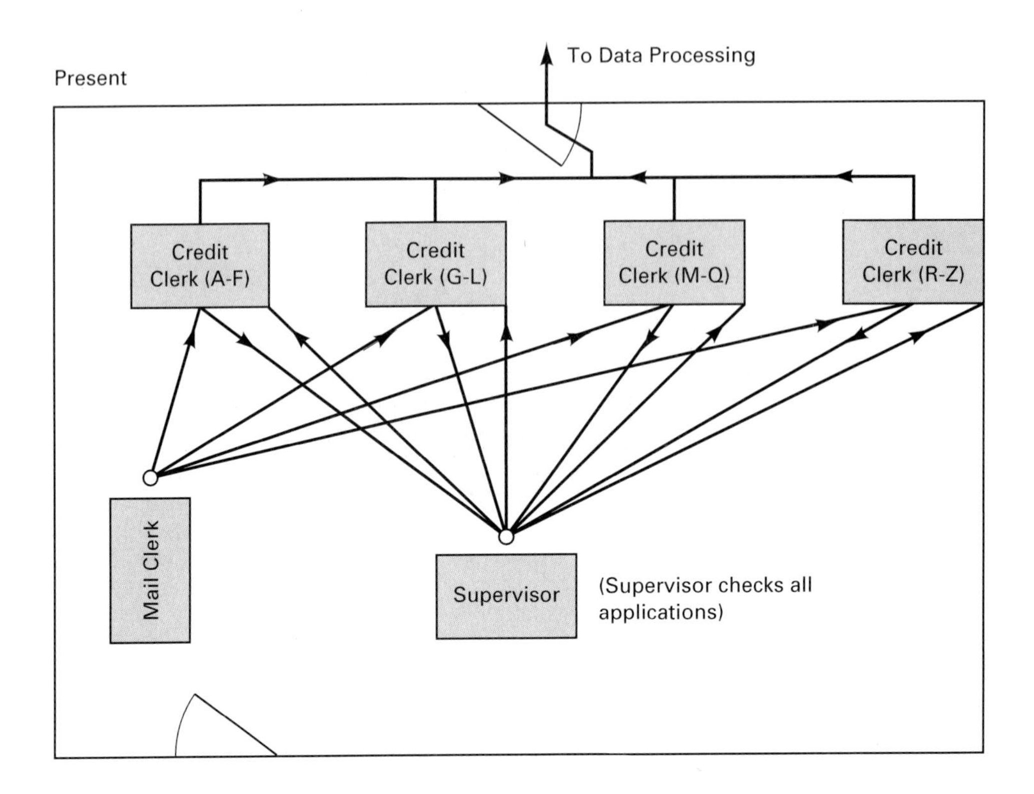

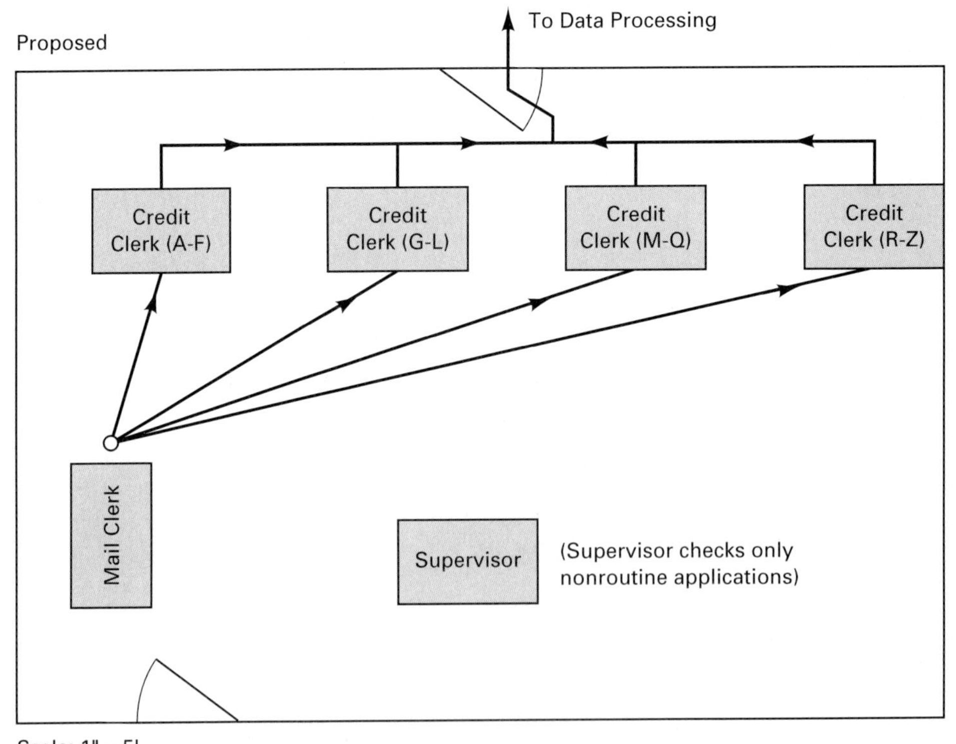

Scale: 1" = 5'

Figure 17-8 Office layout chart.

ment of materials involved in the work process. For example, in Figure 17-9, which illustrates the manual collation of five sheets of paper, the five sheets are identified as 1, 2, 3, 4, and 5.

The upper-right corner of the chart provides space for identifying the nature of the job being analyzed. The summary section appears below the layout and identification sections. Space is provided for summarizing the present process, the proposed process, and the differences between the two processes.

The lower two-thirds of the form is used to summarize the movement of the right and left hands in relation to one another. Space is provided for a brief description of each motion, and the symbols representing the various motions are connected with lines.

Following the careful outlining of the present work process, the necessity and efficiency of each step in the process is considered. After the process has been analyzed and the various motions have been appropriately eliminated, combined, or simplified, the proposed process is outlined on a second right- and left-hand chart. The various motions are then summarized in the proposed area of the summary section. The differences between the present and proposed methods are also noted in the summary section.

Operator-Machine Process Chart

The **operator-machine process chart** is used to study the relationship between an operator and the machine used by the operator. Its use is primarily limited to analyzing high-volume, repetitive work processes.

As is true with the other process charts discussed in this chapter, the primary reason for using this chart is to analyze a work process, focusing on opportunities to eliminate, simplify, or combine as many steps as possible. By reducing idle time, higher levels of productivity can be realized.

What information do operator-machine process charts provide?

Illustrated in Figure 17-10 is the operator-machine process chart, which consists of a summary section, an identification section, a layout section, a parts section, and the section used to illustrate the various steps in the work process. The left-hand activity column is used for operator activities; the right-hand activity column is used for machine activities.

Found in the middle of the chart is the time column used to depict the amount of time each activity consumes. The lines in the time column represent a standard unit of time, perhaps one to six seconds. The columns on either side of the time column are darkened to identify inactivity either on the part of the operator or the machine.

Horizontal Flow Process Chart

What information do horizontal-flow process charts provide?

The **horizontal flow process chart** is useful for illustrating work processes that involve multicopy forms (such as purchase orders, invoices, and credit applications). These charts follow the movement of each copy of the form, starting with the point of origin, moving through the various steps in the flow of work, and ending with the disposition of each copy of the form. The symbols used in the horizontal flow process chart are similar to those illustrated in Figure 17-12.

Figure 17-11 is a horizontal flow process chart that illustrates a purchasing subsystem, including the preparing of the purchase requisition and the purchase order, sending the purchase order to the vendor, and transmitting copies of the purchase order to the receiving and accounting departments. Horizontal flow process charts will also be prepared by these two departments to illustrate the flow of work through them.

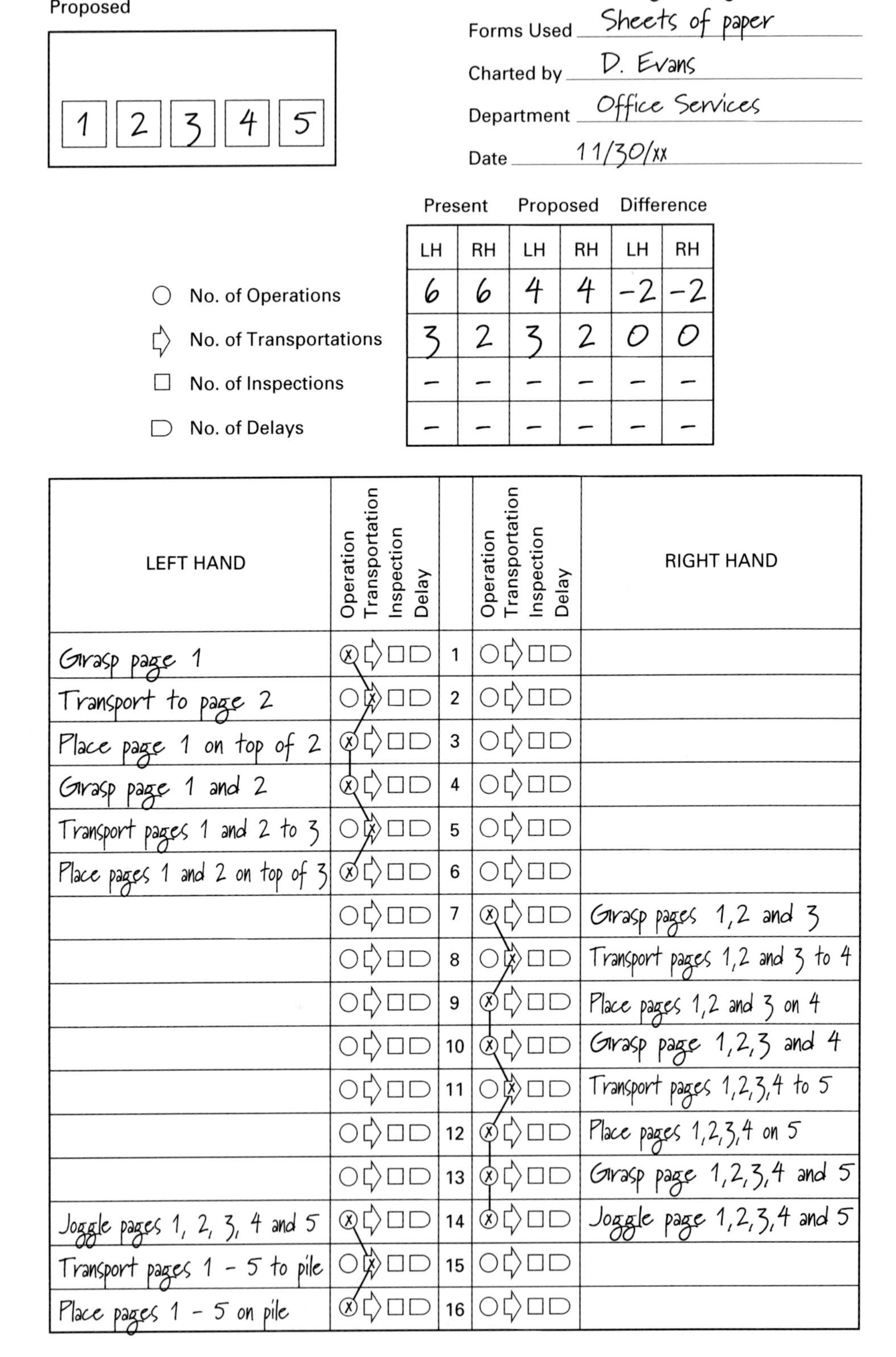

Proposed

1	2	3	4	5

Job Collating 5 pages
Forms Used Sheets of paper
Charted by D. Evans
Department Office Services
Date 11/30/xx

	Present LH	Present RH	Proposed LH	Proposed RH	Difference LH	Difference RH
○ No. of Operations	6	6	4	4	−2	−2
⇨ No. of Transportations	3	2	3	2	0	0
□ No. of Inspections	–	–	–	–	–	–
D No. of Delays	–	–	–	–	–	–

LEFT HAND	Operation / Transportation / Inspection / Delay		Operation / Transportation / Inspection / Delay	RIGHT HAND
Grasp page 1	Operation	1		
Transport to page 2	Transportation	2		
Place page 1 on top of 2	Operation	3		
Grasp page 1 and 2	Operation	4		
Transport pages 1 and 2 to 3	Transportation	5		
Place pages 1 and 2 on top of 3	Operation	6		
		7	Operation	Grasp pages 1,2 and 3
		8	Transportation	Transport pages 1,2 and 3 to 4
		9	Operation	Place pages 1,2 and 3 on 4
		10	Operation	Grasp page 1,2,3 and 4
		11	Transportation	Transport pages 1,2,3,4 to 5
		12	Operation	Place pages 1,2,3,4 on 5
		13	Operation	Grasp page 1,2,3,4 and 5
Joggle pages 1, 2, 3, 4 and 5	Operation	14	Operation	Joggle page 1,2,3,4 and 5
Transport pages 1 – 5 to pile	Transportation	15		
Place pages 1 – 5 on pile	Operation	16		

Figure 17-9 Right- and left-hand chart.

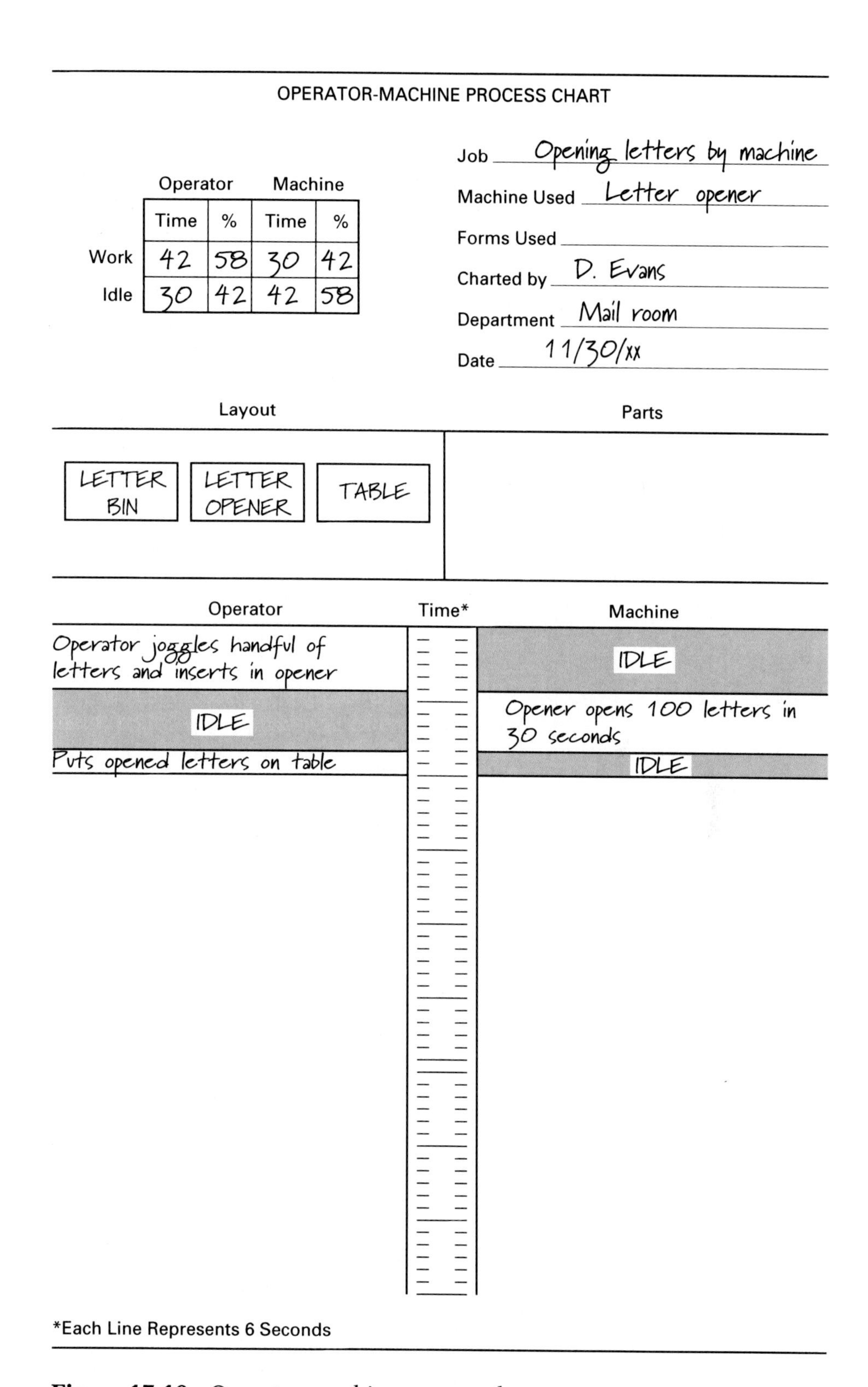

OPERATOR-MACHINE PROCESS CHART

	Operator Time	Operator %	Machine Time	Machine %
Work	42	58	30	42
Idle	30	42	42	58

Job Opening letters by machine

Machine Used Letter opener

Forms Used

Charted by D. Evans

Department Mail room

Date 11/30/xx

Layout

LETTER BIN | LETTER OPENER | TABLE

Parts

Operator	Time*	Machine
Operator joggles handful of letters and inserts in opener		IDLE
IDLE		Opener opens 100 letters in 30 seconds
Puts opened letters on table		IDLE

*Each Line Represents 6 Seconds

Figure 17-10 Operator-machine process chart.

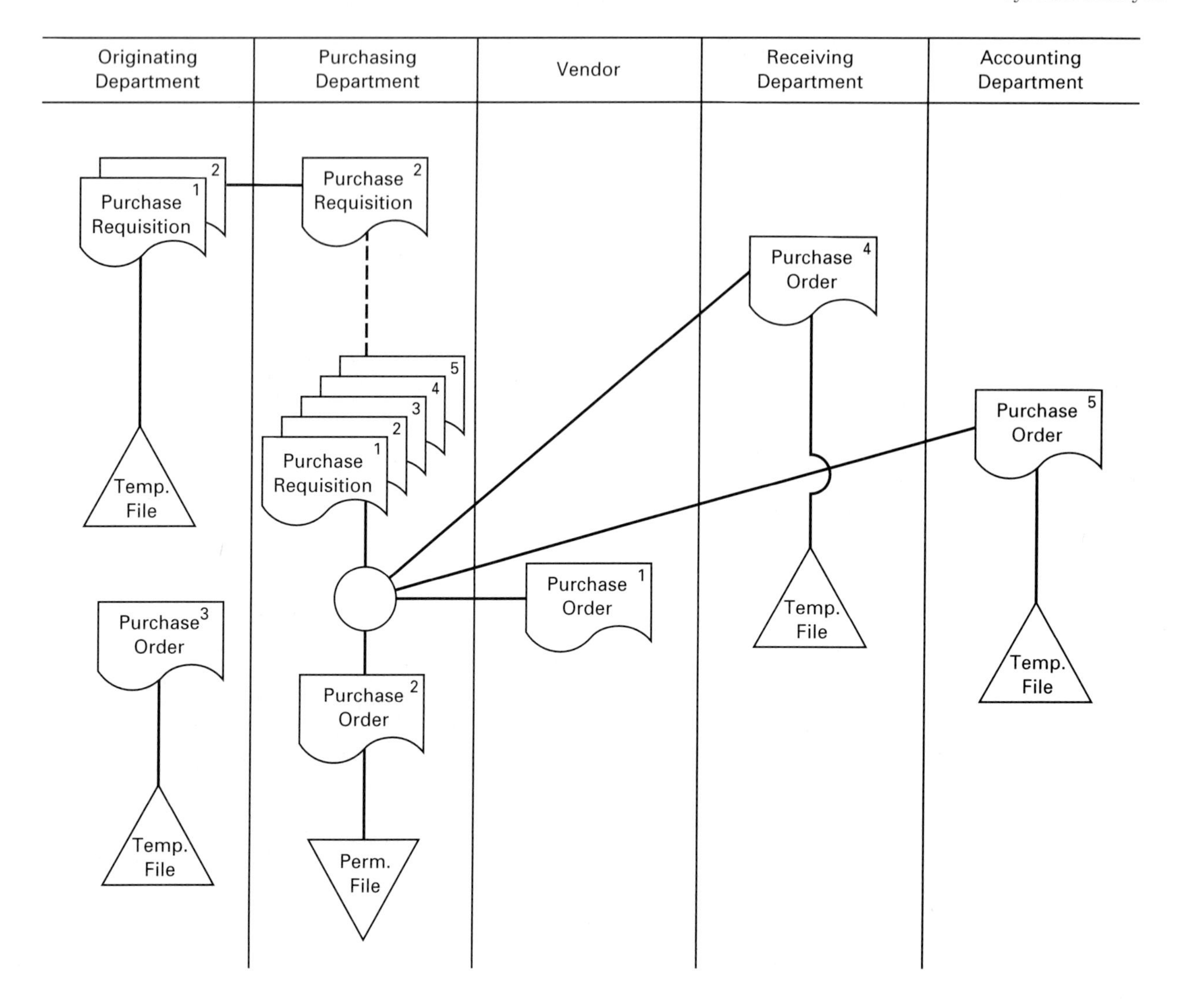

Figure 17-11 Horizontal flow process chart.

When designing new systems, the horizontal flow process chart is useful for outlining the various procedures in each subsystem. It is also useful when modifying an existing system.

EDP Block Diagram

For what are EDP block diagrams used?

Because many systems are computer based, a variety of programs must be prepared to facilitate the orderly processing of data and information.

Before preparing a computer program, an **EDP block diagram** is frequently prepared to assist the programmer in organizing ideas about solving business problems in an efficient, sequenced manner. The diagrams are also useful when a program malfunctions or has to be modified. EDP block diagrams use standardized symbols, such as those illustrated in Figure 17-12.

Although the EDP block diagram illustrated in Figure 17-13 is not readily transferable into a computer program, the basic fundamentals of the diagram are illustrated. The processes that a student may go through in getting ready to go to class, in getting ready for the class to start, and in getting ready to leave the class are illustrated in the diagram.

Depicted by diamond-shaped symbols, the decision steps of the diagram

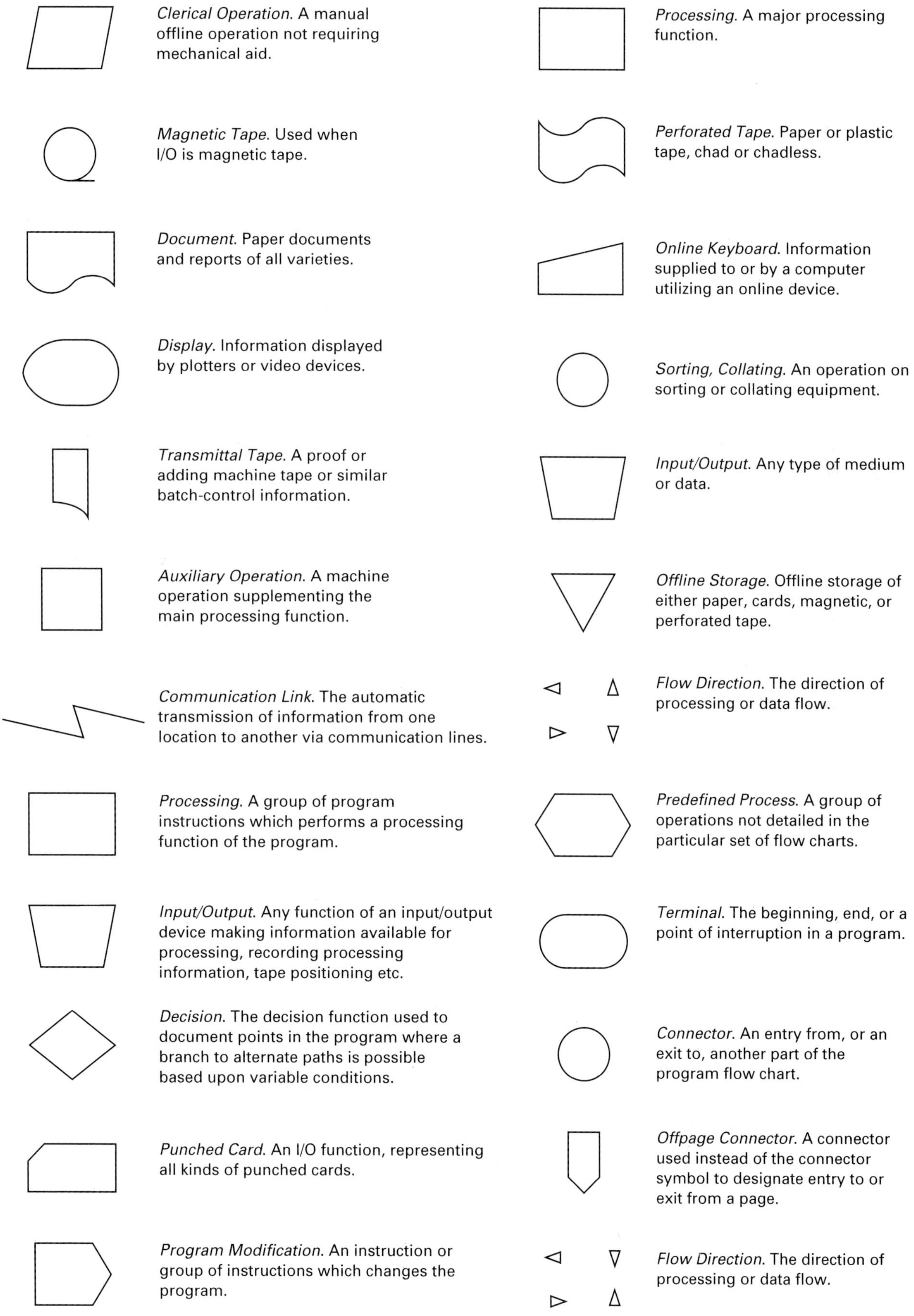

Clerical Operation. A manual offline operation not requiring mechanical aid.

Processing. A major processing function.

Magnetic Tape. Used when I/O is magnetic tape.

Perforated Tape. Paper or plastic tape, chad or chadless.

Document. Paper documents and reports of all varieties.

Online Keyboard. Information supplied to or by a computer utilizing an online device.

Display. Information displayed by plotters or video devices.

Sorting, Collating. An operation on sorting or collating equipment.

Transmittal Tape. A proof or adding machine tape or similar batch-control information.

Input/Output. Any type of medium or data.

Auxiliary Operation. A machine operation supplementing the main processing function.

Offline Storage. Offline storage of either paper, cards, magnetic, or perforated tape.

Communication Link. The automatic transmission of information from one location to another via communication lines.

Flow Direction. The direction of processing or data flow.

Processing. A group of program instructions which performs a processing function of the program.

Predefined Process. A group of operations not detailed in the particular set of flow charts.

Input/Output. Any function of an input/output device making information available for processing, recording processing information, tape positioning etc.

Terminal. The beginning, end, or a point of interruption in a program.

Decision. The decision function used to document points in the program where a branch to alternate paths is possible based upon variable conditions.

Connector. An entry from, or an exit to, another part of the program flow chart.

Punched Card. An I/O function, representing all kinds of punched cards.

Offpage Connector. A connector used instead of the connector symbol to designate entry to or exit from a page.

Program Modification. An instruction or group of instructions which changes the program.

Flow Direction. The direction of processing or data flow.

Figure 17-12 Flow charting symbols.

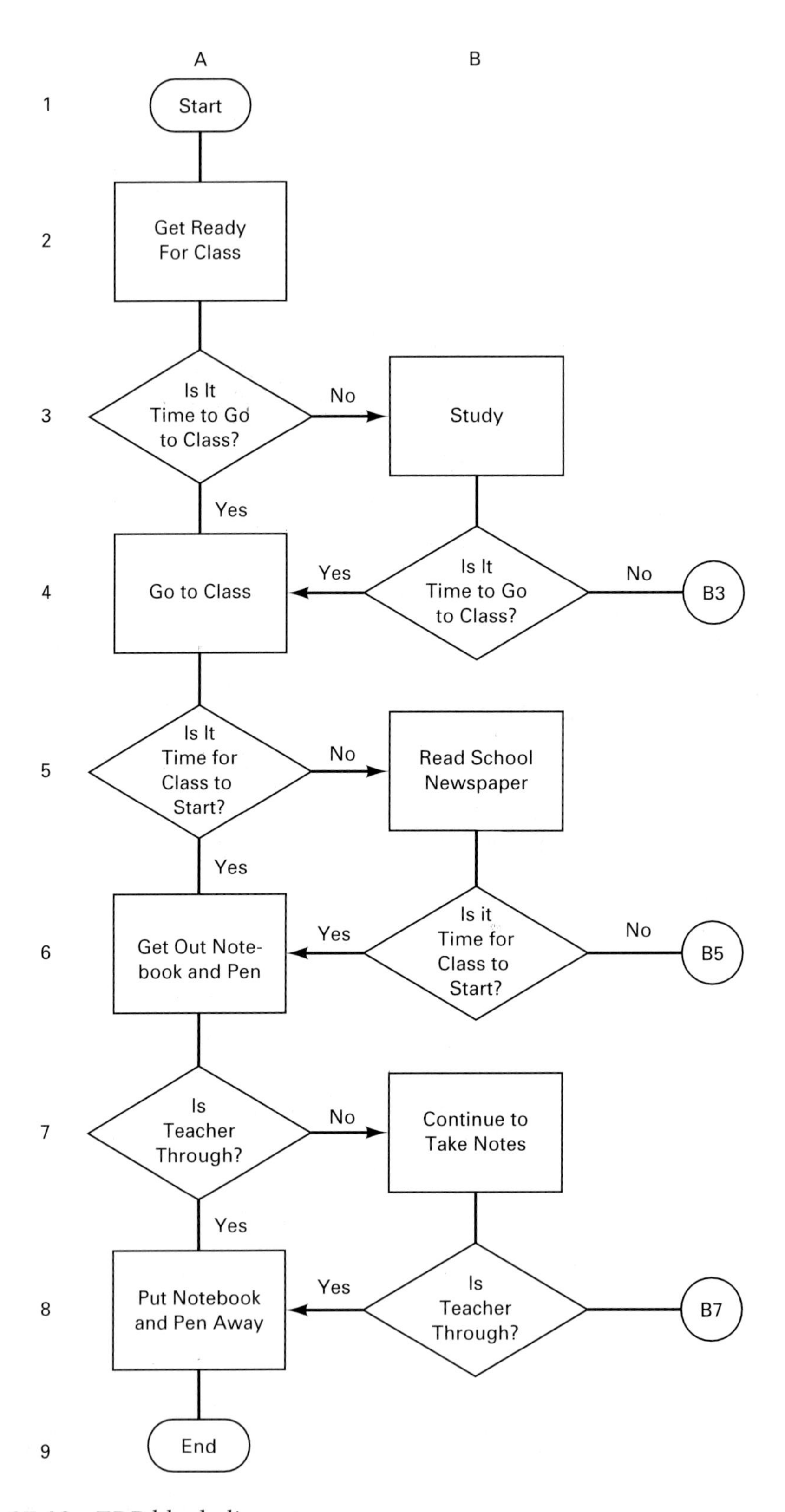

Figure 17-13 EDP block diagram.

	Work Load Chart	Flow Process Chart	Right- and Left-Hand Chart	Operator-Machine Chart	Horizontal Flow Process Chart	EDP Block Diagram
Analysis of employee or departmental activities	x					
Useful for nonintricate work processes	x	x				
Identification and analysis of steps in specific work processes		x	x	x	x	x
Identify nature of each step in work process		x	x	x	x	x
Identify distance that objects or employees move		x				
Identify amount of time of each step	x			x		
Identify ways to eliminate, combine, simplify steps	x	x	x	x	x	x
Identify hand movement in work process		x	x	x		
Identify relationship between operator and machine				x		
Identify activity of each copy of a multicopy form					x	
Identify steps of a computer program						x

Figure 17-14 Uses of systems analysis tools.

involve either a *yes* or *no* decision. In the case of a *yes* decision, the process then proceeds to the next step in the vertical sequence of the diagram. In the case of a *no* decision, an alternative step (called branching) is used until the appropriate situation occurs that allows the process to continue sequencing through the vertical listing of steps. For example, in Figure 17-13, the student will continue to study until the time arrives to leave for class.

Figure 17-14 summarizes some of the characteristics of each of the systems analysis tools.

IMPLICATIONS FOR THE ADMINISTRATIVE OFFICE MANAGER

The level of responsibility that administrative office managers have for systems analysis varies from organization to organization. Generally, the alternative used by the organization for staffing its systems analysis function determines the administrative office manager's level of responsibility for this area. The greatest amount of involvement tends to be in organizations that use a part-time staff headed by the administrative office manager.

Familiarity with the organization's operating units is crucial for those involved with systems analysis and design. This is especially true nowadays because of the trend toward developing and implementing integrated systems. Those who are involved in systems development also should be familiar with work flow, data processing, and fundamentals of analysis and design.

Like several of the other areas for which administrative office managers are responsible, systems analysis provides an opportunity to specialize for those who wish to do so. Some prefer the more specialized nature of systems analysis and design over the more general nature of administrative office management.

REVIEW QUESTIONS

1. What is meant by the integrated systems concept?
2. What are the objectives of the systems concept?
3. What are the characteristics of a well-designed system?
4. What advantages result from using outside consultants for designing a system?
5. Explain the use of the daily log sheet.
6. In a flow process chart, why is the elimination of the *do* steps in a work process advantageous?
7. What special situations are identified by office layout charts?
8. For what type of systems analysis is the horizontal flow process chart especially suited?

DISCUSSION QUESTIONS

1. When a group of employees in your unit recently heard that the company in which you work was going to implement several systems designed to reduce operating costs, they became quite concerned. Their basic complaint was that systems tend to standardize or make uniform operating procedures—and how could several people who perform the same tasks be expected to perform those tasks in the same manner? They also indicated that they each have their special "shortcuts" for performing these tasks and that, as individuals, their own procedures are the most efficient for each of them. What is your reaction to the thinking of these employees?
2. The organization in which you work is presently undertaking a systems analysis project that will culminate in the design and implementation of one or more systems. The group that you supervise was selected to participate in the data-collection process, using a daily log to collect the data. When you attempted to collect the log from one of your subordinates, she said, "I am not going to complete that stupid thing. As long as I do my work well—and you keep telling me that I do—how I spend my day is no one's business. Besides, I know management is doing this just to try to prove that the company is not getting its money's worth from the employees." Discuss how you plan to deal with this situation.
3. You are a senior systems analyst/designer in a consulting firm that has clients all over the country. The president of a company you worked with two years ago just called you to say that the system you installed in his company is producing less-than-desirable results. Instead of helping the company reduce its operating costs, the system seems to be having the opposite effect. This puzzles you very much as you had collected more information than you usually do before you design and implement systems. You noticed during your data-collection efforts that many of the employees seemed to be skeptical of management's intentions, prompting you to collect more information than you otherwise would have. While discrepancies existed in some of the data you collected, you resolved the differences with managers/supervisors before you began designing the system. Identify some of the possible reasons why the system is not producing the results you expected.

4. You are the administrative office manager in the organization in which you work. One of your responsibilities is the coordination of the systems design and implementation project. You have recently discovered that a number of the employees are becoming more resistive to systems utilization, perhaps because of the fear of the unknown. What can you do to help employees become less resistive to systems utilization?
5. The organization in which you work is in the process of designing and implementing several new subsystems. One of these new subsystems will be implemented in your department. Your secretary told you this morning that she overhead several employees talking about purposely distorting their daily logs. These employees claim it takes them longer to do their work than it actually does. Discuss the implications of this situation for the design of the new subsystem for your department. As the manager of the department, what do you plan to do about this situation?
6. The organization in which you work is in the process of designing a new system that will be used to help expedite the paperwork in the purchasing department. The present system, which is quite inefficient, is responsible for a month's backlog in the processing of the department's paperwork. What analysis tool would be useful in collecting data for use in designing the new system? Justify its use.

STUDENT PROJECTS AND ACTIVITIES

1. Talk with a systems analyst who has been intricately involved in the development of a system used in an organization. Have this individual discuss with you the development of the system—from the beginning to the end.
2. Compare the purchasing subsystem presented earlier in this chapter with the purchasing subsystem found in an organization. What are the similarities and differences between the two?
3. Collect examples of the systems analysis tools used in two different organizations. What are their similarities and differences?
4. Using the common flow charting symbols found in Figure 17-12, prepare an EDP block diagram for one of your frequent routine tasks.
5. Make arrangements with one of the offices on your campus to allow you to prepare an office layout chart that depicts the movement of a frequently processed document through the office.

MINICASE

The Hutchinson Oil Company was founded seven years ago. It is still a rather small organization, although its growth during the last five years has been steady. The management recently decided that the organization is now large enough to justify systems utilization. You, a consultant, have been hired by the organization's president to provide badly needed direction in systems design and implementation. He wants to know what is involved in the design and implementation of a system. Accordingly, you decide to prepare a report in which you

1. Identify the steps involved in the design and implementation of a new system.
2. Identify the activities involved in each of these steps.

CASE

Recently, the Merrimac Insurance Company, which is located in Hartford, Connecticut, completed several cost analysis studies and found an alarming increase in the cost of processing insurance claims. Merrimac's rates are about 15 percent higher than the national average.

A recent study completed by several systems analysis experts indicated that much of the cost can be attributed to inefficient work flow. Part-time employees are frequently hired to help process the backlog.

The following outlines the steps involved in processing the claims:

1. The claim is received in the mailroom.
2. The claim is transported to the claims department, a distance of 401 feet.
3. The claim is opened and then assigned to a claims clerk according to an alphabetic sequence.
4. The claim is transported to a claims clerk, a distance of 15 feet.
5. The claims clerk briefly scans the claim.
6. The customer's file is retrieved from the file area, a distance of 50 feet.
7. After checking the customer's folder for coverage, premium status, and history of claims, the claims clerk approves the claim and makes a notation on the folder.
8. The claim is transported for final authorization to the supervisor, a distance of 20 feet. (Because of the backlog, this regularly results in a two-day delay before the supervisor gives final approval.)
9. The authorized claim is transported to data processing, a distance of 160 feet.
10. The customer's folder is refiled.

You have been assigned the responsibility of charting the process as it presently exists.

1. What analysis tool or tools would be appropriate for charting the process?
2. Chart the proposed process, using an appropriate tool.

TELECOMMUNICATIONS

CHAPTER AIM

After studying this chapter, you should be able to design an effective telecommunications system for an organization.

CHAPTER OUTLINE

CHAPTER TERMS

Analog mode
Bandwidth
Baseband channels
Baud
Broadband channels
Bus network
Call processing
Cellular phone technology
Centrex
Closed-circuit television
Coaxial cable
Communication channels
Communication networks
Computer phone
Data-Phone
Digital mode
Duplexing
Electronic mail
Facsimile (fax) devices
Fiber optics
FX line
Grade of service
Interconnect
Interoffice messaging
Intrafax
Key system telephones
Local area network (LAN)
Microwaves
Modem
PABX
Paging systems
PBX
Picturephone
Ring network
Satellites
Star network
Telecommunications
Teleconferencing
Teletypewriter
Telewriter
Twisted-pair wiring
Videoconferencing
Voice messaging
Voiceband channels
WATS
Wide area network (WAN)
Wideband Data Service
Wireless radio frequencies

To carry out their job responsibilities, many employees make extensive use of **telecommunications**. In many organizations, especially smaller ones, the administrative office manager is often responsible for determining the need for and function of telecommunications equipment. In larger organizations, this function may be performed by the manager of telecommunications services. Of the various areas comprising the administrative office management field, telecommunications is now one of the most technical.

Automated office systems, the topic of Chapter 22, make extensive use of communications technology; therefore, additional related information is included in that chapter.

As the technology continues to develop in the near future, telecommunications will be viewed as a network comprised of a number of multimedia components. Among the components built into the network will be video, text, voice, information processing, and computer processing. Because the telephone will be a common means of accessing the network, desired information will be as close as a telephone, regardless of where one is located throughout the world.

THE NATURE OF TELECOMMUNICATIONS

Telecommunications involves the transmission of voice, data, and images from one location to another. Before computers were readily available, telecommunications primarily involved voice communication over telephone lines. However, during the last several years, telecommunications has since expanded to include additional channels and formats, with future expansion making it a multimedia system. This section provides a discussion of several topics related to telecommunications, including communication channels, transmission modes, networking, transmission speeds, duplexing, and modems.

Communication Channels

For what are communication channels used?

The primary function of **communication channels** is to facilitate the transmission of voice, data, or images to computers or other remotely located peripheral equipment. Among the communication channels are twisted-pair wire, coaxial cable, microwaves, satellites, fiber optics, and wireless radio frequencies. If the telecommunications potential is to be maximized, special consideration has to be given to selecting an appropriate channel for specific situations. The various channels are not all equally suited for all situations.

For what type of communication process is twisted-pair wiring typically used?

Twisted-pair wire The oldest of the communication channels is **twisted-pair wiring**. It uses two insulated copper wires twisted around one another. Twisted-pair wiring is used for voice and data communication over standard-grade telephone lines.

Static on standard-grade lines is sometimes excessive, which may result in the transmission of data errors. When this occurs, a special conditioned line may need to be leased. These lines reduce transmission errors and increase data transmission rates. Today, many organizations lease dedicated lines, which provide them with exclusive, full-time use of these lines.

The use of twisted-pair wire requires a physical connection between the sender and receiver. Compared with microwave, satellite channels, and wireless radio frequencies that do not require a physical connection, this requirement is seen by some as a disadvantage.

Coaxial cable Comprised of either copper or aluminum wires, **coaxial cable** is another of the communication channels. The outer surface of coaxial cable is typically a metallic sheathing covered with a plastic coating that protects the data transmission wires from electrical interference. A coaxial cable measuring three inches in diameter may contain as many as one hundred different wires. Large-diameter coaxial cable is used for underwater intercontinental communication systems.

Small-diameter coaxial cable is often used in local area networks, which are discussed in the "Transmission Modes" section of this chapter. The small-size cable also has widespread use in cable television systems.

What are the characteristics of microwave technology?

Microwaves While twisted-pair wiring and coaxial cable require a physical connection, microwave technology does not. Transmitted as high-frequency radio waves, **microwaves** are sent from the sending location to the receiving location, using a series of antennas located not more than 40 miles from one another. Microwave technology is used extensively in sections of the country where the antennas have been installed. The antennas are located on tall towers.

Because microwaves travel in a straight-line path, the sending and receiving antennas have to be located in a precise line of sight. Even a small variance can cause an interruption of service.

What are the characteristics of satellite technology?

Satellites Located approximately 22,300 miles above the earth's surface are a number of earth-orbiting **satellites** used to transmit voice, data, and image signals. These satellites are geosynchronous, meaning that they travel the same orbital speed as the earth. Therefore, they are always positioned above the same earth location. Satellite technology is similar to microwave technology in that it is also a line-of-sight medium. Compared with twisted-pair wire and coaxial cable technologies, satellite transmission is much faster and less expensive.

Satellites that support organizational telecommunications efforts are all privately owned by such carrier companies as AT&T, COMSAT, RCA, and Western Union. Users of the satellite pay a fee for its use. In the future, an increasing number of businesses will have their own satellites. Some organizations are likely to enter into a cooperative arrangement with a handful of other businesses in the joint ownership of a satellite.

With satellite technology, a signal is transmitted from an earth station to the satellite, from which the signal is transmitted back to another earth station. The signal may return directly to the recipient's location, or it may have to travel through another channel (such as microwave) before it reaches the recipient's location.

What are the characteristics of fiber optics technology?

Fiber optics One of the newest of the communication channels is **fiber optics**, a technology that uses hair-sized glass fibers that transmit high-frequency laser (light) pulses. Although the signal is transmitted as a beam of light, the nature of fiber optics allows the beam to round corners. Repeaters are used to strengthen signals transmitted over distances of more than 50 miles.

Fiber optics, when compared with other communication technologies, enjoys the following advantages: (1) it is safer to use in some installations because it involves the transmission of light rather than electrical current; (2) it is not subject to electromagnetic interference or radio frequency interference; (3) it provides greater security for the transmission of data because fiber optics cannot be "bugged"; and (4) the fiber optics cable is lightweight and compact. A fiber optics cable comprised of approximately 150 fibers can carry nearly 100,000 simultaneous two-way phone conversations in a cable measuring an inch in diameter and weighing less than six ounces per foot. Fiber optics cables carry ten times as many signals as a three-inch coaxial cable and 1,000 times as many signals as a microwave system.

Wireless radio frequencies Technology using **wireless radio frequencies** transmits data and/or telephone signals through the air. An antenna attached to the device (whether it be a telephone, a local area network, or a pen-based handwriting recognition device) enables it to send and receive signals.

Employees who are typically away from their desks for a considerable time during the workday will find useful the convertible cellular phone that uses radio frequencies. Being a pocket phone, the employee will use cellular technology outside the organization's premises, with these calls being assessed the usual cellular call charge. However, once the employee enters the building, the convertible phone automatically transforms into a wireless PBX-system-based device that enables any caller to get in phone contact with the employee any time the employee has the phone in his/her possession. Calls made/received on the phone within the premises are not subject to the cellular call charge because the phone is simply functioning as a cordless telephone.

What advantages result from the use of wireless radio frequency devices?

Two primary advantages result from the use of wireless radio frequency devices: (1) the ease with which contact between two individuals can be maintained and (2) the avoidance of having to install wires, cables, or fibers to facilitate telecommunications. Disadvantages include (1) transmission is not secure, meaning that it can be intercepted by others; (2) transmission is subject to static and other types of interference.

Transmission Modes

Data are technologically communicated in either of the following two modes: digital and analog. The differences between the two are explained and illustrated.

Digital Because most business computers are digital in nature, they transmit data as digital signals. Data are transmitted as discrete pulses of electrical current (approximately five volts) through a communication medium. However, before data can be transmitted, they have to be converted into binary code. This means that each alphabetic character, number, and symbol is converted to a series of 1's or 0's capable of being understood by the computer. A more detailed discussion of binary code is found in Chapter 20. A binary code of 1 is transmitted as an electrical pulse, while a binary code of 0 is transmitted as the absence of a pulse.

How do digital and analog modes differ from one another?

Over longer distances, the use of the **digital mode** for transmission of data has the following disadvantages: (1) the strength of the signals tend to weaken as they are transmitted over distance; (2) the presence of static or noise on the line can affect the accuracy of the data that are transmitted; and (3) the longer the distance that data are transmitted, the greater power that is required. These disadvantages are overcome somewhat by using an analog mode, which is the common mode used in telephone systems.

Analog While the digital mode transmits data as electrical pulses, the **analog mode** transmits data as low- and high-pitched sounds. The binary code of 1 is transmitted as a low-pitched sound, while the 0 is transmitted as a high-pitched sound. This is the means by which the disadvantages of the digital mode are eliminated.

Most significant among the disadvantages of the analog mode is its inability to accept digital signals. This problem is remedied by using a modem at the sending location that converts digital signals into analog signals and reconverts the analog signals into digital signals at the receiving location.

Figure 18-1 illustrates the difference between the digital and analog modes.

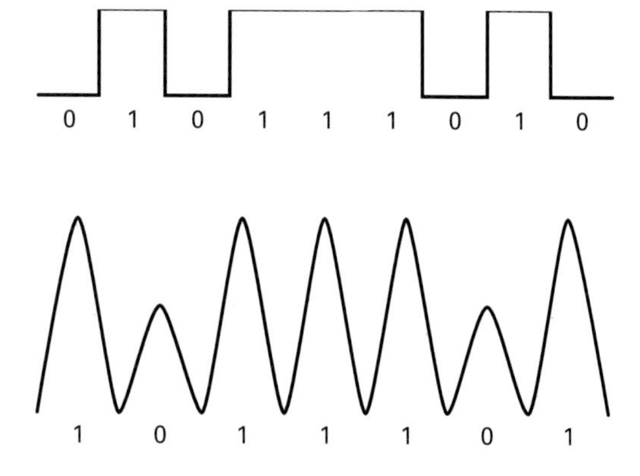

Figure 18-1 Transmission modes.

Networks

The availability of **communication networks** has facilitated the development of the automated office systems, which is the content of Chapter 22. The ability to transmit data and information between two sites makes office automation a reality.

Two types of networks are found: local area networks (commonly called LANs) and wide area networks (WANs; also called long-haul networks). While LANs are used to interconnect computers and peripheral equipment located up to a few hundred feet from one another, wide area networks are used to interconnect computers and peripheral devices located thousands of miles from one another. A greater need exists for LANs than exists for WANs, which is the likely explanation that LAN technology has developed faster than WAN technology.

Although wires, cables, or fibers are typically used to interconnect the devices to a LAN, a new system uses infrared technology. Devices interconnected to the LAN by means of infrared technology need to be positioned in a line of sight to one another or within close proximity to one another. This technology is similar to that used by remote control televisions and stereo devices.

Local area networks A discussion of **local area networks** follows, including these topics: the functions for which LANs are used and the types of LANs that are found.

Among the uses of LANs are to

What are the common functions for which local area networks are used?

1. *Expedite communication.* Increasingly, employees in organizations are able to communicate with one another using their computer terminals. This communication mode is used as an alternative to face-to-face conversations or telephone calls. The use of computers to communicate with another individual is commonly known as electronic mail or electronic messaging. The LAN is used to interconnect the computer devices, thus facilitating their ability to communicate.
2. *Share computer and peripheral devices.* The cost of today's equipment makes desirable the sharing of as many computer and peripheral devices as possible. Not only is shared equipment likely to be used more efficiently, but also it is likely to have more extensive use. To illustrate, rather than installing a hard disk in each of several microcomputers, a LAN can produce the same level of functionalism because several users are able to share one hard disk.
3. *Share computer files.* Increasingly, organizations are storing their data and information electronically. Through the LAN, these stored computer files are available to all authorized users. Electronic filing is discussed more fully in Chapter 21.
4. *Reduce software costs.* The vast majority of software packages are available today for use on mainframe computers. A LAN makes the connection between the mainframe and the user, which allows him or her to use the software package. Having to purchase a separate package for each microcomputer would be considerably more expensive.

The three common types of local area networks are star networks, ring networks, and bus networks. The differences between each are considerable. Figure 18-2 illustrates each type of network.

Using coaxial cable to interconnect computer terminals and other pe-

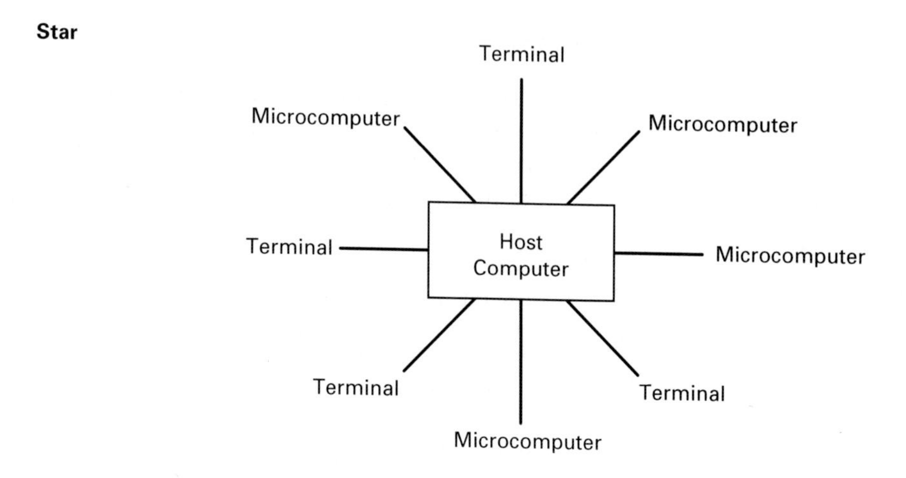

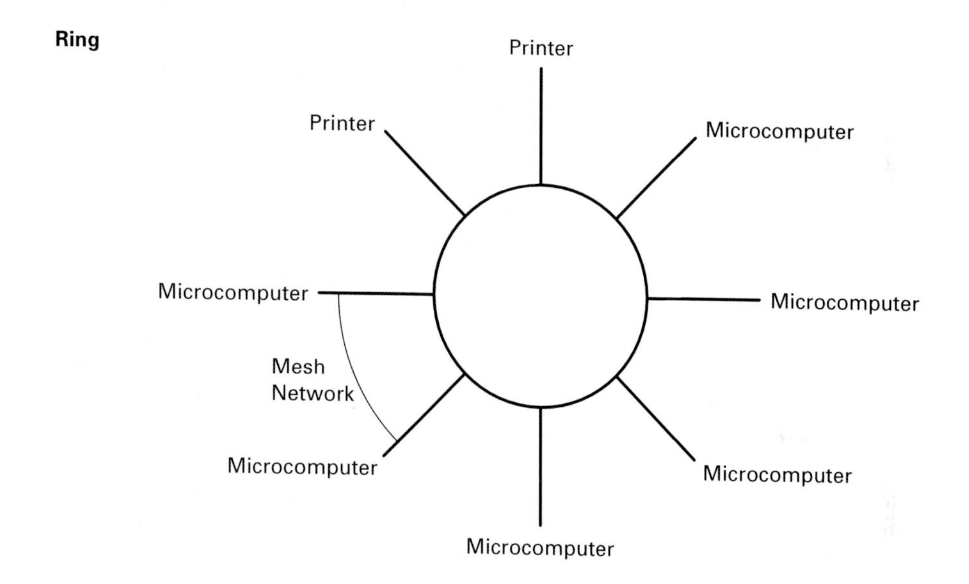

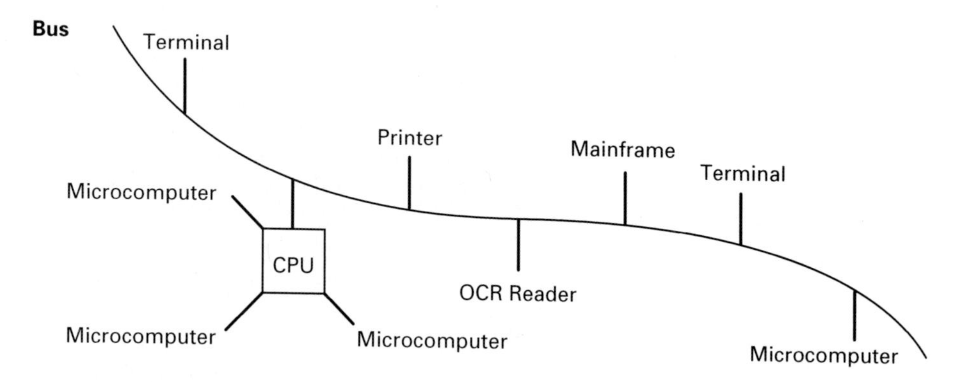

Figure 18-2 Types of local area networks.

What are the characteristics of the star network?

ripheral devices with the host computer, the **star network** acts as a switcher for the various functions that are performed. Data files and software are stored in the host computer. The LAN facilitates accessing both stored data/information and software.

Among the advantages of the star network are the following:

1. Data/information as well as software and certain hardware devices are centralized. User sharing of hardware and software is cost effective.
2. Users can be given the type of terminal that best meets their needs. Those whose job responsibilities can be performed on a terminal that does not possess its own operating intelligence can generally use what is known as a "dumb" terminal. The operating intelligence of these terminals originates from a host computer. Those whose job responsibilities require a device containing its own operating intelligence (called a smart terminal) can be provided a microcomputer interconnected to a host computer. Giving users the type of equipment they need results in reduced operating costs.

Two disadvantages of the star network are the following:

1. The devices are generally interconnected by coaxial cable, which means that significant amounts of cabling must be installed in floors, walls, and ceilings. Installing coaxial cable after a building has been constructed is typically quite expensive.
2. If the host computer fails, the devices that depend on the host for their operating intelligence will be inoperable. The devices that possess their own operating intelligence may continue to be operable, although not for tasks that require software or data/information stored in the host computer.

What are the characteristics of the ring network?

A **ring network** interconnects a number of devices to a continuous network cable. The various devices attached to the ring are all of equal importance; therefore, the ring network differs significantly from the star network that uses a host computer with significantly more importance than any of the other interconnected devices. Certain devices in the ring may also have an exclusive interconnection (called a mesh network) with one another.

The most significant advantage of the ring network is its reliability. This network does not require a host computer; therefore, individual computer workstations will continue to be operable even if a problem occurs in the network. The most significant disadvantage of the ring network is the special care that needs to be exercised in coordinating communication so messages do not become garbled because of signal intermixing during their transmission. Communication controllers are used to prevent the garbling.

What are the characteristics of the bus network?

In a **bus network**, computers and peripheral devices are connected to a network cable. The cable is not continuous as it is with the ring network, nor does the bus network depend on a host computer, as the star network requires. For these reasons, some consider the bus network to be the most ideal of the three types of networks.

Two advantages of the bus network are (1) the reduced amount of network cable that is required, especially when compared with the ring network, and (2) its ability to function without a host computer. Both result in cost reductions.

The most significant disadvantage of the bus network results from timing or scheduling the transmittal of data/information through the channel. Mistiming can result in data collision. This problem is eliminated by using a device that assures the availability of a channel before beginning the transmission of data.

Available now is wireless LAN technology. Microcomputers can send data to peripheral equipment, such as printers, as far away as 150 feet. Using radio signals that can be transmitted through walls, the connected devices are not limited to a line-of-sight arrangement.

Wide area networks Organizations typically use a **wide area network** to interconnect computer equipment and peripheral devices at their headquarters with the equipment at remotely located branches. The interconnection facilitates communication between employees and equipment at the two locations. Contrasted with LANs, WANs typically have more users, and they are more multifunctional.

WANs are used for

What are the common functions for which wide area networks are used?

1. *Centralized electronic filing.* Data/information generated at the remote sites that might be of value to individuals at other sites are often transmitted to the headquarters where they are stored in the organization's database. Users at other sites are then able to access and use this information.
2. *Remote data entry.* The use of a WAN allows data to be entered at a remote site but transmitted to a centralized location where it is processed. For example, point-of-sale terminals are often interconnected to a WAN that transmits data to a centralized computer where processing and storage take place. Using this type of system may be considerably less expensive than purchasing a computer for each remote site.
3. *Centralized software storage.* Some organizations store the software at the centralized location from where it is transmitted through the WAN each time it is needed at a remote site. This is an alternative to providing a separate package at each remote site.
4. *Electronic communication.* The WAN is used for electronic communication in much the same way as the LAN is used for electronic communication. The WAN facilitates computer conferencing (a conference between two individuals in which their computers are used for sending and receiving their "conversation"), electronic mail, and electronic messaging.

Among the types of communication channels typically used in wide area networks are conditioned telephone lines, microwaves, and satellites. A common type of WAN is the hierarchical network in which local microcomputers and terminals are interconnected with regional minicomputers or a mainframe computer. The regional computers are interconnected with a national mainframe.

Transmission Speeds

An important determinant of how well computer applications function is the speed with which data are transmitted from one location to another. The transmission speed is especially significant when an application has many users, such as in an airline reservation system or with automatic teller machines. As the number of users increases, so must the data transmission speed. Otherwise, the users will have to wait for their response, which diminishes the cost effectiveness and efficiency of the system.

The two important determinants of data transmission speed are baud and bandwidth. Information about each is presented in the paragraphs that follow.

Baud By definition, **baud** refers to the number of signal changes per second that a communication channel will allow. Common baud rates are 2,400, 4,800, 9,600, 14,400, and 28,800. A baud of 2,400, for example, means that 2,400 signal changes occur each second.

What is bandwidth?

Bandwidth **Bandwidth** refers to the data transmission capacity of the channel. Generally, the wider the band, the more data it can carry during a specific unit of time. Three bandwidths are found: baseband, voiceband, and broadband.

Because **baseband channels** are narrow, only small amounts of data can be transmitted each second. The upper transmission speed of baseband channels is generally 30 characters per second. Telegraph lines typically are baseband channels.

Commonly found used with telephone lines, **voiceband channels** are capable of transmitting up to 1,000 characters per second. Voiceband channels are likely to interconnect terminals with a minicomputer or a mainframe computer.

Generally using coaxial cable, microwaves, satellites, and fiber optics, **broadband channels** are capable of transmitting millions of characters per second. To accomplish these speeds, digital data are converted to and transmitted as analog signals.

Duplexing

In telecommunications, **duplexing** determines how messages are sent—on a discrete basis or on a simultaneous basis. In a half-duplexing arrangement, data are sent and received between two locations on a discrete basis. Therefore, while the equipment at one location "sends," equipment at the other location "receives." In a full-duplexing arrangement, data can be both sent and received simultaneously. Therefore, "sending" and "receiving" can occur at the same time.

Modems

What is the function of a modem?

Because most business computers are digital and most telephone systems are analog, a **modem** (acronym for modulator-demodulator) is needed. The modem converts digital signals into an analog format so they can be transmitted over phone lines, microwaves, satellites, and so on. At the receiving location, a modem reconfigures the analog signals into a digital format so they can be accepted by a digital computer. Because some intraorganizational phone systems are now able to accept data in digital format, a modem may not always be necessary.

TELEPHONE SYSTEMS

Included in this section is a discussion of the various types of telephone systems, as well as alternate telephone services, grade of service, telephone features and options, other related telephonic devices, interconnect, and telegraphy.

Types of Telephone Systems

Each of the types of telephone systems used in organizations—key system, PBX, PABX, and Centrex—has its own special characteristics and uses.

Key system **Key system telephones**, an inexpensive alternative to PBX, PABX, and Centrex systems, use handsets that are equipped with buttons or keys. The user, therefore, is able to perform a number of functions rather than depending on a receptionist or operator to perform these functions. Key system telephones are becoming much more sophisticated, often possessing a number of the features found in other more expensive systems.

PBX In a **PBX** system, which is the acronym for private branch exchange, all incoming and outgoing calls go through the switchboard. However, a PBX system does not require the use of an operator for making interoffice calls.

PABX The **PABX** system, or private automatic branch exchange, also uses a switchboard or console. The operator receives incoming calls and connects the caller with the call recipient. With a PABX system, employees dial their own outgoing and interoffice calls. PABX systems are more widely used than either PBX or Centrex systems.

What are the characteristics of Centrex telephone systems?

Centrex The **Centrex** system, the acronym for central exchange, requires neither a switchboard nor console for the completion of calls. All employees have their own telephone number. Employees also make their own interoffice calls, typically by dialing the last four or five digits of the telephone number of the individual or department they wish to contact.

Of the three systems, Centrex is the most private because employees do not share telephone lines with others. Also possible is obtaining an itemized list of call charges for each telephone in the organization. Thus, fewer long-distance nonbusiness telephone calls are likely to be made. In Centrex systems, operators are generally used to provide number information service.

Several types of Centrex equipment are available. With Centrex I equipment, operators are needed to transfer calls. Centrex II does not require an operator to transfer calls, and it enables the user to make three-party calls and place a caller on hold while consulting another person.

Centrex tends to be the most expensive telephone system discussed in this chapter. Some organizations, as a cost-cutting measure, have replaced their Centrex system with a PABX system.

Alternative Telephone Services

Over the years, several alternative telephone services have been developed: WATS (wide area telecommunications service); FX (foreign exchange) lines; Wideband Data Service; and cellular phone systems.

What advantages result from the use of WATS lines?

WATS The use of **WATS** by many organizations has resulted in a substantial reduction of long-distance call charges. Before an organization installs a WATS system, though, the use of and need for such a system must be determined. The installation of a system on some basis other than need may result in excessive telephone costs.

WATS lines are available on an inward and outward basis. An inward

WATS line can be used only to call the organization that leases the line. Many organizations lease inward lines as a service to their customers or to provide telephone service between a home office and its regional branches. Telephone numbers with an "800" prefix are inward WATS lines. Outward WATS lines, on the other hand, can be used to make outward calls but cannot be used to receive inward calls.

In many organizations that have a switchboard, the WATS line originates at the switchboard. The operator is responsible for dialing WATS line calls and for keeping a user waiting list when several employees wish to use the line at the same time. Also possible is rigging employees' telephones so they can access the WATS line without using the switchboard or console.

WATS lines are leased on a full-time basis or on a measured-time basis. A flat monthly toll is charged when leasing the line on a full-time basis; the line can be used an unlimited number of hours each month. The measured-time basis entitles the user to a given amount of talking time each month—usually 600 minutes. When a line is used for more than the given amount, the user is charged for the excess minutes at a lower rate and in units of tenths of hours. No refunds are made when the line is used less than the minimum time.

WATS lines are leased by bands. The United States is divided into six bands, and each band serves specific area codes. To obtain coast-to-coast WATS-line service, Band 6 must be leased, which also entitles the user to Bands 1-5. Leasing Band 3 entitles the user only to Bands 1, 2, and 3. Separate WATS lines are used for interstate and intrastate calls; therefore, an interstate call may not be made on an intrastate WATS line.

For what situation is an FX line used?

FX lines When calls are frequently made to the same city, many organizations have found the use of an **FX line** more economical than a WATS line. FX lines can be obtained either from the phone company or from a specialized common carrier that competes with the phone company.

Wideband Data Service The function of **Wideband Data Service** is to select the appropriate band for the type of data or image being transmitted. For example, the slower that words or data are being transmitted through the lines, the narrower the band can be; however, faster transmission rates require wider bands. Rather than leasing a band sufficiently wide to handle the transmission of all types of data, Wideband Data Service provides several band widths. Thus, the user has access to the appropriate band for a specific type of data. For example, computers that are communicating with one another at rates of 200,000 words per minute need a wider band than teletypewriters transmitting at 100 words a minute. The wider the band, the more costly it is to use. Image transmission typically requires a wider band than does either data or voice transmission.

Cellular phone systems The advent of **cellular phone technology** makes possible the use of phones from almost any location. As the technology continues to develop, a wrist-size cellular telephone is inevitable.

Cellular phone systems use radio transmitters. In the more populated areas of the country, radio transmitters are located in designated service areas (cells) that have a radius of eight to ten miles. At the center of each service area is a transmitter.

When a call is placed on a cellular phone, the signal "informs" the transmitter in the service area that a phone channel is needed. Once the connection is made with the phone channel, the signals are transmitted using conventional telephone lines, microwave technology, and so forth.

When a call is placed from a mobile phone to another mobile phone in the same service area, the transmitter serves as both the transmitter and receiver. If the call is made from a conventional phone to a mobile phone in a distant service area, conventional technology is used between the sending location and the transmitter in the area serving the location of the mobile phone. Once the signals reach the service area, the radio transmitter makes the "connection" between the transmitter and the mobile telephone.

The critical component of cellular phone systems is the radio transmitter. If a transmitter is within eight to ten miles of a call's origin, a cellular phone can be used to make local, long-distance, and even international phone calls.

Cellular technology is developing rapidly to accommodate traveling employees and/or telecommuters. Now available are cellular devices that allow the user to plug into a cellular phone for devices such as a modem, laptop computer, or facsimile (fax) device. Some providers of cellular service now offer an encryption feature that provides a totally private voice and data transmission. The lack of a secure transmission channel destroys the confidentiality of a phone conversation.

Grade of Service

What is meant by grade of service?

The number of telephone circuits available is known as **grade of service**. An insufficient grade of service means that the organization does not have an adequate number of trunk lines on its PBX and PABX system to handle the volume of calls it receives. Grade of service is not a concern with Centrex systems. Three or fewer busy signals per one hundred call attempts provides a sufficient grade of service.

Grade of service not only applies to incoming calls, but also to outgoing and interoffice calls. For example, if busy signals are heard often when the outgoing call access (usually 9) is dialed, more outgoing trunk lines may have to be installed. On telephone systems other than Centrex, an insufficient number of links will produce a busy signal when attempting to make interoffice calls.

By attaching to telephone lines special meters that record the number of times busy signals occur during a given period, an organization can assess the adequacy of its grade of service. The ratio of busy signals to completed calls can be calculated to determine the adequacy of grade of service.

Telephone Features and Options

A variety of telephone features and options are now available.

Automatic route selection The system automatically selects the best, most economical route for long-distance phone calls.

Automatic station restriction The system prohibits making long-distance calls from certain phones.

Automatic identification of outward dialing The AIOD system identifies the phone extension that was used to make long-distance phone calls.

Call forwarding The system automatically routes externally originated incoming calls and internally originated calls to other designated on-premises or off-premises phones.

Call pickup The system permits an individual to receive an incoming call on any phone. The call recipient, after being paged over the PA system, uses any convenient phone to dial the appropriate code, thus being able to access the call.

Call return This feature enables the system to redial the last number that called the employee.

Call tracing This feature enables the local phone company to determine the phone number from which an unidentified caller placed a call.

Call waiting The system sounds a tone or lights up a lamp to indicate that another call is awaiting the individual whose phone is currently in use. In the more sophisticated systems, call waiting maintains a running log of the number of waiting calls a person has. When necessary, the employee, with the push of a button, can obtain supervisory assistance to help reduce the backlog.

Distinctive ringing The system uses a distinctive ringing to signal the user of the special status of certain calls (such as return calls).

Direct inward dialing The system automatically completes incoming calls without the assistance of an operator.

Direct outward dialing The system automatically transfers outgoing calls without the assistance of the operator.

In-conference transfers The system automatically transfers an individual's calls to another person when the former is in conference or does not wish to be interrupted.

Repeat dialing This feature allows the system to keep dialing a busy phone number at a predetermined time (perhaps every minute).

Speed dialing The system allows users to make frequently called local or long-distance calls by dialing a prescribed two- or three-digit number.

Station billing system The system provides a printout of the phone numbers called by each user, the date of each call, and the duration of each call.

Station hunting The system automatically transfers calls to another person when the phone is not answered within a specified number of rings.

User code The system matches the services an employee is entitled to use with the service he or she is attempting to use. Unless the required code is provided and the service is within the employee's authorized service limits, the call cannot be completed.

Other Devices Using Telephone Lines

In addition to telephones, several other communication devices found in offices also require the use of telephone lines. While some of these devices use "voice grade" lines, others require the use of heavier-duty lines capable of transmitting high-speed data communication. The following are other devices that use telephone lines: teletypewriter devices, teleconference and videoconference devices, Data-Phone, Picturephone, computer phones, fax devices, e-mail, interoffice messaging, and voice messaging.

What is the function of a teletypewriter?

Teletypewriter devices Whereas the telephone is used to transmit oral communication, **teletypewriters** are used to transmit written messages from one location to another. A teletypewriter is required at both the sending and receiving locations. To transmit a message, the telephone number of the receiving party is dialed, which activates the receiver's teletypewriter. As the sender types the material on the teletypewriter keyboard, impulses carried through the telephone lines reproduce the same material on the receiver's teletypewriter.

Teleconference and videoconference devices As an alternative to holding face-to-face conferences among an organization's executives, a growing number of firms use **teleconferencing** and **videoconferencing**, especially organizations that have executives in several locations throughout the United States.

Teleconferencing uses telephones to connect any number of remotely located individuals, which enables them to communicate by voice only. Videoconferencing transmits images of these individuals as well as their voice communication.

Videoconferencing technology continues to be an expensive investment. The most costly equipment component of a videoconferencing system is the coder-decoder used to translate video images from an analog mode into a digital mode. After translation, the digital computerized signals are transmitted over either high-speed digital lines or satellites. Two types of coder-decoder are used: full motion and limited motion. Full-motion transmission provides on the television screen a real-time image just as it appears to the camera. Limited-motion transmission is much slower, with fast or sudden movement (including rapid lip movement) either appearing at the receiving location as a blur or not appearing.

A videoconference is shown in Figure 18-3.

Figure 18-3 Videoconference. Courtesy: American Telephone and Telegraph.

For what is a Data-Phone used?

Data-Phones Used to transmit and receive data that are coded for computer processing, the **Data-Phone** functions by converting data into tones suitable for transmission by telephone. At the receiving location, the tones are reconverted to coded data and are recorded on such media as punched cards, perforated tape, magnetic tape, and magnetic disks.

The system is activated when the sender calls the receiver and provides proper identification. Transmission begins once the sender's telephone handset is in place. These devices are capable of transmitting data at rates in excess of 3,000 words per minute.

Picturephones Another of the devices that uses telephone lines is the **Picturephone**. This device, which incorporates a televisionlike screen and a telephone, enables the sender and receiver of a call to see one another as they talk.

Computer phones Used to transmit voices and images between two or more individuals in conference with one another, the **computer phone** consists of a camera, microphone, and speaker unit that sits atop one's desktop computer. The computer monitor is used to display the images of the individuals in conference. The most sophisticated units deliver real time, full-motion color video and synchronized audio.

Computer phones are capable of handling as many as thirty-two individuals in conference with one another at the same time. They can be installed on networked computers as well as remotely located computers using high-speed telephone lines.

What is a dedicated fax line?

Facsimile (fax) devices Telephone lines are also used to interconnect **facsimile (fax) devices**. Generally, organizations are using dedicated fax lines to which their fax devices are attached. Doing so eliminates having to call the recipient to tell him or her to activate the fax device so the material can be transmitted. If a dedicated line is not used, a fax/tel switch will be useful. This switch can determine if the incoming call is a fax call or a telephone call. If it is a fax call, the switch activates the fax device to receive the document. If it is a voice call, the telephone rings in the normal manner.

Some of the more sophisticated fax devices can operate unattended. Such devices are capable of automatically dialing up to fifty phone numbers stored in memory. An advantage of such units is their operability at night when long-distance toll charges are the least expensive.

Another option many individuals are having installed in their desktop computers is a fax card, which enables their computer to become a fax device. Any material held in memory or on a storage medium (such as a hard disk drive or a floppy disk) can be transmitted to a remote location. The recipient can either read it on his/her computer monitor or have a hard copy of the material prepared on a printer.

Fax devices in use today use three types of print technology: thermal-transfer (some use plain paper while others use special paper), ink-jet, and laser and light-emitting-diode (LED) machines. The thermal devices are the least expensive while the laser and LED devices are the most expensive.

A fax device is pictured in Figure 18-4.

E-mail The use of **electronic mail** is being found as an efficient way to distribute messages from the sender to the receiver(s) in the same organization. However, if the sender and receiver also have an Internet address and the ability to access the Internet, electronic messages can be sent between individuals regardless of their location throughout the world.

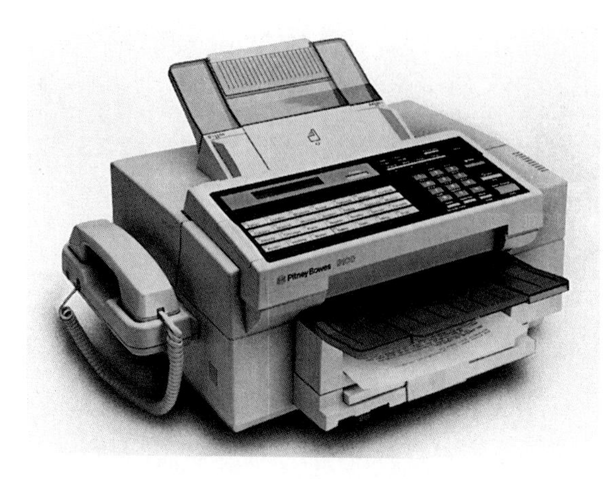

Figure 18-4 Facsimile. Courtesy: Pitney Bowes.

Today, most organizations that use e-mail extensively use a software program specifically designed for that purpose. Two common ones are cc:Mail (Lotus) and Microsoft Mail (Microsoft). Keyboarding the message is as easy as keyboarding material using a word processing software program. Electronic mail software programs function by enabling the sender to keyboard the message after entering the recipient's name and the message subject. Depending on the system traffic and the physical distance between the sender and the receiver, the receiver may receive the message in a matter of seconds or in several hours. The message is "stored" in the system until accessed by the reader.

What are some of the common features found in e-mail software programs?

E-mail software programs are rapidly becoming more versatile. Some of the features commonly found are the following: spell checking, message forwarding, message archiving, attaching of other files to e-mail message, notifying recipient of awaiting messages, and notifying the sender that the message has reached the receiving location. Another desirable feature is the ability to reply to the original sender without having to re-enter his/her e-mail address or subject into the system. Each subsequent reply to the original message simply "builds" on the original message.

For employees who have access to a computer with a modem at a remote location and the necessary e-mail companion software, they are able to access the e-mail sent to the office. This feature is especially desirable for employees who travel extensively, for those who work at home, and for those who telecommute.

Interoffice messaging One of the rapidly developing services in the low-cost area of telecommunications is **interoffice messaging**, which is designed to provide the message recipient with a printed message. Some devices used in interoffice messaging are computer driven while other devices are dedicated to the messaging function. While some interoffice messaging devices use telephone lines, others send messages over the building's electrical lines, thus eliminating the need for additional wiring.

Illustrated in Figure 18-5 is an interoffice messaging device that enables employees to send instant written messages to one another. The device can be used to send keyed messages or such preprogrammed messages as "Have them hold," "Take a message," "No," "Yes," "Send them in," or "Have them wait." An employee can also leave a preprogrammed status message ("Please have John Smith take all my calls while I am in a meeting the remainder of the morning") on his or her unit. Priority messages can also be so identified

Figure 18-5 Interoffice messaging device. Courtesy: Omninote/Teleautograph Corporation.

by using a beeping sound to signal the recipient. Some devices produce the message on paper while others display the message on an LED screen.

Voice messaging One of the newer features of telecommunications systems is **voice messaging**, which allows individuals to send and receive phone messages when they are not in their office or when they are in their office but don't want to be disturbed.

What are the characteristics of voice messaging systems?

Voice messaging systems convert spoken words into digitally encoded information recorded on a magnetic medium. The computer technology that drives the system allows the messages to be transmitted according to the sender's instructions or holds the messages in memory until they are accessed by the recipient. The telephone keypad is used to control basic operational functions, such as recording, playing back, forwarding, saving, and erasing messages.

Two types of voice messaging systems are found: One type uses an add-in board in personal computers while the other uses equipment, added to the telephone system, that is dedicated to voice messaging. The add-in board type is less expensive but is also less versatile than the dedicated system.

Voice messaging can be used in a number of ways. As the sophistication of the system increases, so does the number of ways in which the system can be used. One use of the system is broadcasting, which transmits the same message to as many as 250 individuals. The individuals to receive the message are identified by an identification code, and each person whose code is entered into the system automatically receives the message. Another use is to transmit a message at a predetermined time, which is automatically done by the system.

Messages can also be automatically redirected to other individuals simply by entering the appropriate directions (most likely pressing 0, 1, 2, or 3 on the keypad) into the system. Depending on the system, an individual may have the ability to use a touch-tone phone to access his or her messages 24 hours a day. This is done simply by dialing the appropriate telephone number and using the keypad to enter a confidential identification number. In some instances, the system periodically calls the user, notifying him or her of waiting messages. A user, in accessing the voice messaging system, has the option of listening to a stored message at that time, having a message permanently stored on a magnetic medium, delaying the playback of any stored message, or erasing the message from the system.

The newest development in voice messaging is a system that integrates voice messaging with electronic mail. Thus, users are able to share text, image, and voice data/information, with all messages being delivered into one electronic mailbox. Voice messages are retrieved by phone or terminal, while the written messages are retrieved only by terminal.

Voice messaging virtually eliminates the "telephone tag" problem that plagues many individuals in many offices. It also accommodates individuals who need to communicate with other individuals in other time zones, and it may reduce the number of secretarial support staff needed through a reduction in the number of handwritten messages that have to be prepared regarding incoming phone calls.

Call Processing

What is meant by call processing?

Designed to improve the manner in which incoming calls are expedited in an organization, **call processing** is becoming a vital function in many organizations. Call processing is typically comprised of several integrated components, including an automated attendant, automated call distribution or queuing, and voice messaging. The caller uses the keypad on his or her phone to activate these components.

The automated attendant, when answering an organization's phone, tells the caller to depress a specified key on the keypad to route the call to the desired individual/department. Should the caller need to talk to a human attendant, the appropriate key is mentioned during the recorded message. Some systems have an audio directory that enables the caller to obtain the recipient's extension simply by entering the first two letters of the recipient's last name.

The automated call distribution feature is activated when all of the organization's employees in a given unit are busy (customer service representatives, for example). This feature locks calls into the queue in the order in which they are received, thus assuring the caller that he or she will be connected with an employee when one becomes available. Music is generally heard by those waiting in queue.

Voice messaging, discussed in detail earlier in this chapter, is another component of an increasing number of call processing systems.

To help the organization better manage its telephone service, some call processing systems also provide weekly management reports that identify the times when the system was its busiest, the average length of calls (in minutes and seconds), and the number of calls received. For systems that use a human attendant rather than an automated attendant, other data often available include the number of calls that were abandoned when the caller hung up, the amount of time callers were placed on hold, and the busy rate.

Telephone Interconnect Equipment and Services

In 1968, a court decision gave individuals the right to obtain telephone equipment and long-distance calling services from sources other than the Bell System. Obtaining such equipment or service in this manner is known as **inter-**

connect. Organizations, as a result, may either lease or purchase telephone equipment from an independent equipment supplier or obtain long-distance calling services from an independent carrier. Some of the long-distance interconnect carriers are MCI, Sprint, and Allnet.

Among the important considerations when selecting interconnect equipment or services are the reliability of the supplier and the quality of equipment and/or service the supplier is able to provide. The system can be no better than the equipment and/or service provided by the supplier.

Telephone interconnect provides the following advantages:

What is likely to be the result of proper management of telecommunications services?

1. Over time, the organization may be able to reduce costs significantly by using interconnect equipment and/or long-distance calling services.
2. Interconnect devices are often more flexible than the equipment leased from a telephone company, which helps the organization maximize the efficiency of its operations.

The disadvantages of using interconnect can be summarized as follows:

1. When purchasing interconnect equipment, the service provided by some suppliers tends to decrease, which may result in a less-than-optimum situation.
2. Equipment that is owned may be difficult to dispose of once it becomes obsolete.
3. The service provided by some interconnect equipment suppliers and/or long-distance calling services compares poorly with the quality of service generally provided by AT&T or a Bell subsidiary.

INTRAORGANIZATIONAL COMMUNICATION DEVICES

Several devices are used to transmit data and information within an organization. Included are such devices as telewriter, intrafax, closed-circuit television, and paging systems.

Telewriter

As an internal device, the **telewriter** is used to transmit handwritten messages between two sites fairly close to one another. This device is especially useful for transmitting messages between an organization's office and warehouse or plant. As the words are written on paper attached to the writing table of the device, they are converted to electrical impulses. At the receiving location, these impulses activate the unit to prepare a duplicate paper copy of the message.

Figure 18-6 illustrates the telewriter device.

Intrafax

What is intrafax?

Another fax device is **intrafax**, which is used internally within an organization. It can be used to transmit duplicate copies of all types of forms, letters, drawings, and other kinds of documents between various offices in an organization.

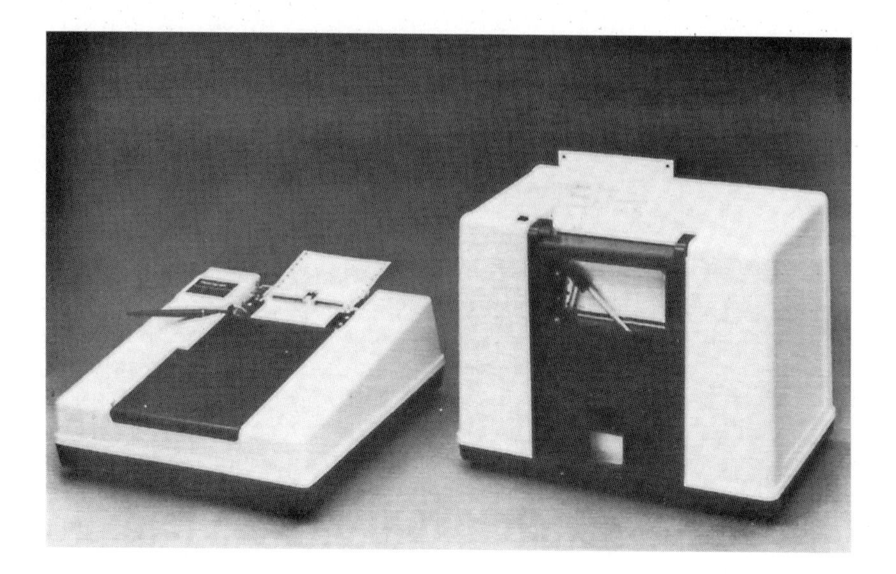

Figure 18-6 Telewriter. Courtesy: Teleautograph.

Closed-Circuit Television

The use of **closed-circuit television** is increasing in organizations. Closed-circuit television is used to transmit information as well as to provide security for the premises. To transmit information between two locations in the organization, information is placed in front of the closed-circuit camera. The image is transmitted instantly to the television monitor at the receiving location.

Paging Systems

A number of **paging systems** are used extensively in organizations. One type uses the organization's public address system. The employee's name or identification code is broadcast through the public address system, along with the message. Another system uses portable pocket-size paging devices. While some of these devices only beep, others permit either one- or two-way audio communication. Some can be used to page a person several miles from the base unit.

MANAGEMENT OF TELECOMMUNICATIONS SERVICES

The growing complexity of telecommunications services within many organizations necessitates the proper management of these services. Therefore, an increasing number of organizations are formally managing their telecommunications systems, generally resulting in the significant reduction of their telecommunication costs.

Among the outcomes of the installation of a management system are the following:

1. An understanding of how the various elements of the telecommunications system fit together, resulting in the most efficient system possible.
2. A consolidation of various technical aspects of the system, resulting in greater efficiency.

3. The use of a system that enables the managers to have the needed information readily available at the time it is needed.
4. The use of a system that is as technologically advanced as the various system components will allow.
5. Coordinated development of the entire system rather than a fragmented approach that affects parts of the system.

Among the benefits of telecommunications services management are the positive impact it has on telecommunications costs and the on-going development of a system that grows with the organization as the technology becomes available. The manager of telecommunications services is a high-level position that provides another career opportunity for the administrative office manager.

CONTROLLING TELECOMMUNICATIONS COSTS

Because telecommunications within an organization is so pervasive and because it is technologically oriented, some effort needs to be expended in controlling telecommunications costs. A number of suggestions can be offered to help control telecommunications costs, including the following:

1. Coordinate all aspects of the telecommunications system, thereby ensuring the compatibility of existing components and the expandability of the system when the need arises.
2. Investigate alternative long-distance call carriers to determine which one can best meet the organization's needs in the most cost-effective manner.
3. Consider the use of reconditioned equipment when new equipment is needed.
4. Determine whether equipment purchasing or leasing is most cost effective.
5. Install a long-distance call monitoring system.
6. Install only the phone features that can be justified from a cost-effective standpoint.
7. When remodeling or building a new facility, design the telecommunications system to accommodate future expansion.

IMPLICATIONS FOR THE ADMINISTRATIVE OFFICE MANAGER

The role of telecommunications in the modern office is becoming more important as organizations develop and install sophisticated office systems. Telecommunications, through a networking arrangement, enables the various devices used within these systems to communicate with one another.

Even in organizations in which these sophisticated office systems have not been installed, the area of telecommunications should be carefully planned. To maximize efficiency, an organization should carefully assess its needs and then select telecommunications devices, services, and functions that best satisfy these needs.

The technical expertise of the administrative office manager is helpful in designing efficient telecommunications systems. In most instances, the efficiency of the system will be affected by the accuracy with which telecommunications needs are assessed. The administrative office manager plays a key role in assessing these needs; and once they have been determined, equipment manufacturing representatives, phone company personnel, and consultants are helpful in determining how these needs can be best fulfilled. The administrative office manager often serves as the liaison between the organization and outside experts.

REVIEW QUESTIONS

1. What types of communication channels are used in telecommunications?
2. How do digital and analog signals differ from one another?
3. For what functions are LANs and WANs used?
4. How do half and full duplexing differ from one another?
5. For what are modems used?
6. In what ways do key systems PBX, PABX, and Centrex telephone systems differ from one another?
7. Under what circumstances are FX lines used?
8. What type of technology do cellular phone systems use?
9. Explain how teleconferencing and videoconferencing differ from one another.
10. What components comprise a computer phone system?
11. Explain how a fax device is used in the transmitting of documents.
12. What are some of the features commonly found on e-mail systems?

DISCUSSION QUESTIONS

1. You were recently appointed to serve on a telephone systems committee in the organization in which you work. At a recent meeting, one of the committee members indicated he thought the present PBX system should be retained. He felt it may be a less expensive system because the company can monitor all outgoing phone calls by having an operator dial these calls. You believe that a PABX system may be a better choice. Explain how a PABX system, over the long run, might be a less expensive system than the present PBX system.
2. The company in which you work has grown quite rapidly the last few years. The number of persons the organization employs has doubled in the last five years. During this time, nothing has been done to enhance the company's telephone system. On several occasions during the last three months, both employees and customers have mentioned that calls cannot be completed because all lines are busy. What problem is being experienced in this company? How can the company obtain needed data to correct the situation?
3. Of all the employees in the organization in which you work, you are the most knowledgeable about telecommunications. The president of the organization discussed with you the rapidly increasing cost of executive travel. He indicated that fewer executives would be able to take trips in the future. He asked you to prepare for him a report in which you discuss telecommunications devices that can be used as an alternative to executive travel. Explain how the devices you plan to present in your report are used.
4. You work in an organization that has its manufacturing facility located next to its headquarters building. Several times each day, written materials have to be transmitted between the two facilities. The organization has been using messengers to hand-carry these materials but is finding that this arrangement is not always satisfactory. What mechanical devices are available for use in transmitting reproductions of materials between buildings? Explain how each works.
5. The telephone charges in the organization in which you work are in-

creasing rapidly. At the present time, no long-distance call services are used. An analysis of the last two monthly statements reveals that 60 percent of the long-distance calls are made to two cities in an adjoining state. What long-distance services might the company use to help control the cost of its phone service? How can the company determine if these services are financially feasible?

6. The organization in which you work has branch offices located in seven major cities throughout the country. Several times each week, the organization has to use an express airmail service to get important documents delivered to the branch offices on time. What type(s) of communication devices are available that would facilitate the rapid transmission of these documents? Explain how each of these devices works.

STUDENT PROJECTS AND ACTIVITIES

1. Talk with a vendor of telephone equipment/systems to determine what new technology is being used in the products manufactured by the vendor's company.
2. Interview a manager of telecommunications, primarily to learn about the nature of his or her job duties.
3. Obtain the service costs from two different interconnect carriers. How comparable are their costs?
4. Tour a videoconferencing facility or studio. Pay particular attention to the various types of equipment you see.
5. Talk with a representative of the local telephone company. What specific types of telephone services are available through the company?

MINICASE

As administrative office manager for the Sanchez Corporation, you are responsible for developing its telecommunications system. The home office is located in New York City, and branch offices are located in six cities throughout the country. The corporate management has recently become quite concerned about its rapidly increasing long-distance phone call charges. At the present, only regular long-distance service is used between the home office and its branches. You decide to prepare a report for the executive vice president in which you discuss

1. The alternatives available to the company to help reduce its long-distance phone call costs.
2. The characteristics of each of the alternatives you identified.

CASE

The Boeckeler Corporation, a distributor of hospital and surgical supplies, is located in New Britain, Connecticut. It is the largest distributor of its kind in the Northeast.

The new president of the corporation, who has now been on the job for 18 months, has asked each unit in the organization to investigate ways of containing its recurring costs. He specifically asked various unit managers to investigate the feasibility of purchasing its present equipment rather than leasing it. Two years ago, the company leased 40 percent of its office equipment.

The reason for leasing so much equipment was to make capital available for expansion of its warehouse.

The organization's purchase of the equipment now appears feasible. This includes the purchase of the telephone equipment presently leased by the company. You decide to prepare a memo for the president in which you discuss

1. The reasons that the purchase of the telephone equipment might be advantageous for the company.
2. The reasons that purchase of the telephone equipment might be disadvantageous for the company.
3. The factors the company should consider in making the decision to purchase versus continue to lease the telephone equipment.

CHAPTER

WORD PROCESSING

CHAPTER AIM

After studying this chapter, you should be able to design an effective word processing system for an organization.

CHAPTER OUTLINE

CHAPTER TERMS

Action paper
Administrative secretaries
Administrative support
Centralized dictation system
Centralized structure
Correspondence secretaries
Decentralized structure
Desktop publishing
Desktop units
Dictation equipment
Discrete analog media equipment
Discrete digital media equipment
Electronic typewriters
Endless loop media equipment
Facsimile (fax) equipment
Feasibility study
Impact printers
Information processing

- Integrated structure
- Integrated system
- Interviews
- Inventory of filed materials
- Line count log
- Memory typewriters
- Microcomputers with word processing software
- Nonimpact printers
- Optical character recognition (OCR) scanner
- Planning committee
- Portable units
- Questionnaires
- Remote transcription
- Self-keyboarding structure
- Shared-logic system
- Shared-resource system
- Special-purpose structure
- Stand-alone devices
- Stand-alone display devices
- Stand-alone nondisplay devices
- Stand-alone partial-line display
- Supervisory console
- Task lists
- Text-editing equipment
- Transcription equipment
- Word originator
- Word processing
- Word processing specialists

Word processing—defined as the mix of people, equipment, and procedures to transform thoughts and ideas into printed copy—is experiencing unprecedented usage today. The word processing concept differs markedly from some of the other more traditional approaches used to transform thoughts and ideas into printed copy. In some ways, the word processing concept has changed considerably during its thirty years of existence, resulting perhaps more from a variety of affordable technological developments than from any other factor.

Almost from the first day of its existence in the mid-1960s, word processing has had a significant impact on the office function. No technological development during this century has done more to revolutionize the way a variety of office methods and procedures are carried out. Expectations are that the technology will continue to change at a moderate rate in the foreseeable future. The next significant technological development affecting word processing is likely to be the ready availability of affordable equipment that allows the user to generate hard copy by speaking into a special type of microphone. The equipment will easily and readily convert the spoken words into printed words.

Recently, certain aspects of word processing have stimulated the evolution of information processing. The section that follows provides a discussion of the information processing concept.

THE EVOLUTION OF INFORMATION PROCESSING

What is information processing?

The end result of the word processing function (preparation of printed copy) has not changed during its existence, although several intermediate elements of the function have changed. Most prominent among these elements is the convergence of data processing and word processing into a new concept commonly referred to as **information processing**. While word processing continues to exist as a text-manipulation function, the information processing function—which involves the manipulation of numbers and text—is becoming increasingly common.

Information processing became a reality because of readily available, affordable equipment and software capable of performing both word processing and data processing functions. While some software can only be used for word processing applications and other software can only be used for data processing applications, integrated software is now available that combines both applications in the same software package. Although the software generally continues to be classified as word processing software, it has both capabilities. Examples of such software are WordPerfect and Microsoft Word, both of which have a spreadsheet component as well as the text-manipulation component.

The continued evolution of information processing will undoubtedly make more difficult the ability to differentiate between word processing and data processing. From an equipment and a procedures standpoint, very little difference exists between the two. Equipment is available that performs both word and data processing applications. Another similarity is in the identical cycles of both word processing and data processing: input, processing, storage and retrieval, and output.

The material presented in the following sections of this chapter treats word processing as a single-component entity. However, most of the material is just as appropriate for a situation in which word processing is considered one of the two components of information processing.

THE WORD PROCESSING CONCEPT ILLUSTRATED

An illustration of a word processing system is an effective way to present the word processing concept. While the basic elements of word processing are briefly discussed in this section, a more detailed discussion of each component is presented in other sections of this chapter.

What is the primary function of a word processing specialist?

In a word processing system, the process of transforming ideas and thoughts into printed copy is performed by expert typists, commonly known as **word processing specialists** or **correspondence secretaries**. They primarily perform such job functions as keyboarding and other related activities. These individuals generally are not responsible for performing such other traditional secretarial or clerical duties as filing, answering the telephone, and receiving office callers.

What is the primary function of an administrative secretary?

The structure of the organization's word processing system determines where the word processing specialists are located. They may all be located in one large centralized area or in several smaller decentralized centers distributed throughout the premises. The nontyping secretarial and clerical duties are performed by **administrative secretaries** who do very little, if any, typing or keyboarding. The administrative secretaries are located near the executives for whom they work. They are commonly responsible for a number of routine executive duties.

In addition to using specialized personnel, word processing also uses specialized **text-editing equipment** capable of storing in coded form all material keyboarded on these devices. Some word processing systems use equipment designed specifically for performing word processing functions while other systems use either microcomputers or computer terminals and appropriate text-editing software and peripheral equipment. Keyboarded material is generally stored in coded form on floppy disks, hard disks, magnetic tapes, or magnetic cards.

Document processing begins with the manual keyboarding of material. Keyboarded strokes are stored temporarily in the internal memory and subsequently stored on a permanent basis on a magnetic medium. Storing the material on a magnetic medium enables it to be retained as long as it is needed.

Therefore, stored material is available for subsequent use without having to rekeyboard the entire document. A hard (paper) copy is obtained simply by giving the machine the appropriate command to print. If the material has already been stored on a magnetic medium, the disk or tape will have to be accessed before the device can begin printing.

When a document needs to be revised, the magnetic medium on which the document is stored is used to "read" the material back into the system. Desired changes are made in the material, and the revised document is stored on the magnetic medium. Another paper copy that contains the revised version of the document is subsequently printed.

Besides using text-editing equipment, word processing also uses **dictation equipment.** The **word originator** dictates material into a recording system, which stores the material for later transcription. The word processing specialist then uses the text-editing equipment to transcribe the stored dictation. In addition to transcribing dictation, specialists may also keyboard from longhand copy, from typewritten copy, or from direct dictation.

The third component of word processing involves procedures. Following the transcription of the material, the document is returned to the originator, who does one of the following: (1) signs the document, (2) revises the document before final printing, or (3) approves and returns the document to the specialist, who prepares it for final distribution.

Word originators sometimes request a rough draft of the material. An originator may make several changes on the draft or may ask that the document be final printed as shown on the draft copy. The word processing specialist uses the rough draft in keyboarding any desired changes, after which the final copy is printed. The magnetic medium is used to store electronically the original keyboarded material as well as the changes requested by the originator.

The use of **administrative support** is found in many word processing systems. While the keyboarding tasks are performed by the employees who use the text-editing equipment, nonkeyboarding tasks are performed by administrative support employees. These personnel perform such functions as filing, telephoning, receiving office callers, writing, and researching, in addition to a variety of other duties assigned them by the word originators for whom they work.

DETERMINING THE NEED FOR WORD PROCESSING

What are the purposes of the feasibility study?

The use of word processing has a widespread effect on the keyboarding and transcription functions in the organization; therefore, the need for a word processing system should be systematically determined before making an installation decision. Installing a system without first determining its need cannot be justified. The **feasibility study** partially helps determine the need for a word processing system. The study can also be used to help determine the types and amount of equipment needed when the installation of a system is justifiable. The information that follows is useful when an organization is considering the installation of a traditional word processing system in which the vast majority of the organization's documents are prepared in a word processing center. Some of the same information will also be useful when an organization is considering the installation of a modified system that puts word processing capability on the desks of word originators and secretaries alike.

Feasibility studies are generally conducted in one of three ways: by employees, by consultants, and by representatives of equipment vendors. At the present, the most common method of conducting the study is the use of employees.

When the feasibility study is conducted, the word originators and the secretarial/clerical employees are generally involved because the installation of a system will directly affect them. Their opinions regarding the suitability of a word processing system may differ widely from one another.

The Feasibility Study

The quality of the feasibility study often determines the success of the word processing system. The ability to install an effective system without first conducting an adequate study is quite unlikely.

What are the functions of the planning committee?

Appointment of a planning committee Before the actual feasibility study gets underway, a **planning committee** should be appointed. Its membership should include employees from the various hierarchical levels of the organization, from vice president to worker, as well as middle management and supervisors.

The functions of the planning committee vary from situation to situation. An important function is to determine if the study should be conducted by organizational employees, by vendor representatives, or by consultants. Each alternative has unique advantages. The committee might also assist with data collection as well as perform an important public relations function.

Because the installation of a word processing system may be resisted by employees, the planning committee can provide an important function by helping them overcome their resistance. Once the decision has been made to install a word processing system, the planning committee may also be involved in providing valuable sessions designed to orient the employees about the word processing concept.

Employees should be informed about the pending feasibility study quickly after the decision is made to conduct the study. Their support at this time is crucial, and one of the most effective ways to get their support is to keep them informed. In addition, employees should be made aware of the benefits of word processing.

Development of a time schedule The feasibility study will be conducted more efficiently when adhering to a realistic time schedule. Identified on the schedule are completion times for the various phases of the study. Although the schedule should be developed with built-in flexibility, every effort should be made to adhere to the approved schedule.

Collection and analysis of data Two integral aspects of the feasibility study are the collection and analysis of data. Several techniques are used for collecting data, including interviews, questionnaires, task analyses, and inventories of stored materials.

What type of information is collected by means of interviews?

Interviews are used to collect data from both word originators and secretaries. The following are likely to be discussed with the originators: their job functions; their duties or tasks that could be assigned to assistants; aspects of their job that could be performed more effectively by additional support staff if it were available; and the nature and number of written documents they create. Also included will be the extent to which the originator (1) uses dictation equipment, (2) dictates to secretaries, or (3) handwrites material to be typed. In addition, originators are asked to assess the frequency with which they presently revise typed drafts of material as well as the extent to which they would likely revise material if it were more convenient to do so.

When interviewing secretaries, the items discussed include the following: the names and titles of originators for whom they work; the nature and quantity of typing tasks they perform; the types (letters, reports, statistical materials) and quantities of written documents with which they work; the quantity of each of the input methods (machine dictation, shorthand, and handwritten) they transcribe; the amount of repetitive material; the nature of revisions; and the nature and quantity of nontyping tasks they perform.

Prior to conducting interviews, a form should be developed on which the interviewees' responses can be recorded. This helps to ensure consistent coverage of all items as well as aid the data-analysis process.

What type of information is collected by means of questionnaires?

When **questionnaires** are used to collect data, different questionnaires should be developed for originators and secretaries. The wording used on the questionnaire often affects the success of the data-collection efforts. The information collected through interviews is quite similar to the data collected by questionnaires.

What type of information is collected by means of task lists?

Analysis of office tasks, officially known as the **task lists** method, is another common data-collection technique. It is used to analyze the nature of tasks performed by the various office employees. A task list provides in summary form all the tasks performed by an employee as well as the amount of time consumed by each task. These lists should be accumulated over a period of one or two weeks.

Although not as commonly used as in the past, an **action paper** is helpful in analyzing the nature of the typing tasks performed by employees. This paper, which is a no-carbon required (NCR) type, is inserted behind the sheet of paper on which a document is typed. This method essentially involves preparing an extra carbon copy of the document being typed. The following kinds of information are also recorded on the sheet: a description of the material, whether the material is a first draft or a revision, and the type of input (dictation, longhand, etc.). The action paper is further analyzed by determining the number of lines typed on the paper.

Another technique for analyzing typing tasks is to count the number of lines typed by each secretary during the data-collection period. These data, in addition to the following information, are recorded on a **line count log**: description of each document, origin of the document and the input method, and whether the document is either revised or repetitive material. As an alternative to line counts, many experts in the field now prefer the use of quarter-page counts because the results are just as accurate, and they are much quicker to compute.

One of the newest techniques used to help determine the feasibility of word processing involves making an **inventory of filed materials**. The inventory will determine the nature of the documents that have been originated in the organization, the quantities in which the documents exist, and who or what department was responsible for the creation of the various documents. This kind of information helps determine the appropriate design of a word processing system.

Once all the data have been collected, the next step involves compiling the data. To expedite this task, summary sheets should be prepared onto which the data/information are transferred. By calculating percentages on the raw data, meaningful relationships can be identified.

After the data have been compiled, the next step involves analyzing the data, which essentially gives them meaning. The primary purpose for analyzing the data is to determine the nature of the tasks performed by both word originators and office employees, a task that must be completed before the need for and/or the feasibility of a system can be determined. This is accomplished by putting the activities into two categories: typing activities and non-typing activities. The nature and quantities of the specific activities also have to be carefully analyzed.

MAKING THE DECISION

The data collected during the feasibility study are just one of the factors considered in determining whether a word processing system is justifiable. If installation cannot be justified on the basis of the work performed in the organization, rarely can it be justified on any other basis.

The installation of a word processing system is likely to be more desirable (1) as the amount of typed letters, reports, and statistical material increases, (2) as the need to revise employee-originated material increases, and (3) as the amount of repetitive typing increases. All but approximately 15 to 25 percent of the typical typing and transcription jobs of an organization are well suited to word processing.

The financial feasibility of the system also has to be determined. The input, output, and equipment costs help determine the financial feasibility of a word processing system. Considerable use of machine dictation (rather than longhand or shorthand input) makes a word processing system more feasible.

Compared with input by machine dictation, shorthand input costs nearly three times more for use by a word originator who makes $20,000 per year. For the same word originator, using longhand is approximately five times more costly than machine dictation. Therefore, if word originators do or will make extensive use of machine dictation, the cost of word processing may not only be less, but also may be much more efficient than traditional systems.

As an alternative to using other types of input nowadays, an ever increasing number of employees who have desktop computers equipped with a word processing software package are able to input a large majority of their own documents. If they have good composition skills and are proficient at keyboarding, self-inputting is a viable alternative.

Input costs are determined by the salaries of the word originators in relation to the type of input they use. Output costs, on the other hand, are determined by the hourly salaries of typists and the amount of their daily keyboarding time.

What factors need to be considered in determining the type and amount of equipment required for an efficient word processing system?

To determine the type and amount of equipment needed for an efficient word processing system, the following factors are considered: the quantity of material typed, the amount of revision, and the quantity of repetitive typing. The traditional typing and transcription processes found in most organizations require that each typist have a typewriter, regardless of how much it is used. In an organization that makes extensive use of word processing, few typewriters will be found.

Although word processing generally involves the use of text-editing devices, equipment outlays may actually be less—especially if most employees already have a desktop computer—because fewer conventional typewriters will be needed. Thus, cost savings may be realized because less additional equipment may be needed. The word processing concept also enables an organization to make more efficient use of equipment because it is used for a large portion of each workday. Also, the employee-specialization characteristic of word processing may result in the need for fewer employees, resulting in salary savings.

The financial cost of the present typing and transcription function should be compared with the cost of the proposed word processing system. Following is a formula helpful in making the comparison:

Input costs + output costs + equipment costs = cost of the system

When the cost of a word processing system is considerably less than the cost of the present system, the management of the organization should seriously consider the installation of a system. However, when a system is not financially feasible, attempting to justify its installation on any other basis is generally impossible. Therefore, no further investigation of the feasibility of a system will likely be undertaken at this time.

Also to be considered in deciding whether to install a word processing system is the perceived acceptance of the system by the word originators and the office employees who do their typing. Even though a word processing system may be needed and is financially feasible, the wisdom of installing a system is questionable if it will not be accepted by employees. Those adamantly opposed to the installation of a system most likely will find it neither effective nor efficient. One reason for the early orientation of the employees to the word processing concept is to help them overcome their resistance.

Why does the ease with which employees' duties can be adjusted and revised need to be considered?

Another factor to be considered is the ease with which the duties of employees can be adjusted and revised. In most word processing systems, office employees either keyboard the greatest portion of the day or they do no keyboarding. Those whose jobs involve nonkeyboarding activities perform such duties as filing, answering the telephone, and receiving callers. In traditional systems, office employees are likely to perform typing duties as well as nontyping duties.

For the word processing system to work well, employees will have to decide which of the two types of jobs are more appealing—the jobs consisting mainly of keyboarding duties or those consisting primarily of nonkeyboarding tasks. Because employees' jobs will have to be adjusted and revised, this factor should be given extensive consideration when deciding if a word processing system should be installed.

ORGANIZATIONAL STRUCTURE OF WORD PROCESSING SYSTEMS

Once the decision has been made to install a word processing system, the appropriate organizational structure of the system will have to be determined. The structure is basically determined by the specific needs of the organization.

The following organizational structures are found in word processing systems:

What are the characteristics of the centralized structure of word processing systems?

Centralized structure, in which all keyboarding and transcription tasks are performed in a large, centralized word processing center, except perhaps for the keyboarding and transcription tasks of top-level executives whose secretaries do most or all of their keyboarding. The nonkeyboarding secretarial/clerical functions are handled by administrative support personnel. Although the centralized structure was the one most commonly used earlier, an increasing number of organizations are now using either the decentralized or integrated structure.

Decentralized structure, in which a number of smaller, decentralized word processing centers, often called satellites, are located throughout the organization. Actually, the decentralized centers are smaller-scale versions of the large centralized centers. The nonkeyboarding secretarial/clerical functions are performed by administrative support personnel.

Special-purpose structure, in which traditional secretaries perform nonkeyboarding secretarial/clerical tasks, as well as light keyboarding tasks. The traditional secretaries use standard electric office typewriters where appropriate, while large jobs or those that require extensive amounts of editing/revising are completed in a centralized word processing center. The physical size of this facility will not be as large as the center found in the centralized structure, nor does this structure use administrative support.

What are the characteristics of the integrated structure of word processing systems?

Integrated structure, in which some secretarial/clerical tasks are performed in traditional ways, but those functions that lend themselves to word processing are performed within the unit by employees who have excellent keyboarding skills. The equipment is likely to be a microcomputer with text-editing software and a letter-quality printer. In some cases, the number of employees who use word processing equipment is greater than the number who use office typewriters. Furthermore, some of the secretaries may perform both keyboarding and nonkeyboarding functions. Neither word processing centers nor administrative support are found in organizations using the integrated structure, which is now one of the five most frequently used structures.

What are the characteristics of the self-keyboarding structure?

The **self-keyboarding structure,** which has become one of the most frequently used, if not the most frequently used structure, puts word processing capability on the desks of most—and perhaps all—white-collar employees in many organizations. The job duties of many of these employees necessitate their already using a microcomputer. All that is needed to provide them with word processing capability is a word processing software program. More likely than not, the employees' computers are already connected to a network. A software site license enables the employees connected to the network to also have access to the word processing software program.

Employees who use the self-keyboarding method do most if not all of their document origination at the keyboard. While some of these originators do all the work in finalizing their documents, others prepare the rough draft and then have an administrative assistant edit their work, correct grammar and punctuation errors, check the spelling, and print the document. In most organizations in which self-keyboarding is found, a certain percentage of the employees will likely resist the use of technology, opting to use a document origination process that allows them to either dictate their documents or handwrite them. At this point, a word processing specialist keyboards their work.

EQUIPMENT USED IN WORD PROCESSING

Equipment commonly found in word processing systems includes text-editing devices, printing equipment, dictation/recording equipment, transcription equipment, and copiers. Other devices/capabilities, such as optical character recognition (OCR) scanners, facsimile (fax) devices, and desktop publishing are also found in some operations.

Text-Editing Devices

Among the common basic characteristics of text-editing devices are electronic storage of material on a magnetic medium—such as a tape, card, cassette, or disk—after it has been keyboarded; depending on the type of equipment, automatic-mode printing speeds ranging from 170 words a minute to approximately 16 pages a minute; and technology that permits the easy revision of material, including deleting, changing, or adding of words. While some equipment used in word processing is capable only of performing text-editing functions, other equipment is multifunctional (such as microcomputers) and requires word processing software.

The revision capability and the ability to store material on a magnetic medium for later playout make the use of text-editing equipment especially suited for word processing applications. Without these two capabilities, text editing is not possible.

Text-editing equipment is capable of performing a number of functions, including those discussed in the listing that follows. However, these features are not found on all equipment dedicated to performing word processing functions nor on all word processing software packages.

What common functions are performed by the devices used in word processing systems?

Arithmetic function: The equipment performs on numerical data the following arithmetic functions: addition, subtraction, multiplication, and division.

Block move and insert: The equipment moves a block of material from one location and inserts that material in another location.

Footnote placement: The equipment automatically moves footnotes from one page to another, which is necessary when the material to which a footnote pertains is moved to another page.

Global search and replace: The equipment automatically searches a document for each occurrence of a word or a phrase. Some equipment will automatically replace the word or words with another word or phrase. Other equipment requires the manual keyboarding of the replacement word at each location.

Grammar checker: The equipment, upon command, processes documents through a grammar checker that identifies such grammar errors as subject-verb disagreement, pronoun-antecedent disagreement, split infinitives, double negatives, and run-on sentences.

Macros: The equipment facilitates the storage of commonly used words, phrases, sentences, or machine functions that may be used several times each day. When the operator provides the appropriate command, the equipment will automatically insert the desired information or the desired function.

Merge: The equipment merges a mailing list and a form letter. Personalized information, such as figures, dates, names, and so forth, can be added to various parts of the letter.

Outline: The equipment is used to prepare an outline of a document.

Page numbering: The equipment automatically numbers the pages. When the number of a page changes because of the adding or deleting of material, page numbers are automatically corrected.

Pagination: The equipment automatically places the prescribed number of lines on a page.

Repagination: The equipment will repaginate with prescribed amounts of material on each page after material is added to or deleted from a document.

Right-hand justification: The equipment automatically produces printed material with an even right margin.

Spelling dictionary: The equipment automatically compares the spelling of keyboarded words with the spelling of words contained in the device's dictionary. Words that cannot be compared because they are misspelled, are a proper noun, or are not stored in the dictionary are highlighted on the display screen. This feature facilitates proofreading.

Thesaurus: The equipment enables the user to identify and select another word as a means of avoiding overuse of the same word too many times in close succession.

Word wraparound: The equipment automatically moves a word that will not fit at the end of one line to the beginning of the next line.

Among the four basic categories of devices used for text editing are the following:

1. Electronic typewriters
2. Stand-alone devices
   a. Dedicated word processors
   b. Microcomputers with word processing software
3. Shared systems
   a. Shared-logic systems
   b. Shared-resource systems
   c. Integrated systems
4. Mainframe systems

What are the characteristics of electronic typewriters?

Electronic typewriters Least sophisticated of the various devices used for text editing are **electronic typewriters**, which are also called **memory typewriters**. In fact, for some office tasks, the electronic typewriter is the device of choice because it can perform certain jobs better and faster than other types of devices used in word processing operations. Examples are such tasks as typing checks, short memos, address labels, and envelopes.

These devices have limited internal storage. Devices at the low end of the market generally do not permit the storage of material on an external medium, such as a floppy disk. The capacity of internal storage ranges from one or two pages, up to 100 pages. When the capacity of the internal storage has been reached, the first-stored material is automatically erased to make room for the newest material. Some of the common text-editing functions are quite difficult, if not impossible, to perform using this equipment.

A growing number of manufacturers of electronic typewriters now offer packages that upgrade the basic device. These packages include an electronic spelling dictionary, a small display monitor, and an external disk drive that permits unlimited storage of material on small floppy disks.

Among some of the features found on the more sophisticated devices are the following: word processing capabilities, spreadsheet capabilities, graphics preparation capability, built-in dictionaries and thesauruses, and grammar checkers.

Figure 19-1 illustrates an electronic typewriter.

How do the various categories of stand-alone devices differ from one another?

Stand-alone devices Commonly used in word processing systems are text-editing devices capable of operating independently of other word processing equipment. These devices are referred to as **stand-alone devices**. They are stand-alone because they are self-contained and do not need other equipment or systems to be operational. Within the stand-alone category are

Figure 19-1 Electronic typewriter. Courtesy: Olivetti Office USA

dedicated word processors and microcomputers that use word processing software.

The earliest equipment used for text editing was **stand-alone nondisplay devices**, which are no longer manufactured. During keyboarding, information was printed on a sheet of paper rather than appearing on a display screen. The correction of keyboarding errors resulted in strikeovers on the paper, thus necessitating the preparation of another printed copy of the document. A significant disadvantage of this equipment was its inability to allow simultaneous inputting and outputting. Therefore, while the device was printing the final copy of a document, it could not be used to keyboard another document. Most of today's equipment permits simultaneous inputting and outputting.

Today's least sophisticated text-editing equipment is classified as **stand-alone partial-line display**. These devices typically have a 20-character buffer. Therefore, errors that appear on the display can be corrected before they are committed to paper. If all errors are found while they reside on the display, the first printed copy is of final-draft quality.

The most sophisticated stand-alone dedicated text-editing equipment is in the **stand-alone display device** category. These devices typically have a large screen capable of displaying one or two pages. As the material is keyboarded, it is displayed on a screen. Errors detected on the screen can be easily and quickly corrected; therefore, the first printed copy is of final-draft quality. These devices are well designed to accommodate the editing/revising process. The operator can easily and quickly locate on the screen the changes desired by the originator. Operator productivity can be maximized because these devices permit simultaneous inputting and outputting.

Most display devices use magnetic disks for the external storage of keyboarded material. Depending on the density of the disk, perhaps as many as three hundred pages can be stored on one floppy disk.

Figure 19-2 illustrates a stand-alone display device.

The other broad category of stand-alone devices includes **microcomputers with word processing software**. Of the various types of devices used for text editing, microcomputers are the newest, as well as the most common. A significant advantage of using microcomputers to perform text-editing func-

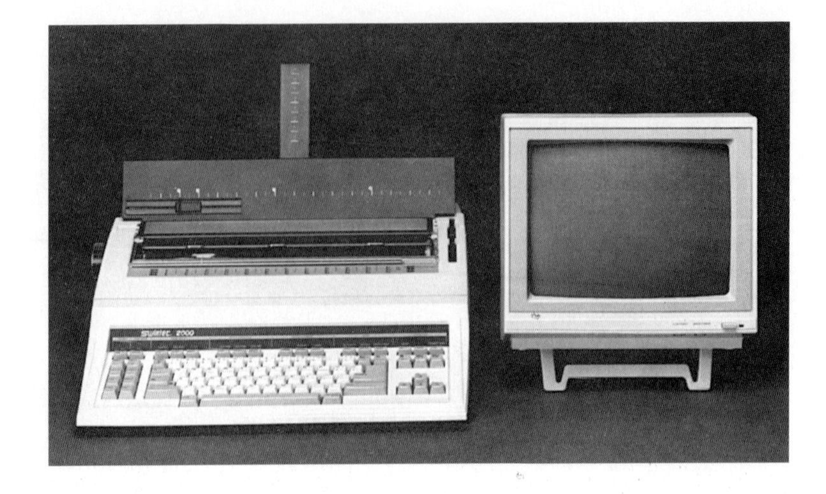

Figure 19-2 Stand-alone display device. Courtesy: Swintec Corp.

tions is the ability to provide rather economical word processing capability for every employee in the organization who needs such capability. Dedicated stand-alone devices can be used only for text editing. Microcomputers, on the other hand, can be used to perform a number of functions other than text editing, including the maintenance of spreadsheet and database information. The software necessary to provide word processing, spreadsheet, and database capability is stored on the microcomputer's hard drive.

To use a microcomputer as a text editor, the operator simply loads the word processing software into the memory of the machine. As the material is keyboarded, it appears on the display screen (most likely a partial-page display). The material can be stored permanently on either a floppy disk or on the system's hard disk. To edit or revise a document, the operator simply reloads the stored material into the machine's memory. After the changes are made, the document is "saved" onto a disk. A printed copy using a printer is subsequently prepared.

What categories of shared systems exist?

Shared systems Three types of shared systems exist: shared logic, shared resource, and integrated systems. Shared systems derive their name from the electronic interlinking of various components of the word processing system. Therefore, these systems tend to be more powerful text-editing devices than some of the other devices discussed earlier in this section, especially electronic typewriters and some word processing software-driven microcomputers.

A **shared-logic system** consists of interlinking several word processing terminals to a host central processing unit of a computer or microcomputer. The number of terminals that share the computer's central processing logic varies from one brand of equipment to another, although most brands accommodate a minimum of four units. Shared-logic systems are generally dedicated to performing only text-editing functions.

Shared-logic system terminals are equipped with a display screen, and the various units share the use of a high-speed printer. Shared-logic systems permit simultaneous input and output.

When the central processing unit of a shared-logic system becomes inoperable, the entire system becomes inoperable because the terminals depend on the CPU for their intelligence.

Figure 19-3 illustrates a shared-logic system.

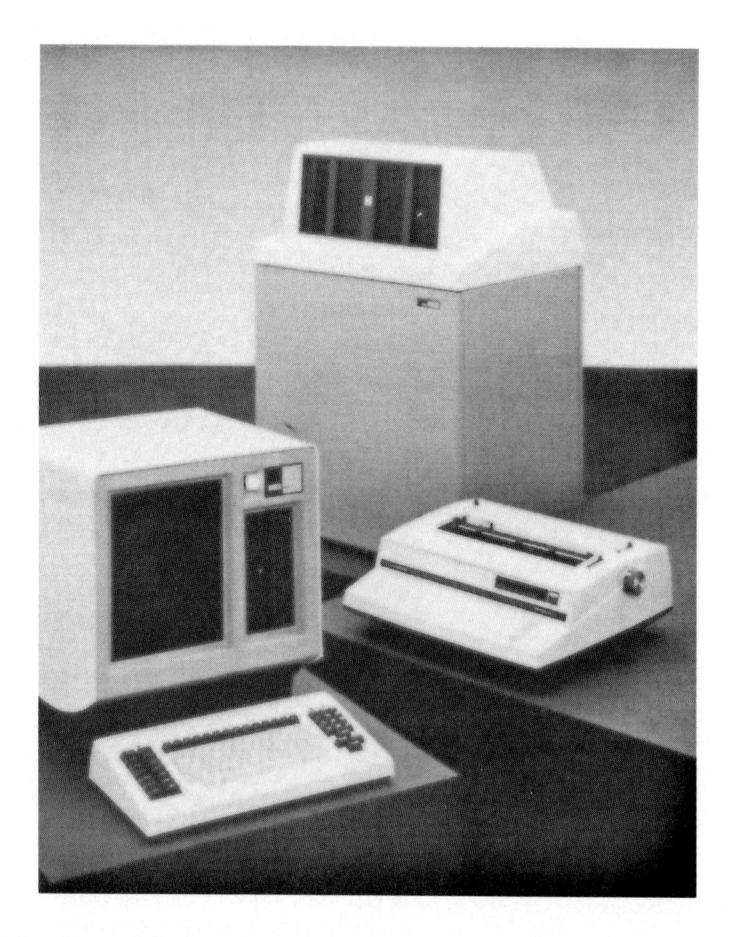

Figure 19-3 Shared-logic system. Courtesy: A. B. Dick Company.

Because a **shared-resource system** uses terminals that have their own intelligence, they do not depend on a host CPU. Therefore, when a portion of the system fails, the other components continue to be operable, although the performance of some functions may not be possible. The terminals share the use of printers as well as occasionally share the use of such peripherals as a data storage unit. Some shared-resource systems are capable of merging word, information, and data processing files into each other. However, most shared-resource systems are dedicated to performing only text-editing functions.

Figure 19-4 illustrates a shared-resource system.

The **integrated system** is the newest of the three types of shared systems and has become the most commonly used. Typically, the equipment used in integrated systems are microcomputers and to a limited extent laptop or notebook computers.

In a microcomputer-based system, the word processing software is stored on a file server, through a site-licensing agreement with the software manufacturer, which makes the software accessible to any employee who is authorized to use it. In addition to being used for word processing, the microcomputers attached to the computer network can perform other functions, including maintenance of database and spreadsheet information. If an integrated software package is being used (such as Microsoft's Works package), word processing, database, and spreadsheet functions can be performed simultaneously. If non-integrated software packages are being used, then the

Figure 19-4 Shared-resource system. Courtesy: A. B. Dick Company.

appropriate software will have to be accessed from the file server in order to perform the desired function.

Mainframe systems The characteristics of mainframe systems are similar to the characteristics of shared-logic systems. Text-editing software is stored in the CPU of the mainframe computer while shared-logic systems typically have their own CPUs.

Mainframe text-editing systems are typically limited to use by large organizations in which word processing capability needs to be provided for many users. When the mainframe terminals are already in place, purchasing the needed word processing software for the mainframe is likely more economical than purchasing a number of dedicated word processing devices or microcomputers. Most of the microcomputer-based word processing software packages also have mainframe versions. Another advantage of this system is that others who need access to keyboarded documents are readily able to gain the access. However, if the terminals receive all their operating intelligence from the mainframe CPU, the entire system will be inoperable if the CPU becomes inoperable.

Printing Equipment

The technology of the printing equipment used in word processing, especially the printing equipment connected to personal computers and microcomputers, is developing rapidly. Two basic categories of computer-interfaced printing equipment are used: **impact printers** and **nonimpact printers**. Examples of impact equipment are dot matrix printers and daisy wheel printers. With impact printers, a mechanical part of the printer strikes against a ribbon, which makes an imprint on the paper. Laser and ink-jet printers are examples of nonimpact equipment. With nonimpact printers, paper is not struck by any of the printer parts.

Many of the documents prepared in word processing need a letter-quality appearance. Therefore, the use of dot matrix printers in word processing systems is typically restricted to the 24-pin category of printers. Although 9-pin printers typically do not produce a letter-quality appearance, daisy wheel printers prepare documents with a letter-quality appearance, especially when the printer is equipped with a carbon ribbon. While impact printers are noisier and typically slower than nonimpact printers, they are also less costly than some nonimpact printers.

Increasingly, nonimpact printers, especially laser printers, are being used in word processing systems. Laser printers possess xerographic technology that typically uses a laser beam to imprint images of the computer data onto a rotating photosensitive drum. The imprinted images on the drum attract magnetically charged toner, which is transferred to a sheet of paper as it makes contact with the drum. The toner, which is heat sensitive, is fused to the paper to prepare the final image.

Affordable desktop laser printers are now available that print from four to seventeen pages per minute and are capable of printing graphics and text material on the same page. The three distinct advantages of laser printers are their printing speed, their quiet operation, and the high-quality images they prepare.

Color laser printers are now available, although their cost is considerably higher than monochrome printers. These printers use the same technology as laser copiers. The appropriate blending of various colors of toner stored in the multi-color cartridge enables the color laser printer to produce high-quality color documents. These printers are slower, more costly to purchase, and more costly to operate than their monochrome counterparts.

Another type of nonimpact printer used in some word processing installations is the ink-jet printer, a device that uses ink cartridges. The sprayed ink is attracted to the paper in the images of the characters they form. Compared with laser printers, ink-jet printers tend to be less costly and slower, although the output quality of some ink-jet printers is quite high. Several of the newer ink-jet printers use solid ink pellets that when heated become liquified. One of the distinct advantages of some ink-jet printers, compared with most laser printers, is their ability to produce output on nonstandard sizes of paper, even paper measuring 17 x 22 inches.

A new type of ink-jet device is the portable battery-operated printer. Generally, it is most useful to individuals who use a battery-operated notebook computer away from a standard electrical source. Although its quality is not as good as other types of less-expensive standard ink-jet printers, it provides a valuable function under certain circumstances.

Dictating/Recording Equipment

The use of dictating/recording equipment is essential in word processing systems. The dictation and transcription process is much more productive for word processing specialists and originators to use than other types of input processes, such as shorthand or longhand. Depending on the originator's keyboarding skills, dictation may also be a quicker means of originating a document than self-keyboarding.

What categories of dictating and recording equipment exist?

The dictation equipment word originators use is classified as portable units, desktop units, and centralized systems. Each classification of equipment has its own special use.

Portable units Especially useful for employees who travel extensively are **portable units**. The magnetic medium, often a minicassette or microcassette, can be mailed to the word processing center; often the material will be transcribed by the time the employee returns to the office. As an alternative to mailing the medium to the office, some originators play back their dictation into a telephone that simultaneously records it in the organization's dictation system.

Desktop units Organizations unable to justify the cost of a centralized dictation system typically use **desktop units**. With the early desktop units, the magnetic media on which dictation was recorded had to be transported to the word processing center before it could be transcribed. Some types of desktop units continue to require the transportation of the magnetic medium to the word processing center.

Available now are desktop units equipped with multiple handsets that accommodate multiple word originators. The recording unit is located in the word processing center, which eliminates having to transport the magnetic media back and forth between word originators' offices and the word processing center.

The majority of the new desktop units are equipped with visual displays that identify the length of each item recorded on the medium, as well as any special instructions to the word processing operator. Some of the more sophisticated units are equipped with automatic telephone answering and message recording mechanisms.

A new development in desktop dictation units allows them to perform both dictation and transcription capabilities. Therefore, the originator and transcriptionist can use the same device. These units are especially useful for employees who have limited dictation needs and whose dictation is transcribed by a secretary located near them rather than in a word processing center.

Centralized Dictation Systems

Generally found in large organizations with a sizable number of originators, **centralized dictation systems** use discrete analog media equipment, discrete digital media equipment, or endless loop equipment.

The **discrete analog media equipment** uses a removable medium, such as disks, belts, cassettes, or cartridges, onto which dictation is recorded. Before beginning the transcription process, the specialist removes the dictation medium from the recording unit and places it in his or her transcription unit.

Some of the discrete media systems use the originator's telephone in the dictation process while other systems require the use of special dictation microphones, commonly referred to as private wire systems. Telephone-based systems are generally functional 24 hours a day, regardless of the originator's location. Therefore, originators need not be on the premises to record dictation. Dictation can even be input using a cellular phone 2,000 miles away from the word processing center. Simply calling the number of the word processing center's dictation unit connects the originator to the system.

When the word originator is connected with the recording equipment in the word processing center, keys on the phone are depressed to activate various functions of the recording equipment. For example, the recording equipment is activated or deactivated by depressing the "1" button on the phone. The "2" button is depressed when the word originator wishes to review material that was just dictated. The "4" button is used to index instructions or corrections in material. By depressing the "5" button, the word originator can talk with an individual in the word processing center.

Discrete digital media equipment operates in much the same way as the analog equipment except that the technology digitizes the dictation, storing it on a hard disk or a floppy disk. Voice quality is often better when using digital technology than when using analog technology, and this technology simplifies the process of locating dictated documents on the medium. This is the same technology used in voice-recognition and voice-activated computer processes.

What are the main advantages of using discrete digital media equipment?

One of the significant advantages of digital dictation is the ability to add material in the middle of a dictated piece. With an analog system, adding material in the middle results in over recording, which results in the erasure of the earlier-dictated material. Digital dictation, on the other hand, opens up a space to accommodate the inserted material. As the inserted material is dictated, the already-dictated material that follows it is moved forward. Thus, no earlier-dictated material is erased unless the originator so wishes. The digital technology also enables the word processing specialist to begin transcribing the document before the originator has completed its dictation.

All **endless loop media equipment**, unlike discrete media equipment, uses magnetic tape as the recording medium. A large quantity of tape is enclosed in the tank component of the unit. Because endless loop equipment has both recording and transcription units, dictation and transcription can take place simultaneously. Therefore, while an originator is dictating mater-

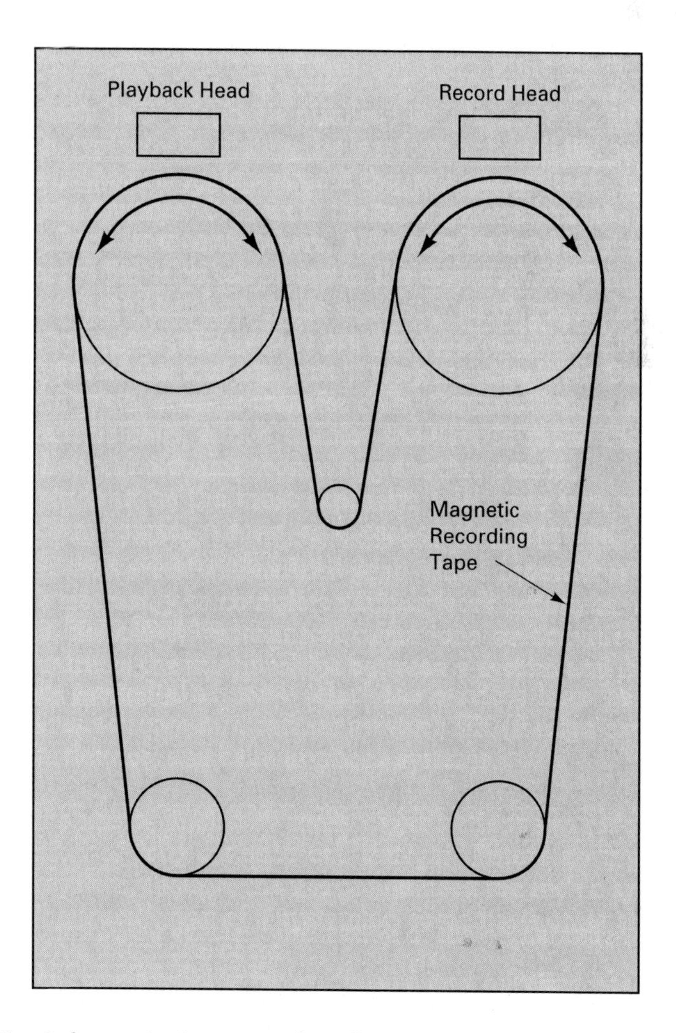

Figure 19-5 Schematic drawing of endless loop equipment.

ial, the word processing specialist can be transcribing. Whereas most discrete media equipment requires a separate transcription unit for each specialist, endless loop equipment systems have built-in transcription units. A schematic drawing of one type of endless loop system is illustrated in Figure 19-5.

For what is a supervisory console used?

Generally found helpful by organizations that use central dictation systems is the use of a **supervisory console**, which functions by monitoring work flow through the word processing center. Using microprocessor technology, consoles provide a variety of information, including the name of the originator of each document, the length of each document, the date and time each document is dictated, the status of the document, the date and time of the transcription, and the name of the word processing specialist who transcribed the document.

The console is also capable of preparing a variety of productivity reports as well as maintaining a record of the charges billed to the various units that use the services of the center.

Figure 19-6 illustrates a supervisory console.

Transcription Equipment

Transcription equipment performs a useful function in word processing systems in which discrete media dictation equipment is used. After the word originator has recorded the dictation, the medium on which the dictation is

Figure 19-6 Supervisory console. Courtesy: Dictaphone Corporation.

stored is used in the transcription process. In some systems, the magnetic medium storing the dictation will be physically removed from the storage device and put into the transcription device, which enables the specialist to listen to the dictation as he or she transcribes the material.

Depending on the nature of the magnetic medium used in the recording equipment, the specialist may not be able to begin transcribing until the medium is filled with dictation. An exception to this occurs when a particular job is classified as a high priority or a rush job, in which case the material is likely to be transcribed immediately.

What is meant by remote transcription?

Available now are devices that permit the **remote transcription** of dictated material. These devices use telephone lines to transmit dictation recorded in the word processing center to a remote site, such as the residence of the word processing specialist. Once the dictation has been keyboarded, the material can be electronically transmitted over telephone lines back to the word processing center, where it is received by a text-editing device that has communication capability. The magnetic medium on which the material is stored as it is received is used to prepare a paper copy of the document, which the word originator reviews. The remote transcription concept is especially attractive to people with disabilities or individuals who desire to be employed but who find working at home more convenient than working in an office.

Copying Equipment

Another type of equipment used extensively in word processing systems is copying equipment. Rather than making carbon copies of keyboarded material, an increasing number of organizations use copying equipment to make copies. The reasons for this procedure include (1) the unit cost of material reproduced on a copier is decreasing; (2) the specialist does not know whether the first draft of keyboarded material will be the final draft, and to make a carbon copy of material that may be revised is not efficient; and (3) the extra human effort required to insert and align carbon paper and second sheets exceeds that required to make copies on copiers. Copying equipment and copying processes are discussed in greater detail in Chapter 24.

Other Types of Equipment Used in Word Processing Systems

How is facsimile equipment used in word processing systems?

Other types of equipment are also used in word processing systems, including **facsimile (fax) equipment**. These devices transmit signals over standard telephone lines—which are usually dedicated to the fax function—to a fax receiver that decodes the signals and prepares a paper copy of the original.

Fax equipment uses either an analog or digital process. Analog devices scan a document line by line at a constant speed. They read the white areas of the document as well as the image areas. Digital devices, on the other hand, operate more rapidly because they scan the image areas but skip the white areas. On an analog machine, a page can be scanned in four to six minutes; on a digital machine, the same document can be scanned in approximately 20 seconds.

Fax technology is developing at a rapid pace. The new technological features available include:

1. A plain-paper digital copier/fax device with an eleven-page-per-minute operating rate.
2. Software that enables laser printers to receive fax messages and then to output these messages onto paper.

3. An add-on fax board that gives microcomputers the ability to transmit material to other microcomputers also equipped with fax capability or to transmit material to fax devices.
4. Canned message printing and automatic address printing that eliminates the need for the cover sheet, which is typically transmitted as part of the document.
5. Integrated units that contain a telephone, answering machine, and convenience copier, some of which are capable of printing in two colors.
6. Fax devices capable of producing various types of voice announcements.

For what is optical character recognition used in word processing systems?

Used primarily to input information into a word processing system, **optical character recognition (OCR) scanners** are becoming quite common. Material that is either printed or typed in an OCR-compatible types style can be read by the equipment and electronically stored at rates of 150 to 300 pages per hour. A beam of light is passed over a page, and the machine digitizes the alphanumeric characters into codes that can be electronically stored on a variety of types of magnetic media. Once stored, the material can be easily and readily revised and edited.

For use in an office, OCR scanners should possess the TWAIN standard, which is a software protocol that allows the scanning of material directly into a software application. This eliminates the need to convert material from one format into another.

ADVANTAGES AND DISADVANTAGES OF WORD PROCESSING

A discussion of the advantages and disadvantages of word processing follows.

Advantages

What are the advantages of word processing?

A distinct advantage of using word processing is the positive impact it has on the productivity of word originators. Prior to the installation of a word processing system, many word originators used longhand to compose documents. At a writing rate of approximately fifteen words per minute, the word originator's time is not efficiently used. With shorthand, the average word originator's dictation rate is approximately thirty-five to forty net words per minute. The use of dictation equipment enables word originators to increase their dictation rates to an average of sixty to eighty words per minute. Therefore, the use of word processing equipment reduces the amount of origination time and increases the amount of time originators have for performing other duties.

The use of word processing also enables word processing specialists to increase their productivity. When shorthand is used in the word origination process, two individuals are involved: the word originator and the transcriber. When dictating equipment is used, on the other hand, transcribers are not involved in the word-origination process, which increases their overall productivity. In addition, if the word originators speak clearly and enunciate properly when dictating, the transcription process is likely to be more rapid than when transcribing shorthand dictation. Because the transcriber does not have to take time to decipher poorly or incorrectly written shorthand characters, transcription rates increase.

The increased efficiency with which equipment is used is another advantage of using word processing. In a traditional system, each secretary or typist has a typewriter that may be used only a few hours each workday. With word processing, on the other hand, the text-editing devices are likely to be used a significant portion of each workday.

In word processing, the recording equipment is likely to be used more efficiently than it is in a traditional system. Even though in a traditional system word originators may have access to recording equipment, they may continue to make extensive use of longhand. Also, individual recording units may only be used a few minutes of each day. In a word processing system, word originators are discouraged from using the longhand form of input.

The division-of-labor characteristic of word processing enhances the level to which employees are able to specialize. Those who use the text-editing equipment have expertise in transcribing and related functions. But those who perform the other secretarial support duties have expertise in the functions they perform. Because of division of labor, the resulting specialization enables an organization to realize greater efficiency in production processes. The division-of-labor concept is discussed in greater detail in the next section of this chapter.

The cost savings resulting from the need for fewer personnel and less equipment is another significant advantage of word processing. After installing a word processing system, most organizations are eventually able to reduce their payroll costs by 15 to 25 percent. Fewer employees are needed to produce the same amount of work because they are used more efficiently. Depending on the word processing structure used, equipment costs can also be reduced because fewer typewriters will be needed.

Another distinct advantage of word processing is the lessened turnaround time needed to get material typed. Some organizations have a maximum turnaround time of two hours, with more rapid turnaround time on rush jobs. In a traditional system in which a typist is likely to be responsible to three or more word originators, turnaround time is likely to be much longer.

In addition, the quality with which work is produced is another distinct advantage of word processing. Office employees are hired and placed in positions that effectively use their special talents and abilities. Thus, less work is likely to have to be retyped as a result of poor keyboarding skills. Only those with excellent skills are likely to be placed in the word processing center. Another dimension of the quality of work is the ease with which material can be revised, which results in better quality work.

Disadvantages

Occasionally, the disadvantages of using word processing will outweigh its advantages. One significant disadvantage is word originator resistance to word processing. When word processing is forced on word originators, some have difficulty overcoming their negative feelings. For this reason, helping these individuals develop a positive attitude about the system before it is installed is strongly recommended.

Another disadvantage of the concept is the lack of job satisfaction that some specialists receive from their jobs. Although they may derive a great amount of job satisfaction for a time, this satisfaction may not be sustained permanently. Their complaints are likely to center around the pressure of the job; the routine, repetitive nature of the work; a lack of familiarity with word originators; a lack of involvement with other employees in the organization; and a lack of promotion opportunities.

In some organizations, a small percentage of the employees who work in their word processing centers after time succumb to the pressure of the job. When this occurs, the organization rotates the employees into another job for a short time. After they have had an opportunity to relax and unwind, they return to their jobs in the word processing center. Organizations that use this rotation plan find a significant decrease in the attrition rates of their employees.

Another distinct disadvantage of word processing results from the inability to perform all jobs in the word processing center. For example, the use of text-editing equipment to enter information on paper forms may be an inefficient use of the equipment because rarely is the information contained on forms either repetitively typed or revised. Special arrangements have to be made for handling work inappropriate for word processing.

In situations where a considerable amount of forms processing is done, either of the following alternatives is preferable to the use of text-editing equipment for forms fill-in. One alternative is to computerize the fill-in process. Another alternative is to use microcomputers with the appropriate forms design/fill-in software. When the latter alternative is used, the constant information and the variable information are printed on blank paper as it passes through a laser printer. Preprinted forms are not used when the second alternative is employed.

EFFECTS OF WORD PROCESSING ON SECRETARIAL PERSONNEL

Word processing usage is frequently thought to provide a variety of new opportunities for secretarial personnel. Several different levels of positions are found within the two secretarial classifications. For example, within the word processing center, an individual may be hired as a word processing specialist, level I. After a period of time, this individual may be promoted to word processing specialist, level II, and then to word processing specialist, senior level. The next promotion may be to word processing specialist, scheduler. The highest-level job within the word processing center is typically the supervisor or manager of the center.

Word processing specialists sometimes are not responsible for the proofreading of their own work. Rather, this task may be the responsibility of the word processing proofreader. Also, some centers have an executive word processing specialist who is responsible for the transcription of materials—especially those of a confidential nature originated by high-level executives.

Just as the word processing specialist category has several different levels, so does the administrative secretary category. Different administrative secretary levels, from the lowest to the highest, may include the following: administrative secretary, level I; administrative secretary, level II; senior administrative secretary; executive administrative secretary; and administrative support supervisor. The word processing supervisor and the administrative support supervisor are likely to be responsible to a manager of word processing/administrative support.

Theoretically, administrative secretaries and word processing specialists have equal opportunities for promotion to middle management positions. However, in practice, the opportunities appear to have been more plentiful for the administrative secretaries. This may be because administrative secretaries work daily with managers while the word processing specialists are not likely to have as much direct communication with the originators. Thus, the administrative secretaries have a distinct advantage because their abilities and the quality of their work are constantly noticed and observed by originators who are in a position to recommend them for promotion to higher-level positions.

THE ADMINISTRATIVE SUPPORT CONCEPT

In many organizations that use word processing, administrative support is also used, which results in a clear and distinct division of labor among the secretarial employees. Those affiliated with word processing perform keyboarding functions while those aligned with administrative support perform the nontyping functions.

Among the more common tasks performed by the administrative support personnel are the following:

1. Assisting in planning and scheduling the workload.
2. Gathering information.
3. Assisting with meetings and conferences.
4. Maintaining records.
5. Preparing travel itineraries and handling arrangements.
6. Processing mail.
7. Supervising work of others.
8. Handling telephone conversations.
9. Requisitioning supplies and equipment.
10. Preparing reports.
11. Greeting office callers.
12. Working with the budget.

Just as word processing has several organizational patterns, so does the administrative support concept. Perhaps the most common pattern is to place the administrative secretaries near the executives for whom they work. An alternative is to provide an administrative support center for each department or work group. A third pattern involves placing both administrative secretaries and word processing specialists in decentralized word processing/administrative support centers located throughout the organization. Because the various patterns are not all equally effective for an organization, the one most suitable should be used.

WORD PROCESSING: ITS PRESENT STATE

The ever-increasing presence of microcomputers on the desktops of virtually all white-collar employees in many organizations has resulted in the decentralization of their word processing operations. Because of the affordability of microcomputers and availability of user-friendly word processing software, an increasing number of employees are self-keyboarding their documents, performing themselves every task from origination to readying them for distribution. But in other cases, originators may give someone else responsibility for proper formatting of their self-keyboarded documents, editing and revising their work, and readying it for distribution after they complete its origination.

In these organizations, the decentralized approach has reduced the amount of work being completed in word processing centers. In such situations, the center will likely be responsible for large jobs (those consisting of multiple pages), complicated jobs (those consisting of formulae and equations and perhaps intricate graphics), jobs requiring the merging of names/addresses in a data base with a form letter, and jobs requiring word processing functions beyond the capability of the originator. The center will also be responsible for doing the work of employees who prefer not to do their own word processing, regardless of its nature.

DESKTOP PUBLISHING

Closely related to the document-preparation function of word processing is **desktop publishing**, a system that uses microcomputers, desktop publishing software, and high-quality printers, such as laser printers. Desktop publishing is typically used to prepare a variety of reports, manuals, booklets, newsletters, and other types of documents. Giving documents a "typeset" appearance, desktop publishing uses a variety of type styles, characteristics, and sizes; format features, such as columns and boxed-in areas; and other design features, such as shadowing, reverse printing, and so forth. Desktop publishing is often used to prepare the master needed when mass duplicating documents.

The advantage of desktop publishing is the in-house ability to prepare documents needing a professional appearance. Therefore, the organization can avoid having to invest in photocomposition equipment or having to contract with an outside typesetter. In many instances, the vast majority of the documents that organizations used to prepare using the photocomposition process are now prepared using desktop publishing.

Two of the more common desktop publishing software packages used in the business world are PageMaker and Ventura. The latest versions of most of the more sophisticated word processing software packages now incorporate some of the more common desktop publishing functions. When desktop publishing functions in an organization are quite extensive or involved, a dedicated software package is generally preferable to the desktop publishing function found in some word processing software packages. Before an organization invests in a software package, a thorough investigation needs to be made of those packages currently available. Thus, the organization is able to obtain a package that best meets its needs.

The more sophisticated desktop publishing software is able to import material from word processing software packages as well as from other types of software, including material scanned through an OCR process. This capability eliminates the need to rekey the material. Once the material has been imported, its format is transformed by desktop publishing software.

IMPLICATIONS FOR THE ADMINISTRATIVE OFFICE MANAGER

The ever-increasing number of organizations using word processing makes this area a common responsibility of administrative office managers. The nature of their involvement varies from situation to situation. In some instances, they design and implement the system. In other instances, they have overall authority and responsibility for the system, while the center's supervisor is responsible for the daily operations.

The rapidly changing nature of word processing technology increases the need for administrative office managers to keep abreast of new developments. This is especially true for those managers who have important responsibilities for the word processing system in the organizations in which they work.

Administrative office managers who are responsible for word processing must also stay abreast of user concerns. In most instances, when a word processing system does not function as well as it should, the problems originate with the users, not the equipment. Therefore, the administrative office manager should attempt to solve these problems as quickly as possible. The longer it takes to overcome these situations or the less effectively they are solved, the more frustrated the users will become with the system.

Well-designed word processing systems make a significant contribution toward increasing word originator and organizational productivity. Administrative office managers can make and often do make a significant contribution to the development of these well-designed systems.

REVIEW QUESTIONS

1. Define word processing.
2. What is information processing?
3. What is undertaken to determine the need for the installation of a word processing system?
4. What data-collection devices are used to determine the feasibility of word processing?
5. How is the financial feasibility of a word processing system determined?
6. Explain the various organizational structures for word processing systems.
7. Why are most copies of materials that are prepared in a word processing center made on an office copier rather than by means of a carbon process?
8. How does a shared-logic system differ from a shared-resource system?
9. Why does the word processing concept result in the lack of job satisfaction for some employees?
10. In practice, why are the promotion opportunities of word processing specialists less than the opportunities for administrative secretaries?
11. What is desktop publishing?

DISCUSSION QUESTIONS

1. You and a friend were discussing recently the word processing concept. Your friend said that he was under the impression that word processing was nothing more than a "glorified secretarial pool." Discuss how word processing is much more than a "glorified secretarial pool."
2. The organization in which you work is in the process of installing a word processing system. You are a member of an advisory committee that was appointed to guide the installation efforts. Several members of the committee favor the installation of a large centralized word processing system. You are committed to the decentralized structure. Explain why you favor the decentralized approach more than the centralized approach.
3. You work in an organization that is in the early stages of investigating the feasibility of installing a word processing system. The planning committee on which you serve will soon be selecting the technique that will be used for collecting data to help determine the feasibility of using word processing. Which of the data-collection techniques are you recommending? Why?
4. You serve on a committee that is guiding the installation of a word processing system in the organization in which you work. The committee will soon have to decide which type of text-editing equipment to recommend. While some believe electronic typewriters should be used, others believe a shared-resource sys-

tem is preferable. What are the advantages and disadvantages of each type of equipment?

5. Several of the word originators in the organization in which you work have expressed reservations about their having to use the word processing system that is being installed. You, as manager of the word processing center, believe that if you could convince these word originators that the use of word processing will save them time and make their jobs easier, they will be more willing to accept its use. Identify specific ways in which the use of word processing saves time and makes a word originator's job easier.
6. You and a person with whom you work recently discussed the word processing concept. This person thought the use of text-editing equipment could be justified in any organization, regardless of the size of the organization or the nature of the work performed in the organization. Discuss the basic fallacy of this person's thinking.

STUDENT PROJECTS AND ACTIVITIES

1. Obtain brochures outlining the functional specifications and capabilities of two competing word processing software packages. How are the packages similar and different?
2. Interview a word processing specialist to determine what he or she likes best and least about the job.
3. Interview a word processing manager who has been involved with the installation of a word processing system. Find out how the need for the system was determined and what techniques were used to overcome any employee resistance to the installation of such a system.
4. Interview an executive or manager whose documents have been prepared using the traditional document-preparation process as well as prepared using the word processing process. Which process does the executive or manager prefer? Why?
5. Talk with a word processing specialist who has used both dedicated word processing equipment as well as a microcomputer with word processing software. What does this individual like best about each type of equipment?

MINICASE

The Winthrop Corporation, manufacturer of antipollution devices used on automobiles, has expanded rapidly during the last few years. The executives of the corporation are especially concerned about the efficiency of various work processes, and they believe the feasibility of installing a word processing system should be investigated. Before they authorize a feasibility study, they have asked you, the administrative office manager, to prepare for them a report that discusses the situations that make word processing desirable and those that make it undesirable. Prepare the report in which you discuss

1. The situations that make word processing desirable and those that make it undesirable.
2. The primary factors (3 or 4) that should be considered in deciding whether or not to install a word processing system.

CASE

Several weeks ago, the Delvin Company, a paint manufacturer located in Old Lyme, Connecticut, hired a consulting firm to conduct a word processing feasibility study. The consulting firm used two basic data-collection techniques: questionnaires completed by word originators and secretarial/clerical employees and an inventory of stored materials. The conclusion reached was that a substantial need existed for the installation of a word processing system.

The consulting firm also recommended a decentralized structure for the system. In addition, a shared-resource system was recommended because certain data processing equipment presently owned by the organization could continue to be used.

While those executives responsible for making decisions about the word processing system are enthusiastic, a number of word originators and office employees are not. The success of the system is dependent on their support, in addition to a number of other factors. You have been asked, as the lead consultant on the consulting project, to prepare a report for management in which you discuss

1. Suggestions that will help assure the success of all aspects of the word processing system.
2. Suggestions that will help the organization overcome employee resistance to the use of word processing.
3. Suggestions for evaluating the success of the system once it is installed (assuming it will be installed).

CHAPTER

20

ELECTRONIC DATA PROCESSING

CHAPTER AIM

After studying this chapter, you should be able to design an effective computer system for an organization.

CHAPTER OUTLINE

CHAPTER TERMS

Analog computers
Arithmetic/logic unit (ALU)
Artificial intelligence
Audio communication
Audio response

AUTOCODER
Bar code input
BASIC
Binary code
Bubble memory
Byte
Cathode ray tubes (CRT)
Central processing unit (CPU)
COBOL
COM
Compiler
Computer viruses
Control unit
Digital computers
Distributed data processing
Expert systems
Floppy disks
FORTRAN
Fourth-generation languages
Handwriting pads
Hardware
Impact printer
Input
Integrated circuits
Light pen
Magnetic cassettes
Magnetic drum
Magnetic hard disks
Magnetic strips
Magnetic tape
Mainframe computers
Mark-sense forms
MICR
Microcomputers
Minicomputers
Monitors
Mouse
Nonimpact printers
Object program
OCR
Optical cards
Optical laser disks
Output
PL/1
Point-of-sale (POS) terminals
Printer-plotters
RPG
Scanners
Software
Source program
SPS
Storage
Supercomputers
Terminals
Touchscreen
Touch-tone phone
Turnkey system
Voice annotation
Voice input

Electronic data processing has a significant impact—either directly or indirectly—on the vast majority of the aspects affecting our working and personal lives. Computers make our jobs easier to perform, in addition to increasing the satisfaction we derive from many aspects of our personal lives.

No invention during this century has had a more revolutionary impact on many of the work processes and procedures used in the business world than has the computer. By installing their own data processing system or by using the services of a computer service bureau, even today's smallest organizations have access to data processing capabilities.

Development of the first electronic computer, the ENIAC (Electronic Numerical Integrator and Computer), was begun at the University of Pennsylvania in 1943 and completed in 1946. This device was developed to solve complex ballistic firing problems of guided missiles and artillery shells. The first commercial electronic computer, the Remington Rand Univac I, was dedicated on June 14, 1951, at the U.S. Bureau of Census and was assigned the task of completing the 1950 census. The first business enterprise to install and use computer applications on a daily basis was the General Electric Company at Appliance Park, Kentucky, which installed a Remington Rand Univac computer in 1954. Since that time, literally hundreds of thousands of computer applications have been developed for use in hundreds of thousands of organizations.

COMPUTER GENERATIONS

Computer technology, which has progressed through three recognizable phases, is presently in a fourth generation or phase. Distinct characteristics of each can be identified.

The first generation of computers, which spanned the years 1952 to 1958, used vacuum tubes that consumed large amounts of electricity and generated considerable heat. Data input was generally restricted to punched cards, and internally stored programs were limited to magnetic cores or rotating drums. The first-generation computers were used primarily by organizations for the mechanical processing of various clerical and accounting procedures. The cost of executing one million instructions on first-generation equipment was approximately $4.50, and the typical maximum capacity of internal memory was 4,000 characters.

How do the characteristics of the second generation of computers differ from the characteristics of the first generation?

The second generation of computers, which were marketed from 1958 through 1963, used solid state transistor cards rather than the vacuum tubes of the first generation. Transistor usage greatly reduced the physical size of computer equipment. Magnetic tape drives were developed during the second generation, and the magnetic core memory devices became much more functional. In addition, the second generation saw the development and use of symbolic computer languages, as well as the use of such random access storage devices as magnetic cards and disk files. The second generation of computers enabled many organizations to develop a systems approach for the processing of data. Processing speeds reached 30,000 instructions per second, the cost of executing one million instructions was reduced to 30 cents, and the maximum capacity of internal memory increased to 30,000 characters.

The third-generation era lasted from 1964 to 1969. During this time, miniature circuitry chips were used in the construction of electronic computers. Other developments of the third generation were (1) unlimited random access storage capability, such as disks, and (2) the availability of many prewritten computer programs. The introduction of minicomputers was one of the major developments of this generation. The impact of the third-generation computer on business applications was most significant in the development and refinement of the total systems approach for the processing of data. The number of instructions that could be executed per second increased nearly seven times (200,000) while the cost of executing one million instructions decreased to 5 cents. Maximum capacity of internal memory increased to 512,000 characters.

The current generation of computers, which appeared in 1970, has resulted in the further simplification and refinement of the systems approach. In addition, fourth-generation computers make greater use of microprogramming, which involves the rapid assembly and use of complex control and processing operations. Fourth-generation computers also use microscopic integrated circuits, which increase equipment operating speeds. Large-scale integration (LSI) and very-large-scale integration (VLSI) allow an ever-increasing number of circuits to be placed on a chip, which significantly reduces equipment manufacturing costs. Today's equipment is capable of executing 80 million instructions per second at less than 1 cent per million of instructions. Maximum capacity of internal memory can exceed 4 million characters.

How do the characteristics of the third generation of computers differ from the fourth generation of computers?

Another characteristic of fourth-generation computers is the associative memory capability, which means that storage locations are identified by their content or subject matter rather than by their position. With the earlier computers, storage locations were identified by the positions.

Data processing equipment has gone from computational speeds of seconds; to milliseconds (one thousandth of a second); to microseconds (one millionth of a second); to nanoseconds (one billionth of a second); to picoseconds (one trillionth of a second). Many computer systems now routinely process data in picoseconds.

What are the characteristics of the fifth generation of computers?

Work on fifth-generation equipment is currently underway. Among the characteristics being speculated for this equipment are the following: widespread use of **artificial intelligence**, megachips, and advanced parallel processing capability. Artificial intelligence will allow computers to learn from their mistakes. The megachips likely to be found in fifth-generation equipment will have over one million storage locations. The parallel processing capability will allow several computers to process numerous instructions simultaneously, unlike today's equipment that is capable of processing only one instruction at a time.

Artificial intelligence allows computers to mimic human behavior, including such behavior patterns as the ability to reason, learn, self-improve, and simulate sensory and mechanical capabilities. The artificial intelligence found in today's fourth-generation systems is quite elementary when compared with the sophistication of the artificial intelligence expected to be found in the fifth-generation systems. Artificial intelligence will give computers the ability to reason, accumulate knowledge, and simulate human sensory capabilities.

Among the categories of artificial intelligence are the following:

1. Expert systems (enables the computer to help with problem solving).
2. Natural languages (allows the user, using a natural human voice, to communicate with a computer).
3. Human sensory simulation (allows a computer to help perform basic human sensory functions, such as speaking, seeing, and hearing).
4. Robotics (uses a computer to operate devices).

Of these various categories, expert systems are seen as having the greatest application for usage in the business world.

What are expert systems?

Expert systems will also be commonly found in the fifth-generation era. These are programs that capture the experiences, decision processes, and thought processes of experts in specific areas, ranging from automobile maintenance, to space planning, to computer systems designing, to surgery.

Expert systems are created by a process that involves interviewing experts in a specific field. The experts' knowledge obtained through the interview process is translated into a series of rules and strategies. Because most expert systems will involve artificial intelligence, the system's knowledge base continually grows because it learns from user feedback. In this sense, the system continues to learn through learning. This technology allows managers and expert systems to become partners in problem solving. The end result is that as knowledge is accumulated by the system, fewer bad decisions will be made.

To illustrate how an expert system works, consider the use of such a system in office space planning. The program might first ask the user to enter several "parameters," such as the number of square feet in a given work area, number of employees to be located in the area, hierarchical level of the various employees, and the typical amount of furniture/equipment each employee has. After this information has been input into the system, the user might be asked to respond to several questions about the following topics: type of lighting system, location of electrical outlets, nature of employee interaction, amount of contact with outsiders, and so forth. Given the needed information, the system will be able to recommend the optimum type of layout structure (open, traditional, etc.) and even the amount of square feet each employee should be allotted as well as the ideal location for each employee.

CLASSIFICATIONS OF COMPUTERS

The backbone of data processing systems is the electronic computer. To understand the electronic data processing concept, an understanding of electronic computers is essential, including their classifications. Computers can be classified by category and by size.

Classification by Category

The categorical classification of computers includes digital computers and analog computers. Each has distinct characteristics and uses.

Digital computers are used primarily to count numbers. Data are represented by strings of numbers, which, in turn, are expressed by electrical impulses. Therefore, the digital computer is most often used for processing business data. The digital computer is capable of calculating and manipulating discrete variables.

Digital computers get their name from the fact that the basic unit of storage is the binary digit or bit. Binary digits have only two settings, usually represented by a "0" or a "1." The use of binary code is explained in the "Storage" section in this chapter.

How do the characteristics of analog computers differ from digital computers?

While digital computers are used to count numbers, **analog computers** are used as measuring devices. The analog computer, which is most appropriate for use in scientific research, operates on continuous values, such as voltages, temperatures, and speeds. While the digital computer is capable of calculating answers with 100 percent accuracy, the analog computer is not as precise. The accuracy of the analog computer is limited by the precision with which the continually variable physical quantities can be controlled.

Classification by Size

Computers can also be classified according to their size. Common computer sizes found are microcomputers, minicomputers, mainframe computers, and supercomputers. The basic differences among the computers in each of the categories are in the computer power each category is able to generate, equipment costs, expansion capabilities, processing speeds, and types of input, output, and storage capacity.

Microcomputers Several types of **microcomputers** are found today: desktop units, handheld units, notebook units, pocket units, and laptop units. Today, the minimum primary storage capacity of microcomputers is 256K bytes. Just a few years ago the minimum storage capacity was 4K bytes. As technology continues to develop, minimum storage will likely increase to 640K bytes. A **byte** usually stores one alphabetic character or two numeric characters. A fully functioning microcomputer can be purchased today for as little as $400.

Microcomputers generally have a limited number of input and output devices. Included are a keyboard used for the inputting of data into the device, a tape recorder or disk drive for data storage, and a monitor used for soft-copy output. A common peripheral device attached to microcomputers is a printer used to prepare hard-copy output. Increasingly, microcomputers are being equipped with hard disks capable of storing up to 500 megabytes.

Microcomputers are used in offices in two basic ways: as a stand-alone device for the processing of data/information or as an intelligent terminal attached to the organization's information network. An increasing number of microcomputers are used as dedicated computers in organizations. This means their use has a specific dedicated function, such as monitoring the organization's environmental control system, controlling the organization's telephone system, or serving as a word processor.

An illustration of a microcomputer is presented in Figure 20-1.

What are the characteristics of minicomputers?

Minicomputers **Minicomputers**, generally free standing in design, are basically mainframe computers in miniature form. These devices are often equipped with a printer, in addition to the keyboard, a monitor, and a disk drive. Both magnetic disks and floppy disks are used for data storage. Prices range from $15,000 to $250,000. Minicomputers are generally multiuser systems that can support as many as 500 on-line terminals. Compared with microcomputers, minicomputers have considerably higher processing speeds.

Like their microcomputer cousins, minicomputers are typically **turnkey** systems. This simply means that all components of the system are bundled, and the user simply has to unpackage the equipment, plug it in, turn it on, and load it with the desired program. The operation of minicomputer systems is easily learned.

Minicomputers are often used for processing business transactions, such as accounts payable and receivable, payroll, inventory control, purchasing, and sales, as well as used to perform complex design (computer-aided design or CAD) functions. The types of transactions processed on minicomput-

Figure 20-1 Microcomputer. Courtesy: International Business Machines Corporation.

ers are often too complex or involved for processing on manual equipment but not sufficiently complex to require the use of more powerful computer equipment. Minicomputers can either be interfaced with more powerful equipment or operate independently of any other equipment.

A minicomputer is illustrated in Figure 20-2.

Mainframe computers In the early 1960s, many organizations began installing **mainframe computer** systems capable of amassing enormous amounts of computing power. These systems use a wide array of input and output devices as well as several types of internal and external memory/storage devices. In comparison to the other sizes of computers, mainframe computers process data at much faster rates. Most are capable of processing as many as several million instructions per second. Mainframe computers typically have a primary storage capacity of millions of bytes. Their cost ranges from $200,000 to $4.5 million. The smallest of the mainframe computers are sometimes called small business computers.

Mainframe computers are often used as host computers, which means they serve as a centralized switching device in a computer network system. They are also capable of supporting thousands of on-line terminals at one time.

Figure 20-3 illustrates a mainframe installation.

Supercomputers The largest of the mainframe computers are referred to as **supercomputers**. Their price ranges from $1 million to $17 million, and they have extremely large primary memories, some as large as hundreds of millions of bytes. Capable of processing hundreds of millions of instructions per second, most organizations are unable to justify the use of such powerful equipment. Only a handful of companies manufacture supercomputers.

COMPONENTS OF COMPUTER SYSTEMS

Computer systems consist of the following components: input unit, storage unit, arithmetic/logic unit (ALU), control unit, and output unit. These components are known as the computer hardware. The computer software, which is discussed in the "Computer Instructions" section of this chapter, consists of

Figure 20-2 Minicomputer. Courtesy: International Business Machines Corporation.

Figure 20-3 Mainframe installation. Courtesy: International Business Machines Corporation.

computer programs and instructions. The relationships between each of the hardware components is illustrated in Figure 20-4.

What are the components of the central processing unit?

Figure 20-4 depicts the flow of information and/or electric pulses between the various components. The **central processing unit (CPU)** consists of three of the five hardware components: control, storage, and arithmetic-logic. Input and output are not part of the CPU of the computer. Each of the five components is discussed in detail in the following sections. Some of the input media and devices are also used for data storage and as output media or devices. The multifunctional media and devices are discussed in detail in the input section of this chapter.

The central processing unit is able to process data much more rapidly than the computer is capable of reading the data from most of the input media or devices. The CPU is also able to process data much more rapidly than the data appear in output form. Buffering the data compensates for the difference between input and processing rates and between processing and output rates. This means that data are temporarily put into storage to compensate for the differences in the operating speeds of the equipment.

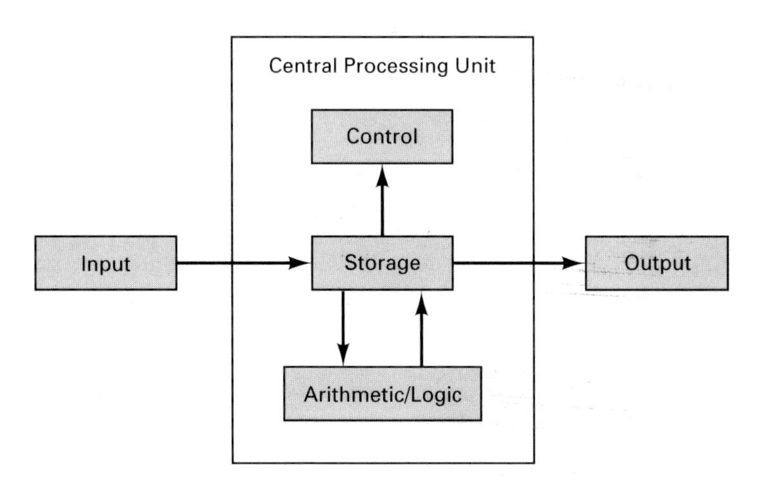

Figure 20-4 Components of electronic computers.

Input

The computer functions by converting letters, numbers, and symbols that humans are capable of reading into data the computer is capable of reading and processing. Paper media, magnetic media, and electronic devices are used to **input** data into computers. The following list identifies the types of media and devices that comprise each of the three main categories of data input:

Paper

What categories of input media exist?

Magnetic ink character recognition
Optical character recognition
Mark-sense forms

Magnetic

Magnetic tapes
Magnetic strips
Magnetic hard disks
Floppy disks
Magnetic cassettes
Magnetic drums

Electronic

Keyboard terminals
Monitors
Point-of-sale terminals
Touch-tone phone
Audio communication
Optical laser disks
Computer mice
Light pen
Touchscreens
Voice input
Handwriting input
Bar code input
Scanners
Optical cards

On what types of documents is the MICR process used?

Magnetic ink character recognition (MICR) Also classified as a paper input medium, **MICR** uses magnetically charged numbers imprinted on paper. MICR is used by banks and other financial institutions as a primary means of processing the millions of checks that are written each day. The numbers on the bottom of checks contain iron oxide magnetizable particles. Blank checks are preimprinted with the routing symbol, the transit number, the individual's account number, and the check number.

The first bank to receive a check after it has been written imprints the check's amount in MICR numbers at the bottom of the check. The check is now ready for processing through regular banking channels. The bank that receives the check may transfer it to a Federal Reserve bank, which then transfers it to the bank on which it was written. Figure 20-5 illustrates the meaning of MICR numbers.

Magnetic ink character recognition reader-sorter units read the imprinted numbers and sort checks by bank number and by account number. Sorting rates range from approximately 180 to 2,000 documents per minute. Before the numbers are read into the reader-sorter, the checks pass through a strong magnetic field, causing the iron oxide to become magnetized. The read heads sense the characters, after which the characters are read into the central processing unit of the computer or transferred to another input medium for later processing.

One advantage of MICR is the high degree of accuracy with which documents are read. Even though they are often folded, contain staple holes, and are covered with a variety of stampings, they are read with a high degree of accuracy. Another advantage of MICR is the readability of characters, which is not possible with some of the other types of input media.

Disadvantages of the MICR system are the following: Because MICR was developed primarily for the banking industry and because it uses only fourteen characters needed by the banking industry, the system, therefore, is not useful for other purposes. Alphabetic characters are not available in the MICR system. Second, clerical involvement is sometimes needed when the preprinted numbers are not sufficiently magnetized with iron oxide particles.

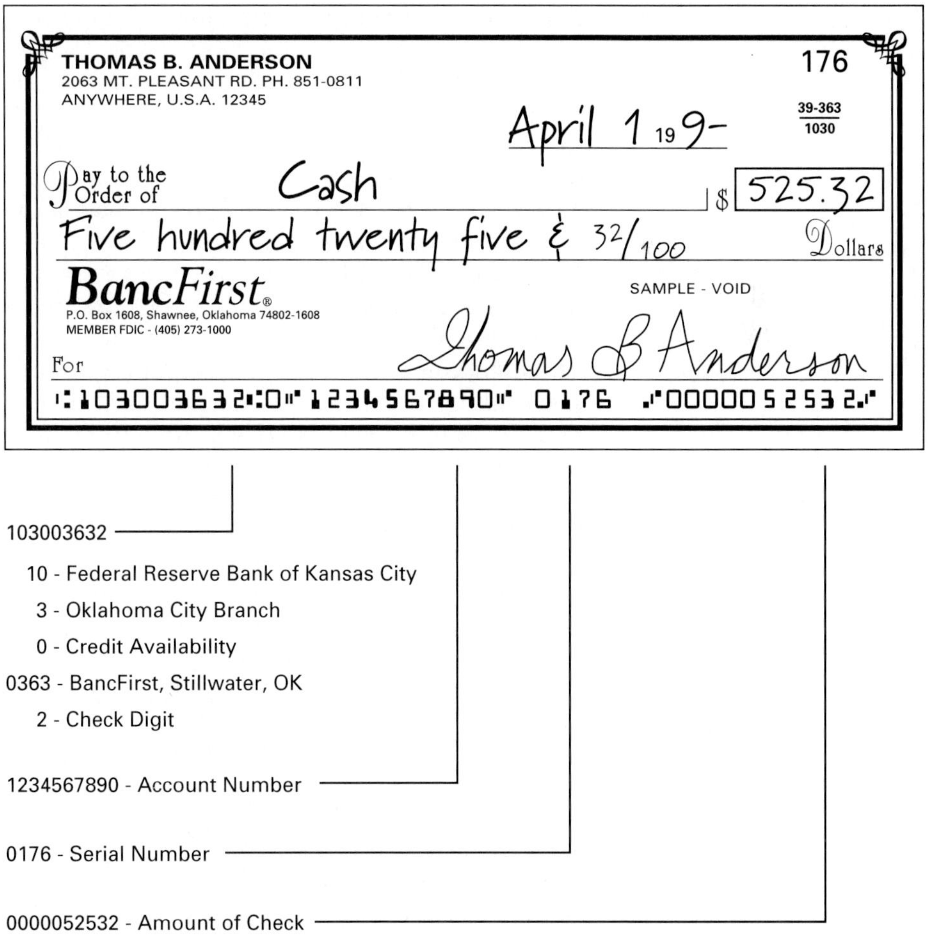

THOMAS B. ANDERSON
2063 MT. PLEASANT RD. PH. 851-0811
ANYWHERE, U.S.A. 12345

176

39-363
1030

April 1 19 9-

Pay to the Order of Cash $ 525.32

Five hundred twenty five & 32/100 Dollars

BancFirst®
P.O. Box 1608, Shawnee, Oklahoma 74802-1608
MEMBER FDIC - (405) 273-1000

SAMPLE - VOID

For Thomas B Anderson

⑆103003632⑆0⑈1234567890⑈ 0176 ⑇0000052532⑇

103003632
10 - Federal Reserve Bank of Kansas City
3 - Oklahoma City Branch
0 - Credit Availability
0363 - BancFirst, Stillwater, OK
2 - Check Digit

1234567890 - Account Number

0176 - Serial Number

0000052532 - Amount of Check

Figure 20-5 MICR numbers. Courtesy: BancFirst, Stillwater, OK.

Therefore, the check has to be reprocessed. In addition, the magnetized numbers on checks are sometimes printed in the wrong location, which requires their reprinting before the check can be processed through the reader.

What are the characteristics of optical character recognition?

Optical character recognition (OCR) Another input medium that uses paper is **OCR**. Whereas MICR consists of only fourteen numbers and symbols, all printed characters can be used in OCR systems. In addition, OCR does not require the use of the special magnetized print that MICR requires. OCR equipment can read data appearing in three formats on source documents: typed, printed, and handwritten. Figure 20-6 illustrates OCR letters, numbers, and symbols.

OCR is frequently used in credit card billings. When a customer charges a purchase, the customer's account number that appears on the plastic credit card is imprinted on the charge slip. If the customer's account number and the total amount of the transaction shown on the charge slip are OCR numbers, the document can then be read directly into the computer's central processing unit or transferred to another input medium for later processing.

Increasingly, OCR is being used to input data/information into organizational data bases, especially externally originated data/information. The content of reports and other business documents, as long as they are printed or typed in an OCR-compatible print/type style, can be scanned by OCR readers. Once the data/information are stored in the data base, they can be used in several different ways. For example, suppose some statistical data stored in the data base are appropriate for inclusion in a report being prepared by a manager. Depending on the type of word processing system on which the report is being prepared, the manager may be able to use the word processing software to access the desired data. After the data have been accessed, they can be easily inserted at the desired location in the report. Thus, the manager will not have to keyboard the desired data.

Like the other types of input media and devices, certain advantages result from using OCR. Among these are the following: The original source document can be used for input into the computer without first having to transfer the information onto some other input medium or device; it reduces the amount of human effort involved in the electronic processing of data; OCR data are easily read by humans; and only a limited amount of rather inexpensive equipment is needed to imprint OCR characters on documents.

To a certain extent, OCR is limited because of the rather strict type fonts and character sizes that must be used, although newer equipment is more flexible. If an incorrect type font is used or if the characters are larger or smaller than those the reader is capable of reading, the system may not work. In addition, when OCR characters are imprinted on paper with a typewriter equipped with a special font, extreme care must be exercised when correcting errors. Another limitation is the high cost of heavy-duty OCR readers. Light-

ABCDEFGHIJKLMNOPQRSTOVWXYZ
abcdefghijklmnopqrstuvwxyz

⑁⑀⑂$%|&*{}——=+█/?'";:.,
1234567890

Figure 20-6 OCR-compatible characters. Courtesy: International Business Machines Corporation.

duty readers that require manual movement of the read head can be purchased for as little as $200.

Common types of OCR scanners are (1) those that scan labels, such as price tags; (2) page scanners that scan material on a typewritten or printed page; and (3) document scanners that scan varying-sized documents, such as billing invoices.

What are the characteristics of mark sense?

Mark-sense forms When using **mark-sense forms**, preprinted shapes (such as squares, rectangles, or circles) are darkened with a writing instrument, most commonly a No. 2 lead pencil. These forms are then run through optical equipment. As the equipment "senses" the darkened areas, the system keeps a tally of the number of each area it reads. The end result is the preparation of a report that identifies the number of times each darkened area appears on a mark-sense form. The use of mark-sense forms in test taking is common. In this situation, a report detailing the number of incorrect responses subtracted from the correct responses will be prepared for each mark-sense form run through the scanning device. An example of a mark-sense form is shown in Chapter 23, Figure 23-4.

Magnetic tape In high-speed, large-volume computer applications, **magnetic tape** is the most widely used type of input. Magnetic tape, which is also the most common external data storage medium, is used as an output medium as well. The iron oxide coating on one side of the magnetic tape receives the electromagnetic pulses, which enables data, appearing as binary digits, to be recorded on the tape. Because the pulses can be erased and new pulses stored on magnetic tape, this input medium is reusable.

How are data entered on magnetic tape?

Data are entered on magnetic tapes either directly or indirectly. For example, data that are transferred by a converter from mark-sense forms to magnetic tape are transferred indirectly, while key-to-tape units, which use a typewriterlike keyboard or a terminal keyboard, are direct. The information contained on the source document is keyed into the unit; and as each key is depressed, two things simultaneously occur: (1) The electromagnetic pulse is recorded as a binary digit in one of the tracks or channels on the tape; and (2) the letter, number, or symbol appears on a screenlike display unit that facilitates verifying its accuracy.

Key-to-tape units prepare either standard-size magnetic tape or smaller-sized magnetic tape found in special cartridges or cassettes. Before the data on the smaller size tape can be fed into the central processing unit, the use of a converter to transfer the data to a standard-sized magnetic tape may be necessary.

Magnetic tape units are used for data input (reading) and for output (recording or writing). Such units, which are referred to as tape drives, must contain as many read-write heads as there are tracks on the magnetic tape being used. If the magnetic tape contains nine tracks, which is a common size, the tape drive must also contain nine read-write heads. As the electromagnets pass over the binary digits stored as pulses on the tape, the data are fed into the CPU. A tape drive is illustrated in Figure 20-7.

What are the advantages and disadvantages of magnetic tape?

Among the advantages resulting from the use of magnetic tape are the following: Data can be stored much more compactly on a tape than on cards or floppy disks (to illustrate, a standard reel of magnetic tape has the same storage capacity as five hundred single-sided, double-density floppy disks); magnetic tape is relatively inexpensive to purchase; magnetic tape is one of the fastest input mediums; and the likelihood of misplacing a magnetic tape is small in comparison to the likelihood of misplacing floppy disks.

Figure 20-7 Magnetic tape drive. Courtesy: Hewlett Packard Company.

Use of magnetic tape results in certain disadvantages, one of which is the inability of people to read the data recorded on the tape. In addition, the environmental conditions for using magnetic tape are more strict than the conditions required for using MICR forms. For example, minute specks of dust can cause the data on the tape to be misread, and tapes can be mistakenly erased.

Furthermore, controlling humidity levels in a computer room where magnetic tape is used may be necessary. When the data needed for a certain processing operation are at the end of the tape, all the data on the tape must first pass through the tape reader. Therefore, because of its sequential nature, information recorded on magnetic tape cannot be accessed randomly. Before self-locking tape systems were invented, tapes were sometimes stretched, crinkled, or contaminated by computer operators. The magnetic nature of the tape means that data can be erased or distorted with a magnet.

Instead of keying data directly onto the magnetic tape, data are sometimes keyed first onto either a hard-disk drive or floppy disks. Before the data are fed into the central processing unit, they are transferred onto magnetic tape.

Magnetic strips Found on the back of credit cards and some ID badges, **magnetic strips** provide a fast, accurate method of data input. The data stored on the strip allows the user to communicate with the computer. In some instances, the data contained on the strip provides an element of security, which prevents the fraudulent use of the card or badge.

Magnetic hard disks Similarly to several of the other input media already discussed, **magnetic hard disks** are used for input, storage, and output. During the inputting process, a keyboard is commonly used. Unlike magnetic tape, which requires sequential accessing, magnetic hard disks permit random accessing of data. Therefore, data can be accessed from a disk without all of the disk contents having to be read to the place where the desired data are stored. Random accessing of data on a disk is much faster than the sequential-accessing nature of magnetic tape.

How does random accessing differ from sequential accessing?

Magnetic disks, the diameters of which range in size from 5 to 36 inches, are made of thin metal plates covered on both sides with a magnetic recording material. A disk pack contains several of these disks, typically ten to twenty. Data are accessed from the disk pack by arms that, upon command from the computer, move to the location of the data to be accessed. The read-write heads located on the arms then read and transfer to the computer the electromagnetic pulses contained in the tracks on the disk. During the read-write process, heads do not come into contact with the disk. If they do, a head crash occurs, which may destroy the readability of the entire disk pack.

While some disk drives contain only permanent access arms with multiple read-write heads for each disk contained in the disk pack, others contain an access arm with an attached read-write head for each disk surface. The arms in a multiple-access unit move simultaneously. Consequently, if the computer directs an access arm to the seventh track on the fourth disk, all the arms move to the seventh track of their respective disks. The read-write heads on the No. 4 access arm will then read and transfer the desired data to the computer. A disk drive is illustrated in Figure 20-8.

What are the advantages and disadvantages of magnetic hard disks?

Several advantages result from the use of magnetic hard disks. One of the most significant is its random-accessing capability, which shortens data retrieval time. Another advantage is that disks in several disk packs can re-

Figure 20-8 Disk drive. Courtesy: Burroughs Corporation.

ceive data from one input operation, which simultaneously updates the data stored on several disks. In addition, related data stored on several disk packs can be accessed as the data are required for a processing operation.

The most significant disadvantage of magnetic hard disks is their cost. When compared with the same amount of data storage space on magnetic tapes, disks are considerably more expensive. However, the cost of storing data on disk packs has decreased from one generation of equipment to the next.

One of the most significant developments in the microcomputer market is the availability of hard disks for this type of equipment. Three types of microcomputer hard disks are found: external, internal, and hard disk cards. The most common are internal hard disks, although hard disk cards are becoming quite popular. Hard disks are used to store both software and data.

Floppy disks **Floppy disks**, which are made of a flexible plastic material, vary in size from 3.5 inches to 8 inches in diameter. They are permanently encased in either a plastic case or an envelope. A keyboard, such as a terminal keyboard, a microcomputer keyboard, or a keyboard attached to a dedicated word processor, is used to input information on a floppy. To correct an error, one simply "backspaces" over the error as it appears on the screen and then depresses the correct keys on the keyboard. After the information is keyboarded, it is "read" from memory onto the disk. This process facilitates permanent disk storage of the keyboarded material.

Perhaps the most significant advantage of floppy disks is the ease with which they are handled. They are easily placed in and removed from the disk drive, they are easily mailed, they permit the easy correction of errors, they can be reused, and they are easily maintained. Another significant advantage is their low cost.

When compared with magnetic disks, the amount of storage capacity on floppy disks may be a potential disadvantage. Although floppy disks can store data in either single or double density (high density) and on one or two sides, they do not store nearly as much information as a magnetic hard disk. Other potential disadvantages are a lack of standardization of various types of floppy disks and their tendency to be somewhat vulnerable to fingerprints, liquids spilled on disks, smoke, close contact with a magnet, and dust.

A new type of floppy disk drive is now available that accommodates very high-density floppy disks capable of storing 20.9 MB of data on a 3.5-inch floppy. These drives are developed around a process that merges optical and magnetic recording technologies.

Magnetic cassettes Resembling a VCR tape cassette, **magnetic cassettes** are another of the magnetic input media. Such cassettes are most commonly used in minicomputer systems. Both four- and eight-track cassettes are available. Keyboards are used to enter the data into system memory, after which they are stored on the tape. The input, utilization, and output processes using magnetic cassettes are much like those for magnetic tape and floppy disks.

Digital audio tape technology (DAT) permits the very high-density storage of data on magnetic tape cassettes. One high-density DAT cassette can store 1.3 billion characters of data. The primary application of DAT is the backup storage of large data files.

What are the advantages and disadvantages of magnetic cassettes?

Advantages of magnetic cassettes are their use as a low-cost storage medium, their ability to be reused, their ability to store large quantities of information, and their compactness. The most significant disadvantage results from their slow reading and writing speeds, especially when compared with other types of media.

What are the advantages of magnetic drums?

Magnetic drums The final magnetic input medium to be discussed in this chapter is the **magnetic drum**, which is a cylinder with a magnetized outer surface. Like several of the other input media already discussed, the magnetic drum is also used for storage and output. As the drum rotates, data are either read from or recorded onto it by the read-write heads. Magnetic drums are erasable; and as new data are being recorded on the drum, the data previously stored in that location are erased. When retrieving data, the read-write heads move to the appropriate location of the stored data, and the reading process begins.

In comparison with disk packs, magnetic drums have a faster access time. The use of magnetic drums for storing data is much less expensive than storing data in the internal memory of the computer. However, drum devices have a more limited storage capacity than disk drives do. Furthermore, drums are quite costly—considerably more so than hard disks. Another disadvantage of magnetic drums is the erasing of old data as the new data are recorded on the drum.

Keyboard terminals Specially equipped typewriters and teletype units can be used as data input devices. **Terminals**, which are connected on-line to the computer, are capable of transforming the letters, numbers, and symbols humans are capable of reading into codes the computer is capable of reading. This type of terminal is not designed for the mass input of data because the data are entered only as rapidly as the operator is able to keyboard.

Keyboards may be located in the same room as the computer or hundreds of miles away. Some keyboards, such as console terminals, are attached on-line to the computer while others are attached off-line (by means of telephone equipment) to computers hundreds of miles away. To illustrate the use of these terminals, consider their use for making hotel and motel reservations. To determine whether or not a room is available, the operator uses the terminal to enter the data into the computer. The appropriate data are retrieved from the computer's storage facility and are then transmitted by the terminal to the operator. If a room is available and if reservations are then desired, the operator uses the terminal to transmit the appropriate data to the computer.

What are the advantages and disadvantages of keyboard terminals as an input medium?

The use of keyboard devices for on-line data input has several distinct advantages. As input devices, they are rather inexpensive. In addition, these terminals can be used to communicate with a computer over a distance of many miles. Another advantage is the ability to obtain hard copies of data input and output. On the other hand, the use of keyboard devices to communicate with the computer is extremely slow. Therefore, they are not suitable for inputting massive amounts of data, which presents another disadvantage.

Monitors As an input/output (I/O) device, **monitors**, which use **cathode ray tubes (CRTs)**, are being used with increasing frequency. An examination of Figure 20-9 reveals that monitors have a televisionlike screen and a keyboard. The keyboard is used for inputting data into the computer, and the screen is used to verify the accuracy of the data being input as well as to display output. Errors are easily corrected by backspacing over the error and then depressing the correct key.

Monitors, like keyboard terminals, can be located a distance from the computer facility. Some of these terminals may be used as input devices (for

Figure 20-9 Monitor. Courtesy: Burroughs Corporation.

on-line update) or as inquiry-response devices (that is, the data are displayed only for inquiry purposes).

For what is an input tablet used?

In some instances, an input tablet, which consists of a grid comprised of hundreds of copper wires, is attached to a monitor. The grid is covered with a glass or plastic shield, and the paper on which the illustration appears is placed on the shield. Using a special pen to trace over the lines on the paper, the copper wires enable the unit to transmit electrical impulses to the storage unit of the computer. To change a line on the electronically stored illustration, the special pen is used to erase the original line prior to moving the new line to the desired location.

An electronic light pen may also be used to transmit illustrations to a computer. This pen, which contains a photocell, is used to trace the illustration directly onto the screen of the monitor. Electronic responses between the terminal screen and the photocell in the light pen are transmitted to the computer. The light pen can also be used to add, delete, or modify lines on illustrations or in tabular information.

The use of monitors results in several distinct advantages: It is a noiseless system, and output is displayed rapidly on the screen. In addition, it is the only input device suitable for the input of the line drawing type of illustrations. Another advantage is the ease with which illustrations can be modified. Disadvantages of the visual display terminal are its inability to operate when the CPU is inoperable, its inability to make backup copies of data that may be lost during the inputting process (which means that such data will have to be rekeyed), and the growing concern of the unhealthy nature of long-term CRT usage. In addition, as an input device, the monitor is not suitable for on-line inputting of large volumes of data into the computer.

When purchasing monitors, several of their attributes need to be considered, including the following:

Interlaced vs. noninterlaced: noninterlaced monitors result in less flickering.

Refresh rate: the higher the refresh rate (70 Hz or higher is recommended), the less flickering that will be noticed.

Dot pitch: refers to how far apart the individual dots of the same color are on the screen. A smaller dot pitch will produce a sharper, more clear image.

Resolution: refers to the amount of information available on a screen. SVGA (800 x 600 resolution)is becoming the standard.

Flat vs. conventional screens: flat screens produce less glare and less distortion, which may be important when using CAD/CAM applications.

Safety standards: the Swedish rating of MPR-II is becoming standard, meaning that the monitor emits radiation in the extra low frequency or very low frequency range.

For what functions are point-of-sale terminals used?

Point-of-sale terminals An increasing number of stores and businesses are using **point-of-sale (POS) terminals** rather than cash registers. In some stores, as much as 70 to 80 percent of the required operating data can be captured at the point of sale. These devices are attached on-line to a computer. As the required data for the sale are captured, they are stored in the system for later use in preparing summary reports. In some companies, the captured data originating from the sales are used to facilitate automatic re-ordering when a sufficient number of specific items have been sold.

In addition to performing the same functions as cash registers, POS terminals have the following capabilities: providing computerized inventory control; providing credit information about a charge customer; printing credit card charge slips; and, by means of a sensing wand, reading and transmitting to the computer the price found on the magnetized price tags that are attached to merchandise. Of the various types of tags, the most common type uses the universal product code, such as the tags found on items in food markets. From an efficiency standpoint, the most significant advantage of POS terminals is their elimination of the need to depend on a mechanical means to input data into the computer. Thus, a time-consuming, labor-intensive step is eliminated. Calculations are performed by the computer, and the terminal prints the results automatically on a sales receipt. The most significant disadvantage of POS terminals is their inoperability when the system's computer is down.

Figure 20-10 illustrates a point-of-sale terminal.

Touch-tone phone The use of a **touch-tone phone** is likely to increase as a data input system. When the various keys on the phone are depressed, the tones can be used to activate devices that input data into a computer. Although still in the experimental stage, this system will undoubtedly be used extensively to facilitate banking transactions, to pay bills, to place orders, and to do accounting-like arithmetic.

Two significant advantages result from using this type of data input device. One advantage is the convenience of the device, and the other is its low cost. Perhaps the most significant disadvantage is that errors can be easily made, especially if people are not totally familiar with the uses of the system.

Audio communication As an input medium, **audio communication** facilitates the transformation of standard telephones into data terminals.

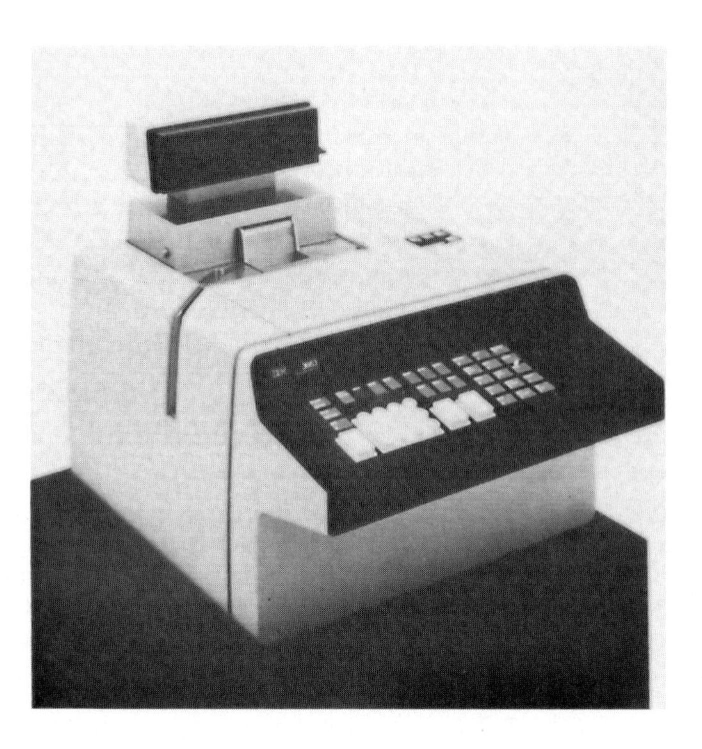

Figure 20-10 Point-of-sale terminal. Courtesy: International Business Machines Corporation.

For what is audio communication used?

Portable audio terminals onto which telephone handsets are placed communicate with computers. These terminals are usually battery operated, and they transmit data through a telephone communication medium (copper lines, fiber optics, and microwaves, for example) to receiving units that ultimately feed data into computers.

Data are input into the system by means of the terminal keyboard. Output is in the form of prerecorded voice responses transmitted through telephone lines to a speaker in the portable terminal.

This terminal device is especially useful for traveling salespeople, who, for example, might need to communicate with the home office about the availability of certain products that a customer wishes to order. The portable terminal is also used to place the order.

Audio communication that uses portable audio terminals is advantageous for several reasons. Electronic equipment can be used to communicate information that individuals previously have had to communicate. It is a convenient system to use because any telephone can be transformed into a terminal. In addition, data can be kept up-to-date, and they are readily obtainable. However, the portable audio terminal is not designed for mass input of data, which, to a certain extent, limits its use.

Optical laser disks Another of the electronic media used to input data into a computer are **optical laser disks**. Using a keyboarding device, data are entered and stored as binary digits on the disk. While some binary digits create pits in the disk surface, others do not. During the process of inputting data into the computer, a laser beam is used to read the configuration of the pit.

Optical laser disks have become more useful with the availability of technology that enables their contents to be erased. Typically, a laser beam is used to erase data that have been magnetically recorded on the disk.

What are the advantages of optical laser disks?

The most significant advantage of optical laser disk technology is the potential storage capacity. A double-sided optical laser disk is capable of storing 4 billion bytes. To store the equivalent amount of information on double-sided floppy disks requires more than 15,000 floppies.

A common application of optical laser disk technology is CD-ROM, the acronym for compact disk read-only-memory. Because of the read-only-memory feature, data on the disk can only be read; they cannot be manipulated or changed. One single CD-ROM has a storage capacity of 680MB. Compared with other technologies, CD-ROM enjoys a significantly more dense storage capacity.

Computer mice An increasingly common type of data/information input into a computer involves the use of a **mouse**, a small plastic box hard-wired to a computer. On the bottom of the box is a ball that rolls as the box is moved. Moving the box moves an arrow or pointer on the screen. Thus, if the user moves the mouse to the left, the arrow moves on the screen to the left. The use of a mouse enables the operator to place the arrow "on top" of his or her desired processing command. Then the operator depresses the "enter" key on the mouse, and the command is read into the computer. The alternative is to enter the same command using a keyboard, which may be more time consuming. In some applications, the mouse can be used to draw lines or objects on the screen.

Light pen The **light pen** has a very useful function in some applications, such as working with engineering or architectural drawings. The pen is used in conjunction with the CRT monitor. When the pen is placed close to the screen, the cursor locks onto the position of the pen. To modify a drawing, the user simply moves the light pen to the desired location, which takes the line on the screen with it, thus adjusting its location.

Touchscreens Another input device is the **touchscreen**. To use this technology, the various alternatives available to the user appear on the screen. The alternatives are often shown as icons on a menu. The user simply touches the desired alternative shown on the screen. The heat-sensitive nature of the screen causes the area being touched to close an electronic circuit, which facilitates the reading of the information in that circuit into the computer.

What is voice input?

Voice input Projected by some to be the most common future input system, **voice input** is currently receiving a fair amount of attention in research and development efforts. Although the technology exists today in a rather rudimentary form, its present limitations do not allow its use on a widespread basis. When using voice input, an employee speaks into a microphone attached to a device that transforms each word into a digitized format. The digitized codes representing each word can then be stored in computer memory.

Voice input equipment is currently available that can accommodate a 30,000-word vocabulary. The equipment interactively learns the vocabulary and speaking style used by an employee. With the required pause between each word, the equipment is capable of creating text at a rate of approximately 35 to 40 words per minute.

Closely related is equipment that enables drivers with cellular telephones to operate their phones with voice recognition commands rather than push button commands. Thus, users can access their voice messaging system while driving a car, without having to take their eyes off the road. The system can also be used to make calls or to have the system call them back if they have voice messages waiting but don't want to take receipt of the messages at this time.

An adaptation of voice input is called **voice annotation**, which allows a user to record a voice message at specific locations in a written document being displayed on a computer monitor. Suppose, for example, as a supervisor, you are on-screen editing a subordinate's report. Rather than handwriting a comment about a change you recommend, you can insert a voice comment at that location. Then, when the subordinate continues revising the document, he or she hears the comment rather than reads the comment.

Handwriting input Available now are **handwriting pads** that recognize handwritten characters when interfaced with a microcomputer. About the size of clipboards, although thicker and heavier, these writing pads can be carried around by the user. Data are entered on the pad by a writing instrument that resembles a pen. After the data are entered, they are downloaded into the computer, thus eliminating data-entry time and effort.

Figure 20-11 illustrates a handwriting pad.

Bar code input An increasing number of applications found in many organizations accommodate **bar code input** of data into the computer. Various units of data/information can be contained in bar code format, which is subsequently entered into the computer by means of a scanning device, such as a light pen. The technology enables the information contained in the bar code to be directly read into the computer.

In organizations that have bar code technology, a common application of bar code input might be departmental checkout of supplies. Each item in supply has a bar code identification. The checkout operation involves scanning the department's bar code identification, followed by the scanning of each item being checked out. Bar code input greatly simplifies the process of charging each department for the supplies it uses.

For what is a scanner used?

Scanners For data/information not originally stored in an organization's computer system, the use of a **scanner** eliminates the need to input the material using a manual procedure. For example, if a report is received from

Figure 20-11 Handwriting pad. Courtesy: GRiD Systems Corp.

someone outside the organization but the information found in the report will be useful to employees within the organization, a scanner is used to digitize the report's content, which then stores it within the system. At that point, the text data can be manipulated by means of a text editor, and numerical data can be placed in a spreadsheet form. Scanners also digitize line drawings, photographs, and other graphics, which facilitate their electronic storage.

Optical cards Used as a storage device as well as an input device, **optical cards**, which are about the size of a credit card, hold 100MB of data, which is roughly equivalent to 40,000 pages. Special readers are used to input the data from the card into the computer system. A less-sophisticated version of the optical card is found on the magnetic strip on the backside of charge cards. The strip includes information such as the cardholder's name and account number. To input the information into the system, the user simply moves the card through a special card reader.

Summary While some of the input media and devices discussed in this section are used only for data input purposes, others are used also for output purposes, while still others are used for input, storage, and output. Several other multipurpose media and devices are identified in the sections that follow.

Storage

The **storage** component of the computer, which is part of the central processing unit, is also known as the computer memory. After the data have been converted into a coded format capable of being read by the computer, they are fed into the CPU by means of one of the input mediums or devices discussed in the preceding section. Data are held in storage until needed.

The storage unit also holds the data being processed; it often holds the final processed results until they are outputted; and it holds the program instructions. While being processed, data are likely to enter and exit storage several times.

Data that humans are capable of reading cannot be read by the computer until they have been converted into an appropriate coded format. **Binary code** converts each letter, number, and symbol into combinations of 0's and 1's. To illustrate, the number 9 is converted to a combination of 0 and 1 codes, as are the letter C and the comma symbol.

How is binary code used?

Computer components operate with their electric switches continually closing (0) and opening (1). Electric pulses are either absent (0) or present (1). Microcircuits are either not conducting (0) or conducting (1).

Data that are converted into binary code are represented by a combination of 0's and 1's. Binary counting involves right-to-left direction, starting with a 1 and each position to the left of 1 doubling in value. In a right-to-left direction, the following represents binary counting:

128, 64, 32, 16, 8, 4, 2, 1

By using a combination of 0 and 1 codes, letters, numbers, and symbols are converted to binary code. The code of 1 is used to represent a *yes* or *on* position, while a 0 is used to represent a *no* or *off* position. The number 13 is represented by a binary code of 001101; 15, by 001111; 19, by 010011; and so on. Figure 20-12 illustrates the binary codes for numbers 1 through 10 and letters A through Z.

Decimal	Binary 32	16	8	4	2	1
1	0	0	0	0	0	1
2	0	0	0	0	1	0
3 (2 + 1)	0	0	0	0	1	1
4	0	0	0	1	0	0
5 (4 + 1)	0	0	0	1	0	1
6 (4 + 2)	0	0	0	1	1	0
7 (4 + 2 + 1)	0	0	0	1	1	1
8	0	0	1	0	0	0
9 (8 + 1)	0	0	1	0	0	1
0 (8 + 2)	0	0	1	0	1	0

Character	Binary
A	11 0001
B	11 0010
C	11 0011
D	11 0100
E	11 0101
F	11 0110
G	11 0111
H	11 1000
I	11 1001
J	10 0001
K	10 0010
L	10 0011
M	10 0100
N	10 0101
O	10 0110
P	10 0111
Q	10 1000
R	10 1001
S	01 0010
T	01 0011
U	01 0100
V	01 0101
W	01 0110
X	01 0111
Y	01 1000
Z	01 1001

Figure 20-12 Binary codes for numerical and alphabetical characters.

Data are either held internally within the computer or stored externally on one of the storage mediums or devices. The following list identifies the various types of internal and external storage. The external storage media/devices on the list that are also used for data input were discussed in the previous section.

Internal Storage

Magnetic thin film
Plate-wire storage
Integrated circuits
Bubble memory

External Storage

Magnetic tape
Magnetic cassettes
Magnetic hard disk packs
Floppy disks
MICR
OCR
Optical laser disks
Optical cards

Unlike external storage, internal storage uses no moving parts in carrying out the storage function. A state-of-the-art memory chip, measuring approximately 1/4-inch square, can store more than 400,000 characters of data.

The amount of data that can be held in internal storage is limited by the amount of storage capacity available in the CPU. Because internal storage equipment is often quite costly and has limited storage space, data have to be stored externally. However, before externally stored data can be processed, they first have to pass through the system's memory unit.

Data held in external storage cannot be accessed as rapidly as internally stored data. Before data that are stored on magnetic tape are accessible, the tape reel has to be retrieved manually from the tape rack and then manually placed on a tape drive machine.

The following discussion of storage components is limited to integrated circuits and bubble memory.

What two common types of internal memory are used?

Integrated circuits Since the introduction of third-generation computers, **integrated circuits** have been used extensively for internal storage. Each circuit consists of a power source and a switch capable of opening and closing.

Bubble memory The development of the **bubble memory** represents a technological breakthrough in computer memory devices. Bubble memory is capable of holding 92,000 bits of data in a device measuring one square inch.

Bubble memory uses garnet chips in which binary digits can be magnetically induced. The presence of a bubble in the chip indicates the binary code of "1," while the "0" is indicated by the absence of a bubble.

In contrast with other memory devices, fluctuations in electrical power, including outages, do not affect the ability of the bubble memory device to hold data.

Figure 20-13 illustrates "0" and "1" binary codes using both integrated circuits and bubble memory.

Several terms associated with the internal memory of microcomputers are the following:

How does RAM differ from ROM?

RAM (random-access memory) Refers to memory used to store data or instructions. The user can alter the data or instructions held in RAM.

ROM (read-only memory) Refers to memory in which permanently encoded data or instructions are stored. The user cannot alter the contents of ROM.

Certain types of hybrid ROM are now available that the user can erase, including the following:

EROM (erasable read-only memory) Can be erased using ultraviolet light.

PROM (programmable read-only memory) Can be programmed with a special device commonly called a ROM programmer.

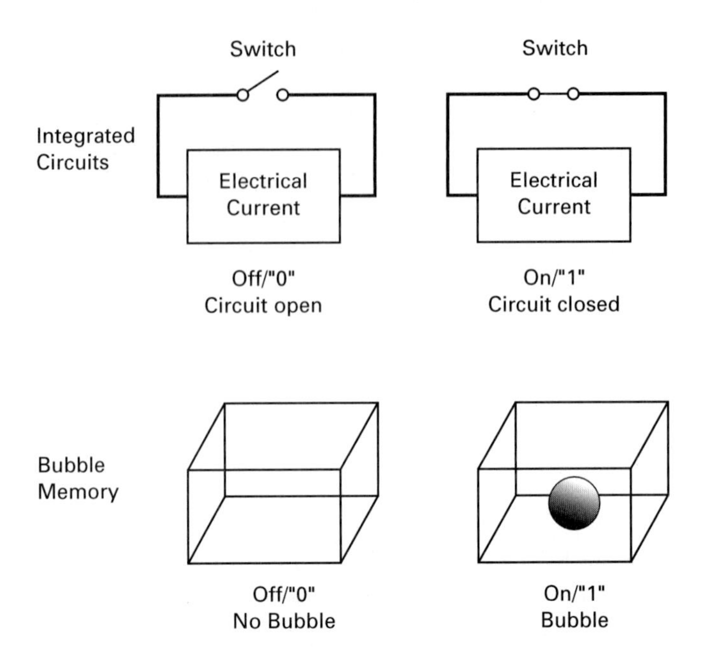

Figure 20-13 Binary codes for integrated circuits and bubble memory.

EPROM (Erasable, programmable read-only memory) Can be erased and programmed with special devices.

Cache memory, found in some computers, is used to increase the throughput of work through the computer. It serves as a high-speed holding area for the program instructions and the data that are being processed. Cache memory, when compared with RAM, is considerably more expensive.

Arithmetic/Logic Unit

What is the function of the arithmetic-logic unit?

The **arithmetic/Logic unit**, another of the components of the central processing unit, is capable of performing addition, subtraction, multiplication, and division operations. The ALU is also capable of comparing the size of data. During processing operations, data are transferred upon command from storage to the ALU where they are manipulated and returned to storage. During one processing operation, data may be transferred back and forth several times between the ALU and storage.

Data that are transferred from storage to the ALU are held during manipulation in either accumulator or storage registers. For example, if the computer is being used to calculate payroll, the number of hours worked is transferred to a register known as the accumulator. The hourly rate of pay is also transferred to a storage register. At this point, the amount in the accumulator (hours worked) and the amount in the storage register (hourly wage) are transferred to the adder, which multiplies the hours by the wage rate to determine the amount of gross wages. This figure is then transferred back to the accumulator, where it is held until again needed. Eventually, this figure will have to be transferred back to the adder, where the amount of deductions is subtracted from gross wages. The amount of net wages is stored until the output operation is performed. The adder is capable of performing all four arithmetic operations.

Control Unit

The **control** unit, which is another of the components of the central processing unit of the computer, performs three main functions: selection, interpretation, and execution of the program instructions. Specifically, the control unit

What is the function of the control unit?

1. Instructs input devices to read data into storage.
2. Locates data held in storage and transfers them to memory.
3. Instructs the arithmetic/logic unit to perform certain operations on the data.
4. Informs the arithmetic/logic unit of the location of data stored in memory.
5. Informs the output devices which information is to be printed or transferred to some other medium where it will be stored.

The control unit is easily recognized because of its vast array of blinking lights and assorted dials. Primarily, the flashing lights indicate that the computer is working, and these lights are used by the customer engineer in servicing the computer. In addition, the control unit typically contains a console keyboard or a visual display terminal that is used to communicate with the computer and to input small amounts of information.

Output

Many of the input media and devices are also used for **output**. Those media and devices with dual input and output functions that were discussed in the input section of this chapter are not discussed again in this section. Rather, they are simply listed, and the discussion in this section is limited to those devices that only perform output functions.

The following are the media and devices capable of performing both input and output functions:

Media

Magnetic tape
Magnetic hard disks
Floppy disks
Magnetic cassettes
Optical laser disks
Optical cards

Devices

Magnetic drums
Keyboard terminals
Monitors
Point-of-sale terminals
Audio communication devices

The discussion of output devices in this section includes impact printers, nonimpact printers, printer-plotters, computer output microfilm (COM), and audio response output.

Impact printers The **impact printer** is a commonly used output device. After the data have been processed in the central processing unit, an impact printer is used to prepare a hard (paper) copy of the results. In comparison to some of the other types of output devices, the impact printer is relatively slow, although some of the newer printers are now capable of printing up to 2,000 lines of 132 characters per minute. The impact printer functions by pressing a typeface against a ribbon that comes in contact with paper. The impact printing process is similar to the typewriting process much although faster. Among the common types of impact printing technology used today are the following: dot matrix, daisy wheel printers, chain printers, band printers, and drum printers.

Figure 20-14 illustrates an impact printer.

Nonimpact printers **Nonimpact printers**, which function without typefaces, are much faster than impact printers. The faster nonimpact printers are capable of printing at rates in excess of 13,000 lines per minute at 8 lines per inch with 136 to 204 characters per line.

Two types of ink-jet printers are found: those using squirts of ink and those using wax that changes from a solid state to a liquid state and back to a solid state on the paper during the printing process. Printers that use liquid ink in the printing process come equipped with small jets through which squirts of ink are forced.

Another type of nonimpact printer—the laser printer—uses a dry toner in the printing process. Of the two, laser printers are now used more often in businesses than ink-jet printers. In the home office market, however, ink-jet printers are more common than laser printers.

Figure 20-14 Impact printer. Courtesy: Centronics Data Computer Corporation.

Color printing is now available with both laser printers and ink-jet printers. Costwise, color ink-jet printers are much more economical to purchase than color laser printers. The primary advantage of using color in the printing process is the impact it creates on the reader.

What is a potential disadvantage of nonimpact printers?

A disadvantage of using nonimpact printing devices is their inability to make multiple copies. And the shape of characters formed on ink-jet printers occasionally lacks uniformity, although the quality of work produced by ink-jet printers has improved dramatically over the years.

Printer-plotters Used primarily to prepare graphic illustrations, such as scientific and engineering drawings, **printer-plotters** are also capable of printing characters. This type of equipment, which is quite expensive, is valuable to a growing segment of the data processing market.

Computer output microfilm When **COM** is used, output is in the form of microfilm rather than paper. Two methods of preparing COM are available. One method uses magnetic tape on which output data are recorded. The tape is processed through equipment that decodes the data and prepares the COM. The other method uses a microfilm recorder that contains a cathode ray tube similar to the screen found on monitors. As data are processed through the central processing unit, the characters are displayed on the CRT and are subsequently photographed by a microfilm camera. Comparatively, COM prepares output much faster than printers.

Audio response Used as a type of computer output, **audio response** involves translating computer output into spoken language. Among the common applications are the following: equipment maintenance or diagnostic instructions or directives; telephone number changes; pay telephone charges; time and temperature readings; proofreading of numbers in spreadsheets and so forth.

In some instances, all messages are prerecorded, and the computer selects the one that is appropriate for the given situation. In other instances, such as when reporting telephone number changes, the computer assembles each message as the need arises.

COMPUTER INSTRUCTIONS

Up to this point, the content discussed in this chapter has pertained to **hardware**—the physical devices, machines, and equipment found in computer installations. **Software**, which is needed for the hardware to be operable, refers to the application programs and the systems programs.

What steps are involved in developing computer programs?

The first step in developing a computer program is to define the problem. To do this, the alternatives for preparing a solution to the problem have to be determined. Identifying the input data needed to solve the problem as well as determining the appropriate ways for processing data are both considered in preparing the solution.

The second step in developing a computer program involves preparing a flow chart, such as the one illustrated in Figure 20-15. Flow charts, which are also known as decision tables, are used to outline what has to be done with the data to obtain the desired output. The information on the flow chart is then usually converted into instructions the computer is capable of understanding.

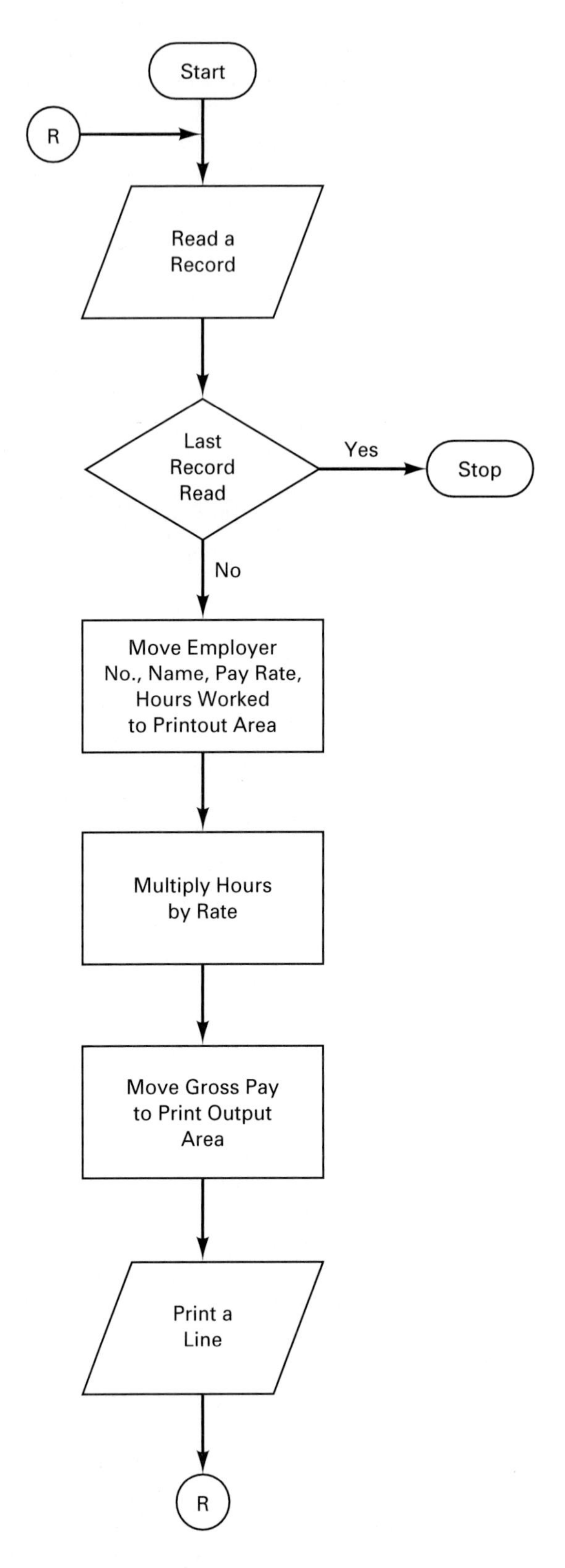

Figure 20-15 Flow chart. Courtesy: Methods Research Corp., Ocean Township, NJ 07712.

What are the functions of a compiler, a source program, and an object program?

Although many programs use words that have meaning to people, these programs have to be translated into instructions the computer is capable of understanding. A **compiler** is used to translate the **source program**, which people are capable of reading, into an **object program**, which the computer is capable of understanding.

Four different types of programming languages have been developed: symbolic languages, procedure-oriented languages, problem-solving languages, and fourth-generation languages. When a symbolic language is used, the translation of the source program into an object program is performed by a third program known as an assembler. When either a procedure-oriented language or a problem-oriented language is used, a compiler translates the source program into an object program.

The following outlines the steps involved in reading a program into the computer and the subsequent processing of the data:

1. The compiler program is read into the central processing unit. The compiler, which may be recorded on such media as magnetic tape or a disk pack, is usually supplied by the computer manufacturer.
2. The source program, which is recorded on an input medium, is read into the CPU.
3. The compiler program translates the source program into an object program, which is subsequently recorded on an output medium or device (tapes and disks, for example).
4. The object program is read into the CPU.
5. Using one of the input media, the data to be processed are read into the CPU.
6. The data are processed according to the object program's instructions and are stored until the control unit directs an output device to record the processed data.

Symbolic languages, which resemble machine instructions, use mnemonic codes to identify various operations. Examples of symbolic languages are **AUTOCODER** and **SPS** (Symbolic Programming System). Symbolic languages and procedure-oriented languages differ from one another in the following way: Procedure-oriented languages involve descriptions of a set of procedures to be used in solving the problem. Some examples are **BASIC** (Beginner's All-purpose Symbolic Instruction Code); **COBOL** (Common Business-Oriented Language); **FORTRAN** (Formula Translation); and **PL/1** (Programming Language 1).

Problem-oriented languages, on the other hand, describe the nature of the problem. The language used in the program is similar to the language of the problem that is to be solved. An example of a problem-oriented language is **RPG** (Report Program Generator).

What are the characteristics of fourth-generation languages?

Developed in the late 1970s and early 1980s, **fourth-generation languages** were developed to overcome some of the problems inherent in the procedure-oriented languages. A prime characteristic of fourth-generation languages is that they allow the user to focus on what is to be accomplished rather than on how it is to be accomplished, which is a trait of the earlier programming languages. Another characteristic of fourth-generation languages is their design for specific applications, such as spreadsheets, graphic presentations, and financial modeling. Some examples of fourth-generation languages are Focus, Ramis II, Microsoft Chart, Encore, and System W.

Although the author's intent is not to provide a detailed discussion of programming languages in this chapter, a short discussion of COBOL is presented to aid the reader's understanding of computer processes.

COBOL was designed primarily for the processing of business data and is now a widely used programming language. Rather than using codes or symbols to represent processing functions, COBOL uses English words. Thus, a source program written in COBOL will contain such words as ADD, SUBTRACT, CALL, and FILE. A compiler is then used to translate the source program into the object program, enabling the computer to understand the instructions contained in the program.

A COBOL program contains four divisions: identification, environment, data, and procedure. The identification section of a program written in COBOL typically includes the following types of information: the name of the program, the author of the program, the date on which the program was written, and the date on which the program was compiled.

The environmental division is used to identify for the compiler the types of equipment available for compiling the source program and for processing the object program. The computer doing the translating may or may not be the same one used to run the object program. The environment division also describes the input/output devices that are to be used in the processing of data.

The data division describes the files from which the program is to retrieve the data that are to be processed. This division also identifies the characteristics and format of the data to be processed.

The procedure division is the location of the actual programming of the problem. This is the part of the program that appears in the flow chart prepared earlier.

DISTRIBUTED DATA PROCESSING

What is distributed data processing?

An increasing number of organizations are using **distributed data processing**, a concept that began evolving in the early- to mid-1970s. Distributed data processing is a network comprised of two or more microcomputers. Each microcomputer has the ability to process data independently of one another at the user site, as well as the ability to communicate with one another. The concept enables computer power to be placed where it is most often needed—at a user site.

Distributed data processing is actually a third-generation data processing system (not to be confused with equipment generations). The first generation involved a totally decentralized data processing system, often using now-obsolete accounting machines. New computer equipment developments provided the impetus for the second generation, which generally involved large centralized computer systems. The third generation, which has become very popular, got its impetus from the development of a new type of computer—the microcomputer. Fourth-generation data processing systems will make extensive use of expert systems.

Essentially, the design of data processing systems has now gone full circle, starting with decentralization and returning to decentralization. Although both the first- and third-generation systems are decentralized, many differences between the two systems exist, especially in terms of equipment, operations, applications, functions, and characteristics.

The equipment used in the second-generation systems—powerful, fast, expensive, and often massive—necessitated centralized operations. In many organizations, the structure of the centralized operations makes the development of management information systems a logical process. MIS is advantageous from the standpoint of providing an enormous data base that managers throughout the organization find useful in their decision-making efforts.

How do third-generation systems differ from second-generation systems?

The equipment found in third-generation systems better meets the needs of some organizations than second-generation systems. Second-generation systems are often unable to meet organizations' needs (1) because the system reaches an ultimate size beyond which it cannot be further expanded, (2) all the users of the system must conform to the parameters of the system, (3) second-generation systems are more costly than third-generation systems, and (3) second-generation systems may not be able to provide managers with the timely information they need to facilitate their decision making.

What reasons exist for implementing distributed data processing?

Four strong cases for implementing distributed data processing are (1) processing control is returned to the user; (2) in contrast to a large centralized computer facility, the use of microcomputers is more economical; (3) the user department can design processing operations that meet its specific needs; and (4) by installing processing equipment at the user site, data do not first have to be transmitted to another location.

Organizations that use distributed data processing will not necessarily have only microcomputers. In fact, most distributed data processing systems use mainframe equipment as well. The four types of distributed data processing systems are (1) microcomputers that communicate with mainframe equipment; (2) microcomputers that communicate with other microcomputers; (3) microcomputers that function in an audit-entry capacity; and (4) microcomputers that function in a stand-alone capacity.

When microcomputers are used to communicate with a mainframe centralized computer, they more often than not function as satellites added to the central system. Perhaps the central system has expanded to the point where adding more equipment to the mainframe is impractical. The microcomputers process data at the user site as well as interact with the central computer system. In many cases, after microcomputers process the data at the user site, they input summary data into the central system.

Systems in which microcomputers communicate with other microcomputers are generally comprised of only microcomputers. Because a mainframe does not exist in most cases, one of the microcomputers functions as the network controller. The organization's data base is maintained in three ways: by one microcomputer, by each microcomputer having its own data base, or by each microcomputer controlling a part of the data base, with all microcomputers having access to it.

Typically, when microcomputers function in an audit-entry capacity, they are used to enter data into the organization's data system. They are also often used to verify the data in an off-line manner. Used in this way, microcomputers provide economical processing of data, as well as a fast and efficient means of data entry.

Microcomputers that are used in a stand-alone capacity process data independently of all other computer equipment. They are not able to communicate with other devices, nor are they used to input data into a centralized data base as they are sometimes used in other types of distributed data processing systems.

The use of distributed data processing results in several distinct advantages:

What are the advantages of distributed data processing?

1. Distributed data processing gives the user department control over the processing of data. Processing data at the point where the results are used is logical. Also, when user departments are made responsible for data processing, more attention is likely to be given to operating efficiency and cost-benefit ratios.
2. Distributed data processing is likely to result in reduced data processing costs. Over the long run, the unit cost per computation is likely to be less than comparable costs incurred when using large centralized facilities. In addition, communications costs involved in computer operations are lower because data will be processed "on site" rather than being transmitted to a centralized facility for processing.
3. Distributed data processing systems can be easily expanded or contracted to meet changing user needs. Whereas large-scale centralized operations are not easily modified to accommodate changing user needs, a distinct advantage of microcomputer systems is the ease with which they are modified. The modular nature of microcomputers is a characteristic generally not found in a large-scale system.
4. User departments are not at the "mercy" of a centralized computer facility. In centralized operations, jobs tend to be processed on a priority basis. When user departments have access to their own microcomputers, data can often be processed more quickly.
5. Decentralized data processing systems are less vulnerable. In contrast to centralized systems that affect the entire organization when they are inoperable, a malfunctioning microcomputer will not have a serious impact on the organization's ability to process data.

The use of distributed data processing in organizations that have a centralized computer facility transfers a considerable amount of responsibility to the user, including data entry, input/output control, and processing, maintenance, and programming. Centralized operations retain the following responsibilities: technical support and control over hardware, software, data bases, and communications. The most successful distributed data processing systems are those in which both centralized and decentralized responsibility are found.

MANAGING COMPUTER PROBLEMS

A number of problems affect the operation of computers. The impact of these problems can be minimized by using appropriate management. Among the most bothersome problems are electrical power problems and computer viruses.

Computer Power Problems

Electrical power problems can have a devastating effect on computers, especially if the power problems cause a total computer crash, resulting in the loss of a significant amount of data/information. Computer equipment requires power that fits rather rigid specifications. When the power fails to conform with these specifications, equipment, software, and data/information can experience varying degrees of damage.

Among the types of power problems are the following:

1. Sags: a short-term significant decrease in voltage, which results in loss of data/information, creates software glitches, and causes keyboard lockup.
2. Brownouts: a longer-term significant decrease in voltage, which will generally result in total computer failure.
3. Oscillations: the superimposing of high frequency noise on the electrical waveform, which results in equipment damage, loss of data/information, and glitches in the software.
4. Surges: a short-term increase in voltage, exceeding the maximum specification, which causes overheating of equipment, sometimes resulting in equipment failure.
5. Spikes: a short-time significant increase in voltage, which can cause massive damage to the equipment.

To avoid the excessive voltage problems, protection devices are useful. These devices simply prevent excessive voltage from reaching the equipment.

Power failure is avoided by installing standby power units, which generate power to replace that which is lost or reduced. Most of these units contain battery backup that protects the system until the generator is activated.

Working with an electrical consultant is recommended when installing a system designed to prevent computer power problems. The specialization these individuals have enables the organization to install a system tailored to its specific needs.

Computer Viruses

Perhaps more annoying to computer users than power problems—especially to microcomputer users—are **computer viruses**. These viruses can destroy massive amounts of data/information in a desktop unit or disrupt an entire network operation.

Suggestions for dealing with viruses include the following:

1. Avoid the use of software obtained from sources other than reliable sources.
2. Avoid exchanging floppy disks between computers.
3. Avoid letting others use your computer, especially if they want to use their own software.
4. Back up the data frequently.
5. Back up new software immediately—and then use only the back up copy.
6. Stop using the computer immediately if abnormal operations begin to occur.
7. Have access to a virus detection/eradication software package.
8. Be especially careful of software downloaded from a bulletin board.

Once viruses become present in a computer system, they multiply very rapidly, sometimes affecting the entire system. In dealing with computer viruses, a proactive posture is much preferred to a reactive posture.

IMPLICATIONS FOR THE ADMINISTRATIVE OFFICE MANAGER

Increasingly, administrative office management functions are becoming computer oriented. Miniaturized computer chips, which are found in much of the new equipment, expands its capability and increase its power. And most of the new operating systems for which the administrative office manager is responsible are now computer driven.

A basic understanding of electronic data processing is crucial for administrative office managers. They also need a basic understanding of the role of electronic data processing in the various systems that impact on the office function. Administrative office managers need this background so they can make intelligent decisions about various aspects of the areas for which they are responsible.

Although the basic electronic data processing concept remains relatively unchanged since its origination, important changes have taken place in equipment capability, power, and cost and in the nature of the systems that use electronic data processing. As the automated office system concept matures, even more changes will take place in the way electronic data processing is used in the office function.

REVIEW QUESTIONS

1. What are the differences between artificial intelligence and expert systems?
2. What are the characteristics of the current generation of electronic computers?
3. How do digital computers differ from analog computers?
4. What are the various size classifications of computers?
5. How do OCR and MICR differ as input media?
6. What is a point-of-sale terminal?
7. What functions does the arithmetic/logic unit perform?
8. How do source programs and object programs differ?
9. What are the four main divisions of a COBOL program, and what is contained in each?
10. Why is distributed data processing desirable?
11. How can the impact of computer viruses be minimized?

DISCUSSION QUESTIONS

1. The organization in which you work is assessing the desirability of converting from its centralized data processing system to a distributed data processing system. What factors should be considered in determining the feasibility of this conversion?
2. You were recently appointed by the president of the company in which you work to chair a committee responsible for investigating the installation of a data processing system. At the present, the company has no data processing equipment. Identify the relevant background qualifications of the other individuals whom you would like to have serve on your committee.
3. You work in a small office that presently uses no computer equipment. Several of your job tasks (typing correspondence, keeping financial records, and so forth) could be performed more efficiently, however, using a microcomputer instead of the manual processes you presently use. When you recently talked with the owner of the company about the purchase of a microcomputer, he said, "Convince me you need one, and I will think about it." Outline the sales pitch you plan to use in persuading the manager to purchase a microcomputer.
4. You have been asked to make a presentation to one of the business class-

es at the local high school. Your suggested topic is a discussion of the various areas of our personal lives that are affected by computer technology. Identify the areas that you plan to discuss during your presentation.

5. The organization in which you work is installing a totally new data processing system. The present facilities are no longer adequate to meet the needs of the organization. A number of employees are a little apprehensive about the new system because of the fear that they will no longer be needed. What can the organization do to eliminate the apprehension being experienced by these employees?
6. The organization in which you work is quite small. Management prefers to train a limited number of its present employees to work with the system rather than hiring several new employees who have specialized data processing training. How might the company determine which size of computer is most ideal for its needs? What concept should the company make use of that will eliminate its having to hire several new employees who have specialized training in computer applications and programming?

STUDENT PROJECTS AND ACTIVITIES

1. Talk with the director/manager of a large-scale computer operation. What are the common job responsibilities of this individual?
2. Obtain the promotional brochures for two competing microcomputers. In what ways are the two devices similar to one another? Different from one another?
3. Talk with a computer operator. What are the common job responsibilities of this individual?
4. Talk with an individual who is responsible for expert systems within an organization. Obtain information about the process used to develop these systems.
5. Compare the specifications of a microcomputer available today with a microcomputer available five years ago. What are the differences in their specifications?

MINICASE

The Durham Company is a large supplier of automobile parts. When the traveling sales representatives receive an order from a customer, they telephone it to the appropriate regional warehouse. Frequently, items in the warehouse have an out-of-stock status. A minimum of two days pass before the sales representative learns that an item is temporarily out of stock. By that time, several other customers may have also ordered the same out-of-stock items. Because the company is greatly concerned about its customer relations, several managers believe that if the customers were to know the availability status of a given item immediately, the negative impact would be less than when the customer finds out two days later that the item is not available. You, a consultant, have been asked by the company to help it with its dilemma. You decide to prepare a report in which you

1. Identify and discuss an input device that will help the company resolve its dilemma.
2. Discuss how the device can be used.

CASE

Jack Hemingway, president of Hemingway Company, recently appointed a group of employees to serve on a computer systems study committee. The Hemingway Company, which manufactures electrical components for automobiles, is interested in upgrading its present computer facilities because they are no longer adequate. The system has been expanded to capacity, primarily because of the organization's recent rapid growth and because of its desire to make greater use of operating systems.

You, the administrative office manager, have been appointed to serve on the computer systems study committee. Your specific responsibilities involve investigating the various types of input media that are presently available for input and storage of data and then writing a report in which you

1. Identify the types of magnetic media that might be appropriate for use by the company.
2. Discuss the advantages and disadvantages of the media.
3. Identify the magnetic medium the committee favors and explain why the committee favors it.

CHAPTER

21

RECORDS MANAGEMENT AND MICROGRAPHICS

CHAPTER AIM

After studying this chapter, you should be able to design an effective records management program for an organization.

CHAPTER OUTLINE

CHAPTER TERMS

- Aperture cards
- Centralized control
- Charge-out system
- Computer-assisted retrieval (CAR)
- Computerized records retrieval
- Computer output microfilm (COM)

- Decentralized control
- Filing
- Film strips
- Finding ratio
- Front-projection readers
- Image processing
- Jacketed film
- Lateral equipment
- Microfiche
- Micrographics
- Microimage format
- Mobile filing equipment
- Open-shelf file
- Performance standards
- Planetary camera
- Power filing equipment
- Processor camera
- Rear-projection readers
- Record processor
- Records
- Records inventory
- Records management
- Records management manual
- Records retention
- Roll film
- Rotary camera
- Rotary power files
- Structural power files
- Transfer
- Use ratio
- Vertical equipment
- Vertical rotary files

The ever-increasing volume of an organization's records that must be maintained requires their efficient management. A well-designed, efficient records management program can significantly reduce an organization's operating costs. Furthermore, an efficient records management program helps ensure the proper care of an organization's records. Improperly maintained records in hard-copy form are more likely to be misplaced or destroyed by mistake. Improperly maintained records stored electronically may become inaccessible. An effective program provides the protection an organization's records accumulation needs.

Records, which refer to informational documents used to carry out various functions, include forms, letters, memoranda, reports, and manuals. **Records management** refers to the activities involved in controlling the life cycle of a record, beginning with its creation and ending with its ultimate disposition. **Filing** refers to the activities involved in rough sorting documents, locating the proper folder for the document, and placing the document in the folder.

The emergence of data processing has resulted in new applications used in storing and retrieving information. Before organizations used data processing, storage and retrieval of information involved hard-copy documents. Increasingly, information is now being stored on magnetic tape, magnetic hard disks, or optical disks, using a process known as **image processing**.

Records management also encompasses **micrographics**, the process of making miniature film images of paper documents. The film on which the microimage appears is available in several different formats. A process known as **computer-assisted retrieval (CAR)** is often used to retrieve microrecords. Micrographics is discussed in detail in a later section of this chapter.

THE RECORDS CYCLE

What stages comprise the records cycle?

Informational documents, including records, typically proceed through the life cycle illustrated in Figure 21-1. One of the most important functions of the *creation stage* involves controlling the development and adoption of new forms. Only when new forms and records can be substantially justified should they be approved for use. The creation stage is also concerned with

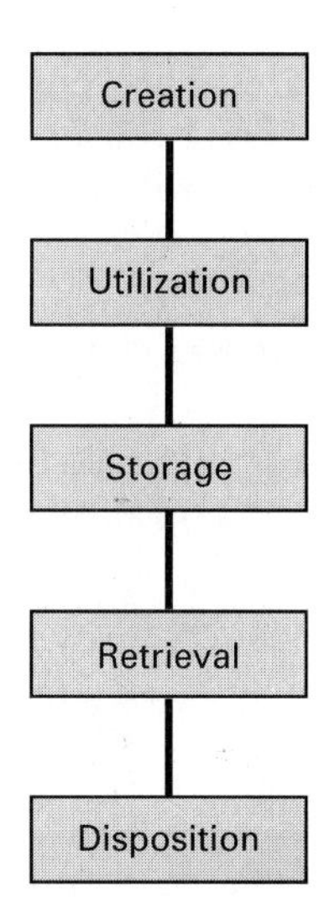

Figure 21-1 Records cycle.

developing efficient methods of entering data on documents, a task of critical importance. Another important function of the creation stage involves determining the length of time records should be stored before they are destroyed.

The *utilization stage* of the records cycle is concerned with developing efficient procedures for use in retrieving and delivering desired records to their desired location at the desired time. Consideration is also given to developing efficient procedures for the movement of documents through their respective work flows. The effectiveness with which a document is used in this stage is greatly affected by the quality of the information it contains. For information stored electronically, utilization involves making accessible to the user the records he or she is authorized to use and making inaccessible those he or she is not authorized to use.

The *storage stage* involves developing efficient procedures for using filing equipment and the space occupied by the equipment. To maximize efficiency and convenience, records should be stored in a location readily accessible to users. Storage is also concerned with protecting records against disaster or unauthorized use.

The *retrieval stage* is concerned with locating requested records. In addition to "signing out" documents removed from the files, retrieval involves tracking down documents not returned to the files within a reasonable time. For records stored electronically, retrieval involves using appropriate keyboard commands to access the desired information.

The *disposition stage* involves preserving valuable documents, especially those that are vital for the smooth operation of the organization. Disposition also involves transferring records from a high-cost storage area to a low-cost storage area as well as properly destroying records no longer having any value to the organization. Microrecording documents is also an important function of this stage. For records stored electronically, they can be permanently archived or purged when they have fulfilled their useful life.

ORGANIZING A RECORDS MANAGEMENT PROGRAM

In addition to becoming increasingly aware of the rapidly growing number of records created and the costs incurred, managers are also becoming more aware of the benefits of implementing an efficient records management program. The following sections provide information about various program components of managing records stored in a nonelectronic (computerized) format.

Objectives of the Records Management Program

One of the first priorities in developing a records management program is a clear identification of a set of program objectives, such as the following:

What are the objectives of records management programs?

1. To provide control over the records cycle, that is, the creation, utilization, storage, retrieval, and disposition of records.
2. To develop efficient procedures for each stage of the cycle.
3. To eliminate needless storage of duplicate records.
4. To reduce costs in each stage of the records cycle.
5. To develop realistic standards for employee performance and program evaluation.
6. To develop employee appreciation for the value of a records management program.
7. To standardize procedures and equipment used in the records management program.

Policies of the Records Management Program

Why are policies needed that are designed to guide the records management program?

After the objectives of the records management program have been developed, general operating policies should be adopted. Policies are used to guide decision making about various aspects of the program. Because vague or ambiguous policies often result in ineffective or improper actions, policies should be clearly worded. The following are examples of the kinds of policies frequently included in records management programs:

1. The records management program, which has management's support, is considered to be an integral organizational function.
2. Each record created in the organization comes under the jurisdiction of the records management program and, therefore, is subject to centralized control.
3. The records management program shall operate under the procedures outlined in the records management manual.
4. Records must receive adequate protection at all times.
5. The administrative office manager has primary responsibility for the records management program, but ultimate responsibility lies with the appropriate functional vice president.
6. Efficiency will have precedence over cost when making decisions about work flow.

Organization of the Program

The type of control and the location of records storage determine the organization of the records management program. Some programs operate under **centralized control** while others operate under **decentralized control**. Records can be stored in a records depository (centralized) in the organization or within the various work units (decentralized).

How does centralized control differ from decentralized control?

Centralized control When a records management program uses centralized control, the overall authority and responsibility for the program is vested in one individual. Centralized control usually increases the formality of the program. In a centrally controlled program, records can be stored either centrally or decentrally.

Centralized storage, which means that records are stored in a central location within the organization, is advantageous for the following reasons:

What are the advantages and disadvantages of centralized storage?

1. The number of duplicate records that are stored is reduced considerably. In some instances, no duplicate records are stored.
2. The equipment is more efficiently used, resulting in the need for fewer file storage units.
3. The organization can take advantage of the cost savings that accrue from the use of standardized equipment and procedures.
4. The program uses trained employees who file documents accurately.
5. The retrieval, retention, and transfer of records is better controlled.
6. The records pertaining to a particular subject are stored in one place.
7. The program operates continuously and is not hampered by employee absence.
8. The records that are obscure are obtained more quickly because their whereabouts are known.

The disadvantages of centralized storage are the following:

1. The records may be more vulnerable because they are stored in one central location.
2. The time spent in transporting frequently used records to and from the central storage area may delay their immediate use.
3. The records that cannot be immediately obtained may result in inconvenience.
4. The confidentiality of records may be more difficult to maintain. More organizations are storing confidential records decentrally.

Decentralized storage means that records are kept within the various work units until the time has arrived for their destruction or transfer to low-cost storage areas. The following are advantages of decentralized storage:

What are the advantages and disadvantages of decentralized storage?

1. Confidential records are stored in work units throughout the organization and, therefore, are less vulnerable.
2. Because the records are stored on site, valuable time is not consumed in transporting records.
3. Because each work unit is primarily responsible for the storage of its own records, flexible procedures can be developed.

The following outlines the disadvantages of decentralized storage:

1. Some work units are likely to develop their own procedures rather than use those of the system.
2. Duplicate filing equipment may be required.
3. Filing equipment may not be efficiently used.

Several factors should be considered when deciding whether to store records centrally or decentrally. Among the more important ones are attitude of top management toward the storage of records, competence of personnel, size and type of the organization, philosophy of the organization with regard to centralization and decentralization, and the number and kinds of records stored.

Decentralized control With decentralized control, each work unit assumes responsibility for the management of its own records. Decentralized control results in duplication of equipment, records, and personnel effort, as well as results in a lack of consistency in methods and procedures. In most cases, when control is decentralized, so is the storage of records.

Filing Systems

Another critical component of the records management program is the filing system or systems that are used. The filing system involves systematically classifying, coding, arranging, and placing records in storage and facilitating their quick and easy retrieval when requested by a user. Most organizations use standardized filing rules approved by the American Records Management Association. Cross-referencing of materials is also frequently involved in the filing process.

What types of indexing systems are used in records management programs?

Two general filing methods exist—alphabetic and nonalphabetic. The alphabetic method consists of three specialized indexing systems—filing by *name*, *subject*, or *geographic area*—while the nonalphabetic method is comprised of *numerical* and *chronological* indexing systems. Figure 21-2 illustrates the various systems.

Most organizations use one of the alphabetic indexing systems. Each of these three systems uses alphabetic sections (A, B, C, D, etc.). Filing rules are used to determine the appropriate alphabetic section under which each record will be filed. Each system also uses two types of folders—individual and miscellaneous—for each alphabetic section. When a specified number of records (usually five) is filed under a particular category, a separate individual folder is then prepared. For example, when the specified number of records pertaining to "Adjustments" has accumulated, a file folder labeled "Adjustments" is prepared. However, until that time, records are placed in the appropriate miscellaneous folder.

Using the foregoing example, until the specified number of records pertaining to "Adjustments" is filed, records pertaining to this subject are filed in the "A" miscellaneous folder, along with other records of insufficient quantity to warrant the use of an individual folder. Records within each miscellaneous folder are filed alphabetically, with the most recent record filed as the first record in each category.

Both numeric systems use a numbering system. Numeric systems are used extensively for filing records that are numbered serially and for records on which the date is an important information item. Examples of records filed by numerical systems are purchase orders, sales slips, and invoices.

When the numerical indexing system is used, each category is assigned an individual number. To illustrate, a separate category is provided for each salesperson in an organization. The records pertaining to the salespersons are filed by their individual numbers. Cross-referencing is crucial in the numerical system. In the example just used, the name of each salesperson and his or her number are recorded on 3- by 5-inch index cards. Because the cards are filed alphabetically, the cross-reference index is used to determine the categorical number under which a particular individual's records are filed. Although time is consumed when having to use the cross-reference index, the system is useful when the secrecy and confidentiality of records must be maintained.

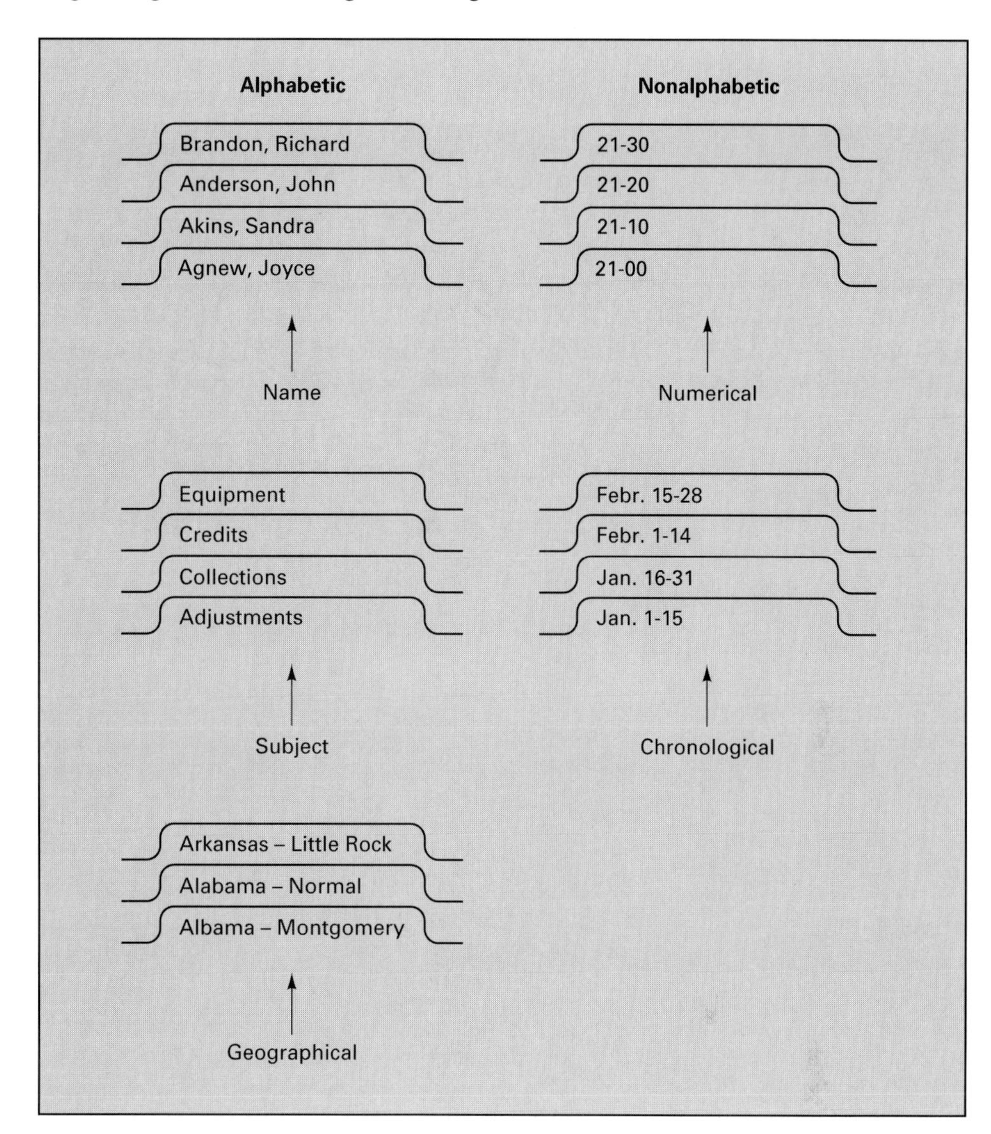

Figure 21-2 Alphabetical and nonalphabetical indexing systems.

With the chronological indexing system, records are filed by a significant date. In some cases, this indexing system is used to follow up situations that require attention by a specific date. In other cases, the system is used for filing such records as daily reports and sales summaries. When the chronological indexing system is used, the record being filed is placed in front of all others in the file folder; thus, the file is arranged with the most recent record on top of the accumulation and the least recent record on the bottom.

Personnel

What types of positions are found in records management programs?

The personnel needs of the records management program are greatly influenced by two factors: the type of program structure used and the size of the organization. Centralized storage uses personnel who work with records on a full-time basis; in decentralized storage, personnel may work with records on a part-time basis. When converting from decentralized storage to centralized storage, some organizations find that more personnel are needed to staff the records management program. Over the long run, the expertise and specialization provided by full-time personnel will most likely offset the increased labor costs.

In small organizations that use centralized control and storage, overall responsibility for the records management program frequently rests with the administrative office manager. All day-to-day operations are likely performed by one employee, usually a file clerk. As organizations increase in size, greater specialization takes place. Responsibility for the program still rests with the administrative office manager, with a file supervisor likely managing the day-to-day operations of the center. The support staff is comprised of file clerks, requisition clerks, and messengers.

The file clerks are responsible for filing and retrieving records. The requisition clerks approve requests after determining whether the requests are valid and whether the individuals making the request have proper authorization to view the requested record. The requisition clerks are also responsible for the follow-up of materials not returned by the due date. Messengers deliver requested records and return records to be refiled.

In extremely large organizations, a records manager—rather than the administrative office manager—assumes responsibility for the management of records. The mechanical aspects of the program are carried out by the support staff.

A growing number of individuals who work with records management are earning the designation of a Certified Records Manager (CRM), a program sponsored by the Institute of Certified Records Managers. Certification requires the passage of a five-part test covering (1) records management principles and program organization; (2) records generation and control; (3) active records retrieval systems, and equipment; (4) records disposition/protection; and (5) technology of records management. In addition, the candidate must have a minimum of three years' full-time or equivalent professional experience in records management; a baccalaureate degree (or an equivalent substitution); and a recommendation from a Certified Records Manager.

Records Retention

What does records retention specify?

Records retention, another important component of the records management program uses retention schedules to specify the length of time that records and documents must be retained by an organization.

Benefits A systematic records retention program is beneficial in several ways:

1. Considerable cost and space savings result from transferring inactive records to low-cost storage areas and from ultimately destroying records no longer useful to the organization.
2. Retrieval of records is simplified because fewer active status records are stored.
3. Systematic destruction of records prevents their being destroyed prematurely.
4. Equipment for storing records—both active status and inactive status—is more efficiently used.

Why is a records inventory conducted?

Conducting the records inventory Prior to developing a records retention schedule, an important task involves determining the nature and volume of all records created. This is the major reason for conducting the **records inventory**. To conduct the inventory by sorting through files, record by

Name or Title of Record	Form Identification No. (if Used)	Type of Copy (Original, Carbon Copy, etc.)	Location	Number of Location of Carbon Copies (if in Existence)	Indexing Method	Volume (in Linear Feet)	Inclusive Dates of Records	Frequency of Use and by Whom

Figure 21-3 Records inventory form.

record, would result in considerable time consumption and effort. An overall view of what has been created and filed is usually sufficient. To facilitate the process, a records inventory form similar to the one illustrated in Figure 21-3 is useful.

If the records are stored decentrally, cooperation of each department head is essential; otherwise, the inventory is likely to be somewhat inaccurate. Often a liaison person is appointed within each department to assist the personnel conducting the inventory.

Classifying the records Upon completing the records inventory, the next step in the development of a comprehensive records management program involves classifying records according to their value or worth to the organization. A widely used classification scheme, which was developed by the National Fire Protection Association[1], uses the following two categories to classify records: vital and important.

How do vital records differ from important records?

Vital records are considered to be irreplaceable. A reproduction of vital records does not have the same value as their originals. Vital records are needed for the continued existence of the organization.

Important records are those for which a reproduction is obtainable, often with considerable expense and labor or delay.

Scheduling retention periods The records retention schedule, which is frequently used in a records management program, specifies the length of time each record is to be kept prior to its destruction. It does not designate when records should be transferred from active status to inactive status. Therefore, if the retention schedule indicates that a certain record has a life of

[1]Reprinted with permission from NFPA 232-1980, Standard for the Protection of Records, Copyright © 1980, National Fire Protection Association, Quincy, Massachusetts 02269. This reprinted material is not the complete and official position of the NFPA on the referenced subject, which is represented only by the standard in its entirety.

three years, the record will be eligible for destruction after that length of time has passed.

The development of the records retention schedule involves several well-defined steps:

What steps are involved in developing a records retention schedule?

1. Getting authorization to develop the schedule.
2. Conducting a records inventory to determine the kinds, volume, and location of records.
3. Developing a records classification scheme to determine the value of each kind of record.
4. Developing a tentative retention schedule.
5. Securing top management's approval of the schedule.
6. Distributing the approved schedule to appropriate individuals.

Generally, a committee is appointed to develop the schedule. In smaller organizations, a representative from each work unit might be appointed to serve on the committee. In larger organizations in which the appointment of a representative from each work unit would be too cumbersome, an individual may represent several work units.

In addition to relying on the judgment of the committee members to develop the records retention schedule, several other factors should be considered. Because some records have a legal life of a specified length, the statute of limitations should be considered. Statutes, which vary from state to state, specify the legal life of certain records. *The Guide to Records Retention Requirements*, published annually by the U. S. Government Printing Office, lists retention periods required by departments of the federal government. The legal life of other records is specified by federal legislative acts—the Walsh-Healey and Fair Labor Standards Acts, for example.

After the tentative records retention schedule has been developed but before it receives final approval, the organization's tax specialist, attorney, and chief financial officer should closely scrutinize the schedule. The insight of these individuals is helpful. In some instances, one or more of these specialists is appointed to serve on the committee that develops the records retention schedule.

As with all programs and policies, the records retention schedule should be reviewed periodically to determine if revision is necessary. As additional legislation is passed and as the use and quantity of records change, the schedule may need to be updated.

An example of a records retention schedule is presented in Figure 21-4.

Storage and Retrieval of Records

Another factor that affects the success of the records management program is the equipment used for storing records. When acquiring storage equipment, every attempt should be made to secure equipment that will be satisfactory for its intended use.

Standardization of storage equipment, a characteristic of centrally controlled programs, helps ensure similarity of equipment size, durability, capacity, and design features. Of particular significance for storing vital and important records is the maximum temperature the equipment is able to withstand.

What factors should be considered in deciding what type of storage equipment to use?

Various criteria should be considered before deciding upon a particular kind of storage equipment, including the following:

1. The nature of the records being stored, including size, quantity, weight, physical composition, and value.

Record Retention Timetable

LEGEND FOR AUTHORITY TO DISPOSE

- AD – Administrative Decision
- ASPR – Armed Services Procurement Regulation
- CFR – Code of Federal Regulations
- FLSA – Fair Labor Standards Act
- ICC – Interstate Commerce Commission
- INS – Insurance Company Regulation
- ISM – Industrial Security Manual, Attachment to DD Form 441

LEGEND FOR RETENTION PERIOD

- AC – Dispose After Completion of Job or Contract
- AE – Dispose After Expiration
- AF – After End of Fiscal Year
- AM – After Moving
- AS – After Settlement
- AT – Dispose After Termination
- ATR – After Trip
- OBS – Dispose When Obsolete
- P – Permanent
- SUP – Dispose When Superseded

*After Disposed ** Normally † Govt R&D Contracts

TYPE OF RECORD	RETENTION PERIOD (YEARS)	AUTHORITY
ACCOUNTING & FISCAL		
Accounts Payable Invoices	3	ASPR-STATE, FLSA
Accounts Payable Ledger	P	AD
Accounts Receivable Invoices & Ledgers	5	AD
Authorizations for Accounting	SUP	AD
Balance Sheets	P	AD
Bank Deposits	3	AD
Bank Statements	3	AD
Bonds	P	AD
Budgets	3	AD
Capital Asset Record	3*	AD
Cash Receipt Records	7	AD
Check Register	P	AD
Checks, Dividend	6	
Checks, Payroll	2	FLSA,STATE
Checks, Voucher	3	FLSA,STATE
Cost Accounting Records	5	AD
Earnings Register	3	FLSA,STATE
Entertainment Gifts & Gratuities	3	AD
Estimates, Projections	7	AD
Expense Reports	3	AD
Financial Statements, Certified	P	AD
Financial Statements, Periodic	2	AD
General Ledger Records	P	CFR
Labor Cost Records	3	ASPR, CFR
Magnetic Tape and Tab Cards	1**	
Note Register	P	AD
Payroll Registers	3	FLSA,STATE
Petty Cash Records	3	AD
P & L Statements	P	AD
Salesman Commission Reports	3	AD
Travel Expense Reports	3	AD
Work Papers, Rough	2	AD
ADMINISTRATIVE RECORDS		
Audit Reports	10	AD
Audit Work Papers	3	AD
Classified Documents: Inventories, Reports, Receipts	10	AD
Correspondence, Executive	P	AD
Correspondence, General	5	AD
Directives from Officers	P	AD
Forms Used, File Copies	P	AD
Systems and Procedures Records	P	AD
Work Papers, Management Projects	P	AD

Figure 21-4 Records retention schedule. Courtesy: Electric Wastebasket Corporation, New York, NY 10036.

TYPE OF RECORD	RETENTION PERIOD (YEARS)	AUTHORITY
COMMUNICATIONS		
Bulletins Explaining Communications	P	AD
Messenger Records	1	AD
Phone Directories	SUP	AD
Phone Installation Records	1	AD
Postage Reports, Stamp Requisitions	1AF	AD
Postal Records, Registered Mail & Insured Mail Logs & Meter Records	1AF	AD, CFR
Telecommunications Copies	1	AD
CONTRACT ADMINISTRATION		
Contracts, Negotiated Bailments, Changes, Specifications, Procedures, Correspondence	P	CFR
Customer Reports	P	AD
Materials Relating to Distribution Revisions, Forms, and Format of Reports	P	AD
Work Papers	OBS	AD
CORPORATE		
Annual Reports	P	AD
Authority to Issue Securities	P	AD
Bonds, Surety	3AE	AD
Capital Stock Ledger	P	AD
Charters, Constitutions, Bylaws	P	AD
Contracts	20AT	AD
Corporate Election Records	P	AD
Incorporation Records	P	AD
Licenses - Federal, State, Local	AT	AD
Stock Transfer & Stockholder	P	AD
LEGAL		
Claims and Litigation Concerning Torts and Breach of Contracts	P	AD
Law Records - Federal, State, Local	SUP	AD
Patents and Related Material	P	AD
Trademark & Copyrights	P	AD
LIBRARY, COMPANY		
Accession Lists	P	AD
Copies of Requests for Materials	6 mos.	AD
Meeting Calendars	P	AD
Research Papers, Abstracts, Bibliographies	SUP, 6 mos. AC	AD
MANUFACTURING		
Bills of Material	2	AD, ASPR
Drafting Records	P	AD †
Drawings	2	AD, ASPR
Inspection Records	2	AD
Lab Test Reports	P	AD
Memos, Production	AC	AD
Product, Tooling, Design, Engineering Research, Experiment & Specs Records	20	STATUE LIMITATIONS
Production Reports	3	AD
Quality Reports	1AC	AD
Reliability Reports	P	AD
Stock Issuing Records	3AT	AD, ASPR
Tool Control	3AT	AD, ASPR
Work Orders	3	AD
Work Status Reports	AC	AD

Figure 21-4 *continued*

TYPE OF RECORD	RETENTION PERIOD (YEARS)	AUTHORITY
OFFICE SUPPLIES & SERVICES		
Inventories	1AF	AD
Office Equipment Records	6AF	AD
Requests for : Services	1AF	AD
Requisitions for Supplies	1AF	AD
PERSONNEL		
Accident Reports, Injury Claims, Settlements	30AS	CFR, INS, STATE
Applications, Changes & Terminations	5	AD, ASPR, CFR
Attendance Records	7	AD
Employee Activity Files	2 or SUP	AD
Employee Contracts	6AT	AD
Fidelity Bonds	3AT	AD
Garnishments	5	AD
Health & Safety Bulletins	P	CFR
Injury Frequency Charts	P	AD
Insurance Records, Employees	11AT	INS
Job Descriptions	2 or SUP	CFR
Rating Cards	2 or SUP	CFR
Time Cards	3	AD
Training Manuals	P	AD
Union Agreements	3	WALSH-HEALEY ACT
PLANT & PROPERTY RECORDS		
Depreciation Schedules	P	AD
Inventory Records	P	AD
Maintenance & Repair, Building	10	AD
Maintenance & Repair, Machinery	5	CFR, AD
Plant Account Cards, Equipment	P	AD
Property Deeds	P	AD
Purchase or Lease Records of Plant Facility	P	AD
Space Allocation Records	1AT	AD
PRINTING & DUPLICATING		
Copies Produced, Tech. Pubs., Charts	1 or OBS	AD
Film Reports	5	AD
Negatives	5	AD
Photographs	1	AD
Production Records	1AC	AD
PROCUREMENT, PURCHASING		
Acknowledgments	AC	AD
Bids, Awards	3AT	CFR
Contracts	3AT	AD
Exception Notices (GAD)	6	AD
Price Lists	OBS	AD
Purchase Orders, Requisitions	3AT	CFR
Quotations	1	AD
PRODUCTS, SERVICES, MARKETING		
Correspondence	3	AD
Credit Ratings & Classifications	7	AD
Development Studies	P	AD
Presentations & Proposals	P	AD
Price Lists, Catalogs	OBS	AD
Prospect Lines	OBS	AD
Register of Sales Order	NO VALUE	AD
Surveys	P	AD
Work Papers, Pertaining to Projects	NO VALUE	AD

Figure 21-4 *continued*

TYPE OF RECORD	RETENTION PERIOD (YEARS)	AUTHORITY
PUBLIC RELATIONS & ADVERTISING		
Advertising Activity Reports	5	AD
Community Affairs Records	P	AD
Contracts for Advertising	3AT	AD
Employee Activities & Presentations	P	AD
Exhibits, Releases, Handouts	2 - 4	AD
Internal Publications	P (1 copy)	AD
Layouts	1	AD
Manuscripts	1	AD
Photos	1	AD
Public Information Activity	7	AD
Research Presentations	P	AD
Tear-Sheets	2	AD
SECURITY		
Classified Material Violations	P	AD
Courier Authorizations	1 mo. ATR	AD
Employee Clearance Lists	SUP	ISM
Employee Case Files	5	ISM
Fire Prevention Program	P	AD
Protection - Guards, Badge Lists, Protective Devices	5	AD
Subcontractor Clearances	2AT	AD
Visitor Clearance	2	ISM
TAXATION		
Annuity or Deferred Payment Plan	P	CFR
Depreciation Schedules	P	CFR
Dividend Register	P	CFR
Employee Withholding	4	CFR
Excise Exemption Certificates	4	CFR
Excise Reports (Manufacturing)	4	CFR
Excise Reports (Retail)	4	CFR
Inventory Reports	P	CFR
Tax Bills and Statements	P	AD
Tax Returns	P	AD
TRAFFIC & TRANSPORTATION		
Aircraft Operating & Maintenance	P	CFR
Bills of Lading, Waybills	2	ICC, FLSA
Employee Travel	1AF	AD
Freight Bills	3	ICC
Freight Claims	2	ICC
Household Moves	3AM	AD
Motor Operating & Maintenance	2	AD
Rates and Tariffs	SUP	AD
Receiving Documents	2 - 10	AD, CFR
Shipping & Related Documents	2 - 10	AD, CFR

Figure 21-4 *continued*

2. The frequency with which records are retrieved.
3. The length of time that records are stored in both active and inactive status.
4. The location of storage facilities (centralized and decentralized).
5. The amount of space allocated for storage and the possibilities for expansion.

6. The type and location of storage facilities for inactive records.
7. The layout of the organization.
8. The degree to which stored records should be protected.

What categories of storage equipment are used in records management programs?

Types of storage equipment Equipment designed for mass storage of records is categorized as vertical, lateral, and power. Each category consists of a variety of different types of equipment.

Vertical equipment is the type most commonly used in records management programs. Of the various types of vertical equipment, standard four-, five-, and six-drawer file cabinets continue to be the most widely used. These cabinets use approximately 2.5 square feet of floor space, and a like amount of additional space must be allowed for opening drawers. A distinct advantage of the standard file cabinet is the ease with which it may be moved with its contents intact. However, in time, the space-wasting feature of the drawered cabinets will likely make them obsolete for storage of large accumulations of records.

Another type of vertical equipment often used in records management programs is the **open-shelf file**. Although it maximizes the use of space (the files frequently extend from floor to ceiling) and improves storage efficiency, this equipment is recommended only for records that are filed and removed with the folders intact. This type of equipment is not well suited for situations where individual documents are frequently removed from folders. Open shelf filing is illustrated in Figure 21-5.

Several types of **vertical rotary files** have also been developed. In a comparable amount of floor space, this type of equipment holds considerably more records than the standard file. Because of the rotary feature, retrieval is fast and convenient. Figure 21-6 illustrates vertical rotary filing.

Vertical equipment is most often used for storing inactive records in low-cost storage areas. Records are frequently stored in cardboard containers on steel shelves that extend from floor to ceiling. The containers are often the same ones used to transfer records from high-cost storage areas to low-cost storage areas.

Figure 21-5 Open shelf filing. Courtesy: Aurora Steel Products, Inc.

Figure 21-6 Rotary filing equipment. Courtesy: Acme Visible Records, Inc., Crozet, VA.

How does lateral equipment differ from vertical equipment?

Although vertical in structure, **lateral equipment** uses lateral pull-out drawers that require considerably less space than standard file cabinets. Storing records in drawers rather than on open shelves may expedite retrieval. Because lateral equipment can be insulated and equipped with doors that lock, some consider lateral equipment to have distinct advantages over open-shelf files. Figure 21-7 illustrates lateral filing equipment.

Power filing equipment, although not necessarily new, is now being used with greater frequency. Comparatively, the initial investment is considerably higher with power filing equipment than with other types of storage equipment. Some types of power equipment reduce the number of personnel needed in the records management function, and the resulting savings from labor costs can be used to offset the cost of the equipment.

The following questions should be assessed when evaluating the suitability of power equipment:

Figure 21-7 Lateral filing equipment. Courtesy: TAB Products Co.

1. Structurally, will the floor withstand the weight of the equipment?
2. Because the installation of this type of equipment is permanent, have future storage space needs received adequate attention?
3. What effect will power outages have on the system; for example, can the system be operated manually, although perhaps not conveniently?
4. Do the equipment and physical environment provide adequate protection and security for the stored records?
5. In the event of equipment malfunction, are service representatives located nearby?

Three types of power equipment are available: (1) rotary power files designed to accommodate a particular size card or form; (2) structural files designed to accommodate all kinds of forms and records; and (3) mobile files. **Rotary power files** are frequently used by organizations for storing information about customers or clients and patient records in hospitals or doctors' offices, for example. Power is used to rotate the mechanism until the desired file bin is accessible; the file clerk then retrieves the requested record. Figure 21-8 illustrates a rotary power file.

Structural power files are typically used to store all types of records—not just one type as is characteristic of rotary power files. Some of the newer heavy-duty files are equipped with an electronic eye. At the push of a button, the transport mechanism scans and locates the desired storage container. A retrieval mechanism then moves the storage container to the console operator, who removes the requested record. Structural power files are often custom designed to meet the special needs of a particular records management program. A structural power file is illustrated in Figure 21-9.

How does one retrieve a document from a mobile file?

For classification purposes, **mobile filing equipment** is classified as a power unit, even though some units are operated manually. Because mobile files eliminate the need for aisle space, they are especially useful where storage space is limited. Shelves are stored back to back against one another. A rail system facilitates the forward or backward movement of shelf units, which creates aisle space between two units. Aisle space has to be created between the shelf on which the desired record is stored and the adjacent shelf.

Figure 21-8 Rotary power files and computer interface. Courtesy: White Office Systems.

Figure 21-9 Structural power file. Courtesy: Supreme Equipment and Systems Corporation.

Only one aisle can exist within the unit at any time, which makes the remainder of the shelves in the unit nonaccessible. Figure 21-10 illustrates a mobile filing system.

Records Retrieval

Records retrieval, which refers to the activities involved in locating and removing tangible records from the files, involves the following steps: (1) the individual who desires a record fills out a request slip, which is transported to the central storage facility (as organizations install e-mail systems, the request more than likely will be sent as an e-mail message), (2) the requisition clerk approves the request and asks the file clerk to retrieve the record, (3) the record is transported either by messenger or by a mechanical device to the individual making the request, and (4) the record is returned to the central storage area when no longer needed. The procedures for manual retrieval are similar for both power and nonpower equipment.

Figure 21-10 Mobile filing system. Courtesy: TAB Products Co.

What is the primary function of charge-out systems?

Many organizations are now using a **computerized records retrieval** and **charge-out system**. The computerized system, which is often powered by a microcomputer, is used to keep an inventory of all checked-out records. The inventory lists the name of the person who checked out the record, the date the record was checked out, the due date, and the names of others who have asked to check out the record upon its return. Before the requisition clerk submits the request to the file clerk, the terminal is used to determine the availability of the record.

These computerized systems can also be used to perform such other tasks as maintaining the records retention schedule, maintaining the transfer schedule, and providing use-analysis statistics.

Disposition of Records

What types of records disposition exist?

Disposition refers to the ultimate fate of records. For example, some records are permanently stored. Some are transferred to low-cost storage areas where they may be permanently stored or eventually destroyed. And some are microrecorded while others are immediately destroyed. The four major methods of records disposition are protection, **transfer**, microrecording, and destruction.

Protection The value attached to vital records is a basic factor in determining the type of protection these records are to receive. Most vital records are protected by storing them in fire-resistant safes and vaults. If this protection is inadequate or unavailable, vital records can be duplicated and the copies stored in secure off-site locations.

Transfer Transfer refers to changing the status of records from active to inactive. In many instances, as soon as the status of records has changed, they are transferred from high-cost to low-cost storage areas.

A basic factor used to determine when records should be transferred is their frequency of use. For example, records that are used at least three times a month should be considered active. If a record is referred to twice a month, it is still considered active but should probably be stored in the less accessible areas of the storage center (for example, in the lower drawers of file cabinets). Records that are referred to not more than once a month are often considered inactive and are, therefore, transferred to low-cost storage areas. In all probability, most of the records found in active status will not be more than two years old.

How do perpetual and periodic transfer differ from one another?

The two most common methods of records transfer are *perpetual* and *periodic*. When the perpetual method is used, records are continuously transferred to low-cost storage areas. The records are constantly examined; and when their age or frequency of use renders them inactive, they are transferred.

When periodic transfer is used, the files are examined at frequent intervals (perhaps every four months), and the inactive materials are transferred. An adaptation of the periodic transfer method is the *duplicate equipment technique* that requires a double set of files and equipment. The current year's records are stored in one set of file cabinets. The previous year's records are filed in the other set of cabinets, which are located beside the current year's files. After a year has passed, transfer takes place. The current year's records (now a year old) become the previous year's records. The previous year's records (now two years old) are transferred to low-cost storage or destroyed, and the now-empty cabinets are used for the filing of the current year's records.

Microrecording Microrecording, a means of records disposition, is used primarily for two reasons: (1) It can significantly reduce the amount of space needed to store records, and (2) it is a means of making duplicate copies of those records sufficiently important to justify keeping duplicate copies.

Destruction When records have been maintained for the length of time stipulated by the records retention schedule, their suitability for destruction should be evaluated. Several destruction methods are available. In warmer climates, the heating requirements of some buildings can be partially or wholly provided by incinerating records. Other organizations shred records and sell the paper for packing and other industrial purposes.

In what ways are records destroyed?

For ecological reasons, many organizations use paper recycling to dispose of records. By 2000, the U. S. paper industry hopes to recover and reuse more than 50 percent of the nation's waste paper. This goal responds to an Environmental Protection Agency guideline that states that printing and writing grades of paper must contain at least 50 percent recycled waste paper. Technology is now available that enables recycled paper to be of sufficient quality that it can be used for good-quality letterhead paper.

When records are destroyed, a certificate of destruction is usually prepared that identifies the date on which the document was destroyed. Special procedures may have to be used when destroying confidential materials.

Evaluating the Records Management Program

Records management programs should be periodically evaluated, especially those that have been implemented recently. The longer a program exists, the less frequently it may need to be evaluated. A new program is typically evaluated six or nine months after implementation.

What information do finding and use ratios provide?

The **finding** and **use ratios** are frequently used to evaluate the condition of the files in which records are stored. The finding ratio is used to determine how many requested records are actually found and is calculated with the following formula:

$$\text{Finding ratio} = 100 - \frac{\text{Number of records not found}}{\text{Number of records found}}$$

Thus, if 200 requested records were found and 2 were not, the finding ratio of 99 percent would result. The suitable range for the finding ratio is 97 percent or higher. Ratios less than 97 percent indicate that one or more of the following conditions may exist: (1) Records are misfiled, (2) records are not properly indexed or coded, (3) records are not promptly returned for refiling, and (4) the whereabouts of records are not known because of improper charge-out procedures.

The use ratio is helpful in assessing the frequency of record use as well as determining if too many unused records are filed and is calculated by using the following formula:

$$\text{Use ratio} = \frac{\text{Number of records used}}{\text{Number of records not used}}$$

A ratio of 20 percent or higher is generally considered satisfactory. The following situations may be responsible for a low use ratio: (1) Too many records are being maintained in active status when they should be transferred to inactive status, and (2) individuals are using duplicate records rather than requesting records from the central storage area.

Using **performance standards** is another means of evaluating the effectiveness of the records management program. Comparing employees' perfor-

Task	*Units per Hour*
Type 3 × 5 inch cards, labels, or tags	100
Code one-page letters	200
Sort 3 × 5 inch cards	300
Sort indexed or coded correspondence	250
File 3 × 5 inch cards	180
File correspondence	250
File vouchers numerically	700
Retrieve 3 × 5 inch cards	180
Retrieve correspondence and prepare charge-out forms	70

Source: Wilmer O. Maedke, Mary F. Robek, and Gerald F. Brown, *Information and Records Management*, 2nd ed. (Encino, CA: Glencoe Publishing Co., 1981), p. 165. Reprinted with permission.

Figure 21-11 Filing standards.

mance against reliable standards provides information about the efficiency of employees in their carrying out various mechanical aspects of the program. Comparison reveals whether or not the employees are performing at an acceptable rate or at an above-average rate. Training in appropriate areas may be desirable for those whose performance is unacceptable.

Figure 21-11 illustrates performance standards for filing and other related activities. These standards were developed under certain conditions; and unless the organization is able to duplicate these conditions, adjustments may need to be made.

Comparing the operating costs of the records management program with standard operating costs is another way to evaluate its effectiveness. Acceptable costs vary among organizations and between geographical areas, but the following guidelines are typical:

Salaries: 75–80 percent

Equipment and supplies: 15–20 percent

Space: 5–10 percent

THE RECORDS MANAGEMENT MANUAL

The **records management manual** is a vital document in the records management program. After the manual has been prepared, it should be approved and then updated periodically as program changes are made. The manual should also be available to each employee who works with the management of records.

Appropriate content sections of the manual are the following:

What content sections are often found in records management manuals?

1. Objectives of the records management program.
2. Statement of policy of the program.
3. Organizational structure of the program.
4. Filing systems used in the program and the types of records filed under each system.
5. Personnel structure of the program.
6. Records retention schedule.
7. Procedures for retrieving records and information.
8. Disposition of records, including protection, transfer, microrecording, and destruction.

9. Procedures for evaluating the program.
10. Document management. (if used)
11. Micrographics usage. (if used)
12. Image processing. (if used)

DOCUMENT MANAGEMENT

What is a common component of document management systems?

Because of the ever-increasing number of records stored in organizations, the need exists to develop efficient ways to manage those documents. As a result, document-management software was developed to aid the process of properly managing an organization's records accumulation. A common component of these management systems is the bar-code labeling of the documents stored within the system, even if the document will be stored as a microform or digitally. As paper records are created and moved into storage, a bar-code label is placed on each record or on the file folder label.

Once the records are bar coded, tracing their movement in and out of the document depository involves scanning the label and keying in either the destination or the recipient's code. If the document or folder is passed from its original recipient to another person before it is returned to the records depository, placing scanners in offices is useful for tracking the movement of the document or folder should follow-up become necessary.

An integral part of document management is the indexing of documents and/or key words within the documents. When employees might find certain documents helpful and if the documents are digitized and stored electronically, a key word search can be undertaken that identifies all the documents within the organization that contain the key word(s). At that time, each of the documents stored in hard-copy format can be retrieved and checked out by scanning the bar code labels attached to the documents or file folders. For paper documents that have been digitized (by scanning), they can be retrieved and displayed on the monitor of a desktop computer. Documents/records created on a microcomputer (word processing, spreadsheets, databases, e-mail messages, and so forth) can bypass the scanning process if they are archived on a magnetic medium or optical disk.

The goal in document management systems is to make them "seamless," regardless of the various types of media used for document storage. Therefore, the procedures would be identical when retrieving records stored in paper form, as a microimage, or on a magnetic or optical medium.

Because new developments are occurring at a rapid pace in document management systems, a careful study of their capabilities and the organization's needs is critical before a purchasing decision is made. Failure to study the situation carefully and thoroughly will likely result in the purchase of a system that provides less than optimum results.

MICROGRAPHICS

Micrographics, a system used to increase the efficiency of a records management program, is used extensively in many organizations. Among the most desirable aspects of using micrographics is the significant amount of space saved when storing documents in microimage format. The contents of one hundred file drawers can be reduced to two drawers when storing contents in microimage format, which results in a 98 percent reduction in the amount of document storage space.

Today, in many organizations, as some records are microrecorded, they are simultaneously scanned using a high-speed image input device. This process digitizes their contents for storage on a magnetic medium or on an optical disk. Once the document has been digitized, it can be used as any other stored information is used. Under these circumstances, the digitized copy of the document likely is the one employees use, while the microrecord is used as a backup and for permanent storage. Once a digitized record is no longer considered to be active or has reached an age when it should be purged from electronic storage, the microrecord provides permanent storage.

Determining the Feasibility of a Micrographics System

How is the feasibility of micrographics usage determined?

Before an organization makes a decision about installing a micrographics system, its feasibility first has to be determined by assessing technical, financial, and efficiency factors.

Technically, microrecording certain documents may not be feasible because of limitations imposed by such factors as document size, physical condition, or readability. Although microrecording certain documents may be feasible in other respects, the inability to overcome certain technical constraints may prohibit their being microrecorded.

To assess the financial feasibility of micrographics, the cost of storing records in hard-copy format is compared with the cost of preparing and storing microimages. Included are equipment costs, materials costs, and labor costs. The financial feasibility of micrographics will also be affected by the break-even point. The point at which greater economy can be achieved by storing a document in microimage format rather than hard-copy format will need to be determined. If the break-even point arrives after a document is eligible for destruction, then converting the document to microimage format is generally not financially feasible.

To determine the efficiency of a micrographics system, the convenience of using micrographics is assessed. Of special concern are the ease and speed with which desired microimages are retrieved and the convenience of magnifying the images, thus making them readable. Some types of equipment streamline the retrieval process, which reduces the amount of manual retrieval effort.

Microimage Formats

What types of microimage formats are available?

Another important decision that will have to be made when installing a micrographics program is which **microimage format** to use. Figure 21-12 illustrates the major types of microimages used today: roll film, aperture cards, jacketed film, microfiche, and **film strips**.

Roll film Of the various types of microimage formats, **roll film** continues to be the most widely used format as well as the most economical. The film may be stored on a reel or in a cassette, cartridge, or magazine.

Crucial to the success of a roll-film system is the indexing procedure used in retrieving the desired image. One of the more sophisticated systems is Miracode, a system developed by Eastman Kodak Company. A binary code index notation is made adjacent to each frame on the filmstrip. To find a specific frame, the film is inserted into a reader, and a keyboard is used to enter the binary code index of the desired frame into the machine. In a matter of seconds, the desired frame is mechanically retrieved and displayed on the screen of the reader.

Another means of indexing microimages involves the use of flash targets, which are suitable for use on reel or cartridge microfilm. The film is divided into segments of twenty feet, and each twenty-foot length is numbered consecutively, beginning with the number 1. When retrieving a microimage, the segment number is used to find the general location of the microimage,

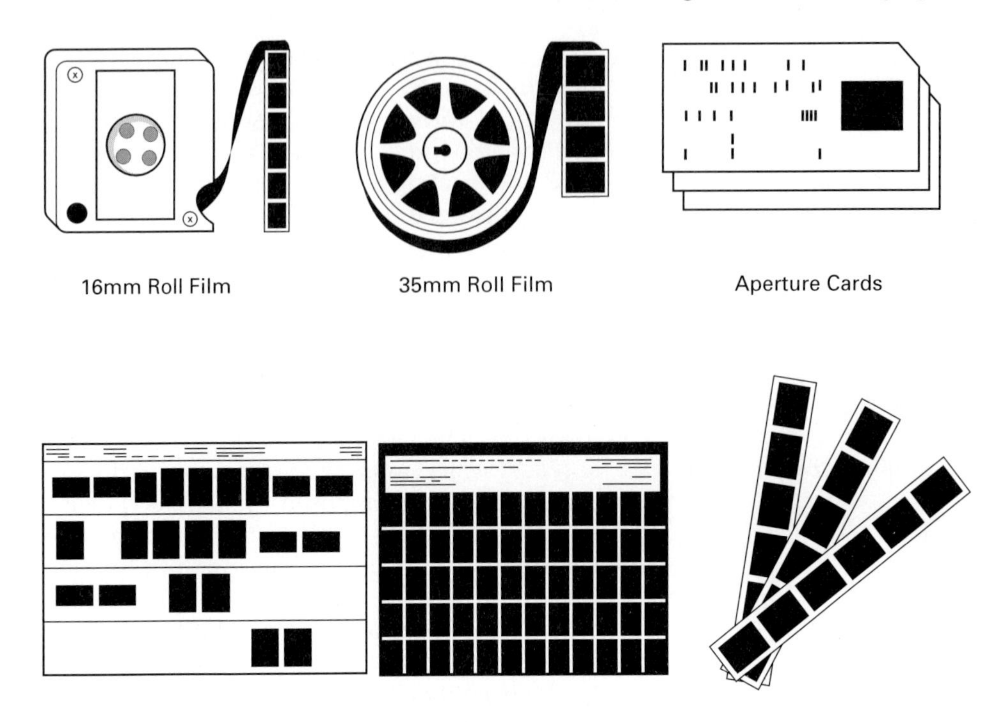

Figure 21-12 Types of microimages. Courtesy: Infosystems Magazine, Hitchcock Publishing Company.

and manual screening is used to find the specific image. The Miracode system locates an image faster than the flash target system.

What are the characteristics of aperture cards?

Aperture cards Although **aperture cards** are generally used to store one image, several images can be affixed on a card. The image is mounted in the hole on the card, and identifying data can be keypunched into the card. The keypunched holes are "read" by the card sorter, thus facilitating the mechanical retrieval of the desired card.

Jacketed film A jacket consists of two thin pieces of clear plastic into which strips of microfilm can be inserted. The jacket, which typically has four channels, holds the strips in place. **Jacketed film** is especially useful for the temporary storage of microimages. Strips can be easily removed from the jacket, which makes it reusable. If a permanent, tamperproof image is desired, a microfiche copy of the jacket can be prepared. Jackets are not suitable for mechanical retrieval.

Microfiche As many as several hundred images can be stored on a **microfiche**, which is a piece of film commonly measuring 4 inches by 6 inches. If a reduction ratio of 24 to 1 is used, 98 images of hard copy, each measuring 8 1/2 inches by 11 inches, can be recorded on one microfiche. But if a reduction ratio of 42 to 1 is being used, 325 pages of material can be recorded on one microfiche of the same size.

Typically, microfiche are indexed by displaying the contents of the fiche in one of the frames, most likely the one in the lower right corner. While letters of the alphabet are used to identify rows, numbers are used to identify columns. To display the contents in frame B-10, the grid coordinate mechanism on the reader is set at B-10.

Other Features of Micrographics Systems

Micrographics systems may use several other features, including computer-assisted retrieval (CAR) and computer output microfilm (COM).

For what is CAR used?

Computer-assisted retrieval The efficiency of a micrographics system is greatly affected by its retrieval process. Generally, organizations that have extensive micrographics systems use computer-assisted retrieval (CAR). A computerized index of each document that is stored in microimage format is maintained.

To retrieve the microrecord, the title of the desired image is entered by terminal keyboard into the computer system. The computerized index is scanned to locate the reel number (or microfiche number) of the desired document; and this number is displayed on the terminal screen. The micrographics clerk then retrieves the appropriate reel (or microfiche) from the storage rack. The reel (or fiche) is inserted into the reader, and the appropriate frame is then located either manually or automatically by a system, such as by the Miracode system that was previously discussed.

An illustration of a CAR system is shown in Figure 21-13.

For what is COM used?

Computer output microfilm A COM system bypasses the paper printout process found in most computer systems. As the data are processed by the computer, the output results are displayed on an internal cathode ray tube. A special camera that produces either microfilm or microfiche is used to photograph each screen display of data/information. The **computer output microfilm (COM)** process prepares output twenty to twenty-five times faster than paper output is prepared on impact or laser printers.

The primary advantages of using COM are its origination and retrieval speed; the increased data availability because microimages are easily and inexpensively created; the decreased cost of data distribution; the reduction of storage space; and thc environmental consideration of not having to dispose of large amounts of paper.

Equipment Used in Micrographics Systems

The equipment used in micrographics is the most costly aspect of installing these systems. Needed equipment includes cameras, image processors, and readers (reader-printers).

Figure 21-13 Computer-assisted retrieval. Courtesy: Canon U.S.A., Inc.

Cameras Two basic types of cameras are used in the microrecording process—rotary and planetary cameras.

How do rotary and planetary cameras differ from one another?

A **rotary camera** automatically feeds documents through the machine. The camera operator places the document on the feed tray, and the document is microrecorded as it moves through the machine. Most rotary cameras have a 12-inch document width restriction.

A **planetary camera** is useful for microrecording large documents, such as engineering drawings and blueprints. The most significant difference between the planetary camera and the rotary camera is in document feeding. While documents are not automatically fed through the planetary camera, they are through the rotary camera. The operator places the document to be microrecorded on the camera's overhead flatbed, makes the exposure, and then removes the document. A document being microrecorded on a rotary camera continually moves through the camera; but on a planetary camera, the document is stationary during the microrecording process.

The **processor camera**, which is a variation of the planetary camera, is useful for microrecording large documents. The unique feature of this camera is its capability of automatically mounting an image in an aperture card. The entire process takes about 40 seconds, which makes this camera especially attractive when an immediate image is required.

New camera technology makes possible the updating of microfiche as well as the ability to obtain an instant image. The camera that possesses these two capabilities is known as a **record processor**. By means of an electrostatic image-fusing system, outdated images can be overprinted with such words as PAID or VOID. At any time, new images can be added to unused frames on the fiche. Two categories of records appear to be well suited for updating: certain personnel records and insurance records.

Figure 21-14 illustrates a micrographics camera.

What is the function of an image processor?

Image processors Most of the new image processors move the film through the following steps: developing, washing, fixing, washing, and drying. Perhaps the biggest difference between the various processors on the market today is the way in which the film is moved through the equipment. Some processors move the film through in a straight-line path while other processors move the film through in a serpentinelike path.

Readers The ultimate usability and acceptability of a micrographics system is often influenced by the image reader. Unless the users of the reader are easily and quickly able to obtain good quality displays of the image, they most likely will not be satisfied with the system.

The two broad categories of readers are **front-projection readers** and **rear-projection readers**. Within each category, a variety of readers are available to accommodate the various types of microimage formats.

Some readers are equipped with a printing device that enables the user to obtain a hard copy of an image. The user simply pushes the "print" button on the reader; and in a matter of seconds, a hard copy can be obtained. Figure 21-15 illustrates such a reader/printer.

What factors need to be considered to determine which documents to microrecord?

Factors to Consider in Determining Which Documents to Microrecord

After the decision has been made to install the micrographics system, decisions about which documents to microrecord will have to be made. Answering the following questions will be useful in making these decisions:

Figure 21-14 Micrographics camera. Courtesy: Eastman Kodak Company.

1. *How long is the record to be kept?* Generally, records must be kept for at least four years before microrecording is financially feasible. For each year longer than four years that records are retained, microrecording becomes increasingly desirable.
2. *Will the physical characteristics of certain records prevent their being microrecorded?* The quality of the microimage will be no better than the quality of the original. Dark colors sometimes do not photograph well when black-and-white film is used.
3. *Will the microimage be admissible as evidence in legal courts?* Increasingly, microimages are becoming admissible as court evidence; but before original copies are destroyed, appropriate laws should be checked.
4. *Does a sufficient volume of certain records exist to warrant their being microrecorded?* Generally, the greater the number of records, the more advantageous microrecording is apt to be.
5. *Considering the frequency of use, would the original record be more convenient to use than a microimage?* If efficient procedures are used, the original record and the microimage should be about equally convenient.

IMAGE PROCESSING

Why is image processing used?

The most significant new development in records management involves image processing, which eliminates much of the information that in the past has been stored on paper. Although paper continues to be the most common medium for storing information—at least in the near future—in the majority

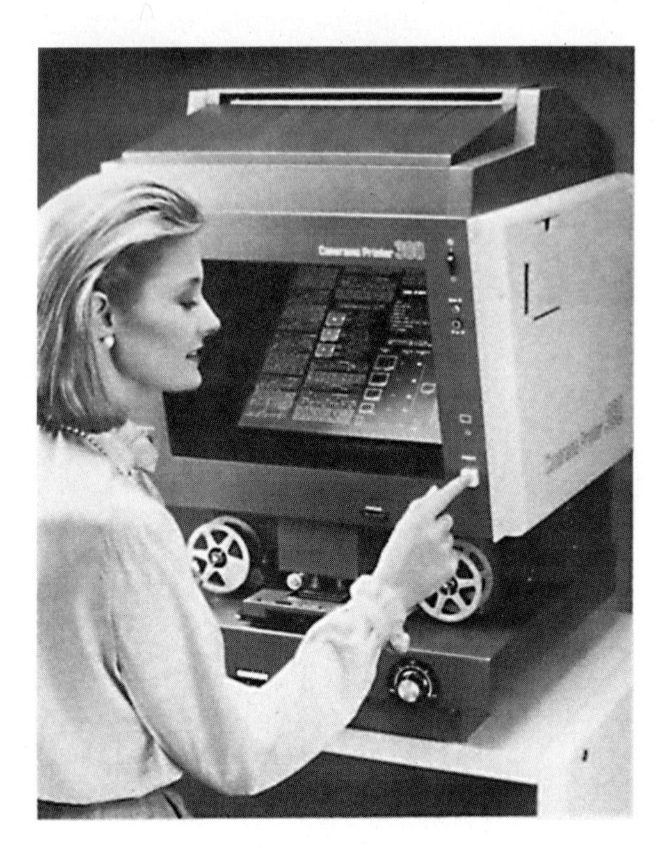

Figure 21-15 Micrographic reader-printer. Courtesy: Canon U.S.A., Inc.

of organizations, its use in the distant future will likely decrease at a rate comparable to the increase in the use of image processing.

Image processing involves the capture, storage, and retrieval of information in two different formats: electronically as digitized documents or as micrographic images. The emergence of new technology is stimulating interest in and growth of this critical area of records management. The new technology permits the simultaneous scanning and microrecording of images, thus making them available in the two formats (microimage and digitized). Other technology permits the digitizing of records previously stored as microimages. Once a record is digitized, it can be manipulated in the same way that any other computer-stored information can be manipulated. Furthermore, stored images subsequently can be moved through other electronic peripherals, such as fax devices and laser printers.

Storing documents in microimage format is more economical than storing them in digitized format. As a rule, converting records to digital form is about five times more costly than converting them to microimage format. However, the ease with which digitized records can be retrieved is the factor that causes many organizations to opt for the more costly digitized format. Depending on the way the digitized records are indexed, a key word search can be conducted that identifies all records in the data base that contain the key word. Thus, if the user wishes to retrieve all records involving "ABC Company," the company's name is entered into the system as a key word. Other documents by their specific file name can also be retrieved (letter to John Brown on December 12, 1995, for example). In this case, the following file name might be entered into the system: Brown, John/letter/12-12-95. The system will then retrieve the letter and display it on the user's desktop computer monitor.

On what type of medium are digitized records typically stored?

Digitized records are often stored on an optical medium, such as a disk, tape, or card. The digitizing process uses lasers to burn minute holes in the medium surface (representing the 1 and 0 of binary code). Of the three media, disks are the most common. Optical disks on which records are stored include (1) read only, (2) write once-read many (WORM), and (3) erasable disks that allow the erasing of data to facilitate the rewriting of new data. Most commonly used for document storage today are WORM disks.

Image processing offers a number of benefits, including the following: the dependablity of microimaging, the sophistication of optical-disk technology, the significant reduction in storage space required, and the lessened opportunity for misplacement of documents or loss of documents. Another advantage results from increased employee efficiency because fewer hours are required to maintain the stored information, and the employees who access the information from the data base enjoy almost instant access to stored information.

IMPLICATIONS FOR THE ADMINISTRATIVE OFFICE MANAGER

The nature of the administrative office manager's responsibility for records management varies from organization to organization. While some managers have day-to-day responsibilities, others have overall responsibility. In the latter situation, the records manager usually has responsibility for the daily activities of the program.

A basic understanding of records management is needed by managers and especially by those who have functional responsibility for the area. No longer can managers hold on to the mistaken notion that records management is solely a clerical task. Like so many other managerial responsibilities, the effectiveness of the records management program is directly related to the amount of attention it receives.

The two most significant challenges facing those who are responsible for records management are electronic filing and micrographics. Both of these areas, because of new developments, are technically oriented and are experiencing significant changes. Managers who have extensive records management responsibilities need to keep abreast of these developments.

The information created and stored within an organization is often considered to be its lifeline. If that information is not effectively managed, organizational success can be hampered.

REVIEW QUESTIONS

1. Review the differences between records management and filing.
2. What is meant by records disposition?
3. In deciding whether the storage of records should be centralized or decentralized, what factors should be considered?
4. What kinds of filing systems are available for use in a records management program?
5. What kinds of employees are likely to be used in a centralized storage facility?
6. Explain the perpetual, periodic, and duplicate equipment methods of records transfer.
7. How can the effectiveness of a records management program be evaluated?
8. What kinds of microimage formats are now available, and what are the characteristics of each?
9. What is CAR?
10. What is COM?
11. What is image processing?

DISCUSSION QUESTIONS

1. The organization in which you work has grown fairly rapidly during the last few years. One area in need of attention is the management of the organization's records. At the present time, each unit is responsible for the management of its own records. You and another employee in the organization were discussing records management programs recently. The other individual said that he felt each unit should be able to continue to maintain its own system because the "uniqueness of each unit can be better accommodated when using the present system." Discuss the implications of this employee's feelings about the appropriate structure of a records management program.
2. You are the records manager in the organization in which you work. The organization uses centralized records storage. A few days ago, one of the unit managers told you that he would like to have control over the records in central storage that pertain to his unit. You indicated that this action would violate the organization's policy with regard to records control. Prepare a defense of why he should not be given control over his unit's records.
3. You are a new assistant to the manager of the department in which you work. One of the duties the manager recently delegated to you was responsibility for straightening out the records "mess." In examining the contents of several folders, you discovered that many documents are fifteen to twenty years old. When you discussed this with the manager, she said that she was aware of this but that she could never decide what to keep, so she kept everything. Explain the process you will use to determine how long each document should be kept.
4. The organization in which you work is revamping its records management program. At the present time, six-drawer file cabinets are used exclusively for records storage. You have been asked to put together a list of factors to consider in assessing other types of storage equipment. What factors do you plan to put on your list that will be used to help determine the other types of storage equipment that should be considered?
5. The organization in which you work recently installed a micrographics system. Those responsible for installing the system were not especially knowledgeable about micrographics. An attempt is now being made to determine which documents to microrecord, as the original thought was to microrecord everything. What can you offer that might be useful in helping decide which documents to microrecord?
6. The organization in which you work has grown fairly rapidly the last few years. Because no more office space is available for expansion, the organization has to make maximum use of the space it presently has. Recently, someone suggested that if all the paper records held in storage were microrecorded, a significant amount of space could be gained. Discuss the implications of the suggestion to microrecord all the records presently stored in paper format. Do other alternatives to microrecording exist that should be investigated? Discuss.

STUDENT PROJECTS AND ACTIVITIES

1. Tour the records storage area of a large organization. What types of filing equipment were used? Does the equipment maximize the efficiency with which records are stored?
2. Tour the records storage area of a small organization. What types of filing equipment were used? Does the equipment maximize the efficiency with which records are stored?
3. Interview a records manager. How did this individual become qualified for the position he or she holds?
4. Obtain promotional brochures about two comparable types of equipment used in microrecording. In what ways are the devices similar? Different?
5. Make arrangements to observe a microrecording system. What system is used to index the microimages? How are the microimages retrieved?

MINICASE

The Mackle Corporation is in the process of installing a new centralized records management program. Because of your expertise in records management, you have been asked to serve on an advisory committee. You are to present a written report at the next committee meeting that outlines the steps involved in preparing a records retention schedule.

1. Prepare your report.

CASE

About five years ago, the Beyer Corporation, which is located in Omaha, Nebraska, designed and implemented a decentralized records management program. Except for confidential records, all documents are stored centrally. The program was designed and implemented by Alan Cole, who left Beyer about two years ago when he accepted a position as vice president for corporate relations in a milling company located in a neighboring state.

Over the past several months, Becky Johnson, Cole's successor, has been hearing a growing number of complaints about the centralized system. The following complaints are heard most frequently.

1. Records cannot be retrieved rapidly enough.
2. Some records that have been requisitioned have not been found.
3. Determining the whereabouts of records that have been checked out from the central storage area is not always possible.
4. Some employees keep in their offices duplicate copies of records, enabling them to avoid waiting for records requisitioned from central storage.
5. Discrepancies exist in the subject categories into which records should be filed.
6. Employees who work in centralized storage find the work boring and monotonous.

The company is now thinking about returning to a decentralized storage system whereby records would be stored in various departments. Because you were Ms. Johnson's instructor in a records management course she took at the local community college, she has decided to seek your input. When you had an on-site visit with her recently, she asked a number of questions, some of which you answered at that time and others you decided to answer in a written report. In your report, you decide to provide answers to the following questions Ms. Johnson asked of you:

1. Do you believe the company should retain centralized storage or return to a decentralized storage system? Why?
2. If the company decides to keep the centralized storage system, what courses of action would you recommend to alleviate the problems that have been cited?
3. What factors should be considered in deciding whether to keep the centralized system or to install a decentralized system?

CHAPTER

22

OFFICE AUTOMATION

CHAPTER AIM

After studying this chapter, you should be able to design an effective automated office system for an organization.

CHAPTER OUTLINE

- The Feasibility Study
  - Feasibility Study Tools
    - Questionnaires
    - Interviews
    - Time Logs
    - Activity Lists
    - Inventories
  - Data Consolidation and Analysis
- Designing and Installing Automated Office Systems
  - Step 1: Develop a Detailed Planning Guide for the Project
  - Step 2: Conceptualize the System
  - Step 3: Design Procedures and Select Appropriate Equipment
  - Step 4: Plan the Human Dimension of the System
  - Step 5: Design the Installation Procedures
  - Step 6: Evaluate the System
- Characteristics of Effective Automated Office Systems
- Suggestions for Improving the Effectiveness of Automated Office Systems
- Barriers to Successful Design/Implementation of Automated Office Systems
- Benefits of Automated Office Systems
- Components of Automated Office Systems
  - Applications
    - E-mail
    - Voice Mail
    - Calendaring
    - Scheduling
    - Image Processing
    - Spreadsheets
    - Data Bases
    - Decision-support Systems
    - Integrated Tasks
    - Computer Conferencing
    - Videotex
    - Audiotex
    - Electronic Document Management
  - Executive Workstations
    - Components
    - An Illustration of Workstation Usage
- Workstation of the Future: A Prototype
- Implications for the Administrative Office Manager

CHAPTER TERMS

Activity lists
Advisory committee
Audiotex
Automated office systems
Calendaring

Computer conference
Data base
Decision-support system
Dedicated equipment operator
Electronic document management (EDM)
E-mail
Executive workstations
Feasibility study
Image processing
Interviews
Inventory
Office automation coordinator
Office of the future
PERT chart
Planning guide
Questionnaires
Scheduling
Spreadsheets
Time logs
User friendly
User need
Videotex
Voice mail

Automated office systems are having a significant impact on the way employees at all levels of the organization—from corporate executives to junior-level office employees—perform many of their job tasks. Other than the widespread installation of computer systems in the 1950s, no development has had a greater impact on the way employees at all levels of the organization carry out their job responsibilities. A significant number of organizations—even smaller ones—have already installed these systems or soon plan to install them. Many others are investigating their feasibility.

A number of the components of automated systems originated in the **office of the future** concept, which was a widely discussed and highly speculative topic of the late 1970s and early 1980s. In fact, several components that comprised the office of the future concept provide the basic framework for many of these automated systems.

Automated office systems affect the way employees carry out a number of their tasks:

What job tasks of office employees does office automation affect?

1. Acquiring, storing, and retrieving written information, including memos, letters, and reports.
2. Preparing and transmitting written information.
3. Acquiring, analyzing, storing, and retrieving data used in making decisions.
4. Receiving and transmitting verbal communication.
5. Participating in conferences and meetings.
6. Scheduling meetings and appointments, maintaining employees' calendars, and making travel arrangements.
7. Monitoring deadlines, determining priorities of tasks that must be completed, and managing a variety of other tasks.

Prior to designing an automated office system, its feasibility has to be determined. After a system has been designed, the next step involves its installation. The extent to which the effectiveness of a system is maximized is largely affected by the way the system's feasibility determination, design, and installation procedures are carried out.

Organizations contemplating the installation of automated office systems typically begin by forming an **advisory committee** and appointing an **office automation coordinator**. Generally, the coordinator chairs the advisory committee; therefore, he or she should have expertise in the various technological areas and in systems design. Members of the advisory committee also should be knowledgeable about these areas. The training and work experience of many administrative office managers make them a strong candidate for either the coordinator's position or membership on the advisory committee. Much of the later success of the automated office systems project can often be attributed to the early efforts of the coordinator and advisory committee.

While many organizations use their own employees for the design and installation of the system, others use the services of outside consultants. The use of outsiders does not diminish the importance of the responsibilities of the automation coordinator or of the advisory committee.

THE FEASIBILITY STUDY

Why are feasibility studies conducted?

When designing an effective automated office system, a well-planned and thoroughly conducted **feasibility study** is a crucial prerequisite. The study has a two-fold purpose: (1) to help determine if an automated system is feasible and (2) to make the information available for use in designing a system if one is found feasible. The coordinator and members of the advisory committee often play an important role in determining the feasibility of an automated office system.

In planning the feasibility study, one of the first tasks to be completed is the selection of the departments or units to be included in the study process. In many instances, areas experiencing information-related problems are the ones singled out for inclusion in the study process.

Typically, a team of employees collects data from each unit being studied. Not only are employees likely to be more familiar than outsiders with what takes place in their respective departments or units, but also early involvement of employees may be crucial to their future acceptance of a new automated system.

Feasibility Study Tools

What types of feasibility study tools are used?

Several tools are available for use in conducting the feasibility study. These tools include questionnaires, interviews, time logs, activity lists, and inventories. The automation coordinator and the advisory committee most likely will determine which tools will be used. More often than not, more than one study tool will be used.

In some cases, the coordinator and committee members prepare the materials (such as questionnaires) used in the study process; in other cases, a specially appointed committee prepares the materials. The appropriate content for these materials is determined by their intended function or purpose. Before the wording and content of the materials are finalized, the documents should be reviewed by a few employees who have job responsibilities similar to those persons for whom the materials are prepared. This step will help identify unclear wording or incomplete sections that need to be reworked.

Questionnaires **Questionnaires** are often used to help determine which departmental activities or functions might be well suited for automating. Data gathered from the questionnaires are useful for determining the importance of various activities or functions, as well as for identifying those that need to be studied in greater depth.

Questionnaire content is determined by the nature of the respondents' job duties. Consequently, the content of questionnaires designed for managers will be quite different from the content of those designed for secretaries.

Examples of items that might be included on questionnaires prepared for executives/managers are as follows:

What type of information is collected by means of a questionnaire?

Nature of job activities and amount of time spent each week performing each activity.

Nature of specific information needed by executives/managers for performing their job functions, including how the information is obtained and identification of problems that need to be corrected.

Nature of specific information communicated by executives/managers to others, including how the information is prepared and transmitted and identification of problems that need to be corrected.

Nature and quantity of key documents and forms used in carrying out job functions and identification of problems that need to be corrected.

Nature of support services used by executives/managers that could be handled more efficiently by new technology, including multifunction terminals or executive workstations.

Questionnaires prepared for secretarial/clerical personnel might include the following items:

Nature of job responsibilities, including amount of time consumed each week in performing responsibilities, key activities involved in carrying out each responsibility, and identification of problems that need to be corrected.

Nature of and amount of time consumed each week performing such specific tasks as capturing, retrieving, processing, receiving, distributing, storing, destroying, and searching for information.

Nature of and frequency with which various tasks require the employee to be away from his or her desk.

Nature of and amount of time spent each week performing the following job functions: typing, calculating, copying, and telephoning.

Nature of and amount of time consumed each week performing a variety of support services.

Nature and quantity of specific documents typed each week, including input format used (dictation, handwriting, and so forth).

Employees who are given work time to complete their questionnaire typically provide more accurate results and respond more frequently than those who are expected to complete their questionnaire on their own time.

What type of information is collected by means of an interview?

Interviews Another tool used to collect information from employees about the nature of their specific job functions are **interviews**. Those conducting the interviews should be skilled in the interviewing process.

The interviewer will generally use a specially prepared document designed with the following dual functions: (1) to provide a list of items to be discussed during the interview and (2) to provide a record sheet on which the employees' responses can be recorded. The items to be discussed during the interview will be determined by the nature of the job functions of the participants. Many of the topics discussed earlier in the questionnaire section are also appropriate for inclusion in the interview.

To help verify the accuracy of the data collected from employees, the interview technique is sometimes used in conjunction with the questionnaire technique. After all the employees have completed their questionnaires, a few employees may be randomly selected to be interviewed. This information is used primarily to verify the accuracy of the questionnaire data, but also may be used to clarify or supplement the questionnaire data.

Time logs When gathering information for the feasibility study, certain employees may also be asked to record how they spend their workdays. They do this by listing on **time logs** the tasks they perform and the amount of time they spend performing each task. This will provide valuable information about the variety of tasks they perform as well as the frequency with which these tasks are performed. Information collected on time logs is useful in identifying activities well suited for automating.

How is the information that is collected by means of activity lists used?

Activity lists When used as a feasibility study tool, **activity lists** compiled by employees provide a record of the steps that comprise various activities they perform. An analysis of this information identifies the following:

1. Steps that can be easily automated.
2. Steps that can be eliminated, simplified, or consolidated with others.
3. Steps that require human involvement that may not be easily automated. Most of the information provided on activity lists can be used as input for improving the efficiency with which employees carry out their tasks.

Inventories In designing automated office systems, the information collected by the **inventory** technique is useful for determining the nature and quantity of documents processed by various departments/units. The inventory also provides valuable information about the amount of duplication and the age of the documents that are stored—information that is helpful when designing an improved, more efficient records storage system.

A document analysis will help reveal which documents should be or can be made part of an automated system. Some documents simply aren't used frequently enough to be included. And the content or design of other documents may preclude their being used in an automated system.

Data Consolidation and Analysis

After all data are collected, the next task involves data consolidation and analysis of the results. These data help determine whether problems exist and, if so, the extent to which the implementation of an automated office system is likely to solve the problems. In most instances, automated office systems probably will not solve all the identified problems. Rather, other strategies will have to be implemented to deal with those problems.

After the problems are clearly identified and analyzed, the feasibility of using an automated system for their solution has to be carefully assessed. The input of the following individuals will be helpful in making decisions about the feasibility of installing an automated system: department/unit employees, department/unit managers and supervisors, the study team members, the advisory committee members, and the automation coordinator.

The effectiveness of the final phase of the feasibility study is largely determined by the care exercised in consolidating, analyzing, and interpreting the data. The more experience individuals have in working with data, the more valid the results are likely to be.

If the data reveal that the installation of an automated office system will be useful in solving identified problems, the next step involves designing the system, the topic of the following section.

DESIGNING AND INSTALLING AUTOMATED OFFICE SYSTEMS

To a large extent, the effectiveness of an automated office system is directly related to the planning that goes into its design and installation. The complex, involved nature of most automated office systems requires the use of systematic, well-designed planning procedures.

Each person involved in the design process should be familiar with the existing problems that the automated office system is intended to eliminate. These individuals should also be familiar with various departmental/unit functions, processes, and procedures. Another area the planning group should be knowledgeable about includes various aspects of human behavior and attitudes, especially those that may impede the effective installation of an automated office system.

What steps are involved in designing and installing an automated office system?

The design and installation of an automated office system involves several steps. A brief, nontechnical discussion of some of the activities involved in each step follows:

Step 1: Develop a Detailed Planning Guide for the Project

The identified goals and objectives of the project are helpful in developing the planning guide. Input from management, the automation coordinator, and the advisory committee is also helpful in formulating goals and objectives.

The intricate nature of the design process makes a **planning guide** helpful. This guide identifies the major tasks that must be completed in the design process, as well as expected task completion dates and the individual or individuals responsible for completing each task. Units or departments that may ultimately become involved in the installation process (such as the training and development department or the personnel department) should also be made fully aware of areas of responsibility and deadlines.

For what is a PERT chart used?

A **PERT chart**, which is discussed in Chapter 25, is a useful scheduling device when designing and installing an automated system. The chart identifies an appropriate amount of time for completing various important project activities. Keeping the completion of certain tasks on schedule is critical; failure to do so may prevent the timely completion of the project.

Step 2: Conceptualize the System

This step involves determining which system concepts are best suited for the system being designed. The nature of the problem being solved helps determine which concepts are well suited for use in the system. For example, anticipating that the system might be expanded at a future date makes expandability an important concern. In conceptualizing the system during this step, the exact nature of **user need** will help determine which procedures to include in the system.

The appropriate location for various components is another important concept in need of thorough study. In some instances, the problem being solved may make the distribution of terminals throughout the building highly desirable. In other instances, centralized location of terminals for use in completing certain tasks might be more effective.

The system's architecture also will be conceptualized during this step.

Architecture refers to the various equipment components needed to enable the system to operate as planned. The system's architecture is affected by the availability and affordability of needed equipment.

Another concept involves the user of the equipment. In some instances, having a **dedicated equipment operator**, which means that a device is used only by one person, may be desirable. In other instances, allowing several individuals to share the use of the equipment may be desirable.

Step 3: Design Procedures and Select Appropriate Equipment

In an automated system, many of the procedures employees use in carrying out their job tasks will change. Every effort should be made to combine and/or simplify the existing procedures as much as possible. Special attention should be focused on the step-by-step sequences as well as on the nature of their relationship with other procedures. In addition, the nature of employee involvement and the functional role of equipment in performing each procedure have to be considered. Expertise in systems design is especially useful to those responsible for developing efficient procedures.

The equipment enables the system to perform prescribed functions. Therefore, the equipment should be selected on the basis of the functions that need to be performed rather than designing the system around the equipment's functional capabilities.

What factors need to be considered in selecting equipment?

Several key considerations affect equipment selection, including availability, cost, flexibility, ease of use, expandability, functional capability, specifications, availability of needed software, feasibility of interconnecting various hardware components, and so forth. Those responsible for equipment selection must be thoroughly familiar with the present technology, and they must continue to stay abreast of new technology. The number of significant changes in the technology and the frequency with which these changes occur compound the difficulty of this task.

Step 4: Plan the Human Dimension of the System

For obvious reasons, some employees will not enthusiastically support the installation of an automated office system. In many instances, their resistance arises from the fear of the unknown. An important aspect of this step involves eliminating any resistance that may exist. The more effort devoted to overcoming resistance throughout the entire planning process, the less employees will resist the system once it becomes operational. Employee resistance to automated office systems is discussed in greater detail in the "Suggestions" section of this chapter.

In some instances, employees will need to be trained to use the new equipment. Consideration should be given to providing early training experiences where needed. Although pretraining all equipment users may not be feasible, as many as possible should be trained early. Otherwise, the system may be only minimally functional when it becomes operable.

This step also involves determining staffing needs. If the system will require employees who have specialized backgrounds or training—and none of the current employees have these qualifications—additional staff may have to be hired.

Step 5: Design the Installation Procedures

A comparable amount of care needs to be exercised in designing the procedures for installing the automated office system as has been exercised in carrying out each of the earlier steps. The intricate nature of most automated systems requires a detailed, step-by-step installation plan. Included in the plan are the name or names of the individual or individuals responsible for each step as well as the date by which each step is to be completed. A PERT chart is useful for guiding the installation of an automated system.

The implementation of an automated office system may require some changes in the basic structure of the organization or in some of the organization's units. Perhaps most common are basic changes in department/unit responsibilities. Appropriate planning will facilitate the implementation of these basic changes.

Although the automated systems developed for many organizations affect a number of units or departments, a gradual phase-in of the system is often used. As soon as the system elements are functioning smoothly in one unit, they are installed in another unit, and so on until the entire system has been installed.

Psychologically, system phase-in is desirable for several reasons. System elements that are causing problems may need to be modified so that identical problems will not be experienced later on in another unit. In addition, a gradual phase-in may produce quicker results than a total phase-in, primarily because skeptical employees can be convinced of the system's merits before they begin its use.

Step 6: Evaluate the System

How can the effectiveness of an automated office system be evaluated?

After the system has been installed and operable for six months or so, its performance should be evaluated. The accomplishments of the system should be evaluated against the goals and objectives that were established in step 1. If any goals or objectives have not been achieved, an attempt should be made to determine the possible reasons for lack of success. Data analysis will be helpful in revealing the nature of any changes that should be made.

Periodic evaluation of the system should be made to determine whether other aspects of the system need to be modified. Inefficient or cumbersome activities are two types of problem situations that need to be remedied.

CHARACTERISTICS OF EFFECTIVE AUTOMATED OFFICE SYSTEMS

What is the function of networking in automated office systems?

Effective automated office systems possess a number of characteristics, which are especially prevalent in the more sophisticated systems. Networking—the electronic interconnecting of various equipment components—is one important characteristic. Networking increases the capabilities of the equipment and allows devices to communicate with one another. Several brands of networks are now available, and most of the major office equipment manufacturers are now selling such technology.

Another important characteristic found in effective automated office systems is the greater ease with which the equipment is used, giving it a **user-friendly** quality. Equipment considered to be user friendly increases the desire of the operator to use it. An effective way to increase employees' acceptance of a system and to reduce their resistance is to provide them with user-friendly equipment, a characteristic that should be considered when selecting the hardware components.

What are multifunctional terminals?

Providing the basic framework for an automated system are the use of multifunctional terminals and electronic terminals, another characteristic of automated office systems. Among the common functions of these terminals and workstations are their use in performing the following: word and data processing, electronic filing, electronic mailing, graphics preparation, calendaring, communications, and scheduling.

Finally, effective automated systems are custom designed around user requirements. Designing the system around employee requirements makes more sense than allowing the design of the system to dictate how employees will use the system. The increasing flexibility of hardware and greater abundance of software facilitate the custom designing of automated systems.

SUGGESTIONS FOR IMPROVING THE EFFECTIVENESS OF AUTOMATED OFFICE SYSTEMS

What suggestions will help improve the effectiveness of automated office systems?

Several of the sections presented earlier in this chapter provide a number of suggestions for improving the effectiveness of automated office systems. This section elaborates on some of these suggestions and provides information about others.

User support is crucial to the success of automated office systems. Because some users will not enthusiastically support an automated system, a fair amount of time and effort will have to be devoted to overcoming employee resistance. One of the most useful techniques for eliminating resistance is for management to keep all employees well informed about the status of the project. Each employee should be made aware of how he or she will personally benefit from the system as well as how the system will affect each person.

In addition, if the system's effectiveness is to be maximized, employees will have to overcome their fears and concerns. The hierarchical levels and job responsibilities of employees influence their fears and concerns. For example, a common concern of office employees is that automation may result in the loss of their jobs or that it will deny them the opportunity to use their skills. Managers, on the other hand, become more concerned about the possibility of losing support personnel. Some managers, especially older ones, may also be concerned about learning to use the technology. Management can help allay these fears and concerns by displaying a cooperative, supportive attitude. Communication is most useful for reducing employees' fears and concerns about office automation.

Another suggestion is to involve the users in the design of the system. In many instances, they know better than anyone else what is needed to solve the problems they encounter. Extensive user involvement in planning and designing an automated office system increases the level of their support. In addition, extensive user involvement will help prevent the belief that management has an "antiemployee" attitude. To maximize the effectiveness of a system, the dynamic nature of the office requires extensive user involvement.

The intricate, complex nature of many automated systems requires a high level of expertise among the key individuals involved in systems design. If none of the key employees has the needed level of expertise, then consideration should be given to their participation in appropriate educational and training programs. Another alternative is to use the services of an outside consultant.

BARRIERS TO SUCCESSFUL DESIGN/IMPLEMENTATION OF AUTOMATED OFFICE SYSTEMS

The design of automated office systems does not always proceed as smoothly as desired. In some cases, barriers, although often surmountable, impede

What barriers prevent the successful design and implementation of automated office systems?

progress. One effective defense against these barriers is to be aware that they can and often do exist.

One of the most significant barriers occurs when those responsible for the design of a system fail to give the user full consideration, often resulting in the design of a system that neither meets personal needs nor is capable of performing desired tasks. One of the best strategies to overcome this barrier is to involve the users throughout the entire design process.

Another barrier occurs when the designers overplan, which will likely result in a more costly, sophisticated system than is needed or desired at the present time. Suggested is giving users what they need for the short range but building in long-term flexibility that expedites expansion when the need arises.

Some organizations also have allowed a handful of employees to dictate the design of the system. The end result is the development of a system that provides what the designers believe is needed—which may be quite different from what users actually want and need. User involvement will help eliminate this barrier.

Another barrier may be created if employees distrust management's motives for installing an automated system. Employees often develop the attitude that management desires to install the system to reduce the size of the organization's workforce. However, this is not a legitimate reason for installing automated systems. Two legitimate reasons—to improve the quality of employees' performance and to increase their productivity—should be communicated to employees from the beginning. The satisfaction of employees with their jobs should also increase as a result of the system.

Another barrier—although it is continually becoming less serious—is the incompatibility of various devices. A few years ago, most of the equipment was incompatible, especially different brands of equipment. The potential need to expand the system makes equipment compatibility crucial, as does the ability to interconnect various devices electronically.

A barrier may be created in those organizations that plan to make extensive use of vendor field support. The amount of free support vendors provide clients is decreasing. Eventually, the training, installation assistance, and design services provided by vendors may virtually disappear as a no-cost item.

In some organizations, management itself may be responsible for creating a barrier when it approves the design and installation of an automated system but then fails to lend crucial, ongoing support. Insufficient commitment of needed financial resources or a basic failure of management to cooperate reflect lack of support.

BENEFITS OF AUTOMATED OFFICE SYSTEMS

What benefits are provided by the use of automated office systems?

Automated office systems provide their users several important benefits, including the positive impact of systems' use on decision-making processes. Systems, therefore, provide the decision makers with better quality, more timely, and more pertinent information.

In addition, these systems often reduce the number of errors that are made because of the increased ability to maintain accurate information throughout the system. The electronic nature of the system reduces considerably the potential for making errors. These systems are also capable of providing increased control over certain operations. This benefit helps ensure that actual results match expected results.

Furthermore, automated office systems are capable of improving employees' productivity. Because more work can be completed in less time and often at a lower cost, employee productivity is increased. Employees are also able to use the automated technology for an increased number of their assigned responsibilities, which gives them more time to spend on those tasks that are not part of the automated system. Essentially, systems usage allows employees to work smarter, not harder.

COMPONENTS OF AUTOMATED OFFICE SYSTEMS

What are the components of automated office systems?

Automated office systems are comprised of three basic components, including applications, equipment/technology, and personnel. The automated office systems concept has not resulted in the development of a significant amount of new equipment or technology. But it has resulted in significant changes in the way various devices interact with one another as they perform automated office applications. Most of the applications can be used on a "stand-alone" basis. However, when they are incorporated into an automated office system, they provide their users with considerably more functional power.

Figure 22-1 illustrates a comprehensive automated office system and its three basic components. The paragraphs that follow contain a discussion of several elements within the applications and equipment/technology components.

Applications

Among the application elements discussed in this section are the following: **e-mail,** voice mail, calendaring, scheduling, image processing, spreadsheets,

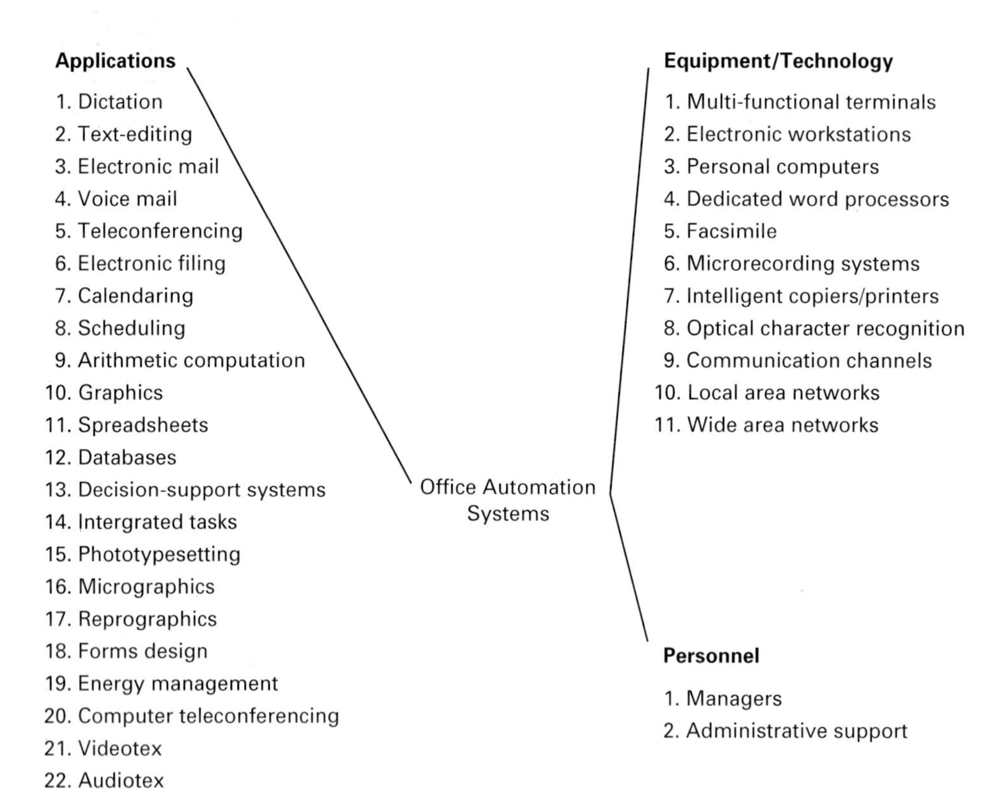

Figure 22-1 Components of an automated office system.

data bases, decision-support systems, integrated tasks, computer conferencing, videotex, audiotex, and electronic document management.

E-mail Automated office systems make extensive use of **e-mail**, which is a technological system that facilitates the electronic transmission of text, data, or images. The recipient receives the document in either hard-copy or soft-copy format. The hard copy most likely is prepared on a computer printer, on a graphics printer, or by an intelligent copier/printer. Soft copy is received on a terminal screen or on a microcomputer monitor.

E-mail can be used internally and externally. It can also be used between remotely located units/branches of an organization as well as between organizations.

E-mail is one of the most frequently used—if not the most frequently used—component of the Internet, the information superhighway, which allows users worldwide to communicate with one other. For those whose employer does not provide e-mail capability, individuals can obtain it through an on-line service to which they subscribe. Examples are Delphi, America Online, Compuserve, and Prodigy.

How is voice mail used in automated office systems?

Voice mail Also known as voice store-and-forward, **voice mail** systems are becoming very common. This system eliminates the telephone tag problem found in traditional telephone systems. Voice mail is a one-way telephone call in which the sender can transmit/record the message in the recipient's voice mailbox. At a convenient time, the recipient listens to the messages stored in his or her mailbox. The more sophisticated voice mail systems not only permit the transmission of a message to one person, but also permit the simultaneous transmission of a message to multiple recipients. Some of the more sophisticated voice mail systems allow a user to access his or her messages from a remote location.

Perhaps the most significant advantage of voice mail is the time it saves the user. An employee no longer has to try several times to reach an individual, and the small talk that frequently occurs between two individuals during a two-way call is eliminated.

Calendaring Automated office systems also facilitate electronic **calendaring**. The times of one's appointments are stored within the system. While the calendar is likely to be displayed most often in soft copy form, a printed copy of the same information can be prepared easily. Some of the more sophisticated electronic calendaring systems use an audible tone (buzzer or chime) as an alarm to notify the user of an imminent appointment. Repetitive appointments (such as a weekly supervisors' meeting at 8 a.m. on Tuesday mornings) only need be entered one time in some systems. They can be marked as repetitive, and the system schedules them indefinitely. Some calendaring systems also provide a to-do function that enables the user to input his or her tasks, along with the dates by which the tasks are to be completed. If tasks are not completed by the due date, they are simply "rolled forward" day by day until they are completed.

How is scheduling used in automated office systems?

Scheduling The inclusion of **scheduling** in an automated office system saves considerable time when planning meetings with other employees. To use the scheduling function, the electronic calendars of the affected individuals are accessed, which enables a person to determine the available times they have in common. The system automatically finds the times that all affected individuals are available. The person scheduling the meeting selects a time from among those times that are available, and the system automatically makes the appointment on the electronic calendars of the affected individuals, as well as reserves the room in which the meeting will be held. The more sophisticated systems also notify the affected individuals that a meeting has been scheduled, using either e-mail or voice mail.

Image processing Common is the use of automated office equipment/software to capture, store, retrieve, or prepare visual or graphic data or images, a concept called **image processing**. Types of visual or graphic data or images used are numeric data, photographs, text, and graphics. Output is prepared by means of color ink-jet printers, plotters, and laser printers. Visual and graphic data have many uses, including the presentation of data (such as pie or bar charts) in text-oriented documents and the visual presentation of data (such as overhead transparencies) during meetings. A large number of image processing software packages are now available that, over the years, have become user friendly.

Spreadsheets Primarily used to "computerize" numerical information, **spreadsheets** have frequent use in the business world. They are commonly used on microcomputers, although they can also be used on mainframe-sized computers. Spreadsheets create a large number of cells of numeric and/or alphabetic data that can be referenced by row and column coordinates. Once the information is stored in the system, it can be manipulated in a variety of ways. Among the common types of information stored in spreadsheets are financial information, budgetary information, and sales data. Spreadsheets facilitate the use of "what if" situations in which certain variables are entered into the system. Changing the nature of the variables provides the user with an answer to a question such as the following: What would be the impact on federal income taxes if we delayed paying real estate taxes until the first day of the next fiscal year?

A number of spreadsheet software packages now incorporate several related applications, such as preparation of graphic or visual aids and preparation of reports. Of the various types of software packages managers use, spreadsheets are among the most common.

Data bases Most automated office systems facilitate the storage of vast amounts of organizational information, including both alphabetic and numeric. Because the information tends to be stored centrally, redundancy is reduced. An advantage of **data base** use is that stored information becomes available to all authorized personnel. Computer terminals and microcomputers are typically used to access the information. Both hard-copy and soft-copy display of output are common. Some of the more sophisticated data base software packages permit the user to program the software to manipulate the stored data in ways other than the predefined instructions that accompany the program. This is done by using a command program.

What is a decision-support system?

Decision-support systems The use of **decision-support systems** reduces the time needed to make business decisions and to project the impact of one action on another. Among the common business functions found in decision-support systems are financial planning, market analysis, complicated arithmetic calculations, tax planning, and financial modeling. In the broadest sense, both data base and spreadsheets are included as part of decision-support systems because they are used in making business decisions.

Integrated tasks The integration of tasks requires the availability of integrated software. This software typically integrates text processing, spreadsheet, data base, image processing, and communication capabilities into one package. Although none of the components of the integrated package is as powerful as a self-contained package, integrated software has a distinct place in automated office systems.

Computer conferencing Instead of communicating with someone by telephone or in person, some individuals prefer a two-way **computer conference**. A terminal or microcomputer keyboard facilitates the inputting of information into the system. Two types of output are common: screen display and paper printout. Computer conferencing uses telecommunications in the transmission of the information.

Videotex The use of **videotex**, although not currently being used extensively in automated office systems, will likely become much more common in the future. Videotex is a terminal-based communication system that combines text and graphics. Functions that can be performed using videotex are the following: electronic messaging, electronic banking, electronic shopping, retrieval of information from public data banks, retrieval of news reports, and expediting stock market transactions. Videotex services are provided on a subscription basis.

Computer terminals and microcomputers are the two common types of equipment used in videotex operations. A modem will likely be used to facilitate the transfer of information between the computer at the host site and the computer at the remote site.

Audiotex Several levels of **audiotex** exist, including the most sophisticated level of voice mail, which has been discussed. A less sophisticated version requires the composition of messages from a prerecorded vocabulary of words, phrases, and sentences. To compose a message, the user simply uses a keyboard terminal to input the identification code (either alphabetic or numeric) of the desired words. To illustrate, "thank you" may have an identification code of "ty" or "123." By entering the appropriate code into the system, the phrase "thank you" is transmitted. The recipient receives the message in an audio format.

What is electronic document management?

Electronic document management The vast amount of information electronically stored within organizations increases the need for its proper management. **Electronic document management (EDM)** integrates several technologies, including those involved in the creation and storage of documents, text, images, and voice resources. EDM is designed to help an organization preserve its information resources and to make them readily available for authorized users. Thus, EDM facilitates the rapid location and retrieval of desired information, even enabling numerous employees to use the same information simultaneously. A distinct characteristic of EDM is its ability to accommodate a variety of information resources in a variety of formats.

Information stored in an EDM system is transmitted and accessed online. Although magnetic media are used to store some information, preference is leaning toward using CD-ROMs, WORMs, erasable optical disks, and videodiscs, primarily because of their much larger storage capacity and faster retrieval.

While much of the information stored within an EDM system is input directly at the time of its origination, other information has to be input by scanning. Information that likely has to be scanned is information originated before the installation of the system or information that was not stored electronically at the time of its origination. Included as part of the EDM system in some organizations is e-mail, voice mail, and personal calendaring and scheduling.

The most sophisticated EDM systems permit employees to use their desktop computers to retrieve desired information. The least sophisticated EDM systems, considered to be stand alone, require that employees go to a microcomputer dedicated to the retrieval of information from the system. Employees are able to retrieve specific documents or use the system to search for all information regarding a certain topic.

EDM technology also is capable of automatically transmitting certain portions of certain documents to certain users. To illustrate, assume that a bank scans for inputting into its EDM system each customer loan application at the time the applicant completes it. Once it is in the system, then certain parts of the application are automatically transmitted to certain employees for data verification, other parts are transmitted to other employees who perform the financial analysis, and so forth. As these employees complete their responsibilities, the system automatically transmits their work to a loan officer who will make the loan decision upon completion of information verification/analysis. Considerable time and effort can be conserved by well-designed EDM systems.

Executive Workstations

Much of the equipment/technology used in automated office systems is discussed in other chapters. This section is used to present information about **executive workstations**, which integrate many of an organization's voice, data, and text functions.

What are the components of an executive workstation?

Components Two basic components comprise the executive workstation: the hardware, which is comprised of several technological devices, and the software, often referred to as executive support systems software. A discussion of each of these two main components follows.

An executive workstation combines several common technological devices, typically dedicated to performing a single function, into one integrated unit. Among the common technological devices integrated into the executive workstation are the telephone, desktop computer, modem, terminal, and a variety of software. A number of nontechnological devices are replaced, including appointment calendars, telephone message pads, telephone and address directories, and so forth.

Some executive workstations permit simultaneous communication of voice, text, image, video, and graphics. Thus, some workstations are capable of teleconferencing and videoconferencing. Executive workstations are able to access the host computer, and they facilitate internal and external voice and data communications. Another feature commonly found is the store-and-forward capability that allows the user to transmit a specific document to a specific individual at a specific time.

How do multifunctional terminals differ from electronic workstations?

Among the features comprising many electronic workstations are the following: automatic redial, directory, unattended messaging, calendaring, signal/alarm function, message logging, touchscreen, calculator, protocol conversion, security interface, word processing, teleconferencing, videoconferencing, multifunction operation, and speakerphone.

The software used on executive workstations, by combining a number of software applications, gives the executive a number of analytical and decision-making tools. It gives the executive an opportunity to obtain answers to "what's best" or "what if" questions. The five components typically comprising executive workstations are (1) data base management, (2) inquiry/analysis functions, (3) electronic mail capability, (4) telecommunications, and (5) graphics and text processing functions.

Executive support systems software facilitates the transformation of large quantities of data into graphs, charts, and text. As a result, the user has almost instantaneous access to compressed data that supports his or her decision-making efforts. Compared with traditional data-acquisition systems, executive support systems provide the executive with more timely, relevant information.

Executive support systems enjoy several advantages. They provide the executive with greater control over various organizational functions and operations, they give the executive the ability to share data with a large number of other employees quickly and easily, they save a considerable amount of executive time, and they enhance the executive's decision-making ability.

While the cost of executive support systems software is high—ranging from $50,000 to several millions—its cost can be easily justified on the basis of the increased productivity of executives. Because of increased productivity and improved decision making, the hardware and software comprising executive workstations generally has a fairly short payback period.

An illustration of workstation usage A description of how an executive might use a workstation in a hypothetical, but realistic, situation will aid reader understanding of the workstation concept. The following narrative explains how the workstation is used to perform a variety of functions, including word processing, information storing and retrieving, graphics displaying, data processing, electronic mailing, electronic filing, scheduling, electronic messaging, voice messaging, conferencing, and telecommuting.

The first thing the executive does upon arriving at the office is to command the workstation to prepare a visual display of the items in his or her electronic mailbox. These items may originate from both internal and external sources. Each item listed on the display is identified by the name of the sender, the date and time of receipt, and the subject of the items. To obtain a visual display of an item, the executive simply depresses the appropriate keys on the terminal keyboard. Or, depending on the type of equipment, the use of an electronic pointer to touch the name of the desired item on the screen will produce an instant screen display of the item. In addition to displaying the item on the screen, the workstation is also capable of printing a hard copy.

Perhaps the executive wishes to prepare an immediate response to the item just displayed on his or her screen. Two options are available to the executive: (1) self-keyboarding of a reply by the executive, using his or her workstation keyboard, or (2) dictating a reply that will be keyboarded on another device by an office support employee. After the response has been prepared using either of these two options, the material can be easily revised. Information electronically stored in the organization's central computer system can be readily retrieved for use in preparing graphic displays of information, such as charts or graphs, that the executive may wish to include in the response. In addition, the workstation is capable of processing any raw data that the executive may need as he or she prepares the response.

Once the executive is satisfied with the content and wording of the response, the workstation can be used for electronically transmitting the document to the recipient. However, in some cases, the executive may choose to send a hard copy of the response rather than use electronic transmission. In other instances, the executive may choose to use the facsimile transmission process. The workstation is also capable of electronically filing any of the items received in the executive's electronic mailbox as well as filing the material he or she originates. These incoming and outgoing items can be held temporarily in an electronic in-out basket or stored permanently in the organization's electronic data management system.

Before working with any other items in the electronic mailbox, the executive decides to examine today's schedule of appointments and events. By using the appropriate keys on the keyboard or the electronic pointer, today's schedule can be displayed on the screen. A hard copy of the schedule can also be readily obtained by depressing the appropriate keys on the keyboard. When individuals wish to make an appointment with the executive, they simply access the executive's electronic calendar and select an available block of time. The executive uses the same process in making appointments with other individuals in the organization who have electronic calendars.

The executive will also use his or her workstation to schedule group meetings. This is easily done by using the software to access the calendars of each individual in a group. The computer provides a list of times that each individual in the group is available and then automatically schedules the meeting on each employee's electronic calendar. The computer is also capable of reserving a room that will accommodate the group.

The executive can also use voice messaging, which essentially is a one-way telephone call. The sender's verbal message is recorded on the recipient's voice mailbox, which likely can be accessed by the recipient from his or her own phone or a remote phone.

Conferencing is another function of the electronic workstation. Perhaps the executive needs to obtain information from individuals in several remotely located branch offices. Information can be obtained from these individuals immediately if they are in their offices at the time of the request. But if not, they can provide the information at their convenience after they return. Information of this type is transmitted back and forth through communication networks. If the two individuals who are communicating with each other have computers equipped with C-phones (computer phones), they will be able to see images of each other as they converse.

The executive may also be able to use two other conferencing techniques, although neither specifically requires the electronic workstation. With audio conferencing, a conference call is placed to each individual in a group with whom the executive wishes to converse. Each participant hears all the conversation that takes place during the call. The other conferencing technique has both visual and audio capability. Video equipment enables the participants to see as well as hear one another. Visual images of paper documents may also be transmitted; and depending on the equipment, providing each participant with a hard copy of the documents transmitted during the conference may be possible. This form of conferencing, which is known as teleconferencing, is being used by organizations to decrease the time and expense of executive travel.

Another function, telecommuting, enables executives to work at home. A modem provides communications linkage between the executive's home personal computer and the organization's central system. This feature is helpful to executives who wish to work at home at night. And depending on the sophistication of the system, the executive may also be able to work at home during the days he or she does not need to be present at the workplace. The equipment will also allow the executive to read at home his or her electronic mail received at the office. The voice messages stored at the office can also be accessed from home.

WORKSTATION OF THE FUTURE: A PROTOTYPE

Illustrated in Figure 22-2 is a prototype of a workstation of the future. This device is expected to reduce significantly the amount of paper that flows through the organization.

Among the specific features of the workstation are the following:

1. A 3′ by 4′ transparent panel that links the station's keyboard with the LAN. The screen displays images, text, and graphics.
2. A flat screen on the work surface that serves as the computer terminal.
3. Voice recognition capability for computer file creation and management.
4. A soft-touch keyboard integrated into the chair and into the work surface.
5. A translucent panel between two workstations that becomes transparent with a voice command.
6. An environmental control system, including lighting, that operates by voice command.
7. A noise-masking system that permits individual control over ambient noise.

Figure 22-2 Electronic workstation. Courtesy: Haworth, Inc.

8. Fax capability integrated into the work surface.
9. A cellular telephone that reduces the need for telephone cabling.

IMPLICATIONS FOR THE ADMINISTRATIVE OFFICE MANAGER

The area of office automation has created a new field in which administrative office managers can specialize. No one is better qualified than administrative office managers to provide leadership in this emerging area.

Automating various office operations is the best means for organizations to have cost-effective office functions. Although a variety of other means can be used to improve the efficiency of the office function, properly designed automated systems can provide a significant contribution.

Anyone involved in any way with automated office systems must keep abreast of new developments. This is not an easy task because of the rate at which these developments are occurring. A variety of trade publications and professional journals provide an abundance of information about office automation. Attending office automation seminars is another excellent way to keep up-to-date in this area.

The amount of progress made in developing sophisticated office systems is largely dependent on the availability of network technology. The hardware and software used in these systems seem to be more readily available at the present than the networks which enable various devices to communicate with one another.

REVIEW QUESTIONS

1. What is the relationship between the office of the future concept and automated office systems?
2. What is the purpose of a feasibility study?
3. What kinds of information are collected on time logs?
4. What use is made of the information collected on activity logs?
5. What factors should be considered when selecting equipment for an automated office system?
6. What are the characteristics of effective automated office systems?
7. How can employee resistance to the use of automated office systems be overcome?
8. What are the benefits of automated office systems?
9. What are the basic components of automated office systems?
10. What is videotex?
11. What is electronic document management?

DISCUSSION QUESTIONS

1. You were recently discussing the electronic workstation concept with a group of your friends. One said that to him the workstation seems to be an expensive executive toy. "Why not just hire more office employees to do the things this toy does?" asked your friend. Defend executive use of the electronic workstation by explaining why it is more than just a toy. Also discuss why your friend's suggestion to hire more office employees as an alternative to installing workstations may not be practical.
2. Of all the employees in the organization in which you work, you are regarded as the one who is most knowledgeable about automated office systems. The president would like to discuss with the board of directors at its next meeting the possibility of installing an automated office system. You are to put together some information about automated

office systems that will be presented at the board meeting. The information you prepare most likely will be instrumental in getting either a "green or red light" from the board. What kinds of information should be presented to the members of the board to convince them of the desirability of automated office systems?

3. As a member of the office automation advisory committee in the organization in which you work, you are responsible for helping ensure the success of the automated office system that is now being developed. You are well aware of the need for conducting a quality feasibility study. What suggestions can you share with the other members of the advisory committee that will be helpful in designing and conducting a quality feasibility study?
4. A discussion about office automation that you had this morning with a coworker convinced you that he did not know much about this topic. When you mentioned to him that the installation of an automated office system often results in fairly significant changes in the procedures employees use to carry out their jobs, he asked, "Why?" He said that he was under the impression that all you had to do was let the equipment do what people once did. Why do procedures have to be changed in most cases when they are automated? Discuss the implications of his comment about letting "equipment do what people once did."
5. You recently read an article written by a leading authority in the area of automated office systems. This authority said, "In the final analysis, the users of the system will most likely be responsible for its success or failure." Do you agree with this statement? Why or why not?
6. The article referred to in question 5 also mentioned that one of the biggest—if not the biggest—roadblock to successful utilization of automated office systems was employee anxiety. According to this authority, "Employees will most likely resist automated office systems more than any other development in the history of the modern office." Do you agree with this authority about the level of employee resistance to automated office systems? Why or why not? How might this level of employee resistance be reduced?

STUDENT PROJECTS AND ACTIVITIES

1. Tour an organization with an automated office system. What kinds of functions is the system able to perform?
2. Talk with an employee in a company that recently installed an automated office system. Compared with the old system, how does this employee like the new system?
3. Talk with an individual who regularly conducts the feasibility studies designed to determine the need for an automated office system. Which tool does he or she use most frequently? What types of information are commonly collected?
4. Obtain promotional brochures on two competing electronic workstations. In what ways are the workstations similar to one another? Different from one another?
5. View a demonstration of a decision-support system. What specific functions was it capable of performing?

MINICASE

Several employees in the Jackman Corporation were recently appointed to serve on an office automation advisory committee. At the present time, they are having difficulty trying to determine which tools to use when studying the feasibility of automating certain secretarial/clerical operations. As the chair of the committee, you decide to prepare a memo to be sent to each committee member for his or her perusal before the next committee meeting. In the memo, you decide to

1. Identify the tools you believe are especially appropriate for studying the secretarial/clerical staff, along with a justification of why you are recommending each one that you identified.
2. Identify the general guidelines you believe should be considered in selecting the appropriate tools for studying the feasibility of installing an automated office system in an organization.

CASE

The Merrimac Publishing Company, which is located in St. Louis, Missouri, is the largest U.S. publisher of college-level humanities texts. During the last few months, the amount of paperwork which has to be processed is creating serious problems that are quite unmanageable at this time.

A conservative management style has prevailed in Merrimac for several decades. Therefore, the company is generally a follower rather than a leader when installing new technology. Perhaps the expressed feeling of the president that much of the new technology that has been introduced during the last few years is "trendy" or "faddish" is also responsible for the company's "follower" status. Once the president is convinced that technology can produce significant results, however, he is supportive of its use.

Several managers in Merrimac believe that if they could devise a strong justification for installing an automated office system, they might be able to get the support of the president. They know that they will have to justify the cost of installing such a system. These members decide to prepare a report for the president in which they

1. Discuss the ways an automated office system might be cost-worthy for Merrimac.
2. Explain why automated office systems are here to stay—that they are not "faddish" or "trendy."
3. Sell the president on the worth or value of an automated office system.

CHAPTER

23

FORMS DESIGN AND CONTROL

CHAPTER AIM

After studying this chapter, you should be able to develop effective forms for use in an organization.

CHAPTER OUTLINE

- Forms Control Program
  - Step 1: Cataloging Forms
  - Step 2: Classifying Forms
  - Step 3: Analyzing Forms
  - Step 4: Eliminating Forms
  - Step 5: Consolidating Forms
  - Step 6: Developing Design Guidelines
  - Step 7: Developing Forms
  - Step 8: Printing Forms
  - Step 9: Maintaining Perpetual Supply Inventory
- Types of Office Forms
  - Continuous Forms
  - Unit-set Forms
  - Carbonless Forms
  - MICR Forms (magnetic ink character recognition)
  - OCR Forms (optical character recognition)
  - Mark-sense Forms
  - Electronic Forms
- Forms Design
  - Design Elements
    - Adequate Identification
    - Alignment of Items
    - Preprinting
    - Prenumbering
    - Instructions
    - Identification Number
    - Type of Carbon
    - Data-entry Method
    - Paper
    - Color
    - Size
    - Print Type Size
    - Shading
    - Adequate Margin Size
  - Forms Design Software
  - Forms Design Illustrated
- Professional Forms Services
- Implications for the Administrative Office Manager

CHAPTER TERMS

Analysis
Ballot-box design
Bar code
Box design
Carbonless forms
Cataloging
Classification
Continuous forms
Data-entry method
Electronic forms
Fan-fold forms
Forms control program

Grade of paper
Grain of paper
Mark-sense forms
MICR
OCR
One-time carbon
Prenumbering
Professional forms services
Removable side strip forms
Roll forms
Statute of limitations
Unit-set forms

The quality of forms used in business transactions often affects the efficiency of the transactions. In many instances, the best way to improve transaction efficiency is quite simple: improve the quality of the forms. Today, increasing numbers of organizations are replacing their paper forms with electronic forms. This trend is likely to become even more common in the future.

Most of the forms used in an organization perform a vital function. Those without a vital function typically are poorly designed, or they have minimal value; the discontinuation of their use should be considered.

Forms are a vital component of the integrated systems discussed in Chapter 17. The design of forms used in integrated systems is especially crucial because of the need for forms to be compatible with the equipment used in the system and with other related forms

FORMS CONTROL PROGRAM

Because administrative office managers are frequently involved with forms design, their involvement with **forms control programs** seems logical. Forms control programs that have the benefit of advisory committees are being used with greater frequency. An essential prerequisite of these programs is top-management support.

The following objectives are typical of forms control programs:

What are the common objectives of forms control programs?

1. To guard against the development of unneeded forms.
2. To eliminate unneeded existing forms.
3. To assist in the development and design of efficient forms.
4. To consolidate and simplify existing forms when appropriate.
5. To provide a continuous review of existing forms.
6. To facilitate the development of efficient work procedures that involve the use of forms.

The implementation of operating systems in an organization generally requires the standardization of organizational forms. Consequently, the systems staff and individuals involved with forms design and control should work together. Otherwise, the effectiveness of the system will be diminished.

Several distinct steps are involved in the design of an efficient forms control program. These steps are presented in chronological order.

Step 1: Cataloging Forms

The **cataloging** of forms enables those individuals responsible for the forms control program to determine the nature, type, and purpose of the forms used throughout the organization. The individuals responsible for forms control collect from each department or work unit several copies of each of its forms. The cataloging procedure will reveal the following:

What information is provided by forms cataloging?

1. The primary purpose of each form.
2. The forms used by each department or work unit.
3. The frequency of use of each form.
4. The number of copies of a multiple-copy form set.
5. The routing of each copy of a multiple-copy form set.
6. The final disposition of each copy of a multiple-copy form set.
7. The primary method of entering data on each of the forms.
8. The relationship among various forms.

Each form is assigned an identification number during Step 1. Generally found in the lower left corner, the number usually appears in a coded format. Typically, each department within an organization is assigned a numerical code. Each form within a given department is then assigned a specific identification number. To illustrate, the following number is coded as follows:

23-010 (The number "23" refers to the marketing department; "010" refers to the tenth form developed in the marketing department.) Some organizations also include in the identification number the month and year that the form was last revised as well as the number of forms printed the last time the supply was replenished. This appears as follows:

> 23-010 Rev. 1/95 4M
> "Rev. 1/95" means the form was revised in January 1995, and "4M" means that 4,000 copies of the form were last printed.

Step 2: Classifying Forms

What is the purpose of forms classification?

The use of a forms **classification** scheme facilitates the analysis of the forms assembled during the cataloging process. Forms are typically classified in two ways: by function and by number.

Classifying forms by function means they are organized according to their specific purpose. For example, all forms pertaining to sales are grouped together, all forms pertaining to accounts receivable are grouped together, and so forth. When completed, the functional classification enables those responsible for forms design and control to analyze the similarities and differences among the various forms.

Classifying forms by number involves assembling the various forms according to the identification number assigned to each form in Step 1. Although using a number classification scheme generally is not helpful when comparing the similarities and differences between forms, it provides a master file useful for cross-referencing purposes as well as for assigning the identification number to new forms.

Step 3: Analyzing Forms

An integral aspect of a forms control program is forms **analysis**, which often results in reducing the cost of creating and processing a form. Forms analysis involves studying each form in terms of its function.

Forms analysis provides answers to the following questions:

What information is provided by forms analysis?

1. What is the primary purpose of the form?
2. Does the form contain the necessary information to fulfill its purpose?
3. Do the design specifications on the form accommodate its data entry, transmittal, filing, and retrieval requirements?
4. Does the form contain any extraneous information?

Forms analysis should take place before a new or revised form is officially approved or before an existing form is restocked. Ideally, each form is subjected to an analysis every two or three years.

Step 4: Eliminating Forms

If the forms analysis reveals that certain forms either are no longer used or need to be used, their elimination should be considered. In some instances, certain forms may not be needed because the purpose for which they were designed is not being served by another form. Or perhaps a form is no longer used because it is not compatible with the organization's systems and procedures.

Step 5: Consolidating Forms

Forms analysis may reveal a similarity of some items on certain forms. In some instances, the development of one new form that consolidates two or more currently existing forms may be possible. The consolidating process is facilitated by the use of a grid similar to the one illustrated in Figure 23-1, which identifies the various items found on several forms.

An examination of the grid reveals several items are found in common on the various forms being analyzed. The greater the number of common items, the more easily forms can be consolidated.

Step 6: Developing Design Guidelines

Before new forms are designed or existing forms are revised, design guidelines should be developed. These guidelines will be helpful in designing forms compatible with one another. The following identifies several design guidelines:

	FIRM NAME AND ADDRESS	SHIP TO	SEND TO	QUANTITY	DESCRIPTION	CATALOG NUMBER	PRICE	TOTAL PRICE	SUGGESTED VENDOR	TERMS	SUB TOTAL	TAX
PURCHASE REQUISITION				X	X	X			X			
PURCHASE ORDER	X	X	X	X	X	X	X	X		X	X	X
RECEIPT OF GOODS				X	X	X	X	X		X	X	X

Figure 23-1 Data comparison grid.

1. When the same information appears on several forms, it should appear in the same location on each form (for example, the name and address of the organization).
2. Information that is to be transferred from one form to another should appear in the same sequence on both forms. (For example, the columns common to both a purchase requisition and a purchase order should appear in the same order on both forms.)
3. When control of forms is important, the forms should be numbered sequentially. (For example, numbering checks helps guard against their misuse.)
4. The design of the form should be guided by such characteristics as simplicity, practicality, and ease of use.

Step 7: Developing Forms

When new forms are being developed, their need has to be justified. In addition, their design should be consistent with the guidelines covered in this chapter.

Step 8: Printing Forms

In the past, many organizations had their forms duplicated by printing companies. Because increasing numbers of organizations are installing extensive reprographics units with the specialized equipment needed to print forms, this step, more than ever before, is likely to be done in-house.

Step 9: Maintaining Perpetual Supply Inventory

What is the primary reason that a perpetual supply inventory is maintained?

The last step in the forms control program is the development of procedures for use in maintaining a perpetual supply inventory. This helps keep a sufficient supply of forms on hand. When the supply reaches the minimum level, it is replenished. Effective inventory procedures also prevent the presence of a surplus of forms.

TYPES OF OFFICE FORMS

Several types of office forms exist. Those presented in this chapter include continuous, unit-set, carbonless, MICR, OCR, mark-sense, and electronic.

Continuous Forms

Many of the forms used in offices today are classified as **continuous forms**. Although these forms are attached to one another, the perforations separating each form facilitate their detachment from one another. Three types of continuous forms are available: **fan-fold**, **roll**, and **removable side strip**.

Figure 23-2 illustrates each of these three types.

The fan-fold type is a multicopy set, the roll type is a single-copy form, and the removable side-strip form may be either a single or multiple copy.

What are the characteristics of fan-fold forms?

Fan-fold forms are distinctive because the copies are made by bellow folding several times a single sheet of paper. Carbon copy is interleaved between the various copies. The forms are generally perforated on the sides and the top and bottom, which facilitates separation of the various copies from one another.

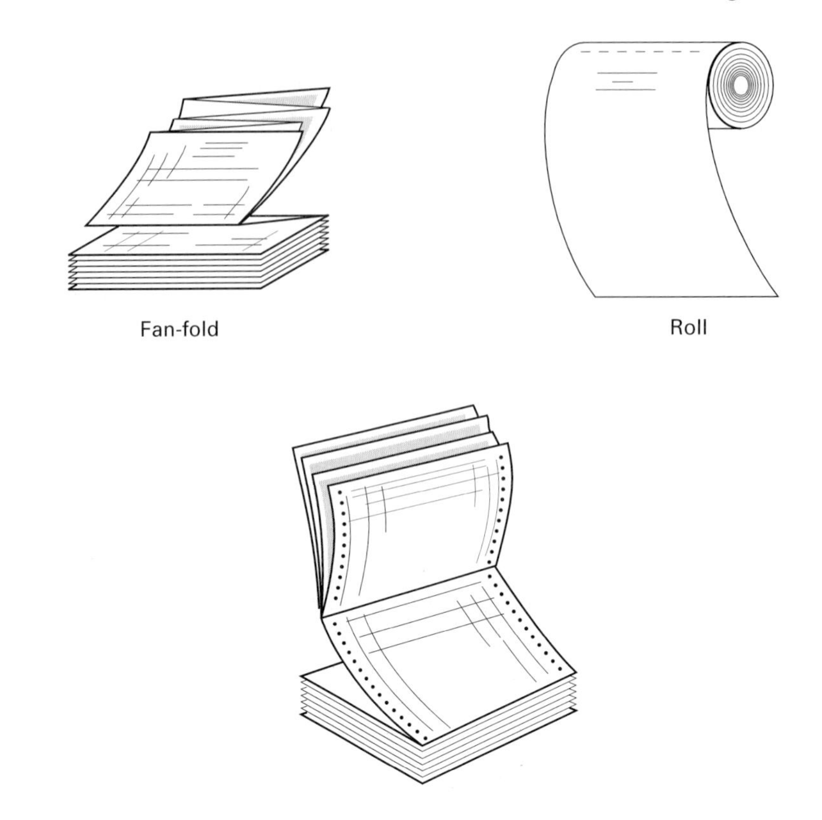

Figure 23-2 Types of continuous forms.

The multiple-copy removable side-strip form has a separate sheet of paper for each copy. The side strip serves two purposes. The holes in the strip are used in feeding the forms through the printing device. They are also helpful in holding the original and the multiple copies of the forms together until the various copies are separated from one another.

The roll type is restricted to single-copy forms because of the tendency for multiple-copy forms to become misaligned when rolled. Continuous letterheads, a type of roll form, can be used on high-speed impact printers. The perforations facilitate the separation of one letterhead from another.

Continuous forms are especially suited for automated printing equipment, such as computer printers and automatic typewriters. A considerable amount of time is saved because continuous forms are automatically fed through the equipment, eliminating the need to insert each form in the equipment.

Cards in a continuous format that can be processed by computer equipment are also now available. These cards, which are commonly used for customer billing, are printed on heavy paper stock. The removable side strips on both sides facilitate automatic feeding through the printing device. After data entry, the cards are separated from one another. The portion of the card that is generally returned with the customer's payment can then again be processed by card-reading equipment.

Unit-set Forms

What are the characteristics of unit-set forms?

Unit-set forms are maintained as separate forms and may be either single or multiple copy. The multiple-copy variety frequently uses a one-step carbon removal technique in which all carbons are removed at one time. At the top of each form set is a perforated strip to which the various sheets of carbon are attached. The carbons are shorter than the copies of the form. Carbon is removed by grasping the perforated strip with one hand and the bottom of the copies with the other. During removal, the carbons remain attached to the perforated strip.

A unit-set form is illustrated in Figure 23-3.

Unit-set forms are versatile. Certain portions of the carbon copies can be deleted in either of two ways: (1) by not carbonizing these portions of the carbon copy or (2) by omitting the section on each copy that is to be deleted. The latter process is easily accomplished by eliminating the paper where the deleted portions would have appeared had paper been there. This is done by using sheets of different sizes to construct the unit-set form.

Carbonless Forms

What advantages result from the use of carbonless forms?

Carbonless forms use a process in which the back side of one copy and the face side of the next copy have special coatings. When pressure is applied to the form, the chemical coatings interact, which causes an image of the information written on the original copy to appear on the carbon copy. Until recently, the images on carbonless copies appeared in blue, a color that does not always photocopy well. New chemicals are available that produce black images, thus facilitating the photocopying of these forms.

Although the cost of making copies by this method is approximately 15 percent higher than with other methods, the carbonless process results in significant advantages. For example, portions of copies can be easily deleted by not applying the coatings to these areas. Because carbon paper does not have to be inserted between the various copies of the form, the form set is thinner. Not only can more copies be made, but also the sets consume less storage space. Furthermore, because carbon paper is not used, the process is cleaner and is less likely to result in smudged copies. The carbonless form also enables one to detect erasures, which decreases the likelihood of unauthorized changes being made on the forms. Furthermore, because no carbon is used, maintaining confidentiality is not the concern that it is with carboned forms.

MICR Forms (Magnetic Ink Character Recognition)

MICR forms are used primarily by banks and other types of lending institutions to expedite the storing and processing of numerical data found on banking documents. Numbers are imprinted on the documents with a magnetic ink. Special equipment reads these numbers and then transmits the data to the computer or to other processing equipment.

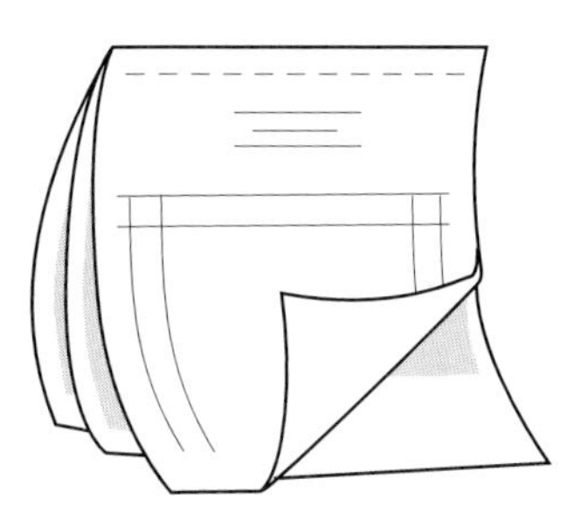

Figure 23-3 Unit-set form.

OCR Forms (Optical Character Recognition)

Whereas the MICR forms are used only for numerical data, **OCR** forms use both alphabetic and numerical data. As the data are read on the OCR form, they are transmitted to the computer where processing takes place. Although machines are generally used to enter data on the OCR forms, handwriting, to a limited extent, can be used. Considerable precision must be used in the development of forms using the OCR concept. Improper alignment can cause the equipment to misread the data.

A related type of form is that which has a **bar code** imprinted on it. A scanner is used to read the bar code, which inputs the scanned information into the organization's information system. A variety of information is included in bar codes. A common one is the form's number.

Mark-sense Forms

How are mark-sense forms processed?

A **mark-sense form**, such as the one illustrated in Figure 23-4, is useful for certain applications. Special scanning equipment reads pencil marks on the form. These forms are especially advantageous for information comprised mostly of numerical characters. The data-entering process becomes quite cumbersome when a considerable amount of alphabetic information has to be entered.

Electronic Forms

Of the various types of forms used widely in organizations, the newest and fastest-growing type are **electronic forms**. The shell or template (constant information) is stored in the organization's computer system (perhaps on the organization's network, making it readily accessible to every employee who uses a particular form). A terminal, most likely a desktop computer, is used to enter the variable information. If a paper copy of the form is needed, a laser printer is used to print the variable and constant information simultaneously. In most cases, the variable information entered on the shell is simultaneously stored in the organization's computerized data base. Thus, it can be later used in a variety of ways and for a variety of purposes. When forms are created electronically, the need for preprinted forms is eliminated, as is the use of handwriting or a typewriter for data entry.

What elements are encompassed in the electronic forms concept?

The electronic forms concept encompasses several elements, including the design of the template or shell (constant information), the fill-in process (variable information), data base linkage, printing, and computer networks. Depending on how electronic forms are used in the organization's operating systems, they may be an integral part of its automated processes. For example, if a branch office routinely needs a paper copy of an electronic form that is created in the home office, the system can be used to print the paper copy automatically—with no human intervention—in the branch office.

Among the advantages of using electronic forms are the following:

What advantages result from using electronic forms?

1. Filling in the variable information on an electronic form is quicker than handwriting or using a typewriter to fill in the variable information on a paper form.
2. The need to keep an inventory of paper forms is greatly diminished because fewer paper copies of forms will likely be prepared.
3. The need to enter redundant information on several different forms is greatly reduced. Once the information has been captured and stored

REGISTRATION SECTION REQUEST FORM — MICHIGAN STATE UNIVERSITY — OFFICEOF THE REGISTRAR

NAME ____________________
LAST FIRST MIDDLE

STUDENT NUMBER

INSTRUCTIONS

1. Using a *2 pencil, *write* and *mark* student number in box at right.
2. Write and mark in the boxes below the sequence number for each lecture, laboratory or recitation (disregard the hyphen printed in the sequence number).
3. Write and mark the number of credits (CR column) for each lecture, laboratory or recitation. For a Variable credit course (VA) write and mark the exact number of credits you are carrying in that course.
4. If you are visiting or repeating a course, mark the visitor or repeat circle.
5. If you are taking a course for Credit-No Credit, use the box designated as such in the lower right corner.
6. See example ar right for proper marking. Be certain to fill in each circle completely.
7. Complete this form by marking the boxes on the far right for the total number of sequence boxes used and the inital of your last name.

EXAMPLE
0 3 0 4 1 2
SEQUENCE NUMBER

MAKE HEAVY BLACK MARKS THAT FILL CIRCLE COMPLETELY

FOR ACCURACY IN YOUR SCHEDULE, AVOID STRAY MAKRS

ERASE COMPLETELY ANY ENTRY CHANGED

Lectures, Labs and Recitations all carry the same credit on this form (not for fee assessment, but for the purpose of early enrollment)

SEQUENCE NUMBER — CR — VISITOR — REPEAT

MARK TOTAL NUMBER OF SEQUENCE BOXES USED: 1 2 3 4 5 6 7 8 9 10 11 12

MARK FIRST INITIAL OF YOUR LAST NAME: A B C D E F G H I J K L M N O P Q R S T U V W X Y Z

USE ONLY FOR CREDIT-NO CREDIT OPTION

MSU is an Affirmative Action/Equal Opportunity Institution

Michigan State University Prining

Figure 23-4 Mark-sense form. Courtesy: Michigan State University.

in the organization's data base, the information can be automatically pulled into other forms as the need arises.

4. The need to file paper copies is greatly reduced, thus reducing filing time and storage space.
5. Information stored on electronic forms can be retrieved more readily than paper copies.
6. The shell of an electronic form can be easily and quickly revised as the need arises.

FORMS DESIGN

The efficiency with which information is entered on a form is affected by its design. Poorly designed forms are difficult to complete, especially for individuals who are unfamiliar with the use to be made of specific forms. Poorly designed forms increase the likelihood that errors will be made.

Extreme care must be exercised when designing forms that are part of an organization's operating system. Forms that are not compatible with the system or that are not compatible with other related forms destroy the efficiency of various work processes. For this reason, many organizations often use the services of professional forms designers when new forms are needed. The expertise of these designers helps ensure the compatibility of the forms with the organization's operating system.

Depending on the qualifications of the organization's internal staff, the services of outside forms designers may not be needed. And because of the limited function of some forms or their infrequent use, trying to justify the cost of hiring professional designers may not be possible.

Before actual work begins on designing the form, the following information is needed:

1. *The purpose of the form.* The purpose of the form must be defined before the following can be determined: the type of information to be included on the form, the number of copies that will be needed, the routing of each copy, and the nature of completion directions or instructions that are needed. In addition, the form's purpose will determine the necessity for using certain control procedures, such as prenumbering or authorization signatures.

Why does the nature of the equipment that will be used in processing a form need to be determined before the form is designed?

2. *The nature of the equipment on which the form will be processed.* The equipment on which the form will be processed may restrict its size. The type of equipment will also determine whether or not automatic feeding of the form is possible. In addition, the nature of the equipment will determine if the paper on which the form is printed has to possess certain characteristics, as well as determine the amount of space needed for inserting the information on the form.
3. *The relationship between the form being studied and any other previously developed forms.* If the form being developed is related in any way to other forms, care must be taken to ensure their compatibility. The sequencing of items should be identical, especially if the information from one form has to be later transferred to another form.

What impact do statutes of limitation have on forms design?

4. *The length of time that various copies must be legally retained.* If the **statute of limitations** requires that a certain form be kept for a long time, the paper on which it is printed must be sufficiently durable to withstand the time element. This will directly influence the quality of paper on which the form is printed.

Design Elements

After the four background characteristics have been considered, the design process may begin. Among the factors to be considered are those discussed in the paragraphs that follow.

Adequate identification The name of the form should be clearly displayed on the form. In addition, if the form is an external one, the organization's name, address, and telephone number should also appear on each copy. Other than printing the organization's logo or trademark on the form, the use of symbols or pictures should be kept to a minimum.

Alignment of items The items on a form should be aligned so that only a minimum number of tab settings have to be made, especially on forms for which a typewriter is commonly used for data entry. Ideal alignment enables one tab set to be used several times. Figure 23-5 illustrates the incorrect and correct way of aligning items on a form.

In the incorrect illustration in Figure 23-5, a single tab set will not accommodate each item. By aligning the items as shown in the correct illustration, one tab set will accommodate all the items. Over time, properly aligned items will conserve considerable physical effort.

Preprinting As much information as possible should be preprinted on forms. Doing so simplifies the task of entering information as well as enhances the completion of the form. When information can be preprinted, the individuals who complete the form simply check the desired items. This is illustrated in Figure 23-6. The use of **ballot-box design** in the correct illustration is a useful time-saving technique.

Why are some forms prenumbered?

Prenumbering The **prenumbering** of forms is advantageous in several respects. Among the advantages are the following: Employee time and effort

Incorrect	*Correct*
Name:	Name:
Address:	Address:
City:	City:
State:	State:

Figure 23-5 Item alignment.

Incorrect	*Correct*
Please state which shipping method you prefer________________	□ Parcel post □ Land freight □ Air freight □ Other________________________

Figure 23-6 Ballot-box design.

are conserved; greater control can be exercised over the use of the form; and if necessary, the processed forms can be easily rearranged in numerical order. Forms are typically prenumbered in the upper right corner.

Types of forms frequently prenumbered are purchase orders, checks, payment vouchers, invoices, and so forth.

Instructions Because of the complexity of some forms or because the individual using a certain form may not be familiar with its completion procedures, the inclusion of instructions on the form is helpful. Generally, external forms are the only ones on which instructions are needed. Employees, either through training or use, are familiar with internal forms, thus eliminating the need for instructions.

When needed, instructions should be placed as close as possible to the items to which they pertain. If this is not possible because of insufficient space, the instructions may be placed on the backside of the form or on a separate sheet. If instructions cannot be placed near the information to which they pertain, their location should be noted so they can be readily found.

Identification number All forms should have an identification number, which is often located in the lower left corner. The number might consist of a department number, the number of the form within the department, the adoption or last revision date, and the quantity of forms printed during the last printing. The following, which contains the four elements just mentioned above, illustrates an identification number:

212:017 Rev. 9/95 4M

Type of carbon When selecting the appropriate type of carbon for making copies of a form, the following factors should be considered:

What factors need to be considered in determining the appropriate carboning method?

1. The frequency of use of the form.
2. The number of copies of the form that must be made.
3. The confidentiality of the form.
4. The opportunity for tampering with the data on the form (erasing and retyping, for example).
5. The method for entering data on the form.
6. The nature of the equipment through which the form has to be processed during completion.

Several methods exist for making carbon copies: carbonless, one-time carbon, carbon roll fastened to the equipment, and single-sheet carbon.

When justified, the use of the carbonless system to make copies results in several advantages that were outlined in the "Types of Office Forms" section.

One-time carbon is the type used in continuous forms or unit-set forms. In terms of quality, one-time carbon is a low-grade type and is used only one time. Because the carbon is inserted between the various sheets of the form during the manufacturing process, considerable employee time is saved.

Although carbon rolls are not used frequently, some machines are equipped with a carbon roll device attached to the equipment. The carbon feeds through the equipment independently of the movement of forms through the machine. Therefore, employees do not have to insert carbon paper between each copy of each form.

Because some forms are not used frequently enough to justify one of the carbonizing methods listed earlier, the single-sheet carbon method is used. High-grade carbon can be reused a number of times. A carbon sheet has to be inserted manually between each copy of the form, which can make this method quite time consuming, depending on the frequency of use.

Why does the primary method of data entry need to be considered in forms design?

Data-entry method The **data-entry method** on a form has a significant impact on the spacing between the items on the form as well as on the design of the form.

1. *Spacing*. The primary method for entering data should be considered when determining the amount of vertical and horizontal space to provide between items. If the typewriter is the primary data-entry method, the vertical spacing between items should be consistent with the regular typewriter spacing. Otherwise, employee time and effort is wasted when having to align the typewriter's printing device with each line of the form. Double spacing (three lines to an inch) is the recommended vertical spacing when using the typewriter as the primary data-entry method.

   Sufficient horizontal space must also be provided when the typewriter is used as the primary data-entry method. Ample space should be provided to accommodate the longest alphabetic or numerical item to be typed in each section of the form.

   When handwriting is used as the primary data-entry method, more horizontal space must be provided on the form than is needed when the typewriter is the primary data-entry method. Three lines to an inch is the recommended vertical spacing when handwriting is the primary data-entry method.
2. *Design format*. The primary data-entry method must also be considered in designing the format of the form. For example, if the primary data-entry method is a typewriter or some other mechanical printing device, a **box design** is preferred. This design, which is shown in Figure 23-7, simplifies aligning the form when it is placed in the typewriter. By placing the identifying tabs in the upper left corner rather than below each box, the typist does not have to space down to read what is to be typed and then space back up to type the desired information.

Line design, which is illustrated in Figure 23-8, is the preferred design format when handwriting is used as the primary data-entry method. In line design, the identifying tabs may appear below the lines.

<table>
<tr><td>Last Name</td><td>First Name</td><td>Middle Initial</td></tr>
<tr><td>House Number</td><td colspan="2">Street</td></tr>
<tr><td>City</td><td>State</td><td>ZIP Code</td></tr>
</table>

Figure 23-7 Box design.

Last Name	First Name	Middle Initial
House Number	Street	
City	State	ZIP Code

Figure 23-8 Line design.

Paper For several reasons, the paper on which forms are to be printed must be considered. The type of paper has a significant impact on the durability of forms, ability of forms to withstand the passage of time, and ease with which forms can be handled. Paper possesses three basic qualities—weight, grade, and grain. The effect that each of these qualities has on forms design is presented in the following sections.

1. *Weight*. The weight of paper on which forms are printed determines their durability. Weight is determined by how much 500 sheets (a ream) of paper stock measuring 17 by 22 inches weigh. If the ream weighs twenty pounds, the paper is referred to as twenty-pound paper. If it weighs sixteen pounds, it is sixteen-pound paper. The ream is then cut into different sizes, depending upon the desired size of the form. A ream of twenty-pound standard-sized letterhead paper (8 1/2 by 11 inches) weighs five pounds. The lightest weight paper suitable for the circumstances should be used.

   Because many forms nowadays have multiple copies, paper weight is especially important because it will determine the number of copies that can be made. The weight of paper may also have an impact on postal costs.

2. *Grade*. The **grade of paper** on which forms are printed determines their durability and how well they will withstand the passage of time. Paper grade is determined by the type of materials—cloth and/or sulphite—used in the manufacturing of paper. As the cloth content increases and the sulphite content decreases, the paper's grade improves. Paper consisting of 100 percent sulphite lasts up to fifteen years; 25 percent cloth, fifteen to twenty-five years; 50 percent cloth, twenty-six to fifty years; and 100 percent cloth, fifty years or longer.

   What impact does the grade of paper on which forms are printed have on forms design?

   The grade of paper on which forms are to be printed should be determined by (1) the number of years the organization is legally required to keep a particular form; (2) the frequency of use of the form (greater cloth content makes the paper less brittle); and (3) the primary data-entry method.

   In addition to the physical content of paper, its finish may also be an important consideration. The finish is apt to determine the ease with which erasures can be made, how rapidly ink will soak into the paper, and the overall appearance of the paper. Although several types of finish are available, a bond finish is one of the most commonly used, if not the most commonly used. Bond paper has greater internal strength than nonbond paper and is relatively easy to erase because of its fairly smooth finish.

   Why does the grain of paper have to be considered in forms design?

3. *Grain*. The **grain of paper** refers to the fibers contained in the paper. Fibers run through paper in either a vertical or horizontal direction, depending on how the paper is cut. When equipment is used for data

entry, special consideration should be given to the direction of the fibers in the form. The grain of paper should be vertical in forms that are fed automatically through the equipment. Therefore, the grain of paper should run the same direction that the paper is fed through the equipment. The paper is more apt to misfeed when the grain is opposite of the direction that it feeds through the equipment.

Color The use of colored paper and ink in printing forms should be kept to a minimum and used only when justifiable. Colored paper is often used in multiple-copy form sets, especially when different copies of the form are to be routed to different places. By printing each copy of the form set on paper of a different color, the sorting process is greatly simplified. Light-colored stock should be used because it provides a better contrast with the ink.

The use of several colors of ink is generally not recommended. Not only does the cost of printing increase, but also the different colors are apt to distract from the form's purpose. Generally, black is the most desirable color of ink, although limited use of other ink colors can be justified when certain sections of a form need to be emphasized.

Size The size of the form is determined largely by the amount of data that will be entered on the form. When a typewriter is used for data entry, forms can generally be smaller than when the primary data-entry method is handwriting. Another factor to consider is the size of the type used to print the form. Also of some importance may be the size of the paper stock from which the forms are cut. To keep trim waste to a minimum, the size of the paper stock should be considered in determining the size of the forms. Another factor to consider are possible restrictions placed on form size by the equipment that will be used in processing the forms.

Print type size While many printing type styles are available, the number used on a form should be kept to a minimum. When several type styles are used, items of equal significance should be printed with the same type size and style. Items needing emphasis can be typed in a bold type style, which will make them more distinctive.

Some states have passed legislation setting minimum type sizes for certain portions or areas of forms. The type size restrictions generally pertain to items having a financial or legal significance, such as the minimum type sizes of conditional sales contracts.

For what is shading used in forms design?

Shading To emphasize certain portions of forms, areas are sometimes shaded. The more distinctive areas draw the user's attention to the emphasized material.

Adequate margin size The method of data entry should be considered in determining adequate margin size. This is especially true when the typewriter is the primary data-entry method. A sufficient bottom margin should be provided to prevent slippage of the form in the typewriter when entering material at the bottom of the form.

Forms Design Software

Increasingly, forms designers are using forms design software in the process of preparing nonelectronic forms. These are the traditional type of forms that use paper, unlike the electronic forms discussed earlier that may or may not appear on paper.

In selecting a forms design software package, the following factors must be considered:

What factors need to be considered in selecting a forms design software package?

1. The hardware on which the software will be used, including its memory capabilities.
2. The ability of the software package to accept scanned information.
3. The format features provided by the software package, including the following:

   a. ability to accommodate variations in vertical and horizontal spacing
   b. availability of a variety of font types and sizes
   c. ability to make "combs," (the putting of vertical lines on a horizontal rule, the result of which serves as dividers for individual letters or numbers)
   d. presence of a zoom feature
   e. ability to accept logos (needs a graphic import capability)
   f. ability to provide a shell into which information is keyed, after which a paper copy of the form is prepared on a laser printer
   g. ability to imprint bar codes on forms.

In some instances, forms design software provides the shell for use in creating electronic forms. In other cases, it is used only to prepare the master needed for the quantity printing of forms on which information is generally either handwritten or typewritten.

Forms Design Illustrated

Figure 23-9 is presented to illustrate several of the forms design factors covered in the preceding discussion. The form is a three-part unit-set form. One-time carbon is used for making carbon copies.

1. *Adequate information*. The name of the form (Components) is clearly presented on the perforated strip at the top of the form. The name of the organization and its phone number appear in the upper left corner, along with the organization's logo.
2. *Alignment of items*. The form illustrates the alignment of items (hospital and city), which reduces the number of tabs that must be set on the equipment.
3. *Preprinting*. A considerable amount of preprinting (method of transporting, components, and use of components) is shown on the form. The form also makes use of ballot-box design for these items.
4. *Prenumbering*. The sequential number of the form (01255) appears on the form.
5. and **13.** *Instructions and shading*. Instructions appear in the lower left corner near the items to which they pertain. The instructions are highlighted by shading and arrows.

GLRP 5500 (6)

RUSSELL BUSINESS FORMS, INC.
LANSING, MICHIGAN R-1874

(1) COMPONENTS

GREAT LAKES REGIONAL
RED CROSS
BLOOD PROGRAM
☐ LANSING, MICHIGAN
(517) 484-7461

MUSKEGON, MICHIGAN
☐ (616) 726-3555

COMPONENT DISTRIBUTION ORDER 27505 (4)		TAKEN BY (2)	HOSPITAL	
DISTRIBUTION DATE	DAILY ORDER NUMBER	CITY	☐ ROUTINE ☐ EMERGENCY	☐ STOCK ☐ SPECIAL
(3) ☐ COURIER ☐ VOLUNTEER ☐ DISPATCHER	☐ POLICE ☐ BUS ☐ AIR	☐ OTHER	ALL UNITS LISTED ON THIS ORDER HAVE BEEN INSPECTED AND ARE NORMAL IN APPEARANCE.	PERSON FILLING ORDER

(11)

	Rh POSITIVE				Rh NEGATIVE				PRODUCT TOTALS
	O	A	B	AB	O	A	B	AB	
CRYOPRECIPITATE									
FRESH FROZEN PLASMA									
(12) PLATELET CONCENTRATE									
PHERESIS ☐ LEUKOCYTES ☐ PLATELETS									
RECONSTITUTED DEGLYCEROLIZED RED CELLS									
WASHED RED CELLS									
SINGLE DONOR PLASMA									
									TOTAL UNITS
SHIPPED									
GROUP TOTALS									

	TOTAL	LOT NUMBER	EXPIRATION
SERUM ALBUMIN			
AHF CONCENTRATE			

UNIT NUMBER	GROUP	Rh	EXPIRATION
(8)			

SPECIAL INSTRUCTIONS

RECEIVED BY	DATE/TIME

(5) (13) REGULATIONS REQUIRE THE HOSPITAL TO COMPLETE, SIGN AND RETURN THIS FORM WITHIN 7 DAYS

PERMANENT COPY

1. Adequate identification
2. Alignment of items
3. Preprinting
4. Prenumbering
5. Instructions
6. Identification number
8. Data entry method
11. Size
12. Print type size
13. Shading
14. Adequate margin size

Figure 23-9 Forms design illustrated. Courtesy: RBF, Inc., Lansing, MI.

6. *Identification number*. The identification number of the form (LRP 5500) appears on the perforated strip in the upper left corner.
8. *Data-entry method*. Because the data-entry method is primarily by typewriter, this fact was considered in the design process. The form accommodates the typical vertical spacing found on typewriters.

The form also illustrates the design format recommended when typewriters are used for data entry.

11. *Size*. The size of the form accommodates the various types of equipment that will be used for processing and storing the form.
12. *Printing type styles*. Items of equal emphasis on the form are presented in equal type sizes.
14. *Adequate margin sizes*. To prevent slippage, an adequate bottom margin appears on the form.

PROFESSIONAL FORMS SERVICES

What functions do professional forms services provide?

The use of **professional forms services** should not be overlooked, especially when the organization has several sophisticated systems. Using professional forms services becomes perhaps even more crucial for designing forms that are an integral part of these systems.

Forms services provide a variety of functions for their clients. The two most common ones are forms design and production. After the purpose of a form and its function within an operating system are identified, the specialist designs the form. Following the design and approval of the form, the service makes arrangements for producing the form. The forms specialist can also offer many suggestions for forms revision, which enables the organization to use forms compatible with one another as well as with its operating systems.

Some professional forms services also provide a variety of other functions. They may provide warehouse facilities for storing their clients' forms supply. They also keep their clients supplied with a sufficient quantity of forms. When the supply of forms stored in the warehouse reaches a certain level, the forms service automatically reorders a new supply. The forms service thus assumes responsibility for the storage and perpetual supply inventory of clients' forms.

IMPLICATIONS FOR THE ADMINISTRATIVE OFFICE MANAGER

The widespread installation of integrated systems is responsible for the design and control of forms becoming a more important administrative office management responsibility. Forms are an integral component of these systems, and every effort should be made to ensure that they enhance rather than destroy the operating efficiency of the systems in which they are used.

The involvement of the administrative office manager in forms design and control can vary from total responsibility to no responsibility. Those who are involved may be responsible for directing the forms control program as well as for designing the forms. Both these responsibilities require a thorough understanding of the elements of forms design and control.

In some instances, professional forms designers are used in the design process. The individual who serves as the liaison between the organization and the professional designer—whether it is the administrative office manager or some other employee—must have a basic understanding of the forms design process. Those who are not familiar with this process may find their liaison role to be a challenging experience.

For those managers who are knowledgeable about the design process, forms simplification, consolidation, and elimination may be a more challenging task than forms design. This task is simplified somewhat, though, when each manager in the organization becomes concerned about the efficiency of the forms for which he or she is responsible.

REVIEW QUESTIONS

1. What are the objectives of a forms control program?
2. What is involved in the cataloging of forms?
3. Why is the prenumbering of forms useful?
4. What device is commonly used in entering data into electronic forms?
5. When instructions are included on forms, where should they be placed?
6. What techniques exist for making carbon copies of forms?
7. Why should the data-entry method be considered when designing forms?
8. How is the weight of paper determined?
9. How do the grade and grain of paper differ?
10. What factors need to be considered in selecting a forms design software package?

DISCUSSION QUESTIONS

1. As the manager of the forms control program in the organization in which you work, you are responsible for selecting seven individuals to serve on the program's advisory committee. What background characteristics should these individuals possess in order to make the maximum contribution to the committee?
2. You and another employee where you work were discussing integrated systems. The individual with whom you were talking said that he was under the impression that a system is designed around the forms that are used in an organization—and not the forms around the system. Discuss the implications of the other employee's ideas about the relationship between systems and forms design.
3. You are working on a special project for your employer. One of your responsibilities is to make a collection of all the forms that are used in the organization and prepare a forms classification. When you explained the nature of this project to one of the department heads, he said, "You've got to be kidding! Someone is allowing you to waste your time doing this?" Defend the importance of the project on which you are working.
4. Six years ago when you were a member of the forms control program advisory committee in the organization in which you work, you were surprised to learn that the organization had 194 official forms. You were again appointed recently to serve on the committee after a four-year absence and were even more shocked to learn that the organization now has 318 official forms. You acknowledge that a number of the new forms are probably unjustifiable. What types of uncontrolled situations may be responsible for some of the increase in the number of official forms?
5. One of your subordinates spends about three hours each day typing purchase orders. Batching these orders so they can be typed continuously during a time span is difficult to do. Therefore, this subordinate might type three or four orders, then type some other material, and then return to typing purchase orders. Yesterday, for example, the typing of purchase orders was interrupted eighteen times with other materials that had to be typed. Your subordinate recently complained to you about the inefficiency of the continuous format of the purchase order. Discuss the legitimacy of her complaint. Under the circumstances, what type of form may be appropriate?
6. You have been asked by your supervisor to design a new purchase order.

After you agreed to accept this responsibility, you told your supervisor that you needed some background information before you could begin the design process. Your supervisor replied, "No, you don't need any other information—just design it." Discuss the implications of this situation. What kinds of background information would you find helpful?

STUDENT PROJECTS AND ACTIVITIES

1. Arrange to have an individual responsible for forms design demonstrate the design process, from beginning to end.
2. Obtain a comparable form from two different organizations (such as a purchase order or an invoice). In what ways are the forms similar? Different?
3. Tour a facility in which forms are printed. Pay particular attention to how some of the more specialized forms are produced.
4. Critique a form, using the design guidelines presented in this chapter.
5. Prepare a form, such as a purchase order or an invoice. Arrange to have the form critiqued by a forms designer.

MINICASE

Jamison Importers is a fairly small wholesaler of items sold in gift stores located throughout the nation. The firm is in the process of developing a new invoice that will be processed on its new microcomputer. The organization is hoping to design an invoice that also incorporates a shipping label. The president of the company has asked you, the office supervisor, for a written report in which you are to

1. Identify the type of form you recommend, along with a rationale for your decision.
2. Identify the kind of carbonizing process you recommend and your reasons for choosing that process.

CASE

The Borowitcz Manufacturing Company, which is located in Memphis, Tennessee, has hired you, a consultant, to help design efficient office procedures. When you were contacted a few weeks ago about this project, you were told that the office function "has several areas of operating inefficiency."

After you spent several hours analyzing various aspects of the organization's operations, you have concluded that a forms control program is badly needed. Forms are continually being developed that seem to lack full justification. Many of the forms are also poorly designed.

In talking with several managers in Borowitcz, you have gotten the impression that they will not be in favor of implementing another regulatory program unless its need can be totally justified. Consequently, you know that if you are to be successful in getting your suggestion approved, you will have to build a strong case for the development of a forms control program. In the report you are to prepare for Borowitcz, you decide to

1. Discuss the benefits of a forms control program as a means of trying to convince management of the need for such a program.
2. Discuss the strategies that can be used to help increase employee acceptance of the program once it is implemented.

OFFICE REPROGRAPHICS AND MAIL SERVICES

CHAPTER AIM

After studying this chapter, you should be able to design an effective reprographics service and a mail service for an organization.

CHAPTER OUTLINE

CHAPTER TERMS

Addresser-printers
Conveyor system
Courier services
Desktop publishing
Diazo copying
Diffusion transfer copying
Electric mail carts
Fiber optics copying
Gelatin transfer copying
Offset process duplication
Pneumatic tube system
Production standards
Reprographics centers
Satellite centers
Spirit process duplication
Stabilization copying
Stamping-sealing equipment
Stencil duplication
Thermography copying
Xerographic process copying

Technologically, the equipment used in **reprographics centers** is undergoing fairly significant change. New technology enables the equipment to produce higher quality work at a faster rate and at a lower per unit cost. The technology also makes the equipment easier to use, and the documents produced using the new technology have a more appealing visual appearance than the early technology was able to provide.

What is the primary function of reprographics centers?

Reprographics centers are designed to provide copying and duplication services. Day-to-day management responsibility is generally assigned to the center supervisor, while the administrative office manager typically has overall managerial responsibility for the center.

This chapter, in addition to covering the topic of reprographics, provides a discussion of several mechanical devices used to transmit internal correspondence as well as provides information about the mailroom. While the mailroom supervisor is typically responsible for the day-to-day operations of the mailroom, the administrative office manager often has overall responsibility for its effective management.

ORGANIZATION OF THE REPROGRAPHICS CENTER

The efficiency of the reprographics center, similarly to most other administrative office management functions, is likely to be determined in part by its organizational structure. Operating efficiency can come closer to its maximum potential when the center is properly organized and managed. The appropriate organization for a reprographics center is determined in part by the various needs it fulfills.

Determining Needs

The administrative office manager and/or the supervisor responsible for the present reprographics unit are generally the individuals responsible for determining the center's needs. To a large extent, the needs are affected by the organization's copying and duplicating requirements. In most cases, these requirements are assessed by analyzing the nature and quantity of copied and duplicated materials.

What factors are considered in determining the needs of the reprographics center?

To determine needs, the following factors should be considered:

1. The number of copies needed of various documents prepared in the organization.

2. Special production requirements of the copying or duplicating process (such as color requirements, reducing or enlarging requirements, and types of paper on which the copies are to be made).
3. The overall quality of the original document (such as typewritten, line drawings, and photographs).
4. The desired quality of the copying or duplicating processes.
5. The turnaround time needed for obtaining copies of original documents.
6. The nature of specialized production jobs.

Unless this phase of the installation of a center is carefully considered, the center most likely will not be efficiently organized nor will the equipment in the center be appropriate for various production jobs.

Centralized Control

A common characteristic of most reprographics centers nowadays is the centralized control of the unit. Typically, the administrative office manager has overall responsibility for and control over the operation of the center. The day-to-day operation of the center, however, is frequently the responsibility of a supervisor.

Primarily to facilitate user accessibility, reprographics centers generally are located centrally in the organization. Because most of the departments are likely to use reprographics services, location is of primary importance. In organizations that occupy several floors of a building, the location of **satellite centers** throughout the premises may be desirable. These centers most likely contain only a portion of the equipment found in the main center. Smaller production jobs are performed in the satellite centers while major jobs are most likely performed in the main center. In some cases, departments that make extensive use of copiers may find essential the installation of their own desktop-sized copiers.

In comparison with decentralized control, centralized control of the center offers the following advantages:

What advantages result from centralized control?

1. Greater control over the reprographics function is possible.
2. The center is likely to operate with greater efficiency.
3. The selection and utilization of the equipment is likely to be more efficient.
4. The process of purchasing and replenishing supplies is likely to be performed more efficiently.

Personnel

The quality of the services produced in the reprographics center is directly related to the care with which personnel produce the work. Because many of the processes are quite specialized, the employment of individuals who are skilled in and knowledgeable about reprographics is critical. Otherwise, maximum use of the equipment may not be possible.

A number of techniques are used to teach personnel how to operate the equipment found in the reprographics center. For the less sophisticated devices, manufacturers generally provide short, comprehensive training sessions. For more sophisticated equipment, the personnel may need to complete a formal education program provided by a variety of schools, including high schools, technical schools, community colleges, and four-year colleges and universities. The participants in these educational programs frequently enroll in a printing or graphics program.

Operators of heavy printing equipment commonly work for several years as a printer apprentice. Heavy equipment is more likely to be used in firms that specialize in printing than in reprographics centers found in organizations.

Layout

Also needing to be considered is the layout of the reprographics center. Because a considerable amount of work produced in the center involves several steps, the flow of work through the center must be planned. The most efficient pattern is to have a straight-line work flow that eliminates backtracking and crisscrossing.

The specialized nature of the equipment found in reprographics centers makes desirable the use of the various services provided by equipment manufacturers. Representatives of these manufacturers are not only able to provide excellent suggestions for the layout of a reprographics center, but also they are able to help an organization develop efficient operating procedures.

What special facilities may need to be provided in the reprographics center?

Planning the layout of the center involves (1) determining the placement of the equipment in the center, (2) providing washroom and darkroom facilities, if needed, and (3) providing adequate storage space for the enormous amount of supplies that are typically needed in printing and duplicating operations. In addition, certain environmental conditions are also important in the center, including adequate ventilation and acoustical control.

Policies and Procedures

The policies and procedures used in operating the center are mainly concerned with the delivery of user services.

The completion of a requisition form is generally required by those who use the services of the reprographics center. The form is a work order that includes the following items: the number or name of the document being reproduced; the desired reproduction method; the number of pages in the master copy; the number of copies needed; special directions (such as color of paper, ink, reduction, collating, and stapling); the name of the department to be charged; the name of the individual making the request; and authorization.

Another important procedure involves the handling of confidential materials. To maintain the integrity of this material, some centers assign the processing of confidential work to certain individuals who can be trusted and who are held responsible for maintaining its confidentiality.

What types of policies should be established for the reprographics center?

The reprographics center must also establish a policy governing the processing of high-priority items. This policy is needed because some employees believe that each item they send to the reprographics center has a high priority, requiring immediate attention. Most centers operate on a first-in, first-out basis, except for legitimate high-priority or rush jobs. For a job to be classified as high priority, some centers require that the job be certified as such by several individuals. This procedure eliminates the likelihood that some employees will abuse the privilege of rush production.

Designing the process for determining the appropriate copying or duplicating method for each job is another procedure that needs to be developed. The basis for determining the appropriate method is influenced by the number of copies that are to be made, the intended use of the copies, and the turnaround time needed.

Maintenance of Equipment

The specialized nature of the equipment found in reprographics centers requires quality maintenance that extends its life and improves the quality with which the work is produced. Improper maintenance is often responsible for increasing the center's operating costs.

Equipment operators are able to provide a wide variety of routine equipment maintenance, which helps keep the equipment clean and properly adjusted. More complex maintenance is provided by specially trained individuals. In some cases, these individuals are employed by the organization; but in most cases, they work for equipment vendors and provide the maintenance service on a request basis.

Standards

For the reprographics center to be financially feasible, its efficiency is paramount. One way to judge the center's efficiency is to determine how well **production standards** are attained. These standards, which can be obtained from many of the manufacturers of the equipment found in the center, identify the per hour number of copies that various devices are reasonably capable of attaining. Without the use of standards, the organization has no way of knowing whether or not the reprographics center is operating efficiently. If the actual results are considerably less than the level of expected results, the administrative office manager and/or the reprographics center supervisor must determine the reasons for the difference. Where needed, appropriate action must be subsequently taken.

In some instances, the reprographics center supervisor will determine the standards rather than using those available from the various equipment manufacturers. To do this, the center's output has to be recorded over a period of time. These records can then be used to determine either hourly or daily output rates for each employee in the center, as well as to determine the need for additional employees. Each time the volume of work increases to the point that one more employee is needed, the reprographics center supervisor can use these data to justify hiring additional help.

In addition to production standards, the reprographics center must also be concerned with cost standards. Factors that must be considered in developing these standards are the following: cost of operating equipment (lease or depreciation); cost of supplies; operator costs; and the cost of the space occupied by the center. When the per unit costs exceed normal costs, the administrative office manager or the reprographics center supervisor should determine the reasons for the excessive costs.

Cost Control

The nature of the reprographics center not only makes cost control desirable, but also crucial. The existence of many potential areas of costly waste in the center requires giving continual attention to cost-control measures. The following suggestions are useful for controlling costs:

How can costs be controlled in the reprographics center?

1. Use the most economical duplicating and copying processes that the jobs will allow.
2. Request or produce only as many copies as are needed.
3. Keep the equipment in proper adjustment so that very few, if any, pages are ruined in the duplicating or copying processes.
4. Print on both sides of the paper when possible.

5. Use the services of the reprographics center for a particular project unless some outside organization is able to provide more economical service.
6. Take advantage of quantity purchasing of supplies.

Equipment

Also having a significant bearing on the efficiency of the reprographics center is the equipment that is used. The center's equipment also determines to a great extent the types of services the center is able to provide. A wide variety of equipment is presently on the market, much of which varies considerably in terms of the operational processes.

Subsequent sections in this chapter provide a detailed discussion of the following: the copying process, the duplicating process, and the imprinting process. Also included is a discussion about some of the auxiliary equipment found in reprographics centers.

THE COPYING PROCESS

The presence of efficient copying equipment has undoubtedly been greatly responsible for the paperwork explosion occurring in organizations. For the most part, the equipment has resulted in significant advantages, although certain disadvantages also result. Perhaps the most significant disadvantage is the ease with which unneeded extra copies of documents are made. Not only does this add to operating costs, but also provisions have to be made for storing and/or disposing of the extra copies.

A common means of categorizing copying equipment is by the type of paper used in the equipment. While some copying equipment requires special sensitized paper, other copying equipment uses plain paper.

Copying Equipment Requiring Sensitized Paper

What types of copying processes use sensitized paper?

Several copying processes require the use of sensitized paper. Among these processes are the following: diffusion transfer, gelatin transfer, stabilization, diazo, and thermography.

Diffusion transfer Also called a wet-copy process, **diffusion transfer** requires the use of two chemically coated sheets of paper for each copy that is made. One of the sheets is a negative coated with a silver halide gelatin, making the sheet sensitive to light. The other sheet is the positive. The face of the document being copied is placed against the gelatin side of the negative sheet. These two sheets are then exposed to an intense light. The image areas of the original absorb light rays while the nonimage areas of the original document reflect light back to the negative, thus forming an image on the negative.

After the negative has been exposed, it is placed face-to-face against the positive sheet; and the two sheets are then passed through a developing solution. A reaction of this solution with the image on the negative sheet causes the image to transfer by diffusion to the positive sheet. The two sheets are then passed through rollers to remove excess developer. The negative is discarded; and after the positive sheet has been allowed to dry for a few minutes, the copy is ready for use.

Compared with some of the other copying processes, this method results in several disadvantages: a developing solution is needed, copies have to dry before they are usable, and the process is quite slow.

What are the characteristics of the gelatin transfer process?

Gelatin transfer Sometimes known as dye transfer, **gelatin transfer** also requires the use of special paper and developing chemicals. The face of the original document is placed against the surface of the negative sheet, which is coated with a gelatin substance. The original and the negative are exposed to light, allowing the nonimage areas of the original to reflect to the negative. The exposed negative is then passed through a chemical solution that causes gelatin in the exposed areas to harden. The unexposed areas of the negative remain soft, and as the negative is passed through the chemical solution, these areas become a dye. As the dye areas of the negative come into contact with the copying paper, the dye transfers to the paper, which creates a likeness of the original on the paper. Up to ten copies of the original can be made before the dye either dries or is spent.

This process has the same disadvantages as the diffusion transfer process.

Stabilization Whereas the diffusion and the gelatin transfer processes require both negative and positive sheets, the **stabilization** process does not. This process involves the reflection of light from the original document onto sensitized paper. The copy paper is first passed through a developing chemical and then through a stabilization chemical, which permanently affixes the image on the copy paper.

Stabilization is especially suited for copying photographs. Like the other processes already discussed, disadvantages of this process are the following: required use of chemicals, copies have to be dry before they are usable, and the process is slow.

Diazo Especially well suited for making copies of architectural and engineering drawings, **diazo** requires the use of an original document in a translucent state. Therefore, it can only be used to copy those documents that have printing on one side of the page. The original document is placed against a copy sheet coated with a diazonium compound. The two sheets are then exposed to light. The nonimage areas allow the light rays to pass through to the coated copy paper, which activates the decomposition of the diazonium compound. The copy paper is then exposed to a chemical; and while the decomposed areas remain neutral, the active areas (image areas on the original) react and cause an image to appear on the copy sheet.

Although it is one of the least expensive copying processes, diazo is marked by several disadvantages, including the use of ammonia fumes in the development process and the slowness with which the process works.

What are the characteristics of the thermography process?

Thermography Another of the copying processes requiring the use of sensitized paper is **thermography**. This process works on the principle that dark areas or substances absorb heat, whereas light areas or substances do not. This process is also known as the infrared or the heat-transfer process. When thermography is used, the original document is placed beneath the copy paper. As the original and the copy paper are exposed to infrared rays, the image or printed areas of the original hold heat, causing the copy paper to darken in these areas. The original images are produced on the copy paper. Because this process requires the use of writing and printing substances that hold heat long enough to transfer the image to the copy paper, some types of ink and colors cannot be used.

Among the more serious disadvantages of this process are the restriction of its use to heat-sensitive substances and the tendency of thermography copy papers to darken and become brittle with age.

Copying Equipment Using Plain Paper

What copying processes use plain paper?

Two copying processes presently available use plain paper: the **xerographic process** and **fiber optics**. For routine types of office copying, these processes are generally considered as being superior to the other processes that require sensitized copy paper or liquid chemicals.

Xerographic process The basis of the xerographic process is the physics principle of unlike electrical charges being attracted to each other but like charges being repelled from each other. The process, by means of a camera, transmits the image of the original document to a selenium-coated drum that is positively charged. The nonimage areas of the original document allow light to strike the drum, which causes the positive charge in those areas to dissipate. The image areas of the drum, on the other hand, hold their positive charge. A negatively charged black powder is then spread over the drum; and because unlike electrical charges attract each other, the powder adheres to the image areas. A plain sheet of paper with a positive charge is then passed over the drum, which transfers the images to the paper and creates a likeness of the original document. The black powder is permanently affixed to the paper by means of a heat transfer process.

Some of the newer, more advanced copiers replace the traditional light source with a laser or CRT light source. A toner is used to produce the image that appears on the drum, and the image is transferred to paper. The toner is affixed to the paper by means of a heat transfer process.

Among the features commonly found on today's plain-paper copiers are image reduction, image enlargement, automatic document feed, duplexing (facilitates copying on both sides of a sheet of paper during one pass through the copier), collating, and stapling.

Other new, less common features found on copiers include automatic paper folding; adhesive binding; automatic hole punching; facsimile; built-in image editing (allows certain areas of the document to be copied and other areas to be deleted); spot color (allows the addition of one color to a portion of a black-and-white copy); digital editing (the copy scans the image to convert it to digital signals, which makes possible the subsequent alteration of the image); and remote monitoring and diagnostics (an internal modem permits the copier to send usage data from a branch office to a home office or, when the copier is malfunctioning, send diagnostic data from the installation site to a service center).

Many new plain-paper copiers use microprocessors to perform a variety of functions. Among these are diagnostic capabilities, density control, and user prompts. For example, the prompt may give the user the following verbal instruction: "Please load with more paper." When the paper supply has been replenished, the microprocessor-controlled prompt will say, "Thank you."

Full-color copier technology is currently developing at a fast rate. This technology, which permits the interfacing of full-color copiers with microcomputers and facsimile machines, is resulting in the continual decrease in the per page cost of full-color copying. Like black-and-white copying, full-color copying also uses xerographic technology. Other technologies used are electrophotographic (image is produced by using chemicals on photographic paper) and thermal transfer (uses heat and pressure to fuse onto the surface of paper the colors that are found on a coated ribbon). The xerographic and electrophotographic technologies produce better quality copies than does the thermal transfer process.

The digital color copying process provides a number of useful features unavailable on nondigital equipment. Among the features are the following: stretching, shrinking, or slanting text material, enlarging (up to 200 percent) and reducing material (down to 50 percent), overlaying one image on another, mirror imaging, color converting, reverse imaging, and deleting of material while copying other material from the same image.

What categories of plain-paper copiers are available?

The following categories of plain-paper copiers are available: low volume, medium volume, and high volume.

Low-volume copiers are designed to produce 1,000 to 20,000 copies per month at rates of 10 to 30 copies per minute. The copiers, which are small enough to fit on a desk top, are found distributed throughout the premises. Some of the low-volume copiers use microprocessor controls.

The medium-volume copiers are used to produce 20,000 to 50,000 copies per month. They operate at a faster rate (30 to 60 copies per minute) than the low-volume copiers, and generally they are centrally located. Medium-volume copiers are likely to possess more functions than their low-volume counterparts.

The high-volume copiers are used to produce 50,000 to 100,000 copies per month and operate at rates exceeding 60 copies per minute. They are always used in a central location. Of the three categories, high-volume copiers perform the greatest number of functions.

The newest generation of plain-paper copiers are the electronic or intelligent printers/copiers, which actually are nonimpact printers and copiers integrated into one device. This equipment may receive digital input from a word processor, computer, or CRT unit, from which it prepares a hard copy. In some cases, the printing will take place immediately. In other instances, the information will be stored in the system's memory that is capable of holding up to 1,000 pages. Printing will be completed later. Another feature of the printer/copier is ability to store for later use a variety of graphics and forms. Color printer/copier devices are also now available that permit printing in color from a computer as well as color copying.

A new copier device is available that combines the following functions: copying, scanning, facsimile, computing, and printing. Eventually, this device will be able to massage, change, and redistribute all of the information received—including paper documents, images, graphics, computer data/information, and mail—in an organization.

Figure 24-1 illustrates a plain-paper copier using the xerographic process.

When selecting or comparing copiers, the following factors should be kept in mind:

What factors should be considered when selecting copiers?

Copier applications
Equipment reliability
Equipment cost
Image quality
Copier volume
Vendor reputation
Vendor service response time

Fiber optics The newest development in copying processes is the use of fiber optics. The process functions in the following way: The conventional mirror lens assembly on a plain-paper copier is replaced with a fiber optics mechanism. The optic tubes transmit light from the original document to a drum. Each fiber carries a minute portion of the document image. The toner, which produces the image, is fused to the paper as the document is prepared.

Figure 24-1 Plain-paper copier. Courtesy: Xerox Corporation.

Monitoring Copier Usage

The accessibility of copiers is directly related to their use for personal copying. Among the suggestions for reducing copier misuse are the following:

1. Set the per page cost of personal copying as low as possible, assuming that if the cost is sufficiently low, employees will be more inclined to pay for personal copying.
2. Restrict copier usage to certain individuals who will do all copying for the organization.
3. Install counter-monitoring equipment on copiers, thus preventing copier usage without the counter cartridge. To use the copier, an employee has to obtain the cartridge from his or her supervisor.
4. Remove convenience copiers and install satellite copy centers, with use being restricted to individuals who work in the centers.

THE DUPLICATION PROCESS

The differentiation between copying and duplicating at one time was fairly clear-cut. The major distinction was in the number of copies the equipment was used to make. To illustrate, a copying process was typically advantageous for making fewer than twenty to thirty copies of an original, while duplicating processes were used for larger-quantity jobs. But because of new copying technology, an increasing number of organizations are now using copiers for all but their largest production jobs.

What types of duplicating processes exist?

The three major types of duplicating processes found today are the spirit process, the stencil process, and the offset process. As time passes, the spirit and stencil processes are used less commonly in offices.

Spirit Process

This process is suitable for making fewer than 300 copies from one master. Of the three duplicating processes, the **spirit process** is the least expensive. It requires the use of a spirit master, which consists of two sheets—the carbon backing sheet and the face of the master. As the master face is written on, drawn on, or typed on, the carbon adheres to its backside (in reverse image). When ready for use, the master is placed carbon side up on the duplicator drum. The master is moistened with a special alcohol solvent, which causes a small portion of the carbon to transfer to each sheet of copy paper upon its passage through the duplicator. The master can be used to print copies until all of the carbon is depleted.

Spirit masters can also be prepared by a thermal process. The original document and a thermal master are fed through a device that causes the image areas of the document to hold heat. The buildup of heat then causes the carbon on the thermal master to adhere to the face of the master. Typically, fewer copies can be made from thermal masters than from the spirit masters prepared in the conventional manner.

The spirit process is quite flexible. Several colors of carbon can be placed on one spirit master, which provides multicolor printing in one pass through the machine. The masters also can be stored and reused. In addition, portions of the master can be removed from it after some of the printing has been done. This facilitates use of the same master for two different production jobs that have identical information appearing within each. To eliminate a section, the portions can either be cut out of the master, can be covered with tape, or the carbon in those areas can be scraped from the master. The colors produced by the spirit process are not as vivid as the colors produced by stencil duplication.

Stencil Duplication

What are the characteristics of the stencil duplication process?

Like the spirit process, **stencil duplication** is also rather inexpensive. Stencil duplication is suitable for making up to 2,500 copies from one master. The stencil consists of a fiber substance coated with wax. When the stencil is typed, written on, or drawn on, the wax is pushed aside, which enables ink to pass through the exposed areas. The stencil is attached to a drum covered with an ink-soaked pad. The ink, which passes through the exposed areas of the stencil, is transferred to the copy paper as the paper and stencil come into contact with one another. If properly cared for, the stencil can be stored and reused.

When color duplicating is desired, a separate stencil may have to be made for each needed color. For example, a stencil may have to be prepared to transfer the red areas to the paper, another for the blue areas, and so forth. Therefore, if a duplicating job involves four different stencils, the paper has to pass through the duplicator four different times.

In some instances, producing multicolor documents may be possible simply by applying the various colors of ink to the appropriate areas of one ink pad. This eliminates having to make separate stencils for each color because all colors will be printed in one pass of the paper through the machine. This technique is not suitable when the various ink colors are near one another on the ink pad as the inks have a tendency to blend with one another.

Stencils can be prepared on an electronic stencil-making device. The same images that are found on the original document are burned into the stencil. Electronic stencil-making devices are also capable of making halftone illustrations.

More copies can be made from a stencil master than can be made from a spirit master. In comparison to the spirit process, the stencil duplication process is less convenient for multicolor duplication.

The advent of digital duplicators has given the stencil-duplication process a renewed life in an increasing number of organizations. These duplicators use a digital scanning process to prepare the required stencil. Once the stencil is prepared, the device automatically mounts it and then unmounts it when the desired number of copies have been printed. As a result, it is cleaner to use than was the case with the old stencil duplicators. Compared with copier technology, digital duplicators provide the following advantages: they produce no ozone or radiation, and they use water-based ink (unlike their predecessors that used a petroleum-based ink). The quality of work produced by digital duplicators makes it suitable for company newsletters, manuals, reports, and so forth.

Offset Process

What are the characteristics of the offset process?

Although more costly and more intricate than either the spirit process or stencil duplication, the **offset process** is more extensively used than either of the other two duplication processes. Depending on the conditions, several thousand copies can be made from one master.

The offset process is based on the chemical principle that water and grease do not mix. The image areas on the printing master hold the greasy printing ink, while the nonimage areas hold water, which repels the ink. The inked images are transferred or offset to a rubber blanket or roller. As the duplicating paper comes into contact with the roller, the image is transferred to the paper.

Offset masters, which are prepared in a variety of ways, are either paper or metal. Some of the paper masters are direct image and can be drawn on, typed on, or written on. Paper masters can also be prepared photographically by a master maker while the metal plates can only be prepared photographically by a plate maker. A much larger number of copies can be produced from a metal plate than from a paper master.

Many offset duplicators are highly automated. Some of the features found on these duplicators are the ability to cut sheets of paper from a paper roll; perforating, slitting, and collating attachments; a counter that stops the duplicator when the desired number of copies have been prepared; automatic insertion and ejection of paper masters; and automated machine cleanup.

Of the three primary duplication processes, offset offers the best quality of work. In most cases, the quality of offset duplication is nearly as high as the quality of the original. Because offset equipment is more specialized, operators need to be well trained. In relation to the spirit and stencil processes, the per unit cost of offset duplication is somewhat higher.

Copy Printer

What are the characteristics of a copy printer?

Copy-printer equipment, which incorporates the offset printing process, is a new development in reprographics equipment. This device is especially well suited for high-volume, short-run, repetitive jobs. It is designed for situations in which five to a thousand copies are needed and is well suited for organizations printing from 150,000 to 500,000 copies per month.

A characteristic of copy-printer equipment is the extensive number of its automated features. The operator simply places the original in the machine and inputs the number of copies to be made. The machine automatically completes the job. The machine, therefore, is capable of electrostatic master making, master feeding, and offset duplicating, all without operator assistance. In addition, most copy printers are also capable of reducing the original to a smaller-sized copy as well as sorting the copies into sets.

THE IMPRINTING PROCESS

The imprinting process is used to add information to an already existing document. Several imprinting processes are available, including those discussed in the following paragraphs.

Signature Machines

Two types of signature machines are presently available. One machine uses a ribbon to imprint a signature on a document. This is the type of machine frequently used to affix signatures to checks. Another type uses a template of the individual's signature. As the stylus follows the signature contained in the template, a mechanical pen produces the signature on the document. This device is especially useful for placing original signatures on important mass mailings, for example.

Impression Stamps

These stamps are used when a small amount of repetitive data needs to be recorded on documents. Examples are date stamps, signature stamps, name and address stamps, and authorization stamps. For small jobs, an impression stamp is generally more convenient than other printing processes.

Numbering Devices

Numbering a series of documents sequentially is often desirable. The use of a mechanical numbering device is much quicker and neater than numbering by hand.

AUXILIARY EQUIPMENT

During the last few years, a considerable amount of auxiliary equipment for use in reprographics centers has been developed. While some of this equipment mechanizes the duplicating process to a greater extent than ever before, other equipment expands the process so a greater variety of jobs can be performed. The following provides a discussion of some of the more significant developments.

Automatic Collators

These devices have considerably reduced the amount of the manual effort expended in many offices. Automatic collators, which can be attached to offset duplicators, copiers, and intelligent copiers/printers, mechanically collate pages as they leave the device. Each page is transported to the appropriate bin in the collator. At the end of the production cycle, the bins will contain one copy of each page that has been duplicated/copied. As the collated sets are removed from the collator, they can be stapled, thus completing the job.

Binders

What is meant by perfect binding?

Instead of binding documents with staples or spirally binding documents, a recent development is the adhesive binding of documents. This process, which is also known as "perfect binding," involves putting a thin layer of adhesive along one edge of the document to be bound. The adhesive holds the pages together.

Photolettering Equipment

A form of photocomposition, photolettering equipment is used to place letters, one at a time, on a strip of film or on photographic paper. The photolettering process is primarily used for setting miscellaneous lines of type, typically in a large-size format.

Desktop Publishing

The newest development in the photocomposition process is known as **desktop publishing**. Primarily used for internal and lower-volume external documents, desktop publishing results in the preparation of documents that have a professional appearance. A microcomputer and desktop publishing software package are used for the inputting of material into the system. The document, the output of which is typically prepared on a laser printer capable of producing high-quality work, has the appearance of a typeset document. When multiple copies are needed, an original of the document is used as a master. The process facilitates the inclusion in a document of graphics, photographs, and various sizes and styles of type.

Phototypesetters

This type of equipment is designed for projects too large for processing on photocomposition equipment. The present phototypesetters are either classified as second-generation or third-generation equipment.

Phototypesetting is used to prepare documents needing a more professional image than provided by typewriters or computer printers. Its uses are extensive, including, for example, preparing documents that will be distributed externally as well as for preparing such internal documents as manuals, reports, newsletters, and announcements.

How do second-generation and third-generation phototypesetters differ from one another?

Second-generation phototypesetters are driven or controlled by other input media, such as perforated tape or magnetic tape produced on a keyboard device. These phototypesetters generate type images by flashing light beams through a photographic master, such as a revolving disk or strip of film. The smaller phototypesetters typically have no more than four different type styles or fonts, and they set type in a minimum number of sizes. The larger phototypesetters have more type fonts, can set type in a greater number of sizes, and are much faster than the smaller versions. Some of the newer second-generation devices also incorporate a microcomputer that can be programmed to hyphenate words automatically at the ends of lines.

Third-generation phototypesetters differ from the second-generation equipment in the manner in which the type is generated. The third-generation equipment creates type characters on the face of a cathode ray tube, and

Figure 24-2 Software-based Modular Composition System (MCS TM). Courtesy: Compugraphic Corporation.

these images are subsequently photographed. This generation of equipment also permits much faster operating speeds than earlier generations did.

Because of the complexity of the phototypesetting process, any organization giving thought to the installation of such equipment should carefully consider all the alternatives. Before an installation decision is made, the cost of the equipment requires a thorough analysis of the need for a phototypesetting system.

Figure 24-2 illustrates a phototypesetter.

MECHANICAL DEVICES FOR TRANSPORTING INTERNAL CORRESPONDENCE

What mechanical devices are used for the internal transmission of documents?

While some of the internally created documents stay within the departments in which they are generated, others must be transported to other departments. In addition to using a messenger service, a variety of mechanical devices are used. The more common types of mechanical devices are pneumatic tubes, conveyor systems, and electric mail carts.

Pneumatic Tubes

The use of a **pneumatic tube system** requires a network of tubes located throughout the premises. To install a tube system after a building has been completed adds greatly to the cost of the system.

Documents to be transported from one department to another are placed in special carriers that travel through the network of tubes. Less sophisticated tube systems generally have a central receiving-distributing point that interconnects the tube network throughout the departments in the organization. More sophisticated pneumatic systems incorporate an automatic dialing tube unit. The user dials the destination point and inserts the carrier into the tube. Once it begins traveling, the carrier is automatically switched from one tube to another until it reaches its destination. The more sophisticated systems eliminate the central receiving-distributing point required in the less sophisticated systems.

Conveyor Systems

An effective mechanical device for transporting documents from one location to another location on the same floor is the **conveyor system**. This device consists of a continuous conveyor belt on which several multilength channels are placed. Each workstation has its own channel. After the document is placed in the appropriate channel, the belt moves it to the desired station where it falls into a receiving tray. The number of workstations that can receive documents by this system is limited to the number of upright channels that are contained in the system.

Electric Mail Carts

Some organizations use **electric mail carts** rather than employees to distribute incoming mail or to collect outgoing mail from the various departments. The carts, which follow copper wires imbedded in the floor or magnetic paint on the floor surface, can be programmed to stop at various locations. These devices automatically stop when an object gets in their way.

Some electric mail carts are equipped with a recorder unit that can be used to broadcast any kind of prerecorded information. The more sophisticated carts are also capable of riding unassisted on elevators. Figure 24-3 illustrates an electric mail cart.

Figure 24-3 Electric mail cart. Courtesy: Bell & Howell, Inc., Automated Systems Division, Zeeland, MI.

THE MAILROOM

Considerable diversity exists among mailrooms found throughout organizations. In fact, of all the areas of administrative office management, the greatest diversity most likely will be found among organizations' mailrooms.

To a large extent, the structure of the mailroom is determined by the size and needs of the organization. Smaller organizations are generally able to function with one individual who has responsibilities other than processing incoming and outgoing mail and delivering internal correspondence. In larger organizations, one or more employees have a full-time responsibility for mail services. The personnel, layout, and equipment requirements of the mailroom are determined by several factors:

What factors determine the personnel, layout, and equipment requirements of the mailroom?

1. The number of employees in the organization.
2. The correspondence volume of the organization. The volume is affected by the type of organization.
3. The speed with which the mail must be handled. Organizations that receive large sums of money through the mail each day may require faster mail-handling procedures than other organizations require.
4. The nature of the outgoing mail that is processed in the mailroom. Correspondence mailed in standard-sized envelopes that does not need to be weighed requires less processing time than materials that must be weighed or that require special handling because of the mailing container.

Typical functions of mailrooms are the processing of incoming and outgoing mail, internal pickup and delivery of mail, distribution of internal correspondence, and receipt and shipment of parcels. The extent to which each of these functions is performed in the mailroom partially determines the number and type of personnel needed in the mailroom, as well as the amount and type of equipment needed to perform the various functions.

Mailroom Personnel

The type and number of personnel required in the mailroom is determined by the size of the organization and the variety of functions performed by the mailroom. When one or more full-time employees are needed, a supervisor is typically responsible for day-to-day operations, while the administrative office manager is more likely to have ultimate responsibility for its operation. Other types of employees found in mailrooms are senior mail clerk, mail clerk, delivery clerk, and messenger.

The senior mail clerk may be responsible for opening and routing to the appropriate recipients mail that is addressed either to the organization or to a position/title (such as manager of human resources) rather than to a named individual. This person needs to have a thorough understanding of the various operational functions of the organization as well as have a familiarity with the individuals who work in each of the functional areas. In addition, the senior mail clerk may be responsible for other routine duties commonly performed in the mailroom.

A primary responsibility of the mail clerk is to rough sort incoming mail into predetermined categories, such as by floor or by department. The mail clerk is also frequently responsible for operating the various mailing machines, in addition to performing other routine duties.

The delivery clerk is generally responsible for the mail for a specific area or group of departments in the organization. This employee may also be responsible for pickup and delivery of internal correspondence as well as for sorting outgoing mail.

The messenger is typically responsible for special-request delivery of materials and mail. In some instances, the messenger may be responsible for transporting the rough-sorted mail from the mailroom to the appropriate delivery clerks. In addition, the messenger may, upon request, be responsible for running errands inside or outside the organization.

As an alternative to an organization's employing its own mailroom staff, some organizations are using outsourcing, which involves having an outside organization perform some or all mailroom functions. Some organizations have all mailroom functions performed by outsourcing. Other organizations have only a few functions performed by outsourcing, such as presorting.

Mailroom Layout

Because of the amount of physical activity involved in the mailroom, layout can have a direct bearing on its efficiency. For this reason, special consideration needs to be given to mailroom layout.

The functions performed by the mailroom determine the areas that should be considered in planning its layout. For example, space should be provided for removing mail from mail sacks. In order to accommodate those who wish to work in a standing position, the dumping table typically has raised sides and may be higher than a normal table. After the mail is dumped, the next process may be to align the various envelopes so they can be run through the mail opener. Mail that is marked "personal" or "confidential" has to be removed before the mail is mechanically opened. In some organizations, the envelopes are opened by the individuals to whom they are addressed.

Another area that needs to be considered in designing the layout of the mailroom is the sorting area. If the mailroom is responsible for the rough sorting of incoming mail but not for the final sorting, less space is needed than when the mailroom is responsible for both sortings. Pigeonhole racks speed up the sorting process. Additional space is also needed for packing and wrapping parcels, in addition to stamping, sealing, and sorting outgoing mail.

When designing the layout of the mailroom, special consideration should be given to its flow of work. The processing of mail should move from one point to the next with a minimum amount of physical effort and distance. The efficiency of the design of the mailroom—typically a U-shape arrangement is recommended—greatly determines the speed and accuracy with which the mail is processed. Figure 24-4 illustrates the layout of a well-designed mailroom.

Mailroom Equipment

Much of the new equipment being manufactured for processing incoming and outgoing mail greatly reduces the amount of physical effort involved in mail processing. Some of these new developments combine several functions into one piece of equipment. For example, equipment is available that performs all of the following functions: stamping, postmarking, sealing, counting, and stacking.

What types of equipment are found in the modern mailroom?

Among the several categories of equipment found in the modern mailroom, are the following:

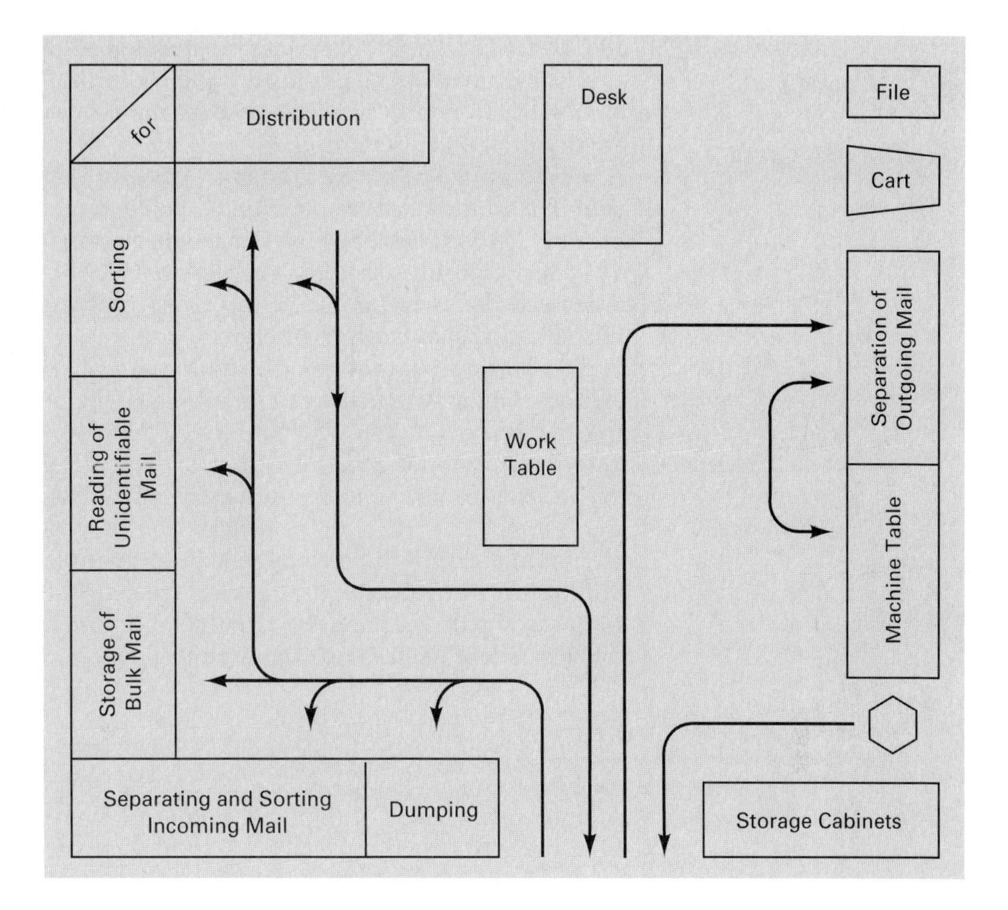

Figure 24-4 Mailroom layout. Courtesy: Pitney Bowes.

Addresser-printer equipment This type of equipment is used to print mailing addresses on envelopes and other types of mailing containers. **Addresser-printers** vary considerably in terms of their mechanical operation. Some are manually operated, but most are electrically powered. All addresser-printers require the use of data plates, which are about the size of a plastic credit card. These plates, which are made of metal, plastic, or foil, are capable of holding at least 320 characters. To imprint names and addresses on mailing containers, a tray containing the data plates is inserted into the addresser-printer. As the plate comes in contact with the mailing container, an impression is made on the envelope when the ribbon inserted between the raised characters on the data plate is pressed against the envelope.

Increasingly, addresser-printer equipment uses a dot matrix printing device or an ink-jet printer interfaced with a computer, rather than the address plates common among earlier equipment. This equipment facilitates the easy maintenance of an up-to-date mailing list.

Opening equipment A considerable amount of employee time can be saved by using automatic opening equipment. The opener trims off a small part of the envelope. Care has to be taken to make sure that the opener does not also cut the contents of the envelopes.

Stamping-sealing equipment A wide variety of **stamping-sealing equipment** is now available. While some of the equipment only stamps and seals envelopes, other more sophisticated equipment performs the following additional functions: postmarking envelopes, stacking envelopes, recording the amount of postage used, and counting the number of envelopes processed. In addition, some postage meters are equipped with attachments for signing and backstamping.

Stamping-sealing equipment typically consists of mechanical components, in addition to the detachable postage meter. To purchase postage, the meter is taken to a U. S. Post Office where it is reset and resealed. The capacity of some postage meters is as high as $9,999.99. Each time an envelope is processed through the meter, the amount of the postage affixed to the envelope is subtracted from the meter.

In addition to reducing the amount of physical effort involved in preparing outgoing mail, the use of stamping-sealing equipment is advantageous for another reason. When this equipment is used, envelopes that require more than the minimum amount of postage are generally weighed, thus assuring the accuracy of the amount of postage affixed to the envelope.

Automatic envelope emptiers Equipment is also available that automatically removes the contents of envelopes. In addition to removing envelope contents, the devices are also capable of automatically disposing of empty envelopes. These devices are adjustable so that envelopes of different sizes can be processed.

Label preparation equipment Another type of equipment often found in the mailroom is equipment used for the rapid preparation of labels. The printing mechanism of the label preparation equipment is typically activated by a magnetic medium, such as that used by data processing equipment. Names and addresses are contained on the medium; and as it is fed through the equipment, names and addresses are printed on labels. Pressure sensitive labels are commonly used, and equipment can be obtained that mechanically affixes the labels to the mailing container.

The most recent technology used in designing label-preparation equipment incorporates ink-jet printing. The printer is attached to a computer, and the outgoing pieces to be addressed are loaded in the printer's hopper. These printers are designed to handle all sizes and thicknesses of mail. In addition to entering the address on each piece, the printer also adds the appropriate bar code for each ZIP code. Compared with using pressure sensitive labels, ink-jet address printers are faster and more economical.

Inserting equipment This type of equipment is used to stuff inserts into envelopes. Some of the equipment being manufactured is also capable of folding up to six sheets of paper before inserting the material into an envelope.

Electronic scale Many organizations have found the use of electronic scales for weighing mail to be an effective cost-saving device. These scales display the actual amount of postage needed on the item being weighed. Electronic scales do not require as much subjective judgment as earlier scales required.

Bundling equipment The purpose of this equipment is to tie and bundle packages. Because this equipment is capable of performing at a much faster rate than humans are, it can save an organization a considerable amount of time in preparing outgoing mail.

Figure 24-5 illustrates a mailroom device.

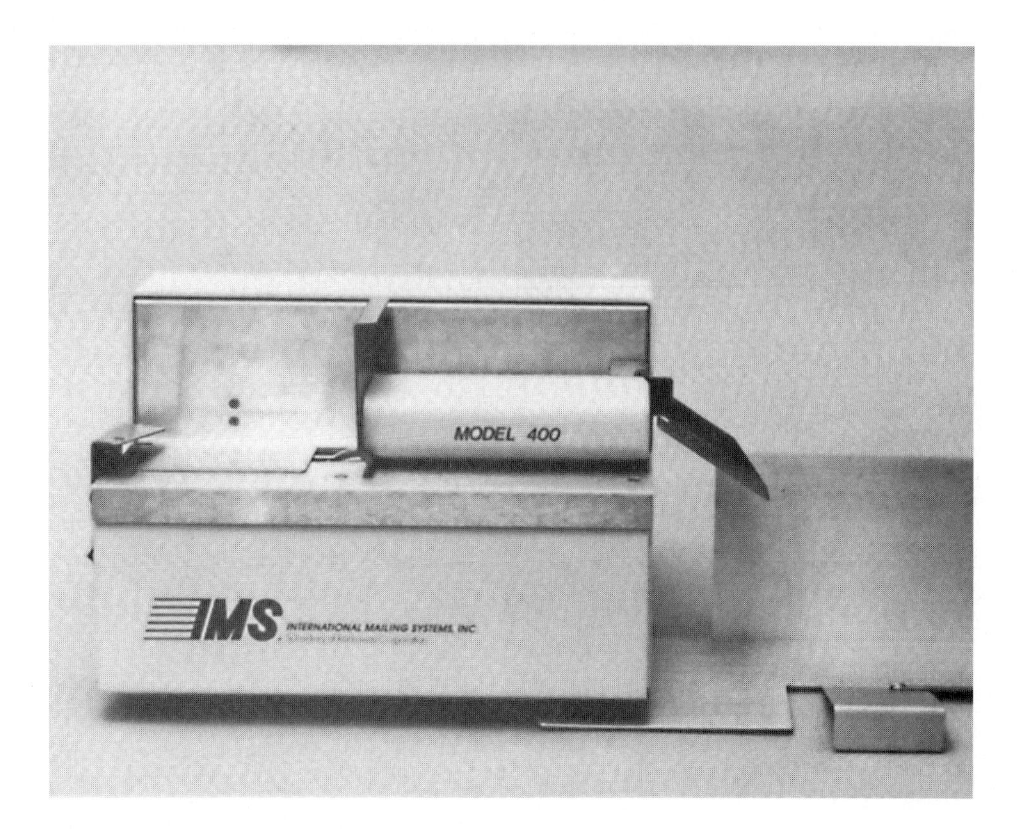

Figure 24-5 Mailroom device. Courtesy: International Mailing Systems, Inc.

Conserving Mailing Costs

Organizations are using a number of techniques to conserve their mailing costs. The majority of these techniques use new mailing technology.

Among the techniques are the following:

1. Imprinting of POSTNET bar codes on the envelope. The use of ZIP + 4 (the original 5-digit ZIP-code number and the newer 4-digit number) on a specified quantity of first-class envelopes entitles the organization to a discount. The bar code must be capable of being read by the U. S. Postal Service's scanning equipment, which means that it needs to be placed in a specified area. Additional discounts are available to users who, in addition to using ZIP + 4, presort their first-class mail before delivering it to their local post office. When designing a ZIP + 4 system, U. S. Postal Service employees should be consulted as a means of incorporating the latest regulations governing the ZIP + 4 program. If a large volume of the 4-digit routing numbers have to be added to an organization's mailing database, the most economical process is to invest in a national ZIP+4 directory on a CD-ROM. With the appropriate software, the system will automatically add the 4-digit numbers to the already stored 5-digit ZIP code.
2. Affixing the proper amount of postage to each piece of mail. The use of new electronic scales helps assure that each mailed item receives a proper amount of postage. This suggestion is especially appropriate when mailing parcels and first-class items weighing more than 1 ounce.

3. Keeping mailing lists up to date. Out-of-date mailing lists are costly, especially when the items cannot be forwarded. Normal forwarding time is one year.
4. Using lightweight mailers. A number of new lightweight mailers are now available, especially those that accommodate unfolded 8 1/2-inch-by-11-inch sheets of paper.
5. Using fax delivery, when possible, rather than an overnight delivery service.
6. Investigating the use of alternative delivery services for parcels.

Courier Services

For what are courier services used?

As an alternative to the traditional delivery method by the U. S. Postal Service, **courier services** are used extensively by some companies. Among these are delivery by Federal Express, Burlington, Purcolator, United Parcel Service, and Greyhound. The advantage of using these services is the speed with which mail and packages can be delivered.

IMPLICATIONS FOR THE ADMINISTRATIVE OFFICE MANAGER

Two areas for which the administrative office manager is commonly responsible are reprographics and mail services. In large organizations, each area is likely to have a full-time supervisor, with the administrative office manager maintaining overall responsibility.

The more extensively these areas are designed around organizational needs, the more efficient they will be. And operational efficiency is directly related to cost efficiency. Among the factors affecting operational efficiency are equipment, procedures, personnel, and layout.

When contrasted with the equipment found a few years ago in these two areas, today's equipment is much easier and simpler to operate. In fact, many of the judgmental decisions that the operator had to make using yesterday's equipment are performed automatically by today's equipment. Another significant change is found in the equipment's operating speed. Today's equipment is much faster.

Regardless of the configuration of either the reprographics area or the mailroom, the administrative office manager, by designing effective operations, can make a significant contribution to organizational efficiency. Doing so will help the organization more readily achieve its profitability goals.

REVIEW QUESTIONS

1. What is a satellite reprographics center and why is it used?
2. What factors need to be considered in determining the layout of the reprographics center?
3. How might the cost of a reprographics center be controlled?
4. Which of the various types of copying processes appear to be the most efficient? Why?
5. What are the various categories of plain-paper copiers?
6. What factors should be considered in selecting copiers?
7. On what chemical principle is the offset process based?
8. What mechanical devices are used for transporting internal correspondence?
9. Explain the uses of the more commonly found equipment in a mailroom.

DISCUSSION QUESTIONS

1. You are an office supervisor in the organization in which you work. You were recently appointed by the president to develop a comprehensive plan for a reprographics center. You plan to begin by determining the needs of the center. Explain how you plan to determine the center's needs.
2. You and a co-worker were recently discussing who should be in control of the satellite copy centers in the organization in which you work. Your co-worker argued for decentralized control because he felt it would be more motivational to the supervisors. You are committed to centralized control. Explain how you plan to convince your co-worker that centralized control is preferable.
3. You are responsible for organizing a small reprographics center in the organization in which you work. You know that the layout of the center will affect its efficiency. Identify the important elements of layout that will guide your planning. What special features do you plan to include in the center?
4. You recently attended a professional association meeting that was concerned with the topic of reprographics. The speaker was asked to suggest ways to control costs in the reprographics center. She replied, "Be hardnosed." The center that you supervise is cost effective, and you don't consider yourself to be especially hardnosed. Explain how you control the costs in the reprographics center for which you have supervisory responsibility.
5. The organization in which you work occupies two floors of a high-rise office building. A medium-volume copier is located on each floor. Lately, management has received several requests to replace these two copiers with several low-volume desktop copiers that would be conveniently located on each floor. Management has been reluctant to do this because of an apparent inability to control how the copiers are used. Identify ways that the organization can control the use of low-volume desktop copiers.
6. You have been asked by your supervisor to determine work standards for the reprographics center. No standards are used at the present time. As you develop these standards, what factors should be kept in mind?

STUDENT PROJECTS AND ACTIVITIES

1. Interview the manager of mail services in an organization. Learn how the needs of the present operation were determined.
2. Obtain promotional brochures for two competing office copiers. Compare and contrast these copiers on the basis of the information contained in the brochures.
3. Interview the manager of the reprographics center in an organization. Learn about the various functions that can be performed in this center.
4. Arrange to see an operational demonstration of various types of equipment found in a mailroom. What kinds of functions is this equipment capable of automatically performing?
5. Follow the receipt of incoming mail through an organization's mailroom. Is the operation efficient, or can you identify areas in which it can be made more efficient?

MINICASE

The Murphy Implement Company has had a 55 percent increase in its copying costs during the last two months. Approximately 25 percent can be attributed to company growth during the last 18 months. Another 15 percent can be attributed to increases in the costs of paper, copier supplies, and equipment rental. As reprographics center supervisor, prepare a report for your boss, the administrative office manager, in which you

1. Identify and discuss factors that may be responsible for the remaining 15 percent increase in copying costs.
2. Identify and discuss suggestions for controlling these costs.

CASE

The Premier Insurance Company, which is headquartered in Kansas City, Missouri, is one of the largest insurance companies in the Midwest. At the present time, approximately 1,800 employees work in the headquarters building.

For several years now, the company has had a policy that all office equipment is to be purchased by bids. The competitive nature of the office equipment vendors in the Kansas City area is responsible for the company's present use of eight different brands of office equipment. The company presently has thirty-five copiers located throughout the premises. In most instances, the supplies/chemicals used by the eight brands of copiers are not interchangeable. Some brands of equipment are found to require greater maintenance than other brands, and some brands have higher repair costs.

You, as administrative office manager, are concerned that the bidding process may be creating some problems. This policy may result in lower purchase prices, and it may also be responsible for higher supplies and maintenance charges. Accordingly, you decide to prepare a report for the executive vice president in which you

1. Discuss how the company can determine whether or not the bidding process over the long run is more costly than a non-bidding process might be.
2. Outline your recommendation for solving this problem.
3. Explain how you will determine the effectiveness of your recommendation once it has been implemented.

CHAPTER

25

QUALITY AND QUANTITY CONTROL

CHAPTER AIM

After reading this chapter, you should be able to design an effective quality and quantity control program for an organization.

CHAPTER OUTLINE

- The Process of Control
- Objectives of Control
- Advantages of Control
- Elements of Control
  - Factors to Control
  - Identification of Anticipated Results
  - Measurement Devices
  - Application of Corrective Measures
- Quality Control
  - Quality Control Techniques
    - Total Inspection
    - Spot Checking
    - Statistical Quality Control
    - Zero Defects
  - Total Quality Management (TQM)
- Quantity Control
  - Controlling Fluctuations
  - Short-interval Scheduling
- Work Scheduling
  - Work Scheduling Devices
    - Schedule Log
    - Work Chart
    - Work Schedule Calendar
    - Gantt Chart
    - Program Evaluation Review Technique
- Implications for the Administrative Office Manager

CHAPTER TERMS

Control limits
Critical path
Gantt Chart
Normal distribution
Performance standards
PERT
Quality control
Quality standards
Quantity control
Quantity standards
Sampling
Schedule log
Short-interval scheduling
Spot checking
Statistical quality control
Total inspection
Total Quality Management (TQM)
Work chart
Work measurement
Work schedule calendar
Work scheduling
Zero defects

Control, one of the five basic management functions, is essential because actual operational results do not always conform with desired or anticipated results. Control facilitates the application of corrective measures when the desired results are not attained.

The administrative office manager, in addition to a wide range of other responsibilities, will find control an important management tool. The absence of control often results in the diminished effectiveness of many office activities, thereby having a negative effect on the quantity and quality of work. The long-term results of the lack of adequate control is seen in reduced output and higher production costs.

Administrative office managers generally have access to several types of control, although this chapter covers two important types: **quality control** and **quantity control**. Two additional types of control—budgetary and cost control—are covered in the following chapter.

Although not a component of quality or quantity control, **work measurement** is an equally important management responsibility. The presence of certain control measures helps assure the timely completion of projects. A discussion of work scheduling is also included in this chapter.

THE PROCESS OF CONTROL

Control, when used for quantity and quality evaluation, involves the following five-step process:

What steps are involved in the process of control?

Step 1: Definition of the parameters of the work being subjected to the control process.

Step 2: Determination of actual results.

Step 3: Evaluation of actual results.

Step 4: Comparison of actual results with expected results.

Step 5: Application of corrective measures when needed.

Because it results in the application of corrective measures, control is considered by some to have disciplinary or punitive overtones. Of the five functions of management, the control function is often viewed the most negatively. The administrative office manager frequently has to apply corrective measures that can have an adverse effect on employer-employee relations. For the individuals responsible for carrying out the control function, such personal qualities as tact, empathy, and helpfulness are important.

OBJECTIVES OF CONTROL

As one of the functions of management, control has several important objectives:

1. To increase the operating efficiency of the organization.
2. To assess the degree to which anticipated results and actual results conform.
3. To coordinate the various elements of a program or a task.
4. To increase the likelihood that the objectives of the organization will be achieved.

5. To assist the office employees in performing their jobs more efficiently.
6. To maximize the profits of the organization by decreasing the amount of work that has to be redone and by reducing the misuse of supplies and materials.

ADVANTAGES OF CONTROL

Among the distinct advantages of applying control to office operations are the following:

What advantages result from the use of control?

1. Control helps maximize the profits of the organization.
2. Control helps employees improve their productivity because they are aware of quantity and quality output requirements.
3. Control provides a yardstick by which an organization can measure its operating efficiency.
4. Control identifies the areas in which actual and anticipated results do not coincide, which facilitates the modification of various work processes.
5. Control helps in the meeting of scheduled deadlines.

ELEMENTS OF CONTROL

The effectiveness of the control process cannot be maximized when certain elements are missing. These elements include factors to control, identification of anticipated results, measurement devices, and application of corrective measures.

Factors to Control

Before beginning the process of controlling an office operation, those responsible for the process must be made aware of which factors within the operation are to be controlled. Factors considered as being insignificant are eliminated from further consideration. Attempting to control insignificant factors typically becomes wasteful of time and energy. On the other hand, inefficiency will likely result if significant factors are not controlled.

The control factors within many office operations are the important documents or forms used in carrying out specific operations. In a purchasing system, for example, the purchase order is likely to be the critical factor to be controlled. By applying control measures to the purchase order, the actual results and the anticipated results of all the other components of the system will likely match one another.

Identification of Anticipated Results

Why must anticipated results be identified?

The absence of a clear identification of anticipated results often makes an attempt to compare actual results and anticipated results impossible. In addition to identifying the anticipated results, their appropriateness should also be determined.

After the anticipated results have been identified and their appropriateness assured, the results must be communicated to the employees whose performance will be evaluated. Employees who are unaware of expected performance levels cannot be held accountable for their failure to reach the desired levels. A primary responsibility of managers and supervisors is communicating the anticipated results to subordinates.

Measurement Devices

Before the actual results and the anticipated results can be compared, the actual results will have to be measured. In some instances, measurement will involve determining quantity output. In this instance, the measurement device will likely be **performance standards**, such as those discussed in Chapter 15. In other instances, the measurement device may involve determining the degree of accuracy with which data are entered on a form.

In organizations that have installed Total Quality Management (TQM), the measurement process is likely to be different than it is in other types of organizations. In some instances, the measurement device focuses on how well the organization's customers believe they are being served. This information is collected by means of a customer survey.

Another difference in the measurement process between TQM-oriented organizations and non-TQM-oriented organizations is in the establishment of baseline goals. An example of a baseline goal is the on-time delivery of a product or service a minimum of 95 percent of the time. By continually tracking the results of the baseline goals and making employees aware of the findings, they become motivated to strive for continual improvement. TQM also employs self-directed work teams that get individuals more diligently committed to effective performance. Because these teams are often considered a small "company within a company," commitment to effective performance is much greater. Coupling the team concept with employee empowerment that gives workers the opportunity to make productivity-related suggestions and then to implement the worthwhile suggestions in their work teams is also having a positive effect in many organizations.

Application of Corrective Measures

When actual results are less than anticipated results, corrective measures become necessary. Suppose, for example, that an office employee fails to produce at the anticipated or expected rate. The manager or supervisor who has the needed authority to take corrective action against the employee will then have to determine if corrective measures should be applied to this situation. Without this authority, the manager's or supervisor's effectiveness will be greatly diminished.

In an organization that uses TQM and that has "empowered" its employees, the corrective action most likely will extensively involve the members of the various work teams rather than management alone in determining the needed corrective action. When employees are able to determine the nature of the correction action that needs to be taken, they are less likely to feel they are being punished than when management alone determines the nature of the correction action.

QUALITY CONTROL

Organizations use quality control to increase their operating efficiency because employees sometimes fail to produce error-free work. Without some form of quality control, errors are likely to go unnoticed. Over time, this results in a negative impact on organizational profit. In addition, if management uses erroneous data, incorrect decisions will likely result, which can affect the well being of the organization.

Quality and quantity control both use standards as a basis for evaluation. Whereas **quality standards** involve evaluating the accuracy with which work is produced, **quantity standards** tend to be more quantifiable. For example, the organizational structure of a document affects its quality. If it deviates too far from the norm, the quality of the document is diminished. The fact that individuals have different perceptions about what constitutes an effective organizational structure makes quality evaluation somewhat subjective. Quantity standards, on the other hand, are more definitive and clear-cut. Either an employee's output equals or exceeds expected output or it doesn't.

A quality control program involves determining minimum standards of acceptability. Once the standards have been determined, the acceptability of the actual work can be compared with the expected standards. When a serious discrepancy exists, corrective measures may be necessary.

Quality Control Techniques

What quality control techniques are available?

Several techniques have been developed for maintaining quality control. Among these are total inspection, spot checking, statistical quality control, and zero defects.

Total inspection As a quality control technique, **total inspection** involves a complete and total inspection of each unit of work that each employee produces. This is done to determine if minimum quality standards have been attained. If not, corrective measures of some type will likely have to be taken.

For certain types of office work, total inspection is quite desirable, if not mandatory. The most common example of total inspection of office work is the proofreading of typed/keyboarded documents. Other examples of office work that frequently receive total inspection are the verification of important arithmetical calculations and the results of compiled statistical data.

Because of the nature of some types of office work, total inspection may not be necessary, especially when the work is of limited importance. In other instances, little opportunity exists for the presence of errors. An example is the filing of clients' correspondence. Although some of the correspondence may be misfiled, ensuring filing accuracy does not warrant the total inspection of the files.

Spot checking The **spot checking** technique involves periodically checking the quality of an employee's work. The desirability of this technique is frequently challenged if work is spot checked without the use of statistical processes to determine how much, who, and when the checks are to be made. However, by adding the statistical dimension, which is a characteristic of statistical quality control, more valid results are likely to be found.

Statistical quality control When total inspection of work is not desirable nor spot checking sufficiently accurate, **statistical quality control** may be a satisfactory alternative. The statistical sampling base this technique uses helps produce accurate and reliable results.

What are the elements of statistical quality control?

Several fundamental statistical elements are found in statistical quality control. These elements include **sampling**, **normal distribution**, and **con-**

trol limits. Sampling, which is based on the laws of probability, is used to determine what percentage of the total output has to be examined in order to be relatively certain that total output is as error-free as the sample. In other words, if proper statistical procedures are used, the quality of the sample should be comparable to the quality of the whole.

Statistical tables, which are available for determining appropriate sample size, take into consideration the following elements: (1) the total number of units from which the sample is being drawn and (2) the minimum accuracy level that is required. If the total output consists of one hundred units and an accuracy level of 90 percent is acceptable, fewer samples will have to be studied than when an accuracy standard of 95 percent is required.

To illustrate the concept, assume that total output consists of one hundred units and that 96 percent accuracy is required. Under these circumstances, the statistical tables indicate that fifteen of the units should be randomly selected for inspection. If no errors are found during the inspection of the fifteen units, the assumption is then made that the one hundred units are also error free. But, according to the law of probability, if one error is found within the sample of fifteen units, seven of the one hundred units can be expected to contain errors. If errors are found in two of the fifteen samples, approximately fourteen of the one hundred units could be expected to contain errors.

What impact does normal distribution have on statistical quality control?

Normal distribution is another of the elements involved in statistical quality control. Normal distribution is based on the principle that randomly observed occurrences of a sufficient quantity tend to be distributed around the mean or average of all the occurrences. For purposes of illustration, assume that the average or mean number of errors made by file clerks is two errors per one hundred units of work. While some clerks will make more than two errors in filing one hundred units and others will make fewer than two errors per one hundred units, the majority will make two errors in filing one hundred units.

The number of errors per total output is important because this factor has a bearing on the number of errors or deviations that are expected to occur within a given number of observations. Deviation is the distance from the mean and is calculated by using the formula for standard deviation. In any normal distribution, 68.3 percent of the total will fall within one standard deviation above and below the mean of the distribution; 95.1 percent will fall within two standard deviations above and below the mean; and 99.7 percent will fall within three standard deviations above and below the mean.

In the foregoing example, the file clerks were found to make an average (mean) of two errors per one hundred units filed. When calculating the standard deviation, assume that a deviation of .53 is found. According to the normal distribution, 68.3 percent of the number of errors made by each file clerk will be within one standard deviation above and below the mean, thus ranging from 1.47 to 2.53 (2.0 –.53 and 2.0 + .53). Two standard deviations above and below the mean (from 0.94 to 3.06 errors) will encompass 95.1 percent of the number of errors made by each file clerk. Three standard deviations will encompass 99.7 percent of the errors. Therefore, all but .3 percent of the number of errors made by each file clerk will be between .41 and 3.59 errors per one hundred units filed. This is illustrated in Figure 25-1.

What is the function of control limits?

The third element of statistical quality control are the control limits. Determining at what point the errors are attributed to chance and at what point they are attributed to some identifiable cause requires the establishment of control limits. For instance, in the foregoing example, if the control limits are set two standard deviations above and below the mean, chance is the cause of

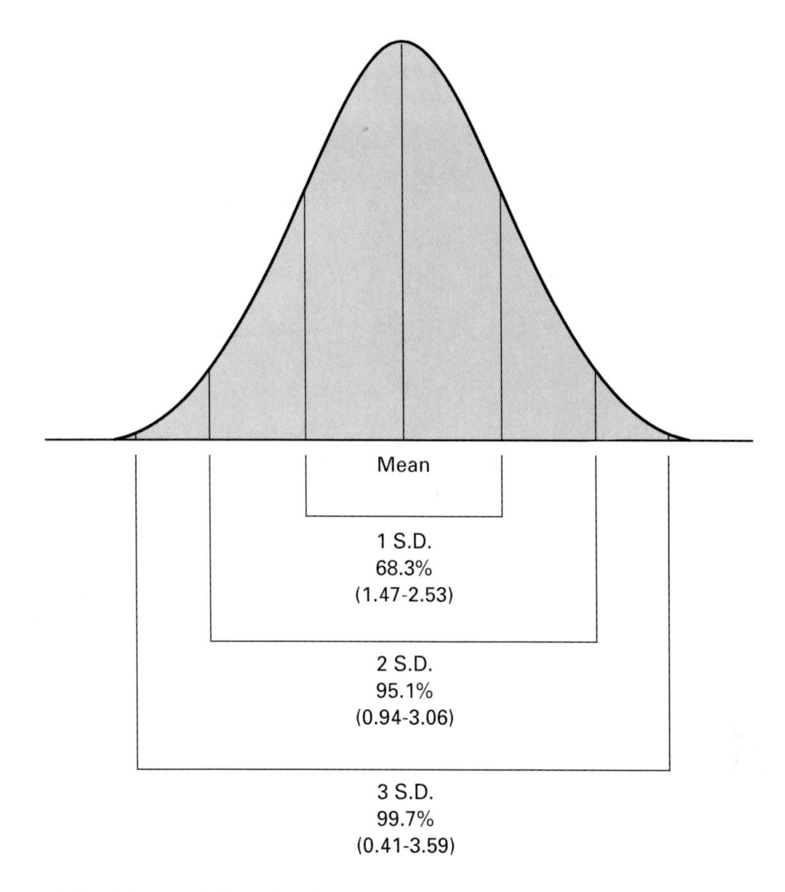

Figure 25-1 Normal distribution.

errors in a situation that ranges from .94 to 3.06 errors per one hundred units. The chance nature of these errors may increase the difficulty of identifying their cause. On the other hand, some identifiable cause is responsible when employees have errors exceeding 3.06 per one hundred units. For example, the errors may be a result of poorly trained employees. Figure 25-2 illustrates the control limits for this particular example.

In Figure 25-2, with the exception of sample 4, all samples fall within the control limits. Therefore, these errors are due to chance. Because the number of errors in sample 4 exceeds the maximum for the upper control limit, some

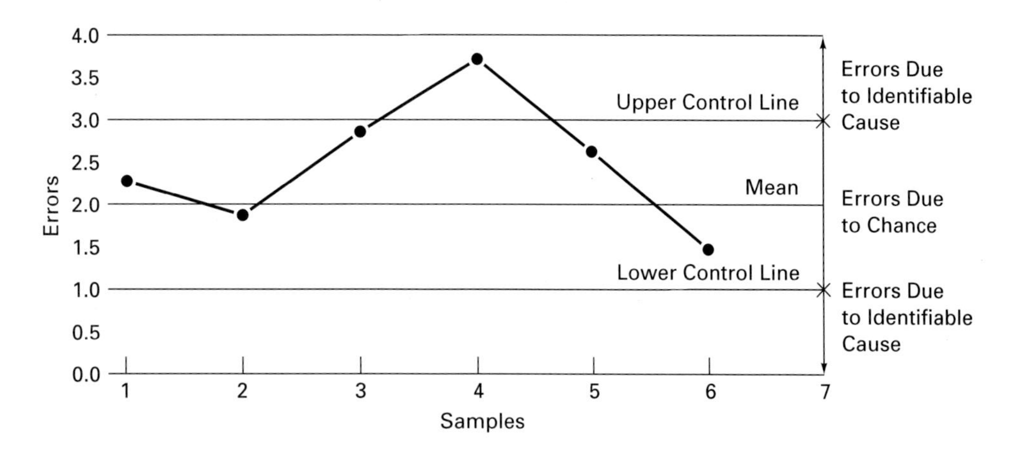

Figure 25-2 Control limits.

factor or factors other than chance are responsible. For example, one might speculate that the sample was taken at the end of the workday when employee fatigue contributed to an increase in their error rate.

What are the characteristics of the zero defects technique?

Zero defects The last quality control technique presented in this chapter is **zero defects**. The fundamental characteristic of this technique is error prevention resulting from employees who do their work correctly the first time. Thus, zero defects involves more than identifying and correcting errors. It also involves motivating employees to do error-free work.

When using the zero defects technique, employees make a pledge to management that they will support the concept by producing error-free work. They also make suggestions to management about ways to eliminate errors. Subsequently, their rewards are based on (1) the quality of the suggestions they submit, (2) the basis of the improvement they make, and (3) the extent of their error-free work.

In some instances, errors are attributable to management rather than to the employees themselves. If nothing is done to eliminate errors attributable to management, the effectiveness of the zero defects program cannot be fully realized.

Total Quality Management (TQM)

Total Quality Management (TQM) programs are being installed in a number of smaller organizations today as well as larger organizations where they first got their hold. In fact, many larger manufacturing organizations today require that the suppliers from which they purchase parts have an effective quality program. Otherwise, the larger organizations will change suppliers rather than risk purchasing parts used in the manufacturing process that have the potential for not meeting quality standards.

TQM is a more encompassing quality program than any other currently being used. Not only is it concerned with the organization's products and/or services, but also with the delivery of the products and/or services and everything involved in getting the products and/or services to the customer. Virtually every employee is involved. As a result, organizations that have implemented TQM programs are even concerned with how their telephones are answered or how a receptionist might greet a visitor.

TQM programs have several critical ingredients, including the following:

1. Customer satisfaction. TQM has a primary focus on customer satisfaction; when customer satisfaction is lacking, regardless of the quality with which the organization's products are manufactured or its services are provided, increasing sales will be difficult. Two types of customers are found: external (the ones who purchase the products and/or services) and internal (an employee who does something with earlier-produced work). For example, a manager will be a customer of a word processing operator who produced the document originated by the manager. Customer dissatisfaction either at the external or internal level has negative implications.
2. Accurate statistical measurement. TQM uses a variety of statistical techniques that measure every critical variable of the organization's operations. When the measuring process identifies problems, effort is immediately expended to eliminate the problems.
3. On-going improvement of products and/or services. Organizations have learned over the decades that satisfied customers are their best

form of advertisement. Satisfied customers are generally repeat customers; dissatisfied customers frequently become customers of the competition. An organization's prime competition is regularly improving the quality of its products and/or services; therefore, the organization also has to improve regularly the quality of its products and/or services.

4. New employee relations. TQM programs make extensive use of work teams and employee empowerment. Because TQM gives employees a greater stake in the organization's success, they have greater commitment to ensuring its success.

QUANTITY CONTROL

Quantity control, like quality control, uses standards that facilitate the comparison of anticipated and actual results. However, unless the standards are fairly accurate, the base for quantity control is not valid.

What provides a basis for developing quantity standards?

Used as the basis for developing quantity standards are the data gathered during the work measurement processes. Several work measurement techniques and the setting of quantity standards are discussed in Chapter 15. Work measurement is designed to determine what constitutes a fair day's work for both the employer and the employee. Therefore, employees have some assurance that their anticipated output levels do not exceed what is reasonably expected, and the employers have some assurance employees are being paid for doing a reasonable amount of work.

Normally in most organizations, the amount of work that needs to be done fluctuates from time to time. Occasionally, employees will have more work to do than they can be reasonably expected to complete. At other times, they will not have enough work to do. Therefore, management's responsibility is to develop ways to compensate for these fluctuations.

Various techniques for measuring work and setting standards are covered in Chapter 15; therefore, these topics will not be repeated in this chapter. Included in this chapter is a discussion of several techniques that are used to control the inevitable fluctuation in the amount of work that has to be completed. In addition, the short-interval scheduling technique is presented. This technique is useful for monitoring how closely actual output levels conform with anticipated results. If a serious lack of conformity occurs, corrective measures may be appropriate.

Controlling Fluctuations

A considerable portion of the time spent by the manager or supervisor in controlling output involves determining the most effective way to handle workload fluctuations. Several techniques are available to handle these fluctuations.

How can fluctuations in excessive amounts of work be controlled?

When fluctuations result in too much work to be done in a given amount of time, one or more of the following may be used:

1. *Employee overtime*. Many organizations use employee overtime as a way of controlling situations when too much work has to be done. If a situation can be remedied by a few hours of employee overtime, this method may result in significant advantages. On the other hand, if a large number of overtime hours will be required, another method of controlling fluctuations is recommended. This will help the organiza-

tion avoid having to compensate employees at the rate of one and one-half times their regular pay rates. Rather than compensate employees for overtime hours, another possibility is to give them time off for the hours they previously worked overtime. If the employees take time off during slack times, the organization also has a satisfactory method for dealing with a situation of having too little work to be done.

2. *Temporary help*. Use of temporary help is another solution for controlling fluctuations when too much work has to be done. In many cities nowadays, temporary employment agencies can be used to obtain office help for one day or for several weeks. Temporary agencies are discussed in greater detail in Chapter 7.
3. *Part-time help*. When fluctuations occur regularly, part-time help may be the most desirable solution to handle work overloads. Hiring the same employees to work part time whenever the workload becomes excessive eliminates the need of having to train temporary employees each time they are needed.

What is a floating work unit?

4. *Floating work unit*. Some organizations have developed a floating work unit as a solution to excessive workload conditions. Employees assigned to these units "float" to wherever they are needed in the organization. Unless these employees are fairly competent in many areas, they may find working under these circumstances somewhat dissatisfying.
5. *Cycle billing*. When this technique is used, one-twentieth of the customers' accounts are due each working day. Instead of having all the customers' payments due on one day, which makes staffing difficult and causes extreme fluctuations in workloads, the receipts are spread over a full month.

Following is a discussion of practices that may be used whenever too little work exists:

1. *Time off*. To compensate employees who work overtime, organizations sometimes allow them to take time off when an insufficient amount of work exists.
2. *Work backlog*. The nature of some work allows it to be postponed indefinitely. If this is possible, the work can be completed during slow times.
3. *Maintenance projects*. Some organizations have employees do maintenance projects when they do not have enough work to do. Examples of maintenance projects are reorganization of files, cleaning of files, review of work procedures, and the like.

Short-interval Scheduling

What are the characteristics of short-interval scheduling?

As a control device, **short-interval scheduling** helps ensure the completion of a given amount of work in a given amount of time. It also provides the mechanism for determining whether or not the work is completed according to schedule. Short-interval scheduling enables managers or supervisors to determine whether or not output standards are being consistently maintained.

Short-interval scheduling is based on the following assumption: When employees are trying to attain production goals, they improve their chances of being successful by using short-range rather than long-range production goals. Employees are motivated to perform at higher levels because of the short-range nature of the goals and because of the frequent evaluation of their success in reaching pre-determined goals.

The following illustrates how short-interval scheduling works. If an employee is expected to produce 400 units per an eight-hour workday, his or her output could be determined at the end of the day. Unfortunately, the employee may not know until the end of the day if his or her production goal has been achieved. With short-interval scheduling, the employee makes frequent checks throughout the day to determine how closely production rates conform with accepted standards. These checks are typically made each hour of the day.

In the foregoing illustration, the employee would have to produce an average of 50 units per hour to be successful in reaching the predetermined goal. If, upon checking, the employee finds that 120 units were produced during the first three hours, the employee then knows that to reach the 400-unit goal, the 30-unit shortage (150 minus 120) will have to be made up during the day. When supervisors discover that employees are failing to meet their expected hourly production levels, corrective measures can be taken.

Before short-interval scheduling can be implemented, expected production levels must be determined. These levels, which are presented as work standards, identify the acceptable amount of time needed to produce one unit of output.

After the standards have been determined and the supervisor is aware of the employees' expected production levels, the work assignments can be made. A record is kept of how closely employees' actual results conform with expected results, using an assignment record such as the one illustrated in Figure 25-3. This information is also entered on the summary sheet, which is

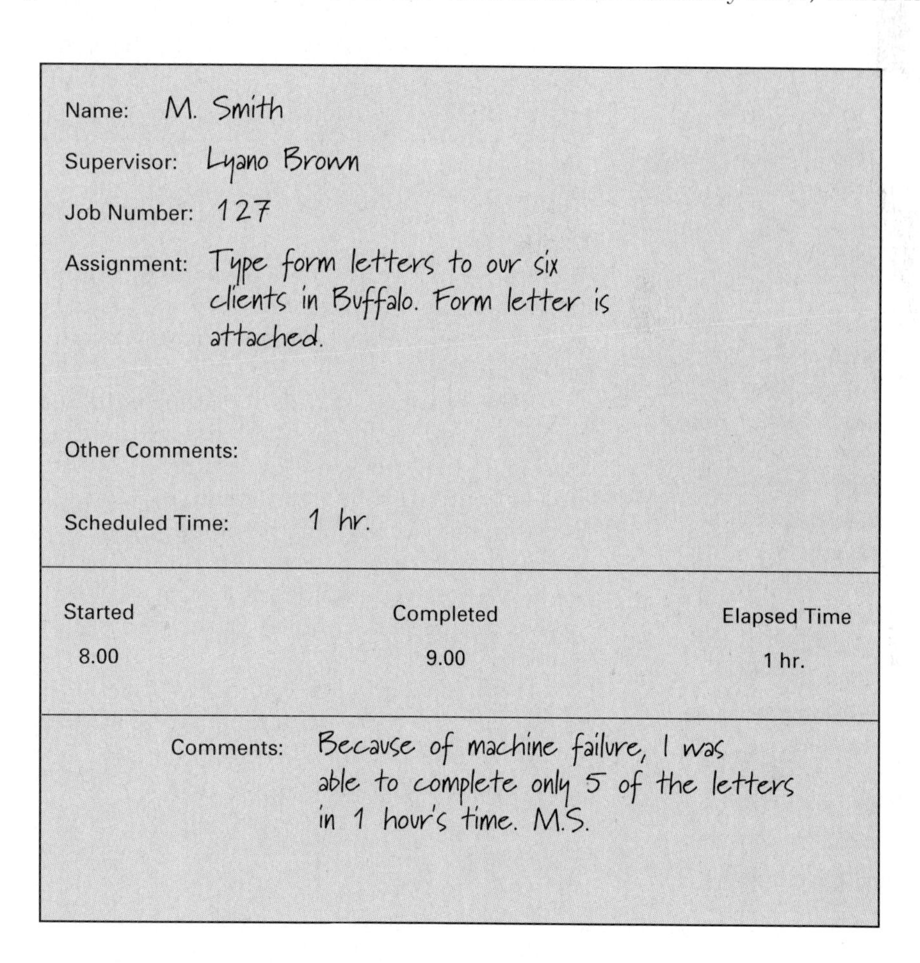

Name: M. Smith

Supervisor: Lyano Brown

Job Number: 127

Assignment: Type form letters to our six clients in Buffalo. Form letter is attached.

Other Comments:

Scheduled Time: 1 hr.

Started	Completed	Elapsed Time
8.00	9.00	1 hr.

Comments: Because of machine failure, I was able to complete only 5 of the letters in 1 hour's time. M.S.

Figure 25-3 Assignment record.

Employee	Results	8-9	9-10	10-11	11-12	12-1	1-2	2-3	3-4	4-5
M. Smith	Expected	6	7	10	8	9	15	20	13	7
	Actual	5*	7	10	8	8*	15	21	13	7
M. Green	Expected	3	5	3	6	10	13	14	7	6
	Actual	4	5	3	7	11	12*	14	8	6

Department: Office Services

Supervisor: D. Brown

Today's Date: 11/15

Figure 25-4 Summary sheet.

illustrated in Figure 25-4. After the work assignment is completed, the employee returns the assignment record, along with the completed work, to the supervisor who then compares actual results with anticipated or expected results.

The number recorded in the "expected" column parallel to each employee's name is the production level that the employee is expected to achieve during a one-hour span. For example, M. Smith was expected to produce six units of output from 8 a.m. to 9 a.m. However, when he "reported in," the supervisor discovered that machine failure enabled him to produce only five units. Therefore, a "5" is entered in the "actual" column parallel to M. Smith's name. When an employee's actual performance fails to coincide with expected performance, an asterisk is entered in the appropriate place on the summary sheet.

By maintaining the summary sheet, the supervisor is readily able to determine at any point during the day if an employee's productivity is ahead of, on, or behind schedule. When the output is consistently behind schedule, corrective measures may be appropriate.

WORK SCHEDULING

In this chapter, **work scheduling** is considered a function of control. Without work scheduling, administrative office managers have little if any control

Name of Project: Prepare proposal			Completion Date: 11/19	
Project Supervisor: Janice Otter				
Task	To be Completed by	Assigned to	Time Started	Time Finished
gather data	11/01	Bill Green	8:00	4:30
process data	11/07	Mary Smith	8:00 (11/2)	2:30 (11/6)
draft proposal	11/17	Bill Green	8:00 (11/7)	4:00 (11/15)
revise proposal	11/18	Bill Green	8:00 (11/18)	3:00 (11/18)
type proposal	11/19	Diane Brown	8:00 (11/19)	4:15 (11/19)

Figure 25-5 Schedule log.

over the completion time of a project. With work scheduling, greater control is possible, which helps ensure the successful completion of a given project.

Work Scheduling Devices

Several devices are available for use in scheduling work to be completed within a given amount of time. Some of the devices are rather simple and can be used for scheduling uncomplicated projects. On the other hand, some of the devices are rather sophisticated and are appropriately used in scheduling more complex projects.

What work scheduling devices are available?

Schedule log A frequently used technique for scheduling office work are **schedule logs**. An example of a schedule log is illustrated in Figure 25-5. Although the schedule log is quite simple, other more complex logs could be developed for the scheduling of a difficult or complex project. The schedule log is generally completed by the project supervisor who has good insight into the status of the project.

Work chart Illustrated in Figure 25-6 is the **work chart**, another of the more simple work scheduling devices. When using this chart, the project supervisor works backward from the completion date. For example, as Figure 25-6 shows, the project is to be completed by November 17. To determine the starting time of the project and the days on which each subproject must be started, the work chart is developed. The illustration, which deals with the writing and submitting of a report, indicates that for the project to be completed by the November 17 deadline, the data must be compiled by November 4, the report must be written by November 10, and so forth.

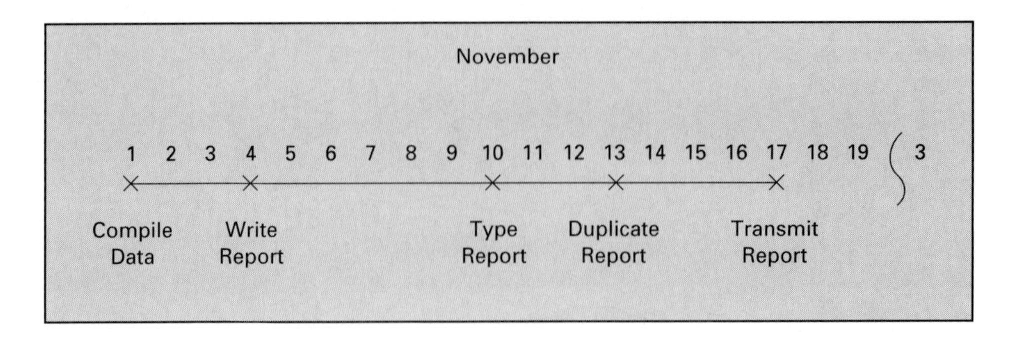

Figure 25-6 Work chart.

Work schedule calendar Another of the more simple work scheduling devices is a **work schedule calendar**, such as the one illustrated in Figure 25-7. The calendar, which is a day-by-day schedule for a week's duration, lists jobs or projects that are to be started each day. Quite often the work schedule calendar also provides a listing of the names of the employees. As jobs or projects are accepted by the work unit, the employee who is responsible for completing each project can be designated. When an employee completes one project, the next one can be started without the supervisor's having to make the assignment at that time.

For what is a Gantt Chart used?

Gantt Chart Used as a work scheduling device, the **Gantt Chart** is more appropriate for longer, more complex projects than is the work schedule calendar. The Gantt Chart and the work schedule calendar are similar because both identify the jobs or projects that are to be completed on any given day. Figure 25-8 illustrates a Gantt Chart. Software packages are now available for use in developing computerized Gantt Charts.

Employee	Monday	Tuesday	Wednesday	Thursday	Friday
Sally B.	Type form letters Type invoices File correspondence				
Jane S	Type report ↓				
Diane	Type manuscript for Mr Jones Sort File cards				
Mary	On vacation				

Figure 25-7 Work schedule calendar.

Figure 25-8 Gantt Chart. Courtesy: Magna Visual, Inc.

The Gantt Chart, which was developed by Henry Gantt, an early management authority, provides a day-by-day list of the jobs that are to be completed, as well as the estimated completion time. Many non-computerized Gantt Charts are now magnetized, which facilitates the movement of the tabs on which the various items are listed.

Although used for scheduling the work found in many offices, the Gantt Chart is especially useful in scheduling work projects involving the use of computer processing.

What are the characteristics of PERT charts?

Program evaluation review technique This scheduling device was originally developed during the Polaris missile program and has been modified for use in scheduling complex projects. Because of its nature, **PERT** is most suitable for projects comprised of many parts or components. Its use in scheduling simple projects cannot be justified.

A PERT chart, which is illustrated in Figure 25-9, is developed to help schedule the component parts of the project. The various components and the estimated amount of time for completing each component must be identified. The numbers within circles on the chart refer to the various components that comprise the total project. The network of lines indicate the various paths that may be followed in completing the project.

In preparing the PERT chart, a **critical path** must be determined. This path, which is also the longest route, consists of the components that must be completed before the project is completed. Each component or activity on the path must be completed on time and in the order in which the activities appear on the chart. A delay in completing a critical component will prevent the project's completion by the deadline. The noncritical components can be completed at any time during the course of the project with no adverse impact on its completion.

Figure 25-9 illustrates a PERT chart that outlines the various components involved in planning a convention. The critical path consists of components or activities 1, 2, 3, 4, 5, 6, 7, 8, 9, and 16. The paths consisting of activi-

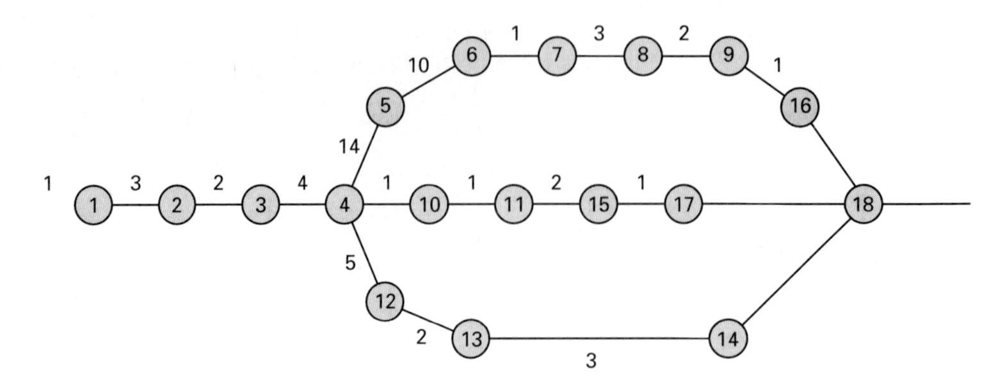

Legend:

1. Set convention date
2. Set convention location
3. Select convention chairman
4. Select convention facilities
5. Develop convention program
6. Select convention speakers
7. Set convention cost
8. Notify members of the convention program
9. Print program
10. Notify convention facility of desired setup of each meeting room
11. Select banquet menu
12. Determine recipient of outstanding member award
13. Prepare citation for outstanding member award
14. Determine honorarium for speakers
15. Arrange for registration booth
16. Make overnight lodging arrangements for members who desire to stay overnight
17. Arrange for transportation of members (from airport)
18. Await convention

Figure 25-9 PERT chart.

ties 1, 2, 3, 4, 10, 11, 15, and 17, and 1, 2, 3, 4, 12, 13, and 14 are not critical. Therefore, the components represented by numbers 10, 11, 15, 17, and 12, 13, and 14 can be completed at any time prior to the opening of the convention. The components on the critical path, on the other hand, must be completed within the scheduled time if the convention is to be planned on time. The numbers above each line represent the estimated number of days needed to complete each component.

IMPLICATIONS FOR THE ADMINISTRATIVE OFFICE MANAGER

Administrative office managers have major responsibilities for quantity and quality control in the areas they manage. This responsibility results from the philosophy that prevails in most organizations whereby unit managers are responsible for quantity and quality control in their specific areas.

Regardless of how efficient and well managed the office area is, the results of certain operations do not always match desired results. The use of quantity and quality control helps ensure conformity of desired results with actual results.

One of the most effective ways for the efforts of administrative office managers to be noticed by top management is for the office function to provide the best quality service that circumstances will allow. Many administrative office managers have enhanced their promotability to higher level positions by establishing a credible quantity and quality control performance.

Although employees often affect the quantity and quality control performance of the office area, inefficient operating procedures and equipment also have a negative impact. The benefits of effective quantity and quality control performance are too great to overlook the implementation of a well-designed control program.

REVIEW QUESTIONS

1. Why is control needed in office situations?
2. What are the objectives of control?
3. What advantages result from implementing control procedures?
4. What is the evaluation basis for both quality and quantity control?
5. As a control technique, how do total inspection and spot checking differ from one another?
6. What steps are involved in developing a statistical quality control program?
7. How does a floating work unit help an organization control fluctuations in its work processes?
8. When used as work scheduling devices, how does the work chart differ from the work schedule calendar?
9. When PERT is used as a work scheduling device, how is the appropriate network to be used chosen?

DISCUSSION QUESTIONS

1. Several of your subordinates reacted negatively to the proposed implementation of a work standards program in your organization. One of your subordinates said, "I work as fast as I can. The use of work standards isn't going to help me produce more. If that is what you want, you'll have to give me another set of arms and hands." What is your reaction to these comments? What will you say in response to this subordinate?
2. Several of the employees in the department that you manage have been complaining to you that more help is needed. However, mathematically, no employee shortage exists. The proper number of employees is available when the number of units of work to be completed in a given time is divided by the expected production rate. What may account for the discrepancy between the number of employees mathematically needed and the number that employees claim is needed?
3. You have been asked to assess the validity of the work standards in the unit you manage. You know that most employees produce more in a given amount of time than what they are expected to produce. Therefore, the standards are too low. Yet, when you were observing several employees' performance recently, you noticed that many were performing at a below-standard rate. How can you get employees to perform at a normal rate while their performance is being measured?
4. Your supervisor, who is responsible for the effective use of the employees in her unit, recently admitted that her work unit (the one in which you work) is probably overstaffed. The supervisor also suggested that everyone always look busy when the "brass" was around. This may prevent any terminations. Discuss the implications of the way your supervisor plans to handle this situation.
5. The organization in which you are a supervisor uses the zero defects quality control technique. Some of your recently hired subordinates indicated that they will do their best to produce error-free work but that doesn't mean that they will always be successful. What essential ingredient of the zero defects technique seems to be lacking in this situation? What should be done to correct the situation?
6. The management in the company in which you work has expressed an interest in installing a short-interval scheduling program. The majority of the employees resist such a program. Management knows that the implementation of a short-interval sched-

uling program may cause the employees to unionize. Management also knows that the use of short-interval scheduling would help the organization become more productive. How can this dilemma be resolved?

STUDENT PROJECTS AND ACTIVITIES

1. Interview an office employee whose output is measured using one of the quantity control techniques discussed in this chapter. Ask this employee about his or her feelings regarding the technique.
2. Interview an administrative office manager who is responsible for the overall quantity and/or quality control in the organization in which he or she works. Try to determine what aspects about the control process create the greatest difficulties for the manager.
3. Make arrangements to talk with a manager who makes extensive use of the PERT technique in carrying out various department responsibilities. Review with the manager the manner in which the critical path is determined in carrying out an actual project.
4. Obtain from two organizations their quantity standards for similar office tasks. Are the standards similar or dissimilar?
5. Talk with an employee whose output is regulated by the short-interval scheduling technique. Assess how the technique affects the employee's motivation to maintain acceptable productivity levels.

MINICASE

The Mitchell Company is the largest office supplies distributor in Colorado. At the present time, all of its accounts receivable billings are mailed out the last working day of the month. This means that a huge volume of payments is received between the first and the tenth of each month. Employees who work in accounts receivable frequently have to put in several hours of overtime during this period each month. Management stresses the need to get these payments processed as quickly as possible because of cash flow. As a consultant who has been asked by Mitchell's management to prepare a report about this situation,

1. Identify and discuss alternatives to the presently used billing system that are available.
2. Identify the alternative you recommend and discuss why it is your preference.

CASE

The Brandy Assurance Company is one of the most rapidly growing insurance companies in the Southwest. Much of its success is attributed to its excellent actuarial department.

At the present time, some departments are unable to get projects completed on time. This situation creates additional problems, especially when an overdue project impedes or slows progress on another project.

A few months ago, all department heads were requested to pay a little more attention to project completion dates. No appreciable difference has been noticed as yet. Obvious is the fact that additional action will have to be taken. Accordingly, you, a consultant, were hired to study the situation. In the written report you are preparing,

1. Identify and discuss suggestions that will be helpful in ensuring the timely completion of the projects.
2. Identify various scheduling devices that may be appropriately used to help ensure the completion of these projects, and discuss how these devices work.
3. Identify the scheduling device you prefer and explain why it is your preference.

CHAPTER

26

BUDGETARY AND COST CONTROL

CHAPTER AIM

After studying this chapter, you should be able to design an effective budgetary and cost control procedure for an organization.

CHAPTER OUTLINE

CHAPTER TERMS

Budgetary control
Budget committee
Budgeting
Budget period
Budget revision
Cost analysis study
Cost breakdown technique
Cost control
Department budget
Direct salaries
Direct supplies
Fixed costs
Indirect salaries
Indirect supplies
Master budget
Moving review
Periodic review
Progressive review
Semivariable costs
Standard cost technique
Variable costs
Zero-based budgeting (ZBB)

In addition to having responsibilities for quality and quantity control, the administrative office manager is also responsible for budgetary and cost control. The absence of effective procedures for controlling the budget or operational costs often results in increased costs of office operations. Therefore, effective cost control techniques need to be used.

BUDGETING

Budgeting is basically a planning process. It facilitates the preparation of a budget, which serves as the organization's financial blueprint. The process of budgeting takes place at several levels within the organization. **Budgetary control**, which is discussed in the next section, is the process of regulating the operating budgets of the organization. Without budgetary control, the preparation and use of budgets is virtually wasted effort.

Purposes of Budgeting

Budgeting has a positive impact on the organization's profitability because the organization's operations are likely to be performed more efficiently. Budgeting also helps management maintain the cost effectiveness of the organization's operations. Unless operations are cost effective, the organization will not be able to maximize its profits. Budgeting also helps the organization better plan for the future.

Advantages of Budgeting

The process of budgeting results in several significant advantages:

What are the advantages of budgeting?

1. Budgeting requires adequate management consideration of the organization's policies.
2. Budgeting requires that departmental-level managers develop practices which facilitate the attainment of budgetary goals.
3. Budgeting requires that managers identify the resources necessary for accomplishing the goals of the organization.
4. Budgeting helps management make accurate, timely decisions regarding various organizational operations.
5. Budgeting helps management determine which functions are not operating efficiently.
6. Budgeting helps management determine which functions are experiencing difficulty in achieving goals and objectives.

Limitations of Budgeting

Although budgeting results in some rather significant advantages for the organization, the administrative office manager also needs to be aware of its limitations.

What are the limitations of budgeting?

1. Because budgeting is based on estimates, the validity of the budget is to a large extent determined by the accuracy with which the estimates are made.
2. The operating effectiveness of an organization is clearly dependent

upon how well management is able to motivate employees to operate within the budgeted allowances.

3. The effectiveness of the budget is to a large extent dependent upon the accuracy with which budget revisions are made.

Prerequisites of Successful Budgeting

What are the prerequisites of successful budgeting?

Successful budgeting does not simply happen. The absence of certain prerequisite conditions—proper organization, financial data, and commitment of top management—will likely result in wasted effort when undertaking the budgeting process. Although the presence of these conditions will not automatically ensure success in budgeting, their presence will improve budgeting efforts.

Proper organization Certain organizational characteristics must be present if the budgeting process is to be successful. These characteristics are (1) the proper grouping of tasks within functions, (2) definitive lines of authority and areas of responsibility, and (3) lines of communication. The absence of any of these characteristics may result in ineffective budgeting. For example, when a manager lacks necessary authority, he or she will not be able to take the necessary corrective action if the costs of various operations exceed the budgeted allowances. Furthermore, individuals who have not been assigned areas of responsibility cannot be held accountable when operations exceed the budgeted allowances.

Financial data The development of a budget requires the use of financial data. Unless these data are available, the base for budget development does not exist. Types of financial data needed include (1) the number of units sold during the previous financial period, (2) the relationship between the units sold and the cost incurred in producing these units, and (3) emerging financial trends. Much of the financial data that are needed can be obtained from the financial records of the previous fiscal period.

Commitment of top management Top management must be committed to the use of the budget as a control mechanism. Without such commitment, the budgeting efforts are likely to produce only minimum worthwhile results. Furthermore, without top management commitment, lower management levels are unlikely to be committed to the attainment of the organization's budgetary goals.

Budget Preparation

Budget preparation consists of several distinct elements, including determination of the budget period, development of the budget, and revision of the budget.

Determining the budget period The length of time covered by the office budget generally coincides with the fiscal period of the organization. Therefore, if the organization's fiscal period begins in January of each year, so does its budget. The length of the **budget period** should be sufficiently long to compensate for any seasonal fluctuations.

Developing the budget The planning involved in developing a budget may consume considerable time. The use of employee participation in the planning process is advantageous.

How do departmental and master budgets differ?

The office budget, which is part of a larger budget, is classified as a **department budget**. The **master budget**, covering the entire organization, is a composite of the various departmental budgets.

Traditionally, after the organization's projected amount of income has been determined, a monetary sum is allocated to each of the departments. From this allocation, each department develops its operating budget. The departmental budgets are then consolidated into the organization's budget.

An alternative to the traditional budgeting process is zero-based budgeting (ZBB), which is discussed later in this chapter.

Figure 26-1 illustrates a portion of a departmental budget.

Before actual work on developing the budget begins, responsibility for budget preparation needs to be assigned. In many larger organizations, overall responsibility is assigned to the controller or treasurer of the organization. In other organizations, responsibility may be assigned to the vice president who is concerned with the organization's financial affairs. In smaller organizations, the administrative office manager may have overall responsibility for the preparation of the budget. Typically, the least amount of responsibility the administrative office manager will have for budget preparation in any size of organization is the development of the budget for the office function.

What are the functions of the budget committee?

Many organizations now use a **budget committee** to provide input into the budget development process. At the organizational level, the budget committee, which is headed by the chief budget official, usually consists of departmental managers. In larger functional departments, a budget committee chaired by the departmental manager and consisting of the various supervisors in the department may also be used. In most cases, budget committees are advisory. Therefore, their primary responsibility is to provide suggestions to the committee's chairperson.

While the chief financial officer is primarily responsible for the budget, several individuals likely will be involved in preparing the budget. The prevailing philosophy is that managers and supervisors who are responsible for various functional areas in the organization should have extensive involvement in the preparation of their departmental budgets. This results from the practice of making the departmental managers and supervisors responsible for organizing their units in a way that maximizes efficient use of organizational resources. Therefore, the budget is typically initiated by the chief budget officer who seeks assistance from other employees in the organization.

The president, chief executive officer, or the chairman of the board frequently authorizes the chief budget officer to begin the development of a budget. This authorization is typically received in a letter in which the president, CEO, or chairman may summarize the condition of the national economy,

	January		*February*		*March*	
	Estimated	*Actual*	*Estimated*	*Actual*	*Estimated*	*Actual*
Salaries	$3,250	$3,140	$3,250	$3,250	$3,250	$3,300
Utilities	80	73	80	84	75	78
Telephone	120	150	120	110	120	125
Postage	50	73	50	75	50	80
Equipment	120	120	120	120	120	120
	3,620	3,556	3,620	3,639	3,615	3,703

Figure 26-1 Portion of departmental budget.

the projected outlook for the industry of which the organization is a part, and the anticipated organizational growth trends.

In most organizations, the office function generates no direct income; therefore, the office budget contains only expenses or costs. But before reasonable projections can be made for each type of expense or cost, an estimate of the cost of each unit of output produced by the office function during the budget period will have to be calculated. An estimate of the number of units of output projected for production by the office function during the budget period is also needed. These estimates are used to determine how much of the organization's financial resources need to be allocated to each type of expense or cost found within the office function.

The common types of expenses or costs found in the office function are the following:

1. Salaries and payroll.
2. Fringe benefits.
3. Equipment rental or purchase.
4. Equipment depreciation.
5. Furniture rental or purchase.
6. Furniture depreciation.
7. Telephone charges.
8. Materials and supplies.
9. Postage and mailing.
10. Utilities.
11. Rent.
12. Taxes.
13. Insurance.
14. Maintenance costs.
15. Training costs.

How do fixed, variable, and semivariable costs vary from one another?

Office costs or expenses can be divided into three groups: fixed costs, variable costs, and semivariable costs. **Fixed costs** are those that remain constant regardless of how many units are produced. For example, rent, insurance, and taxes are fixed costs. These costs are constant, and they do not fluctuate in relation to the output levels.

Variable costs, on the other hand, vary proportionately in relation to the output levels. Examples of variable costs are materials or supplies. Except when discounts are offered for quantity buying, the cost of materials or supplies generally increases in direct proportion to the amount used. For example, two computer printers typically cost twice as much as one computer printer.

Semivariable costs increase as production increases, but not in direct proportion to production increases. An example of a semivariable cost is the rental of copy equipment, which is frequently based on the number of copies made during a given period. As the number of copies increases, the per unit cost generally decreases. To illustrate, if 500 copies are made on a copier during a given time, the per unit cost may be 4.8 cents. But if 750 copies are made during the same period, the per unit cost may be 4.2 cents.

To facilitate budget preparation, certain guiding principles should be followed:

What principles should guide budget preparation?

1. *Employee participation in budget preparation is advantageous.* When employees are allowed to participate, they are given an opportunity to become directly involved in the fiscal affairs of the department in which they work. By giving them an opportunity to participate, they generally develop a feeling of greater commitment, and they are more likely to show greater concern for the budgetary allowances.
2. *The budget should reflect realistic estimates of operating costs.* Some individuals, in preparing budgets, believe the mark of a good manager is keeping operating costs at a low level. While this is theoretically desirable, the practical results of this situation are not always desirable. In some instances, the amounts budgeted for certain operating costs are so minimal that operating efficiency is actually impeded. The budget should reflect estimates that are realistic and that take into consideration operating cost increases resulting from inflation, greater volumes of work, and the like.
3. *The budget must provide for unforeseen circumstances.* Because budgets are sometimes prepared as much as one year in advance, predicting the unforeseen circumstances that may have an adverse effect on the budget may be impossible or nearly impossible. For this reason, the budget must have built-in flexibility to compensate for these circumstances. For example, a contingency fund may be used for this purpose.
4. *The employees should feel committed to the budget.* Unless employees have committed themselves to use of the budget as a guide for certain of their actions, the budget may not be successful. A lack of commitment is likely to result in employees' being wasteful, their misusing organization facilities, and their failing to exert the amount of effort for which they are being paid.

Revising the budget Even though considerable effort may be involved in the preparation of a budget, a variety of uncontrolled circumstances may require periodic **budget revision**. For example, costs of materials may increase, which can have an impact on the organization's profit. In addition, operating costs may increase, which creates difficulties for the organization as it attempts to produce output at a constant level.

What techniques are used to revise budgets?

Among the various techniques used to revise budgets are periodic review, progressive review, and moving review. The review technique that is used depends on the policies of the organization, the organization's financial picture, and the emphasis the organization places on budget revision.

When **periodic review** is used, the budget is revised at predetermined times for the remainder of the year. Depending on the organization, the budget may be reviewed each month for the remainder of the year, every two months for the remainder of the year, or perhaps every quarter for the remainder of the year. Figure 26-2 illustrates periodic review.

The **progressive review** technique uses standard-length time spans of perhaps six months. Therefore, the progressive technique revises the budget at specified times and for a constant length of time. Figure 26-3 illustrates the progressive review technique.

When the **moving review** technique is used, the budget is revised each month; and as one month is completed, the same month in the next year is included. Therefore, when the moving review technique is used, the budget is revised monthly, using the next twelve months in the process. The moving review technique is illustrated in Figure 26-4.

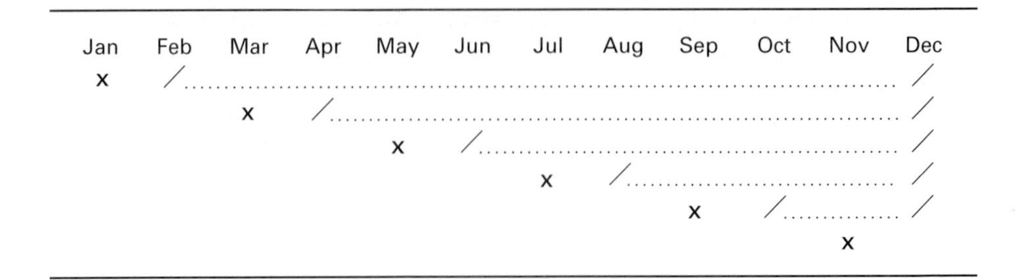

Figure 26-2 Periodic review.

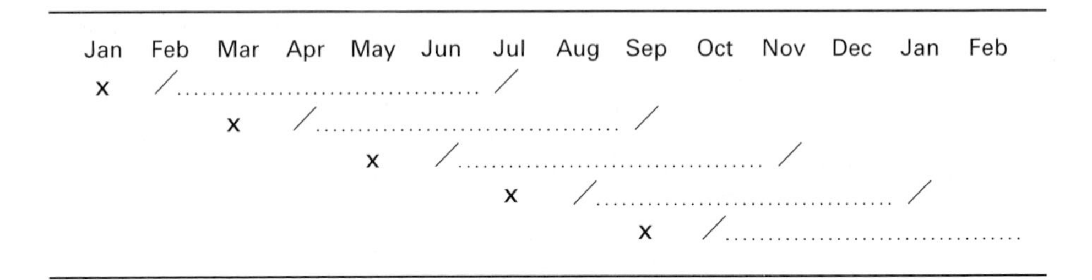

Figure 26-3 Progressive review.

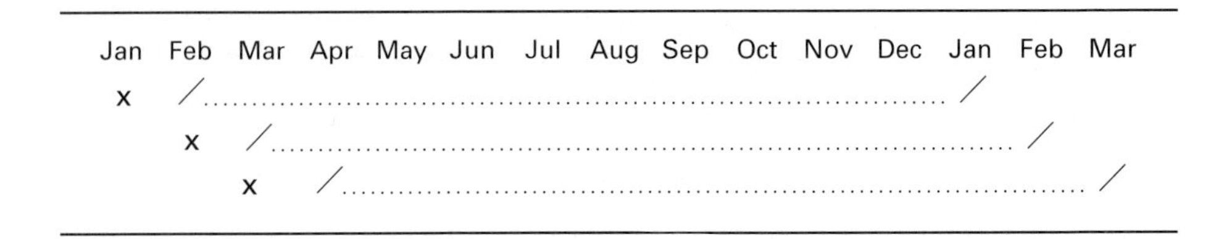

Figure 26-4 Moving review.

ZERO-BASED BUDGETING

What are the characteristics of zero-based budgeting?

As an alternative to traditional budget preparation, **zero-based budgeting (ZBB)** is being used by an increasing number of organizations and government units. According to its proponents, ZBB helps contain operating expenses.

Traditionally, annual budgets have been prepared by increasing the current year's budget by a certain amount, usually a percentage. This practice makes two assumptions: (1) that all current expenditures are necessary and (2) that only the amount of budget increase needs to be substantiated. The traditional budgeting process may be erroneous because certain of the current year's expenses may not be justified. The continued use of an unjustified base in budget preparation perpetuates operating and cost ineffectiveness. Zero-based budgeting eliminates the "add-on" characteristic of traditional budgeting.

With zero-based budgeting, all programs and expenditures are reevaluated each budget period. This method requires that each department manager justify the department's existence each time a budget is prepared. When justification is not sufficient, reductions or even program elimination are possible.

Zero-based budgeting involves three steps:

What are the steps involved in zero-based budgeting?

1. Describing each discrete organizational activity in a decision package.
2. Evaluating and ranking these decision packages in terms of a cost-benefit analysis.
3. Allocating revenues on the basis of need.

Decision packages provide management with a mechanism for evaluating and comparing various organizational operations. They also identify and describe a functional activity or departmental structure. These packages enable management to evaluate and rank an activity against other activities that are competing for the same limited resources.

The preparation of the decision packages begins with a manager's analyzing in detail the status of the department's current operations. At this point, the manager considers alternatives that might be available for performing these existing functions. Once the alternatives have been evaluated, the manager selects the most appropriate course of action.

After the preliminary steps have been completed, the manager begins to analyze the function from a base of zero. While the most important service/activity is selected and assigned a top-priority rating, the less important services/activities are assigned decreased priority ratings.

The ranks prepared by each department manager are then forwarded to higher-level managers who merge the various rankings. At this point, a determination can be made about which services/activities will be funded and which will not be funded because of their low-priority status. Only the justifiable services/activities are included in the budget, which helps eliminate waste of financial resources.

BUDGETARY CONTROL

After the budget has been prepared and approved, budgetary control becomes important. While the preparation process takes place once during the financial year, budgetary control is a continual process.

The budget report is used frequently as a mechanism to coordinate, assess, and control various office operations. The detail needed in the budget report of the office function will be determined by the report's intended use. Because department reports are frequently consolidated to make a larger budget report, less detail will perhaps be needed than if such a consolidation does not take place.

A fundamental purpose of budgeting is the enhancement of the organization's profitability. In many instances, the organization's profit is improved because of the use of skillfully written, carefully prepared budget reports. Several types of reports might be prepared by the administrative office manager. Examples are summaries of actual and budgeted expenses; divisional or departmental summary cost reports; and daily or weekly labor reports comparing actual and standard worker hours.

When preparing budget reports, the following guidelines are suggested:

What guidelines are helpful in preparing budget reports?

1. *Exception situations should be pointed out*. Because managers and executives have an increasing number of job responsibilities, they have less time to devote to operations that are functioning smoothly and

according to plan. Therefore, much of their time has to be devoted to operations that are not progressing according to plan. These operations are known as exception situations. Operations that exceed budgetary allowances should be identified in the budget report.

2. *When presenting figures in a report, a comparison base should be given.* Presenting figures without also presenting a base against which to compare the numbers renders the figures virtually useless. For example, to indicate in a report that the monthly telephone cost was $83.74 is meaningless. But to indicate that the budgeted amount was $70.00 or that the last month's bill was $67.29 provides a base against which comparisons can be made.
3. *Assist the reader by summarizing as much report information as possible.* The report writer can help the busy executive or manager by summarizing much of the information presented in the report. Generally, as reports are presented to higher management levels, fewer details and more summary information is desirable.
4. *When appropriate, reports should include interpretative information.* To assist the reader as much as possible, inclusion of interpretative information in the report may be quite useful. Perhaps the report writer is aware of the reasons why a particular expense exceeded the budgeted allowance. Unless the report reader is quite familiar with a particular situation, providing a valid explanation for the overrun may not be possible.
5. *Reports should be standardized as much as possible.* Preparing identical reports in the same format from one time to the next will help the reader. When reading a standardized format, the reader is able to recall more rapidly important facts or information regarding similar situations in earlier reports. Furthermore, standardizing the report format enables the reader to compare the information contained in one report with related information contained in other reports.

Department: *Office Services* *For Month Ending* *June 30, 19XX*

Expenses	*Amount Budgeted*	*Actual*	*Over*	*Variance %*	*Under*	*%*
01. Salaries	$6,500.00	$6,500.00				
02. Supplies	300.00	320.00	20.00	6.25		
03. Telephone	260.00	220.00			40.00	15.40
04. Xerox	280.00	340.00	60.00	17.65		
05. Postage	150.00	150.00				
06. Repairs	60.00	40.00			20.00	33.34
Totals	$7,550.00	$7,570.00	80.00		60.00	

Variances over or under allocation:

Expense	*Percentage*	*Explanation*
Supplies	+6.25	Significant increase in volume of work
Telephone	−15.40	Employees encouraged to correspond by mail rather than make long-distance phone call
Xerox	+17.65	Significant increase in volume of work
Repairs	−33.34	Better equipment maintenance results in fewer breakdowns

Figure 26-5 Monthly budget report.

Depending upon the nature of the budget report and its use, sections that may be included are (1) purpose of the report, (2) presentation of financial data, (3) summary, (4) conclusions, and (5) recommendations.

In some instances, the summary is presented first, followed by the recommendations and the three remaining sections. Consequently, if the report reader believes the first two sections contain a sufficient amount of information on which to make a decision, the remaining sections may not need to be read. If additional information is needed, however, it is available for the use of the report reader.

Increasingly, unit budget reports prepared on a monthly basis resemble the one illustrated in Figure 26-5. This type of report is an alternative to the narrative type discussed earlier. The variances are clearly identified and explained.

COST CONTROL

In an office, cost control is concerned with the expenses incurred in performing various office operations. **Cost control** is also concerned with keeping expenditures as low as possible. A considerable amount of the administrative office manager's time will involve cost control activities.

The following list identifies several important objectives of cost control:

What are the objectives of cost control?

1. To develop standard costs for various office operations.
2. To develop within the employees a desire to be cost conscious.
3. To assist in the development of efficient operating procedures.
4. To allocate the costs of operations to the appropriate functions.
5. To identify inefficient operations.

Controlling the costs of some office operations is not warranted. For example, spending many dollars only to recommend that the cost of a particular operation be reduced only a few cents is evidence of poor management. When identifying operations for which costs should be determined, the administrative office manager should take into consideration the following: (1) the volume of the operations; (2) the degree to which the operations are standardized; (3) the number of tasks involved in the operations; (4) the efficiency with which the operations are performed; and (5) the level of costs incurred in performing the operations.

The information used to determine operating costs can also be used in a variety of ways:

1. Identifying how closely the costs of office operations conform with accepted operating costs.
2. Identifying ways in which various operations are inefficient.
3. Helping determine the type of new equipment needed when mechanizing office operations.
4. Helping determine which work methods should be revamped or revised.
5. Identifying which alternative office procedures are the most efficient in view of the costs involved.

Techniques for Controlling Office Operating Costs

Several techniques are available for use in controlling the cost of office operations. While some of these techniques are rather simple to use, others are more complex, requiring certain prerequisite knowledges on the part of the administrative office manager.

What techniques are available for controlling office costs?

Cost breakdowns An easy-to-use technique for controlling office costs is the **cost breakdown technique**. This technique involves determining what percentage of the total cost of an operation is classified as a salary or labor cost, a materials or supplies cost, and an overhead cost. The following percentages are generally regarded as being standard for most office operations:

- Salaries, including fringe benefits: 60–70 percent
- Supplies and/or services, including forms, postage, stationery, telephone, telegraph, and so on: 15–20 percent
- Overhead, including maintenance and depreciation of equipment, rent, utilities, taxes, and insurance: 15–20 percent

Some administrative office managers believe the salaries and supplies categories should be divided further into direct and indirect costs, as illustrated in the following:

How do direct salaries differ from indirect salaries?

- **Direct salaries**: the salaries paid to those individuals directly concerned with the production of office work. Examples include the typists, keyboarding specialists, administrative assistants, and secretaries.
- **Indirect salaries**: the salaries paid to those individuals who help make the production of office work possible, although not directly involved in the production process. An example is the janitorial staff.
- **Direct supplies**: the actual supplies used in the production of office work. Examples include stationery and forms.
- **Indirect supplies**: the supplies used in producing office work that are not part of the work being produced. An example is a magnetic disk and equipment depreciation.

To control office costs, the expenditures of actual operations are compared with standard cost breakdowns. If the actual costs exceed the projected cost breakdowns, the administrative office manager should make an attempt to determine the reasons for the excessive costs. After the reasons have been determined, the administrative office manager can develop a cost reduction plan.

Standard costs The **standard cost technique** for controlling office costs involves determining the unit cost of various office operations. As long as the operation can be broken down into the various component parts and the cost of each part can be determined, the unit cost of the operation can be determined.

The following example illustrates the use of the standard cost technique. Assume that the standard cost for processing claims in the health insurance industry is $2.56 per claim. In a particular insurance company, the financial data revealed that the processing of one hundred claims cost $310. Therefore, the unit cost incurred by the company was $3.10. Because this amount is significantly greater than the industry's standard cost, an investigation should be made to determine why the insurance company's cost exceeded the standard cost.

What information is provided by cost analysis studies?

Cost analysis studies The last cost control technique to be discussed in this chapter is the **cost analysis study**. This type of study is used to compare the costs of a current period's operations with the operational costs of a prior period. For example, the office salaries for the current month might be compared with the office salaries for the same month a year ago. If the current figure is considerably higher than the previous figure, the reason for the increase should be determined.

Because the cost analysis study technique is greatly influenced by inflation and increases in operating costs, certain adjustments may have to be made when it is used during inflationary times. To have a comparable base, for example, the consumer price index may be used to adjust the figures.

Taking Corrective Action

Control is necessary, especially when actual results fail to conform to anticipated results. Corrective action is necessary when the cost of an office operation exceeds an acceptable level.

The administrative office manager or office supervisors are responsible for undertaking the appropriate course of action when such action is necessary. Because many employees consider control to be a punitive measure, the individual responsible for taking the corrective action must use a considerable amount of discretion and judgment. Not all individuals respond in the same way to the corrective action.

The following is a composite of some of the reasons actual costs exceed anticipated costs:

1. Work procedures are not efficient.
2. Employees are not properly trained to perform their assigned tasks.
3. Equipment does not function properly.
4. Supplies are not the appropriate quality for the situation.
5. Employees are not cost conscious.
6. Employees lack motivation to perform at accepted levels.

Controlling Office Costs

An important element of cost control is determining if actual costs exceed anticipated costs. When actual costs exceed anticipated costs, corrective action may be necessary. The most expedient way to control office costs may be to implement practices that prevent excessive costs. The following suggestions are offered.

How can personnel costs be controlled?

Personnel costs Because personnel salaries account for the major portion of office costs, controlling personnel salaries provides greater flexibility than controlling costs in other areas.

Personnel costs can be controlled in several ways. One suggestion is to make sure the number of personnel in each work unit is appropriate for the amount of work that needs to be done. If outside employees are needed because of a shortage of personnel in the organization, hiring additional full-time, permanent employees may be less expensive in the long run. Because turnover is likely to increase if employees believe their output expectations are too great, the cost of frequent selection, placement, and training of new employees may actually exceed the cost of hiring additional help.

Other suggestions include the following:

1. Hire employees who are qualified for the jobs they are expected to perform.
2. Train employees who are not qualified for the jobs they perform.
3. Determine which of the following alternatives results in the greatest cost savings to the organization when the amount of work to be done exceeds the number of personnel available: employee overtime, part-time employees, employees from temporary help agencies, or floating work units.
4. Inform employees of the output levels they are expected to maintain. Employees who are aware of expected output levels are more likely to reach their levels than employees who are not aware of the expected output levels.

How can supplies and materials costs be controlled?

Supplies and materials costs Because most office work involves the use of supplies, forms, and materials, the cost of these items is another area of concern. One of the most significant ways to control these costs is to keep the wasting of supplies to a minimum. Waste occurs because employees are careless, make uncorrectable errors, or do not know how the supplies are to be used. In most instances, a desirable way to control waste of supplies is either to hire properly trained employees or to train employees.

Another way to control costs of supplies, and more specifically the cost of forms, is to minimize the number of forms that are used. Before the use of a new form is approved, its need should be thoroughly justified.

Office costs can also be controlled to a certain extent by using equipment that uses interchangeable supplies rather than using equipment needing a particular brand of supplies. With the exception of copiers, most office equipment uses interchangeble supplies.

The cost of supplies can also be controlled by implementing an efficient inventory system. The absence of an effective inventory system may result in overstocking some supplies while understocking others. By reordering supplies before they are all consumed, the extra cost of rush orders can be kept to a minimum. Taking advantage of discounts on quantity buying will also help the organization control the cost of office supplies.

How can equipment costs be controlled?

Equipment costs Because some office equipment is not as reliable as other equipment, maintenance costs increase. Before purchasing an expensive piece of equipment, the administrative office manager should investigate the dependability of several types of equipment. After a piece of equipment has been purchased, maintenance records should be kept. When a particular piece of equipment has a considerably higher-than-average maintenance record compared with other machines, its trade-off should be considered even if the equipment has not been used the specified number of years.

Equipment costs can also be controlled by obtaining equipment appropriate for its intended use. Some office equipment is rather sophisticated; and if extra features are not needed for the efficient processing of present work, its purchase should be discouraged. If, however, the more sophisticated equipment may be needed in the future, its purchase is more justifiable.

Work process costs Work processes are not always developed with the same degree of efficiency. Because some processes are inefficient, their modification should be considered. Some of the inefficiency of work processes can be identified by work measurement, work simplification, and systems and procedures analysis. Rather than controlling the costs of an inefficient work process, greater economy may result in first revising the work processes.

How can work process costs be controlled?

In many work processes, any inefficiencies that are present are multiplied during each step of the process. Therefore, inefficient processes demand immediate attention.

In developing work processes designed to minimize costs, one should consider the following:

1. The cost of smooth-flowing work processes is less than the cost of erratic work processes.
2. Controlling the cost of work processes should focus on the greatest number of employees.
3. Work processes involving considerable backtracking and crisscrossing are more costly than processes in which the work flows in a straight line.

How can overhead costs be controlled?

Overhead costs Because some overhead costs are variable—for example, lighting, air conditioning, and electricity—these costs can be controlled by making employees more conscious of their excessive use. As a result of increased energy consciousness among employees, specific programs designed to result in energy conservation are being developed. In many instances, all that is needed is an energy conservation awareness on the part of employees.

Some organizations have brought about the conservation of energy by establishing contests in each department of the organization. The employees in the department who achieve the greatest net reduction in consumption over a specified period receive special recognition. In some instances, financial awards are presented to the employees in the winning unit.

IMPLICATIONS FOR THE ADMINISTRATIVE OFFICE MANAGER

Just as administrative office managers become noticed as a result of their performance in quantity and quality control efforts, they can also become noticed as a result of their performance and achievements in budgetary and cost control. For many years, top management focused only minimally on budgetary and cost control of the office function. This is no longer the case.

Nowadays, top management is well aware of the large percentage of organizational administrative costs that originate in the office area. By controlling these costs more effectively, the organization can increase its profitability.

Administrative office managers often have to make compromises between maximizing the efficiency of various office operations and allocating costs to these areas. For example, because managers have to operate within budgetary constraints, they are not always able to purchase equipment that will enable them to maximize the efficiency of the office function. Rather, a compromise approach is used in which they maximize efficiency as much as they can—given the resources with which they have to work.

REVIEW QUESTIONS

1. Why is budgeting important in budgetary control?
2. What are the advantages and limitations of budgeting?
3. Who is generally responsible for the preparation of the office budget?
4. What are the differences among fixed, variable, and semivariable costs?

5. Why is employee participation in budget preparation so useful?
6. Why must a budget provide for unforeseen circumstances?
7. What steps are involved in using the zero-based budgeting process?
8. Why should exception situations be pointed out in the budget report?
9. What advantages result from cost control?
10. As cost control techniques, how do cost breakdowns, standard costs, and cost analysis studies differ from one another?

DISCUSSION QUESTIONS

1. You are an assistant to the department manager in the organization in which you work. One of your responsibilities is to keep the account balances up-to-date. Your manager told you recently that at the end of the budget period, he likes to have a minimum balance of 10 percent in each of the department's accounts "because it makes him look good as a manager." Discuss the implications of this comment.
2. Although the organization for which you work has an "informal policy" of sharing appropriate budget data with employees, your manager does not believe in sharing any of this type of information. When your manager was asked why he didn't share this information, he said, "Employees will keep requesting more and more." He also made the comment that employees who don't have access to this information will make fewer requests. Discuss the pros and cons of sharing budget information with employees.
3. Certain managers in the company in which you work are allowed to overspend their budgets. When this happens, their manager simply gives them unspent allocations from other managers' budgets. As a consequence, top management does not realize this is happening. Discuss the implications of this situation.
4. As a supervisor of several office employees, you find that you are having difficulty getting employees committed to your unit's budget. You have shared budget information with them, but that has not helped much. Discuss ways that you can increase the commitment of employees to a budget.
5. You, a department manager in the organization in which you work, are responsible for maintaining your unit's budget. For each of the last five years, your budget has been increased by the percentage amount equal to the previous year's inflation rate. Therefore, if inflation increased by 8 percent last year, this year's budget was increased by 8 percent. Discuss the implications of using this method for making budget adjustments.
6. One of your managerial responsibilities is budgeting. You find that of all the accounts that comprise your budget, the supplies and services account gives you the greatest amount of difficulty. At the end of some budget periods, you have a fairly large deficit while at the end of other budget periods, you have quite a surplus. What situations are likely to make the activity of the supplies and services account quite unpredictable?

STUDENT PROJECTS AND ACTIVITIES

1. Interview a manager who has budgeting responsibilities as part of his or her position. Find out about the budget review process used by the manager.
2. Interview a manager in an organization that uses zero-based budgeting. What advantages and disadvantages does the manager see for the ZBB technique?
3. Talk with an administrative office manager or office supervisor who is

responsible for controlling costs within his or her unit of responsibility. How does this individual deal with situations in which expenditures greatly exceed approved costs?

4. Compare the office budgets of two organizations. In what ways are they similar and dissimilar?
5. Talk with an administrative office manager or office supervisor to learn about the techniques he or she uses to control such costs as office supplies, equipment costs, and overhead costs.

MINICASE

When she took office, one of the first actions of the new president of the Data Methods Corporation was to embark on a cost-cutting campaign. Costs in a number of areas were not well controlled during the presidency of her predecessor. The new president has asked each department head to provide the following information in a written report:

1. A list of suggestions for controlling the cost of office supplies.
2. A list of suggestions for controlling equipment and equipment maintenance costs.

CASE

The Metropolitan Publishing Company, located in St. Louis, Missouri, is the publisher of the largest daily newspaper in the Greater St. Louis area. The management of the organization has become quite concerned about rapidly increasing office costs.

One of the vice presidents recently undertook an informal study. She discovered that during certain times of the month, some employees are idle because of an insufficient amount of work. Some of the office supervisors she talked with also indicated that greater waste of office supplies seems to be occurring now than was the case earlier. An examination of energy consumption data also revealed that consumption has increased quite dramatically—and for no apparent reason.

The vice president who undertook the informal study has asked you, the administrative office manager, to prepare a report for her regarding the installation of a cost control program. Specifically, she has asked that the following information be included in the report:

1. Benefits that will result from the installation of a cost control program.
2. Suggestions/guidelines that will facilitate the installation of such a program.
3. Suggestions for evaluating the effectiveness of the program once it becomes functional.

INDEX

A

B

D

E

F

G

H

I

J

K

L

M

N

O

P

Q

R

S